UNIVERSITY CASEBOOK SERIES®

AGENCY, PARTNERSHIPS, AND LIMITED LIABILITY ENTITIES

CASES AND MATERIALS ON UNINCORPORATED BUSINESS ASSOCIATIONS

FIFTH EDITION

STEPHEN M. BAINBRIDGE
William D. Warren Distinguished Professor of Law
University of California, Los Angeles

FOUNDATION PRESS

444 Cedar Street, Suite 700
St. Paul, MN 55101
1-877-888-1330

Printed in the United States of America

ISBN: 978-1-64708-575-9

PREFACE

In editing this casebook, I followed the same principles used in my Business Associations casebook. First, given the right material, this is a course that is fun both to teach and to study. So, unless the case has some interesting element, I leave it out.

Second, I follow the cases with notes, problems, and questions that clarify the case's key points. But this is not a textbook. If you or your students want more textual explanation, I suggest supplementing the book with my *Agency, Partnership, and LLCs* treatise (Foundation Press Concepts and Insights 3rd edition 2018).

In this field, planning is especially crucial. Accordingly, I structured the notes, problems, and questions with an eye to how a good lawyer might have mitigated the risk of litigation after-the-fact with better planning up-front.

Finally, I edit the cases mercilessly. One iteration of the law is enough. If a panel seems to lack the guts to say something once and stop, I stop the opinion for them.

I enjoy teaching this subject and detest repetitious text. I have tried to embody those preferences in this book.

STEPHEN M. BAINBRIDGE

Spring 2022

EDITORIAL NOTE AND ACKNOWLEDGMENTS

Footnote numbers in cases are as in the original, with no renumbering to take account of omitted footnotes. Citations in cases are generally omitted, except where the authority cited might be familiar to the student, provides the source of quoted language, or otherwise seemed noteworthy.

I am grateful for permission to reprint copyrighted material from the following:

- The American Law Institute for selected portions of the Restatement of the Law (Second) of Agency. © 1958 by the American Law Institute. Reprinted with permission.
- The American Law Institute for selected portions of the Restatement of the Law (Third) of Agency. © 2000 by the American Law Institute. Reprinted with permission.
- The National Conference of Commissioners on Uniform State Laws for the Uniform Partnership Act (1914).
- The National Conference of Commissioners on Uniform State Laws for Selected Portions of the Uniform Partnership Act (1997, Last Amended 2013). © 2014 National Conference of Commissioners on Uniform State Laws.
- The National Conference of Commissioners on Uniform State Laws for Uniform Limited Partnership Act (2001, Last Amended 2014). © 2014 National Conference of Commissioners on Uniform State Laws.
- The National Conference of Commissioners on Uniform State Laws for Uniform Limited Liability Company Act (1997, Last Amended 2013). © 2014 National Conference of Commissioners on Uniform State Laws.

SUMMARY OF CONTENTS

PREFACE III

EDITORIAL NOTE AND ACKNOWLEDGMENTS V

TABLE OF CASES XVII

Chapter 1. Agency 1
1. Who Is an Agent? 1
2. Liability of Principal to Third Parties in Contract 26
3. Liability of Principal to Third Parties in Tort 85
4. Fiduciary Obligation of Agents 142
5. Appendices 178

Chapter 2. Partnerships 209
1. What Is a Partnership? And Who Are the Partners? 209
2. Partnership Property 245
3. The Rights of Partners in Management 252
4. The Fiduciary Obligations of Partners 271
5. Partners at Loggerheads: The Dissolution Solution Under the UPA (1914) 325
6. Partners at Loggerheads: The Dissolution Solution Under the UPA (1997) 366
7. Buyout Agreements 381
8. Limited Partnerships 386
9. Appendices 417

Chapter 3. Limited Liability Entities 479
1. Limited Liability Companies 479
2. Securities Regulation Issues 575
3. Appendix 596

INDEX 627

TABLE OF CONTENTS

PREFACE III

EDITORIAL NOTE AND ACKNOWLEDGMENTS V

TABLE OF CASES XVII

Chapter 1. Agency 1
1. Who Is an Agent? 1
   Gorton v. Doty 1
   Analysis 6
   MJ & Partners Restaurant Limited Partnership v. Zadikoff 7
   Note 10
   Aftermath 12
   Analysis 12
   Rose v. Giamatti 13
   Note 14
   Aftermath 18
   Analysis 18
   Introductory Note 19
   A. Gay Jenson Farms Co. v. Cargill, Inc. 19
   Note 25
   Analysis 25
   Planning 25
2. Liability of Principal to Third Parties in Contract 26
   A. Authority 26
      Mill Street Church of Christ v. Hogan 26
      Note 27
      Analysis 28
      Karl Rove & Co. v. Thornburgh 29
      Analysis 36
   B. Apparent Authority 37
      Lind v. Schenley Industries, Inc. 37
      Note 42
      Planning 42
      Analysis 42
      Ackerman v. Sobol Family Partnership, LLP 42
      Analysis 49
      Planning 49
   C. Inherent Authority 50
      Watteau v. Fenwick 50
      Note 52
      Analysis 53
      Kidd v. Thomas A. Edison, Inc. 54
      Analysis 57
      Nogales Service Center v. Atlantic Richfield Company 57
      Analysis 62

Problems 62
D. Ratification 63
Botticello v. Stefanovicz 63
Problems 66
Ercanbrack v. Crandall-Walker Motor Company, Inc. 67
Analysis 71
E. Estoppel 72
Hoddeson v. Koos Bros. 72
Analysis 75
Trustees of the American Federation of Musicians and Employers' Pension Fund v. Steven Scott Enterprises, Inc. 75
Note 77
Analysis 81
F. Agent's Liability on the Contract 82
Atlantic Salmon A/S v. Curran 82
Analysis 85
3. Liability of Principal to Third Parties in Tort 85
A. Servant (Employee) Versus Independent Contractor 85
Introductory Note 85
Humble Oil & Refining Co. v. Martin 86
Hoover v. Sun Oil Company 89
Planning 91
Analysis 91
Policy Questions 92
Murphy v. Holiday Inns, Inc. 93
Parker v. Domino's Pizza 96
Analysis 100
B. Tort Liability and Apparent Agency 101
Miller v. McDonald's Corp. 101
Analysis 105
Problem 106
C. Scope of Employment 106
Brill v. Davajon 106
Analysis 109
Ira S. Bushey & Sons, Inc. v. United States 109
Note 113
Analysis 114
Manning v. Grimsley 115
Analysis 117
Lamkin v. Brooks 118
Analysis 120
D. Statutory Claims 121
Arguello v. Conoco, Inc. 121
Analysis 128
E. Liability for Torts of Independent Contractors 129
Majestic Realty Associates, Inc. v. Toti Contracting Co. 129

Analysis 133
Anderson v. Marathon Petroleum Co. 133
Analysis 138
Kleeman v. Rheingold 139
Analysis 142
4. Fiduciary Obligation of Agents 142
Introductory Note 142
A. Duties During Agency 142
Reading v. Regem 142
Note 142
Problems 145
Analysis 145
General Automotive Manufacturing Co. v. Singer 146
Analysis 150
Rash v. J.V. Intermediate, Ltd. 151
Analysis 154
B. Duties During and After Termination of Agency: Herein of "Grabbing and Leaving" 154
Bancroft-Whitney Company v. Glen 154
Analysis 166
Problems 166
Town & Country House & Home Service, Inc. v. Newbery 167
Analysis 169
Corroon & Black-Rutters & Roberts, Inc. v. Hosch 170
Analysis 177
Planning 177
5. Appendices 178
Restatement of the Law (Second) Agency 178
Restatement of the Law (Third) Agency 192
Note 197

Chapter 2. Partnerships 209
1. What Is a Partnership? And Who Are the Partners? 209
A. Partners Compared with Employees 209
Fenwick v. Unemployment Compensation Commission 209
Analysis 213
Clackamas Gastroenterology Associates v. Wells 214
Analysis 218
Davis v. Loftus 219
Questions 220
Equal Employment Opportunity Commission v. Sidley Austin Brown & Wood 220
Note 221
Analysis 228
Frank v. R.A. Pickens & Son Company 228
Analysis 231

B. Partners Compared with Lenders 232
Introductory Note 232
Martin v. Peyton 232
Notes 235
Planning 237
Analysis 237
Background 237
Kaufman-Brown Potato Co. v. Long 238
Analysis 242
C. Partnership by Estoppel 242
Young v. Jones 242
Analysis 245
2. Partnership Property 245
In re Fulton 245
Note 245
Note 247
Analysis 247
Putnam v. Shoaf 248
Analysis 252
3. The Rights of Partners in Management 252
Introductory Note 252
National Biscuit Company v. Stroud 253
Analysis 255
Summers v. Dooley 255
Note 256
Planning 256
Analysis 256
Moren ex rel. Moren v. Jax Restaurant 256
Analysis 258
Problem 259
RNR Investments Ltd. Partnership v. Peoples First Community Bank 259
Analysis 263
Day v. Sidley & Austin 263
Note 270
Analysis 270
4. The Fiduciary Obligations of Partners 271
A. Introduction 271
Meinhard v. Salmon 271
Planning 276
Analysis 277
Sandvick v. LaCrosse 277
Analysis 283
Singer v. Singer 283
Analysis 287
Nemec v. Shrader 287
Note 289

Analysis ... 295
B. After Dissolution ... 296
Bane v. Ferguson ... 296
Analysis ... 297
C. Grabbing and Leaving ... 298
Meehan v. Shaughnessy ... 298
Problem ... 304
Analysis ... 304
Gibbs v. Breed, Abbott & Morgan ... 305
Analysis ... 310
D. Expulsion ... 311
Lawlis v. Kightlinger & Gray ... 311
Analysis ... 316
Bohatch v. Butler & Binion ... 317
Analysis ... 324
5. Partners at Loggerheads: The Dissolution Solution Under the UPA (1914) ... 325
A. The Right to Dissolve ... 325
Owen v. Cohen ... 325
Analysis ... 328
Note and Question ... 329
Collins v. Lewis ... 329
Note ... 334
Analysis ... 334
Introductory Note ... 334
Planning ... 334
Page v. Page ... 334
Problems ... 337
B. The Consequences of Dissolution ... 337
Prentiss v. Sheffel ... 337
Analysis and Planning ... 340
Disotell v. Stiltner ... 341
Analysis ... 348
Monin v. Monin ... 349
Note ... 349
Analysis ... 351
Pav-Saver Corporation v. Vasso Corporation ... 352
Analysis and Planning ... 357
Note ... 358
C. The Sharing of Losses ... 358
Kovacik v. Reed ... 358
Note ... 358
Notes and Questions ... 360
D. Law Partnership Dissolution ... 361
Meehan v. Shaughnessy ... 361
Note ... 363
Analysis ... 365

6. Partners at Loggerheads: The Dissolution Solution Under the UPA (1997) ... 366
Note ... 366
Giles v. Giles Land Company ... 367
Note ... 370
Analysis ... 373
Creel v. Lilly ... 374
Analysis ... 381
7. Buyout Agreements ... 381
Introductory Note ... 381
G & S Investments v. Belman ... 382
Note ... 385
8. Limited Partnerships ... 386
Introduction ... 386
Frigidaire Sales Corporation v. Union Properties, Inc. ... 387
Analysis ... 389
Jerman v. O'Leary ... 389
Analysis ... 393
Sonet v. Plum Creek Timber Co., L.P. ... 394
Note ... 394
Note ... 395
Analysis ... 399
Cincinnati SMSA L.P. v. Cincinnati Bell Cellular Systems Co. ... 401
Analysis ... 404
In re: El Paso Pipeline Partners, L.P. Derivative Litigation ... 405
Note ... 410
Note ... 413
Analysis ... 415
Note on Subsequent Related Decisions ... 415
Note on Contractual Nature of Partnerships ... 416
9. Appendices ... 417
Uniform Partnership Act (1914) ... 417
Uniform Partnership Act (1997, Last Amended 2013) (selected provisions) ... 434
Uniform Limited Partnership Act (2001) (Last Amended 2013) ... 463

Chapter 3. Limited Liability Entities ... 479
1. Limited Liability Companies ... 479
Introductory Note ... 479
A. Formation ... 479
Water, Waste & Land, Inc. d/b/a Westec v. Lanham ... 479
Analysis ... 484
B. The Operating Agreement ... 484
Introductory Note ... 484
Duray Development, LLC v. Perrin ... 485
Analysis ... 490
Elf Atochem North America, Inc. v. Jaffari ... 491

Analysis ... 498
Fisk Ventures, LLC v. Segal ... 498
Note ... 500
Note ... 504
Analysis ... 504
C. Piercing the LLC Veil ... 505
Introductory Note ... 505
Tom Thumb Food Markets, Inc. v. TLH Properties, LLC ... 506
Analysis ... 508
NetJets Aviation, Inc. v. LHC Communications, LLC ... 509
Note ... 509
Analysis ... 517
D. Fiduciary Obligation ... 517
McConnell v. Hunt Sports Enterprises ... 517
Analysis ... 523
VGS, Inc. v. Castiel ... 523
Analysis ... 529
Gottsacker v. Monnier ... 530
Note ... 530
Note ... 531
Analysis ... 535
E. Additional Capital ... 535
Racing Investment Fund 2000, LLC v. Clay Ward Agency, Inc. ... 535
Analysis ... 539
Planning: Additional Capital ... 539
F. Expulsion ... 540
Walker v. Resource Development Co. ... 540
Analysis ... 554
G. Dissolution ... 555
The Dunbar Group, LLC v. Tignor ... 555
Analysis ... 559
Investcorp, L.P. v. Simpson Investment Co. ... 560
Note ... 562
Analysis ... 563
Aftermath ... 563
R & R Capital, LLC v. Buck & Doe Run Valley Farms, LLC ... 564
Note ... 566
Analysis ... 568
Fisk Ventures, LLC v. Segal ... 568
Analysis ... 574
2. Securities Regulation Issues ... 575
Introductory Note ... 575
Great Lakes Chemical Corp. v. Monsanto Co. ... 578
Analysis ... 589
Koch v. Hankins ... 589
Note ... 589

Note 593
3. Appendix 596
Uniform Limited Liability Company Act (1997, Last Amended 2013) 596

INDEX 627

TABLE OF CASES

The principal cases are in bold type.

A. Gay Jenson Farms Co. v. Cargill, Inc., 19
Abbott Laboratories v. Norse Chemical Corp., 171
Abetter Trucking Co. v. Arizpe, 153
Acheson v. White, 46
Ackerman v. Sobol Family Partnership, LLP, 42
Albright v. Stegeman Motor Car Company, 70
Allen v. Encore Energy P'rs, P.P., 411
Allied Capital Corp. v. GC-Sun Holding, LP, 504
Anderson v. Marathon Petroleum Co., 133
Ansonia v. Cooper, 65
Arguello v. Conoco, Inc., 121
Atlantic Salmon A/S v. Curran, 82
Bakalis v. Bressler, 269
Bancroft-Whitney Company v. Glen, 154
Bane v. Ferguson, 296
Billops v. Magness Const. Co., 103
Bohatch v. Butler & Binion, 317
Botticello v. Stefanovicz, 63
Brennan v. Brennan Associates, 371
Brill v. Davajon, 106
Callier v. Callier, 574
Cardullo v. Landau, 302
Carolin Paxson Advertising, Inc., In re, 33
Chandler v. Kelley, 94
Charles O. Finley & Co., Inc. v. Kuhn, 14
Chelsea Indus. v. Gaffney, 303
Cincinnati SMSA Ltd. P'ship v. Cincinatti Bell Cellular Sys. Co., 290, **401**
Cities Service Co. v. State, 135
Clackamas Gastroenterology Associates v. Wells, 214
Clover v. Snowbird Ski Resort, 113
Collins v. Lewis, 329
Community for Creative Non-Violence v. Reid, 215
Comptroller of Treas. v. Thompson Tr. Corp., 377
Contemporary Health Management, United States v., 33
Continental Ins. Co. v. Rutledge & Co., Inc., 291, 404
Cook v. Lauten, 219
Cooper v. Isaacs, 384
Corporate Prop. Assocs. 14 Inc. v. CHR Holding Corp., 504
Corroon & Black-Rutters & Roberts, Inc. v. Hosch, 170
Creel v. Lilly, 374
Davis v. Loftus, 219, 227
Day v. Avery, 263
Day v. Sidley & Austin, 263
Delaney v. Fidelity Lease Ltd., 388
Dieckman v. Regency GP LP, 413
Disotell v. Stiltner, 341
Dreifuerst v. Dreifuerst, 344
Dunbar Group, LLC, The v. Tignor, 555
Dunlap Investors Ltd. v. Hogan, 392
Dunlap v. State Farm Fire & Cas. Co., 290, 293, 503
Duray Development, LLC v. Perrin, 485
E.I. DuPont de Nemours & Co. v. Pressman, 290
Edin v. Josten's, Inc., 508
El Paso Pipeline Partners, L.P. Derivative Litigation, In re, 405
Elf Atochem North America, Inc. v. Jaffari, 491, 552, 566, 567
Equal Employment Opportunity Commission v. Sidley Austin Brown & Wood, 220
Ercanbrack v. Crandall-Walker Motor Company, Inc., 67
Escobedo v. Conoco, Inc., 121
Estey Mfg. Co. v. Runnells, 487, 489
Feliberty v. Damon, 140
Fenwick v. Unemployment Compensation Commission, 209
Fisk Ventures, LLC v. Segal, 498, **568**, 569, 573
Fitz-Gerald v. Hull, 319
Fleer Corp. v. Topps Chewing Gum, Inc., 293
Fortugno v. Hudson Manure Co., 268
Fountain v. Metcalf, Zima & Co., P.A., 224
Frank v. R.A. Pickens & Son Company, 228
Frigidaire Sales Corporation v. Union Properties, Inc., 387
Fulton, In re, 245
G & S Investments v. Belman, 382
Gary Van Zeeland Talent, Inc. v. Sandas, 171, 174
Gelder Med. Group v. Webber, 319
General Automotive Manufacturing Co. v. Singer, 146
General Building Contractors Association v. Pennsylvania United Engineers and Constructors, 123
Geyer v. Ingersoll Publications Co., 511

Gibbs v. Breed, Abbott & Morgan, 305
Giles v. Giles Land Company, 367
Gochee v. Wagner, 6
Goldberg v. Whitaker House Cooperative, Inc., 217
Gorton v. Doty, 1
Gottsacker v. Monnier, 530
Great Lakes Chemical Corp. v. Monsanto Co., 578
Green v. H & R Block, Inc., 18
Grynberg v. Dome Petroleum Corp., 280
Gumpert v. Bon Ami Co., 40
Guth v. Loft, 161
Haley v. Talcott, 565, 571
Harco National Insurance Co. v. Green Farms, Inc., 511
Harper v. Delaware Valley Broadcasters, Inc., 512
Hartford Accident & Indemnity Co. v. Cardillo, 112
Haynes Family Trust, The v. Kinder Morgan G.P., Inc., 416
Hishon v. King & Spalding, 222, 226
Hocking v. Dubois, 593
Hoddeson v. Koos Bros., 72
Holman v. Coie, 316
Hoover v. Sun Oil Company, 89
Humble Oil & Refining Co. v. Martin, 86
Hurst v. Hurst, 393
Hyland v. New Haven Radiology Associates, P. C., 214
Investcorp, L.P. v. Simpson Investment Co., 560
Ira S. Bushey & Sons, Inc. v. United States, 109
Jackson Nat. Life Ins. Co. v. Kennedy, 293
Jerman v. O'Leary, 389
Jewel v. Boxer, 364, 365
Johnson v. Bernheim, 253
Johnson v. Brewer & Pritchard, P.C., 151
Karl Rove & Co. v. Thornburgh, 29
Kaufman-Brown Potato Co. v. Long, 238
Keith v. Black Diamond Advisors, Inc., 584
Kidd v. Thomas A. Edison, Inc., 54, 61
Klee v. United States, 5
Kleeman v. Rheingold, 139
Koch v. Hankins, 589
Kovacik v. Reed, 358
Kurtzon v. Kurtzon, 355
Lafayette Trust Co. v. Beggs, 377
Lamkin v. Brooks, 118
Landreth Timber Co. v. Landreth, 583
Lawlis v. Kightlinger & Gray, 311
LeBrane v. Lewis, 119
Lind v. Schenley Industries, Inc., 37
Lois Grunow Memorial Clinic v. Davis, 61
Maharishi School of Vedic Sciences, Inc. (Connecticut) v. Connecticut Constitution Associates Ltd. Partnership, 45, 46
Majestic Realty Associates, Inc. v. Toti Contracting Co., 129
Manning v. Grimsley, 115
Martin v. Peyton, 232
McCallum v. Asbury, 268
McConnell v. Hunt Sports Enterprises, 517
McLaughlin v. Chicken Delight, Inc., 64
Meehan v. Shaughnessy, 298, 307, 361
Meinhard v. Salmon, 271, 281
Mill Street Church of Christ v. Hogan, 26
Miller v. Federated Department Stores, Inc., 116
Miller v. McDonald's Corp., 101
Minskoff v. American Express Travel Related Services Co., 78
Mist Properties, Inc. v. Fitzsimmons Realty Co., 392
MJ & Partners Restaurant Limited Partnership v. Zadikoff, 7
MJ & Partners Restaurant Limited v. Zadikoff, 10
Monarch Ins. Co. of Ohio v. Ins. Corp. of Ireland. Ltd., et al., 80
Monin v. Monin, 349
Moreland v. Mason, 5
Moren ex rel. Moren v. Jax Restaurant, 256
Murphy v. Holiday Inns, Inc., 93
National Biscuit Company v. Stroud, 253
Nationwide Mut. Ins. Co. v. Darden, 215, 227
Neff v. American Dairy Queen Corporation, 124
Nelson v. American-West African Line, 110
Nelson v. United States, 138
Nemec v. Shrader, 287
NetJets Aviation, Inc. v. LHC Communications, LLC, 509
Newcomb-Endicott Co. v. Fee, 488
Nogales Service Center v. Atlantic Richfield Company, 57
Owen v. Cohen, 325, 335
Page v. Page, 334
Palsgraf v. Long Island R.R. Co., 113
Parker v. Domino's Pizza, 96

Pauley Petroleum Inc. v. Continental Oil Co., 511
Pav-Saver Corporation v. Vasso Corporation, 352
PC Tower Ctr., Inc. v. Tower Ctr. Dev. Assoc. Ltd. P'ship, 571
Peeples v. Kawasaki Heavy Indust., Ltd., 103
Personnel Decisions, Inc. v. Bus. Planning Sys., Inc., 567
Prentiss v. Sheffel, 337, 340
Prisco v. State of New York, 80
Putnam v. Shoaf, 248
R & R Capital, LLC v. Buck & Doe Run Valley Farms, LLC, 564, 570
Racing Investment Fund 2000, LLC v. Clay Ward Agency, Inc., 535
Rash v. J.V. Intermediate, Ltd., 151
Reading v. Regem, 142
RNR Investments Ltd. Partnership v. Peoples First Community Bank, 259
Rose v. Giamatti, 13
Sandvick v. LaCrosse, 277
Sarno v. Gulf Refining Co., 132
Scott v. Walton, 71
SEC v. C.M. Joiner Leasing Corp., 591
SEC v. Glenn W. Turner Enters., Inc., 592
SEC v. Parkersburg Wireless LLC, 584
SEC v. R.G. Reynolds Enterprises, Inc., 586
SEC v. Shreveport Wireless Cable Television Partnership, 585
SEC v. W.J. Howey Co., 582, 591
Segal v. Fisk Ventures, LLC, 498
Shenandoah Life Ins. Co. v. Valero Energy Corp., 504
Simpson v. Ernst & Young, 221, 224
Singer v. Singer, 283
Smith v. Gross, 577
Sonet v. Plum Creek Timber Co., L.P., 394
SPW Associates, LLP v. Anderson, 279
Strother v. Southern California Permanente Medical Group, 224
Summers v. Dooley, 255
Svihl v. Gress, 281
Texas Company v. Wheat, 88
Tisch Auto Supply Co. v. Nelson, 488
Tom Thumb Food Markets, Inc. v. TLH Properties, LLC, 506
Tomlinson v. Board of Education, 46, 47, 48
Touchstone v. G.B.Q. Corp., 136
Town & Country House & Home Service, Inc. v. Newbery, 167
TravelCenters of Am., LLC v. Brog, 565, 570
Trustees of the American Federation of Musicians and Employers' Pension Fund v. Steven Scott Enterprises, Inc., 75
Union Producing Co. v. Allen, 34
United Housing Foundation, Inc. v. Forman, 583, 588
United Teachers Ass'n Ins. Co. v. MacKeen & Bailey, Inc., 153
Van Hooser v. Keenon, Ky., 350
VGS, Inc. v. Castiel, 523
Voorhees v. Jones, 212
Walker v. Resource Development Co., 540
Wasserman v. Wasserman, 392
Water, Waste & Land, Inc. d/b/a Westec v. Lanham, 479
Watteau v. Fenwick, 50
Wells v. Whitaker, 96
Wendt v. Fischer, 273
Wheeler v. Hurdman, 224
Wilgus v. Salt Pond Inv. Co., 503
Willi v. Schaefer Hitchcock Co., 3
Williamson v. Tucker, 592
Witkop & Holmes Co. v. Boyce, 168
Wurtz v. Fleischman, 534
Young v. Jones, 242
Zajac v. Harris, 230

UNIVERSITY CASEBOOK SERIES®

AGENCY, PARTNERSHIPS, AND LIMITED LIABILITY ENTITIES

CASES AND MATERIALS ON UNINCORPORATED BUSINESS ASSOCIATIONS

FIFTH EDITION

CHAPTER 1

AGENCY

1. WHO IS AN AGENT?

Gorton v. Doty

57 Idaho 792, 69 P.2d 136 (Idaho 1937).

In September, 1935, an action was commenced by R. S. Gorton, father of Richard Gorton, to recover expenses incurred by the father for hospitalization, physicians', surgeons', and nurses' fees, and another by the son, by his father as guardian ad litem, to recover damages for injuries sustained as a result of an accident. By stipulation the actions were consolidated for trial. Upon the trial of the cases so consolidated, the jury returned a verdict in favor of the father for $870 and another in favor of the son for $5,000. Separate judgments were then entered upon such verdicts. Thereafter a motion for a new trial was made and denied in each case. The cases come here upon an appeal from each judgment and order denying a new trial.

. . .

It appears that in September, 1934, Richard Gorton, a minor, was a junior in the Soda Springs High School and a member of the football team; that his high school team and the Paris High School team were scheduled to play a game of football at Paris on the 21st. Appellant was teaching at the Soda Springs High School and Russell Garst was coaching the Soda Springs team. On the day the game was played, the Soda Springs High School team was transported to and from Paris in privately owned automobiles. One of the automobiles used for that purpose was owned by appellant. Her car was driven by Mr. Garst, the coach of the Soda Springs High School team.

One of the most difficult questions, if not the most difficult, presented by the record, is, Was the coach, Russell Garst, the agent of appellant while and in driving her car from Soda Springs to Paris, and in returning to the point where the accident occurred?

Briefly stated, the facts bearing upon that question are as follows: That appellant knew the Soda Springs High School football team and the Paris High School football team were to play a game of football at Paris September 21, 1934; that she volunteered her car for use in transporting some of the members of the Soda Springs team to and from the game; that she asked the coach, Russell Garst, the day before the game, if he had all the cars necessary for the trip to Paris the next day; that he said he needed one more; that she told him he might use her car if he drove it; that she was not promised compensation for the use of her car and did not receive any; that the school district paid for the gasoline used on the trip to and from the game; that she testified she loaned the car to Mr. Garst; that she had not employed Mr. Garst at any time and that she had not at any time "directed his work or his services, or what he was doing."

. . .

Broadly speaking, "agency" indicates the relation which exists where one person acts for another. It has these three principal forms: 1. The relation of principal and agent; 2. The relation of master and servant; and, 3. The relation of employer or proprietor and independent contractor. While all have points of similarity, there are, nevertheless, numerous differences. We are concerned here with the first form only.

Specifically, "agency" is the relationship which results from the manifestation of consent by one person to another that the other shall act on his behalf and subject to his control, and consent by the other so to act. [Restatement of Agency § 1.]

[In a subsequent passage, the court indicated that the principal is responsible for the acts of his or her agent: "After having given the jury a correct definition of the term 'agency,' the [trial] court . . . instructed the jury that if they found from the evidence that Russell Garst was, at the time of the accident, the agent of appellant, then that she was chargeable with the acts of her agent as fully and to the same extent as though she had been driving the automobile herself . . ., which is unquestionably the law."]

. . . [This court has not held] that the relationship of principal and agent must necessarily involve some matter of business, but only that where one undertakes to transact some business or manage some affair for another by authority and on account of the latter, the relationship of principal and agent arises.

To enable the Soda Springs football team to play football at Paris, it had to be transported to Paris. Automobiles were to be used and another car was needed. At that juncture, appellant volunteered the use of her car. For what purpose? Necessarily for the purpose of furnishing additional transportation. Appellant, of course, could have driven the car herself, but instead of doing that, she designated the driver (Russell Garst) and, in doing so, made it a condition precedent that the person she designated should drive her car. That appellant thereby at least consented that Russell Garst should act for her and in her behalf, in driving her car to and from the football game, is clear from her act in volunteering the use of her car upon the express condition that he should drive it, and, further, that Mr. Garst consented to so act for appellant is equally clear by his act in driving the car. It is not essential to the existence of authority that there be a contract between principal and agent or that the agent promise to act as such (Restatement Agency, §§ 15, 16, pp. 50–54), nor is it essential to the relationship of principal and agent that they, or either, receive compensation (Restatement Agency, § 16, p. 53).

Furthermore, this court held in Willi v. Schaefer Hitchcock Co., 53 Idaho 367, 25 P.2d 167, in harmony with the clear weight of authority, that the fact of ownership alone (conceded here), regardless of the presence or absence of the owner in the car at the time of the accident, establishes a prima facie case against the owner for the reason that the presumption arises that the driver is the agent of the owner. . . .

It is vigorously contended, however, that the facts and circumstances bearing upon the question under discussion show appellant loaned her car to Mr. Garst. A determination of that question makes it necessary to quote appellant's testimony. She testified as follows:

"Q. On or about the 21st day of September, 1934, state whether or not you permitted Russell Garst to use that car?

"A. I did.

"Q. Under what circumstances?

"A. I loaned it to him.

"Q. When did you loan it to him? Was it that day, or the day before?

"A. On the day before I told him he might have it the next day.

"Q. Did you receive any compensation, or were you promised any compensation, for its use?

"A. No, sir.

"Q. What were the circumstances under which you permitted him to take it?

"A. Well,—"

After having so testified, appellant was then asked:

"Q. You may relate the conversation with him, if there was such conversation.

"A. I asked him if he had all the cars necessary for his trip to Paris the next day. He said he needed one more. I said that he might use mine if he drove it. That was the extent of it."

While it appears that appellant first testified that she permitted Russell Garst to use her car and also that she loaned it to him, it further appears that when she was immediately afterward asked to state the conversation she had with the coach about the matter, she stated that she asked him if he had all the cars necessary for the trip to Paris the next day, that he said he needed one more, that she said he might use her car if he drove it, and, finally, she said that that was the extent of it. It is clear, then, that appellant intended, in relating the conversation she had with the coach, to state the circumstances fully, because, after having testified to the conversation, she concluded by saying, "That was the extent of it." Thus she gave the jury to understand that those were the circumstances, and all of the circumstances, under which Russell Garst drove her car to the football game. If the appellant fully and correctly related the conversation she had with the coach and the circumstances under which he drove her car, as she unquestionably undertook to, and did, do, it follows that, as a matter of fact, she did not say anything whatever to him about loaning her car and he said nothing whatever to her about borrowing it.

We therefore conclude the evidence sufficiently supports the finding of the jury that the relationship of principal and agent existed between appellant and Russell Garst.

. . .

During the course of the closing argument of counsel for respondent, an objection was made by counsel for appellant to certain remarks addressed to the jury. Thereupon the trial court ordered a brief recess and took up such objection in chambers with counsel for the respective parties, whereupon the following proceedings took place outside of the presence of the jury:

> "Mr. GLENNON: What I said, your Honor, was in response to counsel's repeated charges that the plaintiff was attempting to mulch [mulct] the defendant in damages, and I stated to the jury in substance, 'That you have a right to draw on your experience as business men in determining the facts in this case, and that you know from your experience as business men that prudent automobile owners usually protect themselves against just such contingencies as are involved in this case.' "

Following that statement by Senator Glennon, counsel for appellant agreed it was substantially correct. Upon returning to the courtroom, the trial judge denied appellant's motion for a mistrial and then instructed the reporter to read the above quoted remarks to the jury, after which the court instructed the jury to disregard the remarks.

Appellant contends that the trial court erred in denying her motion for a mistrial.

Funk & Wagnalls New Standard Dictionary defines the word mulct: "1. To sentence to a pecuniary penalty or forfeiture as a punishment; fine; hence, to fine unjustly, as, to mulct the prisoner in $100. 2. To punish." Appellant had testified during the trial that she volunteered the use of her car. To charge, then, that respondent was attempting to "mulct" her in damages carried the inference that respondent was attempting to punish her in damages for having volunteered the use of her car for the commendable purpose of supplying additional transportation for the home town football team.

And it will be noted that Mr. Glennon stated, and the record shows no denial, that the above-quoted remarks were made by him only in response to repeated charges by appellant's counsel that respondent was attempting to mulct appellant in damages. There is no evidence whatever in the record justifying such charges. They were made during the course of the argument of counsel for appellant, and were as fully and clearly outside the record as the remarks of counsel for respondent. It was a case of meeting improper argument with improper argument. The remarks complained of were provoked by the conduct of counsel for appellant. Hence, we conclude that appellant has no just cause for complaint. Having reached that conclusion, we find it unnecessary to review the cases cited by counsel for the respective parties.

. . .

The judgments and orders are affirmed with costs to respondents.

■ BUDGE, J., dissenting.—I am unable to concur in the majority opinion.

As I read the entire record there is a total lack of evidence to support the allegation in the complaint that Garst was the agent of appellant Doty at or prior to the time of the accident in which respondent Richard Gorton was injured and as such agent was acting within the scope of his authority. An agent is one who acts for another by authority from him, one who undertakes to transact business or manage some affair for another by authority and on account of the latter. (Moreland v. Mason, 45 Idaho 143, 260 P. 1035.) Agency means more than mere passive permission. It involves request, instruction or command. (Klee v. United States, 53 F.2d 58.) . . . As I read the record [Ms. Doty] simply loaned her car to Garst to enable him to furnish means of transportation for the team from Soda Springs to Paris. It was nothing more or less than a kindly gesture on her part to be helpful to Garst, the athletic coach, in arranging transportation for the team. The mere fact that she stated to Garst that he should drive the car was a mere precaution upon her part that the car should not be driven by any one of the young boys, a perfectly natural thing for her to do. It is principally and particularly upon this statement of fact that the majority opinion holds that the relationship of principal and agent was created and that Garst became the agent of Miss Doty, authorized by her to undertake the transportation of the boys from Soda Springs to Paris for her and on her behalf. In other words, Miss Doty is held legally liable for each and every act done or performed by Garst as though she had been personally present and personally performed each and every act that was done or performed by Garst, this in the absence of any contractual relationship between her and Garst or between her and the school district. The rule would seem to be that one who borrows a car for his own use is a gratuitous bailee and not an agent of the owner. (Gochee v. Wagner, 257 N.Y. 344, 178 N.E. 553.). . . .

I am also of the opinion the judgment should be reversed because of the prejudicial remarks of one of counsel for respondent while making his closing argument to the jury as follows:

"That you have a right to draw on your experience as business men in determining the facts in this case and what you know from your experience as business men that prudent automobile owners usually protect themselves against just such contingencies as are involved in this case."

Upon the making of the above-quoted remarks by respondent's counsel appellant moved for a mistrial basing his motion upon the theory that they suggested that the appellant was carrying insurance and would not have to pay any judgment the jury might render, and, that there was no evidence to support such a theory. The court refused to declare a mistrial but directed counsel for respondent not to argue the point further and directed the jury to disregard that part of counsel's argument. However, the prejudicial effect of the remarks was not cured by the court instructing the jury to disregard that part of counsel's argument. Nothing can be gleaned from the remarks made by learned counsel other than that he, intentionally or otherwise, clearly and unmistakably impressed upon the minds of the jurors that appellant carried insurance on her car and that she personally would not be called upon to pay any verdict that might be rendered against her. Error for injecting the question of insurance in a case of this character is quite clearly stated in [citing numerous authorities]. . . .

The judgment should be reversed and the cause remanded for further proceedings as herein indicated.

ANALYSIS

1. **Definition or Application.** The dissent obviously disagreed with the majority as to the existence of an agency relationship between Doty and the Coach. Did the dissent disagree as to the test to be applied or merely as to the way in which the test should be applied?

2. **Necessity of Contract.** The majority stated: "It is not essential . . . that there be a contract between principal and agent." What did the court mean by that?

3. **Implications.** Suppose that you were Ms. Doty's attorney and that a few months after the decision was handed down she stopped by your office. She tells you that the new football coach wants to use her car to take some players to another game. She asks for your advice as to how

she could avoid liability in the event of an accident. What do you tell her?

4. **Judicial Purpose.** Was the court using agency concepts to impose liability on the alleged principal in order to achieve some desired outcome? If so, what policy outcome was the court trying to implement?

MJ & Partners Restaurant Limited Partnership v. Zadikoff

10 F.Supp.2d 922 (N.D.Ill.1998).

Plaintiffs MJ & Partners Restaurant Limited Partnership (MJ & Partners) and 23 Food, Inc. (23 Food) filed their original complaint against defendant David Zadikoff (Zadikoff) seeking injunctive and monetary relief for alleged acts of trademark infringement in violation of the Lanham Act, 15 U.S.C. § 1125(a) (Count I), . . . [and] breach of fiduciary duty (Count V). At issue is Zadikoff's motion to dismiss the original complaint under Fed.R.Civ.P. 12(b)(6).[1]

Background

. . .

[Michael] Jordan is a resident of Illinois and president of plaintiff Jump, a District of Columbia corporation with its principal place of business in Illinois. 23 Food, Inc. (23 Food) is an Illinois corporation with its principal place of business in Illinois. MJ & Partners is an Illinois limited partnership with its principal place of business in Illinois. Zadikoff is an individual residing and conducting business in this judicial district.

Jump and 23 Food are signatories to a restaurant license agreement dated September 12, 1990 (restaurant license agreement). The agreement grants 23 Food the right to use Jordan's name, likeness, voice, and persona (collectively, Name), providing in relevant part as follows:

> Subject to the terms and conditions hereinafter set forth, Jump hereby grants to [23] Food, and Food hereby accepts from Jump, the exclusive right and license in the Chicago metropolitan area (herein defined as in the Cook, Lake, DuPage, Will, Kane and McHenry Counties, Illinois) to use the Name directly or through a partnership, joint venture or other entity of which Food is a partner, joint venturer, owner, or other equity holder (a

[1] After the original complaint was filed, plaintiff-intervenors Michael Jordan (Jordan) and Jump, Inc. (Jump) filed a complaint seeking declaratory judgment. In our February 25, 1998 memorandum and order, we granted Jump's summary judgment motion, declaring that under the terms of the restaurant licensing agreements, Jump was entitled to withhold approval of the opening of additional restaurants in Chicago based on the Name. Thereafter, plaintiffs filed an amended complaint adding Jordan and Jump as defendants, including a seventh count for declaratory judgment against them, and adding additional specific allegations. . . .

"Restaurant Entity") to own and operate the Restaurant Business.

The restaurant license agreement further stated that Jump "will not take any action or enter into any new agreements in the restaurant industry that in any manner violates or interferes with the rights granted to Food by Jump hereunder." MJ & Partners is a sublicensee under the agreement. Jump and 23 Food also entered into a side agreement dated September 12, 1990, that supplements the restaurant license agreement. This agreement states that

> during the term of the Restaurant License Agreement neither Jump nor any of its affiliates shall grant, sell, assign or otherwise entitle any person, firm, corporation or other entity the right to open any restaurant based on the Name within Cook, Lake, DuPage, Will, Kane and McHenry Counties, Illinois.

In April 1993, plaintiffs opened Michael Jordan's Restaurant at the corner of LaSalle and Illinois Streets in Chicago. The restaurant has become one of the most visited tourist attractions in Chicago and Jordan has personally received significant monetary benefits in the form of royalty payments, pursuant to the restaurant licensing agreement. Based on the success of the restaurant plaintiffs have been planning to open several additional restaurants and nightclubs based on the Name in the Chicago metropolitan area, which they believe could result in sales of approximately 60 to 80 million dollars per year.

Since its opening, Zadikoff has performed the duties of chief executive for Michael Jordan's Restaurant.[2] Zadikoff's responsibilities include, but are not limited to, determining the hours of operation, selecting vendors and suppliers, determining the restaurant's menu, selecting prices for goods and services, setting labor policies (including wages, hiring, supervising, assigning, promoting, and discharging of employees), formulating marketing and advertising plans, establishing quarterly and annual budgets, handling on-site relations with private investors and relations with celebrities, and planning promotional events. Zadikoff also has the authority to sign corporate checks on the restaurant's bank accounts.

As chief executive, Zadikoff received the following information: the price and cost to plaintiffs of products and goods purchased from suppliers for the restaurant, the sales and employee history of the restaurant and retail store, the terms and conditions offered by suppliers

---

[2] Of course, Zadikoff disputes this characterization, claiming the contracts that govern his employment (which should be incorporated as part of plaintiffs' complaint) demonstrate that he is merely an independent contractor. However, since Zadikoff raises this argument as part of his substantive response to plaintiffs' breach of fiduciary duty claim, we will address it below as we evaluate the merits of the motion to dismiss.

from which plaintiffs purchased products, the gross profit for every item sold in the restaurant, the restaurant's revenues and expenses, financing agreements, the list of investors in 23 Food and MJ & Partners, the restaurant's marketing plans, and special customer relationships.

Plaintiffs allege that while continuing to work on behalf of Michael Jordan's Restaurant, Zadikoff has made plans with Jordan to open a new restaurant in Chicago using the Name. According to plaintiffs this restaurant is to be located at 160 North Loomis Street in Chicago (hereinafter referred to as the Loomis restaurant). The ownership of the Loomis restaurant is structured in the following way. Jordan and Jump own 100 percent of JCI, L.L.C. (JCI), a Delaware limited liability company. Jump and JCI own 100 percent of Treadwater, L.L.C. (Treadwater), a Delaware limited liability company which owns the land and the building where the Loomis restaurant is located. Treadwater leased the building where the Loomis restaurant is located to Emanon, L.L.C. (Emanon), a Delaware limited liability company. Emanon is owned 95 percent by Jump and JCI, and 5 percent by Cornerstone Management & Consulting, Inc. (Cornerstone). Zadikoff is the chairman of Cornerstone and has absolute discretion to act on behalf of Cornerstone in connection with its dealings with Jordan. Emanon entered into a management agreement with Cornerstone to provide and control the overall management of the Loomis restaurant.

. . .

Plaintiffs allege that Zadikoff has taken the following actions with respect to the Loomis restaurant: he initiated a "whispering campaign" regarding the opening of the Loomis restaurant in Chicago; he released information to the media regarding the opening of the Loomis restaurant; he and Jordan once intended to name the restaurant "Restaurant J"; and he and Jordan strategically selected the Ogden Avenue location to benefit from its proximity to the United Center, home of the Chicago Bulls, the large number of sports fans that use that thoroughfare to the United Center from the north and northwest, the location's neighbor, Hoops, a highly regarded basketball facility used regularly by visiting NBA teams, and its proximity to the James Jordan Boys Club. Plaintiffs further allege that Zadikoff and Jordan plan to utilize the Name in the following ways: by serving "Carolina Style Food," to take advantage of the fact that Jordan is from North Carolina; by modeling the Loomis restaurant after other celebrity-owned restaurants such as "Georgia" in Los Angeles, which is owned by a retired NBA star; by having Jordan personally appear to promote the restaurant, and displaying Jordan's name on a publicly-displayed personal humidor inside the restaurant; and by making Jordan's vehicles, many of which bear vanity license plates, "clearly visible" outside the Loomis restaurant when Jordan is visiting.

NOTE

Jordan's position was that under the terms of the contract, despite the fact that MJ & Partners had the exclusive right to use his name in the Chicago metropolitan area, it could not open any additional restaurants without his approval, and that he could withhold approval without any justification or reason. The court agreed. MJ & Partners Restaurant Limited v. Zadikoff, 995 F.Supp. 929 (N.D.Ill.1998). So Jordan could not open a restaurant using his name (since MJ & Partners had the exclusive right), nor could MJ & Partners (since Jordan refused to approve).

Plaintiffs have not consented to the use of the Name in connection with any restaurant other than Michael Jordan's Restaurant. Plaintiffs have demanded that Zadikoff cease his activities with respect to the Loomis restaurant, but Zadikoff has not done so.

Discussion

[The court dismisses the Lanham Act claim. The Lanham Act is a federal statute that provides, in the court's words, "a cause of action to plaintiffs who believe that another person's use of the same mark will likely cause confusion as to the affiliation of that person with the plaintiff." The court concludes that there is "no likelihood of confusion" in this case between the two restaurants. It is the Lanham Act that supplied federal jurisdiction. At the end of the opinion, after considering the pendant state-law causes of action, the court states, "we question whether we continue to have subject matter jurisdiction since we have dismissed plaintiffs' Lanham Act claim. Although we do not decide that issue here, we note that a dismissal of plaintiffs' case without prejudice might require them to revisit their state law claims in state court under the state's separate pleading standards."]

Count V alleges a claim for breach of fiduciary duty. Specifically, plaintiffs allege that as "Chief Executive of Michael Jordan's Restaurant, with access to and knowledge of confidential and proprietary information." Zadikoff owed plaintiffs fiduciary duties which he breached by (1) appropriating plaintiffs' trade secrets for use in connection with the Loomis restaurant, (2) soliciting plaintiffs' private partners to invest in the Loomis restaurant, (3) soliciting employees of Michael Jordan's Restaurant to work at the Loomis restaurant, and (4) by using Michael Jordan's Restaurant to meet with plaintiffs' partners and employees to discuss the Loomis restaurant venture.

In Illinois, certain relationships are considered fiduciary relationships as a matter of law. . . . One such relationship is that of principal and agent. To determine whether an agency relationship exists the court must consider two factors: (1) whether the principal has the right to control the manner and method in which agent performs his services, and (2) whether the agent has the power to subject the principal to personal liability. . . .

Zadikoff argues that plaintiffs cannot state a claim for breach of fiduciary duty because they cannot establish that he is plaintiffs' agent. Specifically, he argues that he is an independent contractor to an unrelated limited partnership responsible for running plaintiffs' restaurant and, as such, cannot be held to have any fiduciary relationship with plaintiffs. Zadikoff strenuously objects to plaintiffs' characterization of him as the "Chief Executive" of Michael Jordan's Restaurant and argues instead that the contracts governing his relationship with plaintiffs clearly demonstrate that he is an independent contractor.

[Certain management] contracts indicate that plaintiffs entered into a Restaurant Management Agreement with RMI Limited Partnership (RMI), which is affiliated with Hyatt Corporation (Hyatt). This agreement appoints RMI as "the sole and exclusive management agent of Owner for the Restaurant" and grants to RMI the "sole and exclusive fight to manage and operate the Restaurant pursuant to the terms of this Agreement." The agreement further provided that RMI may not operate or manage any other restaurant "incorporating a sports or sports celebrity theme" within a one-mile radius of plaintiffs' restaurant. Hyatt, on behalf of RMI, entered into a Consulting and Administrative Services Agreement with Cornerstone Management & Consulting, Inc. (Cornerstone), which states that Cornerstone is an "independent consultant" that is to provide "consulting, administrative and other services" to RMI (among other "Hyatt Entities"). Zadikoff is a principal of Cornerstone.

On the basis of these contracts Zadikoff asserts that he is simply an independent contractor for RMI and has no direct contractual relationship with plaintiffs—certainly not one pursuant to which he acts as "Chief Executive" of Michael Jordan's Restaurant. However, the existence of an agency relationship is determined based on the actual practices of the parties, and not merely by reference to a written agreement. . . . Plaintiffs allege that Zadikoff had significant responsibilities in managing Michael Jordan's Restaurant, including determining hours of operation, selecting vendors and suppliers, determining the menu, setting prices, establishing labor policies and the restaurant's budget, and signing corporate checks. We cannot say that these allegations are insufficient as a matter of law to establish the existence of an agency relationship. Whether or not Zadikoff actually carried out these duties, the degree of control plaintiffs exerted over his actions, and the extent to which these actions could be imputed to plaintiffs for the purposes of determining liability, are factual issues that should not be resolved on a motion to dismiss.

Zadikoff's argument that the contracts contradict plaintiffs' complaint and clearly establish that plaintiffs did not exert the requisite degree of control is unavailing. That the contracts defined the scope of

Cornerstone's authority as limited to "consulting, administrative and other services" does not demonstrate the authority plaintiffs actually reposed in Zadikoff or how much plaintiffs supervised Zadikoff on a day-to-day basis. We thus find that the contracts, while shedding light on the relationship between Zadikoff and plaintiffs, do not contradict the allegations contained in plaintiffs' complaint, which we are obligated to accept as true for the purposes of this motion.

We also refuse to dismiss Count V based on Zadikoff's argument that he was merely a "subagent" whose duties to plaintiffs were limited by the terms of the Restaurant Management Agreement with RMI. It is true, as Zadikoff notes, that a subagent "stands in a fiduciary relation to the principal, and is subject to all the liabilities of an agent to the principal. . . ." Restatement (Second) of Agency § 5(1) cmt. d. On this basis Zadikoff argues that his duty to plaintiffs could have been no greater than RMI's duty to plaintiffs. Thus, Zadikoff claims that he was only limited by RMI's promise not to open a sports-theme restaurant within one mile of Michael Jordan's Restaurant. Because the Loomis restaurant is outside this one-mile radius, he claims that he has not violated any rights he owed to plaintiffs as a subagent. However, we do not think that, on the basis of the factual allegations detailing Zadikoff's myriad responsibilities, we can say that plaintiffs could prove no set of facts that would support their claim that Zadikoff was plaintiffs' agent, despite the parties' contractual arrangement. . . . Again, it is conceivable that Zadikoff's actual relationship with plaintiffs took the form of an agency relationship, even though the contractual language would indicate otherwise. Accordingly, we deny Zadikoff's motion to dismiss Count V.

. . .

AFTERMATH

The LaSalle Street restaurant (called "Michael Jordan's Restaurant"), lasted 14 years, then, lacking Michael Jordan's support, in 2012 it shut down. The North Loomis restaurant (called "160 Blue," after a play used by the Bulls) is still (as of 2018) in business. Unlike the tourist attraction on LaSalle Street, it is decidedly upscale and expensive.

ANALYSIS

1. **Nature of Relationship—Jordan and MJ & Partners.** What seems to be the practical or economic relationship between Michael Jordan and MJ & Partners? What is the legal relationship?

2. **Nature of Relationship—Zadikoff and MJ & Partners.** What seems to be the practical or economic relationship between Zadikoff and MJ & Partners? What is the legal relationship? What is the chain of entities between the two?

3. **Evidence Necessary.** What evidence should MJ & Partners hope to produce to recover ultimately against Zadikoff?

Rose v. Giamatti

721 F. Supp. 906 (S.D. Ohio 1989).

Plaintiff, Peter Edward Rose, is the Field Manager of the Cincinnati Reds baseball team. In February of this year, then Commissioner of Baseball Peter V. Ueberroth and then Commissioner of Baseball-elect A. Bartlett Giamatti initiated an investigation regarding allegations that Rose wagered on major league baseball games. . . . Commissioner Giamatti ultimately scheduled a hearing concerning the allegations for June 26, 1989.

In an effort to prevent Commissioner Giamatti from conducting the June 26 hearing, Rose filed an action in the Court of Common Pleas of Hamilton County, Ohio, on June 19, 1989, seeking a temporary restraining order and preliminary injunction against the pending disciplinary proceedings. Named as defendants in that action were A. Bartlett Giamatti, Major League Baseball, and the Cincinnati Reds. The crux of the complaint[1] is Rose's contention that he is being denied the right to a fair hearing on the gambling allegations by an unbiased decisionmaker. The complaint requests permanent injunctive relief, which, if granted, would prevent Commissioner Giamatti from ever conducting a hearing to determine whether Rose has engaged in gambling activities in violation of the Rules of Major League Baseball. Rose asks that the Court of Common Pleas of Hamilton County, Ohio determine whether he has wagered on major league baseball games, including those of the Cincinnati Reds. . . .

On July 5, 1989, Rose filed a motion to remand this action to the Court of Common Pleas of Hamilton County, Ohio, asserting that there is a lack of complete diversity of citizenship between himself and the defendants . . . .

The United States district courts are courts of limited jurisdiction, and the federal statute permitting removal of cases filed in state court restricts the types of cases which may be removed from state court to federal court. . . . Defendant Giamatti contends in his notice of removal that the district court has original jurisdiction of this action by virtue of . . . "diversity" jurisdiction. . . . If diversity of citizenship is found to exist among the parties to this action and none of the defendants in interest properly joined and served is a citizen of Ohio, then the action is properly

---

1 The complaint alleges seven causes of action based upon state law claims of breach of contract, breach of an implied covenant of good faith and fair dealing, breach of fiduciary duty, promissory estoppel, tortious interference with contract, negligence, and the common law of "due process and natural justice."

removable from the state court. If the required diversity of citizenship does not exist, then the action is not properly removable and must be remanded to the state court.

With regard to the citizenship of the parties to this controversy, the complaint contains the following allegations concerning their identity and citizenship. Rose is alleged to be a resident of Hamilton County, Ohio. Commissioner Giamatti's residence is not stated in the complaint; in the notice of removal, however, he is alleged to be a citizen of the State of New York. Defendant Major League Baseball is alleged in the complaint to be an unincorporated association headquartered in New York and consisting of the two principal professional baseball leagues (National and American) and their twenty-six professional baseball clubs. The Cincinnati Reds, dba the Cincinnati Reds Baseball Club, is identified in the complaint as an Ohio limited partnership (hereinafter referred to in the singular as the "Cincinnati Reds"). . . .

NOTE

For purposes of diversity jurisdiction, both a limited partnership and an unincorporated association are considered to be citizens of each state in which one or more of its partners or members are citizens.

In the present case, it appears from the allegations of the complaint that defendant Cincinnati Reds and defendant Major League Baseball are citizens of the same state as plaintiff Rose. . . . [The court determined that the Ohio citizenship of the Cincinnati Reds could be disregarded, because the Reds were a nominal defendant whose interests were not adverse to those of Rose. In order to determine whether the Ohio citizenship of Major League Baseball likewise could be disregarded, the court was obliged to examine the nature of the relationship between Major League Baseball and its Commissioner. In particular, if Commissioner Giamatti's conduct could result in liability on the part of Major League Baseball to Rose, Major League Baseball would not be a mere nominal defendant and its Ohio citizenship thus would preclude removal of the case to federal court.]

. . .

If Major League Baseball were a typical unincorporated association, its jurisdictional status would be more easily determined. The reality, however, is that Major League Baseball is a unique organization. A brief history of the background of the Major League Agreement and the extraordinary powers vested in the Commissioner by the association is set forth in Charles O. Finley & Co., Inc. v. Kuhn, 569 F.2d 527 (7th Cir.), cert. denied, 439 U.S. 876, 99 S.Ct. 214, 58 L.Ed.2d 190 (1978).

> Prior to 1921, professional baseball was governed by a three-man National Commission formed in 1903 which consisted of the presidents of the National and American Leagues and a

third member, usually one of the club owners, selected by the presidents of the two leagues. Between 1915 and 1921, a series of events and controversies contributed to a growing dissatisfaction with the National Commission on the part of players, owners and the public, and a demand developed for the establishment of a single, independent Commissioner of baseball.

On September 28, 1920, an indictment issued charging that an effort had been made to 'fix' the 1919 World Series by several Chicago White Sox players. Popularly known as the 'Black Sox Scandal,' this event rocked the game of professional baseball and proved the catalyst that brought about the establishment of a single, neutral Commissioner of baseball.

In November, 1920, the major league club owners unanimously elected federal Judge Kenesaw Mountain Landis as the sole Commissioner of baseball and appointed a committee of owners to draft a charter setting forth the Commissioner's authority. In one of the drafting sessions an attempt was made to place limitations on the Commissioner's authority. Judge Landis responded by refusing to accept the office of Commissioner.

On January 12, 1921, Landis told a meeting of club owners that he had agreed to accept the position upon the clear understanding that the owners had sought 'an authority . . . outside of your own business, and that a part of that authority would be a control over whatever and whoever had to do with baseball.' Thereupon, the owners voted unanimously to reject the proposed limitation upon the Commissioner's authority, they all signed what they called the Major League Agreement, and Judge Landis assumed the position of Commissioner. . . . The agreement, a contract between the constituent clubs of the National and American Leagues, is the basic charter under which major league baseball operates.

The Major League Agreement provides that '[t]he functions of the Commissioner shall be . . . to investigate . . . any act, transaction or practice . . . not in the best interests of the national game of Baseball' and 'to determine . . . what preventive, remedial or punitive action is appropriate in the premises, and to take such action. . . .' Art. I, Sec. 2(a) and (b).

The Major League Rules, which govern many aspects of the game of baseball, are promulgated by vote of major league club owners. . . .

The Major Leagues and their constituent clubs severally agreed to be bound by the decisions of the Commissioner and by the

> discipline imposed by him. They further agreed to 'waive such right of recourse to the courts as would otherwise have existed in their favor.' Major League Agreement, Art. VII, Sec. 2.

Id. at 532–33 (footnotes omitted). . . .

The Commissioner's jurisdiction under the Major League Agreement to investigate violations of Major League Rules, or any activity he believes is "not in the best interests" of baseball, is exclusive. The major leagues and the twenty-six major league clubs have absolutely no control over such an investigation or the manner in which the Commissioner conducts it.[10] Rose does not challenge any provision of the Major League Agreement or the Major League Rules, including the rule prohibiting wagering on major league baseball games, nor does he challenge the Commissioner's authority under Article I, Section 2(e) of the Major League Agreement to promulgate his own rules of procedure dealing with investigations of suspected violations of the Major League Rules. What Rose challenges is Commissioner Giamatti's conduct of the investigation and disciplinary proceedings in his particular case. In short, Rose's controversy is not with Major League Baseball, but is with the office of the Commissioner of Baseball for the Commissioner's alleged failure to follow his own procedural rules in conducting the investigation of Rose's alleged gambling activities. Clearly, complete relief can be afforded with regard to the primary relief sought in the complaint-preventing Commissioner Giamatti from conducting a disciplinary hearing-without the need for any order against Major League Baseball or its constituent major league professional baseball clubs.

There is nothing in Rose's contract with the Cincinnati Reds or in the Major League Agreement which gives to the Cincinnati Reds or any other member of Major League Baseball any right, much less a duty, to prevent the Commissioner from conducting hearings concerning conduct "deemed by the Commissioner not to be in the best interests of Baseball." Major League Agreement, Art. I, Sec 3. The Major League Agreement empowers the Commissioner to formulate his own rules of procedure which, as previously noted, are not a part of the Major League Agreement, the Major League Rules, or Rose's contract with the Cincinnati Reds. Accordingly, disregard of those procedural rules by the Commissioner, while it may be the basis for an action against the Commissioner, would not impose contractual liability on the Cincinnati Reds or the other members of Major League Baseball based on either the Major League Agreement or Rose's own contract.

Rose contends that Commissioner Giamatti, in conducting disciplinary proceedings, is acting as the agent for Major League

[10] One indicia of the complete independence of the Commissioner is Art. IX of the Major League Agreement, which provides that neither the Commissioner's powers nor his compensation may be diminished during the term of his office.

Baseball, and that Major League Baseball is therefore liable for any violation of a duty owed by the Commissioner to Rose to follow his own procedural rules. If Major League Baseball were a typical business organization, Rose's contention might have merit. However, as noted in the *Finley* case, "baseball cannot be analogized to any other business. . . . Baseball's management through a commissioner is . . . an exception, anomaly and aberration. . . ." 569 F.2d at 537. Whatever other activity the Commissioner may be authorized to perform as an agent on behalf of Major League Baseball, it is clear that with regard to disciplinary matters, the major league baseball clubs have made the Commissioner totally independent of their control. Under the Major League Agreement, the Commissioner's status with respect to disciplinary matters is analogous to that of an independent contractor, a person employed by Major League Baseball to act as an arbitrator and judge independent of any control by the members of Major League Baseball. Under Ohio law, it is clear that a party cannot be held liable for the conduct of such a person over whom the party has no control.

. . .

The Court recognizes, of course, that in this case it was Major League Baseball itself that placed the conduct of the Commissioner beyond the scope of its control, and had Rose not agreed to this unique delegation of absolute authority to the Commissioner, his claim against Major League Baseball might have some substance. It is undisputed, however, that the Major League Agreement, which deprives its members of control over the Commissioner in disciplinary matters and requires that its members "be finally and unappealably bound by [all actions taken by the Commissioner under the authority of the Agreement] and severally waive such right of recourse to the courts as would otherwise have existed in their favor," is incorporated as a part of Rose's contract with the Cincinnati Reds, and Rose necessarily has agreed to its terms and conditions.

. . . As neutral bystanders to the battle between Rose and the Commissioner which is the subject of this action, the member clubs of Major League Baseball have no legal interest in the controversy, and at most would be considered to be nominal parties for the purpose of determining diversity of citizenship. . . . Therefore, the citizenship of Major League Baseball may be disregarded for diversity purposes . . ., diversity of citizenship exists between Rose, a citizen of Ohio, and Commissioner Giamatti, a citizen of New York, and . . . the action was properly removable from the Court of Common Pleas of Hamilton County, Ohio. . . .

AFTERMATH

There is little doubt that Pete Rose was one of Major League Baseball's greatest players. He still holds career records for hits and games played, among others, and is among the all-time leaders in such statistics as runs, doubles, hitting streaks, and all-star appearances. He had 10 seasons with 200 or more hits (the most ever) and led the league in various hitting statistics numerous times, including seven season hitting titles and five doubles titles.

Following the court's decision, in August 1989, Rose and Commissioner Giamatti entered into a settlement pursuant to which Rose agreed to a lifetime ban from baseball. In response, the Baseball Hall of Fame adopted a rule stating that individuals banned from baseball are ineligible for induction into the Hall. In 2004, Rose admitted to having bet on baseball games, including having bet on the Reds, while denying that he ever bet against the Reds. As of this writing (mid-2006), he remains banned from baseball and from the Hall of Fame.

ANALYSIS

1. **Implications of Contract.** Two parties enter into a contract that expressly states "A is not the agent of B." Does *Rose* stand for the proposition that, as against third parties, A is not B's agent as a matter of law? Suppose that the contract instead expressly stated that "Y has no power or right to control the actions of Z pursuant to this contract" and that the contract in fact denied Y any meaningful power to control Z. Does Rose stand for the proposition that, as against third parties, Z is not Y's agent as a matter of law?

2. **Extent of Control.** It doesn't take a lot of control by the principal in order for an agency relationship to exist. A "principal need not exercise physical control over the actions of its agent" so long as the principal may direct "the result or ultimate objectives of the agent relationship." Green v. H & R Block, Inc., 735 A.2d 1039, 1050 (Md. 1999). Hence, for example, the requisite level of control may be found so long as the principal is able to specify the task the agent is to perform, even if the principal is unable to ensure that the agent carries out that task. In determining whether Giamatti was an agent of Major League Baseball, should the court have focused narrowly on the question of whether Major League Baseball had the power to control Giamatti's actions in disciplining players? Put another way, can Giamatti be Major League Baseball's agent for some purposes and not for others?

3. **Alternative Arrangements.** Suppose that, under the Major League Agreement, the teams could at any time by majority vote amend the agreement to restrict or eliminate the Commissioner's exclusive jurisdiction over disciplinary matters. Would that change the result in this case? Alternatively, suppose that, under the Major League

Agreement, the teams could at any time by majority vote terminate the Commissioner with or without cause. Would that change the result?

INTRODUCTORY NOTE

In the next case, A. Gay Jenson Farms Co. v. Cargill, Inc., the context is that of a creditor exercising control over its debtors after the debtor has experienced financial difficulties. The plaintiffs were farmers who sold their grain crops to Warren Grain & Seed Co. (Warren). Warren was a local firm that operated a grain elevator (a storage facility). Cargill is a large, worldwide dealer in grain. On Cargill's view of the facts, Warren bought grain from the farmers and sold it to Cargill. On the farmers' view of the facts, Warren bought grain as an agent for Cargill. Warren became insolvent without having paid the farmers for their grain and they sued Cargill. The case offers a nice illustration of a legal issue of considerable importance to business firms like Cargill that provide trade credit to other firms, as well as to banks and other financial intermediaries.

A. Gay Jenson Farms Co. v. Cargill, Inc.

309 N.W.2d 285 (Minn.1981).

Plaintiffs, 86 individual, partnership or corporate farmers, brought this action against defendant Cargill, Inc. (Cargill) and defendant Warren Grain & Seed Co. (Warren) to recover losses sustained when Warren defaulted on the contracts made with plaintiffs for the sale of grain. After a trial by jury, judgment was entered in favor of plaintiffs, and Cargill brought this appeal. We affirm.

This case arose out of the financial collapse of defendant Warren Seed & Grain Co., and its failure to satisfy its indebtedness to plaintiffs. Warren, which was located in Warren, Minnesota, was operated by Lloyd Hill and his son, Gary Hill. Warren operated a grain elevator and as a result was involved in the purchase of . . . grain from local farmers. The cash grain would be resold through the Minneapolis Grain Exchange or to the terminal grain companies directly. Warren also stored grain for farmers and sold chemicals, fertilizer and steel storage bins. In addition, it operated a seed business which involved buying seed grain from farmers, processing it and reselling it for seed to farmers and local elevators.

Lloyd Hill decided in 1964 to apply for financing from Cargill. Cargill's officials from the Moorhead regional office investigated Warren's operations and recommended that Cargill finance Warren.

Warren and Cargill thereafter entered into a security agreement which provided that Cargill would loan money for working capital to Warren on "open account" financing up to a stated limit, which was originally set as $175,000.[2] Under this contract, Warren would receive funds and pay its expenses by issuing drafts drawn on Cargill through Minneapolis banks. The drafts were imprinted with both Warren's and Cargill's names. Proceeds from Warren's sales would be deposited with Cargill and credited to its account. In return for this financing, Warren appointed Cargill as its grain agent for transaction with the Commodity Credit Corporation. Cargill was also given a right of first refusal to purchase market grain sold by Warren to the terminal market.

A new contract was negotiated in 1967, extending Warren's credit line to $300,000 and incorporating the provisions of the original contract. It was also stated in the contract that Warren would provide Cargill with annual financial statements and that either Cargill would keep the books for Warren or an audit would be conducted by an independent firm. Cargill was given the right of access to Warren's books for inspection.

In addition, the agreement provided that Warren was not to make capital improvements or repairs in excess of $5,000 without Cargill's prior consent. Further, it was not to become liable as guarantor on another's indebtedness, or encumber its assets except with Cargill's permission. Consent by Cargill was required before Warren would be allowed to declare a dividend or sell and purchase stock.

Officials from Cargill's regional office made a brief visit to Warren shortly after the agreement was executed. They examined the annual statement and the accounts receivable, expenses, inventory, seed, machinery and other financial matters. Warren was informed that it would be reminded periodically to make the improvements recommended by Cargill.[3] At approximately this time, a memo was given to the Cargill official in charge of the Warren account, Erhart Becker, which stated in part: "This organization [Warren] needs *very strong* paternal guidance."

In 1970, Cargill contracted with Warren and other elevators to act as its agent to seek growers for a new type of wheat called Bounty 208. Warren, as Cargill's agent for this project, entered into contracts for the growing of the wheat seed, with Cargill named as the contracting party. Farmers were paid directly by Cargill for the seed and all contracts were performed in full. In 1971, pursuant to an agency contract, Warren contracted on Cargill's behalf with various farmers for the growing of sunflower seeds for Cargill. The arrangements were similar to those made in the Bounty 208 contracts, and all those contracts were also

---

[2] Loans were secured by a second mortgage on Warren's real estate and a first chattel mortgage on its inventories of grain and merchandise in the sum of $175,000 with 7% interest. . . .

[3] Cargill headquarters suggested that the regional office check Warren monthly. Also, it was requested that Warren be given an explanation for the relatively large withdrawals from undistributed earnings made by the Hills, since Cargill hoped that Warren's profits would be used to decrease its debt balance. Cargill asked for written requests for withdrawals from undistributed earnings in the future.

completed. Both these agreements were unrelated to the open account financing contract. In addition, Warren, as Cargill's agent in the sunflower seed business, cleaned and packaged the seed in Cargill bags.

During this period, Cargill continued to review Warren's operations and expenses and recommend that certain actions should be taken.[4] Warren purchased from Cargill various business forms printed by Cargill and received sample forms from Cargill which Warren used to develop its own business forms.

Cargill wrote to its regional office in 1970 expressing its concern that the pattern of increased use of funds allowed to develop at Warren was similar to that involved in two other cases in which Cargill experienced severe losses. Cargill did not refuse to honor drafts or call the loan, however. A new security agreement which increased the credit line to \$750,000 was executed in 1972, and a subsequent agreement which raised the limit to \$1,250,000 was entered into in 1976.

Warren was at that time shipping Cargill 90% of its . . . grain. When Cargill's facilities were full, Warren shipped its grain to other companies. Approximately 25% of Warren's total sales was seed grain which was sold directly by Warren to its customers.

As Warren's indebtedness continued to be in excess of its credit line, Cargill began to contact Warren daily regarding its financial affairs. Cargill headquarters informed its regional office in 1973 that, since Cargill money was being used, Warren should realize that Cargill had the right to make some critical decisions regarding the use of the funds. Cargill headquarters also told Warren that a regional manager would be working with Warren on a day-to-day basis as well as in monthly planning meetings. In 1975, Cargill's regional office began to keep a daily debit position on Warren. A bank account was opened in Warren's name on which Warren could draw checks in 1976. The account was to be funded by drafts drawn on Cargill by the local bank.

In early 1977, it became evident that Warren had serious financial problems. Several farmers, who had heard that Warren's checks were not being paid, inquired or had their agents inquire at Cargill regarding Warren's status and were initially told that there would be no problem with payment. In April 1977, an audit of Warren revealed that Warren was \$4 million in debt. After Cargill was informed that Warren's financial statements had been deliberately falsified, Warren's request for

[4] Between 1967 and 1973, Cargill suggested that Warren take a number of steps, including: (1) a reduction of seed grain and cash grain inventories; (2) improved collection of accounts receivable; (3) reduction or elimination of its wholesale seed business and its speciality grain operation; (4) marketing fertilizer and steel bins on consignment; (5) a reduction in withdrawals made by officers; (6) a suggestion that Warren's bookkeeper not issue her own salary checks; and (7) cooperation with Cargill in implementing the recommendations. These ideas were apparently never implemented, however.

additional financing was refused. In the final days of Warren's operation, Cargill sent an official to supervise the elevator, including disbursement of funds and income generated by the elevator.

After Warren ceased operations, it was found to be indebted to Cargill in the amount of $3.6 million. Warren was also determined to be indebted to plaintiffs in the amount of $2 million, and plaintiffs brought this action in 1977 to seek recovery of that sum. Plaintiffs alleged that Cargill was jointly liable for Warren's indebtedness as it had acted as principal for the grain elevator.

. . .

The major issue in this case is whether Cargill, by its course of dealing with Warren, became liable as a principal on contracts made by Warren with plaintiffs. Cargill contends that no agency relationship was established with Warren, notwithstanding its financing of Warren's operation and its purchase of the majority of Warren's grain. However, we conclude that Cargill, by its control and influence over Warren, became a principal with liability for the transactions entered into by its agent Warren.

Agency is the fiduciary relationship that results from the manifestation of consent by one person to another that the other shall act on his behalf and subject to his control, and consent by the other so to act. . . .

In order to create an agency there must be an agreement, but not necessarily a contract between the parties. . . . An agreement may result in the creation of an agency relationship although the parties did not call it an agency and did not intend the legal consequences of the relation to follow. The existence of the agency may be proved by circumstantial evidence which shows a course of dealing between the two parties. . . . When an agency relationship is to be proven by circumstantial evidence, the principal must be shown to have consented to the agency since one cannot be the agent of another except by consent of the latter. . . .

Cargill contends that the prerequisites of an agency relationship did not exist because Cargill never consented to the agency, Warren did not act on behalf of Cargill, and Cargill did not exercise control over Warren. We hold that all three elements of agency could be found in the particular circumstances of this case. By directing Warren to implement its recommendations, Cargill manifested its consent that Warren would be its agent. Warren acted on Cargill's behalf in procuring grain for Cargill as the part of its normal operations which were totally financed by Cargill.[7] Further, an agency relationship was established by Cargill's

[7] Although the contracts with the farmers were executed by Warren, Warren paid for the grain with drafts drawn on Cargill. While this is not in itself significant . . . it is one factor to be taken into account in analyzing the relationship between Warren and Cargill.

interference with the internal affairs of Warren, which constituted de facto control of the elevator.

A creditor who assumes control of his debtor's business may become liable as principal for the acts of the debtor in connection with the business. Restatement (Second) of Agency § 14 O (1958). It is noted in comment a to section 14 O that:

> A security holder who merely exercises a veto power over the business acts of his debtor by preventing purchases or sales above specified amounts does not thereby become a principal. However, if he takes over the management of the debtor's business either in person or through an agent, and directs what contracts may or may not be made, he becomes a principal, liable as a principal for the obligations incurred thereafter in the normal course of business by the debtor who has now become his general agent. The point at which the creditor becomes a principal is that at which he assumes de facto control over the conduct of his debtor, whatever the terms of the formal contract with his debtor may be.

A number of factors indicate Cargill's control over Warren, including the following:

> (1) Cargill's constant recommendations to Warren by telephone;
>
> (2) Cargill's right of first refusal on grain;
>
> (3) Warren's inability to enter into mortgages, to purchase stock or to pay dividends without Cargill's approval;
>
> (4) Cargill's right of entry onto Warren's premises to carry on periodic checks and audits;
>
> (5) Cargill's correspondence and criticism regarding Warren's finances, officers salaries and inventory;
>
> (6) Cargill's determination that Warren needed "strong paternal guidance";
>
> (7) Provision of drafts and forms to Warren upon which Cargill's name was imprinted;
>
> (8) Financing of all Warren's purchases of grain and operating expenses; and
>
> (9) Cargill's power to discontinue the financing of Warren's operations.

We recognize that some of these elements, as Cargill contends, are found in an ordinary debtor-creditor relationship. However, these factors cannot be considered in isolation, but, rather, they must be viewed in light of all the circumstances surrounding Cargill's aggressive financing of Warren.

It is also Cargill's position that the relationship between Cargill and Warren was that of buyer-supplier rather than principal-agent. Restatement (Second) of Agency § 14K (1958) compares an agent with a supplier as follows:

One who contracts to acquire property from a third person and convey it to another is the agent of the other only if it is agreed that he is to act primarily for the benefit of the other and not for himself.

Factors indicating that one is a supplier, rather than an agent, are:

> (1) That he is to receive a fixed price for the property irrespective of price paid by him. This is the most important. (2) That he acts in his own name and receives the title to the property which he thereafter is to transfer. (3) That he has an independent business in buying and selling similar property.

Restatement (Second) of Agency § 14K, comment a (1958).

Under the Restatement approach, it must be shown that the supplier has an independent business before it can be concluded that he is not an agent. The record establishes that all portions of Warren's operation were financed by Cargill and that Warren sold almost all of its market grain to Cargill. Thus, the relationship which existed between the parties was not merely that of buyer and supplier.

. . .

The amici curiae assert that, if the jury verdict is upheld, firms and banks which have provided business loans to county elevators will decline to make further loans. The decision in this case should give no cause for such concern. We deal here with a business enterprise markedly different from an ordinary bank financing, since Cargill was an active participant in Warren's operations rather than simply a financier. Cargill's course of dealing with Warren was, by its own admission, a paternalistic relationship in which Cargill made the key economic decisions and kept Warren in existence.

Although considerable interest was paid by Warren on the loan, the reason for Cargill's financing of Warren was not to make money as a lender but, rather, to establish a source of market grain for its business. As one Cargill manager noted, "We were staying in there because we wanted the grain." For this reason, Cargill was willing to extend the credit line far beyond the amount originally allocated to Warren. It is noteworthy that Cargill was receiving significant amounts of grain and that, notwithstanding the risk that was recognized by Cargill, the operation was considered profitable.

On the whole, there was a unique fabric in the relationship between Cargill and Warren which varies from that found in normal debtor-creditor situations. We conclude that, on the facts of this case, there was sufficient evidence from which the jury could find that Cargill was the principal of Warren within the definitions of agency set forth in Restatement (Second) of Agency §§ 1 and 14O.

NOTE

Warren, Minnesota was a town with a population of about 2,000 at the time this case was tried. Warren is located in Marshall County, which is in the northwest corner of Minnesota, on the North Dakota border, with a population of about 15,000. The plaintiffs were local farmers and the defendant was a corporate giant. The case was tried to a jury.

ANALYSIS

1. **Why Did Cargill Lend?** Why do you suppose Cargill kept extending more and more credit to Warren?
2. **What Should the Farmers Have Done?** What could the farmers have done to protect themselves from the risk of nonpayment?
3. **What Should Cargill Have Done?** What could Cargill have done to ensure that the grain it bought from Warren was paid for?
4. **Who Should Bear the Risk of Loss?** In light of your answers to questions 2 and 3, does the result in the case place responsibility for avoiding loss on the person with the lower cost of doing so?

> **PLANNING**
>
> Suppose you are Cargill's lawyer. The chief executive officer (CEO) of the company, after hearing about the decision in the case involving Warren Grain & Seed Co., asks for your recommendations about how Cargill should change the way it does business to avoid liability in the future. She also wants your views on whether, with a supplier like Warren, at the time that its financial condition became desperate, it would have been advisable for Cargill to (a) call in its loans and force the supplier into bankruptcy or (b) notify all other potential creditors that Cargill would not be liable for any purchases by the supplier. What would you say? Bear in mind that you are expected to exercise sound business, as well as legal, judgment, but that your role is to offer alternatives, not to make decisions.

5. **The Court's Test.** If Peter says to Amy, "Go out and buy a thousand bushels of corn for me and I'll pay you the usual commission," Amy is Peter's nonservant agent (that is, she acts on behalf of Peter but is not subject to his control over how the objective is achieved). Peter is bound to contracts made by Amy to buy the corn. Control of the manner in which Amy accomplishes the assignment is not an issue. In the *Cargill* case, however, there seems to have been no evidence to support that

kind of ordinary nonservant principal/agent relationship. Presumably that is why the court focuses on control and on the Restatement (Second) of Agency § 140. Examine the nine factors listed by the court as supporting a conclusion that Cargill exercised control over Warren. How, if at all, does each of these factors tend to establish a principal/agent relationship rather than a relationship of creditor to debtor or buyer to supplier?

2. LIABILITY OF PRINCIPAL TO THIRD PARTIES IN CONTRACT

A. AUTHORITY

Mill Street Church of Christ v. Hogan

785 S.W.2d 263 (Ky.1990).

Mill Street Church of Christ and State Automobile Mutual Insurance Company petition for review of a decision of the New Workers' Compensation Board [hereinafter "New Board"] which had reversed an earlier decision by the Old Workers' Compensation Board [hereinafter "Old Board"]. The Old Board had ruled that Samuel J. Hogan was not an employee of the Mill Street Church of Christ and was not entitled to any workers' compensation benefits. The New Board reversed and ruled that Samuel Hogan was an employee of the church.

. . . In 1986, the Elders of the Mill Street Church of Christ decided to hire church member, Bill Hogan, to paint the church building. The Elders decided that another church member, Gary Petty, would be hired to assist if any assistance was needed. In the past, the church had hired Bill Hogan for similar jobs, and he had been allowed to hire his brother, Sam Hogan, the respondent, as a helper. Sam Hogan had earlier been a member of the church but was no longer a member. . . .

Dr. David Waggoner, an Elder of the church, soon contacted Bill Hogan, and he accepted the job and began work. Apparently Waggoner made no mention to Bill Hogan of hiring a helper at that time. Bill Hogan painted the church by himself until he reached the baptistry portion of the church. This was a very high, difficult portion of the church to paint, and he decided that he needed help. After Bill Hogan had reached this point in his work, he discussed the matter of a helper with Dr. Waggoner at his office. According to both Dr. Waggoner and Hogan, they discussed the possibility of hiring Gary Petty to help Hogan. None of the evidence indicates that Hogan was told that he had to hire Petty. In fact, Dr. Waggoner apparently told Hogan that Petty was difficult to reach. That was basically all the discussion that these two individuals had concerning hiring a helper. None of the other Elders discussed the matter with Bill Hogan.

On December 14, 1986, Bill Hogan approached his brother, Sam, about helping him complete the job. Bill Hogan told Sam the details of the job, including the pay, and Sam accepted the job. On December 15, 1986, Sam began working. A half hour after he began, he climbed the ladder to paint a ceiling corner, and a leg of the ladder broke. Sam fell to the floor and broke his left arm. Sam was taken to the Grayson County Hospital Emergency Room where he was treated. He later was under the care of Dr. James Klinert, a surgeon in Louisville. The church Elders did not know that Bill Hogan had approached Sam Hogan to work as a helper until after the accident occurred.

After the accident, Bill Hogan reported the accident and resulting injury to Charles Payne, a church Elder and treasurer. Payne stated in a deposition that he told Bill Hogan that the church had insurance. At this time, Bill Hogan told Payne the total number of hours worked which included a half hour that Sam Hogan had worked prior to the accident. Payne issued Bill Hogan a check for all of these hours. Further, Bill Hogan did not have to use his own tools and materials in the project. The church supplied the tools, materials, and supplies necessary to complete the project. Bill purchased needed items from Dunn's Hardware Store and charged them to the church's account.

It is undisputed in this case that Mill Street Church of Christ is an insured employer under the Workers' Compensation Act. Sam Hogan filed a claim under the Workers' Compensation Act. . . .

NOTE

If Bill Hogan had authority to hire Sam, then Sam would be deemed the Church's agent (technically, a sub-agent) and its employee for purposes of the Worker's Compensation Act.

As part of their argument, petitioners argue the New Board also erred in finding that Bill Hogan possessed implied authority as an agent to hire Sam Hogan. Petitioners contend there was neither implied nor apparent authority in the case at bar.

It is important to distinguish implied and apparent authority before proceeding further. Implied authority is actual authority circumstantially proven which the principal actually intended the agent to possess and includes such powers as are practically necessary to carry out the duties actually delegated. Apparent authority on the other hand is not actual authority but is the authority the agent is held out by the principal as possessing. It is a matter of appearances on which third parties come to rely.

Petitioners attack the New Board's findings concerning implied authority. In examining whether implied authority exists, it is important to focus upon the agent's understanding of his authority. It must be determined whether the agent reasonably believes because of present or past conduct of the principal that the principal wishes him to act in a certain way or to have certain authority. The nature of the task or job may be another factor to consider. Implied authority may be necessary in order to implement the express authority. The existence of prior similar practices is one of the most important factors. Specific conduct by the principal in the past permitting the agent to exercise similar powers is crucial.

The person alleging agency and resulting authority has the burden of proving that it exists. Agency cannot be proven by a mere statement, but it can be established by circumstantial evidence including the acts and conduct of the parties such as the continuous course of conduct of the parties covering a number of successive transactions. . . .

In considering the above factors in the case at bar, Bill Hogan had implied authority to hire Sam Hogan as his helper. First, in the past the church had allowed Bill Hogan to hire his brother or other persons whenever he needed assistance on a project. Even though the Board of Elders discussed a different arrangement this time, no mention of this discussion was ever made to Bill or Sam Hogan. In fact, the discussion between Bill Hogan and Church Elder Dr. Waggoner, indicated that Gary Petty would be difficult to reach and Bill Hogan could hire whomever he pleased. Further, Bill Hogan needed to hire an assistant to complete the job for which he had been hired. The interior of the church simply could not be painted by one person. Maintaining a safe and attractive place of worship clearly is part of the church's function, and one for which it would designate an agent to ensure that the building is properly painted and maintained.

Finally, in this case, Sam Hogan believed that Bill Hogan had the authority to hire him as had been the practice in the past. To now claim that Bill Hogan could not hire Sam Hogan as an assistant, especially when Bill Hogan had never been told this fact, would be very unfair to Sam Hogan. Sam Hogan relied on Bill Hogan's representation. The church treasurer in this case even paid Bill Hogan for the half hour of work that Sam Hogan had completed prior to the accident. Considering the above facts, we find that Sam Hogan was within the employment of the Mill Street Church of Christ at the time he was injured.

The decision of the New Workers' Compensation Board is affirmed.

ANALYSIS

1. **Subjective Belief.** Is Sam Hogan's belief that his brother Bill had authority to hire Sam relevant to the issue of whether Bill had actual authority to do so?

2. **Hypotheticals.** The following problems are based on a simple fact pattern in which Paul owns an apartment building and has hired Ann to manage it.

   a. Paul tells Ann to hire a company to cut the grass. Ann does it. Is Paul bound by the contract?

   b. Without express instructions, Ann hires a janitor to clean the building. Is Paul bound by the employment contract with the janitor? See Restatement (Second) of Agency § 35; Restatement (Third) of Agency, § 2.01(1).

   c. Suppose Paul specifically instructed Ann not to hire a janitor, but that local custom gives apartment managers the power to hire janitors. Would Paul be bound by the contract?

Karl Rove & Co. v. Thornburgh

39 F.3d 1273 (5th Cir.1994).

I. Facts and Proceedings

A. Background

. . .

In 1991, [Richard] Thornburgh ran in a special election to fill the U.S. Senate seat that had become vacant when Pennsylvania Senator John Heinz was killed in an aircraft accident. [Murray] Dickman, a longtime Thornburgh aide, agreed to the offer of [Karl] Rove & Company to provide direct mail fundraising services for the campaign, upon Thornburgh's entering into the U.S. Senate race and establishment of a principal campaign committee. The instant dispute arose when, after Thornburgh lost the election, the then-insolvent ["Thornburgh for Senate Committee"] failed to pay Rove & Company for services that it had provided pursuant to a contract with the Committee, dated September 18, 1991 (the "September Contract").

There is no longer any dispute regarding the existence or quantum of the Committee's liability to Rove & Company on the September Contract. On appeal, therefore, the only issue is whether Thornburgh personally has joint and several liability with the Committee for the debt to Rove & Company. . . .

The September Contract was between Rove & Company and the Committee, not Thornburgh. That agreement contained a signature line for both parties and identified "Murray Dickman" as the proposed signatory for the Committee. Rove signed the contract and forwarded it to Bob Mason ("Mason"), the Financial Director of the Committee, who, in turn, delivered it to Dickman. But neither Dickman nor anyone else ever signed the document for the Committee. The district court found nonetheless that Rove & Company and the Committee thereafter conducted business according to the terms of the September Contract. There is no evidence in the record, however, that Thornburgh ever saw this agreement or knew of its terms and conditions.

Dickman is a longtime Thornburgh aide, who, according to the district court, was widely known to be Thornburgh's spokesman. Karl Rove ("Rove"), the president of Rove & Company, initiated the contact with Dickman when Rove learned that Thornburgh was interested in running in the special election to select Heinz' successor. Rove contacted Dickman because Rove was aware of Dickman's association with Thornburgh and knew that Dickman was the person who had been in primary control of Thornburgh's previous campaigns.

True to form, Dickman also played a prominent role during this senatorial campaign. He took part in the Committee's decision to hire Michele Davis ("Davis") as campaign manager, a position characterized as the chief executive officer of the Committee. Dickman was the primary point of contact between the Committee and Thornburgh; Dickman was also one of the persons involved in the Committee's decisions to hire Rove & Company, then whether to pay Rove & Company, and, if so, when to pay Rove & Company.

Dickman conducted the initial negotiations with Rove & Company on behalf of the Committee and, in the early stages of the campaign, delivered much of the material that Rove & Company needed to conduct the direct mail campaign. . . . In his discussions with Rove, however, Dickman never expressly represented himself as an agent for either Thornburgh or the Committee.

Thornburgh's direct interactions with Rove and with Rove & Company were more limited than Dickman's. In fact, the district court found that Rove's only personal contact with Thornburgh occurred on September 23 or 24, 1991, when Rove accidentally ran into Thornburgh in an airport. Rove stated that he identified himself to Thornburgh as the person running the direct mail fundraising campaign, and that Thornburgh responded by telling Rove that he was doing a good job and to keep up the good work. At no time, however, was Rove or anyone else told by Thornburgh that he intended to be personally liable to Rove & Company for the September Contract or any other debt incurred with regard to the services provided by Rove & Company.

Thornburgh denied that he knew whom the Committee had retained to provide direct mail fundraising services. He did acknowledge, however, that he was aware that the Committee had contracted to have such services provided and that the Committee was being charged for these services. Neither did Thornburgh object to the Committee's decision to purchase direct mail fundraising services; in fact, he testified that: "I assisted the Committee in whatever way that I could in helping them to raise money through a direct mail effort" and "I cooperated with [the Committee] and facilitated with them and facilitated their efforts to see that the contract [for direct mail services] went forward."

In support of those fundraising efforts, Thornburgh authorized the Committee to use his signature on the solicitation letters; he made available his political donors' list; and, he reviewed and edited the content and language of several fundraising letters. . . . Finally, Thornburgh admitted that he had the authority, if he desired, to stop completely all direct mail fundraising efforts on his behalf at any time.

Thornburgh also testified regarding his knowledge of and interactions with the Committee. On his statement of candidacy, Thornburgh designated the Committee as his only "principal campaign committee." . . .

Thornburgh testified, however, that he did not know who was on the Committee, did not select or approve its members, and did not know who had authority to act for the Committee. He further testified that he was not familiar with the inner workings of the Committee, was not involved in the management of Committee finances, did not know how the Committee spent its funds, and played no part in the Committee's selection of vendors in general or Rove & Company in particular.

In light of the fact that Thornburgh is a "very experienced and intelligent politician with intimate knowledge of the inner workings of political campaigns," the district court found that Thornburgh's testimony regarding his attenuation from the Committee lacked credibility. The district court commented that "there is no way a man of his intellect—a man who was entrusted with the governorship of his home state and who served as Attorney General for his nation—did not have control of the organization running his campaign either directly or through persons in his confidence and of his choosing." The district court found more credible the testimony of Mason, who had stated that Thornburgh was "ultimately in control" of the campaign.

In all, Rove & Company completed 28 separate projects, mailed 695,094 letters, and raised over $750,000, netting $425,000 for the Thornburgh campaign. . . . All of the money received by the Committee was used exclusively to fund Thornburgh's campaign for the Senate. Of Rove's total billings to the Committee, $169,732.48 went unpaid, excluding interest and attorneys' fees.

B. Procedural History

Rove & Company filed the instant suit in federal district court against Thornburgh, Dimuzio, and the Committee, seeking recovery for breach of contract, quantum meruit, fraud, and theft of services. A bench trial was held on April 1 and 2, 1993. On June 17, 1993, the district court . . . held Thornburgh and the Committee jointly and severally liable for breach of contract. Having found liability under this breach of contract, the district court did not address Rove & Company's other theories of liability.

Thornburgh—but not the Committee—timely filed a notice of appeal. Thornburgh complains to us that the district court erred in holding him liable based on the finding that he, personally and through his general agent, Dickman, authorized, assented to, or ratified the September Contract between Rove & Company and the Committee. In particular, Thornburgh challenges the district court's conclusions that he assented to the September Contract and that Dickman was his general agent, vested with authority to enter into contracts on behalf of Thornburgh personally.

Not unexpectedly, Rove & Company responds that the district court got it right. . . .

II. Analysis

. . .

A. The Legal Framework of this Dispute

We have never before been called upon to consider the extent to which—or under what circumstances—a candidate for federal office, or the treasurer of such a candidate's unincorporated principal campaign committee, may be held personally liable for a contractual debt incurred by such a committee. . . .

[The court next concluded that (1) federal election law does not preempt state law, (2) a uniform federal common law governing disputes over election debts was not appropriate, and (3) state common law therefore controlled. The court ducked the question of whether the law of Pennsylvania (Thornbugh's home) or that of Texas (Rove's base) applied, asserting that they were essentially identical.]

3. The Applicable Law

a. The Law of Unincorporated Nonprofit Associations

As noted, the common law has neither applied nor created a separate legal regime to resolve disputes concerning the liability of persons affiliated with unincorporated political campaign committees; rather, such disputes have been adjudicated by analogical extension of the law of unincorporated nonprofit associations. That kind of association typically includes such entities as churches, labor unions, and social clubs.

Pursuant to this law, an individual is not liable for the debts of the association merely because of his status as a member or officer of the association. Rather, principles of the law of agency are applied to the particular facts on a case by case basis to decide whether the individual in question is liable. Fundamentally, a member is personally responsible for a contract entered into by the nonprofit association only if—viewing him as though he were a principal and the association were his agent—that member authorized, assented to, or ratified the contract in question. Both Texas and Pennsylvania have long embraced this rule. . . .

B. Liability of Thornburgh for the September Contract with the Committee

[The court held that Thornburgh was a member of the Committee or, at least, was estopped to deny his membership. The court further held that Thornburgh had assented to the contract. It then went on to consider an alternative theory of liability based on agency law.]

3. Thornburgh's Liability Resulting From Dickman's Acts

The district court also found Thornburgh liable "as a result of Dickman's authorization of, and assent to, the contract." Thornburgh does not contest the district court's finding that Dickman authorized or assented to the contract; rather, Thornburgh takes issue only with the court's conclusion that Dickman acted as Thornburgh's general agent with authority to enter into a contract with Rove & Company on Thornburgh's personal behalf.

"Under Texas law, agency is a mixed question of law and fact. To the extent that the facts are undisputed, the trial court's ruling is freely reviewable on appeal. However, where . . . the facts are disputed, the clearly erroneous standard applies."[105] As Thornburgh does not contest the factual findings upon which the district court based its conclusion that Dickman acted as Thornburgh's general agent, we review de novo that court's legal conclusion.

Agency is a legal relationship created by an express or implied agreement or by operation of law whereby the agent is authorized to act for the principal, subject to the principal's control. As in the formation of any contract, the consent of both parties is necessary to establish an agency relationship. Agency is never to be presumed; it must be shown affirmatively. The party who asserts the existence of agency relationship has the burden of proving it. To prove an agency relation under Texas law, there must be evidence from which the court could conclude that "the alleged principal [had] the right to control both the means and the details of the process by which the alleged agent [was] to accomplish the task."[108] . . . .

---

[105] In re Carolin Paxson Advertising, Inc., 938 F.2d 595, 598 n. 2 (5th Cir.1991). . . .

[108] In re Carolin Paxson Advertising, Inc., 938 F.2d 595, 598 (5th Cir.1991); see United States v. Contemporary Health Management, 807 F. Supp. 47, 49 (E.D.Tex.1992) ("Under Texas agency law, the essential element is the 'right of control' of the purported agent by the purported principal.").

a. Dickman As Thornburgh's Agent

Although both Thornburgh and Dickman testified that Thornburgh had not constituted Dickman as Thornburgh's agent for any purpose, agency can be implied from the conduct of the parties under the circumstances. In the instant case, Dickman (the person authorized to answer interrogatories on behalf of the Committee) admitted in the Committee's answers to Rove & Company's interrogatories that he was "the primary point of contact between the Committee and Defendant Richard Thornburgh." Dickman also acknowledged that he was known as "an intermediary" to Thornburgh regarding, inter alia, the running and organizing of Thornburgh's campaign. Thornburgh solicited Dickman's opinion on a "day-to-day basis" about campaign activities, including broad campaign strategies, where Thornburgh should speak, and what issues Thornburgh should address. Thornburgh used Dickman as his go-between to provide mailing lists, a signature exemplar, and edited solicitation letters to the Committee to facilitate the Committee's direct mail contract with Rove & Company. Thornburgh testified that Dickman was a "loyal friend," who had served as a high-level assistant to Thornburgh during several of Thornburgh's campaigns and while Thornburgh served in various government positions.[114]

Consistent with a principal's role, Thornburgh retained the ultimate authority over Dickman and Dickman's activities within the Committee. For example, even though Dickman took part in the Committee's decision to hire Davis as the Committee's Campaign Manager, Dickman acknowledged that, had Thornburgh disapproved of this choice, another campaign manager would have been selected. In addition, although Dickman authorized and assented to the Committee's contract with Rove & Company, Thornburgh retained control over the content of the fundraising letters and whether the letters would be mailed at all. Finally, Thornburgh was the only person authorized to grant the Committee (and thus its employees, one of whom was Dickman) the authority to raise and spend funds on Thornburgh's behalf. Thornburgh thus had the right to withhold his authorization of the Committee, a decision that would have halted all Committee activities—including Dickman's. Consequently, the evidence supports the district court's finding that Dickman served as Thornburgh's agent acting under Thornburgh's control. Nevertheless, we still must determine the scope of Dickman's authority.

---

[114] Contrary to Thornburgh's assertions, it was proper for the district court to consider Dickman's relationship to Thornburgh in determining whether Dickman acted as Thornburgh's agent. Although agency cannot be proven by evidence of the alleged agent's general reputation as the agent of the alleged principal, this does not mean that a court cannot look to the relationship between the parties and their conduct concerning the transaction in controversy as competent evidence of an agency relationship. See Union Producing Co. v. Allen, 297 S.W.2d 867 (Tex.Civ.App.1957); Restatement (Second) of Agency § 34.

b. The Scope of Dickman's Authority

An agent has only as much authority as the principal has either expressly or impliedly conferred.[116] The extent of an agent's authority is determined in light of all surrounding circumstances, including, inter alia, the parties' relations to one another, the undertaking in which the parties are engaged, and the general usages and practices of those engaged in such undertakings. . . .

Although we recognize that there is some evidence and authority to support the district court's conclusion that Dickman was acting as Thornburgh's general agent, authorized to enter into the September Contract for Thornburgh personally, we need not go that far to hold Thornburgh liable here. The record makes clear that Dickman acted as Thornburgh's agent to the Committee and was authorized to represent Thornburgh in all Committee activities, including whether to enter into the September Contract. This finding alone is sufficient to hold Thornburgh personally liable, given Thornburgh's acknowledgement that Dickman authorized and assented to that Committee's contract with Rove & Company.

. . . [F]or Thornburgh to be liable for the September Contract, Rove & Company had only to prove that Thornburgh authorized, assented to, or ratified the Committee's decision to enter into the agreement. Thornburgh could manifest his authorization or assent personally or through an agent. In the instant case, the record is clear that Dickman, as Thornburgh's representative to the Committee, authorized or assented to the September Contract.

Much of the same evidence that establishes that Dickman acted as Thornburgh's agent also supports the district court's findings that Dickman was Thornburgh's "primary point of contact" with the Committee and that "Dickman's role in the Committee was obviously to assure Thornburgh's interests would best be served and to be Thornburgh's voice." There is no indication that these findings by the district court were clearly erroneous. We also note that Thornburgh testified that it is customary during a political campaign for a candidate to rely on others, such as Dickman, to manage the day-to-day operations of the campaign—which operations would include such things as the purchase of services necessary to support the candidacy. As it is customary to rely on others for such services, and as the district court found that Dickman was the primary person upon whom Thornburgh relied during his senatorial campaign, we are led to but one conclusion: Dickman, as Thornburgh's representative to the Committee, had either actual or apparent authority to bestow Thornburgh's blessings on

[116] See Restatement (Second) of Agency § 33 ("An agent is authorized to do, and to do only, what it is reasonable for him to infer that the principal desires him to do. . . .").

Committee activities, which included the Committee's decision to contract with Rove & Company. As Dickman had such authority, and as Thornburgh concedes (and the record substantiates with uncontroverted evidence) that Dickman authorized and assented to the September Contract, Thornburgh can also be found liable for the September Contract as a result of Dickman's authorization and assent to the Committee's decision to enter into that agreement. Consequently, we need not, and do not, reach the issue whether Thornburgh also is personally liable because Dickman acted as Thornburgh's general agent vis-à-vis Rove & Company, vested with authority to enter into pacts such as the September Contract and bind Thornburgh personally. . . .

III. Conclusion

. . . For the reasons detailed above, we AFFIRM the district court judgment to the extent it holds Thornburgh liable for the debts of the Committee. . . .

ANALYSIS

1. **Contracting Around Liability.** How could a candidate for office structure the business relationship between the candidate, the election committee, and contractors so as to minimize the candidate's potential liability?

2. **The Restatement Standard.** According to Restatement (Second) of Agency § 26 (see also Restatement [Third] of Agency § 2.02(2), actual "authority to do an act can be created by written or spoken words or other conduct of the principal which, reasonably interpreted, causes the agent to believe that the principal desires him so to act on the principal's account." Under that standard, did Dickman have actual authority to bind Thornburgh?

3. **Political Calculus.** According to former President Ronald Reagan's famous dictum, the 11th Commandment reads, "Thou shall not speak ill of a fellow Republican." Why then is a GOP operative like Rove suing one of the party's most prominent candidates? What downside, if any, is there to a suit by Rove?

B. APPARENT AUTHORITY

Lind v. Schenley Industries, Inc.

278 F.2d 79 (3d Cir.1960) (en banc).

■ BIGGS, CHIEF JUDGE.

This is a diversity case. Lind, the plaintiff-appellant, sued Park & Tilford Distiller's Corp.,[1] the defendant-appellee, for compensation that he asserts is due him by virtue of a contract expressed by a written memorandum supplemented by oral conversations as set out hereinafter. Lind also sued for certain expenses he incurred when moving from New Jersey to New York when his position as New Jersey State Manager of Park & Tilford terminated on January 31, 1957. The evidence, including Lind's own testimony, taking the inferences most favorable to Lind, shows the following. Lind had been employed for some years by Park & Tilford. In July 1950, Lind was informed by Herrfeldt, then Park & Tilford's vice-president and general sales-manager, that he would be appointed assistant to Kaufman, Park & Tilford's sales-manager for metropolitan New York. Herrfeldt told Lind to see Kaufman to ascertain what his new duties and his salary would be. Lind embarked on his new duties with Kaufman and was informed in October 1950, that some "raises" had come through and that Lind should get official word from his "boss," Kaufman. Subsequently, Lind received a communication, dated April 19, 1951, signed by Kaufman, informing Lind that he would assume the title of "District Manager." The letter went on to state: "I wish to inform you of the fact that you have as much responsibility as a State Manager and that you should consider yourself to be of the same status." The letter concluded with the statement: "An incentive plan is being worked out so that you will not only be responsible for increased sales in your district, but will benefit substantially in a monetary way." The other two district managers under Kaufman received similar memoranda. Lind assumed his duties as district sales manager for metropolitan New York. . . .

In July 1951, Kaufman informed Lind that he was to receive 1% commission on the gross sales of the men under him. . . . Lind was also informed by Herrfeldt in the autumn of 1952 that he would get a 1% commission on the sales of the men under him. Early in 1955, Lind negotiated with Brown, then president of Park & Tilford, for the sale of Park & Tilford's New Jersey Wholesale House, and Brown agreed to apply the money owed to Lind by reason of the 1% commission against

---

1 Park & Tilford Distiller's Corp. was merged into Schenley Industries, Inc., a Delaware corporation, before the commencement of this action, with Schenley assuming all of Park & Tilford's obligations. Schenley was substituted in this action on March 31, 1958, by order of Judge Wortendyke.

the value of the goodwill of the Wholesale House. The proposed sale of the New Jersey Wholesale House was not consummated.

Notice to produce various records of Lind's employment was served on Park & Tilford but one slip dealing with Lind's appointment as district manager was not produced and is presumed to have been lost. The evidence was conflicting as to the character of the "incentive compensation" to be offered Lind in connection with his services as a district manager. Herrfeldt designated the incentive an "added incentive plan with a percentage arrangement." Kaufman characterized the plan as "bonuses and contests." Weiner, Park & Tilford's Secretary, said that the incentive was a "pension plan." Kaufman testified, however, that the pension plan had nothing to do with the bonus incentive he referred to.

The record also shows that Lind commenced his employment with Park & Tilford in 1941, that from 1942 to 1950 he worked on a commission basis, that on August 31, 1950, he became an assistant sales manager for the New York metropolitan area at $125 a week, which was raised to $150 a week on October 1, 1950, plus certain allowances. After Lind became district manager on April 19, 1951, he continued to receive the same salary of $150 a week but this was increased to $175 in January 1952. On February 1, 1952, Lind was transferred from New York to New Jersey to become state manager of Park & Tilford's business in New Jersey. He retained that position until January 31, 1957, when he was transferred back to New York.

Park & Tilford moved for but was denied a directed verdict at the close of all the evidence. . . . However, the court . . . submitted the case to the jury subject to a later determination of the legal questions raised by Park & Tilford's motion to dismiss. The court then requested the jury to answer [certain] questions. . . .

The answers provided by the jury amounted to a determination that Kaufman did offer Lind a 1% commission on the gross sales of the men under him; that the agreement commenced April 19, 1951; that the agreement terminated February 15, 1952, the date of Lind's transfer to New Jersey; that Park & Tilford did cause Lind to believe that Kaufman had authority to offer him the one percent commission; and that Lind was justified in assuming that Kaufman had the authority to make the offer. [The jury found in favor of Lind in the amount of $37,000, but the trial court entered a judgment notwithstanding the verdict and, in the event of a reversal, an order for a new trial.]

The decision to reverse the verdict for Lind with respect to the 1% commission was based on two alternative grounds. First, the court found that Lind had failed to prove a case of apparent authority in that the evidence did not disclose that Park & Tilford acted in such a manner as to induce Lind to believe that Kaufman had been authorized to offer him the 1% commission. Also the court concluded that the issues of "actual" and "implied" authority had somehow been eliminated from the case. Second, the court reasoned, that even if the jury could find apparent authority, the alleged contract was not sufficiently definite nor specific to be enforceable against Park & Tilford. The trial judge rejected a contention by Park & Tilford that a document signed by Lind on January 31, 1957, upon receiving his last pay check as New Jersey State Manager, should be construed as a release of his claims for commissions.

. . .

The problems of "authority" are probably the most difficult in that segment of law loosely termed, "Agency." Two main classifications of authority are generally recognized, "actual authority," and "apparent authority." The term "implied authority" is often seen but most authorities consider "implied authority" to be merely a sub-group of "actual" authority. . . . An additional kind of authority has been designated by the Restatement, Agency 2d, §§ 8A and 161(b) as "inherent agency." Actually this new term is employed to designate a meaning frequently ascribed to "implied authority."

"Actual authority" means, as the words connote, authority that the principal, expressly or implicitly, gave the agent. "Apparent authority" arises when a principal acts in such a manner as to convey the impression to a third party that an agent has certain powers which he may or may not actually possess. "Implied authority" has been variously defined. It has been held to be actual authority given implicitly by a principal to his agent. Another definition of "implied authority" is that it is a kind of authority arising solely from the designation by the principal of a kind of agent who ordinarily possesses certain powers. It is this concept that is called "inherent authority" by the Restatement. In many cases the same facts will support a finding of "inherent" or "apparent agency." Usually it is not necessary for a third party attempting to hold a principal to specify which type of authority he relies upon, general proof of agency being sufficient. . . .

In the case at bar Lind attempted to prove all three kinds of agency; actual, apparent, and inherent, although most of his evidence was directed to proof of "inherent" or "apparent" authority. From the evidence it is clear that Park & Tilford can be held accountable for Kaufman's action on the principle of "inherent authority." Kaufman was Lind's direct superior, and was the man to transfer communications from the upper executives to the lower. Moreover, there was testimony tending to prove that Herrfeldt, the vice-president in charge of sales, had told Lind to see Kaufman for information about his salary and that Herrfeldt himself had confirmed the 1% commission arrangement. Thus Kaufman, so far as Lind was concerned, was the spokesman for the company.

It is not necessary to determine the status of the New York law in respect to "inherent agency" for substantially the same testimony that would establish "inherent" agency under the circumstances at bar proves conventional "apparent" agency. The Restatement, Agency 2d § 8, defines "apparent agency" as "the power to affect the legal relations of another person by transactions with third persons, professedly as agent for the other, arising from and in accordance with the other's manifestations to such third persons." There is some uncertainty as to whether or not the third person must change his position in reliance upon these manifestations of authority, but this is of no consequence in the case at bar since Lind clearly changed his position when he accepted the job of district manager with its admittedly increased responsibilities.

The opinion of the court below and the argument of the appellee here rely heavily on Gumpert v. Bon Ami Co., 2 Cir., 1958, 251 F.2d 735, a diversity case decided under New York law, upholding the lower court's reversal of a jury verdict for the plaintiff. The facts in that case showed that Gumpert had been hired by Rosenberg, a director and member of the executive board of the Bon Ami company for a salary of $25,000 in cash plus $25,000 worth of the company's common stock. The Court of Appeals found that the jury could not properly find that the Bon Ami company had clothed Rosenberg with apparent authority to offer Gumpert $25,000 in common stock. This decision is inapposite for here we deal with an offer made by an employee's immediate superior, the man who represented the company to those under him, not a contract offered by one not an officer of a corporation to prospective employee. Furthermore a salary of $25,000 in cash and $25,000 in common stock might well be deemed unusual enough to put the prospective employee on notice as to a possible lack of authority in the director to make the offer but the same may not be said of an offer of a commission to a salesman who had been habitually working on that basis, in a corporation that confined itself to selling others' products. It should be borne in mind also that a director, even if he be a member of the executive board, does not ordinarily hire employees. Moreover in the case at bar there was evidence by an employee of Schenley that at least some state managers received 1% commissions.

Testimony was adduced by Schenley tending to prove that Kaufman had no authority to set salaries, that power being exercisable solely by the president of the corporation, and that the president had not authorized Kaufman to offer Lind a commission of the kind under consideration here. However, this testimony, even if fully accepted, would only prove lack of actual or implied authority in Kaufman but is irrelevant to the issue of apparent authority.

The opinion below seems to agree with the conception of the New York agency law as set out above but the court reversed the jury's verdict and the judgment based on it on the conclusion, as a matter of law, that Lind could not reasonably have believed that Kaufman was authorized to offer him a commission that would, in the trial judge's words "have almost quadrupled Lind's then salary." But Lind testified that before he had become Kaufman's assistant in September 1950, the latter position named being that which he had held before being "promoted" to district manager in April 1951, he had earned $9,000 for the period from January 1, 1950 to August 31, 1950, that figure allegedly representing half of his expected earnings for the year. Lind testified that a liquor salesman can expect to make 50% of his salary in the last four months of the year owing to holiday sales. Thus Lind's salary two years before his appointment as district manager could have been estimated by the jury at $18,000 per year, and his alleged earnings, as district manager, a position of greater responsibility, do not appear disproportionate. On the basis of the foregoing it appears that there was sufficient evidence to authorize a jury finding that Park & Tilford had given Kaufman apparent authority to offer Lind 1% commission of gross sales of the salesmen under him and that Lind reasonably had relied upon Kaufman's offer.

. . .

The judgment of the court below will be reversed and the case will be remanded with the direction to the court below to reinstate the verdict and judgment in favor of Lind.

■ HASTIE, CIRCUIT JUDGE, with whom KALODNER, CIRCUIT JUDGE, joins (dissenting).

I agree that the order granting judgment for the defendant notwithstanding the verdict for the plaintiff must be set aside. However, I think the majority make a serious mistake when they take the extraordinary additional step of reversing the alternative order of the trial judge, granting a new trial because he considered the verdict against the weight of the evidence.

. . .

The present record discloses a sharp conflict of testimony whether Kaufman, the metropolitan sales manager, ever promised plaintiff, his subordinate district manager, a 1% commission on all gross sales of agents working under plaintiff. There are several remarkable aspects of this alleged promise which could reasonably have influenced the trial judge on this decisive issue. This commission would have more than quadrupled plaintiff's salary of $150 per week, making him much higher paid than his immediate superior, Kaufman, or any other company executive, except the president. No other sales manager or supervisor received any such commission at all. Moreover, after the alleged promise was made, month after month elapsed with no payment of the 1% commission or indication of any step to fulfill such an obligation. Yet plaintiff himself admits that he made no formal demand for or inquiry about the large obligation for several years, and said nothing even informally about it to anyone for many months save for an occasional passing verbal inquiry said to have been addressed to Kaufman. . . .

NOTE

This case introduces two theories of liability of principals for the acts of their agents: inherent agency (also referred to as inherent agency power) and apparent authority. These are both theories under which the principal may be held liable for the acts of an agent where (as in the present case) there is no (actual) authority. Inherent agency is a puzzling doctrine that is used to impose liability on the principal when there is neither authority nor apparent authority. As the court says, it arises "solely from the designation by the principal of a kind of agent who ordinarily possesses certain powers." The primary focus here will be on apparent authority. Subsequent cases will focus on the doctrine of inherent agency power.

PLANNING

1. **Incentive to Park and Tilford.** What should firms like Park & Tilford (Schenley) do to avoid the problem that gave rise to this decision?

2. **Incentive to Lind.** What could Lind have done to avoid the problem?

ANALYSIS

The court quotes the Restatement (Second) of Agency § 8 (see also Restatement (Third) of Agency § 2.03), which makes the issue of apparent authority turn on the principal's "manifestations." (a) What were the manifestations by Park & Tilford that led Lind to believe that Kaufman had authority to enter into the contract for his (Lind's) services? (b) If the contract had been for ten years, would Park & Tilford still have been liable? What if it had been for Lind's lifetime?

Ackerman v. Sobol Family Partnership, LLP

298 Conn. 495 (2010).

The principal issue in this consolidated appeal, which arises out of a series of disputes concerning the management and oversight of a family partnership and various family trusts, is whether the plaintiffs' attorney had apparent authority to make settlement proposals, engage in settlement discussions and bind the plaintiffs to a global settlement agreement with the defendants. . . .

In the underlying cases, the plaintiffs alleged, inter alia, breach of contract, breach of fiduciary duty, unjust enrichment, civil conspiracy and violation of the Connecticut Unfair Trade Practices Act. On July 3, 2008, however, the Sobol defendants and the defendant Bank of America each filed a motion to enforce a settlement agreement purportedly reached with the plaintiffs on July 1, 2008. On July 8, 2008, the trial court, *Eveleigh, J.*, conducted a hearing . . . to determine whether the settlement agreement was enforceable, at which the plaintiffs argued that there was no agreement and the defendants argued that there was. On July 9, 2008, the court issued an oral decision from the bench containing the following findings of fact and conclusions of law.

"[T]he parties met for a mediation, which was held on May 29, 2008, before the Honorable Michael Sheldon. The plaintiffs' attorney, Glenn Coe, represented the plaintiffs at this mediation.

"At the time the mediation was concluded, a settlement had not been reached . . . although Judge Sheldon did remain active in further negotiations between the parties. These negotiations continued to the point where [Coe] made a detailed offer of settlement . . . by way of letter dated June 16, 2008, which was addressed to Attorneys [Robert] Wyld, [Dina] Fisher, and [Steven] Ecker representing the defendants in this action other than Bank of America.

"That particular letter was responded to by [Wyld] . . . in which he rejected the proposal. . . . After that rejection, negotiations continued in the matter to the point where [Coe] made an offer to settle the litigation in a series of conversations with [Wyld] and [Attorney David] Schneider [who represented the Bank of America] on Thursday, June 26, and Friday, June 27, 2008.

"[Coe] had been speaking on behalf of all [the] plaintiffs regarding settlement with the knowledge and authority of his own client[s], as well as [Attorney William Horan], who [had] represented the other two plaintiffs . . . [Rakoszynski] . . . and Mann, and that situation had continued since the time of the mediation on May 29, 2008. During that two day period of June 26 and June 27, 2008, [Coe] expressly assured [the] defendants' attorneys on separate occasions in response to direct questioning on the issue that the settlement offer proposed by him at that time was fully authorized by his client[s] as well as [Horan]; [and] that if accepted by the defendants, [it] would resolve the litigation in all respects.

"[Wyld], who was negotiating the settlement on behalf of . . . the Sobol defendants . . . notified [Coe] on Monday, June 30, 2008, that the offer of settlement made by [Coe] on behalf of all [of the] plaintiffs was accepted by the Sobol defendants. The Sobol defendants understood that the settlement between the plaintiffs and the Sobol defendants was part of a global settlement proposal made by [the] plaintiffs' counsel, and, therefore, both [Wyld] and [Coe] awaited word from [Schneider], who represented the Bank of America in the separate actions in which Tamar Ackerman . . . and [Rakoszynski] were named plaintiffs.

. . .

"... The Bank of America, through [Schneider], accepted the $1.1 million settlement proposal in the early afternoon of July 1, 2008, prior to the 5 p.m. deadline. The global settlement offer thus [had] been accepted by all [of the] defendants.

"The plaintiffs Rena Ackerman, [Rakoszynski], and [Mann], were all present on the day that the Bank of America accepted the offer, July 1, 2008. Beginning at 9:30 that morning, the parties had convened at the Hartford offices of Shipman and Goodwin for the deposition of [Rakoszynski] and [Mann], [the] plaintiffs in [one of] the ... cases. In particular, Rena Ackerman was present from the outset of the deposition.

"At no time prior to the acceptance of the settlement proposal on July 1, 2008, were [the] defendants or their attorneys notified that the offer had been withdrawn, unauthorized, or otherwise ineffective. During that same period [Rena] Ackerman never manifested to [the] defendants or their attorneys that the settlement authority of her attorney was limited or had been terminated.

"[Coe] is a very experienced, highly regarded lawyer. He's been representing plaintiffs and parties for over thirty years. [Coe], again, [has been] the lead negotiator in settlement discussions since May 29, 2008, in an ongoing sustained and intense series of negotiations. It was certainly clear that by May 29, 2008, he was authorized to negotiate settlement terms on the plaintiffs' behalf.

"Defense counsel had observed [Rena] Ackerman in [Coe's] presence during the mediation process and knew that [Coe] was consulting with her concerning negotiations based upon [Coe's] feedback. [Rena] Ackerman was very involved in every aspect ... of the case, including settlement. She [is] found by the court to be a very bright person who is vigilant in pursuing and protecting her interests in these lawsuits.

"[Coe] expressly and unambiguously assured both [Wyld] and [Schneider] in separate conversations that he had authorization from [Rena] Ackerman to offer the specific settlement terms at issue....

"It further appears to the court that there was no challenge at the time of the hearing from the testimony of [Coe] himself. It was clearly expressed to Bank of America that $1.1 million would resolve the case. They came up with $1.1 million. The offer was accepted. It's further clear to the court that although there are numerous issues as testified to by [Wyld] regarding the settlement of the Sobol defendants, the one remaining issue to be resolved was the amount of money to be paid and the demand in that regard was that the Sobol defendants pay $1.4 million. They came up with the money. The proposal was accepted....

"... Apparent authority exists, one, where the principal held the agent out as possessing sufficient authority to embrace the act in question and knowingly permitted him to act as having such authority;

and, two, in consequence thereof, the person dealing with the agent acting in good faith reasonably believed under all the circumstances that the agent had the necessary authority. . . .

"Based upon the court's prior findings in this matter, the court finds that [Coe] certainly did have apparent authority from his client[s]. Further . . . the defendants' counsel reasonably believed that [Coe] was, in fact, authorized by the plaintiffs to make the settlement offer at issue, and . . . were acting in good faith in their respective efforts to settle the case on the terms proposed by [Coe].

"As noted earlier, [Coe] had been, in fact, engaged in settlement discussions with his client's obvious assent. [Rena Ackerman] had accompanied him to the mediation for over [one] month prior to the time the settlement was reached. [Coe] was certainly held out as being authorized to negotiate settlement on behalf of the plaintiffs and the defendants acted reasonably in believing that he had authority to do so. . . . Further, there was no evidence at all that [Coe's] apparent authority had been terminated at any time by [Rena] Ackerman. . . .

"The court understands the plaintiffs' attorney to indicate that there was a misunderstanding and that he did not appreciate the clients' wishes with regard to the proposal. That testimony, while unfortunate, does not change the fact that he had apparent authority to enter into these discussions and bind his client[s]. . . .

"With regard to . . . the testimony of Rena . . . Ackerman regarding the settlement discussions and her authority to [Coe] indicating that he had no authority to enter into this settlement, the court finds that her testimony is not credible.[6]

. . . [T]he plaintiffs appealed from the July 9 decision enforcing the settlement agreement to the Appellate Court. . . .

I

. . .

With respect to the governing legal principles, "it is a general rule of agency law that the principal in an agency relationship is bound by, and liable for, the acts in which his agent engages with authority from the principal, and within the scope of the agent's employment. . . . An agent's authority may be actual or apparent. . . . Actual authority exists when [an agent's] action [is] expressly authorized . . . or . . . although not authorized, [is] subsequently ratified by the [principal]." . . . *Maharishi School of Vedic Sciences, Inc. (Connecticut) v. Connecticut Constitution Associates Ltd. Partnership,* 260 Conn. 598, 606–607, 799 A.2d 1027

[6] Rena Ackerman testified that she was "in shock" after Coe explained on July 1, 2008, the terms of the settlement that he had negotiated with the defendants because she purportedly had never agreed to such terms.

(2002). In contrast, "[a]pparent authority is that semblance of authority which a principal, through his own acts or inadvertences, causes or allows third persons to believe his agent possesses. . . . The issue of apparent authority is one of fact to be determined based on two criteria. . . . First, it must appear from the principal's conduct that the principal held the agent out as possessing sufficient authority to embrace the act in question, or knowingly permitted [the agent] to act as having such authority. . . . Second, the party dealing with the agent must have, acting in good faith, reasonably believed, under all the circumstances, that the agent had the necessary authority to bind the principal to the agent's action. . . .

"Apparent authority terminates when the third person has notice that: (1) the agent's authority has terminated; (2) the principal no longer consents that the agent shall deal with the third person; or (3) the agent is acting under a basic error as to the facts. Unless otherwise agreed, there is a notification by the principal to the third person of revocation of an agent's [apparent] authority or other fact indicating its termination: (a) when the principal states such fact to the third person; or (b) when a reasonable time has elapsed after a writing stating such fact has been delivered by the principal . . . to the other personally. . . ." . . . *Tomlinson v. Board of Education,* 226 Conn. at 734–35, 629 A.2d 333 . . . .

The same principles apply to the relationship between attorneys and their clients. Thus, an attorney with apparent authority may enter into a settlement agreement that is binding on the client. Although reviewing courts in Connecticut have acknowledged that "[a]n attorney who is authorized to represent a client in litigation does not *automatically* have either implied[7] or apparent authority to settle or otherwise to compromise the client's cause of action"; (emphasis added) *Acheson v. White,* 195 Conn. 211, 213 n. 4, 487 A.2d 197 (1985); they also have repeatedly held that an agent with implied or apparent authority may bind the principal to an enforceable settlement agreement.

. . . Both the Restatement of Agency and the Restatement of the Law Governing Lawyers provide that the mere act of retaining an attorney, without more, is insufficient to create apparent authority to bind the client to a settlement. Rather, manifestations of apparent authority must take the form of "conduct by a person, observable by others, that

[7] "Implied authority is actual authority circumstantially proved. It is the authority which the principal intended his agent to possess. . . . Implied authority is a fact to be proven by deductions or inferences from the manifestations of consent of the principal and from the acts of the principal and [the] agent." (Citation omitted; internal quotation marks omitted.) Maharishi School of Vedic Sciences, Inc. (Connecticut) v. Connecticut Constitution Associates Ltd. Partnership, supra, 260 Conn. at 607, 799 A.2d 1027. Thus, implied authority is determined by examining the conduct of the principal and the agent, whereas apparent authority is determined by examining the conduct of the principal as manifested to the third party and which leads the third party reasonably to believe that the agent has authority to represent the principal.

expresses meaning." 1 Restatement (Third), Agency, supra, at § 1.03, comment (b), p. 56. Such conduct, however, "is not limited to spoken or written words. . . . Silence may constitute a manifestation when, in light of all the circumstances, a reasonable person would express dissent to the inference that other persons will draw from silence. Failure then to express dissent will be taken as a manifestation of affirmance." Id., at p. 57. Apparent authority also may be conveyed to the third person "from authorized statements of the agent, from documents or other indicia of authority given by the principal to the agent, or from third persons who have heard of the agent's authority through authorized or permitted channels of communication. Likewise . . . apparent authority can be created by appointing a person to a position . . . which carries with it generally recognized duties . . . to do the things ordinarily entrusted to one occupying such a position. . . ." 1 Restatement (Second), Agency, supra, at § 27, comment (a), p. 104. The Restatement (Third) of Agency similarly explains that "[a] principal may . . . make a manifestation by placing an agent in a defined position in an organization or by placing an agent in charge of a transaction or situation. Third parties who interact with the principal through the agent will naturally and reasonably assume that the agent has authority to do acts consistent with the agent's position or role unless they have notice of facts suggesting that this may not be so. . . .

A

We begin by considering whether the plaintiffs held Coe out as possessing sufficient authority to settle the litigation as required under the first prong of *Tomlinson v. Board of Education,* supra, 226 Conn. at 734, 629 A.2d 333. . . .

The plaintiffs do not dispute the trial court's finding that Coe represented all of the plaintiffs at the court-ordered mediation on May 29, 2008, during which settlement terms were discussed and Rena Ackerman and the other plaintiffs were present. Moreover, it was Coe, acting on behalf of all of the plaintiffs, who subsequently rejected the defendants' written offer in a conference telephone call scheduled by Judge Sheldon and who stated that a counteroffer might be forthcoming. Thereafter, Coe made the anticipated counteroffer on behalf of all of the plaintiffs in his June 16 letter to the Sobol defendants. It is clear that Coe was authorized to make this offer, which would have settled the litigation if accepted, because the letter contained language indicating that it pertained to all of the pending litigation and was "for settlement purposes only." . . .

Furthermore, after the Sobol defendants rejected the counteroffer, Wyld observed Rena Ackerman conferring with Coe at a hearing on June 25, 2008, to determine which issues would be tried to a jury. Thereafter, Coe made the global settlement offer to the defendants in a series of conversations with Schneider and Wyld, repeatedly assuring them that he had authority to settle the litigation for the terms under discussion. On July 1, one day after the Sobol defendants accepted the offer, the plaintiffs Rena Ackerman, Rakoszynski and Mann were present with Coe at the Hartford offices of Shipman and Goodwin for the depositions of Rakoszynski and Mann. . . . Wyld and Schneider both observed Rena Ackerman and her husband at the offices, where they met with Coe from time to time and were seen conferring with Coe before Schneider called to inform them that the Bank of America had accepted the offer, thus settling the litigation. There was no apparent discord or distance in the relationship between Coe and Rena Ackerman . . . . In other words, Ackerman manifested by her conduct during the times she was observed with Coe prior to the offer's acceptance that she was aware of, and fully supported, the global settlement offer.

. . . Specifically, there is no evidence that the plaintiffs notified any third person that they had revoked Coe's authority following the defendants' rejection of their counteroffer, or that Coe no longer was representing Rakoszynski and Mann during the negotiations in June. This conclusion is supported by Rena Ackerman's testimony that she had authorized Coe to engage in settlement discussions with other counsel, and that she never notified any other person involved in the negotiations that she had limited or revoked Coe's authority after June 16 to reach a settlement on her behalf. . . .

B

As previously noted, the second prong of the test set forth in *Tomlinson* requires evidence that "the party dealing with the agent must have, acting in good faith, reasonably believed, under all the circumstances, that the agent had the necessary authority to bind the principal to the agent's action." (Internal quotation marks omitted.) *Tomlinson v. Board of Education,* supra, 226 Conn. at 734–35, 629 A.2d 333. In the present case, it is undisputed that Coe represented all of the plaintiffs when he rejected the defendants' written settlement offer and when he made the counteroffer to the defendants in his letter of June 16. Thereafter, the plaintiffs gave no notice to the defendants or their counsel that Coe no longer had authority to continue settlement negotiations or to make settlement offers on their behalf. Rather, Rena Ackerman was seen conferring with Coe at a court proceeding in late June and at the depositions on July 1, when settlement negotiations intensified. Thus, simply on the basis of this course of dealing among the parties, the defendants reasonably could have believed that Coe continued to have authority to discuss settlement terms and to make settlement offers during the middle and latter part of June.

To the extent that the defendants did not have a reasonable belief that Coe had apparent authority to bind the plaintiffs, they testified at the hearing to enforce the settlement agreement that they not only had queried Coe repeatedly on June 26 and 27, to obtain such assurances, but that Coe had answered their questions plainly and directly and told them at various times throughout the negotiations whether he did or did not have such authority. . . . After Schneider returned to his Bank of America office, Coe telephoned at approximately 4 p.m. to inform him that the settlement number was $1.2 million. When Schneider pressed him for a lower number, Coe responded that $1.1 million would be acceptable but that he had no room to maneuver below that amount. He also assured Schneider that he was acting on behalf of all of the plaintiffs in the cases in which the Bank of America was a party. On the basis of these conversations, Schneider thus reasonably believed that Coe had authority to settle the litigation for the financial terms they had discussed during the last days of June.

Wyld gave similar testimony. . . .

ANALYSIS

1. Rule 1.2(a) of the Connecticut Rules of Professional Conduct provides in relevant part: "A lawyer shall abide by a client's decision whether to settle a matter. . . ." Did Coe violate that rule? Should lawyers be subject to a special rule limiting their apparent authority to settle cases without express client approval?

2. In footnote 7, the court defines implied authority as "actual authority circumstantially proved." Can apparent authority be proven circumstantially? If so, would that not also be a form of implied authority?

3. Why didn't Coe have actual authority to settle the case?

4. How would you resolve the following cases?

   a. Paul owns an apartment building. He hires Ann to manage it. Paul says nothing to Ann about cleaning the building. Ann hires a janitor to clean the building. Did Ann have authority (of any sort) to do so?

   b. Paul owns an apartment building. He hires Ann to manage it. Paul gave Ann no instructions about hiring a janitor, but local custom gives apartment managers the power to hire janitors. Would Ann have authority?

PLANNING

1. What should plaintiffs have done to protect themselves against the problem that arose in this case?

2. What else could the defendants have done to protect themselves?

3. In light of your answer to questions 1 and 2, does the result in the case place responsibility for avoiding loss on the person with the lower cost of doing so?

c. Paul owns an apartment building. He hires Ann to manage it. Paul specifically instructed Ann not to hire a janitor, but local custom gives apartment managers the power to hire janitors. Would Ann have authority?

C. INHERENT AUTHORITY

Watteau v. Fenwick

[1893] 1 Queen's Bench 346 (1892).

From the evidence it appeared that one Humble had carried on business at a beerhouse called the Victoria Hotel, at Stockton-on-Tees, which business he had transferred to the defendants, a firm of brewers, some years before the present action. After the transfer of the business, Humble remained as defendants' manager; but the licence was always taken out in Humble's name, and his name was painted over the door. Under the terms of the agreement made between Humble and the defendants, the former had no authority to buy any goods for the business except bottled ales and mineral waters; all other goods required were to be supplied by the defendants themselves. The action was brought to recover the price of goods delivered at the Victoria Hotel over some years, for which it was admitted that the plaintiff gave credit to Humble only: they consisted of cigars, bovril, and other articles. The learned judge allowed the claim for the cigars and bovril only, and gave judgment for the plaintiff for 22*l.* 12*s.* 6*d.* The defendants appealed.

1892, Nov. 19. *Finlay, Q.C.* (*Scott Fox,* with him), for the defendants. The decision of the county court judge was wrong. The liability of a principal for the acts of his agent, done contrary to his secret instructions, depends upon his holding him out as his agent—that is, upon the agent being clothed with an apparent authority to act for his principal. Where, therefore, a man carries on business in his own name through a manager, he holds out his own credit, and would be liable for goods supplied even where the manager exceeded his authority. But where, as in the present case, there is no holding out by the principal, but the business is carried on in the agent's name and the goods are supplied on his credit, a person wishing to go behind the agent and make the principal liable must show an agency in fact.

[Lord Coleridge, C.J. Cannot you, in such a case, sue the undisclosed principal on discovering him?]

Only where the act done by the agent is within the scope of his agency; not where there has been an excess of authority. Where any one has been held out by the principal as his agent, there is a contract with the principal by estoppel, however much the agent may have exceeded his authority; where there has been no holding out, proof must be given of an agency in fact in order to make the principal liable.

Boydell Houghton, for the plaintiff. The defendants are liable in the present action. They are in fact undisclosed principals, who instead of carrying on the business in their own names employed a manager to carry it on for them, and clothed him with authority to do what was necessary to carry on the business. The case depends upon the same principles as *Edmunds v. Bushell*, where the manager of a business which was carried on in his own name with the addition "and Co." accepted a bill of exchange, notwithstanding a stipulation in the agreement with his principal that he should not accept bills; and the Court held that the principal was liable to an indorsee who took the bill without any knowledge of the relations between the principal and agent. In that case there was no holding out of the manager as an agent; it was the simple case of an agent being allowed to act as the ostensible principal without any disclosure to the world of there being any one behind him. Here the defendants have so conducted themselves as to enable their agent to hold himself out to the world as the proprietor of their business, and they are clearly undisclosed principals: *Ramazotti v. Bowring*. All that the plaintiff has to do, therefore, in order to charge the principals, is to show that the goods supplied were such as were ordinarily used in the business—that is to say, that they were within the reasonable scope of the agent's authority. . . .

Dec. 12. Lord Coleridge, C.J. The judgment which I am about to read has been written by my brother Wills, and I entirely concur in it.

■ WILLS, J. The plaintiff sues the defendants for the price of cigars supplied to the Victoria Hotel, Stockton-upon-Tees. The house was kept, not by the defendants, but by a person named Humble, whose name was over the door. The plaintiff gave credit to Humble, and to him alone, and had never heard of the defendants. The business, however, was really the defendants', and they had put Humble into it to manage it for them, and had forbidden him to buy cigars on credit. The cigars, however, were such as would usually be supplied to and dealt in at such an establishment. The learned county court judge held that the defendants were liable. I am of opinion that he was right.

There seems to be less of direct authority on the subject than one would expect. But I think that the Lord Chief Justice during the argument laid down the correct principle, viz., once it is established that the defendant was the real principal, the ordinary doctrine as to principal and agent applies—that the principal is liable for all the acts of the agent which are within the authority usually confided to an agent of that character, notwithstanding limitations, as between the principal and the agent, put upon that authority. It is said that it is only so where there has been a holding out of authority—which cannot be said of a case where the person supplying the goods knew nothing of the existence of a principal. But I do not think so. Otherwise, in every case of undisclosed principal, or at least in every case where the fact of there being a principal was undisclosed, the secret limitation of authority would prevail and defeat the action of the person dealing with the agent and then discovering that he was an agent and had a principal.

But in the case of a dormant partner it is clear law that no limitation of authority as between the dormant and active partner will avail the dormant partner as to things within the ordinary authority of a partner. The law of partnership is, on such a question, nothing but a branch of the general law of principal and agent, and it appears to me to be undisputed and conclusive on the point now under discussion.

The principle laid down by the Lord Chief Justice, and acted upon by the learned county court judge, appears to be identical with that enunciated in the judgments of Cockburn, C.J., and Mellor, J., in Edmunds v. Bushell, the circumstances of which case, though not identical with those of the present, come very near to them. There was no holding out, as the plaintiff knew nothing of the defendant. I appreciate the distinction drawn by Mr. Finlay in his argument, but the principle laid down in the judgments referred to, if correct, abundantly covers the present case. I cannot find that any doubt has ever been expressed that it is correct, and I think it is right, and that very mischievous consequences would often result if that principle were not upheld.

In my opinion this appeal ought to be dismissed with costs.

Appeal dismissed.

NOTE

The Restatement (Second) of Agency included a broad concept called "inherent agency power," which Section 8A of the Restatement defined as follows:

> Inherent agency power is a term used in the restatement of this subject to indicate the power of an agent which is derived not from authority, apparent authority or estoppel, but solely from the agency relation and exists for the protection of persons harmed by or dealing with a servant or other agent.

The Restatement (Second) of Agency § 194 states that an undisclosed principal is liable for acts of an agent "done on his account, if usual or necessary in such transactions, although forbidden by the principal."

Under the Restatement (Second) of Agency § 195, "An undisclosed principal who entrusts an agent with the management of his business is subject to liability to third persons with whom the agent enters into transactions usual in such business and on the principal's account, although contrary to the directions of the principal."

Although some set of rules for dealing with cases like *Watteau* is necessary, the vaguely defined concept of inherent agency power attracted more than its share of critics. The Restatement (Third) of Agency rejected the concept of inherent agency power in favor of a rule more narrowly targeted at cases like *Watteau*:

> **§ 2.06 Liability of Undisclosed Principal.**
>
> (1) An undisclosed principal is subject to liability to a third party who is justifiably induced to make a detrimental change in position by an agent acting on the principal's behalf and without actual authority if the principal, having notice of the agent's conduct and that it might induce others to change their positions, did not take reasonable steps to notify them of the facts.
>
> (2) An undisclosed principal may not rely on instructions given an agent that qualify or reduce the agent's authority to less than the authority a third party would reasonably believe the agent to have under the same circumstances if the principal had been disclosed.

The comments to § 2.06 claim that it reflects the rule of *Watteau* and Restatement (Second) § 195, but the Restatement (Third) rule in fact may be substantially narrower. It concludes with the qualification that the principal is liable "if the principal, having notice of the agent's conduct and that it might induce others to change their position, did not take reasonable steps to notify them of the facts." This makes the rule seem more akin to estoppel than to the old inherent agency power. It seems that the defendants in Watteau were not aware that Humble was buying cigars from *Watteau* and therefore would not be liable under the Restatement (third) rule—contrary to the actual result in *Watteau*.

ANALYSIS

1. **Is There Apparent Authority?** Is there any basis in this case for holding the defendants liable on a theory of apparent authority?
2. **Why the Result?** Humble had authority to buy "ales and mineral waters" from third parties but not "cigars, bovril, and other articles." (Bovril is a nonalcoholic drink.) The court claims that "mischievous consequences" would result from a decision for the defendants. What are those mischievous consequences? In responding to this question, ask yourself if there is any basis for distinguishing between ales and mineral waters, on the one hand, and cigars and bovril, on the other hand. Bear in mind that the plaintiffs seek recovery from the personal assets of the defendants, not just the assets (if any) invested by the defendants in the Victoria Hotel.

3. **Hypothetical.** The Restatement (Third) offers the following hypothetical:

> P Corporation produces musical recordings and employs A to engage performers. A's counterparts in the recording industry have authority to make unconditional contracts with performers, but B, who is A's superior within P Corporation, directs A to condition all payments to performers on the sales revenues that P Corporation receives from their work. B's direction to A is not known outside P Corporation.

Consider this hypothetical in light of the case that follows. Note that Restatement (Third) § 1.03 states:

> A person manifests assent or intention through written or spoken words or other conduct.

The drafters then explain:

> [A]n agent is sometimes placed in a position in an industry or setting in which holders of the position customarily have authority of a specific scope. Absent notice to third parties to the contrary, placing the agent in such a position constitutes a manifestation that the principal assents to be bound by actions by the agent that fall within that scope. . . . P Corporation has made a manifestation to performers with whom A deals on its behalf that it assets to be bound by contracts made by A on terms that are standard in the industry.

Kidd v. Thomas A. Edison, Inc.

239 Fed. 405 (S.D.N.Y.1917).

At Law. Action by Mary Carson Kidd against Thomas A. Edison, Incorporated. On defendant's motion to set aside, on exceptions, a verdict for plaintiff. Motion denied.

This is a motion by the defendant to set aside a verdict for the plaintiff on exceptions. The action was in contract, and depended upon the authority of one Fuller to make a contract with the plaintiff, engaging her without condition to sing for the defendant in a series of "tone test" recitals, designed to show the accuracy with which her voice was reproduced by the defendant's records. The defendant contended that Fuller's only authority was to engage the plaintiff for such recitals as he could later persuade dealers in the records to book her for all over the United States. The dealers, the defendant said, were to agree to pay her for the recitals, and the defendant would then guarantee her the dealers' performance. The plaintiff said the contract was an unconditional engagement for a singing tour, and the jury so found.

The sole exception of consequence was whether there was either any question of fact involved in Fuller's authority, or a fortiori whether there was no evidence of any authority. In either event the charge was erroneous, and the defendant's exception was good. The pertinent testimony was that of Maxwell, and was as follows: He intrusted to Fuller particularly the matters connected with the arranging of these "tone test" recitals. He told him to learn from the artists what fees they would expect, and to tell them that the defendant would pay the railroad fares and expenses. He also told Fuller to explain to them that the defendant would book them, and act as booking agent for them, and would see that the money was paid by the dealers; in fact, the defendant would itself pay it. He told him to prepare a form of contract suitable for such an arrangement with such artists as he succeeded in getting to go into it, and that he (Maxwell) would prepare a form of booking contract with the dealers. He told him to prepare a written contract with the artists and submit it to him (Maxwell), which he did. He told him that he was himself to make the contracts with the artists by which they were to be booked, that he was not to bring them to him (Maxwell), but that he should learn what fees they would demand, and then confirm the oral agreement by a letter, which would serve as a contract.

This is all the relevant testimony.

■ LEARNED HAND, DISTRICT JUDGE (after stating the facts as above).

The point involved is the scope of Fuller's "apparent authority," as distinct from the actual authority limited by the instructions which Maxwell gave him. The phrase "apparent authority," though it occurs repeatedly in the Reports, has been often criticized (Mechem, Law of Agency, §§ 720–726), and its use is by no means free from ambiguity. The scope of any authority must, of course, in the first place, be measured, not alone by the words in which it is created, but by the whole setting in which those words are used, including the customary powers of such agents. . . . This is, however, no more than to regard the whole of the communication between the principal and agent before assigning its meaning, and does not differ in method from any other interpretation of verbal acts. In considering what was Fuller's actual implied authority by custom, while it is fair to remember that the "tone test" recitals were new, in the sense that no one had ever before employed singers for just this purpose of comparing their voices with their mechanical reproduction, they were not new merely as musical recitals; for it was, of course, a common thing to engage singers for such recitals. When, therefore, an agent is selected, as was Fuller, to engage singers for musical recitals, the customary implication would seem to have been that his authority was without limitation of the kind here imposed, which was unheard of in the circumstances. The mere fact that the purpose of the recitals was advertisement, instead of entrance fees, gave no intimation to a singer dealing with him that the defendant's promise would be conditional upon so unusual a condition as that actually imposed. Being concerned to sell its records, the venture might rightly be regarded as undertaken on its own account, and, like similar enterprises, at its own cost. The natural surmise would certainly be that such an undertaking was a part of the advertising expenses of the business, and that therefore Fuller might engage singers upon similar terms to those upon which singers for recitals are generally engaged, where the manager expects a profit, direct or indirect.

Therefore it is enough for the decision to say that the customary extent of such an authority as was actually conferred comprised such a contract. If estoppel be, therefore, the basis of all "apparent authority," it existed here. Yet the argument involves a misunderstanding of the true significance of the doctrine, both historically (Responsibility for Tortious Acts: Its History, Wigmore, 7 Harv.L.Rev. 315, 383) and actually. The responsibility of a master for his servant's act is not at bottom a matter of consent to the express act, or of an estoppel to deny that consent, but it is a survival from ideas of status, and the imputed responsibility congenial to earlier times, preserved now from motives of policy. While we have substituted for the archaic status a test based upon consent, i.e., the general scope of the business, within that sphere the master is held by principles quite independent of his actual consent, and indeed in the face of his own instructions. . . . It is only a fiction to say that the principal is estopped, when he has not communicated with the third person and thus misled him. There are, indeed, the cases of customary authority, which perhaps come within the range of a true estoppel; but in other cases the principal may properly say that the authority which he delegated must be judged by his directions, taken together, and that it is unfair to charge him with misleading the public, because his agent, in executing that authority, has neither observed, nor communicated, an important part of them. Certainly it begs the question to assume that the principal has authorized his agent to communicate a part of his authority and not to disclose the rest. Hence, even in contract, there are many cases in which the principle of estoppel is a factitious effort to impose the rationale of a later time upon archaic ideas, which, it is true, owe their survival to convenience, but to a very different [one] from the putative convenience attributed to them.

However it may be of contracts, all color of plausibility falls away in the case of torts, where indeed the doctrine first arose, and where it still thrives. It makes no difference that the agent may be disregarding his principal's directions, secret or otherwise, so long as he continues in that larger field measured by the general scope of the business intrusted to his care. . . .

The considerations which have made the rule survive are apparent. If a man select another to act for him with some discretion, he has by that fact vouched to some extent for his reliability. While it may not be fair to impose upon him the results of a total departure from the general subject of his confidence, the detailed execution of his mandate stands on a different footing. The very purpose of delegated authority is to avoid constant recourse by third persons to the principal, which would be a corollary of denying the agent any latitude beyond his exact instructions. Once a third person has assured himself widely of the character of the agent's mandate, the very purpose of the relation demands the possibility of the principal's being bound through the agent's minor deviations. Thus, as so often happens, archaic ideas continue to serve good, though novel, purposes.

In the case at bar there was no question of fact for the jury touching the scope of Fuller's authority. His general business covered the whole tone test recitals; upon him was charged the duty of doing everything necessary in the premises, without recourse to Maxwell or any one else. It would certainly have been quite contrary to the expectations of the defendant, if any of the prospective performers at the recitals had insisted upon verifying directly with Maxwell the terms of her contract. It was precisely to delegate such negotiations to a competent substitute that they chose Fuller at all.

The exception is without merit; the motion is denied.

ANALYSIS

1. **What Legal Basis?** What is a better legal theory for liability in Kidd v. Thomas A. Edison, Inc., apparent authority or inherent agency power? As to apparent authority, what manifestations did the defendant make to the plaintiff?
2. **What Should the Parties Have Done?** What could each of the parties have done to avoid the problem that arose in this case and how does that bear on the wisdom of the decision?
3. **How Has the Law Changed?** How has the law changed under the Third Restatement, as discussed after the *Watteau* case?

Nogales Service Center v. Atlantic Richfield Company

126 Ariz. 133, 613 P.2d 293 (1980).

The trial below was on Nogales Service Center's (NSC) claim for breach of contract against Atlantic Richfield Company (ARCO). This is an appeal from the judgment entered on a jury verdict in favor of ARCO. NSC contends the trial court erred in denying certain instructions and in the admission and rejection of evidence.

Prior to June 1969, Albert F. Cafone and Angus McKenzie were produce brokers in Nogales, Arizona. They decided that profits could be derived from the operation at Nogales of a facility to sell fuel to the great number of trucks which seasonally came to Nogales, loaded with produce to be transported to points in the United States and Canada. No such enterprise was operating in Nogales at that time.

Before contacting ARCO, Cafone and McKenzie approached Texaco and Shell. They were looking for a supplier to lend them a large sum of money to be applied towards the construction and equipment of a suitable facility. They finally contacted ARCO, which was itself looking for a truck stop in the area. Cafone and McKenzie organized a corporation, Nogales Service Center, and entered into an agreement with ARCO for construction of the facility. The total estimated cost of the facility, which was to include an auto/truck service station, coffee shop, motel and brokerage offices, was $508,000. ARCO lent the corporation $300,000 to help finance construction.

Construction of the truck stop began in 1969 and was finished in early 1970. Operations began in April or May of 1970. As originally built, the facility did not include the motel and restaurant, a factor which created a definite problem. The funds which ARCO lent to NSC were not put in escrow and some were spent for a cantaloupe crop which failed, therefore the restaurant was not constructed.

NSC and ARCO also entered into a products agreement on November 4, 1969. It was to be effective for a period of 15 years, subject to termination by mutual agreement after the 10th year, and provided for the sale of fuel at prices to be fixed by ARCO, subject to change by the latter at any time without notice. It called for the purchase of at least 50 percent of NSC's fuel from ARCO.

NSC's operation was in financial difficulty from the beginning of its operation. Among other things, its price for diesel fuel was not competitive with truck stops in the Tucson area. In May of 1972, Cafone's brother-in-law, William Terpenning, bought out McKenzie and assumed his liability on the $300,000. In July and August, Cafone and Terpenning met in Los Angeles, California with Joe Tucker who was then ARCO's manager of truck stop marketing. The problem of competitive pricing was discussed. It was at these meetings that, according to Terpenning, NSC and ARCO entered into an oral agreement which formed the basis of NSC's claim. Terpenning testified that Tucker told him that the construction of a motel and restaurant at the truck stop was a "must"; that if NSC constructed these facilities, which were estimated to cost $400,000, it would lend $100,000; that ARCO would give NSC a 1 cent per gallon across the board discount on all diesel fuel; and that it would keep NSC "competitive." In reliance on Tucker's promise, Terpenning bought out Cafone, borrowed money and used his own funds to construct the motel and restaurant. ARCO approved the loan application after the construction was commenced and lent the $100,000 but the 1 cent per gallon discount was disapproved. According to Terpenning, ARCO never made NSC "competitive."

Terpenning and NSC defaulted on the original note and on the $100,000 note. ARCO then brought a foreclosure action and prevailed. This suit involves a counterclaim filed by NSC which was tried after the foreclosure judgment. For convenience in the trial court, NSC, the counterclaimant, was designated the plaintiff and the original plaintiff, ARCO, was designated the defendant.

At trial ARCO contended that Tucker never agreed to make NSC competitive or to give it an across-the-board 1 cent discount; that if such an agreement were made by Tucker it was outside his authority and that the statute of frauds barred any action on the alleged oral contract.

The trial court, *without objection* [emphasis supplied], gave the following instructions relating to the authority of an agent:

> An employee-agent has apparent authority to make an agreement binding on his employer-principal, if, but only if, the latter through officers or other agents authorized to do so has held out that [the] employee-agent . . . has such authority. In this case, in order to find Joe Tucker had apparent authority to make an agreement for ARCO, you must find that ARCO had actually or by necessary implication, represented to the officers of Nogales Service Center that Tucker had such authority; and you must find further that such representations were made by officers or other agents of ARCO having authority from the company to make them.
>
> If you find by a preponderance of all the evidence that such an agreement was made, then you shall consider whether those making it were authorized by their respective companies to do so. An employee-agent can legally bind his employer-principal only when he has actual or apparent authority to do so. Authority of either type, actual or apparent, can be derived only from acts of the employer-principal. An employee-agent cannot confer authority upon himself merely by claiming it for himself. If you find that Joe Tucker had no actual authority to enter into any agreement for ARCO, then he could do so in such a way as to bind ARCO if, but only if, you find that he had apparent authority to make an agreement.

The trial court refused to give the following instruction offered by the appellant:

> Requested Jury Instruction No. 21: ARCO's employees who dealt with Service Center in the claimed oral agreements made

> ARCO responsible for any such agreements if they are acts which usually accompany or are incidental to transactions which the agent is authorized to conduct, even if the employees were forbidden to make such agreements, if persons from Nogales Service Center reasonably believed that ARCO's employees were authorized to make them, and has no notice that ARCO's employees were not so authorized.

. . .

Appellee contends that No. 21 was covered by the instructions which were given. We do not agree. The instructions given covered only actual or apparent authority. Inherent authority depends upon neither of these concepts since it may make the principal liable because of conduct which he did not desire or direct, to persons who may or may not have known of his existence or who did not rely upon anything which the principal said or did. . . .

The Restatement (Second) of Agency § 8A (1957) defines inherent agency power:

> Inherent agency power is a term used in the restatement of this subject to indicate the power of an agent which is derived not from authority, apparent authority or estoppel, but solely from the agency relation and exists for the protection of persons harmed by or dealing with a servant or other agent.

The rationale of inherent agency power is explained in Comment b to § 8A:

> The other type of inherent power subjects the principal to contractual liability or to the loss of his property when an agent has acted improperly in entering into contracts or making conveyances. Here the power is based neither upon the consent of the principal nor upon his manifestations. There are three types of situations in which this type of power exists. First is that in which a general agent does something similar to what he is authorized to do, but in violation of orders. In this case the principal may become liable as a party to the transaction, even though he is undisclosed. As to such cases, see Sections 161 and 194. Second is the situation in which an agent acts purely for his own purposes in entering into a transaction which would be authorized if he were actuated by a proper motive. See §§ 165 and 262. The third type is that in which an agent is authorized to dispose of goods and departs from the authorized method of disposal. See §§ 175 and 201.

In many of the cases involving these situations the courts have rested liability upon the ground of 'apparent authority,' a phrase which has been used by the courts loosely. If the meaning of the term is restricted, as is done in Section 8, to those situations in which the principal has manifested the existence of authority to third persons, the term does not apply to the above situations. No theory of torts, contract or estoppel is sufficient to allow recovery in the cases. But because agents are fiduciaries acting generally in the principal's interests, and are trusted and controlled by him, it is fairer that the risk of loss caused by disobedience of agents should fall upon the principal rather than upon third persons.

Appellant's offered Instruction No. 21 is a paraphrase of § 161 of the Restatement (Second) of Agency which states:

> A general agent for a disclosed or partially disclosed principal subjects his principal to liability for acts done on his account which usually accompany or are incidental to transactions which the agent is authorized to conduct if, although they are forbidden by the principal, the other party reasonably believes that the agent is authorized to do them and has no notice that he is not so authorized.

As explained in Comment b to § 161, inherent power is to be distinguished from apparent authority:

> The Rule stated in this Section applies to cases in which there is apparent authority, but includes also cases in which there is no apparent authority. Thus, the principal may be liable upon a contract made by a general agent of a kind usually made by such agents, although he had been forbidden to make it and although there had been no manifestation of authority to the person dealing with the agent.

The rule set forth in § 161 was apparently followed by the court in Lois Grunow Memorial Clinic v. Davis, 49 Ariz. 277, 66 P.2d 238 (1937) although the court at times used the term "implied authority" for inherent authority and confused "apparent authority" with inherent authority.

Sec. 161 uses the term "general agent." The Restatement (Second) of Agency defines a "general agent" as an agent authorized to conduct a series of transactions involving a continuity of service. Restatement (Second) of Agency § 3 (1957). Tucker dealt with the various truck stops accounts in the area of special problems, on matters of investment and discounts. Although the evidence was that he did not have authority to grant the alleged across-the-board discount, he did have authority to grant certain discounts such as volume discounts, gasoline merchandising discounts and dealer temporary aid discounts. On the subject of an agent disobeying the principal it was observed by Judge Learned Hand in the case of Kidd v. Thomas A. Edison, Inc., 239 F. 405 (S.D.N.Y.1917), aff'd, 242 F. 923 (2d Cir.1917) that:

> It makes no difference that the agent may be disregarding his principal's directions, secret or otherwise, so long as he continues in that larger field measured by the general scope of the business intrusted to his care.

239 F. at 407. However, there are two reasons why there was no error in refusing [Instruction 21]. First, [this instruction] conflict[s] with and contradict[s] the instruction given, without objection, which told the jury the agreement was binding only if there was actual or apparent authority. The second reason is the form of objection [was insufficiently specific].

. . .

Affirmed.

ANALYSIS

1. **Does the Distinction Matter?** Is the distinction between apparent authority and inherent agency power a useful one in a case such as *Nogales Service Center*?

2. **What Evidence?** What proof might the plaintiff have offered in support of each theory?

3. **Necessary Protections.** What can reasonably be expected of a person like Terpenning to assure himself that the person with whom he was dealing had authority to make the deal that Tucker offered?

4. **How Has the Law Changed?** Again, how has the law changed under the Third Restatement, discussed after the *Watteau* case?

PROBLEMS

1. Suppose Professor Paula Potter has a student research assistant, Allie. Allie is about to graduate and Paula asks her to hire a successor. Paula says that she is willing to pay $9 per hour for 100 hours of work. Allie finds another student, Zelda, who wants the job but points out that the going rate is $10 per hour. Allie says, "Well, if that's the going rate, that's O.K. You have the job." Thereafter Paula tells Zelda that she will pay only $9 and Zelda (who has turned down other job offers) seeks to enforce the contract that she thinks she has for $10 per hour. Who wins? Why? Suppose Paula had said to Allie, "Find the best available person, tell that person what the job is and how much I am willing to pay, and send her or him to me so I can offer the job if I am satisfied with your choice." Same result?

2. Suppose you are the lawyer for M/M Records, a small record company with good management and exciting prospects. The head of the company, Millie Mogul, has just hired a woman named Sheena Swiftie, who is friendly with a number of leading recording stars and hopes some day to establish herself as an independent agent in the entertainment industry, but wants to start out as an employee (largely

because she needs a steady income). Sheena's job is to line up recording stars to make records for M/M Records. Sheena will be paid a salary plus bonuses based on what she produces. Millie tells you, "Sheena seems a bit flaky, but I think she can deliver." In recent years, in the recording business, it has become common for record companies to offer substantial guarantees to star performers, But M/M Records does not do so, because it cannot afford to take the risk. Instead, it offers higher royalties than its competitors do. Millie wants Sheena to have authority to pin artists down to contracts when the moment is right, but has emphasized to Sheena the M/M Records policy of no guarantees. Millie asks you if she has anything to worry about and, if she does, what suggestions you might have. You are aware that Millie tends to resent lawyers in general because she thinks they are "deal breakers." What is your response to her?

D. RATIFICATION

Botticello v. Stefanovicz

177 Conn. 22, 411 A.2d 16 (1979).

This case concerns the enforceability of an agreement for the sale of real property when that agreement has been executed by a person owning only an undivided half interest in the property. . . .

The finding of the trial court discloses the following undisputed facts: The defendants, Mary and Walter Stefanovicz (hereinafter "Mary" and "Walter") in 1943 acquired as tenants in common a farm situated in the towns of Colchester and Lebanon. In the fall of 1965, the plaintiff, Anthony Botticello, became interested in the property. When he first visited the farm, Walter advised him that the asking price was $100,000. The following January, the plaintiff again visited the farm and made a counteroffer of $75,000. At that time, Mary stated that there was "no way" she could sell it for that amount. Ultimately the plaintiff and Walter agreed upon a price of $85,000 for a lease with an option to purchase; during these negotiations, Mary stated that she would not sell the property for less than that amount.

The informal agreement was finalized with the assistance of counsel for both Walter and the plaintiff. The agreement was drawn up by Walter's attorney after consultation with Walter and the plaintiff; it was then sent to, and modified by, the plaintiff's attorney. The agreement was signed by Walter and by the plaintiff. Neither the plaintiff nor his attorney, nor Walter's attorney, was then aware of the fact that Walter did not own the property outright. The plaintiff, although a successful businessman with considerable experience in real estate never requested his attorney to do a title search of any kind, and consequently no title search was done. Walter never represented to the plaintiff or the plaintiff's attorney, or to his own attorney, that he was acting for his wife, as her agent. Mary's part ownership came to light in 1968, when a third party sought an easement over the land in question.

Shortly after the execution of the lease and option-to-purchase agreement, the plaintiff took possession of the property. He made substantial improvements on the property and, in 1971, properly exercised his option to purchase. When the defendants refused to honor the option agreement, the plaintiff commenced the present action against both Mary and Walter, seeking specific performance, possession of the premises, and damages.

The trial court found the issues for the plaintiff and ordered specific performance of the option-to-purchase agreement. In their appeal, the defendants [claim] that Mary was never a party to the agreement, and its terms may therefore not be enforced as to her. . . .

The plaintiff alleged, and the trial court agreed, that although Mary was not a party to the lease and option-to-purchase agreement, its terms were nonetheless binding upon her because Walter acted as her authorized agent in the negotiations, discussions, and execution of the written agreement. The defendants have attacked several findings of fact and conclusions of law, claiming that the underlying facts and applicable law do not support the court's conclusion of agency. We agree.

Agency is defined as " 'the fiduciary relationship which results from manifestation of consent by one person to another that the other shall act on his behalf and subject to his control, and consent by the other so to act. . . .' Restatement (Second), 1 Agency § 1." McLaughlin v. Chicken Delight, Inc., 164 Conn. 317, 322, 321 A.2d 456 (1973). Thus, the three elements required to show the existence of an agency relationship include: (1) a manifestation by the principal that the agent will act for him; (2) acceptance by the agent of the undertaking; and (3) an understanding between the parties that the principal will be in control of the undertaking. Restatement (Second), 1 Agency § 1, comment b (1958).

The existence of an agency relationship is a question of fact. The burden of proving agency is on the plaintiff and it must be proven by a fair preponderance of the evidence. Marital status cannot in and of itself prove the agency relationship. Nor does the fact that the defendants owned the land jointly make one the agent for the other.

The facts set forth in the court's finding are wholly insufficient to support the court's conclusion that Walter acted as Mary's authorized agent in the discussions concerning the sale of their farm and in the execution of the written agreement. . . . The finding indicates that when the farm was purchased, and when the couple transferred property to their sons, Walter handled many of the business aspects, including making payments for taxes, insurance, and mortgage. The finding also discloses that Mary and Walter discussed the sale of the farm, and that

Mary remarked that she would not sell it for $75,000, and would not sell it for less than $85,000. A statement that one will not sell for less than a certain amount is by no means the equivalent of an agreement to sell for that amount. Moreover, the fact that one spouse tends more to business matters than the other does not, absent other evidence of agreement or authorization, constitute the delegation of power as to an agent. What is most damaging to the plaintiff's case is the court's uncontradicted finding that, although Mary may have acquiesced in Walter's handling of many business matters, Walter never signed any documents as agent for Mary prior to 1966. Mary had consistently signed any deed, mortgage, or mortgage note in connection with their jointly held property.

. . .

The plaintiff argues, alternatively, that even if no agency relationship existed at the time the agreement was signed, Mary was bound by the contract executed by her husband because she ratified its terms by her subsequent conduct. The trial court accepted this alternative argument as well, concluding that Mary had ratified the agreement by receiving and accepting payments from the plaintiff, and by acquiescing in his substantial improvements to the farm. The underlying facts, however, do not support the conclusion of ratification.

Ratification is defined as "the affirmance by a person of a prior act which did not bind him but which was done or professedly done on his account." Restatement (Second), 1 Agency § 82 (1958). Ratification requires "acceptance of the results of the act with an intent to ratify, and with full knowledge of all the material circumstances." Ansonia v. Cooper, 64 Conn. 536, 544, 30 A. 760 (1894). . . .

The finding neither indicates an intent by Mary to ratify the agreement, nor establishes her knowledge of all the material circumstances surrounding the deal. At most, Mary observed the plaintiff occupying and improving the land, received rental payments from the plaintiff from time to time, knew that she had an interest in the property, and knew that the use, occupancy, and rentals were pursuant to a written agreement she had not signed. None of these facts is sufficient to support the conclusion that Mary ratified the agreement and thus bound herself to its terms. It is undisputed that Walter had the power to lease his own undivided one-half interest in the property and the facts found by the trial court could be referable to that fact alone. Moreover, the fact that the rental payments were used for "family" purposes indicates nothing more than one spouse providing for the other.

The plaintiff makes the further argument that Mary ratified the agreement simply by receiving its benefits and by failing to repudiate it. See Restatement (Second), 1 Agency § 98 (1958). The plaintiff fails to recognize that before the receipt of benefits may constitute ratification, the other requisites for ratification must first be present. "Thus if the original transaction was not purported to be done on account of the principal, the fact that the principal receives its proceeds does not make him a party to it." Restatement (Second), 1 Agency § 98, comment f (1958). Since Walter at no time purported to be acting on his wife's behalf, as is essential to effective subsequent ratification, Mary is not bound by the terms of the agreement, and specific performance cannot be ordered as to her.

PROBLEMS

Ratification is a means by which the principal can say, "my agent didn't have the right to enter into this contract, but I'm glad she did so. Accordingly, I'll affirm the transaction and agree to be bound by the contract." Any ratification case involves two critical questions: First, what types of acts constitute an affirmation by the principal? Second, what effect should we give to that affirmation?

Obviously, one can expressly affirm a contract. The principal can say something like: "Gosh, what a wonderful deal. I'll go forward with it." Harder questions arise in implied affirmation cases. Consider the following examples:

1. Suppose Pam is a writer. Her husband Alex enters into a contract with ABC Book Publishers under which Pam's next book is to go to ABC. Pam gets a check from ABC, representing the advance on the contract, which she cashes. She then spends the proceeds on a new computer for her office. Some months later Pam tries to sell her new book to another publisher. ABC claims the book. Pam correctly points out that Alex had no authority to act as her agent. ABC responds by saying that she had ratified the contract. Who wins?

2. Suppose Pam argues that she thought the check was for royalties on one of her previous books, which ABC had published. She asserts that she neither knew nor had reason to know that it was an advance on her next book. Who wins?

3. Alan is a slightly deranged fan of Pam's books. Alan goes to a local landscaping company. Pretending to be Pam's butler, he asks the company to cut Pam's grass. Pam arrives home just after the men finished up. Pam thanks them and goes inside. The company sues her for refusing to pay. Pam correctly points out that Alan had no authority to enter into this contract. The company claims she ratified the contract by accepting and retaining its benefits. Who wins?

4. Paula is an investor who has opened an account at a local brokerage. She instructs Al, her broker, only to purchase U.S. treasury bonds for the account. Al disregards those instructions and buys stock in a new very risky high-tech company. Paula does not learn about this until her first monthly statement arrives. She decides to take a wait and see attitude. When her next monthly statement arrives she notices that the stock's price has dropped rather drastically. She calls Al and demands that he close the account and reimburse her for the money she lost. She correctly claims he had no authority to buy the stock. Al closes the account, but refuses to make Paula's losses good. Al claims Paula ratified the purchase by waiting. Who is right: Paula or Al?

5. Paula owns a mansion called Whiteacre Manor. Alan, having no authority to do so, enters into a sale contract with Ted by which Ted is to purchase Whiteacre Manor. The next day the mansion burns to the ground. Paula then expressly affirms the contract. Ted says she's too late. Who wins?

. . .

We turn now to the question of relief. In view of our holding that Mary never authorized her husband to act as her agent for any purpose connected with the lease and option-to-purchase agreement, recovery against her is precluded. As to Walter, the fact that his ownership was restricted to an undivided one-half interest in no way limited his capacity to contract. He contracted to convey full title and for breach of that contract he may be held liable. The facts of the case are sufficient to furnish a basis for relief to the plaintiff by specific performance or by damages.

There is error as to the judgment against the defendant Mary Stefanovicz; the judgment as to her is set aside and the case remanded with direction to render judgment in her favor. As to the defendant Walter Stefanovicz, there is error only as to the remedy ordered. The judgment as to him is set aside and the case remanded for a new trial limited to the form of relief.

Ercanbrack v. Crandall-Walker Motor Company, Inc.

550 P.2d 723 (Utah Sup.Ct.1976).

■ TAYLOR, DISTRICT JUDGE: Plaintiff appeals from an order of the trial court granting defendant's motion to dismiss the complaint and dismissing plaintiff's complaint. Plaintiff initially filed a complaint for specific performance of an alleged contract for the purchase of a Ford pickup truck.

. . .

On the 25th day of October, 1973, plaintiff signed a "Vehicle Buyer's Order" which was also signed by a salesman for the defendant company. The salesman advised the plaintiff that the truck would have to be ordered from the factory. From time to time the plaintiff contacted the salesman as to when the new truck would arrive. In March of 1974 the plaintiff met an officer of the company off the premises and casually asked him if his black truck had gotten there yet. The officer responded "No, we haven't heard on it yet." There was no further conversation. The record indicates that no further contact was made by the plaintiff with any officer of the defendant company until May of 1974 when the plaintiff did talk to an officer of the corporation who advised him that the price of the truck had increased and offered to sell the truck to the plaintiff for the increased price. The plaintiff refused to take the new truck. At this time an officer of the defendant company advised the plaintiff that the "Vehicle Buyer's Order" had never been signed or accepted by the company's sales manager or any officer of the company.

The "Vehicle Buyer's Order" was introduced into evidence and showed that just above the plaintiff's signature appeared the following words: "THIS ORDER IS NOT VALID UNLESS SIGNED AS ACCEPTED HERE BY SALESMANAGER OR OFFICER OF THE COMPANY." The plaintiff testified that he knew that the sales manager or officer of the company had not signed the agreement but that he thought it was sufficient for the salesman who made out the order to sign the order. The trial court held that the "Vehicle Buyer's Order" was not a valid contract between the parties since it had not been accepted by the sales manager or an officer of the defendant company. The plaintiff, appellant herein, seeks a reversal of the judgment of the trial court and cites [the] grounds therefor . . . listed as follows:

> 1. Failure on the part of the company or an officer of the company to notify plaintiff of nonacceptance amounts to a ratification of the contract.
>
> 2. The defendant is estopped to deny the agency of the salesman and ratified the salesman's act in stating to the plaintiff that the order had been accepted by failure of the defendant to take some positive action to inform the plaintiff to the contrary.
>
> 3. The defendant was bound by the terms of the "Vehicle Buyer's Order" even if an officer of the company did not sign said order where it led the plaintiff to believe that the offer had been accepted by the acts of the salesman.

. . .

In support of plaintiff's contention that failure to notify or silence amounts to an affirmance of the contract the plaintiff cites Restatement of Agency, Second, p. 244, § 94 [comment]:

> Failure to Act as Affirmance:
>
> a. Silence under such circumstances that, according to the ordinary experience and habits of men, one would naturally be expected to speak if he did not consent, is evidence from which assent can be inferred. Such inference may be made although the purported principal had no knowledge that the other party would rely upon the supposed authority of the agent; his knowledge of such fact, however, coupled with his silence would ordinarily justify an inference of assent by him.

Plaintiff's reliance upon this section is not justified. The balance of [the comment to] § 94, which was not quoted by the plaintiff, reads as follows:

> Whether or not such an inference is to be drawn is a question for the jury, unless the case is so clear that reasonable men could come to but one conclusion.

The trial court after hearing the evidence and observing the witnesses concluded that an inference from silence was not justified and ruled against the plaintiff. While this was not a jury question, it was a question for the trier of the fact and the trial court having rejected the contention, such ruling should not be upset upon appeal.

In further support of plaintiff's contention with regard to failure to notify of nonacceptance of the contract or ratification of the contract, plaintiff cites 3 Am.Jur.2d 565–6, Agency, § 179. This section discusses the failure to promptly repudiate the agent's acts but points out that this duty arises only after information of the transaction is received by the principal. There is no evidence in the record that the defendant company knew of the acts of their agent. Therefore, plaintiff's first contention must be rejected.

The argument made with respect to estoppel to deny the agency of the salesman is this: The company ratified the salesman's act by stating to the plaintiff that the order had been accepted by failing to take some positive action to inform the plaintiff to the contrary.

Plaintiff's contention in this regard is without merit. The evidence in the record shows that the only notification to plaintiff that the order had been accepted came from the salesman of the defendant company and not from an officer or sales manager of the company. The company cannot be estopped by failing to take some positive action about a matter which the evidence shows the defendant's officer or sales manager had no knowledge. The authorities cited by plaintiff assume that the principal knows that another has purported to act as his agent, or after receiving information that an act had been done without actual or apparent authority is not bound by that act under the law of agency unless he ratifies the act. Ratification of an act about which the principal knows nothing is inherently impossible.

With regard to plaintiff's contention that the defendant was bound by the terms of the "Vehicle Buyer's Order" even though an officer did not sign said order the plaintiff contends:

It is fundamental contract law that the parties may become bound by the terms of a contract even though they did not sign the contract, where they have otherwise indicated their acceptance of the contract, or led the other party to so believe that they have accepted the contract.[2]

This is a sound principle of contract law but has no application in this case.

Plaintiff relies on the case of Albright v. Stegeman Motor Car Company, 168 Wis. 557, 170 N.W. 951 (1919), which case adopts the foregoing principle of contract law. Albright is easily distinguished from this case. The order form in the Albright case contained the clause:

This proposal, if accepted, constitutes a contract, subject to the approval of the Stegeman Motor Car Company, at its office in Milwaukee, and must be countersigned by an officer of the company to be valid and in force.

This clause was placed in the order form for the same reason that the clause in the order form involved herein, to wit, that to make a binding contract that an officer of the company must accept the order form. [Sic.] In Albright there was no question of agency involved as there is in this case. The Stegeman Motor Car Company was a manufacturer of motor cars and trucks at Milwaukee. The plaintiff ordered the truck from the defendant and on one occasion paid the sum of $450 and on another occasion the sum of $500, took the company's receipt therefor and on the same date deposited in a like manner $1,150 more. After the order was placed the company entered upon the building on the truck, the plaintiff secured employment at the factory of the company in order that he could work on his truck and become familiar with its construction. The order required the truck to be delivered on or about April 1st. It was not completed April 1st nor for some time thereafter. On three different occasions the plaintiff served notice on the company that unless the truck was completed on various dates he would cancel the order. A final agreement between the plaintiff and the officers of the company was that if the truck should be delivered on the 12th of May, the plaintiff would be satisfied. On the 10th day of May the plaintiff left the factory and notified the company that he was going to cancel the order. The company refused to accept or honor the cancellation. The Supreme Court of Wisconsin held:

Conceding that the order was never countersigned by an officer of the company as required by its terms, the inquiry is whether the company otherwise became bound thereon. It is undisputed that shortly after the date of the order the company started work on the truck to be delivered in fulfillment thereof, that the appellant was cognizant of the fact, that he secured work in the factory in order that he might work on 'his' truck and become familiar with its construction, that delay in its completion was the subject of frequent complaint and discussion, and

[2] 17 Am.Jur.2d, § 70, pp. 408–409.

that he even had the truck out on trial trips. If this is not sufficient to indicate an acceptance of the order by the company, the receipt and retention by it of $450 down payment is certainly sufficient to estop it from denying its acceptance of the order.

. . .

The defendant's motion to dismiss and dismissal of plaintiffs complaint were properly granted by the trial court. The decision below is affirmed. Costs to respondent.

■ HENRIOD, C.J., and TUCKETT, J., concur.

■ CROCKETT, JUSTICE (dissenting): It was the defendant who selected its salesman and entrusted him with the responsibility of procuring the plaintiff to sign the buyer's order, and he signed it himself, upon a representation to the plaintiff that he had a contract to purchase the truck.[1] In subsequent conferences about changes in price, similar representations were made to the plaintiff from October 25, 1973 until December of 1974, under the assumption that there was a binding contract. It was not until the impasse and disagreement occurred that the defendant then sprung the defense that the contract had not been accepted by an authorized company officer. It is a sound principle of law that one who claims a right to repudiate a contract must act with reasonable promptness or be deemed to waive that right. See Scott v. Walton, 32 Or. 460, 52 P. 180 (1898) where it is stated that a party "cannot retain the fruits of the contract awaiting future development to determine whether it will be more profitable for him to affirm or disaffirm it." . . .

It is repugnant to my sense of justice to permit the defendant to thus delude the plaintiff and keep him committed on a contract for all those months, then when the showdown comes, spring the proposition that the defendant was never bound anyway. I would reverse the judgment. MAUGHAN, J., concurs in the dissenting opinion of CROCKETT, J.

ANALYSIS

1. **Imputation.** The salesman was an employee of the defendant. For purposes of estoppel, why wasn't his knowledge of the existence of the contract imputed to the defendant?
2. **Buyer's Options.** How was the plaintiff to know that the salesman was not somehow authorized to act on behalf of the salesmanager or an officer of the defendant? What was he supposed to do when the salesman signed the contract and told him that they had a deal?

---

1 Where loss must fall on one of two parties, it should be borne by the one who chose the party who created the circumstances out of which the loss arose. . . .

3. **Documentation.** What do you suppose the salesman did with the "Vehicle Buyer's Order"?

4. **Law vs. Fact.** Do the majority and dissenting opinions seem to be relying on the same set of facts?

E. ESTOPPEL

Hoddeson v. Koos Bros.

47 N.J.Super. 224, 135 A.2d 702 (App.Div.1957).

The occurrence which engages our present attention is a little more than conventionally unconventional in the common course of trade. Old questions appear in new styles. A digest of the story told by Mrs. Hoddeson will be informative and perhaps admonitory to the unwary shopper.

The plaintiff Mrs. Hoddeson was acquainted with the spacious furniture store conducted by the defendant, Koos Bros., a corporation, at No. 1859 St. George Avenue in the City of Rahway. On a previous observational visit, her eyes had fallen upon certain articles of bedroom furniture which she ardently desired to acquire for her home. It has been said that "the sea hath bounds but deep desire hath none." Her sympathetic mother liberated her from the grasp of despair and bestowed upon her a gift of $165 with which to consummate the purchase.

It was in the forenoon of August 22, 1956 that Mrs. Hoddeson, accompanied by her aunt and four children, happily journeyed from her home in South River to the defendant's store to attain her objective. Upon entering, she was greeted by a tall man with dark hair frosted at the temples and clad in a light gray suit. He inquired if he could be of assistance, and she informed him specifically of her mission. Whereupon he immediately guided her, her aunt, and the flock to the mirror then on display and priced at $29 which Mrs. Hoddeson identified, and next to the location of the designated bedroom furniture which she had described.

Upon confirming her selections the man withdrew from his pocket a small pad or paper upon which he presumably recorded her order and calculated the total purchase price to be $168.50. Mrs. Hoddeson handed to him the $168.50 in cash. He informed her the articles other than those on display were not in stock, and that reproductions would upon notice be delivered to her in September. Alas, she omitted to request from him a receipt for her cash disbursement. The transaction consumed in time a period from 30 to 40 minutes.

Mrs. Hoddeson impatiently awaited the delivery of the articles of furniture, but a span of time beyond the assured date of delivery elapsed, which motivated her to inquire of the defendant the cause of the unexpected delay. Sorrowful, indeed, was she to learn from the defendant that its records failed to disclose any such sale to her and any such monetary credit in payment.

. . .

Although the amount of money involved is relatively inconsiderable, the defendant has resolved to incur the expense of this appeal. . . .

It eventuated that Mrs. Hoddeson and her aunt were subsequently unable positively to recognize among the defendant's regularly employed salesmen the individual with whom Mrs. Hoddeson had arranged for the purchase, although when she and her aunt were afforded the opportunities to gaze intently at one of the five salesmen assigned to that department of the store, both indicated a resemblance of one of them to the purported salesman, but frankly acknowledged the incertitude of their identification. The defendant's records revealed that the salesman bearing the alleged resemblance was on vacation and hence presumably absent from the store during the week of August 22, 1956.

As you will at this point surmise, the insistence of the defendant at the trial was that the person who served Mrs. Hoddeson was an impostor deceitfully impersonating a salesman of the defendant without the latter's knowledge.

. . .

Where a party seeks to impose liability upon an alleged principal on a contract made by an alleged agent, as here, the party must assume the obligation of proving the agency relationship. It is not the burden of the alleged principal to disprove it.

Concisely stated, the liability of a principal to third parties for the acts of an agent may be shown by proof disclosing (1) express or real authority which has been definitely granted; (2) implied authority, that is, to do all that is proper, customarily incidental and reasonably appropriate to the exercise of the authority granted; and (3) apparent authority, such as where the principal by words, conduct, or other indicative manifestations has "held out" the person to be his agent.

Obviously the plaintiffs' evidence in the present action does not substantiate the existence of any basic express authority or project any question implicating implied authority. The point here debated is whether or not the evidence circumstantiates the presence of apparent authority, and it is at this very point we come face to face with the general rule of law that the apparency and appearance of authority must be shown to have been created by the manifestations of the alleged principal, and not alone and solely by proof of those of the supposed agent. Assuredly the law cannot permit apparent authority to be established by the mere proof that a mountebank in fact exercised it.

The plaintiffs here prosecuted an action in assumpsit, alleging a privity of contract with the defendant through the relationship of agency between the latter and the salesman. The inadequacy of the evidence to prove the alleged essential element of agency obliges us to reverse the judgment.

But prelude, as we may do here, a case in which a reconciliation of the factual circumstances disclosed by the evidence of both the plaintiffs and the defendant exhibits an unalleged and an undetermined justiciable cause of action, should the plaintiffs, by our reversal of the judgment, be conclusively denied the opportunity, auspicious or not, appropriately and not mistakenly, to seek judicial relief?

Let us hypothesize for the purposes of our present comments that the acting salesman was not in fact an employee of the defendant, yet he behaved and deported himself during the stated period in the business establishment of the defendant in the manner described by the evidence adduced on behalf of the plaintiffs, would the defendant be immune as a matter of law from liability for the plaintiffs' loss? The tincture of estoppel that gives color to instances of apparent authority might in the law operate likewise to preclude a defendant's denial of liability. It matters little whether for immediate purposes we entitle or characterize the principle of law in such cases as "agency by estoppel" or "a tortious dereliction of duty owed to an invited customer." That which we have in mind are the unique occurrences where solely through the lack of the proprietor's reasonable surveillance and supervision an impostor falsely impersonates in the place of business an agent or servant of his. Certainly the proprietor's duty of care and precaution for the safety and security of the customer encompasses more than the diligent observance and removal of banana peels from the aisles. Broadly stated, the duty of the proprietor also encircles the exercise of reasonable care and vigilance to protect the customer from loss occasioned by the deceptions of an apparent salesman. The rule that those who bargain without inquiry with an apparent agent do so at the risk and peril of an absence of the agent's authority has a patently impracticable application to the customers who patronize our modern department stores.

Our concept of the modern law is that where a proprietor of a place of business by his dereliction of duty enables one who is not his agent conspicuously to act as such and ostensibly to transact the proprietor's business with a patron in the establishment, the appearances being of such a character as to lead a person of ordinary prudence and circumspection to believe that the impostor was in truth the proprietor's agent, in such circumstances the law will not permit the proprietor defensively to avail himself of the impostor's lack of authority and thus escape liability for the consequential loss thereby sustained by the customer.

. . .

Let it not be inferred from our remarks that we have derived from the record before us a conviction that the defendant in the present case was heedless of its duty, that Mrs. Hoddeson acted with ordinary prudence, or that the factual circumstances were as represented at the trial.

In reversing the judgment under review, the interests of justice seem to us to recommend the allowance of a new trial with the privilege accorded the plaintiffs to reconstruct the architecture of their complaint appropriately to project for determination the justiciable issue to which, in view of the inquisitive object of the present appeal, we have alluded. We do not in the exercise of our modern processes of appellate review permit the formalities of a pleading of themselves to defeat the substantial opportunities of the parties.

Reversed and new trial allowed.

ANALYSIS

1. **Reasons for Litigation.** This is one of several cases in this text in which parties vigorously litigated disputes involving seemingly trivial amounts. Why on earth would Koos Bros. have gone to such lengths and expense?
2. **Proof on Remand.** What will plaintiff need to prove on remand to justify an estoppel-based verdict in her favor?
3. **Executory Contract.** What result if plaintiff and the alleged imposter had merely entered into a contract for the purchase of the furniture, rather than exchanging money?

Trustees of the American Federation of Musicians and Employers' Pension Fund v. Steven Scott Enterprises, Inc.

40 F.Supp.2d 503 (S.D.N.Y.1999).

I. Factual Background

Plaintiffs [are] the Trustees of the American Federation of Musicians and Employers' Pension Fund (the "Pension Fund"), [a multi-employer pension fund]. . . . Steven Scott is a company that employs musicians to perform for its clients at various engagements, typically single engagements such as weddings or bar mitzvahs. Steven Scott has been a signatory to various collective bargaining agreements with Local 802, the local union for musicians in New York City. Under these collective bargaining agreements, Steven Scott is required to make certain contributions to the Pension Fund at specified rates. [William] Moriarity has been the President of Local 802 and a Trustee of the Pension Fund since January 1, 1993.

Plaintiffs [seek an audit of] Steven Scott's records under Article 9, Section 8 of the Agreement and Declaration of Trust of the American Federation of Musicians and Employers' Pension Fund ("Trust Agreement"), the collective bargaining agreement that requires an employer to make contributions on behalf of its covered employees. . . .

At the core of Steven Scott's motion for summary judgment are fifteen settlement agreements that defendant entered into with Moriarity, Local 802 President and Pension Fund Trustee, over the course of a three year period, from 1993 to 1996. The substance of each agreement includes the following terms: (1) that Steven Scott agrees to pay a certain sum of money to the Pension Fund for certain employees; (2) that the agreement is in full settlement of all monetary claims against Steven Scott through a specified date; (3) that the agreement binds Local 802, the Pension Fund, and Steven Scott; and (4) that each party, including Moriarity, "acknowledges, represents, and warrants that they are authorized to enter into, execute, deliver, perform, and implement the agreement." In addition, each agreement contains a ratification clause that provides:

[Local 802] and the [Pension Fund] agree to accept the aforesaid payment by [Steven Scott] in full satisfaction of all pension benefit contributions due the [Pension Fund] on behalf of the aforesaid individuals for the period ending [on a specified date]. Negotiation of check for pension benefit contributions shall be deemed ratification of this Agreement.

Each agreement is signed by two parties: Joseph Mileti, an officer and duly authorized agent for Steven Scott, and Moriarity. Moriarity's signature block appears as follows:

ASSOCIATED MUSICIANS OF GREATER NEW YORK, LOCAL 802, A.F. of M

By ___________

William Moriarity An Officer and Duly Authorized Agent

Steven Scott tendered each of the fifteen settlement checks, accompanied by a three-page settlement agreement and a list of employee names and contribution amounts, to Local 802, [which] then forwarded the agreements and checks to the Pension Fund. The checks were processed by Pension Fund clerical workers who were in charge of processing all contributions to the Pension Fund from various employers. . . .

The procedure for handling checks and remittance forms is as follows: (1) Pension Fund clerical workers review the checks to determine whether the signature on the check matches a signatory employer; (2) then they deposit the checks in a bank; and (3) they forward the accompanying remittance forms to an outside agency for data processing. . . .

Eight of the settlement checks and seven of the fifteen settlement agreements were found in plaintiffs' files. Although the settlement checks bear no special legend on the face of the check stating that the checks are in full satisfaction of any disputed or owing debt, each check was accompanied by a settlement agreement, which unequivocally stated that the check was in full settlement of all obligations owed by Steven Scott through a specified date. The Pension Fund admitted that it received a settlement agreement along with each of the fifteen checks. It is also undisputed that all fifteen settlement checks were cashed by the Pension Fund.

> **NOTE**
>
> At least as to the checks, presumably the court meant the defendant's files.

As a Pension Fund Trustee and Local 802 President, Moriarity was authorized to collect Pension Fund contributions from employers. However, Moriarity was not authorized to unilaterally enter into settlement agreements that were in full satisfaction of any owing debts to the Pension Fund. Under the terms of the Trust Agreement that governs the Pension Fund, only the Board of Trustees of the Pension Fund has the authority to enter into such agreements. . . . However, the Pension Fund acknowledges that Steven Scott was not mailed a copy of the Trust Agreement until June 1995, and thus could not have known of the Board's exclusive authority to enter into such agreements prior to executing a majority of settlement agreements at issue. Furthermore, the Pension Fund has not alleged any facts to show that Steven Scott had any reason to know of the Board's exclusive authority in such matters. Although each settlement agreement covers varying periods of time, it is undisputed that the agreements, if enforceable against the Pension Fund, would estop the Pension Fund from auditing Steven Scott for 1992, 1993, and 1994. Thus, the only question for the court to decide is whether these agreements bind the Pension Fund.

II. Discussion

. . .

B. Equitable Estoppel and Apparent Authority

Steven Scott argues that the Pension Fund should be estopped from denying that it is bound by the settlement agreements. Steven Scott asserts that it reasonably relied on Moriarity's repeated written representations that he was authorized to bind the Pension Fund when it entered into fifteen settlement contracts with Moriarity. Steven Scott bases its arguments on the principles of equitable estoppel and apparent authority.

. . . [D]efendant must prove all four elements of equitable estoppel, which are (1) a promise, (2) reliance on that promise, (3) injury caused by the reliance, and (4) an injustice if the promise is not enforced.

Apparent authority shares some of the same elements that comprise equitable estoppel. "[A] principal may be estopped from denying apparent authority if (1) the principal's intentional or negligent acts, including acts of omission, created an appearance of authority in the agent, (2) on which a third party reasonably and in good faith relied, and (3) such reliance resulted in a detrimental change in position on the part of the third party." See Minskoff v. American Express Travel Related Services Co., 98 F.3d 703, 708 (2d Cir.1996) (citations omitted). Here, the Pension Fund is the principal and Moriarity is its agent. Thus, in order to find that Moriarity acted with apparent authority, it is necessary to show that some conduct by the Pension Fund led Steven Scott to reasonably believe that Moriarity was authorized to enter into the fifteen settlement agreements.

Turning first to the estoppel argument, there was a clear and unambiguous promise made by Moriarity. Moriarity represented that he could bind the Pension Fund. This promise was clearly articulated in each of the fifteen settlement agreements at issue. . . .

Plaintiffs propose that despite the clear and unambiguous contractual language, Moriarity did not represent that he could bind the Pension Fund. Plaintiffs allege that Moriarity's signature block, which only refers to his position as Local 802 President, demonstrates that Moriarity acted solely as an agent of Local 802. However, the plain meaning of the contractual language belies this conclusion. Moriarity explicitly represented that he was authorized to "enter into, execute, deliver, perform and implement" these settlement agreements. Thus, to make any sense out of the clause that binds the Pension Fund, the court must infer that Moriarity represented that he could bind the Pension Fund.

Similarly, plaintiffs contend that the inclusion of ratification language shows that the parties intended to bind the Pension Fund only if it ratified the settlement agreements. The court finds, however, that the Pension Fund has not refuted the explicit language of the settlement agreements that supports the contrary conclusion that the Pension Fund is bound without reservation. . . .

There is also little doubt that Steven Scott relied to its detriment on Moriarity's promises. Steven Scott asserts that it would not have entered into the settlement agreements and paid additional contributions to the Pension Fund if the agreements were not considered a full and final settlement of all monetary claims against it. Furthermore, Steven Scott has acknowledged that it has not kept adequate records of its past contributions to the Pension Fund for the time period that the Pension Fund seeks to audit. Given Steven Scott's presumptions about the binding force of the settlement agreements and its failure to keep accurate records, it is plausible to assume injustice would result if the agreements were not enforced, provided that Steven Scott was reasonable in relying on Moriarity's representations.

Did Steven Scott reasonably rely on Moriarity's representation that he could bind the Pension Fund? A rational fact finder could only conclude that Steven Scott was justified in its reliance given the circumstances involved in this case. Moriarity was a Pension Fund Trustee whose duties included the collection of contributions from employers.[2] He entered into fifteen agreements with Steven Scott over the course of three years. A settlement agreement accompanied each check that was sent to the Pension Fund. It is undisputed that all fifteen settlement checks were received and later cashed by the Pension Fund. Steven Scott asserts that it had no reason to believe that Moriarity (a Pension Fund Trustee) lacked the requisite authority to enter into such agreements nor that the Pension Fund was not fully aware of the terms and conditions of the settlement agreements. The Pension Fund never repudiated Moriarity's actions at any point during the three years when the fifteen settlement agreements were being executed. By its own admissions, the Pension Fund concedes that it was on constructive notice of at least seven settlement agreements negotiated by Moriarity, which were found in plaintiffs' possession. Moreover, the Pension Fund's counsel admitted during oral argument that a settlement agreement accompanied each of the fifteen checks that the Pension Fund cashed.

However, a finding of reasonable reliance also depends on whether Steven Scott had notice of the Board's exclusive power to settle claims with employers. As a matter of law, it is unreasonable for an employer to rely on the representations of a union or pension fund agent if an employer has knowledge of the agent's proper scope of authority. . . .

Here, Steven Scott was not mailed a copy of the Trust Agreement until June 1995. . . . The Trust Agreement explicitly states that only the Board of Trustees at the Pension Fund has the authority to compromise claims with contributing employers. . . . As such, Steven Scott's reliance on any representations made by Moriarity after June 1995 were unreasonable as a matter of law. After June 1995, Steven Scott was on

[2] The court finds that Moriarity's position as a Pension Fund Trustee renders plaintiffs' argument that a local union cannot bind the Pension Fund irrelevant for the purposes of deciding defendant's motion. Although there is ample precedent for the proposition that a local union cannot waive a pension fund's rights to collect contributions, . . . the issue is not, as plaintiffs contend, whether Moriarity as Union President can bind the Pension Fund, but rather can a Trustee of the Pension Fund bind the Pension Fund.

constructive notice of the proper scope of Moriarity's authority. Therefore, neither estoppel nor apparent authority may be used as defenses to bind the Pension Fund to the settlement agreements entered into on September 8, 1995 and April 6, 1996, respectively. However, for reasons articulated in Section II(C) infra, the court finds that these latter two agreements, along with the initial thirteen, were ratified by the Pension Fund.

. . .

As for Moriarity's exercise of apparent authority, the court concludes that the Pension Fund's acts of continually cashing all fifteen settlement checks while failing to repudiate Moriarity's unauthorized actions after receiving notice of at least seven settlement agreements created the appearance of authority that Steven Scott reasonably relied on. . . .

However, as noted supra, Steven Scott's reliance on Moriarity's exercise of apparent authority was no longer reasonable after June 1995, the date in which it received notice of the actual scope of Moriarity's agency as outlined in the Pension Fund's Trust Agreement. Thus, any reasonable fact-finder would conclude that Moriarity was acting with apparent authority when he negotiated the first thirteen settlement agreements that are binding on the Pension Fund.

C. Ratification and Accord and Satisfaction

Steven Scott relies on the alternative grounds of ratification and accord and satisfaction to further support its motion for summary judgment. It argues that regardless of Moriarity's ability to bind the Pension Fund to the terms of the settlement agreements, the Pension Fund has nevertheless ratified the agreements by cashing all fifteen settlement checks and by failing to inform Steven Scott that Moriarity was acting outside the scope of his authority. Moreover, Steven Scott also alleges that the agreements represent a valid accord and satisfaction between the parties.

"Ratification of the acts of an agent only occurs where the principal has full knowledge of all material facts and takes some action to affirm the agent's actions." Prisco v. State of New York, 804 F.Supp. 518, 523 (S.D.N.Y.1992). Affirmance of the intent to ratify may be inferred from "knowledge of the principal coupled with a failure to timely repudiate, where the party seeking a finding of ratification has in some way relied upon the principal's silence. . . ." Monarch Ins. Co. of Ohio v. Ins. Corp. of Ireland. Ltd., et al., 835 F.2d 32, 36 (2d Cir.1987) (citations omitted).

Plaintiffs attempt to deny knowledge of the terms of the settlement agreements by arguing that: (1) the agreements were never presented to the Board of Trustees, the principal, (2) the clerical workers who processed the settlement checks did not, and were not authorized to, knowingly accept the agreements by negotiating the checks in the normal course of ordinary business, and (3) Moriarity's knowledge of the agreements cannot be imputed to the Board because he was acting outside the scope of his agency.

Despite the Pension Fund's assertions, knowledge of the settlement agreements is inferred from the undisputed fact that seven settlement agreements were found within plaintiffs' possession. In fact, the Pension Fund admitted to having received copies of all fifteen settlement agreements during oral argument. . . .

Once the Pension Fund had knowledge of the settlement agreements, its failure to repudiate Moriarity's actions constituted ratification of the agreements. . . .

Furthermore, the Pension Fund cannot deny knowledge of the agreements simply because its clerical workers failed to read the settlement agreements prior to cashing the checks. A three-page settlement agreement accompanied each of the fifteen settlement checks. The ratification clause was explicit. The Pension Fund cannot now complain that it failed to read or inquire into the meaning of this clause simply because its clerical workers did not notice the settlement agreements or chose not to read the agreements. . . .

[T]he court declines to address defendant's arguments regarding accord and satisfaction since the court has found the Pension Fund is bound by all fifteen agreements under alternative principles of estoppel, apparent authority, and ratification.

III. Conclusion

Steven Scott's motion for summary judgment is granted . . . and plaintiffs' complaint is dismissed.

ANALYSIS

1. **What Should They Have Done?** What should Steven Scott have done to avoid the problem that gave rise to this litigation? What should the Trustees have done?

2. **What if Copies Had Not Been Sent?** Suppose that Steven Scott had not sent copies of the settlement agreement with its checks. What result?

3. **Why Is Reliance Justified?** The court asserts that "[a] rational fact finder could only conclude that Steven Scott was justified in its reliance given the circumstances involved in this case" on "Moriarity's representation that he could bind the Pension Fund." How does the court know this?

F. AGENT'S LIABILITY ON THE CONTRACT

Atlantic Salmon A/S v. Curran

32 Mass.App.Ct. 488, 591 N.E.2d 206 (1992).

These are the plaintiffs' appeals from a Superior Court judgment for the defendant. The issue presented is as to the personal liability of an agent who at the relevant times was acting on behalf of a partially disclosed or unidentified principal. . . .

The facts are not in dispute,. . . . The defendant began doing business with the plaintiffs, Salmonor A/S (Salmonor) and Atlantic Salmon A/S (Atlantic), Norwegian corporations and exporters of salmon, in 1985 and 1987, respectively. At all times, the defendant dealt with the plaintiffs as a representative of "Boston International Seafood Exchange, Inc.," or "Boston Seafood Exchange, Inc." The salmon purchased by the defendant was sold to other wholesalers. Payment checks from the defendant to the plaintiffs were imprinted with the name "Boston International Seafood Exchange, Inc.," and signed by the defendant, using the designation "Treas.," intending thereby to convey the impression that he was treasurer. Wire transfers of payments were also made in the name of Boston International Seafood Exchange, Inc. The defendant gave the plaintiffs' representatives business cards which listed him as "marketing director" of "Boston International Seafood Exchange, Inc." Advertising placed by the defendant appeared in trade journals under both the names "Boston Seafood Exchange, Inc.," and "Boston International Seafood Exchange, Inc." (indicating in one instance as to the latter that it was "Est: 1982"). At the relevant times, no such Massachusetts or foreign corporation had been formed by the defendant or had existed.

On May 31, 1977, a Massachusetts corporation named "Marketing Designs, Inc.," was organized. It was created for the purpose of selling motor vehicles. As of 1983, the defendant was the president, treasurer, clerk, a director and the sole stockholder of that corporation. The extent of activity or solvency of the corporation is not shown on the record. On October 19, 1983, however, Marketing Designs, Inc., was dissolved, apparently for failure to make requisite corporate filings. . . . On December 4, 1987, a certificate was filed with the city clerk of Boston declaring that Marketing Designs, Inc. (then dissolved), was conducting business under the name of Boston Seafood Exchange (not with the designation "Inc." and not also under the name Boston International Seafood Exchange, Inc.). . . .

Salmonor is owed $101,759.65 and Atlantic $153,788.50 for salmon sold to a business known as Boston International Seafood Exchange or Boston Seafood Exchange during 1988. Marketing Designs, Inc., was dissolved at the time the debt was incurred. In that year, advertising in a trade journal appeared in the name of "Boston Seafood Exchange, Inc.," and listed the plaintiffs as suppliers, and the defendant delivered to representatives of the plaintiffs his business card on which he was described as "marketing director" of "Boston International Seafood Exchange, Inc." On July 8, August 19 and 30, and September 9, 1988, the defendant made checks, imprinted with the name "Boston International Seafood Exchange, Inc.," to one or the other of the plaintiffs as payments for shipments of salmon.

The defendant never informed the plaintiffs of the existence of Marketing Designs, Inc., and the plaintiffs did not know of it until after the commencement of the present litigation on November 25, 1988. Marketing Designs, Inc., was revived for all purposes on December 12, 1988. . . .

In the course of his direct testimony, the defendant said: "We do business in seafood, and we're only in seafood. Boston Seafood Exchange is the name we use because it identifies us very closely with the industry and the products that we deal in. 'Marketing Designs, Inc.,' in the seafood business, would have absolutely no bearing or no recall or any factor at all. I picked the name Boston Seafood Exchange, Inc., because it defines where we are, who we deal with, the type of product we're into, and where our specialties are. The reason we have 'Inc.' on there is because also it seemed to me at the time—obviously it seemed to me at the time that it's incumbent upon me to tell people that I'm dealing with and to let them know that they're dealing with a corporation. So, we used 'Inc.' just to notify them; and I signed all my checks 'Treasurer' and so forth."

At trial and on appeal the defendant argues that he was acting as an agent of Marketing Designs, Inc., in 1988 when he incurred the debt which the plaintiffs seek to recover from him individually. It makes no difference that the plaintiffs thought they were dealing with corporate entities which did not exist, the defendant contends, because they were "aware" that they were transacting business with a corporate entity and not with the defendant individually. The judge essentially adopted the defendant's position. . . .[2]

---

[2] On the evidence in this case, one might view with considerable skepticism the good faith of the defendant's claim that he was in fact acting as the agent of Marketing Designs, Inc. His use of "Inc." in the description of the two fictitious corporations (a criminal violation, . . .), the methods by which the business was conducted and advertised, the late filing of the business certificate, the purpose of Marketing Designs, Inc., and that in the defendant's own words that name "in the seafood business, would have absolutely no bearing or no recall or any factor at all," the use of only one fictitious name on the doing business certificate, the continuation thereafter of the use of business cards and checks in the other fictitious name of Boston International Seafood Exchange, Inc., and the suggestion to the plaintiffs of the reorganization of that nonentity strongly suggest manipulation and the attempted convenient illusion of personal liability by means of a corporation (then dissolved) never intended to conduct or be responsible for the business of salmon importing. Nevertheless, the judge found that the defendant was not culpable of any relevant "fraud or other reprehensible conduct."

"If the other party [to a transaction] has notice that the agent is or may be acting for a principal but has no notice of the principal's identity, the principal for whom the agent is acting is a partially disclosed principal." Restatement (Second) of Agency § 4(2) (1958). Here, the plaintiffs had notice that the defendant was purporting to act for a corporate principal or principals but had no notice of the identity of the principal as claimed by the defendant in this litigation. "Unless otherwise agreed, a person purporting to make a contract with another for a partially disclosed principal is a party to the contract." Id. at § 321.

It is the duty of the agent, if he would avoid personal liability on a contract entered into by him on behalf of his principal, to disclose not only that he is acting in a representative capacity, but also the identity of his principal. . . .

The judge reasoned that since the defendant had filed a certificate with the city of Boston in December, 1987, that Marketing Designs, Inc., was doing business as Boston Seafood Exchange, the plaintiffs could have discerned "precisely with whom they were dealing by reference to public records before the 1988 credits were extended."[3] But the defendant had dealt with Salmonor, and probably Atlantic, before that date, continued to deal with both under the name Boston International Seafood Exchange, Inc., thereafter, and even proposed to the plaintiffs a corporate restructuring of that nonentity. In any event, it was not the plaintiffs' duty to seek out the identity of the defendant's principal; it was the defendant's obligation fully to reveal it. . . .

It is not sufficient that the plaintiffs may have had the means, through a search of the records of the Boston city clerk, to determine the identity of the defendant's principal. Actual knowledge is the test. . . . "The duty rests upon the agent, if he would avoid personal liability, to disclose his agency, and not upon others to discover it. It is not, therefore, enough that the other party has the means of ascertaining the name of the principal; the agent must either bring to him actual knowledge or, what is the same thing, that which to a reasonable man is equivalent to knowledge or the agent will be bound. There is no hardship to the agent in this rule, as he always has it in his power to relieve himself from personal liability by fully disclosing his principal and contracting only in the latter's name. If he does not do this, it may well be presumed that he intended to make himself personally responsible." 1 Mechem on Agency § 1413 (2d ed. 1914).

Finally, the defendant's use of trade names or fictitious names by which he claimed Marketing Designs, Inc., conducted its business is not in the circumstances a sufficient identification of the alleged principal so

[3] Of course, had the plaintiffs checked the public corporate records, they would have found that Marketing Designs, Inc., had been dissolved.

as to protect the defendant from personal liability.... Indeed, the defendant's own testimony expresses the impossibility of any rational connection....

The judgment is reversed, and new judgments are to be entered against the defendant for Atlantic in the amount of $153,788.50 and for Salmonor in the amount of $101,759.65, both with appropriate interest and costs.

ANALYSIS

1. **What if the Firm Existed?** Suppose that before dealing with the plaintiffs, Curran had reinstated Marketing Designs, Inc. as a lawful corporation and had lawfully and effectively changed its name to Boston International Seafood Exchange, Inc. What result?
2. **A Windfall?** Does it seem that the plaintiffs got more than they bargained for?
3. **What Should Curran Have Done?** What should Curran have done to protect himself from liability.
4. **What Should the Plaintiffs Have Done?** What should the plaintiffs have done to protect against the need for litigation to enforce their claims?

3. LIABILITY OF PRINCIPAL TO THIRD PARTIES IN TORT

A. SERVANT (EMPLOYEE) VERSUS INDEPENDENT CONTRACTOR

INTRODUCTORY NOTE

The first two cases that follow, Humble Oil & Refining Co. v. Martin and Hoover v. Sun Oil Company, again present the issue of organization within the firm versus organization across markets. Here we have large oil companies faced with the business issue of how to sell their principal products, gasoline and oil. One possibility is to sell through independently owned and operated gasoline filling stations. Another possibility is to sell through stations that they own and operate through employees. As the cases illustrate, in practice the arrangements have some characteristics of each of these possibilities.

In the era in which these cases arose, most gasoline stations performed three functions. (1) They sold gasoline, with service. There were no self-serve pumps. (2) They sold tires, batteries, and accessories (TBA). And (3) they performed repair services. The oil companies wanted to supply the gasoline and oil and the tires, batteries, and accessories. The repair services were provided by, or under the direction of, the operator of the station, who generally was himself an automobile mechanic.

The cases involve the liability of the oil companies for personal injuries negligently inflicted by gasoline station personnel. The legal issue turns on whether the operator of the station was an employee—a "servant" in the language of the law—or an independent operator (independent contractor) or, in more modern language, a franchisee. Under the doctrine of respondeat superior, a "master" (employer) is liable for the torts of its servants (employees). A master-servant relationship exists where the servant has agreed (a) to work on behalf of the master and (b) to be subject to the master's control or right to control the "physical conduct" of the servant (that is, the manner in which the job is performed, as opposed to the result alone). See Restatement (Second) of Agency §§ 1 and 2.

Servants are distinguished from independent contractors. The latter are of two types, agents and non-agents. An agent-type independent contractor is one who has agreed to act on behalf of another, the principal, but not subject to the principal's control over how the result is accomplished (that is, over the "physical conduct" of the task). A non-agent independent contractor is one who operates independently and simply enters into arm's length transactions with others. For example, if a carpenter is hired to build a garage for a homeowner, and if it is agreed or understood that the carpenter is simply responsible for getting the job done and is not to take directions from the homeowner, the carpenter is an independent contractor and is not acting as an agent. If the carpenter agrees to buy lumber for the project, on the credit account of the homeowner, the carpenter will still be acting as an independent contractor (assuming again that the homeowner does not have the right to tell the carpenter how to accomplish the task), but, because the carpenter is now acting on behalf of the homeowner in the purchase of the lumber, the carpenter is an (independent-contractor-type) agent of the homeowner. These cases are concerned only with the distinction between servants and independent contractors.

Humble Oil & Refining Co. v. Martin

148 Tex. 175, 222 S.W.2d 995 (1949).

Petitioners Humble Oil & Refining Company and Mrs. A.C. Love and husband complain here of the judgments of the trial court and the Court of Civil Appeals in which they were held [liable] in damages for personal injuries following a special issue verdict at the suit of respondent George F. Martin acting for himself and his two minor daughters. The injuries were inflicted on the three Martins about the noon hour on May 12, 1947, in the City of Austin, by an unoccupied automobile belonging to the petitioners Love, which, just prior to the accident, had been left by Mrs. Love at a filling station owned by petitioner Humble for servicing and thereafter, before any station employee had touched it, rolled by gravity off the premises into and obliquely across the abutting street, striking Mr. Martin and his children from behind as they were walking into the yard of their home, a short distance downhill from the station.

The trial court rendered judgment against petitioners Humble and Mrs. Love jointly and severally and gave the latter judgment over against Humble for whatever she might pay the respondents. The Court of Civil Appeals affirmed the judgment after reforming it to eliminate the judgment over in favor of Mrs. Love, without prejudice to the right of contribution by either defendant under Article 2212, Vernon's Ann.Civ.Stat., 216 S.W.(2d) 251. The petitioners here respectively complain of the judgment in favor of the Martins, and each seeks full indemnity (as distinguished from contribution) from the other.

The apparently principal contention of petitioner, Humble, is that it is liable neither to respondent Martin nor to petitioner Mrs. Love, since the station was in effect operated by an independent contractor, W.T. Schneider, and Humble is accordingly not responsible for his negligence nor that of W.V. Manis, who was the only station employee or representative present when the Love car was left and rolled away. In this connection, the jury convicted petitioner Humble of the following acts of negligence proximately causing the injuries in question: (a) Failure to inspect the Love car to see that the emergency brake was set or the gears engaged; (b) failure to set the emergency brake on the Love car; (c) leaving the Love car unattended on the driveway. The verdict also included findings that Mrs. Love "had delivered her car to the custody of the defendant Humble Oil & Refining Company, before her car started rolling from the position in which she had parked it"; that the accident was not unavoidable; and that no negligent act of either of petitioners was the sole proximate cause of the injuries in question. We think the Court of Civil Appeals properly held Humble responsible for the operation of the station, which admittedly it owned, as it did also the principal products there sold by Schneider under the so-called "Commission Agency Agreement" between him and Humble which was in evidence. The facts that neither Humble, Schneider nor the station employees considered Humble as an employer or master; that the employees were paid and directed by Schneider individually as their "boss," and that a provision of the agreement expressly repudiates any authority of Humble over the employees, are not conclusive against the master-servant relationship, since there is other evidence bearing on the right or power of Humble to control the details of the station work as regards Schneider himself and therefore as to employees which it was expressly contemplated that he would hire. The question is ordinarily one of fact, and where there are items of evidence indicating a master-servant relationship, contrary items such as those above mentioned cannot be given conclusive effect. . . .

Even if the contract between Humble and Schneider were the only evidence on the question, the instrument as a whole indicates a master-servant relationship quite as much as, if not more than, it suggests an arrangement between independent contractors. For example, paragraph 1 includes a provision requiring Schneider "to make reports *and perform other duties in connection with the operation of said station that may be required of him from time to time by Company.*" (Emphasis supplied). And while paragraph 2 purports to require Schneider to pay all operational expenses, the schedule of commissions forming part of the agreement does just the opposite in its paragraph (F), which gives Schneider a 75% "commission" on "the net public utility bills paid" by him and thus requires Humble to pay three-fourths of one of the most important operational expense items. Obviously the main object of the enterprise was the retail marketing of Humble's products with title remaining in Humble until delivery to the consumer. This was done under a strict system of financial control and supervision by Humble, with little or no business discretion reposed in Schneider except as to hiring, discharge, payment and supervision of a few station employees of a more or less laborer status. Humble furnished the all important station location and equipment, the advertising media, the products and a substantial part of the current operating costs. The hours of operation were controlled by Humble. The "Commission Agency Agreement," which evidently was Schneider's only title to occupancy of the premise, was terminable at the will of Humble. The so-called "rentals" were, at least in part, based on the amount of Humble's products sold, being, therefore, involved with the matter of Schneider's remuneration and not rentals in the usual sense. And, as above shown, the agreement required Schneider in effect to do anything Humble might tell him to do. All in all, aside from the stipulation regarding Schneider's assistants, there is essentially little difference between his situation and that of a mere store clerk who happens to be paid a commission instead of a salary. The business was Humble's business, just as the store clerk's business would be that of the store owner. Schneider was Humble's servant, and so accordingly were Schneider's assistants who were contemplated by the contract. Upon facts similar to those at bar but probably less indicative of a master-servant relationship, the latter has been held to exist by respectable authority, which seems to reflect the prevailing view in the nation. . . .

The evidence above discussed serves to distinguish the instant case from The Texas Company v. Wheat, 140 Texas 468, 168 S.W.(2d) 632, upon which petitioner Humble principally relies. In that case the evidence differed greatly from that now before us. It clearly showed a "dealer" type of relationship in which the lessee in charge of the filling station purchased from his landlord, The Texas Company, and sold as his own, and was free to sell at his own price and on his own credit terms, the company products purchased, as well as the products of other oil companies. The contracts contained no provision requiring the lessee to perform any duty The Texas Company might see fit to impose on him, nor did the company pay any part of the lessee's operating expenses, nor control the working hours of the station. . . .

Hoover v. Sun Oil Company

58 Del. 553, 212 A.2d 214 (1965).

This case is concerned with injuries received as the result of a fire on August 16, 1962 at the service station operated by James F. Barone. The fire started at the rear of plaintiff's car where it was being filled with gasoline and was allegedly caused by the negligence of John Smilyk an employee of Barone. Plaintiffs brought suit against Smilyk, Barone and Sun Oil Company (Sun) which owned the service station.

Sun has moved for summary judgment as to it on the basis that Barone was an independent contractor and therefore the alleged negligence of his employee could not result in liability as to Sun. The plaintiffs contend instead that Barone was acting as Sun's agent and that Sun may therefore be responsible for plaintiff's injuries.

Barone began operating this business in October of 1960 pursuant to a lease dated October 17, 1960. The station and all of its equipment, with the exception of a tire-stand and rack, certain advertising displays and miscellaneous hand tools, were owned by Sun. The lease was subject to termination by either party upon thirty days' written notice after the first six months and at the anniversary date thereafter. The rental was partially determined by the volume of gasoline purchased but there was also a minimum and a maximum monthly rental.

At the same time, Sun and Barone also entered into a dealer's agreement under which Barone was to purchase petroleum products from Sun and Sun was to loan necessary equipment and advertising materials. Barone was required to maintain this equipment and to use it solely for Sun products. Barone was permitted under the agreement to sell competitive products but chose to do so only in a few minor areas. As to Sun products, Barone was prohibited from selling them except under the Sunoco label and from blending them with products not supplied by Sun.

Barone's station had the usual large signs indicating that Sunoco products were sold there. His advertising in the classified section of the telephone book was under a Sunoco heading and his employees wore uniforms with the Sun emblem, the uniforms being owned by Barone or rented from an independent company.

Barone, upon the urging of Robert B. Peterson, Sun's area sales representative, attended a Sun school for service station operators in 1961. The school's curriculum was designed to familiarize the station operator with bookkeeping and merchandising, the appearance and proper maintenance of a Sun station, and the Sun Oil products. The course concluded with the operator working at Sun's model station in order to gain work experience in the use of the policy and techniques taught at the school.

Other facts typifying the company-service station relationship were the weekly visits of Sun's sales representative, Peterson, who would take orders for Sun products, inspect the restrooms, communicate customer complaints, make various suggestions to improve sales and discuss any problems that Barone might be having. Besides the weekly visits, Peterson was in contact with Barone on other occasions in order to implement Sun's "competitive allowance system" which enabled Barone to meet local price competition by giving him a rebate on the gasoline in his inventory roughly equivalent to the price decline and a similarly reduced price on his next order of gasoline.

While Peterson did offer advice to Barone on all phases of his operation, it was usually done on request and Barone was under no obligation to follow the advice. Barone's contacts and dealings with Sun were many and their relationship intricate, but he made no written reports to Sun and he alone assumed the overall risk of profit or loss in his business operation. Barone independently determined his own hours of operation and the identity, pay scale and working conditions of his employees, and it was his name that was posted as proprietor.

Plaintiffs contend in effect that the aforegoing facts indicate that Sun controlled the day-to-day operation of the station and consequently Sun is responsible for the negligent acts of Barone's employee. Specifically, plaintiffs contend that there is an issue of fact for the jury to determine as to whether or not there was an agency relationship.

The legal relationships arising from the distribution systems of major oil-producing companies are in certain respects unique. As stated in an annotation collecting many of the cases dealing with this relationship:

> "This distribution system has grown up primarily as the result of economic factors and with little relationship to traditional legal concepts in the field of master and servant, so that it is perhaps not surprising that attempts by the court to discuss the relationship in the standard terms have led to some difficulties and confusion." 83 A.L.R.2d 1282, 1284 (1962).

In some situations traditional definitions of principal and agent and of employer and independent contractor may be difficult to apply to service station operations, but the undisputed facts of the case at bar make it clear that Barone was an independent contractor.

Barone's service station, unlike retail outlets for many products, is basically a one-company outlet and represents to the public, through

Sunoco's national and local advertising, that it sells not only Sun's quality products but Sun's quality service. Many people undoubtedly come to the service station because of that latter representation.

However, the lease contract and dealer's agreement fail to establish any relationship other than landlord-tenant, and independent contractor. Nor is there anything in the conduct of the individuals which is inconsistent with that relationship so as to indicate that the contracts were mere subterfuge or sham. The areas of close contact between Sun and Barone stem from the fact that both have a mutual interest in the sale of Sun products and in the success of Barone's business.

The cases cited by both plaintiffs and defendant indicate that the result varies according to the contracts involved and the conduct and evidence of control under those contracts. Both lines of cases indicate that the test to be applied is that of whether the oil company has retained the right to control the details of the day-to-day operation of the service station; control or influence over results alone being viewed as insufficient. . . .

The facts of this case differ markedly from those in which the oil company was held liable for the tortious conduct of its service station operator or his employees. Sun had no control over the details of Barone's day-to-day operation. Therefore, no liability can be imputed to Sun from the allegedly negligent acts of Smilyk. Sun's motion for summary judgment is granted.

> **PLANNING**
>
> 1. **Why focus on hours?** In *Humble Oil* the court states, "The hours of operation were controlled by Humble." In *Sun Oil* the court states, "Barone independently determined his own hours of operation." What do you suppose is the practical difference in the control of each of the oil companies over hours of operation? What do you suppose would happen to Barone if the people at Sun Oil concluded that he was not staying open late enough and that, as a result, Sun Oil was losing sales?
>
> 2. **Contracting around the result.** If you were advising Humble Oil and wanted to improve the prospects of avoiding liability for personal injuries, what changes would you suggest in the manner in which Humble Oil structured its relationship with its operators? What would be the likely substantive effect of these changes?

ANALYSIS

1. **Why the Different Outcomes?** Important elements of business relationships include duration, control, risk of loss, and return. Which of these becomes the key issue in the two cases? How can the outcomes in the two cases be reconciled?

2. **Why the Terms We Observe?** Pretend you know nothing about the legal rules that distinguish between employees (servants) and people working for themselves (independent contractors).

a. If you were a person like Schneider (the gas station operator in the Humble Oil case), which terms or elements of the relationship with Humble Oil would make you feel like an employee? Which terms would make you feel that you were independent, working for yourself?

b. If you were a person like Barone (the operator in the Sun Oil case), would you feel less like an employee and more like an independent business person than a person like Schneider? Why?

c. Focus on those terms of each relationship that suggest that the operator is independent. Assume that the oil companies could have changed those terms to make them consistent with an employment relationship. What would the new terms be? Why do you suppose the oil companies chose what may be thought of as a hybrid set of terms?

3. The Restatement (Third) of Agency discarded the terms servant and master, replacing them with the terms employee and principal:

> A principal is subject to vicarious liability to a third party harmed by an agent's conduct when (a) as stated in § 7.07, the agent is an employee who commits a tort while acting within the scope of employment; or (b) as stated in § 7.08, the agent commits a tort when acting with apparent authority in dealing with a third party on or purportedly on behalf of the principal.

Restatement (Third) of Agency § 7.03(2). Employee is defined as "an agent whose principal controls or has the right to control the manner and means of the agent's performance of work, and . . . the fact that work is performed gratuitously does not relieve a principal of liability." Id., § 7.07(3)(a). Many statutes that apply to employees use the Restatement definition to determine whether someone is an employee for purposes of the statute, but many others do not do so. Should they?

POLICY QUESTIONS

In the *Sun Oil* situation, presumably Sun Oil could have insisted that Barone take out a policy of liability insurance, protecting both him and Sun Oil, or that he agree to indemnify Sun Oil for damages and show that he had enough assets to meet his obligation.

1. Do you think that it was irresponsible for Sun Oil to fail to do that?

2. Assume that your answer to part 1 was yes. What if Barone had operated ten gas stations, under his own name (but still bought most of his gasoline and oil and tires, batteries, and accessories from Sun Oil)?

3. Should the law somehow impose an obligation on Sun Oil to ensure that Barone is able to pay his debts?

4. Assume your answer to part 3 was yes. How would you frame the law?
5. What is your general theory of when people who do business with one another should and should not be liable for each other's tort, or contract, damages?

Murphy v. Holiday Inns, Inc.

216 Va. 490, 219 S.E.2d 874 (1975).

On August 21, 1973, Kyran Murphy (plaintiff) filed a motion for judgment against Holiday Inns, Inc. (defendant), a Tennessee Corporation, seeking damages for personal injuries sustained on August 24, 1971, while she was a guest at a motel in Danville. Plaintiff alleged that "Defendant owned and operated" the motel; that "Defendant, its agents and employees, so carelessly, recklessly, and negligently maintained the premises of the motel that Plaintiff did slip and fall on an area of a walk where water draining from an air conditioner had been allowed to accumulate"; and that as a proximate result of such negligence, plaintiff sustained serious and permanent injuries.

Defendant filed grounds of defense and a motion for summary judgment "on the grounds that it has no relationship with regard to the operator of the premises . . . other than a license agreement permitting the operator of a motel on the same premises to use the name 'Holiday Inns' subject to all the terms and conditions of such license agreement." That agreement, filed as an exhibit with defendant's motion for summary judgment, identifies defendant's licensee as Betsy-Len Motor [Hotel] Corporation (Betsy-Len).

Upon a finding that defendant did not own the premises upon which the accident occurred and that "there exists no principal-agent or master-servant relationship between the defendant corporation and Betsy-Len Motor Hotel Corporation," the trial court entered a final order on April 25, 1974, granting summary judgment in favor of defendant.

Plaintiff's sole assignment of error is that the trial court erred "in holding that no principal-agent or master-servant relationship exists."

On brief, plaintiff argues that the license agreement gives defendant "the authority and control over the Betsy-Len Corporation that establishes a true master/servant relationship." . . .

Actual agency is a consensual relationship.

> "Agency is the fiduciary relation which results from the manifestation of consent by one person to another that the other shall act on his behalf and subject to his control, and consent by the other so to act." Restatement (Second) of Agency § 1 (1958).

. . .

> "It is the element of continuous subjection to the will of the principal which distinguishes the agent from other fiduciaries and the agency agreement from other agreements." Id., comment (b).

. . .

When an agreement, considered as a whole, establishes an agency relationship, the parties cannot effectively disclaim it by formal "consent." "[T]he relationship of the parties does not depend upon what the parties themselves call it, but rather in law what it actually is." Chandler v. Kelley, 149 Va. 221, 231, 141 S.E. 389, 391–92 (1928). . . . Here, plaintiff and defendant agree that, if the license agreement is sufficient to establish an agency relationship, the disclaimer clause[1] does not defeat it.

Plaintiff and defendant also agree that, in determining whether a contract establishes an agency relationship, the critical test is the nature and extent of the control agreed upon.

The subject matter of the license defendant granted Betsy-Len is a "system." As defined in the agreement, the system is one "providing to the public . . . an inn service . . . of distinctive nature, of high quality, and of other distinguishing characteristics." Those characteristics include trade names using the words "Holiday Inn" and certain variations and combinations of those words, trade marks, architectural designs, insignia, patterns, color schemes, styles, furnishings, equipment, advertising services, and methods of operation.

In consideration of the license to use the "system," the licensee agreed to pay an initial sum of $5000; to construct one or more inns in accordance with plans approved by the licensor; to make monthly payments of 15 cents per room per day (5 cents of which was to be earmarked for national advertising expenditures); and "to conduct the operation of inns . . . in accordance with the terms and provisions of this license and of the Rules of operation of said System".

Plaintiff points to several provisions and rules which he says satisfy the control test and establish the principal-agent relationship. These include requirements:

> That licensee construct its motel according to plans, specifications, feasibility studies, and locations approved by licensor;

---

1 That clause provides that "Licensee, in the use of the name 'Holiday Inn' . . . shall identify Licensee as being the owner and operator [and] . . . the parties hereto are completely separate entities, are not partners, joint adventurers, or agents of the other in any sense, and neither has power to obligate or bind the other."

> That licensee employ the trade name, signs, and other symbols of the "system" designated by licensor;
>
> That licensee pay a continuing fee for use of the license and a fee for national advertising of the "system";
>
> That licensee solicit applications for credit cards for the benefit of other licensees;
>
> That licensee protect and promote the trade name and not engage in any competitive motel business or associate itself with any trade association designed to establish standards for motels;
>
> That licensee not raise funds by sale of corporate stock or dispose of a controlling interest in its motel without licensor's approval;
>
> That training for licensee's manager, housekeeper, and restaurant manager be provided by licensor at licensee's expense;
>
> That licensee not employ a person contemporaneously engaged in a competitive motel or hotel business; and
>
> That licensee conduct its business under the "system," observe the rules of operation, make quarterly reports to licensor concerning operations, and submit to periodic inspections of facilities and procedures conducted by licensor's representatives.

The license agreement of which these requirements were made a part is a franchise contract. In the business world, franchising is a crescent phenomenon of billion-dollar proportions.

> "[Franchising is] a system for the selective distribution of goods and/or services under a brand name through outlets owned by independent businessmen, called 'franchisees.' Although the franchiser supplies the franchisee with know-how and brand identification on a continuing basis, the franchisee enjoys the right to profit and runs the risk of loss. The franchiser controls the distribution of his goods and/or services through a contract which regulates the activities of the franchisee, in order to achieve standardization." R. Rosenberg, *Profits From Franchising* 41 (1969). (Italics omitted).

The fact that an agreement is a franchise contract does not insulate the contracting parties from an agency relationship. If a franchise contract so "regulates the activities of the franchisee" as to vest the franchiser with control within the definition of agency, the agency relationship arises even though the parties expressly deny it.

Here, the license agreement contains the principal features of the typical franchise contract, including regulatory provisions. Defendant owned the "brand name," the trade mark, and the other assets associated with the "system." Betsy-Len owned the sales "outlet." Defendant agreed to allow Betsy-Len to use its assets. Betsy-Len agreed to pay a fee for that privilege. Betsy-Len retained the "right to profit" and bore the "risk of loss." With respect to the manner in which defendant's trade mark and other assets were to be used, both parties agreed to certain regulatory rules of operation.

Having carefully considered all of the regulatory provisions in the agreement, we are of opinion that they gave defendant no "control or right to control the methods or details of doing the work," Wells v. Whitaker, 207 Va. 616, 624, 151 S.E.2d 422, 429 (1966), and, therefore, agree with the trial court that no principal-agent or master-servant relationship was created.[2] As appears from the face of the document, the purpose of those provisions was to achieve system-wide standardization of business identity, uniformity of commercial service, and optimum public good will, all for the benefit of both contracting parties. The regulatory provisions did not give defendant control over the day-to-day operation of Betsy-Len's motel. While defendant was empowered to regulate the architectural style of the buildings and the type and style of furnishings and equipment, defendant was given no power to control daily maintenance of the premises. Defendant was given no power to control Betsy-Len's current business expenditures, fix customer rates, or demand a share of the profits. Defendant was given no power to hire or fire Betsy-Len's employees, determine employee wages or working conditions, set standards for employee skills or productivity, supervise employee work routine, or discipline employees for nonfeasance or misfeasance. All such powers and other management controls and responsibilities customarily exercised by an owner and operator of an ongoing business were retained by Betsy-Len.

We hold that the regulatory provisions of the franchise contract did not constitute control within the definition of agency, and the judgment is

Affirmed.

Parker v. Domino's Pizza

629 So.2d 1026 (Fla.Dist.Ct. of Appeal, 4th Dist., 1993).
Rehearing, Rehearing En Banc and Certification Denied, 1994.

. . . The complaints filed in those consolidated actions alleged that Jeffrey Todd Hoppock (Hoppock), while within the course and scope of

---

[2] Because defendant had no such control or right to control, the distinction between a principal-agent and a master-servant relationship is not relevant here. . . .

his employment delivering pizza for J & B Enterprises, Inc., d/b/a Domino's Pizza (J & B Enterprises), operated a vehicle in a reckless, negligent and careless manner, causing it to strike another vehicle. The Parkers, who were both pedestrians at the time of the incident, allege that they were injured when a third vehicle hit them while they were helping the victims of the accident caused by Hoppock. . . . It was further alleged that at the time of the accident J & B Enterprises and Hoppock, employer and employee, were operating as the agents, apparent agents, servants and/or employees of Domino's Pizza, Inc. (Domino's), and that Domino's exercised control over all of the activities of its franchisee, J & B Enterprises, and thus was vicariously liable for the negligence of J & B Enterprises and Hoppock.

Domino's moved for summary judgment based upon its position that at the time of the accident Hoppock was an employee of J & B Enterprises, not Domino's, and that neither J & B Enterprises nor Hoppock were employees of Domino's nor acting within the scope of any employment or agency relationship with Domino's. . . .

The trial court determined that, as a matter of law, J & B Enterprises was an independent contractor, as provided in paragraph forty-five of the franchise agreement between the parties. Consequently Domino's could not be held vicariously liable for the negligence of J & B Enterprises, its agents and employees. . . .

. . .

Whether one party is a mere agent rather than an independent contractor as to the other party is to be determined by measuring the right to control and not by considering only the actual control exercised by the latter over the former. . . .

. . .

The relationship between Domino's and J & B Enterprises is established by a franchise agreement and an operating manual. We have summarized the requirements that best seem to illustrate the extent of control Domino's retains over the performance of its franchisees.

The "preambles" section of the franchise agreement states in relevant part:

Franchisee has applied to the Company for a franchise to operate a Domino's pizza store selling the products and services authorized and approved by the Company and utilizing the Company's business format, methods, specifications, standards, operating procedures, operating assistance, advertising services and the Marks.

The franchise agreement itself contains, *inter alia*, the following:

(1) Sales quotas;

(2) Franchise renewal dependent upon compliance with Domino's specific prescriptions;

(3) Location sites and guidelines for changing locations;

(4) Domino's approval of site and architectural plans, including the dimension requirements for all furniture, fixtures, and equipment;

(5) Specific rules for pizza and beverage preparation, including the minimum standards for delivery, performance, appearance;

(6) Specific signage and decorating requirements;

(7) Guidelines for a mandatory training program completion of which is a precondition to employment;

(8) A reservation of the rights Domino's retains to advise the franchisee on improvements, food preparation, hiring, advertising and general operational procedures;

(9) Company inspections;

(10) A prohibition on selling any products or services other than those authorized by Domino's;

(11) A requirement that delivery service zones may not extend to areas where pizza could not feasibly be delivered within 30 minutes;

(12) Specifications and quality standards by which every single item in the restaurant must abide, including though not limited to the pizza ingredients, packaging, uniforms, cleaning supplies and advertisements;

(13) That each store must contribute 3% of its weekly royalties to a fund administered by Domino's for its advertising and promotions;

(14) Strict advertising restrictions and requirements;

(15) Strict Domino's prescribed book-keeping requirements;

(16) That each franchisee submit weekly, monthly and annual reports of their sales and profits, all which are open to audit by Domino's to check for understatements in earnings;

(17) Specifications for operating procedures including but not limited to employee grooming, delivery techniques, advertising, signage, handling of customer complaints, etc.;

(18) That the franchisee will abide by the Domino's operating manual;

(19) That all new ideas or improvements in products or services conceived by franchisee must be divulged to Domino's without compensation;

(20) Managers must spend no less than 40 hours per week at the store;

(21) The franchisee is responsible for obtaining motor vehicle and comprehensive general liability insurance naming Domino's as an additional insured;

(22) That Domino's has control over the use of trademarks, and may prohibit a franchisee from using them provided the franchisee is compensated for costs;

(23) The franchisee must pay Domino's a 5½ royalty fee of the store's weekly net sales (the franchisee is, however, given the freedom to determine the prices for the products and services it sells);

(24) Random inspections of the inventory, records and assets which may be conducted any time during business hours.

The second item of documentary evidence demonstrating Domino's control over its franchisees is its operations manual. As "Domino's Concept and Objectives," the manual states:

> Our phrase depicts the Domino's concept, "The Domino's People are Pizza People, Period." Thus, the Domino's purpose is: make the finest pizza possible and deliver it fast, hot, and free. . . . Specifically, every pizza is hot, tasty, and good-looking. Ingredients are in the proper proportion to insure a balance of flavor. They are also in the proper amounts to insure a fair value. The product is consistant (sic) throughout the chain. Service is fast and courteous. Specifically, a Domino's pizza is delivered within 30 minutes after the order is taken. Pick-up pizzas are ready in 10 minutes. At all times, the customer receives courteous service . . . [and the] customer is assured that his pizza is prepared only from wholesome ingredients, in sanitary facilities, by clean personnel.

The manual which Domino's provides to its franchisees is a veritable bible for overseeing a Domino's operation. It contains prescriptions for every conceivable facet of the business: from the elements of preparing the perfect pizza to maintaining accurate books; from advertising and promotional ideas to routing and delivery guidelines; from order-taking instructions to oven-tending rules; from organization to sanitation. The manual even offers a wide array of techniques for "boxing and cutting" the pizza, as well as tips on running the franchise to achieve an optimum profit. The manual literally leaves nothing to chance. The complexity behind every element of the operation gives new meaning to the familiar slogan that delivery is to be, "Fast, Hot and Free."

The foregoing leads us to the self-evident conclusion that it was error to determine as a matter of law that Domino's does not retain the right to control the means to be used by its franchisee to accomplish the required tasks. At the very least a genuine and material question of fact is raised by the documentation. We reverse and remand for such other and further proceedings as may be appropriate.

ANALYSIS

1. **The Restatement's Factors.** Restatement (Second) of Agency § 219(1) (see also Restatement [Third] of Agency § 7.03) provides: "A master is subject to liability for the torts of his servants committed while acting in the scope of their employment." The comments to that section make clear that, as a general rule, a principal is not liable for the torts of his non-servant agents—i.e., independent contractors. See also Restatement (Second) § 250. Restatement (Second) § 1 indicates, as stated by the Holiday Inns court, that control is an essential element of the definition of an agency relationship, whether one is dealing with a servant or an independent contractor.

    A key distinction between the servant and independent contractor types of agents, however, is the differing natures and degrees of control exercised by the principal. See Restatement (Second) § 220(1): "A servant is a person employed to perform services in the affairs of another and who with respect to the physical conduct in the performance of the services is subject to the other's control or right to control." Did Holiday Inns have sufficient control over Betsy-Len to make the latter a servant? Are the factors set forth in Restatement § 220(2) helpful in this regard?

    Note that the Restatement (Third) of Agency § 2.04 drops the use of the "master" and "servant" terms, and uses "employer" and "employee" instead. Section 7.07(3)(1) defines an employee as "an agent whose principal controls or has the right to control the manner and means of the agent's performance of work."

2. **Possible Other Factors.** According to the court in *Holiday Inns,* "Plaintiff and defendant agree that, in determining whether a contract establishes an agency relationship, the critical test is the nature and extent of the control agreed upon." Is it possible for a franchiser to have a degree of control consistent with the master-servant relationship without that master-servant relationship arising as a matter of law? What other requirement, if any, must be satisfied? See Restatement (Second) of Agency § 1, quoted by the court. To put the issue another way, in either the *Holiday Inns* case or the *Domino's Pizza* case, does it seem to you that the defendant might have prevailed even if it had lost on the control issue? In other words, did the defendant have another, unused, string to its bow?

3. **Which Factors Matter to the Franchisers?** How do firms like Holiday Inns, Inc. and Domino's Pizza make their profit? What are their risks? In their relationships with franchisers, what legal rights are likely to be important to them?

4. **Which Factors Matter to the Franchisees?** How do the franchisees make their profit? What are their risks? In their relationship with the franchisers, what legal rights are likely to be important to them?

5. **What Real Power Do the Franchisers Have?** How much freedom does a franchisee like Betsy-Len have to run its business? Suppose that a field representative of Holiday Inns, Inc. visits the Betsy-Len motor hotel and finds that the desk clerk, who is a son of one of the owners of the franchise, is surly and inefficient, and that the restaurant, managed by the other owner, is badly run, with poor food and slow service. What are the various steps that Holiday Inns, Inc. can take to induce its franchisee to improve its performance? What do your answers to these questions tell you about drafting a franchise contract? Would your answers to these questions be significantly different for the Domino's Pizza franchise?

B. TORT LIABILITY AND APPARENT AGENCY

Miller v. McDonald's Corp.

150 Or.App. 274, 945 P.2d 1107 (1997).

Plaintiff seeks damages from defendant McDonald's Corporation for injuries that she suffered when she bit into a heart-shaped sapphire stone while eating a Big Mac sandwich that she had purchased at a McDonald's restaurant in Tigard. The trial court granted summary judgment to defendant on the ground that it did not own or operate the restaurant; rather, the owner and operator was a non-party, 3K Restaurants (3K), that held a franchise from defendant. Plaintiff appeals, and we reverse.

. . . 3K owned and operated the restaurant under a License Agreement (the Agreement) with defendant that required it to operate in a manner consistent with the "McDonald's System." The Agreement described that system as including proprietary rights in trade names, service marks and trade marks, as well as "designs and color schemes for restaurant buildings, signs, equipment layouts, formulas and specifications for certain food products, methods of inventory and operation control, bookkeeping and accounting, and manuals covering business practices and policies." . . .

The Agreement described the way in which 3K was to operate the restaurant in considerable detail. It expressly required 3K to operate in compliance with defendant's prescribed standards, policies, practices, and procedures, including serving only food and beverage products that defendant designated. 3K had to follow defendant's specifications and blueprints for the equipment and layout of the restaurant, including adopting subsequent reasonable changes that defendant made, and to maintain the restaurant building in compliance with defendant's standards. 3K could not make any changes in the basic design of the building without defendant's approval.

The Agreement required 3K to keep the restaurant open during the hours that defendant prescribed, including maintaining adequate supplies and employing adequate personnel to operate at maximum capacity and efficiency during those hours. 3K also had to keep the restaurant similar in appearance to all other McDonald's restaurants. 3K's employees had to wear McDonald's uniforms, to have a neat and clean appearance, and to provide competent and courteous service. 3K could use only containers and other packaging that bore McDonald's trademarks. The ingredients for the foods and beverages had to meet defendant's standards, and 3K had to use "only those methods of food handling and preparation that [defendant] may designate from time to time." In order to obtain the franchise, 3K had to represent that the franchisee had worked at a McDonald's restaurant; the Agreement did not distinguish in this respect between a company-run or a franchised restaurant. The manuals gave further details that expanded on many of these requirements.

In order to ensure conformity with the standards described in the Agreement, defendant periodically sent field consultants to the restaurant to inspect its operations. 3K trained its employees in accordance with defendant's materials and recommendations and sent some of them to training programs that defendant administered. Failure to comply with the agreed standards could result in loss of the franchise.

Despite these detailed instructions, the Agreement provided that 3K was not an agent of defendant for any purpose. Rather, it was an independent contractor and was responsible for all obligations and liabilities, including claims based on injury, illness, or death, directly or indirectly resulting from the operation of the restaurant.

Plaintiff went to the restaurant under the assumption that defendant owned, controlled, and managed it. So far as she could tell, the restaurant's appearance was similar to that of other McDonald's restaurants that she had patronized. Nothing disclosed to her that any entity other than defendant was involved in its operation. The only signs that were visible and obvious to the public had the name "McDonald's,"[2] the employees wore uniforms with McDonald's insignia, and the menu was the same that plaintiff had seen in other McDonald's restaurants. The general appearance of the restaurant and the food products that it sold were similar to the restaurants and products that plaintiff had seen in national print and television advertising that defendant had run. To

---

[2] This is plaintiff's testimony in her affidavit. Representatives of 3K testified in their depositions that there was a sign near the front counter that identified Bob and Karen Bates and 3K Restaurants as the owners. There is no evidence of the size or prominence of the sign, nor is there evidence of any other non-McDonald's identification in the restaurant.

the best of plaintiff's knowledge, only McDonald's sells Big Mac hamburgers.

In short, plaintiff testified, she went to the Tigard McDonald's because she relied on defendant's reputation and because she wanted to obtain the same quality of service, standard of care in food preparation, and general attention to detail that she had previously enjoyed at other McDonald's restaurants. . . .

The kind of actual agency relationship that would make defendant vicariously liable for 3K's negligence requires that defendant have the right to control the method by which 3K performed its obligations under the Agreement. . . .[3]

A number of other courts have applied the right to control test to a franchise relationship. The Delaware Supreme Court, in Billops v. Magness Const. Co., 391 A.2d 196 (Del.1978), stated the test as it applies to that context:

> "If, in practical effect, the franchise agreement goes beyond the stage of setting standards, and allocates to the franchisor the right to exercise control over the daily operations of the franchise, an agency relationship exists." 391 A.2d at 197–98.

This statement expresses the general direction that courts have taken. . . . We therefore adopt it for the purposes of this case.

. . . [We] believe that a jury could find that defendant retained sufficient control over 3K's daily operations that an actual agency relationship existed. The Agreement did not simply set standards that 3K had to meet. Rather, it required 3K to use the precise methods that defendant established. . . . Defendant enforced the use of those methods by regularly sending inspectors and by its retained power to cancel the Agreement. That evidence would support a finding that defendant had the right to control the way in which 3K performed at least food handling and preparation. In her complaint, plaintiff alleges that 3K's deficiencies in those functions resulted in the sapphire being in the Big Mac and thereby caused her injuries. Thus, . . . there is evidence that defendant had the right to control 3K in the precise part of its business that allegedly resulted in plaintiff's injuries. That is sufficient to raise an issue of actual agency.

Plaintiff next asserts that defendant is vicariously liable for 3K's alleged negligence because 3K was defendant's apparent agent.[4] The relevant standard is in Restatement (Second) of Agency, § 267 . . .:

---

[3] Under the right to control test it does not matter whether the putative principal actually exercises control; what is important is that it has the right to do so. See Peeples v. Kawasaki Heavy Indust., Ltd., 288 Or. 143, 149, 603 P.2d 765 (1979).

[4] Apparent agency is a distinct concept from apparent authority. Apparent agency creates an agency relationship that does not otherwise exist, while apparent authority expands

> "One who represents that another is his servant or other agent and thereby causes a third person justifiably to rely upon the care or skill of such apparent agent is subject to liability to the third person for harm caused by the lack of care or skill of the one appearing to be a servant or other agent as if he were such."

. . . We have not applied § 267 to a franchisor/franchisee situation, but courts in a number of other jurisdictions have done so in ways that we find instructive. In most cases the courts have found that there was a jury issue of apparent agency. The crucial issues are whether the putative principal held the third party out as an agent and whether the plaintiff relied on that holding out. . . .

In each of these cases, the franchise agreement required the franchisee to act in ways that identified it with the franchisor. The franchisor imposed those requirements as part of maintaining an image of uniformity of operations and appearance for the franchisor's entire system. Its purpose was to attract the patronage of the public to that entire system. The centrally imposed uniformity is the fundamental basis for the courts' conclusion that there was an issue of fact whether the franchisors held the franchisees out as the franchisors' agents.

In this case, for similar reasons, there is an issue of fact about whether defendant held 3K out as its agent. Everything about the appearance and operation of the Tigard McDonald's identified it with defendant and with the common image for all McDonald's restaurants that defendant has worked to create through national advertising, common signs and uniforms, common menus, common appearance, and common standards. The possible existence of a sign identifying 3K as the operator does not alter the conclusion that there is an issue of apparent agency for the jury. There are issues of fact of whether that sign was sufficiently visible to the public, in light of plaintiff's apparent failure to see it, and of whether one sign by itself is sufficient to remove the impression that defendant created through all of the other indicia of its control that it, and 3K under the requirements that defendant imposed, presented to the public.

Defendant does not seriously dispute that a jury could find that it held 3K out as its agent. Rather, it argues that there is insufficient evidence that plaintiff justifiably relied on that holding out. It argues that it is not sufficient for her to prove that she went to the Tigard McDonald's because it was a McDonald's restaurant. Rather, she also had to prove that she went to it because she believed that McDonald's

the authority of an actual agent. . . . In this case, the precise issue is whether 3K was defendant's apparent agent, not whether 3K had apparent authority. . . .

Corporation operated both it and the other McDonald's restaurants that she had previously patronized. It states:

> "All [that] the Plaintiff's affidavit proves is that she went to the Tigard McDonald's based in reliance on her past experiences at other McDonald's. But her affidavit does nothing to link her experiences with ownership of those restaurants by McDonald's Corporation."

Defendant's argument both demands a higher level of sophistication about the nature of franchising than the general public can be expected to have and ignores the effect of its own efforts to lead the public to believe that McDonald's restaurants are part of a uniform national system of restaurants with common products and common standards of quality. A jury could find from plaintiff's affidavit that she believed that all McDonald's restaurants were the same because she believed that one entity owned and operated all of them or, at the least, exercised sufficient control that the standards that she experienced at one would be the same as she experienced at others.

Plaintiff testified in her affidavit that her reliance on defendant for the quality of service and food at the Tigard McDonald's came in part from her experience at other McDonald's restaurants. Defendant's argument that she must show that it, rather than a franchisee, operated those restaurants is, at best, disingenuous. A jury could find that it was defendant's very insistence on uniformity of appearance and standards, designed to cause the public to think of every McDonald's, franchised or unfranchised, as part of the same system, that makes it difficult or impossible for plaintiff to tell whether her previous experiences were at restaurants that defendant owned or franchised. . . .

ANALYSIS

1. **What's Going on Here?** Why is the franchisor fighting this case? Isn't it in the franchisor's interest to ensure that plaintiffs like Miller will not have to worry about finding a solvent defendant?
2. **Agency or Authority.** If the jury finds that an apparent agency relationship exists between the franchisee and McDonald's, would that suffice for vicarious liability, or would plaintiff also have to show that the franchisee had apparent authority?
3. **What Should McDonald's Do?** Should McDonald's reduce the amount of control it exercises over its franchisees, so as to avoid the risk of liability in cases such as this one?
4. **A Better Way?** Franchising as a way of organizing economic activity arose after the servant/independent contractor dichotomy was well-established. In many ways, the franchisor-franchisee relationship is a hybrid having attributes of both servant and independent contractor

status. Accordingly, case outcomes often appear inconsistent and even arbitrary. What might be a better way of handling these cases doctrinally?

5. **Reliance.** In its ruling on apparent agency, the court adopts the Restatement's requirement that the plaintiff must have relied on a manifestation by the apparent principal (here, McDonald's) and it must have been that reliance that exposed the plaintiff to harm. In most cases, this requirement makes good sense. Are there cases, however, in which requiring proof of justifiable reliance might seem unfair or inefficient?

PROBLEM

Suppose that the owners of twenty-five motels in a certain state decide that in order to compete they need a trade name and some statewide advertising. They realize that in order to benefit from the trade name they must ensure that each motel maintains high standards and that all the motels set room rates at a figure that is consistent with their intended image. They agree that they will remodel their lobbies to create a common attractive appearance and will require their employees to wear an agreed-upon uniform. They form a corporation called Finest Motels Corp., in which they share ownership. They are required to make periodic payments to Finest Motels Corp. to pay for advertising and for policing compliance with standards. They hire a former executive of Hilton Inns, Inc. and tell her that they want their motels to live up to Hilton standards. Each of the motels is to change its name, with the new name beginning with the location, followed by "Finest Motel"—for example, "Anaheim Finest Motel." If any of the motels become insolvent, is Finest Motel Corp., or any of the other motels, liable for its debts? What suggestions would you offer to protect against that outcome?

C. SCOPE OF EMPLOYMENT

Brill v. Davajon

51 Ill.App.2d 445, 201 N.E.2d 253 (1964).

This action was brought by David M. Brill to recover damages for injuries arising out of a collision between his automobile and a cab owned by the Checker Taxi Company and an automobile driven by Joel Davajon. The jury returned a verdict in his favor. The defendant, Checker Taxi Company, appeals from a judgment entered against it. The defendant, Joel Davajon, is not involved in this appeal.

On January 7, 1957, at approximately 1:00 A.M., David Brill was driving his automobile east on Foster Avenue, Chicago. It was a cold night, the street was icy and Brill was proceeding slowly. As he approached the intersection of Foster and Ashland Avenue he noticed a Checker cab trying to push another car, which apparently had stalled. There was a conflict in the evidence as to whether the cab and the stalled car were at the south curb line of Foster Avenue, or whether they were in the center of the street in the eastbound left turn lane. Brill testified that he was in the middle of the street and that the cab was at the south curb; that the cab pushed the stalled car outward from the curb into his path and that both vehicles collided with his automobile. The driver of the cab, Frank McFarland, testified that the cab and the stalled car were in the left-hand turn lane and that Brill sideswiped them while attempting to pass them to the left on the slippery street. The driver of the stalled car, Joel Davajon, was not in court and did not testify.

In any event, whatever may have been the relative positions of the vehicles at the time of the occurrence and whatever may have been the actual point of impact between them, it was undisputed that the automobiles collided while McFarland was pushing Davajon's car and that Davajon had offered McFarland one dollar to do this favor for him. Checker contended that McFarland was not acting as its agent at the time of the occurrence and produced proof that what he did was in direct violation of specific orders issued to him by the company. The president of Checker, Michael Sokoll, testified that taxi drivers are instructed not to use the cabs for any purpose other than hauling passengers for hire. McFarland, who had been a Checker driver for 12 years, admitted that he had violated a company regulation in using his cab to aid Davajon and said he had received "a good tongue lashing" for doing so. He stated that he had been given detailed instructions as to his duties by the garage superintendent and had been told that it was against the company rules to push other automobiles. This testimony was in no way controverted. At the close of all the evidence Checker moved for a directed verdict on the ground that McFarland had been acting in his own behalf and that it was not liable under the doctrine of respondeat superior. The denial of the motion is the principal error urged by the defendant in this appeal.

Generally, a party injured by the negligence of another must seek his remedy against the person who caused his injury. The doctrine of respondeat superior is an exception to this general rule. Under this exception the negligence of an employee is imputable to his employer if the relationship of principal and agent existed at the time of and in respect to the particular transaction out of which the injury arose.... Thus it matters little that the negligent employee was usually the agent of his employer if, at the time he injured the third party, the relationship of principal and agent was temporarily suspended. If he was not acting as his employer's agent at the time of the injury, the employer cannot be held liable for his tort. The burden of proving that an employee was acting as the agent of his employer is upon the party who asserts the agency.

The same general principles apply if the injury is caused by an automobile owned by the employer and driven by the employee....

The plaintiff cites many cases both from Illinois and other jurisdictions to the effect that an employer may be liable even though the employee's conduct violated established rules. Upon examination of each of these authorities, however, we find that in one way or another each is distinguishable from the present case. In several of the cases the employer had pursued some course of conduct which amounted to an acquiescence in previous rule-breaking by the employee; under such circumstances, the courts would not allow the employer to use breach of those same rules as a defense when the employee's action resulted in injury to a third party. . . . In other cases cited, though the conduct of the employee was not authorized, he was found never to have departed completely from the business of his employer. . . . Still others, cited by appellees from other jurisdictions, are based on principles of law different from those of Illinois and cannot serve as authority here. Many were decided as they were because an automobile was found to be a dangerous instrumentality, and it was held as a matter of policy that one who places a dangerous instrument in the hands of another should be answerable for injuries caused thereby. . . . These cases cannot serve as authority here since in Illinois an automobile is not a dangerous instrumentality per se. . . .

The plaintiff in this case offered no evidence to show that pushing other automobiles was a practice accepted as within the normal course of a driver's employment. No evidence was offered that the defendant had acquiesced in such actions in the past or that there were circumstances which implied knowledge by the defendant of such acts. As the case came to a close, the evidence of the defendant remained uncontradicted either directly or indirectly, while the plaintiff's case on the indispensable element of agency rested on either a presumption, which had ceased to exist, or on inferences favorable to him, if any there were, which could be drawn from the whole evidence.

The test to be applied to a defendant's motion for a directed verdict at the close of the evidence is whether there is any evidence or reasonable inferences arising from the evidence, tending to prove the cause of action alleged in the complaint. . . .

If there were some dispute as to whether McFarland was in fact pushing Davajon's car, or if there were some doubt whether the gratuity he was to have received would not have been his own but would have been registered on the meter of the cab as the company's income, or if there were some doubt about the company's rules, or if the company had closed its eyes to past dereliction's of duty by its drivers and thus had countenanced infractions of its rules, reasonable men might disagree whether or not McFarland was the company's agent at the moment of impact with Brill's automobile. But under the evidence as presented, we believe all reasonable men would conclude that at the time of this occurrence McFarland had departed from his employer's business and that in pushing Davajon's car he was performing an act which caused a temporary lapse in the agency relationship of employer and employee.

In view of the plaintiff's complete failure to establish the material element of agency, the trial court should have directed a verdict for the defendant or allowed its motion for judgment notwithstanding the verdict. The plaintiff may have had a case against McFarland, whom he did not sue, or against Davajon, whom he did, but he has no case against the defendant Checker Taxi Company, and the judgment is therefore reversed.

ANALYSIS

1. **The $1 Payment.** What would the result have been if Davajon had not promised to pay McFarland $1 and McFarland had not expected to receive any payment?
2. **Derivative Liability.** Suppose that Checker had been held liable and had paid damages. Under black letter agency law, its liability would have been derivative, McFarland would still be the prime tortfeasor, and Checker would have been legally entitled to recover the amount of its loss from McFarland. What do you suppose is the likelihood that Checker would actually seek recovery from McFarland? Why?

Ira S. Bushey & Sons, Inc. v. United States

398 F.2d 167 (2d Cir.1968).

■ FRIENDLY, CIRCUIT JUDGE:

While the United States Coast Guard vessel Tamaroa was being overhauled in a floating drydock located in Brooklyn's Gowanus Canal, a seaman returning from shore leave late at night, in the condition for which seamen are famed, turned some wheels on the drydock wall. He thus opened valves that controlled the flooding of the tanks on one side of the drydock. Soon the ship listed, slid off the blocks and fell against the wall. Parts of the drydock sank, and the ship partially did—fortunately without loss of life or personal injury. The drydock owner sought and was granted compensation by the District Court for the Eastern District of New York in an amount to be determined, 276 F.Supp. 518; the United States appeals.

. . .

The Tamaroa had gone into drydock on February 28, 1963; her keel rested on blocks permitting her drive shaft to be removed and repairs to be made to her hull. The contract between the Government and Bushey provided in part:

(*o*) The work shall, whenever practical, be performed in such manner as not to interfere with the berthing and messing of personnel attached to the vessel undergoing repair, and provision shall be made so that personnel assigned shall have access to the vessel at all times, it being understood that such personnel will not interfere with the work or the contractor's workmen.

Access from shore to ship was provided by a route past the security guard at the gate, through the yard, up a ladder to the top of one drydock wall and along the wall to a gangway leading to the fantail deck, where men returning from leave reported at a quartermaster's shack.

Seaman Lane, whose prior record was unblemished, returned from shore leave a little after midnight on March 14. He had been drinking heavily; the quartermaster made mental note that he was "loose." For reasons not apparent to us or very likely to Lane,[4] he took it into his head, while progressing along the gangway wall, to turn each of three large wheels some twenty times; unhappily, as previously stated, these wheels controlled the water intake valves. After boarding ship at 12:11 A.M., Lane mumbled to an off-duty seaman that he had "turned some valves" and also muttered something about "valves" to another who was standing the engineering watch. Neither did anything; apparently Lane's condition was not such as to encourage proximity. At 12:20 A.M. a crew member discovered water coming into the drydock. By 12:30 A.M. the ship began to list, the alarm was sounded and the crew were ordered ashore. Ten minutes later the vessel and dock were listing over 20 degrees; in another ten minutes the ship slid off the blocks and fell against the drydock wall.

The Government attacks imposition of liability on the ground that Lane's acts were not within the scope of his employment. It relies heavily on § 228(1) of the Restatement of Agency 2d which says that "conduct of a servant is within the scope of employment if, but only if: * * * (c) it is actuated, at least in part, by a purpose to serve the master." Courts have gone to considerable lengths to find such a purpose, as witness a well-known opinion in which Judge Learned Hand concluded that a drunken boatswain who routed the plaintiff out of his bunk with a blow, saying "Get up, you big son of a bitch, and turn to," and then continued to fight, might have thought he was acting in the interest of the ship. Nelson v. American-West African Line, 86 F.2d 730 (2 Cir.1936), cert. denied, 300 U.S. 665 (1937). It would be going too far to find such a purpose here; while Lane's return to the Tamaroa was to serve his employer, no one

---

[4] Lane disappeared after completing the sentence imposed by a courtmartial and being discharged from the Coast Guard.

has suggested how he could have thought turning the wheels to be, even if—which is by no means clear—he was unaware of the consequences.

In light of the highly artificial way in which the motive test has been applied, the district judge believed himself obliged to test the doctrine's continuing vitality by referring to the larger purposes respondeat superior is supposed to serve. He concluded that the old formulation failed this test. We do not find his analysis so compelling, however, as to constitute a sufficient basis in itself for discarding the old doctrine. It is not at all clear, as the court below suggested, that expansion of liability in the manner here suggested will lead to a more efficient allocation of resources. As the most astute exponent of this theory has emphasized, a more efficient allocation can only be expected if there is some reason to believe that imposing a particular cost on the enterprise will lead it to consider whether steps should be taken to prevent a recurrence of the accident. Calabresi, The Decision for Accidents: An Approach to Non-fault Allocation of Costs, 78 Harv.L.Rev. 713, 725–34 (1965). And the suggestion that imposition of liability here will lead to more intensive screening of employees rests on highly questionable premises. . . .[5] The unsatisfactory quality of the allocation of resource rationale is especially striking on the facts of this case. It could well be that application of the traditional rule might induce drydock owners, prodded by their insurance companies, to install locks on their valves to avoid similar incidents in the future,[6] while placing the burden on shipowners is much less likely to lead to accident prevention.[7] It is true, of course, that in many cases the plaintiff will not be in a position to insure, and so expansion of liability will, at the very least, serve respondeat superior's loss spreading function. . . . But the fact that the defendant is better able to afford damages is not alone sufficient to justify legal responsibility . . . and this overarching principle must be taken into account in deciding whether to expand the reach of respondeat superior.

A policy analysis thus is not sufficient to justify this proposed expansion of vicarious liability. This is not surprising since respondeat superior, even within its traditional limits, rests not so much on policy grounds consistent with the governing principles of tort law as in a deeply rooted sentiment that a business enterprise cannot justly disclaim responsibility for accidents which may fairly be said to be characteristic of its activities. It is in this light that the inadequacy of the motive test becomes apparent. Whatever may have been the case in the past, a

[5] We are not here speaking of cases in which the enterprise has negligently hired an employee whose undesirable propensities are known or should have been. . . .

[6] The record reveals that most modern drydocks have automatic locks to guard against unauthorized use of valves.

[7] Although it is theoretically possible that shipowners would demand that drydock owners take appropriate action, see Coase, The Problem of Social Cost, 3 J.L. & Economics 1 (1960), this would seem unlikely to occur in real life.

doctrine that would create such drastically different consequences for the actions of the drunken boatswain in *Nelson* and those of the drunken seaman here reflects a wholly unrealistic attitude toward the risks characteristically attendant upon the operation of a ship. We concur in the statement of Mr. Justice Rutledge in a case involving violence injuring a fellow-worker, in this instance in the context of workmen's compensation:

> Men do not discard their personal qualities when they go to work. Into the job they carry their intelligence, skill, habits of care and rectitude. Just as inevitably they take along also their tendencies to carelessness and camaraderie, as well as emotional make-up. In bringing men together, work brings these qualities together, causes frictions between them, creates occasions for lapses into carelessness, and for fun-making and emotional flare-up. * * * These expressions of human nature are incidents inseparable from working together. They involve risks of injury and these risks are inherent in the working environment.

Hartford Accident & Indemnity Co. v. Cardillo, 72 App.D.C. 52, 112 F.2d 11, 15, cert. denied, 310 U.S. 649 (1940);. . . .

Put another way, Lane's conduct was not so "unforeseeable" as to make it unfair to charge the Government with responsibility. We agree with a leading treatise that "what is reasonably foreseeable in this context (of respondeat superior) * * * is quite a different thing from the foreseeably unreasonable risk of harm that spells negligence * * *. The foresight that should impel the prudent man to take precautions is not the same measure as that by which he should perceive the harm likely to flow from his long-run activity in spite of all reasonable precautions on his own part. The proper test here bears far more resemblance to that which limits liability for workmen's compensation than to the test for negligence. The employer should be held to expect risks, to the public also, which arise 'out of and in the course of' his employment of labor." 2 Harper & James, The Law of Torts 1377–78 (1956). . . . Here it was foreseeable that crew members crossing the drydock might do damage, negligently or even intentionally, such as pushing a Bushey employee or kicking property into the water. Moreover, the proclivity of seamen to find solace for solitude by copious resort to the bottle while ashore has been noted in opinions too numerous to warrant citation. Once all this is granted, it is immaterial that Lane's precise action was not to be foreseen. . . . Consequently, we can no longer accept our past decisions that have refused to move beyond the Nelson rule, . . . since they do not accord with modern understanding as to when it is fair for an enterprise to disclaim the actions of its employees.

One can readily think of cases that fall on the other side of the line. If Lane had set fire to the bar where he had been imbibing or had caused an accident on the street while returning to the drydock, the Government would not be liable; the activities of the "enterprise" do not reach into areas where the servant does not create risks different from those attendant on the activities of the community in general.... We agree with the district judge that if the seaman "upon returning to the drydock, recognized the Bushey security guard as his wife's lover and shot him," 276 F.Supp. at 530, vicarious liability would not follow; the incident would have related to the seaman's domestic life, not to his seafaring activity, and it would have been the most unlikely happenstance that the confrontation with the paramour occurred on a drydock rather than at the traditional spot. Here Lane had come within the closed-off area where his ship lay, ... to occupy a berth to which the Government insisted he have access, ... and while his act is not readily explicable, at least it was not shown to be due entirely to facets of his personal life. The risk that seamen going and coming from the Tamaroa might cause damage to the drydock is enough to make it fair that the enterprise bear the loss. It is not a fatal objection that the rule we lay down lacks sharp contours; in the end, as Judge Andrews said in a related context, "it is all a question (of expediency,) * * * of fair judgment, always keeping in mind the fact that we endeavor to make a rule in each case that will be practical and in keeping with the general understanding of Mankind." Palsgraf v. Long Island R.R. Co.,248 N.Y. 339, 354–355, 162 N.E. 99, 104, 59 A.L.R. 1253 (1928) (dissenting opinion).

...

Affirmed.

NOTE

In Clover v. Snowbird Ski Resort, 808 P.2d 1037 (Utah 1991), Chris Zulliger, an employee of the ski resort, was skiing, at high speed, down an intermediate slope. He had ignored a sign instructing skiers to ski slowly. He reached a crest in the slope and used it to launch himself into a jump. From where he began the jump he was unable to see his landing area, and by the time he was able to see where he would land, he was airborne. He struck and severely injured the plaintiff.

The trial court granted summary judgment in favor of the ski resort, on the theory that the employee was not acting within the scope of his employment. The employee was a chef at one of the resort's restaurants and a supervisor of others. He was expected to ski between restaurant locations. Like many other employees, he had a season ski pass. He was an expert skier. After monitoring the Mid-Gad Restaurant on the mountain, he took about four runs and then started to head for the bottom of the mountain, where he was to begin work as a chef at the resort's Plaza Restaurant. It was on his way down the mountain that he took the reckless and fateful jump.

The Supreme Court concluded that summary judgment should not have been granted in favor of the ski resort and remanded for trial. According to the court, the only doubt about scope of employment arose because Zulliger did not return to the Plaza immediately after monitoring the Mid-Gad. It reasoned, however, that a jury could reasonably find that "Zulliger had resumed his employment and that [his] deviation was not substantial enough to constitute a total abandonment of his employment." The court rejected an alternative argument by the plaintiff, based on *Bushey*, that the employer's liability should depend "not on whether the employee's conduct is motivated by serving the employer's interest, but on whether the employee's conduct is foreseeable." The Utah court noted simply that this is not the test under Utah case law.

ANALYSIS

1. **Friendly vs. Restatement.** Restatement (Second) of Agency § 228 (see Restatement [Third] of Agency § 7.07(2)) provides that a servant's conduct "is not within the scope of employment if it is . . . too little actuated by a purpose to serve the master." In *Bushey*, Judge Friendly acknowledged that no purpose to serve the master could be found in this case—no matter how hard one tried. Apparently, the trial court had likewise concluded that no such purpose could be found. Accordingly, the district court opined, the law should be changed. No longer would plaintiffs be required to show that the agent was motivated by a purpose to serve the master. Instead, it would suffice to show that the conduct arose out of and in the course of the employment. The district court's analysis amounted to virtually a rule of strict liability for the torts of an employee as long as any connection in time and space could be made between the conduct and the employment. Judge Friendly affirmed the district court's result but rejected its rationale, noting that it was not at all clear that the proposed rule would lead to a more efficient allocation of resources. On the other hand, does Judge Friendly articulate a standard different from that of the Restatement?

2. **Basis for Decision.** Judge Friendly declines to base the decision on considerations of "policy"—that is, economic incentives and deterrence. Instead, he states that respondeat superior derives from "deeply rooted sentiment that a business enterprise cannot justly disclaim responsibility for accidents which may fairly be said to be characteristic of its activities." What is the significance of the court's use of the word "sentiment"? Where does the court find evidence of this sentiment?

3. **Scene of the Employment.** In what way was Lane's conduct "characteristic of [the] activities" of the Coast Guard?

4. **Drawing the Line.** In the last paragraph of the opinion, the court states, "If Lane had set fire to the bar where he had been imbibing or

had caused an accident on the street while returning to the drydock, the Government would not be liable. . . ." Why not? What if Lane and other crew members had gone to the bar to relax after a long and arduous voyage and Lane had acted along with several other crew members in setting the fire negligently?

Manning v. Grimsley

643 F.2d 20 (1st Cir.1981).

In this diversity action involving the law of Massachusetts the plaintiff, complaining that he as a spectator at a professional baseball game was injured by a ball thrown by a pitcher, sought in a battery count and in a negligence count to recover damages from the pitcher and his employer. The district judge directed a verdict for defendants on the battery count and the jury returned a verdict for defendants on the negligence count. The district court having entered judgment for defendants on both counts, the plaintiff appeals from the judgment on the battery count.

(1) In deciding whether the district court correctly directed a verdict for defendants on the battery count, we are to consider the evidence in the light most favorable to the plaintiff. That evidence was to the following effect.

On September 16, 1975 there was a professional baseball game at Fenway Park in Boston between the defendant, the Baltimore Baseball Club, Inc. playing under the name the Baltimore Orioles, and the Boston Red Sox. The defendant Ross Grimsley was a pitcher employed by the defendant Baltimore Club. Some spectators, including the plaintiff, were seated, behind a wire mesh fence, in bleachers located in right field. In order to be ready to pitch in the game, Grimsley, during the first three innings of play, had been warming up by throwing a ball from a pitcher's mound to a plate in the bullpen located near those right field bleachers. The spectators in the bleachers continuously heckled him. On several occasions immediately following heckling Grimsley looked directly at the hecklers, not just into the stands. At the end of the third inning of the game, Grimsley, after his catcher had left his catching position and was walking over to the bench, faced the bleachers and wound up or stretched as though to pitch in the direction of the plate toward which he had been throwing but the ball traveled from Grimsley's hand at more than 80 miles an hour at an angle of 90 degrees to the path from the pitcher's mound to the plate and directly toward the hecklers in the bleachers. The ball passed through the wire mesh fence and hit the plaintiff.

We, unlike the district judge, are of the view that from the evidence that Grimsley was an expert pitcher, that on several occasions immediately following heckling he looked directly at the hecklers, not just into the stands, and that the ball traveled at a right angle to the direction in which he had been pitching and in the direction of the hecklers, the jury could reasonably have inferred that Grimsley intended (1) to throw the ball in the direction of the hecklers, (2) to cause them imminent apprehension of being hit, and (3) to respond to conduct presently affecting his ability to warm up and, if the opportunity came, to play in the game itself.

The foregoing evidence and inferences would have permitted a jury to conclude that the defendant Grimsley committed a battery against the plaintiff. This case falls within the scope of Restatement Torts 2d § 13, which provides, inter alia, that an actor is subject to liability to another for battery if, intending to cause a third person to have an imminent apprehension of a harmful bodily contact, the actor causes the other to suffer a harmful contact. . . . It, therefore, was error for the district court to have directed a verdict for defendant Grimsley on the battery count.

[The court holds that the plaintiff is not collaterally estopped by the jury verdict and non-appealed judgment for the defendants on the negligence count.]

It follows that the plaintiff is entitled to a vacation of the judgment on the battery count in favor of the defendant Grimsley.

The plaintiff is also entitled to a vacation of the judgment on the battery count in favor of the Baltimore Club, Grimsley's employer.

(5) In Massachusetts "where a plaintiff seeks to recover damages from an employer for injuries resulting from an employee's assault . . . [w]hat must be shown is that the employee's assault was in response to the plaintiff's conduct which was presently interfering with the employee's ability to perform his duties successfully. This interference may be in the form of an affirmative attempt to prevent an employee from carrying out his assignments. . . ." Miller v. Federated Department Stores, Inc., 364 Mass. 340, 349–350, 304 N.E.2d 573 (1973).

(6) The defendant Baltimore Club, relying on its reading of the *Miller* case, contends that the heckling from the bleachers constituted words which annoyed or insulted Grimsley and did not constitute "conduct" and that those words did not "presently" interfere with his ability to perform his duties successfully so as to make his employer liable for his assault in response thereto. Our analysis of the *Miller* case leads us to reject the contention. There a porter, whose duties consisted of cleaning the floors and emptying the trash cans in Filene's basement store, slapped a customer who had annoyed or insulted him by a remark that "If you would say 'excuse me,' people could get out of your way." The Massachusetts Supreme Judicial Court held that while the employee "may have been annoyed or insulted by" the customer's remark, "that

circumstance alone does not justify imposition of liability on" the employer. 364 Mass. 350–351, 304 N.E.2d 573.

Miller's holding that a critical comment by a customer to an employee did not in the circumstances constitute "conduct" interfering with the employee's performance of his work is obviously distinguishable from the case at bar. Constant heckling by fans at a baseball park would be, within the meaning of *Miller*, conduct. The jury could reasonably have found that such conduct had either the affirmative purpose to rattle or the effect of rattling the employee so that he could not perform his duties successfully. Moreover, the jury could reasonably have found that Grimsley's assault was not a mere retaliation for past annoyance, but a response to continuing conduct which was "presently interfering" with his ability to pitch in the game if called upon to play. Therefore, the battery count against the Baltimore Club should have been submitted to the jury.

Vacated and remanded for a new trial on the battery count.

ANALYSIS

1. **Grimsley vs. Restatement.** Restatement (Second) of Agency § 231 provides that a servant's acts "may be within the scope of employment although consciously criminal or tortious," but the comments to that section indicate that "serious crimes" are outside the scope. Why? Is Manning v. Grimsley inconsistent with the Restatement?

2. **Use of Force.** Restatement § 228(2) provides that a servant's use of force against another is within the scope of employment if "the use of force is not unexpectable by the master." Consequently, for example, the owner of a nightclub probably would be held liable for injuries inflicted by a bouncer in ejecting someone from the bar. After all, the owner presumably hired the bouncer for the very purpose of using force to eject drunken or otherwise undesirable patrons. Was Grimley's conduct a use of force that should have been foreseeable by the Club?

3. **Preventative Steps.** What could the Club have done to prevent the injury?

4. **Derivative Liability.** Once again (see the Analysis following Brill v. Davajon, above), if Manning recovers from the Club, what is the likelihood that it would try to recover from Grimsley?

5. **Compensation.** Suppose the jury verdict is that Grimsley is liable, but not the Club, and that Grimsley asks the Club to pay the amount he owes. What would you advise the Club?

Lamkin v. Brooks

498 So.2d 1068 (La. Sup. Ct. 1986).

. . .

On the night of November 19, 1982, Officer Robert Brooks was on patrol as a police officer for the Town of Lecompte when he saw a truck and a car parked on the shoulder of State Highway 112, just inside the Lecompte town limits. Donnal Lamkin, his son Lonnie, and Lonnie's date were sitting in the vehicles. Lonnie Lamkin, sitting in the driver's seat of the car, was vomiting out of the window. Donnal Lamkin informed Brooks that they did not need assistance and Brooks continued on patrol.

Shortly thereafter, Brooks came upon the Lamkins arguing in the parking lot of the Bayou Lounge, a Lecompte bar. Lonnie's date was sitting in the car. Donnal was obviously intoxicated and Lonnie was trying to persuade his father to leave his truck and ride home with him. Brooks informed the Lamkins that if Donnal insisted on driving while intoxicated, he would have to arrest him. After considerable discussion, Brooks agreed to "look the other way" so that Donnal could drive a short distance to the place where he was to stay that night. Lonnie reportedly assured Brooks that "he would see to it that [Donnal] got to the house." Brooks returned to his patrol.

A few hours later, between three and four o'clock in the morning, Lecompte's police radio operator dispatched units driven by Brooks and Officer Riley Williamson to investigate a complaint of "two drunks" blocking Highway 112 west of Lecompte. Officer Brooks had about one year of experience as a police officer, while Williamson had only been on the job for about two weeks. Brooks and Williamson found the Lamkins parked at the intersection of Humpy Strange Road and Highway 112. This location was outside the jurisdiction of the town. One or both of the Lamkin vehicles at least partially obstructed the intersection. Although Donnal informed the officers that they should get back to town because they were outside their jurisdiction, Lonnie Lamkin and his date voluntarily moved the car and the truck off the road as they were requested to do. Donnal told Brooks that he would "whip his ass" if he did not return to town. Brooks and Williamson then left in their respective vehicles to return to Lecompte. Williamson drove down Highway 112 while Brooks proceeded down Humpy Strange Road. Both routes led back to Lecompte. However, after driving a short distance, Brooks turned his car around and drove back to the intersection where the Lamkins were still parked. Brooks testified in deposition that he went back because he needed to record Donnal's license number on an "incident report." While he was sitting in his car writing down the license number, Donnal approached the car and repeated his threats. When Donnal made what Brooks perceived as a menacing motion, Brooks got out of the car "to defend himself" and hit Donnal once in the face. On the other hand, the Lamkins and Lonnie's date testified that when Brooks returned to the intersection, he got out of the police car and hit Donnal without saying a word. The blow broke several bones in Donnal's face, requiring surgery and hospitalization.

[Donnal sued Brooks, the Town of Lecompte, and the Town's insurance carrier. Donnal won a judgment against Brooks, who did not appeal, but lost his case against the Town and the insurance carrier. Donnal lost again in the court of appeal. The supreme court granted Donnal's petition for writ of certiorari.]

. . . The fact that Brooks wrongfully injured Lamkin outside the town limits does not automatically absolve the Town of Lecompte from liability for its employee's tort. . . . Questions of whether an officer who commits a wrongful act outside his jurisdiction left the jurisdiction knowingly or inadvertently, was dispatched there by his superiors or left it in pursuit of a vehicle are only some of the factors to be considered in determining whether the officer acted in the course and scope of his employment.

We must therefore consider whether Brooks was acting within the course and scope of his employment at the time of his wrongful act in order to determine if the town can be held vicariously liable under the theory of respondeat superior. An employer's vicarious liability in Louisiana derives from La. Civ. Code art. 2320, which provides in pertinent part:

> Masters and employers are answerable for the damage occasioned by their servants and overseers, in the exercise of the functions in which they are employed.

In LeBrane v. Lewis, 292 So.2d 216 (La.1974), we held that the test for an employer's liability is whether "the tortious conduct of the [employee is] so closely connected in time, place, and causation to his employment-duties as to be regarded a risk of harm fairly attributable to the employer's business, as compared with conduct instituted by purely personal considerations entirely extraneous to the employer's interests." In *LeBrane,* Lewis, LeBrane's supervisor, had fired him for cause. While he was waiting to collect his final pay, LeBrane and his supervisor engaged in a violent argument and "more or less invit[ed] each other outside." On the way out, the two began fighting. It is unclear who was the initial aggressor, but Lewis stabbed LeBrane as he tried to run away from the business premises. The trial court found that the supervisor was liable in tort due to his use of excessive force. Both lower courts denied LeBrane recovery against the employer on the ground that by the time that the actual stabbing occurred the altercation had become "a purely personal matter between LeBrane and Lewis." We reversed, reasoning that the dispute that erupted into violence was primarily employment rooted. We found that the tort was sufficiently within the scope of the supervisor's employment for his employer to be held liable to the victim.

In the present case, the altercation between Brooks and Donnal clearly had its roots in Brooks' performance of his duties as a Lecompte police officer. The record indicates that before the night in question no bad blood existed between the two men. All of Brooks' contacts with Donnal that evening occurred in the course of his police duties. The radio operator instructed him to proceed outside the town's jurisdiction to investigate a complaint. Brooks' incident report, which was introduced into evidence, includes Donnal's truck's license number, supporting Brooks' contention that he returned to the scene to record this information. Brooks wore a police uniform, carried a gun and drove a Lecompte police car. Under these circumstances, we find that Brooks' tortious conduct was so closely connected in time, place and causation to his employment duties as to be regarded as a risk of harm fairly attributable to his employer's business. Therefore, Brooks was within the course and scope of his employment at the time he hit Donnal Lamkin and the Town of Lecompte is vicariously liable to plaintiff for his damages.

. . .

We next consider whether the town's insurer, American Home Assurance Company, is required to indemnify the town under the terms of its policy. . . . The policy . . . specifically excludes coverage for "damages arising out of the willful violation of a penal statute or ordinance committed by or with the knowledge or consent of any Insured, or claims or injury arising out of the willful, intentional or malicious conduct of any Insured."

. . . The record fully supports that [Brooks's] unprovoked attack on Lamkin was a willful and intentional act on his part. Therefore, his conduct clearly falls within this exclusion. Because the town's vicarious liability is based on the intentional act of its employee (Brooks), we reject the town's contention that the exclusion does not apply to it. Hence, the policy affords no coverage to the Town of Lecompte.

. . .

ANALYSIS

1. **Recording the License.** What would the result have been if Brooks, when he decided to return to the accident scene, had not had a bona fide intent to "record Donnal's license number"?

2. **Reconciling the Cases.** Would the result have been the same under the doctrine of either of the two preceding cases (*Ira S. Bushey & Sons* and *Manning*)?

3. **Insurance Industry Policy.** Why do you suppose the insurance policy excluded intentional torts? What does your answer suggest about how the case should have been decided?

D. STATUTORY CLAIMS

Arguello v. Conoco, Inc.

207 F.3d 803 (5th Cir.2000),
cert. denied, sub. nom. Escobedo v. Conoco, Inc., 531 U.S. 874 (2000).

The appellants, a group of Hispanic and African-American consumers, filed suit against appellees, Conoco, Inc. ("Conoco" or "Conoco, Inc.") alleging that they were subjected to racial discrimination while purchasing gasoline and other services. Appellants challenge the district court's 12(b)(6) dismissal of their disparate impact claim under 42 U.S.C. § 2000a, and the district court's grant of summary judgment to Conoco on the appellants remaining 42 U.S.C. §§ 1981 and 2000a claims. For the following reasons we affirm in part, and reverse in part.

Factual and Procedural Background

There are three different incidents which form the background for this appeal. In March 1995, Denise Arguello ("Arguello"), and her father Alberto Govea ("Govea"), along with various other members of their family stopped at a Conoco-owned store[1] in Fort Worth, Texas. After pumping their gasoline Arguello and Govea entered the store to pay for the gasoline and purchase other items. When Arguello approached the counter she presented the store cashier, Cindy Smith ("Smith"), with her items and a credit card. Smith asked to see Arguello's identification. When Arguello gave Smith her Oklahoma driver's license Smith stated that an out-of-state driver's license was not acceptable identification. Arguello disagreed with Smith and Smith began to insult Arguello using profanity and racial epithets. Smith also knocked a six-pack of beer off the counter toward Arguello. After Arguello retreated from the inside of the store, Smith used the store's intercom system to continue yelling racial epithets. Smith also made obscene gestures through the window.

Moments after the incident occurred Arguello and Govea used a pay phone outside the station to call a Conoco customer service phone number and complain about Smith's conduct. Govea also attempted to reenter the store to discover Smith's name. When Govea attempted to reenter the store, Smith and another store employee locked the doors. Linda Corbin ("Corbin"), a district manager, received Arguello and Govea's complaints. Corbin reviewed video tape from the store, which had no audio, and concluded that Smith had acted inappropriately. When she was

[1] We will use the term "Conoco-owned" to denote stores that are owned and operated by Conoco, Inc. "Conoco-branded" stores are stores which are independently owned marketers of Conoco products and are subject to the Petroleum Marketer Agreements.

confronted by Corbin, Smith admitted to using the profanity, racial epithets, and obscene gestures. Corbin counseled Smith about her behavior but did not suspend, or terminate Smith. Several months after the incident Corbin transferred Smith to another store for Smith's protection after receiving phone calls that a group was planning to picket the store at which the incident took place.

In September 1995, Gary Ivory ("Ivory"), Anthony Pickett ("Pickett"), and Michael Ross ("Ross") visited a Conoco-branded store in Fort Worth, Texas. While inside the store they allege that they were followed by a store employee and after complaining about this treatment a store employee told them "we don't have to serve you people" and "you people are always acting like this." The employee refused to serve them and asked them to leave. Eventually the police were summoned and the policeman ordered the store employee to serve the group.

In November 1996, Manuel Escobedo ("Escobedo") and Martha Escobedo ("Mrs. Escobedo") stopped at a Conoco-branded store in San Marcos, Texas. Escobedo claims that while visiting this store the store employee refused to provide toilet paper for the restroom, shouted profanities at his wife, and said "you Mexicans need to go back to Mexico." Escobedo called Conoco to complain about this incident, and was told by a Conoco customer service supervisor, Pamela Harper, that there was nothing Conoco could do because that station was not owned by Conoco. In a separate incident at a Conoco-branded store in Grand Prairie, Texas Escobedo was allegedly told by the store clerk that "you people steal gas." Finally, Escobedo claims that at two Conoco-branded stores in Laredo, Texas he was required to pre-pay for his gasoline while Caucasian customers were allowed to pump their gas first and then pay.

In March 1997, Arguello, Govea, the Escobedos, Ivory, Pickett, and Ross ("plaintiffs" or "appellants") filed suit against Conoco, Inc.... The plaintiffs alleged that Conoco was in violation of 42 U.S.C. §§ 1981[4] and 2000a ("Title II")[5] and state law for refusing to serve Hispanic and African-American customers, and subjecting this class of customers to substandard service and racially derogatory remarks. The plaintiffs also claimed that Conoco had illegal policies and practices which disparately impacted Hispanics and African-Americans.

In July 1997, the district court issued an order dismissing all claims based on the plaintiffs' allegations of disparate impact and the plaintiffs'

---

[4] 42 U.S.C. § 1981 provides that "[a]ll persons within the jurisdiction of the United States shall have the same right in every State and Territory to make and enforce contracts, to sue, be parties, give evidence, and to full and equal benefit of all laws . . . as is enjoyed by white citizens."

[5] Title II states that "[a]ll persons shall be entitled to the full and equal enjoyment of the goods, services, facilities, privileges, advantages, and accommodations of any place of public accommodation . . . without discrimination or segregation on the ground of race, color, religion, or national origin." 42 U.S.C. § 2000a.

state law claims. In October 1998, the district court granted summary judgment to Conoco on all of the plaintiffs' remaining claims.

Discussion

Appellants raise several issues on appeal. First, appellants contend that the district court erred in finding no agency relationship between Conoco, Inc. and the Conoco-branded stores. Appellants also argue that the district court erred in finding no agency relationship between Conoco, Inc. and Cindy Smith because Smith acted outside the scope of her employment. Appellants argue in the alternative that even if Smith was outside the scope of her employment Conoco had a nondelegable duty to prevent racial discrimination, and further that Conoco should be held liable because it ratified Smith's conduct. Finally, appellants contend that the district court improperly dismissed their disparate impact claims under Title II.

. . .

B. Agency Relationship between Conoco, Inc. and Conoco-branded Stores

The incidents involving Ivory, Ross, Pickett and the Escobedos occurred at Conoco-branded stores. These Conoco-branded stores are independently owned, and have entered into Petroleum Marketing Agreements ("PMA") that allow them to market and sell Conoco brand gasoline and supplies in their stores. The district court held that no agency relationship existed between Conoco, Inc. and the Conoco-branded stores. The district court found that Conoco, Inc. did not control the details of the daily operations of the Conoco-branded stores, including personnel decisions.

The Supreme Court has suggested that in order to impose liability on a defendant under § 1981 for the discriminatory actions of a third party, the plaintiff must demonstrate that there is an agency relationship between the defendant and the third party. General Building Contractors Association v. Pennsylvania United Engineers and Constructors, 458 U.S. 375, 393 (1982). Agency is a fiduciary relation which results from the manifestation of consent by one person to another that the other shall act on his behalf and subject to his control, and consent by the other so to act. Id. at 391 (citing Restatement (Second) of Agency § 1 (1958) ("Restatement")). At the core of agency is a "fiduciary relation" arising from the "consent by one person to another that the other shall act on his behalf and subject to his control . . . equally central to the master-servant relation is the master's control over or right to control the physical activities of the servant." Id. at 393 (citing Restatement § 1). Therefore, to establish an agency relationship between Conoco, Inc. and the branded stores the plaintiffs must show that Conoco, Inc. has given consent for the branded stores to act on its behalf and that the branded stores are subject to the control of Conoco, Inc.

Appellants argue that the PMAs establish that Conoco, Inc. has an agency relationship with the branded stores. They argue that the PMAs give Conoco, Inc. control of the branded stores because the PMAs require the branded stores to maintain their businesses according to the standards set forth in the PMAs. Plaintiffs further contend that Conoco, Inc. controls the customer service dimension of the Conoco-branded stores. As evidence the plaintiffs point to a statement in the PMA that instructs the branded stores that "all customers shall be treated fairly, honestly, and courteously." Furthermore, the plaintiffs assert that Conoco, Inc. has the power to debrand the Conoco-branded stations for not complying with the contractual terms of the PMA. Thus, because of this debranding power the plaintiffs reason that Conoco controls the operations of their brand marketers in all areas which are discussed in the PMA, including customer service. The plaintiffs also produced summary judgment evidence that Conoco, Inc. conducts random, bi-yearly inspections of the branded stores to determine if business is being conducted in accordance with the standards of the PMA.[6]

Despite the plaintiffs' interpretation of the PMAs and the evidence of inspections, the plain language of the PMA defines the relationship between Conoco, Inc. and its branded stores. The PMA states:

> Marketer [Conoco-branded store] is an independent business and is not, nor are its employees, employees of Conoco. Conoco and Marketer are completely separate entities. They are not partners, general partners . . . nor agents of each other in any sense whatsoever and neither has the power to obligate or bind the other.

The facts of the present case are similar to the facts which formed the basis of the claim in Neff v. American Dairy Queen Corporation, 58 F.3d 1063 (5th Cir.1995). In Neff, the plaintiff appealed summary judgment of her claims against American Dairy Queen Corporation ("ADQ") for violation of the Americans with Disability Act ("ADA"). Neff claimed that ADQ violated the ADA by failing to make its San Antonio stores wheel chair accessible. We held that ADQ was a franchiser and the franchise agreement specifically stated that ADQ did not own or operate the San Antonio stores. The only summary judgment evidence presented by Neff was the franchise agreement. Neff argued that contrary to franchise agreement's statement disclaiming operation of the franchisee establishments, other clauses in the franchise agreement demonstrated that ADQ did in fact "operate" the San Antonio stores. Neff did not allege

[6] These inspections normally focus on product displays and labeling. Customer service is not considered a main focus of the random inspections.

that the franchise agreement was ambiguous, instead she disputed whether the control over franchisee facilities which was provided for in the agreement made ADQ an "operator." The franchise agreement stated that the franchise building should be constructed and equipped in accordance with the ADQ's specifications, and that the building should be maintained in accordance with the ADQ's requirements. We held that this language in the franchise agreement "[did] not establish sufficient control on ADQ's part such that ADQ can be said to 'operate' the San Antonio stores." Id. at 1067.

In the present case, our review of the record and pleadings do not reveal any allegation by the plaintiffs that the language in the PMA is ambiguous as to its meaning. The clauses of the PMA which state that the franchisee's business operations should be conducted in a consistent manner with the standards of Conoco, Inc., and that customers should be treated fairly and courteously are similar to the language of the franchise agreement in Neff which required that building specifications be approved by the franchiser. . . . The language of the PMA, while offering guidelines to the Conoco-branded stores, does not establish that Conoco, Inc. has any participation in the daily operations of the branded stores nor that Conoco, Inc. participates in making personnel decisions.

Therefore, we find that there is no agency relationship between Conoco, Inc. and the branded stores in question, and that Conoco, Inc. as a matter of law cannot be held liable for the unfortunate incidents which happened to Ivory, Pickett, Ross, and the Escobedos at the Conoco-branded stores.

C. Scope of Employment

Arguello and Govea complain of discriminatory treatment at a Conoco-owned store. Appellants argue that the district court erred in finding that Conoco could not be held liable . . . for the acts of its store clerk, Smith. The district court found that as a matter of law there was no agency relationship between Smith and Conoco because Smith's acts of discrimination towards Arguello and Govea were outside the scope of Smith's employment.

[The court reviews several decisions raising agency principles as applied to employment discrimination and concludes that the standard adopted in such cases should not be applied in public-accommodation cases.]

Under general agency principles a master is subject to liability for the torts of his servants while acting in the scope of their employment. See Restatement § 219. Some of the factors used when considering whether an employee's acts are within the scope of employment are: 1) the time, place and purpose of the act; 2) its similarity to acts which the servant is authorized to perform; 3) whether the act is commonly performed by servants; 4) the extent of departure from normal methods; and 5) whether the master would reasonably expect such act would be performed.

First, we must consider the time, place and purpose of Smith's actions. Smith's behavior toward Arguello and Govea occurred while she was on duty inside of the Conoco station where she was employed. The plaintiffs also put forth summary judgment evidence that Smith asked Arguello to present identification for credit card purchases. The purpose of Smith's interaction with Arguello was to complete the sale of gas and other store items. The initial confrontation and subsequent use of racial epithets occurred while Smith was completing Arguello's purchase of her items and processing the credit card transaction.

Second, we must consider whether Smith's actions were similar to those she was authorized by Conoco to perform. The sale of gasoline, other store items, and the completion of credit card purchases are the customary functions of a gasoline store clerk. The plaintiffs presented summary judgment evidence that Smith also used the intercom, which is also a customary action of gasoline store clerks.

Third, we will examine the extent of Smith's departure from normal methods. It is self-evident that Smith did not utilize the normal methods for conducting a sale. There was no summary judgment evidence presented that Conoco expected or anticipated that Smith would perform her functions in this manner. The appellees would have this court adopt the position that because Smith's use of racial epithets is comparable to the commission of an intentional tort, Conoco should not be held liable for Smith's behavior. However, the fact that an employee engages in intentional tortious conduct does not require a finding that the employee was outside the scope of his employment. . . . [A]lthough Conoco could not have expected Smith to shout racial epithets at Arguello and Govea, Smith's actions took place while she was performing her normal duties as a clerk. Conoco, Inc. had authorized Smith to interact with customers as they made purchases. Therefore, although Smith did depart from the normal methods of conducting a purchase this does not lead to the conclusion that as a matter of law she was outside the scope of her employment.

Finally, we must consider whether Conoco could have reasonably expected Smith to act in a racially discriminatory manner. There is no evidence in the record on this prong of the test. However, we note that even if Conoco is able to show that they could not have expected this conduct by Smith, the jury is entitled to find that the other factors outweigh this consideration.

In assessing whether Smith was within the scope of her employment the district court found that the only summary judgment evidence presented by the plaintiffs was that Smith was working in her job as cashier when the offensive behavior occurred. The district court concluded that the summary judgment evidence was insufficient to "overcome the common-sense conclusion" that Smith's offensive actions were not within the scope of her employment. However, we reject the presumption that because Smith behaved in an unacceptable manner that she was obviously outside the scope of her employment. The plaintiffs did present summary judgment evidence that Smith was on duty as a clerk, and that she was performing authorized duties such as conducting sales. This summary judgment evidence is not insignificant. Smith's position as clerk, and her authorization from Conoco to conduct sales allowed her to interact with Arguello and Govea, and put Smith in the position to commit the racially discriminatory acts. The plaintiffs also presented summary judgment evidence that Smith used her authority to conduct credit card transactions and use the gas station intercom system to commit the acts in question.

It is also important to note that Conoco does not challenge whether this incident occurred. Smith admitted to a Conoco district manager that she did subject Arguello and Govea to the use of racial epithets, profanity, and obscene gestures. The only dispute is whether there is a legal remedy for Arguello and Govea by holding Conoco liable for Smith's actions. The plaintiffs contend that the inference that should be drawn from Smith's actions is that Smith was authorized by Conoco to perform the actions of a clerk and that this meant that her actions while on duty as clerk were within the scope of her employment. Conoco, utilizing the same facts asks us to draw the inference that because Smith was acting on personal racial bigotry and animosity that she was outside the scope of her employment.

[The court holds that summary judgment should not have been granted in favor of Conoco on the agency relationship and scope of employment.]

D. Non-Delegable Duty

Appellants argue in the alternative that even if Smith was outside the scope of her employment Conoco should still be held liable because it had a non-delegable duty not to discriminate against minority consumers. . . . The argument that an employer has a non-delegable duty under § 1981 not to discriminate has been largely foreclosed by the Supreme Court in General Building Contractors, 458 U.S. at 395. In General Building Contractors, the Supreme Court stated that § 1981 is meant to prohibit employers from intentional discrimination and not intended to make them guarantors of rights against all third parties. . . . Therefore, it follows that the duty not to discriminate is not a non-delegable duty, instead a plaintiff must establish a close connection between the employer and the third party who engages in the intentional discrimination.

Plaintiffs also argue in the alternative that Conoco ratified the actions of Smith by not suspending or firing her. In order for an employer to be found to have ratified the actions of an employee the employer must know of the act and adopt, confirm, or fail to repudiate the acts of its employee. . . . In the present case, after Conoco was notified of Smith's actions, a customer service supervisor, Linda Corbin, told Arguello and Govea that she agreed that Smith had acted inappropriately and she counseled Smith about her behavior. While Conoco did not fire or suspend Smith, it does not appear that Conoco ratified Smith's actions.

E. Disparate Impact Claims under Section 2000a

Appellants argue that the district court erred in finding that as a matter of law the plaintiffs could not state a claim for redress under 42 U.S.C. § 2000a ("Title II") based on a disparate impact theory. . . .

In the present case, even assuming arguendo that disparate impact claims are cognizable under Title II, the plaintiffs did not establish a prima facie case of discrimination of the type required in disparate impact claims. The plaintiffs failed to allege that there was a specific Conoco policy which had a negative disparate effect on minority customers.

Conclusion

We hold that the district court did not err in finding that no agency relationship existed between Conoco, Inc. and its branded stores, and properly entered summary judgment against the Escobedos, Ivory, Pickett, and Ross. We also affirm the district court's dismissal of the plaintiffs' disparate impact claims for failure to state a claim upon which relief could be granted. We reverse the district court's determination that Cindy Smith acted outside the scope of her employment as a matter of law and remand for further proceedings consistent with this opinion.

ANALYSIS

1. **Reconciling the Cases.** Do you agree with the court's conclusion that the Conoco-branded stores were not agents of Conoco? Is that decision here consistent with the franchise cases studied in Section 1—i.e., Murphy v. Holiday Inns, Inc., and Parker v. Domino's Pizza? Is the decision here consistent with the gas station cases studied earlier in this section—i.e., Humble Oil & Refining Co. v. Martin and Hoover v. Sun Oil Company?

2. **Scope of the Employment.** Do you agree with the court's conclusion that Smith acted within the scope of her employment?

E. LIABILITY FOR TORTS OF INDEPENDENT CONTRACTORS

Majestic Realty Associates, Inc. v. Toti Contracting Co.

30 N.J. 425, 153 A.2d 321 (1959).

Plaintiffs Majestic Realty Associates, Inc., and Bohen's Inc., owner and tenant, sought compensation from defendants Toti Contracting Co., Inc. and Parking Authority of the City of Paterson, New Jersey, for damage to Majestic's building and to Bohen's goods. The claim arose out of the activity of Toti in demolishing certain structures owned by the Authority. . . .

Majestic is the owner of the two-story premises at 297 Main Street, Paterson, New Jersey. Bohen's is the tenant of the first floor and basement thereof in which it conducted a dry goods business. The Authority acquired properties along Main Street beginning immediately adjacent to Majestic's building on the south and continuing to Ward Street, the next intersecting street, and then east on the latter street for 150 feet. The motive for the acquisition was to establish a public parking area. Main Street is one of the principal business arteries of the city and the locality was completely built up.

Accomplishment of the Authority's object required demolition of the several buildings on both streets. Some time prior to October 26, 1956, a contract was entered into by the Authority with Toti to do the work. The razing began on the Ward Street side and moved northwardly until the structure next to Majestic's premises was reached. It was at least a story (about 20 feet) higher than Majestic's roof; the northerly wall of the one was 'right up against' the southerly wall of the other and the two walls ran alongside each other for 40 feet.

In the process of leveling this adjacent building, the contractor first removed the roof, then the front and south sidewalls and all of the interior partitions and floors. Thus, the north wall of brick and masonry next to Majestic's structure was left standing free. Expert testimony was adduced to show that the proper method of demolition under the existing circumstances would have been to remove the roof, leaving the interior partition work for support, and to begin to take the north wall down "never leaving any portion (of it) at a higher point than the interior construction of the building would form a brace."

In demolishing the walls, Toti used a large metal ball, said to weigh 3,500 pounds, suspended from a crane which was stationed in the street. There was testimony that during the week prior to the accident, every time the ball would strike a wall, debris and dirt would fly and the Majestic building "rocked." Further expert testimony indicated that in dealing with the free-standing north wall, the ball should have been made to hit the very top on each occasion so as to level it a few bricks at a time. This course was followed at first; the ball was swung from north to south and the dislodged bricks were catapulted away from Majestic's building and onto the adjoining lot. After a time, work ceased for a few minutes. On resumption, the operator of the crane swung the ball in such a manner that it struck at a point some 15 feet below the top of the wall. The impact propelled the uppermost section of the wall back in the direction from which the blow had come with the result that a 15 by 40 foot section fell on Majestic's roof, causing a 25 by 40 foot break therein. One of Bohen's employees, who saw the incident, asked the crane operator in the presence of Toti's president: "What did you do to our building?" He replied, "I goofed."

In characterizing a demolition undertaking of this type in a built up and busy section of a city, and in particular where one building to be razed adjoined another which was to remain untouched, plaintiffs' expert witness said it was "hazardous work"; "one of the most hazardous operations in the building business." And with reference to the leveling of a building so close to another structure which was not to be harmed, he asserted that the recognized procedure is to take it down in small sections so as not to lose control of the operation. This standard conforms with N.J.S.A. 34:5–15 which specifies that "(i)n the demolition of buildings, walls shall be removed part by part."

On the proof outlined, the trial court recognized that the work was hazardous in its very nature, but did not feel that it constituted a nuisance per se. Therefore, he ruled that the Authority, not having had or exercised control over the manner and method or means of performing the demolition operation, could not be held for the negligent act of its independent contractor. [The Appellate Division reversed.]

The problem must be approached with an awareness of the long settled doctrine that ordinarily where a person engages a contractor, who conducts an independent business by means of his own employees, to do work not in itself a nuisance (as our cases put it), he is not liable for the negligent acts of the contractor in the performance of the contract. . . . Certain exceptions have come to be accepted, i.e., (a) where the landowner retains control of the manner and means of the doing of the work which is the subject of the contract; (b) where he engages an incompetent contractor, or (c) where, as noted in the statement of the general rule, the activity contracted for constitutes a nuisance per se. . . .

As to exception (b), noted above, it is not claimed that the proof makes out a jury question on the charge that an incompetent contractor was hired for the task of demolition. Incidental comment thereon, however, may be fruitful.

It has been intimated that the matter of the competency of a contractor should not be restricted to considerations of skill and experience but should encompass financial responsibility to respond to tort claims as well. Research has not disclosed a case where the proposal has been applied. . . .

Inevitably the mind turns to the fact that the injured third party is entirely innocent and that the occasion for his injury arises out of the desire of the contractee to have certain activities performed. The injured has no control over or relation with the contractor. The contractee, true, has no control over the doing of the work and in that sense is also innocent of the wrongdoing; but he does have the power of selection and in the application of concepts of distributive justice perhaps much can be said for the view that a loss arising out of the tortious conduct of a financially irresponsible contractor should fall on the contractee. Professor Morris, in "Torts of Independent Contractors," [29 Ill. L. Rev. 339, 344 (1934)], put it this way:

> If the contractee has to look out for the interests of others by using due care to pick a man with requisite skill to whom to entrust his enterprises, why should he not also have to look out for the interests of others by selecting a man with sufficient financing? And since there is usually a fool proof method of assuring himself that the contractor will meet all tort obligations in requiring an indemnity bond signed by responsible sureties, it would seem that in most cases the contractee would only measure up to the standard of due care so as to avoid responsibility when the contractor is able to discharge tort claims arising out of the enterprise.

This passage was written in 1934. At the present time it is a matter of common knowledge that liability insurance to cover such demolition operations is available to contractors and it may be assumed fairly that procurement of that type coverage is regarded as an ordinary business expense. Financial responsibility has nothing to do with legal liability of the contractor. . . .

But this precise facet of the problem of Toti's competency was not raised at the trial or in the briefs. It arose as an emanation of the oral argument. Consequently, no decision is rendered with respect to it and the matter is expressly reserved.

Under exception (c), on which plaintiffs rely principally, liability will be imposed upon the landowner in spite of the engagement of an independent contractor if the work to be done constitutes a nuisance per se. The phrase "nuisance per se," although used with some frequency in the reported cases, is difficult of definition. . . .

Without undertaking an exhaustive review of the cases in our State where the expression appears, it seems proper to say that the legal content of "nuisance per se" and the application thereof in a factual framework such as that now before us, is anything but clear. . . . In Sarno v. Gulf Refining Co., 99 N.J.L. 340, 342 (Sup. Ct. 1924), affirmed 102 N.J.L. 223 (E. & A. 1925), the court equated it with "inherently dangerous" and this appears to have set in motion a trend toward the view now espoused by the Restatement, Torts, §§ 835(e), 416.

Section 416 of the Restatement propounds a rule which would impose liability upon the landowner who engages an independent contractor to do work which he should recognize as necessarily requiring the creation during its progress of a condition involving a peculiar risk of harm to others unless special precautions are taken, if the contractor is negligent in failing to take those precautions. Such work may be said to be inherently dangerous, i.e., an activity which can be carried on safely only by the exercise of special skill and care, and which involves grave risk of danger to persons or property if negligently done. . . .

It is important to distinguish an operation which may be classed as inherently dangerous from one that is ultra-hazardous. The latter is described as one which "(a) necessarily involves a serious risk of harm to the person, land or chattels of others which cannot be eliminated by the exercise of the utmost care, and (b) is not a matter of common usage." Restatement, supra, § 520. The distinction is important because liability is absolute where the work is ultra-hazardous,. . . .

There is no doubt that the line between work which is ordinary, usual and commonplace, and that which is inherently dangerous because its very nature involves a peculiar and high risk of harm to members of the public or adjoining proprietors of land unless special precautions are taken, is somewhat shadowy. . . . For the present, we need deal only with the case before us.

There is some conflict in the decisions as to whether demolition activity is one which necessarily involves a peculiar risk of harm to members of the public or to adjoining property. The current New York rule is that the razing of buildings in a busy, built up section of a city is inherently dangerous within the contemplation of section 416 of the Restatement. . . .

In our judgment, the doctrine adopted by New York . . . represents the sound and just concept to be applied. And within the broad outlines thereof, where the minds of reasonable men might differ as to whether the activity contracted for by the landowner is inherently dangerous or involves a peculiar risk of harm to others unless special precautions are taken, the issue is for jury determination. . . .

For the reasons stated herein, the judgment of the Appellate Division is affirmed and the matter is remanded for a new trial against the Parking Authority.

ANALYSIS

1. **The Doctrinal Basis.** Under exception (b), for cases in which the principal retained an incompetent contractor, is the principal liable simply upon a showing that the contractor was incompetent? Or should plaintiff be obliged to show that the principal was negligent in selecting an incompetent contractor?

2. **Explaining the Doctrine.** Do you agree with the court's dicta implying that hiring a financially irresponsible contractor is tantamount to hiring one who is incompetent? If not, why not? In answering that question, it may be helpful to consider the following: As between Majestic and the Authority, which was best able to monitor Toti's conduct? As between Majestic and the Authority, which was in the best position to insure against these sorts of accidents?

3. **Inherently Dangerous Activities.** Under exception (c), for inherently dangerous activities, is the principal liable simply because the contractor was negligent in failing to take adequate precautions? Or should plaintiff be obliged to show negligence on the principal's part?

4. **Contracting Around the Case.** In light of this decision, what should the Authority do in the future when hiring independent contractors to conduct hazardous activities?

5. **Reconciling the Case with Independent Contractor Status.** Do the exceptions recognized by the *Majestic* opinion swallow the rule that principals are not liable for the tortious acts of their independent contractors?

Anderson v. Marathon Petroleum Co.

801 F.2d 936 (7th Cir.1986).

■ POSNER, CIRCUIT JUDGE.

. . .

Donald Anderson was an employee of Tri-Kote, Inc., which had a contract with Marathon to clean the inside of Marathon's oil storage tanks by sandblasting. The evidence, viewed most favorably to the Andersons, shows that sandblasting in a confined space creates clouds of silicon dust, which if breathed in over a long period of time cause silicosis, a serious lung disease from which, in fact, Anderson died. Anderson began working for Tri-Kote in 1970 as a sandblaster, mostly on the Marathon contract, and quit in 1983 when he was diagnosed as suffering from silicosis. During this period he averaged three or four days a week sandblasting Marathon storage tanks. Until 1980 the only form of mask that Tri-Kote supplied Anderson to protect him from silicon dust was a so-called "desert hood." It had no fresh-air hose but only a wire mesh in front of the nose and mouth, and the dust could get in through the mesh. Supervisory personnel of Marathon often saw Anderson coming out of a storage tank with dust on his face after sandblasting and they knew that Tri-Kote had supplied him with just the patently inadequate "desert hood." Yet Marathon did nothing to try to get Tri-Kote to protect its workers better. The two employees of Tri-Kote who sandblasted Marathon's storage tanks before Anderson came on the scene also died of silicosis.

The issue is the tort duty of a principal to the employees of his independent contractor. . . .

Generally a principal is not liable for an independent contractor's torts even if they are committed in the performance of the contract and even though a principal is liable under the doctrine of respondeat superior for the torts of his employees if committed in the furtherance of their employment. The reason for distinguishing the independent contractor from the employee is that, by definition of the relationship between a principal and an independent contractor, the principal does not supervise the details of the independent contractor's work and therefore is not in a good position to prevent negligent performance, whereas the essence of the contractual relationship known as employment is that the employee surrenders to the employer the right to direct the details of his work, in exchange for receiving a wage. The independent contractor commits himself to providing a specified output, and the principal monitors the contractor's performance not by monitoring inputs—i.e., supervising the contractor—but by inspecting the contractually specified output to make sure it conforms to the specifications. This method of monitoring works fine if it is feasible for the principal to specify and monitor output, but sometimes it is not feasible, particularly if the output consists of the joint product of many separate producers whose specific contributions are difficult (sometimes impossible) to disentangle. In such a case it may be more efficient for the principal to monitor inputs rather than output—the producers rather than the product. By becoming an employee a producer in effect submits himself to that kind of monitoring, receiving payment for the work he puts in rather than for the output he produces.

Since an essential element of the employment relationship is thus the employer's monitoring of the employee's work, a principal who is not knowledgeable about the details of some task is likely to delegate it to an independent contractor. Hence in general, though of course not in every case, the principal who uses an independent contractor will not be as well placed as an employer would be to monitor the work and make sure it is done safely. This is the reason as we have said for not making the principal vicariously liable for the torts of his independent contractors. See Calabresi, Some Thoughts on Risk Distribution and the Law of Torts, 70 Yale L.J. 499, 545 (1961).

The rule is not applied, however, when the activity for which the independent contractor was hired is "abnormally dangerous," see Restatement (Second) of Torts § 427A (1964), or in an older terminology "ultrahazardous," see, e.g., Cities Service Co. v. State, 312 So. 2d 799, 802 (Fla.Dist.Ct.App.1975)—i.e., if the activity might very well result in injury even if conducted with all due skill and caution. When an activity is abnormally dangerous, it is important not only that the people engaged in it use the highest practicable degree of skill and caution, but also—since even if they do so, accidents may well result—that the people who have authorized the activity consider the possibility of preventing some accidents by curtailing the activity or even eliminating it altogether. On both scores there is an argument for making the principal as well as the independent contractor liable if an accident occurs that is due to the hazardous character of the performance called for by the contract. The fact that a very high degree of care is cost-justified implies that the principal should be induced to wrack his brain, as well as the independent contractor his own brain, for ways of minimizing the danger posed by the activity. And the fact that the only feasible method of accident prevention may be to reduce the amount of the activity or substitute another activity argues for placing liability on the principal, who makes the decision whether to undertake the activity in the first place. The electrical utility that has to decide whether to transport nuclear waste materials by motor or rail may be influenced in its choice by the relative safety of the modes—if it is liable for the consequences of an accident.

True, the principal would in any event be liable indirectly if the price it paid the independent contractor fully reflected the dangers of the undertaking; but this condition would be fulfilled only if the contractor were fully answerable for an accident if one occurred. And though fully liable in law, the independent contractor would not be fully liable in fact if a damage judgment would exceed his net assets. The likelihood of the independent contractor's insolvency is greater the more hazardous the activity; by definition, expected accident costs are greater. Another thing making them greater is that the contractor will be strictly liable for accidents caused by the abnormally dangerous character of his activity, and therefore his expected legal-judgment costs will be higher than those of a contractor liable only for negligence. With the exposure of the independent contractor to liability so great, it may be necessary to make the principal liable as well in order to ensure that there is a solvent defendant. This is important not only to provide compensation for accident victims but also to reduce the number of accidents. Without such liability a principal might hire judgment-proof independent contractors to do his dangerous jobs, knowing that the contractors would have an incentive to cut corners on protecting safety and health and that this would reduce the cost of the contract to him.

Is sandblasting abnormally dangerous? A district judge in Louisiana, in the only case we have found on the question, held not. Touchstone v. G.B.Q. Corp., 596 F. Supp. 805, 815 (E.D.La.1984). In the absence of any precedent establishing the abnormal dangerousness of sandblasting, the plaintiffs in this case were obliged to lay a factual basis for an inference that people engaged in sandblasting cannot prevent a serious risk of injury by taking precautions. They did not do this. So far as the record shows (an important qualification), if the sandblaster is equipped not with the ridiculous "desert hood" but with a proper face mask to which a fresh-air hose is attached, so that the worker is breathing fresh air rather than air filled with silicon dust, the worker is in no danger, nor anyone else. The design of an effective hood may be more difficult than we are assuming it to be, but in the absence of precedent or data we cannot just assume that the protection of the worker is so difficult that sandblasting should be classified as abnormally dangerous.

Mrs. Anderson [decedent's widow] impresses on us cases which suggest that something less than abnormal danger may be enough to take a case out of the rule that a principal is not liable for the torts of its independent contractors. . . .

. . . With rare exceptions, some based on statutes such as the omnipresent scaffolding acts that impose strict liability on contractors for injuries to their subcontractors' employees caused by hazardous working conditions, the cases that make principals vicariously liable for the torts of their independent contractors involve injuries to third parties rather than employees; and the general though not uniform view is that the employee has no common law tort right against his employer's principal in such a case. . . .

There is a reason for the distinction between the plaintiff who is an employee of the independent contractor and the plaintiff who is not. If a nuclear reactor blows up and thousands of people are irradiated, we would not allow the reactor company to slough off all liability for the accident onto a careless independent contractor, who, not having the resources to compensate the victims of his tort, had lacked adequate incentives to take care. Similarly, we would not want Marathon to be able to avoid liability to its neighbors caused by its hiring contractors, who turn out to be careless, to perform abnormally dangerous jobs. But the only people endangered in this case were the contractor's employees; and they are compensated for the risks of their employment by a combination of wages, benefits, and entitlement to workers' compensation in the event of an accident. The principal pays for the package indirectly, in the contract price, which is calculated to cover the contractor's labor as well as other costs. Moreover, as we shall see, if the contractor does not carry workers' compensation insurance and proves unable to pay benefits out of its own pocket, the principal must pay the benefits. The principal thus has every incentive to assure safe working conditions in order to reduce its contract costs and its contingent liability for workers' compensation; so there is no danger of the shell game that is played when the firm causing the accident is insolvent and its principal is not liable because the tortfeasor was an independent contractor rather than an employee.

Since the principal is the indirect employer of its contractor's employees, to make the principal liable in common law tort for the accidents befalling those employees would be inconsistent with the bedrock principle that workers' compensation rights are exclusive of common law tort rights. . . .

The position urged by Mrs. Anderson would bring about profound changes in liability for industrial accidents. Firms engaged in activities that are dangerous if proper precautions are not taken (and which activity is not?) would become the virtual insurers of their contractors' employees. Indeed, imagine a case where a homeowner hired a contractor to fix the roof, and one of his workers fell off the roof and was injured. The risk of falling would be in some sense inherent in or peculiar to the work; could the worker therefore sue the homeowner? That would be a revolution in liability. . . .

Up to now we have treated the case as one in which the principal is alleged to be vicariously liable for its contractors' torts, but Mrs. Anderson also argues that there was enough evidence of Marathon's negligence to make the directed verdict improper even if Tri-Kote's negligence cannot be imputed to Marathon. Supervisory employees of Marathon testified that on occasion they had seen Mr. Anderson coming out of the storage tanks with dust on his face, and they knew he did not have an adequate mask. Even so, this does not show that Marathon was negligent in hiring Tri-Kote initially; so this conventional avenue of principal's liability is cut off.

But suppose that a principal, having hired an independent contractor after a careful investigation which showed that the contractor was careful and responsible, discovers that the contractor is careless yet takes no steps to correct the contractor's unsafe practices or terminate him; can the victim of the contractor's carelessness get damages from the principal? We assume the answer is "yes" if the victim is a third party, but Mrs. Anderson has cited no case in which an Illinois court has allowed an employee of the independent contractor to recover damages on this basis. The majority view is that he may not. Again the reason is that the employee is protected by his workers' compensation rights; again there is a division of authority (see the comprehensive discussion in Nelson v. United States, 639 F.2d 469 (9th Cir.1980)); again we have no reason to think that Illinois would adopt the minority view. It might; but federal court is not the place to press innovative theories of state law. This precept is particularly apropos in a case such as this where residents file suit in federal court against a nonresident defendant. The choice of the federal forum in such a case cannot be laid to fear of prejudice against a nonresident. The plaintiff is not the nonresident—the defendant is. (It would be different if the Andersons had filed this suit in state court and Marathon had removed it to federal court.) The plaintiffs' appellate counsel could not remember why this suit was brought in federal rather than state court, so we take this occasion to remind that resident litigants who seek adventurous departures in state common law are advised to sue in state rather than federal court.

AFFIRMED.

ANALYSIS

1. **Does the Logic Matter?** The substantive portion of Judge Posner's opinion begins with a short essay on the economic justification for the general rule that principals are not vicariously liable for the tortious conduct of independent contractors. What relevance, if any, does that essay have to the ultimate decision in the case?

2. **Reconciling *Majestic*.** Is Judge Posner's "abnormally dangerous" exception to the general rule of principal immunity for torts of an independent contractor the same as *Majestic's* "inherently dangerous" version of that exception? If not, what doctrinal consequences follow from that distinction?

3. **Is the Doctrine Right?** Is there any logical reason for the distinction, or any natural boundary, between "abnormally dangerous" activities and any other activity causing injury?

4. **Incompetent Contractors.** Does Judge Posner's cost-benefit analysis suggest a rationale for the rule imposing liability upon a principal who selects an incompetent independent contractor?

5. **Is Control All That Matters?** Part of Judge Posner's justification for the general rule of principal immunity for tortious acts of independent contractors is that the principal is unable to control the contractor's performance of the assigned task. Does it necessarily follow that control, standing alone, should result in vicarious liability?

6. **Market Adjustments.** Do you agree with Judge Posner's argument that "the contractor's employees . . . are compensated for the risks of their employment by a combination of wages, benefits, and entitlement to workers' compensation in the event of an accident"? Put another way,

do you think Marathon and/or Mr. Anderson rationally calculated the risk that he would contract silicosis? Does the market for labor set a price on that risk in setting wages?

Kleeman v. Rheingold

81 N.Y.2d 270, 598 N.Y.S.2d 149, 614 N.E.2d 712 (Court of Appeals 1993).

. . . According to the allegations in the present complaint, plaintiff, a victim of alleged medical malpractice, had originally retained defendant and his law firm to pursue her claim against Dr. Neils Lauersen. With only five days remaining before the Statute of Limitations on the claim would expire, defendant promptly prepared a summons and complaint. On November 5, 1978, two days before the Statute of Limitations was to run, defendant delivered the prepared documents to Fischer's Service Bureau, a process service agency regularly used by defendant's law firm, with the instruction that process was to be served "immediately." It is undisputed that Fischer's, not defendant, selected the licensed process server who would actually deliver the papers and that Fischer's and the process server, rather than defendant, determined the precise manner of effecting service.

Although the process server used by Fischer's apparently delivered the papers on time, plaintiff's medical malpractice claim was ultimately dismissed when a traverse hearing revealed that the process server had given the papers to Dr. Lauersen's secretary rather than Dr. Lauersen himself. By the time the traverse hearing was held, the Statute of Limitations had expired and plaintiff had no further legal recourse against the allegedly negligent doctor. . . .

Plaintiff subsequently commenced the present legal malpractice action against defendant and his law firm, claiming that they should be held liable for the negligence of the process server who had been retained to serve Dr. Lauersen on plaintiff's behalf. Defendants moved for summary judgment and plaintiff cross-moved. Plaintiff . . . argued that the process server was defendants' agent and that, under settled agency law principles, they could therefore be held accountable for the process server's wrongful acts . . . .

The trial court rejected all of plaintiff's arguments. . . .

On plaintiff's appeal, a divided Appellate Division affirmed. . . . We now modify by denying defendants' motion for summary judgment. As plaintiff's attorneys, defendants had a nondelegable duty to her and, accordingly, they cannot evade legal responsibility for the negligent performance of that duty by assigning the task of serving process to an "independent contractor."

The general rule is that a party who retains an independent contractor, as distinguished from a mere employee or servant, is not liable for the independent contractor's negligent acts. . . . Although several justifications have been offered in support of this rule, the most commonly accepted rationale is based on the premise that one who employs an independent contractor has no right to control the manner in which the work is to be done and, thus, the risk of loss is more sensibly placed on the contractor. . . .

Despite the courts' frequent recitation of the general rule against vicarious liability, the common law has produced a wide variety of so-called "exceptions" . . . These exceptions . . . fall roughly into three basic categories: negligence of the employer in selecting, instructing or supervising the contractor; employment for work that is especially or "inherently" dangerous . . .; and, finally, instances in which the employer is under a specific nondelegable duty. . . .

The exception that concerns us here—the exception for nondelegable duties—. . . is often invoked where the particular duty in question is one that is imposed by regulation or statute. . . . However, the class of duties considered "nondelegable" is not limited to statutorily imposed duties . . . .

The most often cited formulation is that a duty will be deemed nondelegable when " 'the responsibility is so important to the community that the employer should not be permitted to transfer it to another' " ([Feliberty v. Damon, 72 N.Y.2d 112], 119, [531 N.Y.S.2d 778, 527 N.E.2d 261] quoting Prosser and Keeton, [Torts (5th ed)]., at 512). This flexible formula recognizes that the "privilege to farm out [work] has its limits" and that those limits are best defined by reference to the gravity of the public policies that are implicated (5 Harper, James and Gray, Torts § 26.11, at 73 (2d ed.); see also, id., at 76–77).

Viewed in the light of these principles, the duty at issue here—that owed by an attorney to his or her client to exercise care in the service of process—fits squarely and neatly within the category of obligations that the law regards as "nondelegable." Manifestly, when an individual retains an attorney to commence an action, timely and accurate service of process is an integral part of the task that the attorney undertakes. . . .

The existence of an extensive and comprehensive Code of Professional Responsibility that governs the obligations of attorneys to their clients reinforces our conclusion. Under the Code, a lawyer may not "seek, by contract or other means, to limit prospectively the lawyer's individual liability to a client for malpractice" (DR 6–102, 22 NYCRR 1200.31). Moreover, the Code forbids lawyers from "[n]eglect[ing] legal matter[s] entrusted to [them]" (DR 6–101(A)(3), 22 NYCRR 1200.30(a)(3)), enjoins them to assist in "secur[ing] and protect[ing] available legal rights" (EC 7–1) and requires them to represent their clients as zealously as the "bounds of the law" permit (Canon 7). All of the latter ethical and disciplinary considerations are implicated when a client's lawsuit is undermined—or even defeated—as a consequence of carelessness in the service of process.

Our conclusion is also supported by the perceptions of the lay public and the average client, who may reasonably assume that all of the tasks associated with the commencement of an action, including its formal initiation through service of process, will be performed either by the attorney or someone acting under the attorney's direction. . . .

Finally, we conclude that permitting lawyers to transfer their duty of care to process servers would be contrary to sound public policy. In this State, licensed attorneys have been granted an exclusive franchise to practice law, with the understanding that they have both the specialized knowledge and the character required to represent clients in a competent, diligent and careful manner. . . .

■ BELLACOSA, J. (concurring).

. . . This case should be more prudently resolved on the narrower ground that questions of fact exist as to whether the defendant law firm was negligent in choosing its process server. . . .

[S]ince attorneys may be liable for their own negligence in selecting a particular process server, and since plaintiff alleges that the entity chosen by defendants, Fischer's Service Bureau, Inc., had a reputation for poor and sloppy service, there are fact issues here which suffice to defeat defendants' summary judgment motion for dismissal.

The Court's result is reached instead by classifying service of process, for the first time, as a nondelegable duty of the attorney. This rationale opens up an unrealistic and undue liability channel not only with respect to the relationship of attorneys to process servers but, by analogous extension, also to many other relationships in which attorneys retain specialists and experts in the discharge of their professional obligations to clients.

This broad new rule requires, in effect, that an attorney inquire beyond any facially sufficient affidavit of service of process to verify personally the facts that underlie it. . . . For practical purposes, [this rule] will compel attorneys to assume the role of process servers themselves. While many large firms already have such in-house operatives, attorneys practicing in small firms and solo practitioners may now also have no choice but to hire in-house process servers so that the lawyers can always maintain direct supervision and control over them. . . .

ANALYSIS

1. **Limitations.** Do the majority's assurances as to the limited scope of its opinion vitiate the concurring judge's concerns?

2. **Reasons for the Doctrine.** Why did the majority prefer to rely on the nondelegable duty doctrine instead of the rule that a principal can be liable for negligence in selecting an incompetent independent contractor?

3. **Expected Responses.** Do you agree with the dissent that attorneys can only avoid liability by hiring in-house process servers? If not, what should attorneys do in response to this decision? What should process servers do in response thereto?

4. FIDUCIARY OBLIGATION OF AGENTS

INTRODUCTORY NOTE

We now shift our attention to the fiduciary obligation, or duty of loyalty, owed by agents to their principals. Note that several of the cases to be examined involve agents of corporate principals. They are included in this text because the fact that the principal is a corporation, rather than an individual, is unimportant.

A. DUTIES DURING AGENCY

Reading v. Regem

[1948] 2 KB 268, [1948] 2 All ER 27, [1948] WN 205.

The plaintiff joined the army in 1936, and at the beginning of 1944 he was a sergeant in the Royal Army Medical Corps stationed at the general hospital in Cairo, where he was in charge of the medical stores.

The plaintiff had not had any opportunities, in his life as a soldier, of making money, but in March, 1944, there were found standing to his credit at banks in Egypt, several thousands of pounds, and he had more thousands of pounds in notes in his flat. He had also acquired a motor car worth £1,500. The Special Investigation Branch of the army looked into the matter, and he was asked how he came by these moneys. He made a statement, from which it appears that they were paid to him by a man by the name of Manole in these circumstances. A lorry used to arrive loaded with cases, the contents of which were unknown. Then the plaintiff, in full uniform, boarded the lorry, and

> **NOTE**
>
> Cognizant of Winston Churchill's dictum that the United States and the United Kingdom are "separated by a common language," we have taken the liberty of converting some British legal terms into their American equivalents.

escorted it through Cairo, so that it was able to pass the civilian police without being inspected. When it arrived at its destination, it was unloaded, or the contents were transferred to another lorry. After the first occasion when this happened, the plaintiff saw Manole in a restaurant in Cairo. Manole handed him an envelope which he put in his pocket. On examining it when he arrived home, he found that it contained £2,000. Two or three weeks later, another load arrived, and another £2,000 was paid. £3,000 was paid after the third load, and so it went on until eventually some £20,000 had gone into the pocket of the suppliant. The services which he rendered for that money were that he accompanied this lorry from one part of Cairo to another, and it is plain that he got it because he was a sergeant in the British army, and, while in uniform, escorted these lorries through Cairo. It is also plain that he was clearly violating his duty in so doing. The military authorities took possession of the money. . . .

In this petition of right, the plaintiff alleges that these moneys are his and should be returned to him by the Crown. In answer, the Crown say: "These were bribes received by you by reason of your military employment, and you hold the money for the Crown. Even if we were wrong in the way in which we seized them, we are entitled to recover the amount of them, and to set off that amount against any claim you may have." In these circumstances, it is not necessary to dwell on the form of the claim. The question is whether or not the Crown is entitled to the money. It is not entitled to it simply because it is the Crown—moneys which are unlawfully obtained are not ipso facto forfeited to the Crown. The claim of the Crown rests on the fact that at the material time it was the plaintiff's employer.

There are many cases in the books where a master has been held entitled to the unauthorized gains of his servant or agent. At law, the action took the form of money had and received. In equity it was put on the basis of a constructive trust due to a fiduciary relationship. Nowadays it is unnecessary to draw a distinction between law and equity. The real cause of action is a claim for restitution of moneys which, in justice, ought to be paid over. In my judgment, it is a principle of law that, if a servant takes advantage of his service and violates his duty of honesty and good faith to make a profit for himself, in the sense that the assets of which he has control, the facilities which he enjoys, or the position which he occupies, are the real cause of his obtaining the money as distinct from merely affording the opportunity for getting it, that is to say, if they play the predominant part in his obtaining the money, then he is accountable for it to his master. It matters not that the master has not lost any profit nor suffered any damage, nor does it matter that the master could not have done the act himself. If the servant has unjustly enriched himself by virtue of his service without his master's sanction, the law says that he ought not to be allowed to keep the money, but it shall be taken from him and given to his master, because he got it solely by reason of the position which he occupied as a servant of his master. Instances readily occur to mind. Take the case of the master who tells his servant to exercise his horses, and while the master is away, the servant lets them out and makes a profit by so doing. There is no loss to the master, the horses have been exercised, but the servant must account for the profits he makes.

The ATTORNEY-GENERAL put in argument the case of a uniformed policeman who, at the request of thieves and in return for a bribe, directs traffic away from the site of the crime. Is he to be allowed to keep the money? So, also, here, the use of the facilities provided by the Crown in the shape of the uniform and the use of his position in the army were the only reason why the plaintiff was able to get this money. It was solely on that account that he was able to sit in the front of these lorries and give them a safe conduct through Cairo. There was no loss of profit to the Crown. The Crown would have been violating its duty if it had undertaken the task, but the plaintiff was certainly violating his duty, and it is money which must be paid over to his master—in this case, the Crown.

. . . There was not, in this case, a fiduciary relationship. The plaintiff was not acting in the course of his employment. In my opinion, however, those are not essential ingredients of the cause of action. The uniform of the Crown and the position of the plaintiff as a servant of the Crown were the only reasons why he was able to get this money, and that is sufficient to make him liable to hand it over to the Crown. The case is to be distinguished from cases where the service merely gives the opportunity of making money. A servant may, during his master's time, in breach of his contract, do other things to make money for himself, such as gambling, but he is entitled to keep that money himself. The master has a claim for damages for breach of contract, but he has no claim to the money. So, also, the fact that a soldier is stationed in a certain place may give him the opportunity, contrary to the King's Regulations, of engaging in trade and making money in that way. In such a case, the mere fact that his service gave the opportunity for getting the money would not entitle the Crown to it, but if, as here, the wearing of the King's uniform and his position as a soldier is the sole cause of his getting the money and he gets it dishonestly, that is an advantage which he is not allowed to keep. Although the Crown, has suffered no loss, the court orders the money to be handed over to the Crown, because the Crown is the only person to whom it can properly be paid. The plaintiff must not be allowed to enrich himself in this way. He got the money by virtue of his employment, and must hand it over.

DISPOSITION: Petition dismissed with costs.

PROBLEMS

How, if at all, would you distinguish the following cases from Reading v. Regem?

1. The facts are the same as in the actual case, except that the sergeant had been discharged by the Royal Army before riding along in the smuggler's truck. Would it make a difference if discharged personnel were permitted to wear their uniforms for 30 days, to ease the transition to civilian life?

2. Imagine a U.S. Army Sergeant who, during a recent war, single-handedly wiped out an enemy machine gun emplacement; earned the Congressional Medal of Honor; received huge coverage in newspapers and magazines and on television; and became a public hero. One night, while in New York, he went to a popular restaurant, in uniform. The owner of the restaurant called reporters, who arrived and took pictures, which appeared in papers across the country the next day. As the sergeant left the restaurant, the owner gave him an envelope with $1,000 in cash and urged him to return. (And, of course, the owner would not let him pay for his food and drinks.) The sergeant returned many times and received a total of $10,000 in cash.

3. General Norman Schwarzkopf, culminating a long, distinguished career in the U.S. Army, became well known to the public as head of the U.S. military forces in the Gulf War. After that war he published his autobiography, "It Doesn't Take a Hero," for which he presumably received substantial royalties. Assume that, to promote the book, he appeared at various gatherings and on television, always in civilian clothes.

4. Suppose that the long-time Chief Executive Officer of a major corporation authored a book about his experience as CEO and about the principles that he followed in guiding the corporation to its enormous success. The CEO earned substantial royalties, which he gave to charity.

5. Suppose Los Angeles Lakers professional basketball player Kobe Bryant received substantial royalties for the use of his name by a restaurant in Los Angeles.

6. Suppose an expert witness appeared in court and was identified as a Harvard Law School professor. Her fee for two days of preparation and one day in court was $100,000.

7. A senior executive in an oil company learned that the company's geologists had discovered a huge oil field, but were required to maintain secrecy until the company could buy the drilling rights. The executive bought shares of stock of the company and, after the announcement of the discovery several months later, sold those shares for a large profit.

ANALYSIS

1. **The Basis for the Rule.** The court opines, the sergeant "must not be allowed to enrich himself in this way." Why not?

2. **Is the U.S. Different?** Would a different result obtain under U.S. agency law? Consider Restatement (Third) of Agency § 8.02: "An agent has a duty not to acquire a material benefit from a third party in connection with transactions conducted or other actions taken on behalf of the principal or otherwise through the agent's use of the agent's position." Restatement (Third) § 8.05 may also be relevant: "An agent has a duty (1) not to use property of the principal for the agent's own purposes or those of a third party . . . ."

3. **Is the Rule Right?** Why should the Crown be able to recover even though it "suffered no loss"? Put another way, why is the remedy disgorgement of secret profits rather than actual damages?

General Automotive Manufacturing Co. v. Singer

19 Wis.2d 528, 120 N.W.2d 659 (1963).

Action commenced by General Automotive Manufacturing Company, hereinafter referred to as "Automotive," against John Singer, a former employee, to account for secret profits received while in its employ. Trial was to the court without a jury, which found defendant liable to plaintiff for $64,088.08 and costs. Appeal is from that judgment.

Automotive, plaintiff-respondent, is a Wisconsin corporation engaged in the machine shop jobbing business and has about five employees. Louis Glavin controlled Automotive and was its secretary.

John Singer, defendant-appellant, is a machinist-consultant and manufacturer's representative. Singer has worked in the machine shop field for over thirty years. He is adept at machine work and had ability not only as a machinist but also as to metal treatment, grinding techniques and special techniques. He enjoys this reputation in machine shop circles. None of Automotive's employees has defendant's ability to handle these machines. He is also known to be qualified in estimating the costs of machine-shop products and the competitive prices for which such products can be sold.

. . .

We have carefully reviewed the evidence and have ourselves reached conclusions as stated by the trial court and set forth in its Findings of Fact, as follows:

> "3. That heretofore and on or about the 28th day of March 1953, the plaintiff hired and employed the defendant as general manager of its business and affairs and the defendant accepted such employment under and pursuant to a written contract.
>
> . . .
>
> "6. That in and by said contract as aforesaid, the plaintiff promised and agreed to pay to the defendant as compensation,

> a fixed monthly salary together with a sum equal to 3% of the gross sales of the plaintiff.
>
> . . .
>
> "8. That in and by said contract, in consideration of compensation to be paid by the plaintiff to the defendant, the defendant promised and agreed:
>
> "A. To devote his entire time, skill, labor and attention to said employment, during the term of this employment, and not to engage in any other business or vocation of a permanent nature during the term of this employment, and to observe working hours for 5 1/2 days.
>
> "B. Not to, either during the term of his employment, or at any time thereafter, disclose to any person, firm or corporation any information concerning the business or affairs of the Employer which he may have acquired in the course of or as incident to his employment hereunder, for his own benefit, or to the detriment or intended or probable detriment of the Employer."
>
> . . .

Although stated as a Finding of Fact, Finding No. 10 is mainly a conclusion of law. It produces the principal issue in the case and deserves further discussion. It reads:

> "10. That the defendant breached his contract of employment with the plaintiff and violated the duty of loyalty which he owed to the plaintiff and his fiduciary duty of general manager thereof during the existence of such employment by engaging in business activities directly competitive with the plaintiff, to-wit by obtaining orders from a customer for his own account."

The record leaves no room for doubt of the correctness of Finding 11, as follows:

> "11. That thereafter, instead of turning such orders over to the plaintiff the defendant turned such orders over to other concerns to be filled, collected the proceeds thereof from the customers for his own account and kept the profits accruing therefrom."

Finding 12 is: "That such activities of the defendant were carried on in secret and without the knowledge of the plaintiff."

The evidence on which Finding 12 is based is in dispute. It is not against the great weight and clear preponderance of the evidence and the finding should not be disturbed.

. . .

Study of the record discloses that Singer was engaged as general manager of Automotive's operations. Among his duties was solicitation and procurement of machine shop work for Automotive. Because of Singer's high reputation in the trade he was highly successful in attracting orders.

Automotive is a small concern and has a low credit rating. Singer was invaluable in bolstering Automotive's credit. For instance, when collections were slow for work done by Automotive Singer paid the customer's bill to Automotive and waited for his own reimbursement until the customer remitted. Also, when work was slack, Singer set Automotive's shop to make parts for which there were no present orders and himself financed the cost of materials for such parts, waiting for recoupment until such stock-piled parts could be sold. Some parts were never sold and Singer personally absorbed the loss upon them.

As time went on a large volume of business attracted by Singer was offered to Automotive but which Singer decided could not be done by Automotive at all, for lack of suitable equipment, or which Automotive could not do at a competitive price. When Singer determined that such orders were unsuitable for Automotive he neither informed Automotive of these facts nor sent the orders back to the customer. Instead, he made the customer a price, then dealt with another machine shop to do the work at a less price, and retained the difference between the price quoted to the customer and the price for which the work was done. Singer was actually behaving as a broker for his own profit in a field where by contract he had engaged to work only for Automotive. We concur in the decision of the trial court that this was inconsistent with the obligations of a faithful agent or employee.

Singer finally set up a business of his own, calling himself a manufacturer's agent and consultant, in which he brokered orders for products of the sort manufactured by Automotive,—this while he was still Automotive's employee and without informing Automotive of it. Singer had broad powers of management and conducted the business activities of Automotive. In this capacity he was Automotive's agent and owed a fiduciary duty to it. . . . Under his fiduciary duty to Automotive Singer was bound to the exercise of the utmost good faith and loyalty so that he did not act adversely to the interests of Automotive by serving or acquiring any private interest of his own. . . . He was also bound to act for the furtherance and advancement of the interest of Automotive. . . .

If Singer violated his duty to Automotive by engaging in certain business activities in which he received a secret profit he must account to Automotive for the amounts he illegally received. . . .

The present controversy centers around the question whether the operation of Singer's side line business was a violation of his fiduciary duty to Automotive. The trial court found this business was conducted in secret and without the knowledge of Automotive. . . .

The trial court found that Singer's side line business, the profits of which were $64,088.08, was in direct competition with Automotive. However, Singer argues that in this business he was a manufacturer's agent or consultant, whereas Automotive was a small manufacturer of automotive parts. The title of an activity does not determine the question whether it was competitive but an examination of the nature of the business must be made. In the present case the conflict of interest between Singer's business and his position with Automotive arises from the fact that Singer received orders, principally from a third-party called Husco, for the manufacture of parts. As a manufacturer's consultant he had to see that these orders were filled as inexpensively as possible, but as Automotive's general manager he could not act adversely to the corporation and serve his own interests. On this issue Singer argues that when Automotive had the shop capacity to fill an order he would award Automotive the job, but he contends that it was in the exercise of his duty as general manager of Automotive to refuse orders which in his opinion Automotive could not or should not fill and in that case he was free to treat the order as his own property. However, this argument ignores, as the trial court said, "defendant's agency with plaintiff and the fiduciary duties of good faith and loyalty arising therefrom."

Rather than to resolve the conflict of interest between his side line business and Automotive's business in favor of serving and advancing his own personal interests, Singer had the duty to exercise good faith by disclosing to Automotive all the facts regarding this matter. . . . Upon disclosure to Automotive it was in the latter's discretion to refuse to accept the orders from Husco or to fill them if possible or to sub-job them to other concerns with the consent of Husco if necessary, and the profit, if any, would belong to Automotive. Automotive would then be able also to decide whether to expand its operations, install suitable equipment, or to make further arrangements with Singer or Husco. By failing to disclose all the facts relating to the orders from Husco and by receiving secret profits from these orders, Singer violated his fiduciary duty to act solely for the benefit of Automotive. Therefore he is liable for the amount of the profits he earned in his side line business.

. . .

During the trial the parties stipulated that in the event the court should find that Automotive was entitled to recover profits realized by Singer in his side line business, Singer should be given a credit equal to three percent of the gross sales of that business. Based upon this stipulation the sum of $64,088.08 would be reduced by $10,183. . . .

Judgment . . . affirmed.

ANALYSIS

1. **Why Report Up?** The court says that when Singer received an order that he thought the corporation could not fill, he was supposed to tell someone higher up about it. What is the point of that observation?

2. **The Contractual Terms.** Paragraph 8A of the employment contract has two parts: "devote his entire time . . ." and "not to engage in any other business. . . ." What is the relationship between these two parts? Are they redundant? What is the effect of the phrase "of a permanent nature"?

3. **Which Legal Theory?** Finding of Fact 10 states that Singer "breached his contract of employment" and "violated [his] duty of loyalty." Would either legal theory be sufficient to support the result (Singer's liability)? What difference would it have made if the court had rested its decision on one or the other of the two theories? Would it have been possible to conclude that Singer had breached his contract without violating his duty of loyalty, or vice versa?

4. **Contracting Around the Rule.** Suppose that before Singer was hired, he and the owner of General Automotive had consciously and expressly addressed the possibility that Singer would receive offers of work that he would consider beyond General Automotive's capability. Suppose further that it was clear that it would not have been feasible for Singer to consult with the owner, or any representative of the owner, on what to do with such offers. It is conceivable that the parties might have agreed that Singer would simply turn down these offers. It is also conceivable that they would have agreed that Singer could act as broker, as he did in the actual case, and keep all the profit. Which of these two alternatives seems more likely? Which is more likely to lead to optimal results for both parties? What other solution might you suggest and why?

5. **The Logic to the Rule.** The rule applied by the court is a default rule—that is, one that applies in the absence of agreement. Some default rules reduce the costs of contracting, and achieve fairness, by approximating as closely as possible the provision that the parties would have adopted had they addressed the matter. Other default rules do not have this characteristic but instead are calculated to induce one or the other party to reveal his or her wishes to the other and seek agreement. Into which category does the rule in this case fall?

Rash v. J.V. Intermediate, Ltd.

498 F.3d 1201 (10th Cir. 2007).

. . .

I. Factual Background

J.V. Intermediate, Ltd. and J.V. Industrial Companies, Ltd. (collectively, "JVIC") are Texas-based companies which build, refurbish, expand and manage assets for industrial process plants worldwide. JVIC hired W. Clayton Rash to start and manage a Tulsa, Oklahoma division of its industrial plant maintenance business, inspecting, repairing, and maintaining oil refineries and power plants. The parties signed an employment agreement providing Rash a base salary of $125,000, a bonus of 20% of JVIC-Tulsa's net profits, and a termination bonus of 20% of the division's equity. The contract stipulated the use of Texas law and required that Rash "devote [his] full work time and efforts" to JVIC. The agreement was to last for two years, from 1999 to 2001. Rash continued to serve as manager of the Tulsa branch until 2004, without any written contract extension.

Starting in 2001, JVIC claims that Rash actively participated in and owned at least four other businesses, none of which were ever disclosed to JVIC. One of those businesses was Total Industrial Plant Services, Inc. (TIPS), a scaffolding business. TIPS bid on projects for JVIC-Tulsa, and JVIC-Tulsa, with Rash as its manager, often selected TIPS as a subcontractor. At some point during Rash's tenure, JVIC started its own scaffolding business. Between 2001 to 2004, JVIC paid over $1 million to TIPS. The Tulsa division never used JVIC's scaffolding services. . . .

III. Analysis

. . .

A. Fiduciary Duty

1. Is there a fiduciary relationship?

. . .

Texas courts ... recognize that certain relationships constitute formal fiduciary relationships as a matter of law. Examples of these fiduciary relationships are trustee to beneficiary, executor to beneficiary of estates, attorney to client, and partner to partner. Johnson [v. Brewer & Pritchard, P.C., 73 S.W.3d 193], 200 [(Tex. 2003)]. Under Texas common law, the agent to principal relationship also gives rise to a fiduciary duty. . . .

With respect to the agent to principal relationship, the Texas Supreme Court has adopted relevant provisions of the Restatement (Second) of Agency. In particular, § 387 provides: "[U]nless otherwise agreed, an agent is subject to a duty to his principal to act solely for the benefit of the principal in all matters connected with his agency." . . .

[The court concludes that Rash was an agent of JVIC, for several reasons.]

First, . . . Rash was hired to build the Tulsa division of JVIC from scratch and had sole management responsibilities for operations at the branch. In Rash's own words, "I did the sales, the operations, and everything out of the Tulsa division." He was charged with finding facilities to operate the business, hiring and training employees, gathering tools and equipment for the branch, and promoting the new venture. Rash solicited and received bids for subcontracts and directly received the invoices for those bids. He set the rates charged to JVIC's customers for work performed by the Tulsa division and kept track of all the costs of the division. In general, Rash conceded that he "ran the shop" and was "responsible for generating business for the Tulsa upstart."

Second, Rash contractually agreed to perform the duties of an agent. . . . In his contract, Rash consented to "devote [his] full work time and efforts to the business and affairs of Joint Venture Piping."

Third, Rash does not deny that he was an agent of JVIC. Instead, he only claims that the scope of his agency did not include scaffolding-related ventures. . . .

2. Did Rash breach his fiduciary duty?

Whether Rash breached his fiduciary duty to JVIC turns on the scope of that duty. In *Johnson,* the Texas Supreme Court cautioned courts to "be careful in defining the scope of the fiduciary obligations an employee owes when acting as the employer's agent in the pursuit of business opportunities." 73 S.W.3d at 201. Courts instead inquire whether a fiduciary duty exists with respect to the particular occurrence or transaction at issue. After careful consideration of the question, we are confident that Texas courts would agree on this record that Rash violated his fiduciary duty in failing to disclose his interest in TIPS to JVIC.

Texas law recognizes several basic duties a fiduciary owes the principal:

> Among the agent's fiduciary duties to the principal is the duty to account for profits arising out of the employment, the duty not to act as, or on account of, an adverse party without the principal's consent, the duty not to compete with the principal on his own account or for another in matters relating to the subject matter of the agency, and the duty to deal fairly with the principal in all transactions between them.

Id. at 200 (citing Restatement (Second) of Agency § 13, cmt. a (1958)). Additionally and most importantly for this appeal, the "employee has a duty to deal openly with the employer and to fully disclose to the employer information about matters affecting the company's business." Abetter Trucking Co. [v. Arizpe], 113 S.W.3d [503], 510 [(Tex. App. 2003)]. Although "an employee does not owe an absolute duty of loyalty to his or her employer," *Johnson*, 73 S.W.3d at 201 (acknowledging the right of employees to make preparations for a future competing business venture while still employed), at the very least, an employee's independent enterprise cannot compete or contract with the employer without the employer's full knowledge.

. . . Here, Rash presents two defenses: (1) as a manager of JVIC's general industrial plant maintenance work, he owed no specific duty to JVIC's relatively minor scaffolding business, and (2) JVIC's president, Joe Vardell, told him that he had no problem with Rash forming a business which might contract with JVIC. Yet, these defenses, even if true, misapprehend the nature of his fiduciary duty. As discussed above, Rash had a "duty to deal fairly with the principal in *all* transactions between them," id. at 200 (emphasis added), and "to fully disclose to the employer information about matters affecting the company's business," *Abetter Trucking Co.*, 113 S.W.3d at 503 (emphasis added).

In other words, Rash had a "general duty of full disclosure respecting matters affecting the principal's interests and a general prohibition against the fiduciary's using the relationship to benefit his personal interest, except with the full knowledge and consent of the principal." United Teachers Ass'n Ins. Co. v. MacKeen & Bailey, Inc., 99 F.3d 645, 650 (5th Cir.1996). Even assuming that Rash had no responsibilities to JVIC regarding the scaffolding division or that Vardell gave him hypothetical permission to engage in other businesses, by failing to inform JVIC specifically of his ownership stake in TIPS, he violated his fiduciary duty. . .

The duty of an agent is to disclose to the principal what the principal should rightly know. The facts are uncontroverted that (1) Rash possessed a significant ownership stake in TIPS, (2) TIPS bid for subcontracts with JVIC-Tulsa, (3) Rash played an instrumental role in selecting JVIC-Tulsa's subcontractors, (4) TIPS was selected as a JVIC-Tulsa subcontractor on several occasions, and (5) Rash never disclosed to JVIC or its president, Vardell, his relationship with TIPS. In fact, Vardell testified that he only learned about Rash's ownership of TIPS through this litigation. In our estimation, this amounts to a breach of his fiduciary duty as a matter of law. . . .

This would be a different case altogether if Rash simply notified Vardell or JVIC about his relationship with TIPS. Since he did not, JVIC was entitled to judgment as a matter of law on its breach of fiduciary claim against Rash.

. . .

ANALYSIS

1. **What if JVIC Had Not Entered the Scaffolding Business?** At the time Rash was hired, JVIC did not have a scaffolding business. If JVIC had never formed a scaffolding business, would Rash have violated his fiduciary obligation to JVIC by contracting on its behalf with his company (TIPS)?
2. **What Should Rash Have Done?** What should Rash have done to satisfy the court's notion of his duty to disclose?
3. **Best Effort Clauses.** The court notes that "Rash consented to 'devote [his] full work time and efforts to the business and affairs of Joint Venture Piping.'" These so-called best efforts clauses are common in many types of employment agreements. A somewhat more detailed example provides that "employees shall devote their full working time, attention and efforts to the Company's business and shall not, directly or indirectly, engage in any other business or commercial activities which shall conflict or interfere with or distract from in any way the performance of the employee's responsibilities to the Company or which involve any activities similar to the business conducted by the Company." Why are these clauses necessary in light of the fiduciary duties of agents?

B. DUTIES DURING AND AFTER TERMINATION OF AGENCY: HEREIN OF "GRABBING AND LEAVING"

Bancroft-Whitney Company v. Glen

64 Cal.2d 327, 49 Cal.Rptr. 825, 411 P.2d 921 (1966).

■ MOSK, JUSTICE.

[The plaintiff in this case, Bancroft-Whitney Company, was a lawbook publisher with its headquarters in San Francisco. The defendants were Judson B. Glen, formerly president of Bancroft-Whitney; Matthew Bender & Co., another lawbook publisher, with headquarters in New York; and John T. Bender, the president of Matthew Bender & Co. In 1961, Matthew Bender & Co. began an ultimately successful effort to set up a west coast division. As part of this effort, it hired Glen to head that division. Glen, in turn, assisted Matthew Bender & Co. in various ways in hiring away some of Bancroft-Whitney's key people. The plaintiff's claim, described more fully below, is that while Glen was free to quit his job at Bancroft-Whitney and go to work for Matthew Bender, he breached his fiduciary duties to Bancroft-Whitney when, while still working for Bancroft-Whitney, he helped Matthew Bender line up Bancroft-Whitney employees who defected to Matthew Bender. The trial court, sitting without a jury, found in favor of the defendants. The Supreme Court reverses.]

The Employment of Glen and Baker by Bender Co.

The majority of the stock of plaintiff corporation is owned by the Lawyer's Co-Operative Publishing Co. (LCP), whose principal place of business is Rochester, New York. Glen was employed by the parent company as an editor from 1938 until 1949, and in 1949 he became the editor-in-chief of plaintiff. From 1958 until his resignation on December 15, 1961, he was also president of plaintiff, chairman of the executive committee of plaintiff, and chairman of the product planning committee of LCP. In April 1960, Thomas Gosnell became president of LCP and exercised direct control and domination over much of the actual business operations of plaintiff. Glen and Baker [sales manager of Bancroft-Whitney] thereafter became dissatisfied with their employment.

Prior to 1961, Bender Co. desired to expand its operations in California. In May of that year Bender directed William Vanneman, a vice president of Bender Co., to attempt to verify circulating reports that Glen was unhappy in his position with plaintiff. On May 12, 1961, Vanneman reported orally and in writing to Bender that he had not been able to confirm the rumors of dissatisfaction in his discussions with Glen, but stated that he had heard from the president of another subsidiary of LCP that Bender could create a substantial western operation using plaintiff's personnel. Bender testified that he discarded this suggestion.

Nevertheless, on July 10, 1961, Bender instructed his assistant, Joseph Billo, to contact Glen in San Francisco privately to explore further the possibilities covered in the Vanneman report. After a meeting with Glen at his office in San Francisco, Billo reported to Bender that Glen had reached retirement age, that his pension had vested and he was open to offers, that he would consider a change of employment if he could build up his estate and direct the new operation himself, that he had been asked to stay on in plaintiff's employ for five to seven years, and that, despite feelings of loyalty to plaintiff, he could be swayed. Bender wrote Glen at his home, arranged to meet him in San Francisco on September 19, and there they discussed the possibility that Glen might head a new western division of Bender Co. following his retirement. They also discussed the need for a sales manager for the new organization, and Glen suggested that Bender contact Gordon Baker, who was the Los Angeles regional sales manager and a director of plaintiff. Glen called Baker and arranged a meeting between Bender and Baker in Los Angeles. At that meeting Baker indicated that he might be interested in serving as sales manager for the new organization, but only if Glen also became associated with it. On October 10 the fact that Bender was interested in hiring Glen and Baker (and a number of editors employed by plaintiff, as will be discussed later) came to the attention of Gosnell, the president of LCP, and other LCP officers. Gosnell met Glen in San Francisco in a series of meetings beginning on October 23, 1961, to discuss the situation with him. Glen testified that at these meetings Gosnell did not ask him about his personal plans, but Gosnell claimed that he asked Glen whether he and Baker had been approached about employment by Bender and that Glen had replied he and Baker were not interested in going to work for Bender Co. More of this meeting is discussed hereinafter.

On November 17, 1961, after further negotiations between Glen, Baker, Bender, and other employees and officers of Bender Co., Glen and Baker signed employment contracts with Bender Co., requiring them to commence work on January 1, 1962. Glen's contract provided that he would share in the profits of the new enterprise. On December 15, 1961, Glen resigned as president and director of plaintiff and as a director of LCP. Baker resigned on the same day, and both men commenced employment with Bender Co. in January 1962.

Before November 16 Glen had personally discussed negotiations concerning his probable future employment by Bender Co. with at least two other directors at LCP, and they did not indicate any objection or reproval of Glen's activities. Glen had no written contract of employment with plaintiff, his employment was terminable at will by either plaintiff or himself, and he was not required by the terms or particular circumstances of his employment to resign from or give notice to plaintiff or its remaining officers, directors, or shareholders before negotiating for or signing an employment contract with Bender Co. for the purpose of establishing a western division.

Defendants rely on evidence showing that Glen was discontented with his employment, that a number of plaintiff's officers and employees knew of Glen's discontent and were aware of his negotiations with Bender, and that Glen would have been required to retire from his position with plaintiff because he had reached the age of 65. The evidence regarding these matters is not set forth in detail because it is tangential to the primary issues in the case as described above.

The Hiring of Employees Other Than Glen and Baker

. . .

From the first meeting on September 19, 1961, between Glen and Bender, Glen had mentioned that a dozen editors might accompany him to the new organization. In subsequent contacts this figure fluctuated between 10 and 15 editors. Indeed, at one point Glen suggested to Bender that he might "take" practically all the personnel in plaintiff's organization, but Bender replied that he did not want them all. . . .

On or before October 10, 1961, Glen spoke with two of plaintiff's four managing editors about the possibility of their coming to work with the new organization, and both of them expressed interest. Jules Kalisch testified that Glen had offered him a salary of $15,000, a five-year contract, and a percentage of the profits, but that Kalisch felt $15,000 was not enough and Glen then offered him $18,000. . . . Kalisch's salary with plaintiff was $12,750. Allan Solie, the second managing editor, testified that he was asked by Glen if he was interested in joining the new organization and that Glen offered him a salary of $15,000 a year, a profit-sharing arrangement, and an opportunity to be a member of the board of directors. Solie was earning $11,000 a year. About the middle or the end of November, Glen approached the treasurer of plaintiff, a man named Lahti, and asked him if he was interested in leaving. He was offered a salary of $17,500, representing a $2,500 increase, a five-year contract, and a position as controller of the new organization.

. . .

As mentioned above, when Gosnell, the president of LCP, became aware in early October that Bender Co. might be interested in employing Glen, Baker, and editorial personnel of plaintiff, he came to San Francisco to discuss the matter in a series of meetings with Glen. There is a sharp conflict in the evidence as to whether Gosnell asked Glen at these meetings whether there was a danger of a raid by Bender Co. on plaintiff's editors. Gosnell testified that he asked Glen if there was any danger that Bender might be taking a group of editors from plaintiff and that Glen replied he didn't think there was any danger of this and thought everyone in the editorial department was happy and pleased. Glen denied that Gosnell asked him specifically about a raid by *Bender Co.* but admitted that the subject of a raid by another company was discussed and that he told Gosnell that if there should be a raid on plaintiff's editorial staff he (Glen) would be the first to know about it and "presumably" he would report the matter immediately. Glen testified that his statements did not refer to a raid by a company with which he, Glen, would become associated, because in that case he would not be there to notify anyone. He stated that he knew at the time that if things worked out for him with Bender he would be seeking editors from plaintiff. . . .

Another matter Gosnell discussed with Glen during his visit to San Francisco was salary raises for plaintiff's editors. Although editorial salaries had been under review since the beginning of 1961, Gosnell had ordered another analysis to be made so that he could propose to Glen that increases in salary be given to the editors. The purpose of the suggestion was to head off any Bender Co. raid of plaintiff's editorial staff by maintaining salaries close to the prevailing market rate.

In his meetings with Glen, Gosnell suggested that the salaries of managing editors be raised $2,000 per year, that of assistant managing editors raised $1,500 per year, and that other editors be given raises of $300, $500, or $700 a year, depending upon their experience and competence. Glen told Gosnell that he wished, for purposes of internal administration of plaintiff, to "not make quite such a large jump at this time" but to cut the $2,000 raises for three of the four managing editors to $1,500 and give the full $2,000 raise only to Solie. He also suggested to Gosnell that the salary raises be given in two stages, half immediately, and the other half after January 1, 1962.

Gosnell agreed to the two-step arrangement, and he testified that he was satisfied with the assurances given by Glen before he returned to Rochester. The first-step raises for some of the editors went into effect in November. There is no evidence that Bender knew of the portion of Glen's conversation with Gosnell relating to the raises.

On November 14, Glen flew to New York to attend a directors' meeting of LCP in Rochester. While in Rochester, he told two LCP directors that he might go to work for Bender Co. and stated to one of them that if he decided to leave, Kalisch and Lahti would go with him. . . .

At the meeting in New York Bender and Glen discussed the two managing editors who were to be hired. Bender testified he knew that Glen had definite people in mind for the jobs, but could not recall if Glen mentioned the names of Kalisch and Solie. However, Glen indicated that the salary range for the persons he wanted would run between $15,000 and $17,000 or $17,500. . . .

At this meeting Glen suggested that Bender come to Carmel, where he could meet the two or three people he had in mind as employees and where these persons could meet Bender.

Glen returned to San Francisco, made hotel reservations in Carmel for the meeting, and informed Kalisch, Solie and Lahti about it. Baker learned of the proposed meeting when he was in New York to sign his contract. On November 27 Bender wrote Glen telling him when he expected to arrive for the meeting and assuring Glen that adequate financing for the new organization would be forthcoming. This letter also stated: ". . . the very first thing is to take immediate steps to put together an editorial organization in the following respects: A) Managing Editors B) Experienced Editors C) Selected Trainees. As to group (A) above, Carmel is for that purpose. Then, thereafter, it is your judgment as to when I should be in the picture and when I should be left out of the picture, having in mind that until you actually resign from your present position and the fact of the new organization is known, we will have to be very deft and at least not overlook the possibility of a Fifth Columnist. . . ."

. . .

Bender explained that the reference to a "Fifth Columnist" meant that he didn't want anyone to come to Carmel who wouldn't want to join the new organization because he felt that potential employees would be embarrassed if they attended the meeting and word got back to LCP about it. He also stated he wanted to keep the meeting secret from another competitor.

Bender and his attorney arrived in San Francisco on Friday afternoon, December 1. Glen met them at the airport and drove them to Carmel, taking Solie along. In Carmel they met Kalisch, Baker, and Lahti. Friday night was devoted to the social amenities. On Saturday morning Lahti, Solie, and Kalisch were sitting in the lobby of the hotel when Glen handed them each a copy of an employment contract . . . Lahti, Solie, and Kalisch read their contracts, Bender and his attorney reviewed them, and they were signed with only minor alterations, Bender signing on behalf of Bender Co. . . .

After the contracts were signed, Glen, Solie, and Kalisch proceeded to choose the other editors employed by plaintiff who would be invited to join the new organization. To facilitate this procedure, Glen had brought with him 56 3 × 5 cards, each designating the name of one of the editors employed by plaintiff, and the editor's salary. Prior to leaving for Carmel, he had requested a record of the editors' salaries from plaintiff's personnel department and had entered the amounts on the cards. At the Carmel session, Glen would read the name of an editor and his salary from a card, the three men would discuss his qualities among themselves, and, if it was decided that he should be invited to join, Kalisch would enter his name on a list, place beside it the salary paid to him by plaintiff, and, after a discussion among the three men, a suggested salary to be offered by the new organization.

There is some dispute as to how the suggested salaries were determined. One witness testified that they were 10 per cent higher than the salaries paid by plaintiff, and another that the salaries were determined "by guess and by golly." In each case, however, the suggested salary was higher than the editor was receiving from plaintiff. Glen testified that, in making the selection, he wanted competent candidates. In some cases, an editor was known to only one of the men. Glen recommended that two of the four indexers employed by plaintiff be invited to join, and he suggested one or two other persons unknown to the others. Solie tried to pick some of the younger men to avoid the necessity of offering high salaries. In some cases capable editors were rejected because of purportedly undesirable personal habits or because of a record of absenteeism. In one instance a man was passed over because it was reported he had a good chance for advancement with plaintiff. Kalisch testified that there was no discussion about choosing the "cream of the crop" of editors and that editors from one of the departments of plaintiff were deliberately passed over because that group was working on a national publication and they did not want to interfere with its work. At the conclusion of the meeting, Glen, Kalisch, and Solie had compiled a list of 14 prospects who were to be invited to join. The list also contained the present and the suggested salaries for each candidate.

Bender and his attorney were in the room during a part of the selection process. Bender informed Glen that he (Bender) wished the choice of editors to be made on the basis of their capabilities and their willingness to come to work for Bender Co., and he believed that the selections made followed these requirements. . . .

After the selection process concluded, there was a discussion as to the method of contacting the candidates. Bender's attorney advised that if persons employed by plaintiff solicited the candidates there was a possibility that a lawsuit would result and that they should keep their "hands off." He advised that the actual contacts be made by someone from Bender Co. . . .

Billo [assistant to Bender] arrived [in San Francisco] on December 9. He did not testify, but his deposition was read at the trial. He could not find the list [prepared at the Carmel meeting] at the time his deposition was taken but when he left New York he had with him the list of candidates, their present salaries, and a suggested salary for each. He met Glen before he contacted the editors, and they discussed some of the persons on the list. . . . Billo called each of the editors, told them briefly about the new organization, and invited them to be a part of it. Glen had provided a picture of the building which had been leased for the western division, and Billo showed it to each editor. Billo had been given absolute discretion as to salaries by Bender and had offered salaries "comparable" to the Bender Co. editorial salary scale. In most cases he offered more than the amount suggested on the list.

One of the editors contacted by Glen, who did not accept employment with Bender Co., testified that in his meeting with Billo the latter had stated that several editors who worked for plaintiff were being contacted for employment, that "they" considered these editors to be the cream of the legal editors on the West Coast, and that Billo was in a position to offer the editor $900 per year more than he was receiving from plaintiff. Another editor testified that Billo had told him that "they were selecting all producers," that they were "the cream of the editors on the West Coast," and that the position he would have with Bender Co. would mean an increase in salary of $1,100.

During the period that Billo was soliciting the editors Glen wrote Bender, "I met with Joe Billo last night and he is starting today on his recruiting program. He will keep in touch with us so that he and we here can cooperate to full advantage." On the 11th, the second day of solicitation, Bender telegraphed Billo as follows: "Stengel and Maris eh! The Yanks need you. Tell Jud we'll settle for a championship western division." Bender testified that he did not know what these references meant, but that he thought the telegram was intended to be congratulatory. On December 12 Glen wrote Bender, "We are making fine progress in getting editors. Eleven have committed themselves in our favor. Two will not come with us. We have not heard from the others. It is now my estimate that we will end up with fourteen editors—not bad for a start."

. . .

On December 15, Glen, Kalisch, Solie, Lahti, Baker, and 12 editors resigned from plaintiff's employ. . . .

At noon the departing editors met at a restaurant for lunch and executed tax information forms previously sent out by Bender for them.

Each of the persons (with the exception of Glen) who resigned from plaintiff's employ was contacted personally before he commenced working for Bender Co. by representatives of plaintiff, who invited him to return to plaintiff's employ. Plaintiff had every opportunity it desired to rehire these employees and utilized this opportunity without interference from any defendant. Plaintiff presented each resigning employee with the most favorable terms it was willing to offer in order to induce him to return to its employ, but it did not offer higher salaries than Bender Co. as an inducement. As a result of the meetings, Solie and two of the editors decided to remain with plaintiff. Subsequently, a number of other employees of plaintiff accepted positions with Bender Co.

In analyzing the legal principles applicable in this case, it should be repeated that we are not concerned with the simple right of one competitor to offer the employees of another a job at more favorable terms than they presently enjoy or the right of an employee (or an officer of a corporation) to seek a better job. The question here is whether the president of a corporation is liable for the breach of his fiduciary duty because of the conduct described above relating to other employees of the corporation and whether, under these facts, those who hire the employees are guilty of unfair competition for acting in concert with the president.

The general rules applicable to the duties of a corporate officer have been frequently stated. In the leading case of Guth v. Loft (1939) 23 Del.Ch. 255, 5 A.2d 503, 510, these obligations were cogently described as follows: "Corporate officers and directors are not permitted to use their position of trust and confidence to further their private interests. While technically not trustees, they stand in a fiduciary relation to the corporation and its stockholders. A public policy, existing through the years, derived from a profound knowledge of human characteristics and motives, has established a rule that demands of a corporate officer or director, peremptorily and inexorably, the most scrupulous observance of his duty, not only affirmatively to protect the interests of the corporation committed to his charge, but also to refrain from doing anything that would work injury to the corporation, or to deprive it of profit or advantage which his skill and ability might properly bring to it, or to enable it to make in the reasonable and lawful exercise of its powers." Section 820 of the Corporations Code provides that an officer must exercise his powers in good faith, with a view to the interests of the corporation.

. . .

The mere fact that the officer makes preparations to compete before he resigns his office is not sufficient to constitute a breach of duty. It is the nature of his preparations which is significant.[10] No ironclad rules as to the type of conduct which is permissible can be stated, since the spectrum of activities in this regard is as broad as the ingenuity of man itself.

. . .

There is broad language in some cases to the effect that protection of the corporation's interest requires full disclosure of acts undertaken in preparation for entering into competition. . . . An analysis of these cases indicates, however, that the liability for breach of fiduciary duty was not predicated on the officer's mere failure to disclose such acts, but upon some *particular circumstance* which rendered nondisclosure harmful to

---

[10] Comment e of section 393 of the Restatement Second of Agency provides that an agent can make arrangements to compete with his principal even before the termination of the agency, but that he cannot properly use confidential information peculiar to his employer's business and acquired therein.

> "Thus, before the end of his employment, he can properly purchase a rival business and upon termination of employment immediately compete. He is not, however, entitled to solicit customers for such rival business before the end of his employment nor can he properly do other similar acts in direct competition with the employer's business. The limits of proper conduct with reference to securing the services of fellow employees are not well marked. An employee is subject to liability if, before or after leaving the employment, he causes fellow employees to break their contracts with the employer. On the other hand, it is normally permissible for employees of a firm, or for some of its partners, to agree among themselves while still employed, that they will engage in competition with the firm at the end of the period specified in their employment contracts. However, a court may find that it is a breach of duty for a number of the key officers or employees to agree to leave their employment simultaneously and without giving the employer an opportunity to hire and train replacements."

The illustration given by the Restatement is as follows:

> "A is employed by P as manager for a year. Before the end of the year, A decides to go into business for himself; in anticipation of this and without P's knowledge, he contracts with the best of P's employees to work for him at the end of the year. At the end of the year, A engages in a competing business and employs the persons with whom he has previously contracted. A has committed a breach of his duty of loyalty to P."

the corporation or upon the officer's wrongful conduct apart from the omission.

There is no requirement that an officer disclose his preparations to compete with the corporation in every case, and failure to disclose such acts will render the officer liable for a breach of his fiduciary duties only where particular circumstances render nondisclosure harmful to the corporation. . . . Conversely, the mere act of disclosing his activities cannot immunize the officer from liability where his conduct in other respects amounts to a breach of duty. The significant inquiry in each situation is whether the officer's acts or omissions constitute a breach under the general principles applicable to the performance of his trust.

In our view, the conduct of Glen in the present case, when assessed by the standards set forth above, amounts to a breach of his fiduciary duties to plaintiff as a matter of law. The undisputed evidence shows a consistent course of conduct by him designed to obtain for a competitor those of plaintiff's employees whom the competitor could afford to employ and would find useful. If Glen while still president of plaintiff had performed these acts on behalf of Bender Co. without also obligating himself to join the company, there could be no doubt that he would have violated his duties to plaintiff. Surely his position in this regard cannot be improved by the fact that he was also to be employed by Bender Co. and was to share in the profits of the new western division. In carrying out his design, Glen misled Gosnell into believing there was no danger that Bender Co. would attempt to hire plaintiff's personnel, suggested a two-step salary increase without informing Gosnell that he had solicited some editors and that he or Bender Co. would solicit others if they successfully consummated their negotiations, and disclosed confidential information regarding salaries to Bender in order to facilitate the solicitation. Ultimately, positions at higher salaries than plaintiff was paying were offered either by Glen or Bender Co. to the treasurer of plaintiff, three of its four managing editors, one or two of the four assistant managing editors, three of the four indexers, and approximately 10 other editors. We need not decide whether any of these acts would constitute a breach of fiduciary duty, taken alone, since there can be little doubt that, in combination, they show a course of conduct which falls demonstrably short of "the most scrupulous observance" of an officer's duty to his corporation.

Misleading Gosnell

The conclusion is inescapable that Glen deliberately misled Gosnell regarding the possibility of a raid by Bender Co. on plaintiff's editorial staff and that his suggestion to Gosnell that half of the proposed salary increases for the editors be postponed until after January 1, 1962, without informing Gosnell of his plan to offer them positions, directly or indirectly, with Bender Co. at higher salaries if his own negotiations with

Bender were successful, amounts at the very least to a deliberate and inexcusable failure to inform Gosnell of a matter of vital interest to plaintiff.

Disclosing the Salaries of Plaintiff's Employees

Another significant aspect of Glen's activities on behalf of Bender relates to the list of employees and their salaries compiled at Carmel. It is beyond question that a corporate officer breaches his fiduciary duties when, with the purpose of facilitating the recruiting of the corporation's employees by a competitor, he supplies the competitor with a selective list of the corporation's employees who are, in his judgment, possessed of both ability and the personal characteristics desirable in an employee, together with the salary the corporation is paying the employee and a suggestion as to the salary the competitor should offer in order to be successful in recruitment. This conclusion is inescapable even if the information regarding salaries is not deemed to be confidential. . . .

Assisting the Solicitation of Plaintiff's Employees

The assistance given by Glen to the solicitation of the editors on the list is also to be condemned as a breach of his fiduciary duty. As we have seen, Glen not only provided the list on which the recruiting was based, but he suggested certain tactics to be followed in discussions with the editors, supplied a picture of the new organization's quarters for use by Billo, discussed the persons on the list with Billo during the recruiting campaign, and, in Glen's own words in his letter to Bender, Billo was to keep in touch with him so that "he and we here can cooperate to full advantage." In addition, Glen personally approached Lahti, Kalisch, Solie, Keesey, and Marquis and offered them employment.

. . .

Another matter relied upon by defendants relates to a letter written by Bender on October 10, 1961, to a man named Briggs, who was a director of LCP but was seeking employment with Bender Co. In this letter, Bender stated that he was interested in employing Glen and Baker and that although he had no intention of conducting a raid on plaintiff's personnel, he would not turn his back on any opportunities offered. Briggs showed this letter to Gosnell, and defendants argue that Bender knew Briggs would do so and that therefore Gosnell had been fully informed by Bender of his plans.

However, *after* seeing this letter Gosnell came to San Francisco and received assurances from Glen that he would report to Gosnell any attempt to raid plaintiff's editorial staff, and Glen told Bender he had assured Gosnell that Bender Co. did not intend such action. Thus, any effect of the notice was dissipated by Glen's deception of Gosnell, a matter of which Bender had knowledge. Moreover, the basis underlying the action against Bender and Bender Co. is their cooperation in Glen's breach of fiduciary duty. Since Glen committed many disloyal acts with Bender's knowledge and cooperation, notice of Bender's interest in plaintiff's employees would have been of little significance, and the letter to Briggs does not materially affect the liability of Bender and Bender Co.

. . .

It is clear from the evidence set forth above that Bender was aware of or ratified Glen's breach of his fiduciary duties in all but a few respects, that he cooperated with Glen in the breach, and that he received the benefits of Glen's infidelity.

Damages

Defendants argue that even if we conclude that Glen breached his fiduciary duty and that the other defendants are guilty of unfair competition, we cannot award any damages for this wrongdoing because plaintiff has failed to show that the departure of the employees was proximately caused by defendants' actions. They admit that the primary reason the employees left was that they were offered higher salaries by Bender Co. As recounted above, it was Glen's breach that enabled Bender to determine the amount of salary which would induce these persons to leave plaintiff's employ. Under these circumstances there is no merit in defendants' contention. The causal relationship between Glen's violation of duty and Bender's persuasive inducement to the plaintiff's personnel is crystal clear.

Defendants urge that plaintiff itself bears responsibility for the ultimate departure of its employees because it failed to offer higher salaries in order to induce them to return after they had reached agreement with Bender Co. We cannot indulge in an assumption that such offers would have been accepted under the circumstances. In any event, the question of plaintiff's conduct subsequent to the successful recruitment campaign of defendants relates to the question of damages rather than to proximate cause. To hold otherwise would suggest that a corporation could not protect itself against an officer's breach of fiduciary duties in this regard, no matter how flagrant his conduct, since it could always be said that the corporation which lost its employees might have offered them additional salary to return and that the departing employees might have accepted these offers.

. . .

The trial court found that plaintiff was not damaged in any amount by any tortious acts of defendants, that by the end of 1962 it had fully recovered from the adverse effects "if any" caused by the loss of personnel, and that the only adverse effect "if any" on plaintiff from this loss was a contribution to a delay in 1962 in the preparation and shipment of its work. The undisputed evidence shows that plaintiff suffered other adverse effects as well, and the trial court's findings in this regard are not supported by the evidence. At the very least, it was shown without contradiction that plaintiff had incurred certain expenses in attempting to persuade the persons who had resigned to return to its employ.

. . .

The judgment is reversed with directions to the trial court to retry the issue of general damages and enter judgment for plaintiff.

ANALYSIS

Suppose you had been Bender's lawyer just before Bender approached Glen and had been asked what Glen could and could not do and what the likely costs (in damages) would be if he violated his obligations. With the benefit of the decision you have just read, what would you have said, specifically with respect to the following?

a. Whether Glen has an obligation to his employer to notify his superiors of (i) the offer to him or (ii) the broader "raid" on LCP employees.

b. Whether Glen may provide information about the salaries and the capabilities of his subordinates.

c. Whether Glen may talk to his subordinates about going to work for Bender.

PROBLEMS

Suppose you are a senior associate in the ABC law firm. You are well thought of by the partners of ABC and have good reason to believe, and do believe, that you will soon be asked to become a partner in the firm. You are approached by a partner, Paula, in the XYZ law firm about the possibility of becoming a partner in that firm. The partners in ABC have a strong commitment to the idea of loyalty to the firm; your position at ABC would be undermined if it were known that you were giving serious consideration to the possibility of joining XYZ, but in fact you are doing so.

1. Do you have a legal obligation to ABC to reveal the possibility of your moving to XYZ? What about a moral obligation? What if one of the senior partners of ABC is your mother?

2. Suppose Paula says that XYZ also has an interest in two or three of the associates working under your direction. You feel that you would be more likely to want to join XYZ if they went with you. What, if anything, can you say to them?

3. Your secretary at ABC does an outstanding job and your decision to join XYZ will to some degree depend on whether she will go with you. What can you say to her?

4. A number of the clients whose work you have been doing might follow you to XYZ. Can you ask them whether they will do so?

Town & Country House & Home Service, Inc. v. Newbery

3 N.Y.2d 554, 170 N.Y.S.2d 328, 147 N.E.2d 724 (1958).

This action was brought for an injunction and damages against appellants on the theory of unfair competition. The complaint asks to restrain them from engaging in the same business as plaintiff, from soliciting its customers, and for an accounting and damages. The individual appellants were in plaintiff's employ for about three years before they severed their relationships and organized the corporate appellant through which they have been operating. The theory of the complaint is that plaintiff's enterprise "was unique, personal and confidential," and that appellants cannot engage in business at all without breach of the confidential relationship in which they learned its trade secrets, including the names and individual needs and tastes of its customers.

The nature of the enterprise is house and home cleaning by contract with individual householders. Its "unique" quality consists in superseding the drudgery of ordinary house cleaning by mass production methods. The house cleaning is performed by a crew of men who descend upon a home at stated intervals of time, and do the work in a hurry after the manner of an assembly line in a factory. They have been instructed by the housewife but work without her supervision. The householder is supplied with liability insurance, the secrets of the home are kept inviolate, the tastes of the customer are served and each team of workmen is selected as suited to the home to which it is sent. The complaint says that the customer relationship is "impregnated" with a "personal and confidential aspect."

The complaint was dismissed at Special Term on the ground that the individual appellants were not subjected to negative covenants under any contract with plaintiff, and that the methods and techniques used by plaintiff in conducting its business are not confidential or secret as in the case of a scientific formula; that house cleaning and housekeeping "are old and necessary chores which accompany orderly living" and that no violation of duty was involved in soliciting plaintiff's customers by appellants after resigning from plaintiff's employ. The contacts and acquaintances with customers were held not to have been the result of a confidential relationship between plaintiff and defendants or the result of the disclosure of secret or confidential material.

By a divided vote the Appellate Division reversed, but on a somewhat different ground, namely, that while in plaintiff's employ, appellants conspired to terminate their employment, form a business of their own in competition with plaintiff and solicit plaintiff's customers for their business. The overt acts under this conspiracy were found by the

Appellate Division to have been that, in pursuance of this plan, they formed the corporate appellant and bought equipment and supplies for their operations—not on plaintiff's time—but during off hours, before they had severed their relations as employees of plaintiff. The Appellate Division concluded that "it is our opinion that their agreement and encouragement to each other to carry out the course of conduct thus planned by them, and their consummation of the plan, particularly their termination of employment virtually en masse, were inimical to, and violative of, the obligations owed by them to appellant as its employees; and that therefore appellant was entitled to relief." . . .

Although the Appellate Division implied more relief than we consider to have been warranted, we think that the trial court erred in dismissing the complaint altogether. The only trade secret which could be involved in this business is plaintiff's list of customers. Concerning that, even where a solicitor of business does not operate fraudulently under the banner of his former employer, he still may not solicit the latter's customers who are not openly engaged in business in advertised locations or whose availability as patrons cannot readily be ascertained but "whose trade and patronage have been secured by years of business effort and advertising, and the expenditure of time and money, constituting a part of the good will of a business which enterprise and foresight have built up" (Witkop & Holmes Co. v. Boyce, 61 Misc. 126, 131, 112 N.Y.S. 874, 878, affirmed 131 App.Div. 922, 115 N.Y.S. 1150, . . .). . . .

The testimony in the instant record shows that the customers of plaintiff were not and could not be obtained merely by looking up their names in the telephone or city directory or by going to any advertised locations, but had to be screened from among many other housewives who did not wish services such as respondent and appellants were equipped to render, but preferred to do their own housework. In most instances housewives do their own house cleaning. The only appeal which plaintiff could have was to those whose cleaning had been done by servants regularly or occasionally employed, except in the still rarer instances where the housewife was on the verge of abandoning doing her own work by hiring some outside agency. In the beginning, prospective customers of plaintiff were discovered by Dorothy Rossmoore, wife of plaintiff's president, by telephoning at random in "sections of Nassau that we thought would be interested in this type of cleaning, and from that we got directories, town directories, and we marked the streets that we had passed down, and I personally called, right down the list." In other words, after selecting a neighborhood which they felt was fertile for their kind of business, they would telephone to all of the residents of a street in the hope of discovering likely prospects. On the first day Mrs. Rossmoore called 52 homes. If she enlisted their interest, an appointment would be made for a personal call in order to sell them the service. At the end of the first year, only 40 to 50 customers had thus been secured. Two hundred to three hundred telephone calls netted 8 to 12 customers. Moreover, during the first year it was not possible to know how much to charge these customers with accuracy, inasmuch as the cleaning requirements of each differed from the others, so that special prices had to be set. In the beginning the customer usually suggested the price which was paid until some kind of cost accounting could demonstrate whether it should be raised or lowered. These costs were entered on cards for every customer, and this represented an accumulated body of experience of considerable value. After three years of operation, and by August, 1952, when the individual appellants resigned their employment by plaintiff, the number of customers amounted to about 240. By that time plaintiff had 7 or 8 crews doing this cleaning work, consisting of 3 men each.

Although appellants did not solicit plaintiff's customers until they were out of plaintiff's employ, nevertheless plaintiff's customers were the only ones they did solicit. Appellants solicited 20 or 25 of plaintiff's customers who refused to do business with appellants and about 13 more of plaintiff's customers who transferred their patronage to appellants. These were all the people that appellants' firm solicited. It would be different if these customers had been equally available to appellants and respondent, but, as has been related, these customers had been screened by respondent at considerable effort and expense, without which their receptivity and willingness to do business with this kind of a service organization could not be known. So there appears to be no question that plaintiff is entitled to enjoin defendants from further solicitation of its customers, or that some profits or damage should be paid to plaintiff by reason of these customers whom they enticed away.

For more than this appellants are not liable. . . .

ANALYSIS

1. **What Could They Have Done?** Just what could the defendants have done to lure away Town & Country customers, without incurring liability to the plaintiffs?

2. **Maneuvering Around the Rule.** Assume (reasonably) that the law would allow a competitor with no prior relationship with Town & Country to follow Town & Country trucks and thereby discover the addresses, and then the names and telephone numbers, of Town & Country customers, and then to solicit those customers. Is there any good reason why the defendants should not be permitted to hire a detective to do the same sleuthing and then use the list put together by the detective as a basis for telephone solicitation?

Corroon & Black-Rutters & Roberts, Inc. v. Hosch

109 Wis.2d 290, 325 N.W.2d 883 (1982).

■ CECI, JUSTICE.

The question presented is whether it is unfair competition for an insurance agent to use his former employer's customer lists to direct clients to the agent's new insurance agency.

A jury found that the defendant, Jack Hosch, had unfairly used confidential information to compete with the plaintiff, Corroon & Black-Rutters & Roberts, Inc. The court of appeals reversed and remanded for judgment notwithstanding the verdict, holding that the verdict was not supported by credible evidence and was contrary to public policy. We conclude that the information gleaned by the defendant from the plaintiff's files does not constitute a trade secret under Wisconsin law and, therefore, affirm the decision of the court of appeals.

Jack Hosch has been an agent licensed to sell insurance since 1958. In that year, he began his employment with the Roberts Company, a general insurance agency. In 1973, the business and assets of Roberts, including all of its insurance accounts, were acquired by Corroon & Black through an exchange of the stock of Roberts with the stock of Corroon & Black.

During his employment, Hosch was responsible for procuring and servicing insurance accounts for a large number of Corroon & Black's customers. Hosch himself brought about half of these accounts to Corroon & Black. Servicing an account involved, among other things, contacting a customer when the policy was about to expire and reviewing and updating the coverages before renewing the policy.

When the two agencies merged in 1973, Hosch and other employees of Roberts who joined Corroon & Black were required to sign a covenant not to compete. Hosch's covenant not to compete terminated on December 31, 1977. He entered into no other such agreement.

When the term of the covenant not to compete ended, Hosch left Corroon & Black to work for a competitor. Shortly thereafter, in January of 1978, Corroon & Black's president learned that numerous agent-of-record letters had been issued in favor of Hosch and his new agency. These letters notified insurance companies that certain accounts were being switched to a different agency. This resulted in substantial losses of commissions for Corroon & Black, since approximately two-thirds of Hosch's Corroon & Black customers changed to his new agency.

It is clear that Hosch actively solicited his former Corroon & Black clients. That he utilized information gained during his employment with Corroon & Black is not in dispute. This information was of help to him in contacting former customers. Corroon & Black presented testimony that Hosch may have taken detailed information in the expiration lists. Such lists contain names and addresses of policyholders, key personnel to contact, renewal dates and amounts of coverage. . . .

Corroon & Black's customer files were kept in filing cabinets, which were never locked. Expiration lists were kept in cabinets which were locked on rare occasions. There were approximately 75 employees, all of whom had access to these files.

. . .

The jury determined that it was unfair competition for Hosch, an insurance agent, to use customer lists of his former employer to divert clients to his new insurance agency. Corroon & Black emphasizes the unfairness of this situation and asserts that Hosch was untrustworthy. The plaintiff in Gary Van Zeeland Talent, Inc. v. Sandas, 84 Wis.2d 202, 267 N.W.2d 242 (1978), made a similar argument. However, any perceived unfairness should not be the determining factor. As we stated in *Van Zeeland*:

> "[S]o long as a departing employee takes with him no more than his experience and intellectual development that has ensued while being trained by another, and no trade secrets or processes are wrongfully appropriated, the law affords no recourse." Id. at 214.

We also feel compelled to point out that there was no covenant not to compete in effect when Hosch began working for a competitor of Corroon & Black.

Since the protection of a covenant not to compete is not available to Corroon & Black, the outcome in this case necessarily turns on the question of whether the information taken by Hosch was a trade secret.

. . .

[Our] conclusion that an insurance agency's customer list is not a trade secret is consistent with current Wisconsin law, as enunciated in our decisions in Abbott Laboratories v. Norse Chemical Corp., 33 Wis.2d 445, 147 N.W.2d 529 (1967), and Gary Van Zeeland Talent, Inc. v. Sandas, 84 Wis.2d 202, 267 N.W.2d 242 (1978).

In Abbott, an employee took, among other things, a customer list for artificial sweeteners and used it to compete against his former employer. In the Abbott opinion, we noted that the law concerning trade secrecy features two basic themes. Some courts have emphasized the breach of confidence aspect of the law of unfair competition. Usually, however, such cases also involve an assumed trade secret. The second theme is the requirement of the existence of an actual trade secret as the sine qua non of a cause of action for unfair competition. The emphasis is on the nature of the ideas and concepts which employees take with them to their new jobs.

Corroon & Black's analysis in the instant case bears close resemblance to the first theory in trade secret law discussed in *Abbott*. As mentioned previously, Corroon & Black emphasizes the alleged confidentiality of its customer lists and apparently equates confidentiality of information with trade secret status. We find this to be an inaccurate statement of existing law. This court in *Abbott* adopted the Restatement view of the law of trade secrets, finding that it:

> ". . . gives proper balance to the two factors that have cropped up throughout the development of the law of trade secrets." Id. at 456.

In discussing the definition of a trade secret, we quoted with approval the following language from Restatement, 4 *Torts*, § 757, comment b (1939):

> "Some factors to be considered in determining whether given information is one's trade secret are: (1) the extent to which the information is known outside of his business; (2) the extent to which it is known by employees and others involved in his business; (3) the extent of measures taken by him to guard the secrecy of the information; (4) the value of the information to him and to his competitors; (5) the amount of effort or money expended by him in developing the information; (6) the ease or difficulty with which the information could be properly acquired or duplicated by others." Id. at 463–64.

Applying the Restatement definition, this court held that Abbott's customer list was not a trade secret, because it was not sufficiently secret or confidential and because it contained only the names and addresses of the individual to be contacted, rather than complicated marketing data concerning the customer's projected market needs or the customer's market habits.

We also noted that customer lists are the periphery of the law of unfair competition. This is because legal protection would not provide the incentive to compile such lists; most are developed in the normal course of business, anyway.

. . .

We are not unmindful of the fact that the Corroon & Black list may have contained more detailed information than the "bare bones" customer lists in *Abbott* and *Van Zeeland*. However, we do not agree with Corroon & Black's contention that this should be a deciding factor. Even though it contains more than just names and addresses of customers, an insurance agency customer list, such as the one in this case, is not entitled to trade secret protection under Wisconsin law.

Corroon & Black contends that the six Restatement elements are not requirements for trade secret status, but rather are factors under which the defendant must show that a trade secret does not exist. It is argued that the expiration lists qualify as trade secrets under this interpretation of the Restatement definition.

We hold that an insurance agency expiration list does not meet the six-factor Restatement definition of a trade secret. Each of the six factors should indicate that a trade secret exists if the information is to be afforded legal protection.

Corroon & Black asserts that considerable time and money were expended in the development of the information on the expiration lists. In *Abbott* and *Van Zeeland,* we stated that the customer lists in those cases were "merely the outgrowth of normal marketing endeavors" and were "nothing unique or confidential that should be protected in order to prevent competition." *Van Zeeland,* 84 Wis.2d at 217. The court of appeals below correctly determined that the time and money expended by Corroon & Black were spent on the development of the market which the customer list represents, rather than on the compilation of the information. Thus, the fourth and fifth elements of the Restatement definition are lacking. To afford protection to insurance agency customer lists, which are developed in the normal course of business anyway, would be contrary to public policy.

Corroon & Black's president testified that the files were, in his opinion, confidential. However, the evidence shows that most, if not all, of Corroon & Black's employees had access to this information. On this basis, the customer lists fail to meet the Restatement definition under the second and third elements.

Finally, there is some evidence which indicates that the information on many of the larger insurance clients could have been obtained by Hosch and others even without the customer lists.

Aside from the Restatement definition of a trade secret, this court also considered the route-nonroute distinction in *Abbott* and *Van Zeeland.* As we explained in *Abbott,* a nonroute customer is likely to purchase from several suppliers. Courts are less likely to afford protection against "unfair" competition by a former employee, because there is no particular relationship developed between a customer and a salesman (the employer) which is enduring. 33 Wis.2d at 467. In *Van Zeeland* we pointed out that certain professionals, for example, dentists, doctors, attorneys and accountants, may be considered to be covered by the route sales rationale, even though they do not meet the traditional definition of "route salesman."[6]

Corroon & Black asserts that insurance agents are in the route salesman category. We disagree. To the extent that the route-nonroute rationale applies[7] in this situation, it appears that insurance agents are nonroute salesmen. It seems clear to us that many insurance customers do not depend on one agency for all of their insurance needs. Moreover, many persons change companies and agents quite frequently in order to save a few dollars in premium.

. . .

The decision of the court of appeals is affirmed.

■ ABRAHAMSON, JUSTICE (dissenting).

I dissent because the majority has departed, without justification or explanation, from the well-accepted legal principles which this court has previously adopted in trade secret cases and because the majority has not given proper deference to the jury verdict.

I.

In order to evaluate the majority's departure from precedent and the majority's new standard of appellate review of jury verdicts, I will set forth the factual dispute which the jury in this case was called upon to resolve and the jury instructions which provide the legal framework for the jury to use in deciding the issues presented to it.

Corroon & Black presented evidence that Hosch had unlawfully taken and used three types of information:

(1) "Customer lists," that is, lists containing names and addresses of 85 commercial and 113 personal customers that Corroon & Black had assigned to Hosch;

(2) "Expiration lists," that is, lists of the customer policies showing their expiration date; and

(3) Information contained in "insurance agency files," such as:

(a) names of key personnel to contact regarding particular insurance policies;

---

6 "The typical and classical case of a route customer is the relationship between a householder and a milk delivery salesman. In that situation, the householder, during the course of the relationship, typically buys exclusively from the particular salesman; and it is assumed that, therefore, a special personal relationship will develop which will continue even though the salesman should commence his own enterprise or switch employers." Gary Van Zeeland Talent, Inc. v. Sandas, 84 Wis.2d 202, 215, 267 N.W.2d 242 (1978).

7 Apparently the route-nonroute rationale is most often employed in cases where there is a covenant not to compete and the enforceability of the covenant is being questioned. See, Trade Secrets, Customer Contacts and the Employer-Employee Relationship, 37 Ind. L.J. 218, 230 (1961–62).

(b) type and amount of coverage under each policy;

(c) name of insurer providing each type of coverage;

(d) summaries of calls made to customers and information discussed during those calls;

(e) suggestions concerning information that might be discussed with the customer on the next call;

(f) memoranda regarding a customer's problems that would affect the customer's insurance coverage;

(g) the names of insurance companies with which Corroon & Black had placed the customer's insurance business;

(h) the premium charge for each policy;

(i) the commissions on the policies;

(j) the customer's claims history and loss experience;

(k) whether any other insurer had refused to write a particular type of policy for the customer;

(*l*) engineering surveys and information on structures insured;

(m) evaluations of the customer's business indicating potential for additional insurance.

Hosch acknowledged that he had access to all of this information when he worked for Corroon & Black and that the information had value to an insurance agent or agency because it gave the agent or agency a competitive advantage over others in the business. He denied that he took either the expiration lists or the information in the insurance agency files.

. . .

The jury found, by special verdict, that the insurance files of Corroon & Black were of a confidential nature and that Hosch had made unauthorized use of the information in the insurance files.

On appeal, the court of appeals remanded the case to the trial court to enter a judgment notwithstanding the verdict, and the majority here has, to a great extent, adopted the reasoning of the court of appeals. The majority concludes that the trial court erred in failing to find, as a matter of law, that the information in issue does not constitute a trade secret. In reaching its conclusion, the majority alters significantly the substantive law of trade secrets and undermines the established standard used to review jury verdicts.

II.

The majority departs in two significant ways from this court's prior cases which analyze trade secrets. First, the majority fails to follow our prior case law which recognizes that a wide spectrum of information may be protected as a trade secret and that the decision to protect information as a trade secret in a particular case must be determined on the basis of the facts of the case. Second, the majority, contrary to this court's interpretation of the *Abbott*-Restatement test, holds that the information sought to be protected must fulfill each prong of the six-factor test.

This court has consistently reviewed each trade secret case on its own facts, refusing to create "generic" categories of information which are or are not trade secrets.

. . .

The *Abbott*-Restatement formulation of trade secrets does not categorically deny trade secrets protection to information generated in the normal course of business. The Restatement describes a trade secret as "any formula, pattern, device or compilation of information which is used in one's business and which gives him [or her] an opportunity to obtain an advantage over competitors who do not know or use it." (Id. at p. 5, emphasis added) In addition, the six factors all relate to business information. 4 Restatement of Torts, § 757, comment b, p. 6 (1939). Since business information and information used in business are often generated in the normal course of business, I do not construe either *Abbott* or the Restatement as precluding protection for information generated in the normal course of business.

Similarly, the Wisconsin legislature's definition of a "trade secret" includes business information used or for use in business. The legislature does not exclude from the definition of "trade secret" information generated in the normal course of business. § 943.205, Stats. 1979–80, which applies to both civil and criminal cases, defines trade secret as follows:

> " 'Trade secret' means the whole or any portion or phase of any scientific, technical, laboratory, experimental, development or manufacturing information, equipment, tooling, machinery, design, process, procedure, formula or improvement, or any business information used or for use in the conduct of a business, which is manifestly intended by the owner not to be available to anyone other than the owner or persons having access thereto with the owner's consent and which accords or may accord the owner a competitive advantage over other persons." § 943.205(2) (a), Stats. 1979–80 (emphasis added).

If the legislature authorizes punishment as a felony for the theft of information which might have been generated in the ordinary course of business, the majority's enunciation of public policy should not preclude civil protection of information generated in the ordinary course of business.

. . .

The evidence in this case did not necessitate the majority's conclusion that the protection of Hosch's mobility outweighs the protection of Corroon & Black's business. There was no evidence that protecting Corroon & Black's information would have had any impact at all on Hosch's employability in another insurance agency. There was much evidence that eliminating trade secret protection for this information resulted in Corroon & Black's loss of the competitive advantage it had built up through its efforts. The jury made this balance, and the majority opinion gives no adequate explanation for the court's substitution of its conclusion for the jury's.

. . .

ANALYSIS

1. **Reconciling the Cases.** How, if at all, can one rationalize the difference in outcomes in *Corroon & Black* and *Town & Country*?

2. **Does the Industry Matter?** Why is a lawyer like a milk-delivery person? (See footnote 6 and related text of the majority opinion in *Corroon & Black*.)

3. **Trade Secrets.** The majority in *Corroon & Black* opined that "the outcome in this case necessarily turns on the question of whether the information taken by Hosch was a trade secret." Is that correct? Was there a viable alternative theory of liability?

4. **Waivable?** Is the rule in *Corroon & Black* a "default" rule—that is, one that applies only in the absence of an agreement to the contrary? If so, is it the right default rule? Why?

5. **Statutory Impact.** The majority in *Corroon & Black* relies on a definition of trade secrets from the Restatement of Torts. The dissent quotes a Wisconsin statute that makes theft of trade secrets a felony and that contains a definition of trade secrets. The Uniform Trade Secrets Act, which has been adopted in a number of jurisdictions (e.g., Ind. Code §§ 24–2–3–1 to 24–2–3–8) contains the following definition:

   "Trade secret" means information, including a formula, pattern, compilation, program, device, method, technique, or process, that:

   (1) derives independent economic value, actual or potential, from not being generally known to, and not being readily ascertainable by proper means

> **PLANNING**
>
> Suppose that you were practicing law in Wisconsin at the time Corroon & Black was decided. Corroon & Black has just fired its lawyer (for good reason?) and seeks your advice on what, if anything, it might do to protect its customer lists and files in the future. What do you say?

by, other persons who can obtain economic value from its disclosure or use; and

(2) is the subject of efforts that are reasonable under the circumstances to maintain its secrecy.

Would the majority have reached the same result using the definitions in the Uniform Trade Secrets Act or in the Wisconsin felony statute?

6. **Behavioral Implications.** The majority states, customer lists are the periphery of the law of unfair competition. This is because legal protection would not provide the incentive to compile such lists; most are developed in the normal course of business, anyway.

   This implies that legal protection would not affect economic incentives and, thus, would not affect anyone's behavior. Does that seem plausible?

7. **Timing.** What should the outcome in Corroon & Black have been if Hosch had solicited customers for his rival business before leaving Corroon & Black's employment?

5. APPENDICES

RESTATEMENT OF THE LAW (SECOND) AGENCY

Sec.		Page
§ 1.	Agency; Principal; Agent	180
§ 2.	Master; Servant; Independent Contractor	180
§ 3.	General Agent; Special Agent	180
§ 4.	Disclosed Principal; Partially Disclosed Principal; Undisclosed Principal	180
§ 5.	Subagents and Subservants	180
§ 6.	Power	181
§ 7.	Authority	181
§ 8.	Apparent Authority	181
§ 8A.	Inherent Agency Power	181
§ 8B.	Estoppel—Change of Position	181
§ 13.	Agent as a Fiduciary	182
§ 14K.	Agent or Supplier	182
§ 14O.	Security Holder Becoming a Principal	182
§ 26.	Creation of Authority; General Rule	182
§ 27.	Creation of Apparent Authority: General Rule	182
§ 33.	General Principle of Interpretation	182
§ 34.	Circumstances Considered in Interpreting Authority	182
§ 35.	When Incidental Authority Is Inferred	183
§ 82.	Ratification	183
§ 83.	Affirmance	183
§ 144.	General Rule [Principal's Liability in Contract]	183

§ 145. Authorized Representations 183
§ 159. Apparent Authority 183
§ 160. Violation of Secret Instructions 184
§ 161. Unauthorized Acts of General Agent 184
§ 186. General Rule [Liability of Undisclosed Principal] 184
§ 194. Acts of General Agents 184
§ 195. Acts of Manager Appearing to be Owner 184
§ 195A. Unauthorized Acts of Special Agents 184
§ 219. When Master is Liable For Torts of his Servants 185
§ 220. Definition of Servant 185
§ 228. General Statement [Scope of Employment] 186
§ 229. Kind of Conduct Within Scope of Employment 186
§ 230. Forbidden Acts 187
§ 231. Criminal or Tortious Acts 187
§ 376. General Rule [Duties of Agent to Principal] 187
§ 377. Contractual Duties 187
§ 378. Gratuitous Undertakings 187
§ 379. Duty of Care and Skill 187
§ 380. Duty of Good Conduct 187
§ 381. Duty to Give Information 188
§ 382. Duty to Keep and Render Accounts 188
§ 383. Duty to Act Only as Authorized 188
§ 384. Duty Not to Attempt the Impossible or Impracticable 188
§ 385. Duty to Obey 188
§ 386. Duties After Termination of Authority 188
§ 387. General Principle [Duty of Loyalty] 188
§ 388. Duty to Account for Profits Arising Out of Employment 189
§ 389. Acting as Adverse Party Without Principal's Consent 189
§ 390. Acting as Adverse Party With Principal's Consent 189
§ 391. Acting For Adverse Party Without Principal's Consent 189
§ 392. Acting For Adverse Party With Principal's Consent 189
§ 393. Competition as to Subject Matter of Agency 189
§ 394. Acting for One With Conflicting Interests 189
§ 395. Using or Disclosing Confidential Information 189
§ 396. Using Confidential Information After Termination of Agency 190
§ 397. When Agent has Right to Patents 190
§ 398. Confusing or Appearing to Own Principal's Things 190
§ 399. Remedies of Principal 190
§ 400. Liability for Breach of Contract 191
§ 401. Liability for Loss Caused 191
§ 402. Liability for Misuse of Principal's Property 191
§ 403. Liability for Things Received in Violation of Duty of Loyalty 192
§ 404. Liability for Use of Principal's Assets 192

§ 1. Agency; Principal; Agent

(1) Agency is the fiduciary relation which results from the manifestation of consent by one person to another that the other shall act on his behalf and subject to his control, and consent by the other so to act.

(2) The one for whom action is to be taken is the principal.

(3) The one who is to act is the agent.

§ 2. Master; Servant; Independent Contractor

(1) A master is a principal who employs an agent to perform service in his affairs and who controls or has the right to control the physical conduct of the other in the performance of the service.

(2) A servant is an agent employed by a master to perform service in his affairs whose physical conduct in the performance of the service is controlled or is subject to the right to control by the master.

(3) An independent contractor is a person who contracts with another to do something for him but who is not controlled by the other nor subject to the other's right to control with respect to his physical conduct in the performance of the undertaking. He may or may not be an agent.

§ 3. General Agent; Special Agent

(1) A general agent is an agent authorized to conduct a series of transactions involving a continuity of service.

(2) A special agent is an agent authorized to conduct a single transaction or a series of transactions not involving continuity of service.

§ 4. Disclosed Principal; Partially Disclosed Principal; Undisclosed Principal

(1) If, at the time of a transaction conducted by an agent, the other party thereto has notice that the agent is acting for a principal and of the principal's identity, the principal is a disclosed principal.

(2) If the other party has notice that the agent is or may be acting for a principal but has no notice of the principal's identity, the principal for whom the agent is acting is a partially disclosed principal.

(3) If the other party has no notice that the agent is acting for a principal, the one for whom he acts is an undisclosed principal.

§ 5. Subagents and Subservants

(1) A subagent is a person appointed by an agent empowered to do so, to perform functions undertaken by the agent for the principal, but for whose conduct the agent agrees with the principal to be primarily responsible.

(2) A subservant is a person appointed by a servant empowered to do so, to perform functions undertaken by the servant for the master and subject to the control as to his physical conduct both by the master and by the servant, but for whose conduct the servant agrees with the principal to be primarily responsible.

§ 6. Power

A power is an ability on the part of a person to produce a change in a given legal relation by doing or not doing a given act.

§ 7. Authority

Authority is the power of the agent to affect the legal relations of the principal by acts done in accordance with the principal's manifestations of consent to him.

§ 8. Apparent Authority

Apparent authority is the power to affect the legal relations of another person by transactions with third persons, professedly as agent for the other, arising from and in accordance with the other's manifestations to such third persons.

§ 8A. Inherent Agency Power

Inherent agency power is a term used in the restatement of this subject to indicate the power of an agent which is derived not from authority, apparent authority or estoppel, but solely from the agency relation and exists for the protection of persons harmed by or dealing with a servant or other agent.

§ 8B. Estoppel—Change of Position

(1) A person who is not otherwise liable as a party to a transaction purported to be done on his account, is nevertheless subject to liability to persons who have changed their positions because of their belief that the transaction was entered into by or for him, if

(a) he intentionally or carelessly caused such belief, or

(b) knowing of such belief and that others might change their positions because of it, he did not take reasonable steps to notify them of the facts.

(2) An owner of property who represents to third persons that another is the owner of the property or who permits the other so to represent, or who realizes that third persons believe that another is the owner of the property, and that he could easily inform the third persons of the facts, is subject to the loss of the property if the other disposes of it to third persons who, in ignorance of the facts, purchase the property or otherwise change their position with reference to it.

(3) Change of position, as the phrase is used in the restatement of this subject, indicates payment of money, expenditure of labor, suffering a loss or subjection to legal liability.

§ 13. Agent as a Fiduciary

An agent is a fiduciary with respect to matters within the scope of his agency.

§ 14K. Agent or Supplier

One who contracts to acquire property from a third person and convey it to another is the agent of the other only if it is agreed that he is to act primarily for the benefit of the other and not for himself.

§ 14O. Security Holder Becoming a Principal

A creditor who assumes control of his debtor's business for the mutual benefit of himself and his debtor, may become a principal, with liability for the acts and transactions of the debtor in connection with the business.

§ 26. Creation of Authority; General Rule

Except for the execution of instruments under seal or for the performance of transactions required by statute to be authorized in a particular way, authority to do an act can be created by written or spoken words or other conduct of the principal which, reasonably interpreted, causes the agent to believe that the principal desires him so to act on the principal's account.

§ 27. Creation of Apparent Authority: General Rule

Except for the execution of instruments under seal or for the conduct of transactions required by statute to be authorized in a particular way, apparent authority to do an act is created as to a third person by written or spoken words or any other conduct of the principal which, reasonably interpreted, causes the third person to believe that the principal consents to have the act done on his behalf by the person purporting to act for him.

§ 33. General Principle of Interpretation

An agent is authorized to do, and to do only, what it is reasonable for him to infer that the principal desires him to do in the light of the principal's manifestations and the facts as he knows or should know them at the time he acts.

§ 34. Circumstances Considered in Interpreting Authority

An authorization is interpreted in light of all accompanying circumstances, including among other matters:

(a) the situation of the parties, their relations to one another, and the business in which they are engaged;

(b) the general usages of business, the usages of trades or employments of the kind to which the authorization relates, and the business methods of the principal;

(c) facts of which the agent has notice respecting the objects which the principal desires to accomplish;

(d) the nature of the subject matter, the circumstances under which the act is to be performed and the legality or illegality of the act; and

(e) the formality or informality, and the care, or lack of it, with which an instrument evidencing the authority is drawn.

§ 35. When Incidental Authority Is Inferred

Unless otherwise agreed, authority to conduct a transaction includes authority to do acts which are incidental to it, usually accompany it, or are reasonably necessary to accomplish it.

§ 82. Ratification

Ratification is the affirmance by a person of a prior act which did not bind him but which was done or professedly done on his account, whereby the act, as to some or all persons, is given effect as if originally authorized by him.

§ 83. Affirmance

Affirmance is either

(a) a manifestation of an election by one on whose account an unauthorized act has been done to treat the act as authorized, or

(b) conduct by him justifiable only if there were such an election.

§ 144. General Rule [Principal's Liability in Contract]

A disclosed or partially disclosed principal is subject to liability upon contracts made by an agent acting within his authority if made in proper form and with the understanding that the principal is a party.

§ 145. Authorized Representations

In actions brought upon a contract or to rescind a contract or conveyance to which he is a party, a disclosed or partially disclosed principal is responsible for authorized representations of an agent made in connection with it as if made by himself, subject to the rules as to the effect of knowledge of, and notifications given to, the agent.

§ 159. Apparent Authority

A disclosed or partially disclosed principal is subject to liability upon contracts made by an agent acting within his apparent authority if made in proper form and with the understanding that the apparent principal is a party. The rules as to the liability of a principal for authorized acts, are applicable to unauthorized acts which are apparently authorized.

§ 160. Violation of Secret Instructions

A disclosed or partially disclosed principal authorizing an agent to make a contract, but imposing upon him limitations as to incidental terms intended not to be revealed, is subject to liability upon a contract made in violation of such limitations with a third person who has no notice of them.

§ 161. Unauthorized Acts of General Agent

A general agent for a disclosed or partially disclosed principal subjects his principal to liability for acts done on his account which usually accompany or are incidental to transactions which the agent is authorized to conduct if, although they are forbidden by the principal, the other party reasonably believes that the agent is authorized to do them and has no notice that he is not so authorized.

§ 186. General Rule [Liability of Undisclosed Principal]

An undisclosed principal is bound by contracts and conveyances made on his account by an agent acting within his authority, except that the principal is not bound by a contract which is under seal or which is negotiable, or upon a contract which excludes him.

§ 194. Acts of General Agents

A general agent for an undisclosed principal authorized to conduct transactions subjects his principal to liability for acts done on his account, if usual or necessary in such transactions, although forbidden by the principal to do them.

§ 195. Acts of Manager Appearing to be Owner

An undisclosed principal who entrusts an agent with the management of his business is subject to liability to third persons with whom the agent enters into transactions usual in such businesses and on the principal's account, although contrary to the directions of the principal.

§ 195A. Unauthorized Acts of Special Agents

A special agent for an undisclosed principal has no power to bind his principal by contracts or conveyances which he is not authorized to make unless:

(a) the agent's only departure from his authority is

(i) in not disclosing his principal, or

(ii) in having an improper motive, or

(iii) in being negligent in determining the facts upon which his authority is based, or

(iv) in making misrepresentations; or

(b) the agent is given possession of goods or commercial documents with authority to deal with them.

§ 219. When Master is Liable For Torts of his Servants

(1) A master is subject to liability for the torts of his servants committed while acting in the scope of their employment.

(2) A master is not subject to liability for the torts of his servants acting outside the scope of their employment, unless:

(a) the master intended the conduct or the consequences, or

(b) the master was negligent or reckless, or

(c) the conduct violated a non-delegable duty of the master, or

(d) the servant purported to act or to speak on behalf of the principal and there was reliance upon apparent authority, or he was aided in accomplishing the tort by the existence of the agency relation.

§ 220. Definition of Servant

(1) A servant is a person employed to perform services in the affairs of another and who with respect to the physical conduct in the performance of the services is subject to the other's control or right to control.

(2) In determining whether one acting for another is a servant or an independent contractor, the following matters of fact, among others, are considered:

(a) the extent of control which, by the agreement, the master may exercise over the details of the work;

(b) whether or not the one employed is engaged in a distinct occupation or business;

(c) the kind of occupation, with reference to whether, in the locality, the work is usually done under the direction of the employer or by a specialist without supervision;

(d) the skill required in the particular occupation;

(e) whether the employer or the workman supplies the instrumentalities, tools, and the place of work for the person doing the work;

(f) the length of time for which the person is employed;

(g) the method of payment, whether by the time or by the job;

(h) whether or not the work is a part of the regular business of the employer;

(i) whether or not the parties believe they are creating the relation of master and servant; and

(j) whether the principal is or is not in business.

§ 228. General Statement [Scope of Employment]

(1) Conduct of a servant is within the scope of employment if, but only if:

(a) it is of the kind he is employed to perform;

(b) it occurs substantially within the authorized time and space limits;

(c) it is actuated, at least in part, by a purpose to serve the master; and

(d) if force is intentionally used by the servant against another, the use of force is not unexpectable by the master.

(2) Conduct of a servant is not within the scope of employment if it is different in kind from that authorized, far beyond the authorized time or space limits, or too little actuated by a purpose to serve the master.

§ 229. Kind of Conduct Within Scope of Employment

(1) To be within the scope of the employment, conduct must be of the same general nature as that authorized, or incidental to the conduct authorized.

(2) In determining whether or not the conduct, although not authorized, is nevertheless so similar to or incidental to the conduct authorized as to be within the scope of employment, the following matters of fact are to be considered:

(a) whether or not the act is one commonly done by such servants;

(b) the time, place and purpose of the act;

(c) the previous relations between the master and the servant;

(d) the extent to which the business of the master is apportioned between different servants;

(e) whether or not the act is outside the enterprise of the master or, if within the enterprise, has not been entrusted to any servant;

(f) whether or not the master has reason to expect that such an act will be done;

(g) the similarity in quality of the act done to the act authorized;

(h) whether or not the instrumentality by which the harm is done has been furnished by the master to the servant;

(i) the extent of departure from the normal method of accomplishing an authorized result; and

(j) whether or not the act is seriously criminal.

§ 230. Forbidden Acts

An act, although forbidden, or done in a forbidden manner, may be within the scope of employment.

§ 231. Criminal or Tortious Acts

An act may be within the scope of employment although consciously criminal or tortious.

§ 376. General Rule [Duties of Agent to Principal]

The existence and extent of the duties of the agent to the principal are determined by the terms of the agreement between the parties, interpreted in light of the circumstances under which it is made, except to the extent that fraud, duress, illegality, or the incapacity of one or both of the parties to the agreement modifies it or deprives it of legal effect.

§ 377. Contractual Duties

A person who makes a contract with another to perform services as an agent for him is subject to a duty to act in accordance with his promise.

§ 378. Gratuitous Undertakings

One who, by a gratuitous promise or other conduct which he should realize will cause another reasonably to rely upon the performance of definite acts of service by him as the other's agent, causes the other to refrain from having such acts done by other available means is subject to a duty to use care to perform such service or, while other means are available, to give notice that he will not perform.

§ 379. Duty of Care and Skill

(1) Unless otherwise agreed, a paid agent is subject to a duty to the principal to act with standard care and with the skill which is standard in the locality for the kind of work which he is employed to perform and, in addition, to exercise any special skill that he has.

(2) Unless otherwise agreed, a gratuitous agent is under a duty to the principal to act with the care and skill which is required of persons not agents performing similar gratuitous undertakings for others.

§ 380. Duty of Good Conduct

Unless otherwise agreed, an agent is subject to a duty not to conduct himself with such impropriety that he brings disrepute upon the principal or upon the business in which he is engaged. If the service involves personal relations, he has a duty not to act in such a way as to make continued friendly relations with the principal impossible.

§ 381. Duty to Give Information

Unless otherwise agreed, an agent is subject to a duty to use reasonable efforts to give his principal information which is relevant to affairs entrusted to him and which, as the agent has notice, the principal would desire to have and which can be communicated without violating a superior duty to a third person.

§ 382. Duty to Keep and Render Accounts

Unless otherwise agreed, an agent is subject to a duty to keep, and render to his principal, an account of money or other things which he has received or paid out on behalf of the principal.

§ 383. Duty to Act Only as Authorized

Except when he is privileged to protect his own or another's interests, an agent is subject to a duty to the principal not to act in the principal's affairs except in accordance with the principal's manifestation of consent.

§ 384. Duty Not to Attempt the Impossible or Impracticable

Unless otherwise agreed, an agent is subject to a duty to the principal not to continue to render service which subjects the principal to risk of expense if it reasonably appears to him to be impossible or impracticable for him to accomplish the objects of the principal and if he cannot communicate with the principal.

§ 385. Duty to Obey

(1) Unless otherwise agreed, an agent is subject to a duty to obey all reasonable directions in regard to the manner of performing a service that he has contracted to perform.

(2) Unless he is privileged to protect his own or another's interests, an agent is subject to a duty not to act in matters entrusted to him on account of the principal contrary to the directions of the principal, even though the terms of the employment prescribe that such directions shall not be given.

§ 386. Duties After Termination of Authority

Unless otherwise agreed, an agent is subject to a duty not to act as such after the termination of his authority.

§ 387. General Principle [Duty of Loyalty]

Unless otherwise agreed, an agent is subject to a duty to his principal to act solely for the benefit of the principal in all matters connected with his agency.

§ 388. Duty to Account for Profits Arising Out of Employment

Unless otherwise agreed, an agent who makes a profit in connection with transactions conducted by him on behalf of the principal is under a duty to give such profit to the principal.

§ 389. Acting as Adverse Party Without Principal's Consent

Unless otherwise agreed, an agent is subject to a duty not to deal with his principal as an adverse party in a transaction connected with his agency without the principal's knowledge.

§ 390. Acting as Adverse Party With Principal's Consent

An agent who, to the knowledge of the principal, acts on his own account in a transaction in which he is employed has a duty to deal fairly with the principal and to disclose to him all facts which the agent knows or should know would reasonably affect the principal's judgment, unless the principal has manifested that he knows such facts or that he does not care to know them.

§ 391. Acting For Adverse Party Without Principal's Consent

Unless otherwise agreed, an agent is subject to a duty to his principal not to act on behalf of an adverse party in a transaction connected with his agency without the principal's knowledge.

§ 392. Acting For Adverse Party With Principal's Consent

An agent who, to the knowledge of two principals, acts for both of them in a transaction between them, has a duty to act with fairness to each and to disclose to each all facts which he knows or should know would reasonably affect the judgment of each in permitting such dual agency, except as to a principal who has manifested that he knows such facts or does not care to know them.

§ 393. Competition as to Subject Matter of Agency

Unless otherwise agreed, an agent is subject to a duty not to compete with the principal concerning the subject matter of his agency.

§ 394. Acting for One With Conflicting Interests

Unless otherwise agreed, an agent is subject to a duty not to act or to agree to act during the period of his agency for persons whose interests conflict with those of the principal in matters in which the agent is employed.

§ 395. Using or Disclosing Confidential Information

Unless otherwise agreed, an agent is subject to a duty to the principal not to use or to communicate information confidentially given him by the principal or acquired by him during the course of or on account of his agency or in violation of his duties as agent, in competition with or to the injury of the principal, on his own account or on behalf of another, although such information does not relate to the transaction in which he is then employed, unless the information is a matter of general knowledge.

§ 396. Using Confidential Information After Termination of Agency

Unless otherwise agreed, after the termination of the agency, the agent:

(a) has no duty not to compete with the principal;

(b) has a duty to the principal not to use or to disclose to third persons, on his own account or on account of others, in competition with the principal or to his injury, trade secrets, written lists of names, or other similar confidential matters given to him only for the principal's use or acquired by the agent in violation of duty. The agent is entitled to use general information concerning the method of business of the principal and the names of the customers retained in his memory, if not acquired in violation of his duty as agent;

(c) has a duty to account for profits made by the sale or use of trade secrets and other confidential information, whether or not in competition with the principal;

(d) has a duty to the principal not to take advantage of a still subsisting confidential relation created during the prior agency relation.

§ 397. When Agent has Right to Patents

Unless otherwise agreed, a person employed by another to do noninventive work is entitled to patents which are the result of his invention although the invention is due to the work for which he is employed.

§ 398. Confusing or Appearing to Own Principal's Things

Unless otherwise agreed, an agent receiving or holding things on behalf of the principal is subject to a duty to the principal not to receive or deal with them so that they will appear to be his own, and not so to mingle them with his own things as to destroy their identity.

§ 399. Remedies of Principal

A principal whose agent has violated or threatens to violate his duties has an appropriate remedy for such violation. Such remedy may be:

(a) an action on the contract of service;

(b) an action for losses and for the misuse of property;

(c) an action in equity to enforce the provisions of an express trust undertaken by the agent;

(d) an action for restitution, either at law or in equity;

(e) an action for an accounting;

(f) an action for an injunction;

(g) set-off or counterclaim;

(h) causing the agent to be made party to an action brought by a third person against the principal;

(i) self-help;

(j) discharge; or

(k) refusal to pay compensation or rescission of the contract of employment.

§ 400. Liability for Breach of Contract

An agent who commits a breach of his contract with his principal is subject to liability to the principal in accordance with the principles stated in the Restatement of Contracts.

§ 401. Liability for Loss Caused

An agent is subject to liability for loss caused to the principal by any breach of duty.

§ 402. Liability for Misuse of Principal's Property

(1) An agent is subject to liability to the principal for the value of a chattel, a chose in action, or money which he holds for the principal and to the immediate possession of which the principal is entitled, together with interest thereon if the amount is liquidated, or damages, if the agent:

(a) intentionally or negligently destroys it or causes its loss;

(b) uses it for his own purposes under an adverse claim;

(c) unreasonably refuses to surrender it on demand;

(d) manifests that he will not surrender it except on conditions which he is not privileged to exact;

(e) makes delivery of it to a person to whom he is not authorized to deliver it;

(f) improperly causes the title or indicia of title to be placed in his own name, if either this is done in bad faith or the thing substantially depreciates in value while the title is so held because of his wrongful conduct;

(g) deviates substantially from his authority in its transfer to a third person in a sale or purchase; or

(h) intentionally and substantially deviates from his authority in dealing with the possession of the thing, and the chattel suffers substantial harm during the course of such wrongful dealing or because of it.

(2) An agent who deviates substantially from his authority in the transfer of land belonging to the principal or who, in bad faith, causes the title of such land to be placed in his own name, is subject to liability to the principal for the value of the land.

§ 403. Liability for Things Received in Violation of Duty of Loyalty

If an agent receives anything as a result of his violation of a duty of loyalty to the principal, he is subject to a liability to deliver it, its value, or its proceeds, to the principal.

§ 404. Liability for Use of Principal's Assets

An agent who, in violation of duty to his principal, uses for his own purposes or those of a third person assets of the principal's business is subject to liability to the principal for the value of the use. If the use predominates in producing a profit he is subject to liability, at the principal's election, for such profit; he is not, however, liable for profits made by him merely by the use of time which he has contracted to devote to the principal unless he violates his duty not to act adversely or in competition with the principal.

RESTATEMENT OF THE LAW (THIRD) AGENCY

Sec.		Page
CHAPTER 1. INTRODUCTORY MATTERS		194
§ 1.01	Agency Defined	194
§ 1.02	Parties' Labeling and Popular Usage Not Controlling	194
§ 1.03	Manifestation	194
§ 1.04	Terminology	194
CHAPTER 2. PRINCIPLES OF ATTRIBUTION		195
§ 2.01	Actual Authority	195
§ 2.02	Scope of Actual Authority	196
§ 2.03	Apparent Authority	196
§ 2.04	Respondeat Superior	196
§ 2.05	Estoppel to Deny Existence of Agency Relationship	196
§ 2.06	Liability of Undisclosed Principal	197
§ 2.07	Restitution of Benefit	197

CHAPTER 3. CREATION AND TERMINATION OF AUTHORITY AND AGENCY RELATIONSHIPS 197
§ 3.01 Creation of Actual Authority 197
§ 3.02 Formal Requirements 198
§ 3.03 Creation of Apparent Authority 198
§ 3.04 Capacity to Act as Principal 198
§ 3.05 Capacity to Act as Agent 198
§ 3.15 Subagency 198
§ 3.16 Agent For Coprincipals 199

CHAPTER 4. RATIFICATION 199
§ 4.01 Ratification Defined 199
§ 4.02 Effect of Ratification 199
§ 4.03 Acts That May Be Ratified 199
§ 4.04 Capacity to Ratify 200
§ 4.05 Timing of Ratification 200
§ 4.06 Knowledge Requisite to Ratification 200
§ 4.07 No Partial Ratification 200
§ 4.08 Estoppel to Deny Ratification 200

CHAPTER 5. NOTIFICATIONS AND NOTICE 200
§ 5.01 Notifications and Notice—In General 200
§ 5.02 Notification Given by or to an Agent 201
§ 5.03 Imputation of Notice of Fact to Principal 201
§ 5.04 An Agent Who Acts Adversely to a Principal 201

CHAPTER 6. CONTRACTS AND OTHER TRANSACTIONS WITH THIRD PARTIES 202
§ 6.01 Agent for Disclosed Principal 202
§ 6.02 Agent for Unidentified Principal 202
§ 6.03 Agent for Undisclosed Principal 202
§ 6.04 Principal Does Not Exist or Lacks Capacity 202
§ 6.10 Agent's Implied Warranty of Authority 202
§ 6.11 Agent's Representations 203

CHAPTER 7. TORTS—LIABILITY OF AGENT AND PRINCIPAL 204
§ 7.01 Agent's Liability to Third Party 204
§ 7.03 Principal's Liability—In General 204
§ 7.04 Agent Acts With Actual Authority 204
§ 7.05 Principal's Negligence in Conducting Activity Through Agent; Principal's Special Relationship With Another Person 205
§ 7.07 Employee Acting Within Scope of Employment 205

CHAPTER 8. DUTIES OF AGENT AND PRINCIPAL TO EACH OTHER 206
§ 8.01 General Fiduciary Principle 206
§ 8.02 Material Benefit Arising Out of Position 206
§ 8.03 Acting as or on Behalf of an Adverse Party 206
§ 8.04 Competition 206

§ 8.05 Use of Principal's Property; Use of Confidential Information 206
§ 8.06 Principal's Consent 206
§ 8.07 Duty Created by Contract 207
§ 8.08 Duties of Care, Competence, and Diligence 207
§ 8.09 Duty to Act Only Within Scope of Actual Authority and to Comply With Principal's Lawful Instructions 207
§ 8.10 Duty of Good Conduct 208
§ 8.11 Duty to Provide Information 208
§ 8.14 Duty to Indemnify 208
§ 8.15 Principal's Duty to Deal Fairly and in Good Faith 208

CHAPTER 1. INTRODUCTORY MATTERS

§ 1.01 Agency Defined

Agency is the fiduciary relationship that arises when one person (a "principal") manifests assent to another person (an "agent") that the agent shall act on the principal's behalf and subject to the principal's control, and the agent manifests assent or otherwise consents so to act.

§ 1.02 Parties' Labeling and Popular Usage Not Controlling

An agency relationship arises only when the elements stated in § 1.01 are present. Whether a relationship is characterized as agency in an agreement between parties or in the context of industry or popular usage is not controlling.

§ 1.03 Manifestation

A person manifests assent or intention through written or spoken words or other conduct.

§ 1.04 Terminology

(1) *Coagents.* Coagents have agency relationships with the same principal. A coagent may be appointed by the principal or by another agent actually or apparently authorized by the principal to do so.

(2) *Disclosed, undisclosed, and unidentified principals.*

(a) *Disclosed principal.* A principal is disclosed if, when an agent and a third party interact, the third party has notice that the agent is acting for a principal and has notice of the principal's identity.

(b) *Undisclosed principal.* A principal is undisclosed if, when an agent and a third party interact, the third party has no notice that the agent is acting for a principal.

(c) *Unidentified principal.* A principal is unidentified if, when an agent and a third party interact, the third party has notice that the agent is acting for a principal but does not have notice of the principal's identity.

(3) *Gratuitous agent.* A gratuitous agent acts without a right to compensation.

(4) *Notice.* A person has notice of a fact if the person knows the fact, has reason to know the fact, has received an effective notification of the fact, or should know the fact to fulfill a duty owed to another person. Notice of a fact that an agent knows or has reason to know is imputed to the principal as stated in § § 5.03 and 5.04. A notification given to or by an agent is effective as notice to or by the principal as stated in § 5.02.

(5) *Person.* A person is (a) an individual; (b) an organization or association that has legal capacity to possess rights and incur obligations; (c) a government, political subdivision, or instrumentality or entity created by government; or (d) any other entity that has legal capacity to possess rights and incur obligations.

(6) *Power given as security.* A power given as security is a power to affect the legal relations of its creator that is created in the form of a manifestation of actual authority and held for the benefit of the holder or a third person. It is given to protect a legal or equitable title or to secure the performance of a duty apart from any duties owed the holder of the power by its creator that are incident to a relationship of agency under § 1.01.

(7) *Power of attorney.* A power of attorney is an instrument that states an agent's authority.

(8) *Subagent.* A subagent is a person appointed by an agent to perform functions that the agent has consented to perform on behalf of the agent's principal and for whose conduct the appointing agent is responsible to the principal. The relationship between an appointing agent and a subagent is one of agency, created as stated in § 1.01.

(9) *Superior and subordinate coagents.* A superior coagent has the right, conferred by the principal, to direct a subordinate coagent.

(10) *Trustee and agent-trustee.* A trustee is a holder of property who is subject to fiduciary duties to deal with the property for the benefit of charity or for one or more persons, at least one of whom is not the sole trustee. An agent-trustee is a trustee subject to the control of the settlor or of one or more beneficiaries.

CHAPTER 2. PRINCIPLES OF ATTRIBUTION

§ 2.01 Actual Authority

An agent acts with actual authority when, at the time of taking action that has legal consequences for the principal, the agent reasonably believes, in accordance with the principal's manifestations to the agent, that the principal wishes the agent so to act.

§ 2.02 Scope of Actual Authority

(1) An agent has actual authority to take action designated or implied in the principal's manifestations to the agent and acts necessary or incidental to achieving the principal's objectives, as the agent reasonably understands the principal's manifestations and objectives when the agent determines how to act.

(2) An agent's interpretation of the principal's manifestations is reasonable if it reflects any meaning known by the agent to be ascribed by the principal and, in the absence of any meaning known to the agent, as a reasonable person in the agent's position would interpret the manifestations in light of the context, including circumstances of which the agent has notice and the agent's fiduciary duty to the principal.

(3) An agent's understanding of the principal's objectives is reasonable if it accords with the principal's manifestations and the inferences that a reasonable person in the agent's position would draw from the circumstances creating the agency.

§ 2.03 Apparent Authority

Apparent authority is the power held by an agent or other actor to affect a principal's legal relations with third parties when a third party reasonably believes the actor has authority to act on behalf of the principal and that belief is traceable to the principal's manifestations.

§ 2.04 Respondeat Superior

An employer is subject to liability for torts committed by employees while acting within the scope of their employment.

Comment:

a. *Terminology and cross-references*. This Restatement does not use the terminology of "master" and "servant." Section 7.07(3) defines "employee" for purposes of this doctrine. Section 7.07(2) states the circumstances under which an employee has acted within the scope of employment. Section 7.08 states the circumstances under which a principal is subject to vicarious liability for a tort committed by an agent, whether or not an employee, when actions taken with apparent authority constituted the tort or enabled the agent to conceal its commission.

§ 2.05 Estoppel to Deny Existence of Agency Relationship

A person who has not made a manifestation that an actor has authority as an agent and who is not otherwise liable as a party to a transaction purportedly done by the actor on that person's account is subject to liability to a third party who justifiably is induced to make a detrimental change in position because the transaction is believed to be on the person's account, if

(1) the person intentionally or carelessly caused such belief, or

(2) having notice of such belief and that it might induce others to change their positions, the person did not take reasonable steps to notify them of the facts.

§ 2.06 Liability of Undisclosed Principal

(1) An undisclosed principal is subject to liability to a third party who is justifiably induced to make a detrimental change in position by an agent acting on the principal's behalf and without actual authority if the principal, having notice of the agent's conduct and that it might induce others to change their positions, did not take reasonable steps to notify them of the facts.

(2) An undisclosed principal may not rely on instructions given an agent that qualify or reduce the agent's authority to less than the authority a third party would reasonably believe the agent to have under the same circumstances if the principal had been disclosed.

NOTE

Comment a to § 3.06 states: "An agent's actual authority is premised upon a manifestation of assent made by the principal, in accordance with which the agent reasonably believes the principal wishes the agent to take action. Several distinct types of events terminate an agent's actual authority. . . . First, a principal and an agent may agree to terminate the agent's actual authority either as of the time of agreement or upon the future occurrence of specified circumstances. Second, notwithstanding any agreement between principal and agent, either may terminate the agent's actual authority by a manifestation to the other. Third, an individual principal's death or loss of legal capacity terminates the agent's actual authority, as does cessation of existence or suspension of powers of a nonindividual principal. An agent's death or cessation of existence or suspension of powers also terminates the agent's actual authority. Finally, a statute may provide that an agent's actual authority will terminate upon the occurrence of circumstances specified by the statute, including the impact of divorce upon a spouse's actual authority to act on behalf of the other spouse. Such statutes are beyond the scope of this Restatement." (Citations omitted)

§ 2.07 Restitution of Benefit

If a principal is unjustly enriched at the expense of another person by the action of an agent or a person who appears to be an agent, the principal is subject to a claim for restitution by that person.

CHAPTER 3. CREATION AND TERMINATION OF AUTHORITY AND AGENCY RELATIONSHIPS

§ 3.01 Creation of Actual Authority

Actual authority, as defined in § 2.01, is created by a principal's manifestation to an agent that, as reasonably understood by the agent, expresses the principal's assent that the agent take action on the principal's behalf.

§ 3.02 Formal Requirements

If the law requires a writing or record signed by the principal to evidence an agent's authority to bind a principal to a contract or other transaction, the principal is not bound in the absence of such a writing or record. A principal may be estopped to assert the lack of such a writing or record when a third party has been induced to make a detrimental change in position by the reasonable belief that an agent has authority to bind the principal that is traceable to a manifestation made by the principal.

§ 3.03 Creation of Apparent Authority

Apparent authority, as defined in § 2.03, is created by a person's manifestation that another has authority to act with legal consequences for the person who makes the manifestation, when a third party reasonably believes the actor to be authorized and the belief is traceable to the manifestation.

§ 3.04 Capacity to Act as Principal

(1) An individual has capacity to act as principal in a relationship of agency as defined in § 1.01 if, at the time the agent takes action, the individual would have capacity if acting in person.

(2) The law applicable to a person that is not an individual governs whether the person has capacity to be a principal in a relationship of agency as defined in § 1.01, as well as the effect of the person's lack or loss of capacity on those who interact with it.

(3) If performance of an act is not delegable, its performance by an agent does not constitute performance by the principal.

§ 3.05 Capacity to Act as Agent

Any person may ordinarily be empowered to act so as to affect the legal relations of another. The actor's capacity governs the extent to which, by so acting, the actor becomes subject to duties and liabilities to the person whose legal relations are affected or to third parties.

* * *

§ 3.15 Subagency

(1) A subagent is a person appointed by an agent to perform functions that the agent has consented to perform on behalf of the agent's principal and for whose conduct the appointing agent is responsible to the principal. The relationships between a subagent and the appointing agent and between the subagent and the appointing agent's principal are relationships of agency as stated in § 1.01.

(2) An agent may appoint a subagent only if the agent has actual or apparent authority to do so.

§ 3.16 Agent For Coprincipals

Two or more persons may as coprincipals appoint an agent to act for them in the same transaction or matter.

CHAPTER 4. RATIFICATION

§ 4.01 Ratification Defined

(1) Ratification is the affirmance of a prior act done by another, whereby the act is given effect as if done by an agent acting with actual authority.

(2) A person ratifies an act by

(a) manifesting assent that the act shall affect the person's legal relations, or

(b) conduct that justifies a reasonable assumption that the person so consents.

(3) Ratification does not occur unless

(a) the act is ratifiable as stated in § 4.03,

(b) the person ratifying has capacity as stated in § 4.04,

(c) the ratification is timely as stated in § 4.05, and

(d) the ratification encompasses the act in its entirety as stated in § 4.07.

§ 4.02 Effect of Ratification

(1) Subject to the exceptions stated in subsection (2), ratification retroactively creates the effects of actual authority.

(2) Ratification is not effective:

(a) in favor of a person who causes it by misrepresentation or other conduct that would make a contract voidable;

(b) in favor of an agent against a principal when the principal ratifies to avoid a loss; or

(c) to diminish the rights or other interests of persons, not parties to the transaction, that were acquired in the subject matter prior to the ratification.

§ 4.03 Acts That May Be Ratified

A person may ratify an act if the actor acted or purported to act as an agent on the person's behalf.

§ 4.04 Capacity to Ratify

(1) A person may ratify an act if

(a) the person existed at the time of the act, and

(b) the person had capacity as defined in § 3.04 at the time of ratifying the act.

(2) At a later time, a principal may avoid a ratification made earlier when the principal lacked capacity as defined in § 3.04.

§ 4.05 Timing of Ratification

A ratification of a transaction is not effective unless it precedes the occurrence of circumstances that would cause the ratification to have adverse and inequitable effects on the rights of third parties. These circumstances include:

(1) any manifestation of intention to withdraw from the transaction made by the third party;

(2) any material change in circumstances that would make it inequitable to bind the third party, unless the third party chooses to be bound; and

(3) a specific time that determines whether a third party is deprived of a right or subjected to a liability.

§ 4.06 Knowledge Requisite to Ratification

A person is not bound by a ratification made without knowledge of material facts involved in the original act when the person was unaware of such lack of knowledge.

§ 4.07 No Partial Ratification

A ratification is not effective unless it encompasses the entirety of an act, contract, or other single transaction.

§ 4.08 Estoppel to Deny Ratification

If a person makes a manifestation that the person has ratified another's act and the manifestation, as reasonably understood by a third party, induces the third party to make a detrimental change in position, the person may be estopped to deny the ratification.

CHAPTER 5. NOTIFICATIONS AND NOTICE

§ 5.01 Notifications and Notice—In General

(1) A notification is a manifestation that is made in the form required by agreement among parties or by applicable law, or in a reasonable manner in the absence of an agreement or an applicable law, with the intention of affecting the legal rights and duties of the notifier

in relation to rights and duties of persons to whom the notification is given.

(2) A notification given to or by an agent is effective as notification to or by the principal as stated in § 5.02.

(3) A person has notice of a fact if the person knows the fact, has reason to know the fact, has received an effective notification of the fact, or should know the fact to fulfill a duty owed to another person.

(4) Notice of a fact that an agent knows or has reason to know is imputed to the principal as stated in § § 5.03 and 5.04.

§ 5.02 Notification Given by or to an Agent

(1) A notification given to an agent is effective as notice to the principal if the agent has actual or apparent authority to receive the notification, unless the person who gives the notification knows or has reason to know that the agent is acting adversely to the principal as stated in § 5.04.

(2) A notification given by an agent is effective as notification given by the principal if the agent has actual or apparent authority to give the notification, unless the person who receives the notification knows or has reason to know that the agent is acting adversely to the principal as stated in § 5.04.

§ 5.03 Imputation of Notice of Fact to Principal

For purposes of determining a principal's legal relations with a third party, notice of a fact that an agent knows or has reason to know is imputed to the principal if knowledge of the fact is material to the agent's duties to the principal, unless the agent

(a) acts adversely to the principal as stated in § 5.04, or

(b) is subject to a duty to another not to disclose the fact to the principal.

§ 5.04 An Agent Who Acts Adversely to a Principal

For purposes of determining a principal's legal relations with a third party, notice of a fact that an agent knows or has reason to know is not imputed to the principal if the agent acts adversely to the principal in a transaction or matter, intending to act solely for the agent's own purposes or those of another person. Nevertheless, notice is imputed

(a) when necessary to protect the rights of a third party who dealt with the principal in good faith; or

(b) when the principal has ratified or knowingly retained a benefit from the agent's action.

A third party who deals with a principal through an agent, knowing or having reason to know that the agent acts adversely to the principal, does not deal in good faith for this purpose.

CHAPTER 6. CONTRACTS AND OTHER TRANSACTIONS WITH THIRD PARTIES

§ 6.01 Agent for Disclosed Principal

When an agent acting with actual or apparent authority makes a contract on behalf of a disclosed principal,

(1) the principal and the third party are parties to the contract; and

(2) the agent is not a party to the contract unless the agent and third party agree otherwise.

§ 6.02 Agent for Unidentified Principal

When an agent acting with actual or apparent authority makes a contract on behalf of an unidentified principal,

(1) the principal and the third party are parties to the contract; and

(2) the agent is a party to the contract unless the agent and the third party agree otherwise.

§ 6.03 Agent for Undisclosed Principal

When an agent acting with actual authority makes a contract on behalf of an undisclosed principal,

(1) unless excluded by the contract, the principal is a party to the contract;

(2) the agent and the third party are parties to the contract; and

(3) the principal, if a party to the contract, and the third party have the same rights, liabilities, and defenses against each other as if the principal made the contract personally, subject to § § 6.05–6.09.

§ 6.04 Principal Does Not Exist or Lacks Capacity

Unless the third party agrees otherwise, a person who makes a contract with a third party purportedly as an agent on behalf of a principal becomes a party to the contract if the purported agent knows or has reason to know that the purported principal does not exist or lacks capacity to be a party to a contract.

* * *

§ 6.10 Agent's Implied Warranty of Authority

A person who purports to make a contract, representation, or conveyance to or with a third party on behalf of another person, lacking power to bind that person, gives an implied warranty of authority to the third party and is subject to liability to the third party for damages for loss caused by breach of that warranty, including loss of the benefit expected from performance by the principal, unless

(1) the principal or purported principal ratifies the act as stated in § 4.01; or

(2) the person who purports to make the contract, representation, or conveyance gives notice to the third party that no warranty of authority is given; or

(3) the third party knows that the person who purports to make the contract, representation, or conveyance acts without actual authority.

§ 6.11 Agent's Representations

(1) When an agent for a disclosed or unidentified principal makes a false representation about the agent's authority to a third party, the principal is not subject to liability unless the agent acted with actual or apparent authority in making the representation and the third party does not have notice that the agent's representation is false.

(2) A representation by an agent made incident to a contract or conveyance is attributed to a disclosed or unidentified principal as if the principal made the representation directly when the agent had actual or apparent authority to make the contract or conveyance unless the third party knew or had reason to know that the representation was untrue or that the agent acted without actual authority in making it.

(3) A representation by an agent made incident to a contract or conveyance is attributed to an undisclosed principal as if the principal made the representation directly when

(a) the agent acted with actual authority in making the representation, or

(b) the agent acted without actual authority in making the representation but had actual authority to make true representations about the same matter.

The agent's representation is not attributed to the principal when the third party knew or had reason to know it was untrue.

(4) When an agent who makes a contract or conveyance on behalf of an undisclosed principal falsely represents to the third party that the agent does not act on behalf of a principal, the third party may avoid the contract or conveyance if the principal or agent had notice that the third party would not have dealt with the principal.

CHAPTER 7. TORTS—LIABILITY OF AGENT AND PRINCIPAL

§ 7.01 Agent's Liability to Third Party

An agent is subject to liability to a third party harmed by the agent's tortious conduct. Unless an applicable statute provides otherwise, an actor remains subject to liability although the actor acts as an agent or an employee, with actual or apparent authority, or within the scope of employment.

* * *

§ 7.03 Principal's Liability—In General

(1) A principal is subject to direct liability to a third party harmed by an agent's conduct when

(a) as stated in § 7.04, the agent acts with actual authority or the principal ratifies the agent's conduct and

(i) the agent's conduct is tortious, or

(ii) the agent's conduct, if that of the principal, would subject the principal to tort liability; or

(b) as stated in § 7.05, the principal is negligent in selecting, supervising, or otherwise controlling the agent; or

(c) as stated in § 7.06, the principal delegates performance of a duty to use care to protect other persons or their property to an agent who fails to perform the duty.

(2) A principal is subject to vicarious liability to a third party harmed by an agent's conduct when

(a) as stated in § 7.07, the agent is an employee who commits a tort while acting within the scope of employment; or

(b) as stated in § 7.08, the agent commits a tort when acting with apparent authority in dealing with a third party on or purportedly on behalf of the principal.

§ 7.04 Agent Acts With Actual Authority

A principal is subject to liability to a third party harmed by an agent's conduct when the agent's conduct is within the scope of the agent's actual authority or ratified by the principal; and

(1) the agent's conduct is tortious, or

(2) the agent's conduct, if that of the principal, would subject the principal to tort liability.

Comment:

. . .

b. *In general.* When an agent acts with actual authority, the agent reasonably believes, in accordance with manifestations of the principal, that the principal wishes the agent so to act. See § 2.01. If a principal ratifies an agent's conduct, the principal assents to be affected by the legal consequences of the action. See § 4.01(2). The legal consequences created by ratification are those of actual authority. . . . If an agent's action within the scope of the agent's actual authority harms a third party, the principal is subject to liability if the agent's conduct is tortious. If the agent's conduct is not tortious, the principal is subject to liability if the same conduct on the part of the principal would have subjected the principal to tort liability. For example, an agent's action may not be tortious because the agent lacks information known to the principal. In either situation, the agent is the instrumentality through which the principal achieves the principal's objective. If the agent uses means other than those intended by the principal, the principal is subject to liability if the agent's choice of means is within the scope of the agent's actual authority. See § 2.02.

§ 7.05 Principal's Negligence in Conducting Activity Through Agent; Principal's Special Relationship With Another Person

(1) A principal who conducts an activity through an agent is subject to liability for harm to a third party caused by the agent's conduct if the harm was caused by the principal's negligence in selecting, training, retaining, supervising, or otherwise controlling the agent.

(2) When a principal has a special relationship with another person, the principal owes that person a duty of reasonable care with regard to risks arising out of the relationship, including the risk that agents of the principal will harm the person with whom the principal has such a special relationship.

* * *

§ 7.07 Employee Acting Within Scope of Employment

(1) An employer is subject to vicarious liability for a tort committed by its employee acting within the scope of employment.

(2) An employee acts within the scope of employment when performing work assigned by the employer or engaging in a course of conduct subject to the employer's control. An employee's act is not within the scope of employment when it occurs within an independent course of conduct not intended by the employee to serve any purpose of the employer.

(3) For purposes of this section,

(a) an employee is an agent whose principal controls or has the right to control the manner and means of the agent's performance of work, and

(b) the fact that work is performed gratuitously does not relieve a principal of liability.

* * *

CHAPTER 8. DUTIES OF AGENT AND PRINCIPAL TO EACH OTHER

§ 8.01 General Fiduciary Principle

An agent has a fiduciary duty to act loyally for the principal's benefit in all matters connected with the agency relationship.

§ 8.02 Material Benefit Arising Out of Position

An agent has a duty not to acquire a material benefit from a third party in connection with transactions conducted or other actions taken on behalf of the principal or otherwise through the agent's use of the agent's position.

§ 8.03 Acting as or on Behalf of an Adverse Party

An agent has a duty not to deal with the principal as or on behalf of an adverse party in a transaction connected with the agency relationship.

§ 8.04 Competition

Throughout the duration of an agency relationship, an agent has a duty to refrain from competing with the principal and from taking action on behalf of or otherwise assisting the principal's competitors. During that time, an agent may take action, not otherwise wrongful, to prepare for competition following termination of the agency relationship.

§ 8.05 Use of Principal's Property; Use of Confidential Information

An agent has a duty

(1) not to use property of the principal for the agent's own purposes or those of a third party; and

(2) not to use or communicate confidential information of the principal for the agent's own purposes or those of a third party.

§ 8.06 Principal's Consent

(1) Conduct by an agent that would otherwise constitute a breach of duty as stated in § § 8.01, 8.02, 8.03, 8.04, and 8.05 does not constitute a breach of duty if the principal consents to the conduct, provided that

(a) in obtaining the principal's consent, the agent

(i) acts in good faith,

(ii) discloses all material facts that the agent knows, has reason to know, or should know would reasonably affect the principal's judgment unless the principal has manifested that such facts are already known by the principal or that the principal does not wish to know them, and

(iii) otherwise deals fairly with the principal; and

(b) the principal's consent concerns either a specific act or transaction, or acts or transactions of a specified type that could reasonably be expected to occur in the ordinary course of the agency relationship.

(2) An agent who acts for more than one principal in a transaction between or among them has a duty

(a) to deal in good faith with each principal,

(b) to disclose to each principal

(i) the fact that the agent acts for the other principal or principals, and

(ii) all other facts that the agent knows, has reason to know, or should know would reasonably affect the principal's judgment unless the principal has manifested that such facts are already known by the principal or that the principal does not wish to know them, and

(c) otherwise to deal fairly with each principal.

§ 8.07 Duty Created by Contract

An agent has a duty to act in accordance with the express and implied terms of any contract between the agent and the principal.

§ 8.08 Duties of Care, Competence, and Diligence

Subject to any agreement with the principal, an agent has a duty to the principal to act with the care, competence, and diligence normally exercised by agents in similar circumstances. Special skills or knowledge possessed by an agent are circumstances to be taken into account in determining whether the agent acted with due care and diligence. If an agent claims to possess special skills or knowledge, the agent has a duty to the principal to act with the care, competence, and diligence normally exercised by agents with such skills or knowledge.

§ 8.09 Duty to Act Only Within Scope of Actual Authority and to Comply With Principal's Lawful Instructions

(1) An agent has a duty to take action only within the scope of the agent's actual authority.

(2) An agent has a duty to comply with all lawful instructions received from the principal and persons designated by the principal concerning the agent's actions on behalf of the principal.

§ 8.10 Duty of Good Conduct

An agent has a duty, within the scope of the agency relationship, to act reasonably and to refrain from conduct that is likely to damage the principal's enterprise.

§ 8.11 Duty to Provide Information

An agent has a duty to use reasonable effort to provide the principal with facts that the agent knows, has reason to know, or should know when

(1) subject to any manifestation by the principal, the agent knows or has reason to know that the principal would wish to have the facts or the facts are material to the agent's duties to the principal; and

(2) the facts can be provided to the principal without violating a superior duty owed by the agent to another person.

* * *

§ 8.14 Duty to Indemnify

A principal has a duty to indemnify an agent

(1) in accordance with the terms of any contract between them; and

(2) unless otherwise agreed,

(a) when the agent makes a payment

(i) within the scope of the agent's actual authority, or

(ii) that is beneficial to the principal, unless the agent acts officiously in making the payment; or

(b) when the agent suffers a loss that fairly should be borne by the principal in light of their relationship.

§ 8.15 Principal's Duty to Deal Fairly and in Good Faith

A principal has a duty to deal with the agent fairly and in good faith, including a duty to provide the agent with information about risks of physical harm or pecuniary loss that the principal knows, has reason to know, or should know are present in the agent's work but unknown to the agent.

CHAPTER 2

PARTNERSHIPS

1. WHAT IS A PARTNERSHIP? AND WHO ARE THE PARTNERS?

A. PARTNERS COMPARED WITH EMPLOYEES

Fenwick v. Unemployment Compensation Commission

133 N.J.L. 295, 44 A.2d 172 (1945).

This is an appeal from a judgment of the Supreme Court reversing a determination of the Unemployment Compensation Commission. The question involved is whether one Arline Chesire was, from January 1, 1939, to January 1, 1942, a partner or an employee of the prosecutor-respondent, John R. Fenwick, trading as United Beauty Shoppe. If she was an employee, then she was the eighth and deciding employee for the purpose of determining the status of the respondent for the year 1939 as an employer subject to the terms of the statute. N.J.S.A. 43:21–1 et seq. [requiring employer payments for unemployment compensation fund]. It is not the contention of the appellant commission that there was a fraudulent intent to avoid the act but the case is submitted as one of legal construction of the relation between Mrs. Chesire and the respondent.

Respondent Fenwick commenced operation of the beauty shop in Newark in November, 1936. In either 1937 or early 1938 he employed Mrs. Chesire as a cashier and reception clerk. Apparently her duties were to receive customers, take their orders for services to be performed by the operators, and collect the charges therefor. The shop did not work on an appointment basis but on a "first come-first served" plan. Mrs. Chesire was employed at a salary of $15 per week and continued at that salary until December, 1938, when she requested an increase. Respondent expressed a willingness to pay higher wages if the income of the shop warranted it. Thereupon an agreement was entered into by the parties. This agreement was drawn by a lawyer who had offices nearby and provided:

1. That the parties associate themselves into a partnership to commence January 1, 1939.
2. That the business shall be the operation of the beauty shop.
3. That the name shall be United Beauty Shoppe
4. That no capital investment shall be made by Mrs. Chesire.

5. That the control and management of the business shall be vested in Fenwick.

6. That Mrs. Chesire is to act as cashier and reception clerk at a salary of $15 per week and a bonus at the end of the year of 20% of the net profits, if the business warrants it.

7. That as between the partners Fenwick alone is to be liable for debts of the partnership.

8. That both parties shall devote all their time to the shop.

9. That the books are to be open for inspection of each party.

10. That the salary of Fenwick is to be $50 per week and at the end of the year he is to receive 80% of the profits.

11. That the partnership shall continue until either party gives ten days' notice of termination.

The relationship was terminated on January 1, 1942, at the request of Mrs. Chesire who desired to cease work and remain at home with her child.

The Commission held that the agreement was nothing more than an agreement fixing the compensation of an employee. The Supreme Court held that the parties were partners. The court apparently gave great weight to the fact that the parties had entered into the agreement, had called themselves partners, had designated the relationship one of partnership, and held that the surrounding circumstances, the conduct of the parties, etc., were not such as to overcome the force and effect to be given the declaration of the agreement.

Most of the cases wherein the courts have undertaken to determine whether or not a partnership existed, or whether certain persons were members of existing partnerships, have been those in which creditors have sought to impose liability upon alleged partners. In most cases, too, there have been no written partnership agreements to assist in fixing the status. However, the principles of law to be applied are the same. We think there can be no doubt of the right of the Commission, in the circumstances of this case, to raise the question and have a determination of the question of whether a partnership exists in law even though there is this agreement which is called a partnership agreement. We need not consider here what the effect of the agreement on the parties inter sese would be, but only its effect on the application of the unemployment compensation law.

There are several elements that the courts have taken into consideration in determining the existence or non-existence of the partnership relation. The first element is that of the intention of the parties and here, of course, the agreement itself is evidential although not conclusive. Light on the intent of the parties is shed by the testimony of the respondent as follows:

> "Q. When was she first hired by you? A. That is what I said, either 1937 or 1938, I can't say definitely what it was without looking it up: I couldn't give you the exact date. And she felt as though she was not getting enough money. Well, we were doing a lot of business, but the prices were very low at the time; it was in the depression and you had to bring your prices down to get business. And I told her I did not want to lose her because she was a very very good girl to me in that office, she was what I needed. I told her I couldn't see where I could afford to give her any more. And I did not want to lose her. So it went back and forth, back and forth. Finally I said, 'I will tell you what I will do: If we make any more money I will pay you more, if you want to go along on that agreement.' And that is where the partnership thing came in; that is how we started to be on the partnership concern at that time; that is when that was all discussed and arranged."

That statement is persuasive that the intention of the parties was to enter into an agreement that would provide a possibility of increase of compensation to Mrs. Chesire and at the same time protect Fenwick from being obliged to pay such increase unless business warranted it. The whole thing was prompted and instigated by the demand of the employee for an increase. The employer valued her services and did not wish to lose her. He wished to retain her in the exact same capacity as before but was afraid to promise a straight increase for fear it might mean loss to him. There is no suggestion that anything but the financial relation between the parties, with respect to compensation for services, was the thing they had in mind. After January 1st, 1939, the date the alleged partnership became effective, the operation of the business continued as before. Mrs. Chesire continued to serve in precisely the same capacity as before and Fenwick continued to have complete control of the management of the business. It would seem that, as far as the intention of the parties is concerned, the effect of the statements in the agreement has been met and overcome by the sworn testimony of Fenwick and by the conduct of the parties.

. . .

Another element of partnership is the right to share in profits and clearly that right existed in this case. However, not every agreement that gives the right to share in profits is, for all purposes, a partnership agreement. . . . Therefore, this point is not conclusive.

Another factor is the obligation to share in losses, and this is entirely absent in this case because the agreement provides that Mrs. Chesire is not to share in the losses.

Another is the ownership and control of the partnership property and business. Fenwick contributed all the capital and Mrs. Chesire had no right to share in capital upon dissolution. He likewise reserved to himself control.

The next is community of power in administration, and the reservation in the agreement of the exclusive control of the management of the business in Fenwick excludes this element so far as Mrs. Chesire is concerned. In Wild v. Davenport, Mr. Justice Depue, speaking for this court, said [48 N.J.L. 129, 7 A. 295]:

> "In Voorhees v. Jones [29 N.J.L. 270], the decision that a servant or agent who had a share of profits simply as compensation for services was neither a partner, nor liable for partnership debts, was placed by Chief Justice Whelpley on the ground that such a person had no control over the operation of the firm, and could not direct its investments, nor prevent the contracting of debts; in other words, had none of the prerogatives of a principal in the management and control of the business."

. . .

Another element is the language in the agreement, and although the parties call themselves partners and the business a partnership, the language used excludes Mrs. Chesire from most of the ordinary rights of a partner.

The conduct of the parties toward third persons is also an element to be considered and the conduct of the parties here does not support a finding that they were partners. They did file partnership income tax returns and held themselves out as partners to the Unemployment Compensation Commission, and Fenwick in his New York state income tax return reported that his income came from the partnership. But to no one else did they hold themselves out as partners. They did not inform the persons they purchased materials from, although Fenwick says this was not necessary since all purchases were for cash and they neither sought nor gave credit. The right to use the trade name had apparently come to Fenwick from one Florence Meola, by lease, and the partnership was given that name by Fenwick. There is no evidence that the trade name was ever registered as that of the partnership.

Another element is the rights of the parties on dissolution and apparently in this case the result of the dissolution, as far as Mrs. Chesire is concerned, was exactly the same as if she had quit an employment. She ceased to work and ceased to receive compensation and everything reverted to the condition it was in prior to 1939, except that Fenwick carried on with a new receptionist.

Under all these circumstances, giving due effect to the written agreement and bearing in mind that the burden of establishing a partnership is upon the one who alleges it to exist, . . ., we think that the partnership has not been established, and that the agreement between these parties, in legal effect, was nothing more than one to provide a method of compensating the girl for the work she had been performing as an employee. She had no authority or control in operating the business, she was not subject to losses, she was not held out as a partner. She got nothing by the agreement but a new scale of wages.

. . .

The Uniform Partnership Act defines a partnership as an association of "two or more persons to carry on as co-owners a business for profit." N.J.S.A. 42:1–6. Essentially the element of co-ownership is lacking in this case. The agreement was one to share the profits resulting from a business owned by Fenwick. He contributed all the capital, managed the business and took over all the assets on dissolution. Ownership was conclusively shown to be in him.

The Act further provides that sharing of profits is prima facie evidence of partnership but "no such inference shall be drawn if such profits were received in payment . . . as wages of an employee," R.S. 42:1–7, N.J.S.A., and it seems that is the legal inference to be drawn from the factual situation here.

The judgment is reversed.

ANALYSIS

1. **Bias?** Near the end of its analysis, the court refers to Mrs. Chesire as "the girl." Fenwick, in his testimony, uses the same description. How might the attitude that may be reflected in this usage affect the decision in a case such as this?

2. **"Deal Points?"** What were the "deal points" (that is, the important terms of the economic relationship) between Mr. Fenwick and Mrs. Chesire?

3. **Sharing Control.** Section 105(a) of the Uniform Partnership Act (1997) provides that, with certain exceptions that are not relevant here, "the partnership agreement governs . . . relations among the partners and between the partners and the partnership." In the absence of agreement among the partners, the rules set forth in the Act apply. Section 401(h) provides, "Each partner has equal rights in the management and conduct of the partnership business." A key finding of the court in the present case seems to have been that "Fenwick continued to have complete control of the management of the business." How might a

lawyer draft a "partnership" agreement to make it appear that Chesire had control consistent with the UPA, without in fact depriving Fenwick of the dominant position that he would no doubt insist upon as a matter of business judgment?

4. **Sharing Losses.** The court states, "Another factor is the obligation to share losses, and this is entirely absent in this case. . . ." How might the agreement be drafted to weaken this argument?

5. **Independent Contractor.** Another possibility that Fenwick might want to consider would be to engage Chesire as an "independent contractor." How would you draft an agreement to achieve this result (without significant change in the substance of the relationship)?

Clackamas Gastroenterology Associates v. Wells

538 U.S. 440 (2003).

■ JUSTICE STEVENS delivered the opinion of the Court.

The Americans with Disabilities Act of 1990 (ADA or Act), 42 U.S.C. § 12101 et seq., like other federal antidiscrimination legislation,[1] is inapplicable to very small businesses. Under the ADA an "employer" is not covered unless its work force includes "15 or more employees for each working day in each of 20 or more calendar weeks in the current or preceding calendar year." § 12111(5). The question in this case is whether four physicians actively engaged in medical practice as shareholders and directors of a professional corporation should be counted as "employees."

I

Petitioner, Clackamas Gastroenterology Associates, P. C., is a medical clinic in Oregon. It employed respondent, Deborah Anne Wells, as a bookkeeper from 1986 until 1997. After her termination, she brought this action against the clinic alleging unlawful discrimination on the basis of disability under Title I of the ADA. Petitioner denied that it was covered by the Act and moved for summary judgment, asserting that it did not have 15 or more employees for the 20 weeks required by the statute. It is undisputed that the accuracy of that assertion depends on whether the four physician-shareholders who own the professional corporation and constitute its board of directors are counted as employees. . . .

A divided panel of the Court of Appeals for the Ninth Circuit . . . held that the use of any corporation, including a professional corporation, " 'precludes any examination designed to determine whether the entity is in fact a partnership.' " 271 F.3d 903, 905 (2001) (quoting Hyland v.

---

[1] See, e.g., 29 U.S.C. § 630(b) (setting forth a 20-employee threshold for coverage under the Age Discrimination in Employment Act of 1967 (ADEA)); 42 U.S.C. § 2000e(b) (establishing a 15-employee threshold for coverage under Title VII of the Civil Rights Act of 1964).

New Haven Radiology Associates, P. C., 794 F.2d 793, 798 (C.A.2 1986)). It saw "no reason to permit a professional corporation to secure the 'best of both possible worlds' by allowing it both to assert its corporate status in order to reap the tax and civil liability advantages and to argue that it is like a partnership in order to avoid liability for unlawful employment discrimination." 271 F.3d, at 905. . . .

We granted certiorari to resolve the conflict in the Circuits, which extends beyond the Seventh and the Second Circuits.

II

"We have often been asked to construe the meaning of 'employee' where the statute containing the term does not helpfully define it." Nationwide Mut. Ins. Co. v. Darden, 503 U.S. 318, 322, 112 S.Ct. 1344 (1992). The definition of the term in the ADA simply states that an "employee" is "an individual employed by an employer." 42 U.S.C. § 12111(4). That surely qualifies as a mere "nominal definition" that is "completely circular and explains nothing." *Darden*, 503 U.S., at 323, 112 S.Ct. 1344. As we explained in *Darden*, our cases construing similar language give us guidance on how best to fill the gap in the statutory text.

In *Darden* we were faced with the question whether an insurance salesman was an independent contractor or an "employee" covered by the Employee Retirement Income Security Act of 1974 (ERISA). Because ERISA's definition of "employee" was "completely circular," 503 U.S., at 323, 112 S.Ct. 1344, . . . we adopted a common-law test for determining who qualifies as an "employee" under ERISA.[5] Quoting [Community for Creative Non-Violence v. Reid, 490 U.S. [730], at 739–740, we explained that " 'when Congress has used the term "employee" without defining it, we have concluded that Congress intended to describe the conventional master-servant relationship as understood by common-law agency doctrine.' " *Darden*, 503 U.S., at 322–323, 112 S.Ct. 1344.

---

5 Darden described the common-law test for determining whether a hired party is an employee as follows:

> "[W]e consider the hiring party's right to control the manner and means by which the product is accomplished. Among the other factors relevant to this inquiry are the skill required; the source of the instrumentalities and tools; the location of the work; the duration of the relationship between the parties; whether the hiring party has the right to assign additional projects to the hired party; the extent of the hired party's discretion over when and how long to work; the method of payment; the hired party's role in hiring and paying assistants; whether the work is part of the regular business of the hiring party; whether the hiring party is in business; the provision of employee benefits; and the tax treatment of the hired party." 503 U.S., at 323–324, 112 S.Ct. 1344 (quoting Community for Creative Non-Violence v. Reid, 490 U.S. 730, 751–752, 109 S.Ct. 2166 (1989), and citing Restatement (Second) of Agency § 220(2) (1958)).

These particular factors are not directly applicable to this case because we are not faced with drawing a line between independent contractors and employees. Rather, our inquiry is whether a shareholder-director is an employee or, alternatively, the kind of person that the common law would consider an employer.

Rather than looking to the common law, petitioner argues that courts should determine whether a shareholder-director of a professional corporation is an "employee" by asking whether the shareholder-director is, in reality, a "partner." . . . The question whether a shareholder-director is an employee, however, cannot be answered by asking whether the shareholder-director appears to be the functional equivalent of a partner. Today there are partnerships that include hundreds of members, some of whom may well qualify as "employees" because control is concentrated in a small number of managing partners. . . . Thus, asking whether shareholder-directors are partners—rather than asking whether they are employees—simply begs the question.

Nor does the approach adopted by the Court of Appeals in this case fare any better. The majority's approach, which paid particular attention to "the broad purpose of the ADA," 271 F.3d, at 905, is consistent with the statutory purpose of ridding the Nation of the evil of discrimination. See 42 U.S.C. § 12101(b).[6] Nevertheless, two countervailing considerations must be weighed in the balance. First, as the dissenting judge noted below, the congressional decision to limit the coverage of the legislation to firms with 15 or more employees has its own justification that must be respected—namely, easing entry into the market and preserving the competitive position of smaller firms. . . . Second, as *Darden* reminds us, congressional silence often reflects an expectation that courts will look to the common law to fill gaps in statutory text, particularly when an undefined term has a settled meaning at common law. . . .

. . . [T]he common law's definition of the master-servant relationship does provide helpful guidance. At common law the relevant factors defining the master-servant relationship focus on the master's control over the servant. The general definition of the term "servant" in the Restatement (Second) of Agency § 2(2) (1957), for example, refers to a person whose work is "controlled or is subject to the right to control by the master." . . . In addition, the Restatement's more specific definition of the term "servant" lists factors to be considered when distinguishing between servants and independent contractors, the first of which is "the extent of control" that one may exercise over the details of the work of the other. Id., § 220(2)(a). We think that the common-law element of control is the principal guidepost that should be followed in this case.

---

[6] The meaning of the term "employee" comes into play when determining whether an individual is an "employee" who may invoke the ADA's protections against discrimination in "hiring, advancement, or discharge," 42 U.S.C. § 12112(a), as well as when determining whether an individual is an "employee" for purposes of the 15-employee threshold. . . . Consequently, a broad reading of the term "employee" would—consistent with the statutory purpose of ridding the Nation of discrimination tend to expand the coverage of the ADA by enlarging the number of employees entitled to protection and by reducing the number of firms entitled to exemption.

This is the position that is advocated by the Equal Employment Opportunity Commission (EEOC), ... We are persuaded by the EEOC's focus on the common-law touchstone of control, . . . and specifically by its submission that each of the following six factors is relevant to the inquiry whether a shareholder-director is an employee:

- Whether the organization can hire or fire the individual or set the rules and regulations of the individual's work
- Whether and, if so, to what extent the organization supervises the individual's work
- Whether the individual reports to someone higher in the organization
- Whether and, if so, to what extent the individual is able to influence the organization
- Whether the parties intended that the individual be an employee, as expressed in written agreements or contracts
- Whether the individual shares in the profits, losses, and liabilities of the organization.

As the EEOC's standard reflects, an employer is the person, or group of persons, who owns and manages the enterprise. The employer can hire and fire employees, can assign tasks to employees and supervise their performance, and can decide how the profits and losses of the business are to be distributed. The mere fact that a person has a particular title—such as partner, director, or vice president—should not necessarily be used to determine whether he or she is an employee or a proprietor. . . . Nor should the mere existence of a document styled "employment agreement" lead inexorably to the conclusion that either party is an employee. . . .

III

Some of the District Court's findings (when considered in light of the EEOC's standard) appear to weigh in favor of a conclusion that the four director-shareholder physicians in this case are not employees of the clinic. For example, they apparently control the operation of their clinic, they share the profits, and they are personally liable for malpractice claims. There may, however, be evidence in the record that would contradict those findings or support a contrary conclusion under the EEOC's standard that we endorse today. Accordingly, as we did in *Darden*, we reverse the judgment of the Court of Appeals and remand the case to that court for further proceedings consistent with this opinion.

■ JUSTICE GINSBURG, with whom JUSTICE BREYER joins, dissenting.

"There is nothing inherently inconsistent between the coexistence of a proprietary and an employment relationship." Goldberg v. Whitaker

House Cooperative, Inc., 366 U.S. 28, 32, 81 S.Ct. 933 (1961). As doctors performing the everyday work of petitioner Clackamas Gastroenterology Associates, P.C., the physician-shareholders function in several respects as common-law employees, a designation they embrace for various purposes under federal and state law. Classifying as employees all doctors daily engaged as caregivers on Clackamas' premises, moreover, serves the animating purpose of the Americans with Disabilities Act of 1990 (ADA or Act). Seeing no cause to shelter Clackamas from the governance of the ADA, I would affirm the judgment of the Court of Appeals.

. . .

The physician-shareholders, it bears emphasis, invite the designation "employee" for various purposes under federal and state law. The Employee Retirement Income Security Act of 1974 (ERISA), much like the ADA, defines "employee" as "any individual employed by an employer." 29 U.S.C. § 1002(6). Clackamas readily acknowledges that the physician-shareholders are "employees" for ERISA purposes. . . . Indeed, gaining qualification as "employees" under ERISA was the prime reason the physician-shareholders chose the corporate form instead of a partnership. . . . Further, Clackamas agrees, the physician-shareholders are covered by Oregon's workers' compensation law, a statute applicable to "person[s] . . . who . . . furnish services for a remuneration, subject to the direction and control of an employer," Ore.Rev.Stat. Ann. § 656.005(30) (1996 Supp.). Finally, by electing to organize their practice as a corporation, the physician-shareholders created an entity separate and distinct from themselves, one that would afford them limited liability for the debts of the enterprise. . . . I see no reason to allow the doctors to escape from their choice of corporate form when the question becomes whether they are employees for purposes of federal antidiscrimination statutes. . . .

ANALYSIS

1. **Defining "Employee."** (a) Why rely on the common law, and Restatement, test for determining the meaning of "employee"? (b) What does the Court have in mind when it says that the common law test provides "helpful guidance"?

2. **Employee vs. Partner.** In the third paragraph of Section II of the opinion, the Court rejects the possibility of relying on the distinction between partners and employees, saying that such an approach would be circular. Is that right?

3. **The Corporate Form and Foolish Consistency.** What do you think of the dissent's view that if one uses the corporate form to gain certain advantages (mainly tax and liability) one should be stuck with that choice for ADA purposes.

Davis v. Loftus

334 Ill.App.3d 761, 778 N.E.2d 1144 (2002).

Terry Davis and several corporations he controlled filed a complaint against Michael Loftus, Donald Engel, and the partners in the law firm of Gottlieb & Schwartz, alleging that Loftus and Engel committed legal malpractice in connection with a real estate transaction. . . .

One of the partners named as a defendant, Anthony Frink, filed a motion to dismiss [the claims] against him because he did not qualify as a "partner" in Gottlieb & Schwartz for purposes of vicarious liability. Frink attached a copy of Gottlieb & Schwartz' partnership agreement listing Frink, Jay Tarshis, Roy Bernstein, and others not named in the complaint, as "Income Partners." According to the agreement, the firm paid each income partner "a fixed level of compensation determined on an annual basis by the Executive Committee," plus a bonus. The agreement expressly added: "Income Partners will not share in Partnership Net Profit or Loss."

Each income partner made a "capital contribution" of $10,000 to the firm. If an income partner withdrew from the firm, or upon dissolution of the firm, the firm would return the $10,000 capital contribution to the income partner, without any adjustment for the growth or profits of the firm from the time of the capital contribution. Income partners also had no voting rights and were not eligible to serve on the executive committee. . . .

Section 13 of the Uniform Partnership Act . . . provides that a partnership is liable for any wrongful act of any partner acting in the course of partnership business. Section 15 makes all partners liable for any such acts. . . . The trial court found Frink and others not liable for the acts of Loftus and Engel based on its finding that the income partners of Gottlieb & Schwartz are not "partners" within the meaning of the Act.

The substance and not the form of a business relationship determines whether the relationship qualifies as a partnership. Thus, we must decide whether the provisions of the partnership agreement pertaining to "Income Partners" make them partners within the meaning of the Act.

Cook v. Lauten, 1 Ill.App.2d 255, 117 N.E.2d 414 (1954), controls our disposition of this appeal. In that case the plaintiff and the defendant signed an "agreement for junior partnership." *Cook*, 1 Ill.App.2d at 258, 117 N.E.2d 414. The agreement named the plaintiff as the managing partner and sole owner of the firm's assets, and established the defendant's compensation as a fixed annual salary plus a bonus. While the defendant could advance money to the firm, the firm would only return the same amount later. The defendant, as a junior partner, had no right to participate in the firm's profits or losses. The court held:

> [T]he agreement for a "junior partnership" negatives every one of the elements essential to constitute a partnership relation. * * * Defendant's salary is fixed regardless of profits or losses of the alleged partnership and plaintiff as managing partner may by unilateral action alter defendant's share of the profit at will. * * * In short, defendant was to have no interest in the so-called 'partnership' except his unpaid salary and one month's bonus.

Cook, 1 Ill.App.2d at 259, 117 N.E.2d 414.

Here, too, the agreement established that income partners, including Frink, received a fixed salary plus a bonus, and the income partners took no share of the partnership's profit or loss. While income partners paid a "capital contribution" to the firm, the firm would repay the same amount, without regard to the firm's profit or loss from the time of the "capital contribution." The executive committee, like the managing partner in *Cook*, set the level of compensation for all income partners. Moreover, the income partners had no right to vote on the management or conduct of the partnership business. . . . Following *Cook*, we find that income partners under Gottlieb & Schwartz' partnership agreement do not qualify as partners within the meaning of the Act, and therefore the Act provides no basis for holding income partners liable for the acts of Loftus and Engel. . . .

QUESTIONS

1. **Representations.** Might the liability of the income partners depend on how the firm represented their status to the public?
2. **Relevance of Type of Liability.** Might the liability of the income partners vary according to the type of partnership liability?
3. **Bonuses and Profit Shares.** How is a salary plus profit-based bonus different from a partner's interest in the profits of the firm, where he or she receives the bulk of those profits as a monthly draw?
4. **Ethical Problems?** Are there any ethical (as in, "legal ethics") problems with the firm's structure?

Equal Employment Opportunity Commission v. Sidley Austin Brown & Wood

315 F.3d 696 (7th Cir. 2002).

■ POSNER, CIRCUIT JUDGE.

In 1999, Sidley & Austin (as it then was) demoted 32 of its equity partners to "counsel" or "senior counsel." The significance of these terms is unclear, but Sidley does not deny that they signify demotion and constitute adverse personnel action within the meaning of the antidiscrimination laws. The EEOC began an investigation to determine whether the demotions might have violated the Age Discrimination in Employment Act. After failing to obtain all the information it wanted without recourse to process, the Commission issued a subpoena duces tecum to the firm, seeking a variety of documentation bearing on two distinct areas of inquiry: coverage and discrimination. The reason for the inquiry about coverage is that the ADEA protects employees but not employers. E.g., Simpson v. Ernst & Young, 100 F.3d 436, 443 (6th Cir.1996); see 29 U.S.C. §§ 623(a)(2), (a)(3), 630(f). To be able to establish that the firm had violated the ADEA, therefore, the Commission would have to show that the 32 partners were employees before their demotion.

Sidley provided most of the information sought in the subpoena that related to coverage (but no information relating to discrimination, though Sidley claims that the demotions were due to shortcomings in performance rather than to age), but not all. It contended that it had given the Commission enough information to show that before their demotion the 32 had been "real" partners and so there was no basis for the Commission to continue its investigation. The Commission applied to the district court for an order enforcing the subpoena. The court ordered the firm to comply in full, and the firm appeals. . . .

> **NOTE**
>
> The ADEA, 29 U.S.C. § 623(a), provides:
>
> (a) Employer practices
>
> It shall be unlawful for an employer—
>
> (1) to fail or refuse to hire or to discharge any individual or otherwise discriminate against any individual with respect to his compensation, terms, conditions, or privileges of employment, because of such individual's age;
>
> (2) to limit, segregate, or classify his employees in any way which would deprive or tend to deprive any individual of employment opportunities or otherwise adversely affect his status as an employee, because of such individual's age; or
>
> (3) to reduce the wage rate of any employee in order to comply with this chapter.
>
> 29 U.S.C. § 630(f) provides (in part):
>
> (f) The term "employee" means an individual employed by any employer. . . .

The firm is controlled by a self-perpetuating executive committee. Partners who are not members of the committee have some powers delegated to them by it with respect to the hiring, firing, promotion, and compensation of their subordinates, but so far as their own status is concerned they are at the committee's mercy. It can fire them, promote them, demote them (as it did to the 32), raise their pay, lower their pay, and so forth. The only firm-wide issue on which all partners have voted in the last quarter century was the merger with Brown & Wood and that vote took place after the EEOC began its investigation. Each of the 32 partners at the time of their demotion by the executive committee had a capital account with the firm, averaging about $400,000. Under the firm's rules, each was liable for the firm's liabilities in proportion to his capital in the firm. Their income, however, was determined by the number of percentage points of the firm's overall profits that the executive committee assigned to each of them. Each served on one or more of the firm's committees, but all these committees are subject to control by the executive committee.

. . .

A remarkable feature of the way the case has been argued is that neither party has addressed the question *why* some or all members of partnerships should for purposes of the federal antidiscrimination laws be deemed employers and so placed outside the protection of these laws. That question might be avoidable if the laws contained an exemption for discrimination against partners; we might then simply look to the definition of the term in federal or state law. And if we looked there, we would find that Sidley was indeed a partnership and the 32 demoted partners were indeed partners before their demotion. Sidley has complied with all the formalities required by Illinois law to establish and maintain a partnership; the 32 were partners within the meaning of the applicable partnership law.

Although the EEOC does not concede that the 32 are bona fide partners even under state law, it is emphatic that their classification under state law is not dispositive of their status under federal antidiscrimination law. . . .

An individual who was classified as a partner-employer under state partnership law might be classified as an employee for other purposes, including the purpose for which federal antidiscrimination law extends protection to employees but not employers. Against this conclusion it can be argued that partners should be classified as employers rather than employees for purposes of the age discrimination law because partnership law gives them effective remedies against oppression by their fellow partners, because partnership relations would be poisoned if partners could sue each other for unlawful discrimination, and because the relation among partners is so intimate that they should be allowed to discriminate, just as individuals are allowed to discriminate in their purely personal relations. This is not the occasion on which to come down on one side or the other of the issue, though we note that in Hishon v. King & Spalding, 467 U.S. 69, 78, 104 S.Ct. 2229 (1984), the Supreme Court rejected the argument that the intimate nature of the partnership relation precludes a challenge under Title VII to a discriminatory refusal to promote an employee to partner.

But we do not understand how Sidley, without addressing the purpose of the employer exemption, can be so certain that it has proved that the 32 are employers within the meaning of the ADEA. They are, or rather were, partners, but it does not follow that they were employers. A firm that under pursuit by the EEOC on suspicion of discrimination redesignated its employees "partners" without changing the preexisting employment relation an iota would not by doing this necessarily buy immunity, even if the redesignation sufficed to make them partners under state law.

This case is not as extreme; it does not involve relabeling. Yet it involves a partnership of more than 500 partners in which all power resides in a small, unelected committee (it has 36 members). The partnership does not elect the members of the executive committee; the committee elects them, like the self-perpetuating board of trustees of a private university or other charitable foundation. It is true that the partners can commit the firm, for example by writing opinion letters; but employees of a corporation, when acting within the scope of their employment, regularly commit the corporation to contractual undertakings, not to mention to tort liability. Partners who are not members of the executive committee share in the profits of the firm; but many corporations base their employees' compensation in part anyway, but sometimes in very large part, on the corporation's profits, without anyone supposing them employers. The participation of the 32 demoted partners in committees that have, so far as appears, merely administrative functions does not distinguish them from executive employees in corporations. Corporations have committees and the members of the committees are employees; this does not make them employers. Nor are the members of the committees on which the 32 served elected; they are appointed by the executive committee. The 32 owned some of the firm's capital, but executive-level employees often own stock in their corporations. . . .

Particularly unconvincing is Sidley's contention that since the executive committee exercises its absolute power by virtue of delegation by the entire partnership in the partnership agreement, we should treat the entire partnership as if it rather than the executive committee were directing the firm. That would be like saying that if the people elect a person to be dictator for life, the government is a democracy rather than a dictatorship. The partners do not even elect the members of the committee. They have no control, direct or indirect, over its composition.

Perhaps the most partneresque feature of the 32 partners' relation to the firm is their personal liability for the firm's debts: not because unlimited liability is a sine qua non of partnership (there can be limited partnerships, and there are other business entities besides partnership that have unlimited liability—a sole proprietorship, for example), but because it is the most salient practical difference between the standard partnership and a corporation. Sidley does not have limited liability, and this means, by the way, that although under the firm's rules each partner is liable for the firm's debts only in proportion to his capital, a creditor of the firm could sue any partner for the entire debt owed it. Is this enough to pin the partner tail on the donkey? Wheeler v. Hurdman, 825 F.2d 257, 274–75 (10th Cir.1987), comes close to saying it is; see also Fountain v. Metcalf, Zima & Co., P.A., 925 F.2d 1398, 1400–01 (11th Cir.1991). Yet it does not quite deny the necessity of considering other factors. And tugging the other way are Strother v. Southern California Permanente Medical Group, 79 F.3d 859, 866–68 (9th Cir.1996) (interpreting a similar provision of state antidiscrimination law), and Simpson v. Ernst & Young, supra, 100 F.3d at 441–42. *Simpson* classified partners as employees in circumstances broadly similar to, though distinguishable from, those of the present case:

> Simpson had no authority to direct or participate in the admission or discharge of partners or other firm personnel; participate in determining partners or other personnel compensation predicated upon performance levels, responsibility, and years of service with the firm, including his own; participate in the vote for the chairman or the members of the Management Committee; or participate in the firm's profits and losses or share in unbilled uncollected client accounts ("UBT's"). Simpson had no right to examine the books and records of the firm except to the extent permitted by the Management Committee. He was required to execute a will which mandated that his heirs accept as binding the accounts provided by Ernst & Young with no right of inspection or verification. He had no authority to sign promissory notes on behalf of the firm, or pledge, transfer, or otherwise assign his interest in the firm. He was refused access to data concerning various client accounts. He was denied participation in annual performance reviews and other indicia of partnership status.
>
> In sum, the firm's business, assets, and affairs were directed exclusively by a 10 to 14 member Management Committee and its chairman. The Management Committee exercised exclusive control over the admission and discharge of all personnel, including Simpson. It could terminate employees without cause and without a right to appeal such decisions. The Management Committee unilaterally determined the compensation of all personnel, which authority was exercised and executed in total secrecy. Simpson and those similarly situated had no vote for the chairman or the members of the Management Committee. Instead, the Management Committee appointed its chairman

> and its chairman appointed the members of the Management Committee. "For all practical purposes [the court is quoting here from the district court's opinion], he was an employee with the additional detriment of having promised to be liable for the firm's losses. Ernst & Young was free to draft its Partnership Agreement and U.S. Agreement in such a way as to generate the belief in its employees that they enjoyed partnership status and to permit them to represent themselves as partners. However, because these individuals actually had no bona fide ownership interest, no fiduciary relationship, no share in the profits and losses, no significant management control, no meaningful voting rights, no meaningful vote in firm decisions, and no job security, they were not bona fide partners. Therefore Ernst & Young was obligated not to discriminate against them because of their age, sex, race, religion, national origin, or handicap."

The matter of liability for partnership debts illustrates the importance of referring the question whether a partner in a particular firm is an employer or an employee to statutory purpose. If implicit in the ADEA's exemption for employers is recognition that partners ordinarily have adequate remedies under partnership law to protect themselves against oppression (including age or other forms of invidious discrimination) by the partnership, then exposure to liability can hardly be decisive. These 32 partners were not empowered by virtue of bearing large potential liabilities! The 32 were defenseless; they had no power over their fate. If other partners shirked and as a result imposed liability on the 32, the 32 could not, as partners in a conventional partnership could do, vote to expel them. They had no voting power. What could be argued but is not is that because the *other* partners are potentially liable for the pratfalls of the 32, the partnership should have greater power over their employment than if the firm were a corporation and so had limited liability. To repeat, the issue is not whether the 32 before their demotion were partners, an issue to which their liability for the firm's debts is germane; the issue is whether they were employers. The two classes, partners under state law and employers under federal antidiscrimination law, may not coincide.

. . . [W]e think the district court acted prematurely in ordering order the subpoena complied with in its entirety. . . . Without having proposed a standard or criterion to guide the determination, the Commission has not earned the right to force the law firm . . .[to] produce the voluminous and sensitive documentation sought relating to the question whether, if these 32 partners were employees, they were demoted on account of their age and therefore in violation of the age discrimination law. We are therefore vacating the district court's order and remanding the case with directions to order the law firm to comply fully with the part of the subpoena that requests documents relating to coverage, but upon completion of those submissions to make a determination whether the 32 demoted partners are arguably covered by the ADEA. . . .

We are not ruling that the 32 demoted partners were in fact employees within the meaning of the age discrimination law. Such a ruling would be premature. Sidley has respectable arguments on its side, not least that the functional test of employer status toward which the EEOC is leaning is too uncertain to enable law firms and other partnerships to determine in advance their exposure to discrimination suits—that it would be better if the courts and the Commission interpreted the employer exclusion to require treating all partners as employers, with perhaps a narrow sham exception. These issues will become ripe when Sidley finishes complying with the coverage part of the subpoena. We hold only that there is enough doubt about whether the 32 demoted partners are covered by the age discrimination law to entitle the EEOC to full compliance with that part, at least, of its subpoena.

VACATED AND REMANDED WITH DIRECTIONS.

■ EASTERBROOK, CIRCUIT JUDGE, concurring in part and concurring in the judgment.

I join my colleagues' exemplary discussion of the law governing agency subpoenas but otherwise concur only in the judgment. I do not think that the scope of the ADEA'S coverage is as unfathomable as the majority makes out, nor do I believe that *if* the law were so ambulatory we should punt the legal question to the district court. Instead we should do our best to reduce uncertainty. Sidley and other large partnerships need to plan their affairs; their members also need to know their legal status. Can large law firms adopt mandatory-retirement rules? It is disappointing that the EEOC should profess, some 30 years after the ADEA's enactment, that it hasn't a clue about the answer. My colleagues' opinion does not help matters, and this is a missed opportunity.

The ADEA's definition of "employee" [at 29 U.S.C. § 630(f), supra] has a circular quality . . . . Yet this does not condemn us to wandering forever through the mist like the Flying Dutchman. . . . [The language of § 630(f)] turns out to be a definition in wide use [in federal legislation]. . . . This means on the one hand that a search for legislative purpose is futile—Congress took off the rack language devised, and often used, for subjects other than employment discrimination—and on the other hand that a definition may be secured from opinions that have addressed these other statutes. For example, in Hishon v. King & Spalding, 467 U.S. 69, 104 S.Ct. 2229 (1984), all of the Justices assumed—and Justice Powell in concurrence was explicit—that a *bona fide* partner of a large law firm is not an "employee" for purposes of Title VII. More recently, when dealing with ERISA, the Court held unanimously that the definition's circularity should be fixed by incorporating into federal law the traditional state agency-law criteria for identifying master-servant relations. Nationwide Mutual Insurance Co. v. Darden, 503 U.S. 318, 322–27, 112 S.Ct. 1344 (1992).

Darden turned on the distinction between an employee and an independent contractor. As they had done when resolving a similar problem in copyright law . . . the Justices looked to the approach in the Restatement (Second) of Agency § 220(2) (1958). . . . As Darden recognized, these bodies of law contain some flexible elements but give ready answers for the great majority of situations.

So too with partnership law. No one believes that a *bona fide* partner is in a master-servant relation with the partnership, or that the partner "is employed by" the partnership. The qualification "*bona fide*" is important . . . . It is neither our duty, nor our privilege, to invent a federal law of employment relations, as my colleagues appear to believe. The law must be federal (because § 630 is a federal statute), but *Darden* tells us that federal law tracks ordinary principles of master-servant relations that come from state law.

Were the 32 lawyers *bona fide* partners? The majority all but concedes that they were. . . . We know that all 32 (i) received a percentage of Sidley's profits and had to pony up if Sidley incurred a loss; (ii) had capital accounts that were at risk if the firm foundered; and (iii) were personally liable for the firm's debts and thus put their entire wealth, not just their capital accounts, on the line. We also know that (iv) no non-partner has an equity interest in the firm. The most important of these is the first (which implies the third): under the Uniform Partnership Act, it is profit-sharing (coupled with the lack of organization as an entity under some other law) that *defines* a partnership and identifies its partners, all of whom are personally liable for the venture's debts. See *Uniform Partnership Act* § 202 (1997 rev.); . . . Illinois, which has enacted the model act into positive law, treats participation in profits as the defining characteristic of a *bona fide* partner. The court in *Davis v. Loftus*, 334 Ill.App.3d 761, 268 Ill.Dec. 522, 778 N.E.2d 1144 (2002), held that a partner who shares in the profits or loss is personally liable for the law firm's debts, while an "income partner" who receives a salary plus a bonus is an employee and not liable for the firm's debts.

The 32 lawyers were real partners and consequently not "employees." . . .

What leads me to concur in the judgment is not any doubt about the right characterization of the 32 demoted partners but uncertainty about that of other lawyers. Sidley has a retirement age for everyone it dubs a partner. Whether this is lawful can be determined only by classifying, as "employee" or not, *every* lawyer who carries a "partner" label. The EEOC is entitled to investigate without knowing in advance how the inquiry will come out. . . .

ANALYSIS

1. **Comparison to *Clackamas*.** Is the opinion of the court in this case consistent with the opinion in the Clackamas case, supra, Sec. 1(A) (which was issued after the *Sidley* opinion)?

2. **Partnership Attributes.** (a) Is it as plain as the court declares that "Sidley was indeed a partnership and the 32 demoted partners were indeed partners before their demotion"? (b) The court also declares that "Sidley has complied with all the formalities required under Illinois law to establish and maintain a partnership." What are the "formalities" to which the court refers?

3. **Legislative Purpose.** The concurring opinion asserts that because the language of § 630(f) "turns out to be a definition in wide use [in federal legislation] . . . a search for legislative purpose is futile." Is that right?

Frank v. R.A. Pickens & Son Company

264 Ark. 307, 572 S.W.2d 133 (1978).

Appellant brought this action seeking an accounting and liquidation of the partnership affairs of appellee R.A. Pickens and Son Company, a farming partnership which leases and farms some 13,000 acres of land owned by another partnership, R.A. Pickens & Son. The partnership in question has existed in one form or another since 1925. Appellee R.A. Pickens has managed the firm since 1937. At the close of business on December 31, 1975, there were 22 partners of which R.A. Pickens & Son owned the largest interest, 31%. R.A. Pickens is not a partner in R.A. Pickens & Son Company but is a partner of R.A. Pickens & Son. Appellant employee was brought into the farming partnership on January 1, 1968, initially acquiring a 2% interest and eventually acquiring a total interest of 3%. His initial investment ($21,600) was made by giving his note to the partnership with the understanding that his share of the profits would apply to its payment. He remained an active partner until May 31, 1976, when appellee Pickens, as manager of the partnership, terminated appellant's partnership interest and tendered him a check in the amount of $35,805.97. This sum represented 3% of the partnership capital account of $1,950,000 as of December 31, 1975, or $58,500 plus 10% interest on this amount from January 1, 1976, until May 31, 1976, less a $17,000 note and 5 months interest owed by appellant to the partnership and less $7,706.53 owed by appellant to the partnership store account. Appellant refused to accept the check. That sum has, to date, been retained by the partnership as part of the partnership capital and carried on the books as a credit due appellant and a partnership liability. Appellant has had no active duties in the partnership affairs since May 31, 1976.

About a month thereafter, appellant filed a petition seeking an accounting of the partnership affairs, alleging that he had been wrongfully excluded. This petition was later amended to seek judicial dissolution and liquidation of the partnership assets. Appellees filed a counter-complaint seeking judicial recognition of the dissolution assertedly effected by appellee R.A. Pickens' notification to appellant on May 31, 1976, of his election to dissolve the partnership, which was a partnership at will. The counter-complaint also alleged the existence of an oral agreement for the purchase and termination of an interest in the partnership. The purchase of an interest in the partnership was based upon book value. Upon termination or dissolution, the value of the outgoing partner's interest was based upon the book value of such an interest as of December 31 of the year preceding such dissolution, plus 10% interest per annum from December 31 of that year to the date of dissolution. As previously indicated, appellees computed the amount due appellant at his partnership termination to be $35,805.97, after reduction of appellant's indebtedness to the partnership.

The trial court found that a partnership existed between the parties; that appellant purchased his 3% interest at book value; that Pickens, as managing partner, had the contractual right to terminate appellant's interest at will; that under the terms of the agreement appellant's contractual interest at termination was 3% of the book value of the partnership, or $58,500 as of December 31, 1975; that termination occurred on May 31, 1976, and the 10% interest on that amount, as alleged in the counter-complaint, was not included within the proved contractual terms relating to the calculation of appellant's partnership interest at termination; that appellant's capital and services were used by the partnership until the date of his termination; and therefore he was entitled to $13,843.48 which was 5/12ths of his 3% interest of the net profit for 1976, plus interest. These amounts were to be reduced by appellant's indebtedness to the partnership on his note and store account which were also ordered to bear interest.

Appellant contends that the court erred in not finding that he was entitled to a full share of the profits of the partnership so long as the partnership retained and used his capital contribution, the court erred in finding that R.A. Pickens had a contractual right to terminate appellant's partnership interest and erred in not ordering a termination and winding up of the partnership affairs. As we understand the thrust of appellant's argument, the Uniform Partnership Act is applicable here and therefore appellant has the right to a forced sale and liquidation of the partnership assets and his proper share of the net proceeds.

We first emphasize:

> The business association that is known in the law as a partnership is not one that can be defined with precision. To the contrary, a partnership is a contractual relationship that may vary, in form and substance, in an almost infinite variety of ways.

Zajac v. Harris, 241 Ark. 737, 410 S.W.2d 593 (1967). Further the Uniform Partnership Act provides that the rights and duties of parties are "subject to any agreement between" the partners. Ark.Stat.Ann. § 65–118 (Repl.1966). The Act also contains a provision that "settling accounts" between partners after a dissolution shall be "subject to any agreement. . . ." § 65–140. The partners here could agree, as the court found, that Pickens had exclusive control over the terms of admission and expulsion of the partners.

Pickens testified that appellant, upon becoming a partner, understood that he purchased his interest at book value. Upon leaving, he would be paid the book value and his status as a partner was dependent upon Pickens' willingness for him to continue in that status. It appears undisputed that at the conclusion of each year Pickens conferred with each partner about their individual equity or earnings in the profit sharing venture.

Numerous past and present partners testified. According to them the understanding was they bought their interest in the partnership at book value. The length of their membership was at the will and pleasure of Pickens, the general manager, and upon leaving the company they would be paid at book value. Although appellant denies the oral agreement asserted by Pickens, he admits he acquired his interest at book value based upon a loan of the purchase funds to him by the company as evidenced by a note. Appellant is a college graduate with a business degree. It appears his duties as an employee with the partnership consisted of general office work and bookkeeping a short time before acquisition of his interests and during the 8½ years he was a partner. He was familiar with transactions at book value with respect to incoming and outgoing partners. As indicated, upon termination he refused a tender of payment of his interest after a settlement of accounts.

Here the chancellor had the advantage of seeing and hearing the witnesses and at the same time studying the exhibits to their testimony. We do not reverse a chancellor's finding unless it is against the preponderance of the evidence. Here the chancellor's finding is clearly supported by the preponderance of the evidence. Therefore, in view of the agreement, the Uniform Partnership Act is not applicable and consequently appellant cannot force a liquidation and sale of the appellee partnership.

Affirmed.

ANALYSIS

1. **Partner vs. Employee.** On your view of the facts, was the plaintiff, Frank, a partner or an employee?
2. **Apparent Authority of Partners.** UPA (1914) § 9 provides in part, "(1) Every partner is an agent of the partnership for the purpose of its business, and the act of every partner, including the execution in the partnership name of any instrument, for apparently carrying on in the usual way the business of the partnership of which he is a member binds the partnership, unless the partner so acting has in fact no authority to act for the partnership in the particular matter, and the person with whom he is dealing has knowledge of the fact that he has no authority." UPA (1997) § 301 is essentially the same. Suppose that you had been R.A. Pickens's lawyer and he had asked you whether he should be concerned about people like Frank incurring obligations on behalf of the partnership. What would your response have been?
3. **Frank's Entitlements.** To what extent was Frank entitled to share in increases in the total value of the farming business of the partnership?
4. **Recasting Frank's Role.** Could the relationship of Frank to the other people involved in the business have been cast in terms of employment, rather than partnership, without changing the basic terms of the economic arrangement?
5. **Legal vs. de Facto Control.** The court states that "there were 22 partners." The rule of partnership control, in the absence of an agreement to the contrary, is that each partner has one vote. Assume that there was no provision in the partnership agreement assuring Pickens of his position as managing partner. Frank and eleven other minor partners could have formed a coalition, demanded a meeting of the partners, and voted to fire R.A. Pickens as manager and replace him with Frank. What power did Pickens have that would have made such a plan futile? What does this tell you about partnership control, legal and de facto, in this case? In a law firm?
6. **Book Value: Uses and Alternatives.** "Book value" is an amount on the books of the firm, reflecting the original cost of assets, less depreciation (an allowance for decline in value of an asset by virtue of the passage of time and wear and tear), plus profits that have not been distributed to the partners. What are the advantages and disadvantages to Frank in the use of book value to determine the amount of his buy-out entitlement, as opposed to, say, appraised value? What other methods of setting the amount might be worth considering? What are their advantages and disadvantages?

B. PARTNERS COMPARED WITH LENDERS

INTRODUCTORY NOTE

The next case, Martin v. Peyton, is important for its discussion of legal doctrine and for what it reveals about business relationships. Beyond that, its facts can evoke thoughts about human relationships and feelings—about friendship, trust and distrust, greed, honesty and dishonesty, self-delusion, anger, fear, and so on—that form the background from which the case emerges. Imagine the tale behind this case being turned into a novel or short story by Henry James, John Cheever, or John Updike. Appreciation of the insights of such authors may be as essential to good lawyering as is mastery of legal doctrine.

In this case the question of who is a partner is important because of the rule of partnership law that makes each partner potentially liable for all of the debts of the partnership. As a consequence of this rule, the wealthy defendants in the case were in jeopardy of losing not just the amounts invested in the partnership but all, or a substantial part, of their individual fortunes.

Martin v. Peyton

246 N.Y. 213, 158 N.E. 77 (1927).

■ ANDREWS, J. . . .

Partnership results from contract, express or implied. If denied, it may be proved by the production of some written instrument, by testimony as to some conversation, by circumstantial evidence.

. . .

In the case before us the claim that the defendants became partners in the firm of Knauth, Nachod & Kuhne, doing business as bankers and brokers, depends upon the interpretation of certain instruments. [The plaintiff was a creditor of the firm of Knauth, Nachod & Kuhne, and claimed that the defendants (respondents here), who had made investments in the firm (described later in the opinion), were partners and, as such, liable for its debts. The defendants claimed that they were creditors, not partners.] There is nothing in their subsequent acts determinative of or indeed material upon this question. And we are relieved of questions that sometimes arise. "The plaintiff's position is not," we are told, "that the agreements of June 4, 1921, were a false expression or incomplete expression of the intention of the parties. We say that they express defendants' intention and that that intention was to create a relationship which as a matter of law constitutes a partnership." Nor may the claim of the plaintiff be rested on any question of estoppel. "The plaintiff's claim," he stipulates, "is a claim of actual partnership, not of partnership by estoppel. . . ."

Remitted then, as we are, to the documents themselves, we refer to circumstances surrounding their execution only so far as is necessary to make them intelligible. And we are to remember that although the intention of the parties to avoid liability as partners is clear; although in language precise and definite they deny any design to then join the firm of K.N. & K.; although they say their interests in profits should be construed merely as a measure of compensation for loans, not an interest in profits as such; although they provide that they shall not be liable for any losses or treated as partners, the question still remains whether in fact they agree to so associate themselves with the firm as to "carry on as co-owners a business for profit."

In the spring of 1921 the firm of K.N. & K. found itself in financial difficulties. John R. Hall was one of the partners. He was a friend of Mr. Peyton. From him he obtained the loan of almost $500,000 of Liberty bonds, which K.N. & K. might use as collateral to secure bank advances. This, however, was not sufficient. The firm and its members had engaged in unwise speculations, and it was deeply involved. Mr. Hall was also intimately acquainted with George W. Perkins, Jr., and with Edward W. Freeman. He also knew Mrs. Peyton and Mrs. Perkins and Mrs. Freeman. All were anxious to help him. He therefore, representing K.N. & K., entered into negotiations with them. While they were pending a proposition was made that Mr. Peyton, Mr. Perkins, and Mr. Freeman, or some of them, should become partners. It met a decided refusal. Finally an agreement was reached. It is expressed in three documents, executed on the same day, all a part of the one transaction. They were drawn with care and are unambiguous. We shall refer to them as "the agreement," "the indenture," and "the option."

We have no doubt as to their general purpose. The respondents [Peyton, Perkins, and Freeman] were to loan K.N. & K. $2,500,000 worth of liquid securities, which were to be returned to them on or before April 15, 1923. The firm might hypothecate them to secure loans totaling $2,000,000, using the proceeds as its business necessities required. To insure respondents against loss K.N. & K. were to turn over to them a large number of their own securities which may have been valuable, but which were of so speculative a nature that they could not be used as collateral for bank loans. In compensation for the loan the respondents were to receive 40 per cent. of the profits of the firm until the return was made, not exceeding, however, $500,000, and not less than $100,000. Merely because the transaction involved the transfer of securities and not of cash does not prevent its being a loan. . . . The respondents also were given an option to join the firm if they, or any of them, expressed a desire to do so before June 4, 1923.

Many other detailed agreements are contained in the papers. Are they such as may be properly inserted to protect the lenders? Or do they go further? Whatever their purpose, did they in truth associate the respondents with the firm so that they and it together thereafter carried on as co-owners a business for profit? The answer depends upon an analysis of these various provisions.

As representing the lenders, Mr. Peyton and Mr. Freeman are called "trustees." The loaned securities when used as collateral are not to be mingled with other securities of K.N. & K., and the trustees at all times are to be kept informed of all transactions affecting them. To them shall be paid all dividends and income accruing therefrom. They may also substitute for any of the securities loaned securities of equal value. With their consent the firm may sell any of its securities held by the respondents, the proceeds to go, however, to the trustees. In other similar ways the trustees may deal with these same securities, but the securities loaned shall always be sufficient in value to permit of their hypothecation for $2,000,000. If they rise in price, the excess may be withdrawn by the defendants. If they fall, they shall make good the deficiency.

So far, there is no hint that the transaction is not a loan of securities with a provision for compensation. Later a somewhat closer connection with the firm appears. Until the securities are returned, the directing management of the firm is to be in the hands of John R. Hall, and his life is to be insured for $1,000,000, and the policies are to be assigned as further collateral security to the trustees. These requirements are not unnatural. Hall was the one known and trusted by the defendants. Their acquaintance with the other members of the firm was of the slightest. These others had brought an old and established business to the verge of bankruptcy. As the respondents knew, they also had engaged in unsafe speculation. The respondents were about to loan $2,500,000 of good securities. As collateral they were to receive others of problematical value. What they required seems but ordinary caution. Nor does it imply an association in the business.

The trustees are to be kept advised as to the conduct of the business and consulted as to important matters. They may inspect the firm books and are entitled to any information they think important. Finally, they may veto any business they think highly speculative or injurious. Again we hold this but a proper precaution to safeguard the loan. The trustees may not initiate any transaction as a partner may do. They may not bind the firm by any action of their own. Under the circumstances the safety of the loan depended upon the business success of K.N. & K. This success was likely to be compromised by the inclination of its members to engage in speculation. No longer, if the respondents were to be protected, should it be allowed. The trustees therefore might prohibit it, and that their prohibition might be effective, information was to be furnished them. Not dissimilar agreements have been held proper to guard the interests of the lender.

As further security each member of K.N. & K. is to assign to the trustees their interest in the firm. No loan by the firm to any member is permitted and the amount each may draw is fixed. No other distribution of profits is to be made. So that realized profits may be calculated the existing capital is stated to be $700,000, and profits are to be realized as promptly as good business practice will permit. In case the trustees think this is not done, the question is left to them and to Mr. Hall, and if they differ then to an arbitrator. There is no obligation that the firm shall continue the business. It may dissolve at any time. Again we conclude there is nothing here not properly adapted to secure the interest of the respondents as lenders. If their compensation is dependent on a percentage of the profits, still provision must be made to define what these profits shall be.

The "indenture" is substantially a mortgage of the collateral delivered by K.N. & K. to the trustees to secure the performance of the "agreement." It certainly does not strengthen the claim that the respondents were partners.

Finally we have the "option." It permits the respondents, or any of them, or their assignees or nominees to enter the firm at a later date if they desire to do so by buying 50 per cent. or less of the interests therein of all or any of the members at a stated price. Or a corporation may, if the respondents and the members agree, be formed in place of the firm. Meanwhile, apparently with the design of protecting the firm business against improper or ill-judged action which might render the option valueless, each member of the firm is to place his resignation in the hands of Mr. Hall. If at any time he and the trustees agree that such resignation should be accepted, that member shall then retire, receiving the value of his interest calculated as of the date of such retirement.

This last provision is somewhat unusual, yet it is not enough in itself to show that on June 4, 1921, a present partnership was created, nor taking these various papers as a whole do we reach such a result. It is quite true that even if one or two or three like provisions contained in such a contract do not require this conclusion, yet it is also true that when taken together a point may come where stipulations immaterial separately cover so wide a field that we should hold a partnership exists. As in other branches of the law, a question of degree is often the determining factor. Here that point has not been reached. . . .

The judgment appealed from should be affirmed, with costs.

NOTES

1. **Speculative Investments in Foreign Exchange.** According to the lower court opinion, K.N. & K. was a large, prominent firm, with substantial foreign banking operations, 300 employees, and total

transactions of over $100 million a year. 219 App.Div. 297, 220 N.Y.S. 29. Hall had "been indebted to Peyton in [sic] a substantial sum of money since 1913" and Peyton had helped Hall in various business matters. The reason for the loan of securities rather than cash was to avoid the usury laws. (If Peyton, Perkins, and Freeman had not had ready access to cash, presumably they could have used their securities as collateral for a bank loan of cash, which they could then have loaned to K.N. & K.) The losses that gave rise to the litigation resulting in the present decision arose from speculative investments in foreign exchange, which were prohibited by the agreement between K.N. & K. and Perkins and the other investors. Though Hall was not directly involved in making these investments, he knew about them and apparently did not tell his friends Peyton, Perkins, and Freeman.

2. **Allowing Others to Gamble with Your Money.** There is an important economic principle relating to risk that may have been at play in the situation described in Martin v. Peyton. Crudely stated, the principle is that you should not allow other people to gamble with your money for their own profit. At the very least, the facts of the case offer a nice opportunity for describing that principle. Suppose that K.N. & K. has suffered losses and has reached a point where its assets have a value of $12 million, including $1 million in a bank account, and its liabilities are $20 million. After about two more weeks of normal operations K.N. & K. will not be able to pay its bills and its creditors will shut it down. K.N. & K. has an opportunity to invest $1 million in a foreign exchange transaction. The expectation is that if the transaction turns out as the K.N. & K. partners hope, the payoff will be $20 million, but the probability of that happening is only one in forty. If the transaction does not turn out as hoped, the entire $1 million will be lost. A one in forty chance of a return of $20 million is worth only $500,000, so the investment appears to be a bad one. But suppose it is K.N. & K.'s last chance. If the investment pays off what is the financial effect for the partners of K.N. & K.? If it does not pay off, what do they lose? If you think this is a rare or trivial phenomenon, consider the story of the billions of dollars of losses in the savings and loan industry in recent years—a classic case of people (managers of insured savings and loan institutions) gambling with someone else's money (mostly, as it turns out, the taxpayers').

3. **Limiting Liability by Incorporation.** The risk of liability for Peyton, Perkins, and Freeman would have been avoided if K.N. & K. had been organized as a corporation. Under that form of organization, the equity investors (the counterparts of partners) enjoy "limited liability"—that is, they are not personally liable for the debts of the firm and therefore stand to lose only the amount they have invested in it. Thus, even if the purported lenders had been treated as shareholders, they would have

been shielded from the personal liability that the creditors sought to enforce. Alternatively, under current law they could have formed a limited liability company, a form we explore at length in Chapter 3.

PLANNING

The court did not reach its decision in the case without difficulty. It seems fair to say that PPF had a close call with financial disaster. What changes in the agreement might have been made to strengthen their legal position (that is, their claim that they were not partners) without depriving them of important protections?

ANALYSIS

1. **Risk and Reward.** What amount of loss were Peyton, Perkins, and Freeman (PPF) prepared to risk? Why were they willing to take a substantial risk? What is the moral of the story of their investment in K.N. & K.?

2. **Elements of Return.** What were the various elements of return on their investment that PPF bargained for? What does their potential return tell you about the degree of risk that they believed they were accepting?

BACKGROUND

The Story Behind Martin v. Peyton

The story behind Martin v. Peyton begins around 1920. The principal characters are a small group of wealthy and socially prominent New Yorkers. Their interaction and its legal consequences could have come from the pages of a novel by their near-contemporaries Henry James or Edith Wharton.

The full story appears at William A. Klein, The Story of Martin v. Peyton: Rich Investors, Risky Investment, and the Line Between Lenders and Undisclosed Partners, in J. Mark Ramseyer, ed., Corporate Law Stories 77–103 (Foundation Press, 2009). It is available at no cost, from: http://www.interactivecasebooks.com/documents/EA7_Ramseyer_Corp_Law_Stories_Chap3.pdf.

3. **Protection Against Loss.** Given the degree of risk to which PPF were exposed, and given the fact that they did not want to be involved in running the business, what kinds of protections would you expect them to want? What protections did they in fact bargain for?

4. **Enforcement of Agreement.** As stated above, K.N. & K. violated their agreement with PPF by speculating in foreign exchange and this produced the losses that led to K.N. & K.'s downfall. Why do you suppose PPF did not enforce the agreement and prevent the speculation? What was the value of the prohibition?

5. **Indicia of Agency.** Apparently PPF relied heavily (and, as it turned out, foolishly) on their friend Hall to protect their interests. Yet the court concludes that Hall was not their agent for the purpose of exercising control over the K.N. & K. operations. Why?

6. **Comparison to *Cargill*.** Can the outcome in this case be reconciled with the outcome in the *Cargill* case?

Kaufman-Brown Potato Co. v. Long

182 F.2d 594 (9th Cir.1950).

[This is a decision in a bankruptcy proceeding. Horton and Althouse were partners in the business of growing and of distributing potatoes, under the names of Gerry Horton Company and Gerry Horton Farms. They entered into an agreement with Kaufman and Brown, who were partners in the business of produce distribution, under the name of Kaufman-Brown Potato Co. Horton and Althouse became bankrupt and Kaufman-Brown filed a claim in the bankruptcy proceeding. The rights of Kaufman-Brown turned on whether it was a creditor of Horton and Althouse or a partner of theirs. The lower court ruled against Kaufman-Brown and this is the decision on its appeal.]

Appellants rely mainly upon these arguments: The dealings between Gerry Horton, J.D. Althouse, Charles H. Kaufman, and Albert H. Brown could not constitute [as is claimed they must under California law to constitute a partnership] an association for the purpose of *jointly* carrying on a business together. The word "partner" used twice in each of the written agreements was inadvertent and is not conclusive. The written contracts or agreements themselves in certain particulars and the conduct of the parties under such written agreements negative both any intent to form a partnership or that a partnership in fact was formed or existed.

It appears from the evidence that Horton and Althouse, prior to any association with Kaufman-Brown Potato Company, were doing business in partnership both as Gerry Horton Company and Gerry Horton Farms, under the former name as farm produce distributors and under the latter name as producers. In 1944 they held two parcels of California farm land under lease. As to each parcel separately Horton and Althouse as Gerry Horton Farms contracted in writing with Kaufman and Brown doing business as Kaufman-Brown Potato Company, who were distributors, relative to planting, raising, and harvesting potatoes on such land.

It was agreed in each contract that Kaufman and Brown would purchase from Horton and Althouse for a certain amount an undivided interest [50% as to one parcel; 40% as to the other parcel] in all potato crops to be planted, raised and harvested upon such leased land during the year 1944. Horton and Althouse agreed to pay all costs and expenses of planting and raising in excess of the amount above mentioned to be paid in by Kaufman and Brown for the above undivided interests. The net proceeds after repayment to Kaufman and Brown of the amount they paid in and of any amounts paid by Horton and Althouse in addition thereto for the expenses of planting and raising were to be divided "between the partners" [quoting from such contracts] in like manner. The over-all losses sustained in the venture were to be borne by the parties in their interest ratio. It was also provided that Horton and Althouse would keep full and accurate accounts of the enterprise at their place of business. The written contracts provided for an option to Kaufman and Brown Potato Company to purchase the crop raised and harvested on each parcel of land for a price equal to the prevailing market price but if there were no prevailing market price upon harvest Kaufman and Brown agreed to handle all the potatoes as agents for Horton and Althouse for a stated commission "for said services rendered on behalf of the partners hereto" and pay to Horton and Althouse all money received from the sale thereof "subject to accounting and distribution as hereinbefore set forth." [Quotations are from each contract.] In the event that Kaufman and Brown exercised their option to purchase, Horton and Althouse could add to the purchase price any markups allowed by O.P.A. regulations but the total amount of such markups [was to] be divided between the parties in the ratio of their interests. Horton and Althouse were to furnish all the necessary farming equipment. The contracts also provided for the execution of a crop mortgage as security for faithful performance by Horton and Althouse and for a promissory note also to be executed in an amount which as above mentioned Kaufman and Brown were to pay in. After each contract had been fully complied with, the mortgage and note were to be surrendered and cancelled. It was declared that the mortgage and note were executed solely as security for performance and that Horton and Althouse were not to be held liable for any losses resulting from causes beyond their control. The contracts did not provide for a firm bank account nor for a firm name of the business to be conducted under the provisions of the contracts. Both agreements were prepared by Horton and Althouse's attorney pursuant to Horton's instructions.

As to their farming activities, during the year 1944 Horton and Althouse devoted themselves solely to operations under and in conformity with the written agreements. Potatoes were farmed, harvested and sold and Kaufman-Brown Potato Company, exercising its option, purchased some and paid to Horton and Althouse the prevailing market price therefor. In the aggregate [as to both leases] Kaufman and Brown in fact advanced to Horton and Althouse some $43,000 and had been repaid $20,000. The latter had issued bank checks for the balance of such advances not repaid but they were not honored for lack of sufficient funds. The total of such dishonored checks represents the amount of the claim asserted by Kaufman and Brown in the instant involuntary petition in bankruptcy. It was testified that such checks were accepted in payment of the mortgages and notes executed by Horton and Althouse pursuant to each contract. Appellants assert their claim here as unsecured.

No assignments of the leases held by Horton and Althouse were ever made to the purported partnership with Kaufman-Brown Potato

Company. No bank account was maintained separate from those kept in the names of each of the partnerships of which Horton and Althouse were the sole members. There was no evidence that any of the creditors of the 1944 farming enterprise were told or knew that Kaufman-Brown Potato Company was a partner in the farming of the leased ground or that any of them knew anything about Kaufman-Brown's association or interest.

Section 2400 of the California Civil Code [now § 15006 of the California Corporations Code] defines a partnership in the language of the Uniform Partnership Act as an "association of two or more persons to carry on as co-owners a business for profit." Rules for determining the existence of a partnership are stated in section 2401 of the California Civil Code [now section 15007 of the California Corporations Code].[4]

A partnership may be formed for a single venture. . . . Whether or not a partnership relationship exists is determinable by the intent of the parties to do things which constitute a partnership. . . . It is immaterial that the parties deign not to call their relationship, or believe it not to be, a partnership, especially where as here the rights of third persons are involved. It is true that a mere agreement to share profits and losses does not make a partnership but both the sharing of profits and losses are usual in partnership agreements and practices.

It is plain that the contracts in question were drawn with some of the usual covenants and conditions both of a straight financing contract with options and of a partnership agreement. Appellants point especially to the provisions for crop mortgages as supporting the former relation but their argument is offset by the proviso that such were to be security only for performance on the part of Horton and Althouse and that Horton

---

[4] California Civil Code section 2401 [California Corporations Code section 15007] reads as follows:

"In determining whether a partnership exists, these rules shall apply:

"(1) Except as provided by Section (2410) persons who are not partners as to each other are not partners as to third persons.

"(2) Joint tenancy, tenancy in common, tenancy by the entireties, joint property, common property, or part ownership does not of itself establish a partnership, whether such co-owners do or do not share any profits made by the use of the property.

"(3) The sharing of gross returns does not of itself establish a partnership, whether or not the persons sharing them have a joint or common right or interest in any property from which the returns are derived.

"(4) The receipt by a person of a share of the profits of a business is prima facie evidence that he is a partner in the business, but no such inference shall be drawn if such profits were received in payment:

"(a) As a debt by installments or otherwise.

"(b) As wages of an employee or rent to a landlord.

"(c) As an annuity to a widow or representative of a deceased partner.

"(d) As interest on a loan, though the amount of payment vary with the profits of the business.

"(e) As the consideration for the sale of a goodwill of a business or other property by installments or otherwise."

and Althouse would not be liable for any losses occasioned by causes beyond their control. The non-mention of capital contribution of each of the parties is stressed, but all partners need not contribute capital in the strict sense of the word; some may invest their labor and skill. . . . These contracts provide that Kaufman and Brown were to put up so much money for initial expense but note that all of it was to be returned out of the product as expense before division of sales returns. Horton and Althouse were to devote themselves to the farming aspect using their own equipment, and Kaufman and Brown were to use their sales organization and experience if necessary to effect distribution of the crop. However, the provision that the amounts paid in by Kaufman and Brown were to be repaid before division of sales returns is consistent with a partnership relationship. . . . There is a provision in each of the contracts that in certain circumstances Kaufman and Brown would act as agents for Horton and Althouse to dispose of the potatoes upon harvest through Chicago markets for a stated commission and would pay to Horton and Althouse money obtained from sales. This provision appears to be more unusual in a partnership contract than inconsistent with one, for Horton and Althouse were to keep the accounts and all such provisions were stated to be "subject to accounting and distribution as hereinbefore set forth." The use of the word "partner" in each agreement could have been but a handy word to include personnel without naming them but the fact-finder, on analyzing the complicated contracts, would not be justified in rejecting its possible bearing on the issue entirely. The contracts also provide that Horton and Althouse keep the "books of account and all other records" of the enterprise at their place of business and that each of the partners hereto "shall at all times have access to and may inspect and copy any of them." The latter quoted language is taken verbatim from California Civil Code section 2413 [California Corporations Code section 15019], which relates to "partnership books".

It is evident that Kaufman and Brown advanced more than was required by the contracts. This fact could be accounted for by their desire to protect their interests in either relation. Further, there is testimony to the effect that both Messrs. Kaufman and Brown came to California and made recommendations relative to operations under the contracts. Of course, their interest in the contracts could have justified their personal presence on the ground, either as partners or joint venturers, but it is consistent with partnership interest.

We are of the opinion that the record contains the essentials of a partnership and also substantial proof that such was the intention at least of Horton and Althouse, the authors of the contracts. Upon a review of the record as a whole we do not find that a mistake has been made. . . .

ANALYSIS

1. **Motivation and Expectation.** What seem to have been the motivations of Kaufman-Brown in entering into the arrangement with Horton and Althouse? How did Kaufman and Brown expect to gain?
2. **Why Partnership?** Why did not Kaufman and Brown simply hire Horton to run the farm, as an employee of Kaufman-Brown?
3. **Control.** What degree of control did Kaufman-Brown have? Was this consistent with the role of a lender?
4. **Comparison to Martin v. Peyton.** How can this case be reconciled with Martin v. Peyton, supra?

C. PARTNERSHIP BY ESTOPPEL

Young v. Jones

816 F.Supp. 1070 (D.S.C.1992).

. . . Plaintiffs are investors from Texas who deposited over a half-million dollars in a South Carolina bank and the funds have disappeared.

PW-Bahamas [Price Waterhouse, Chartered Accountants, a Bahamian partnership] issued an unqualified audit letter regarding the financial statement of Swiss American Fidelity and Insurance Guaranty (SAFIG). Plaintiffs aver that on the basis of that financial statement, they deposited $550,000.00 in a South Carolina bank. Other defendants, not involved in the motions herein, allegedly sent the money from the South Carolina Bank to SAFIG. The financial statement of SAFIG was falsified. The plaintiffs' money and its investment potential has been lost to the plaintiffs and it is for these losses that the plaintiffs seek to recover damages.

. . .

The letterhead [used for the SAFIG audit] identified the Bahamian accounting firm only as "Price Waterhouse." The audit letter also bore a Price Waterhouse trademark and was signed "Price Waterhouse."

Plaintiffs assert that it was foreseeable to the accounting firm that issued the letter that third-parties would rely upon the financial statement, the subject of the audit letter. According to the plaintiffs, the stamp of approval created by Price Waterhouse's audit letter of SAFIG's financial statement lent credence to the defrauders' claims so that plaintiffs were induced to invest to their detriment.

. . .

Plaintiffs assert that PW-Bahamas and PW-US [the Price Waterhouse partnership in the United States] operate as a partnership, i.e., constitute an association of persons to carry on, as owners, business for profit. In the alternative, plaintiffs contend that if the two associations are not actually operating as partners they are operating as partners by estoppel.

Defendants PW-US and PW-Bahamas flatly deny that a partnership exists between the two entities and have supplied, under seal, copies of relevant documents executed which establish that the two entities are separately organized. Counsel for plaintiffs admits that he has found nothing which establishes that the two entities are partners in fact. The evidence presented wholly belies plaintiffs' claims that PW-Bahamas and PW-US are operating as a partnership in fact. Thus, the court finds that there is no partnership, in fact, between PW-Bahamas and PW-US.

. . . [T]he argument for estoppel seems to be that if the two partnerships are partners by estoppel then PW-US can be held liable for the negligent acts of its partner PW-Bahamas, so the claim against PW-Bahamas operates as a claim against PW-US. . . .

As a general rule, persons who are not partners as to each other are not partners as to third persons. S.C.Code Ann. § 33–41–220 (Law. Co-op 1976) [U.P.A. (1914) § 7(1)]. However, a person who represents himself, or permits another to represent him, to anyone as a partner in an existing partnership or with others not actual partners, is liable to any such person to whom such a representation is made who has, on the faith of the representation, given credit to the actual or apparent partnership. S.C.Code Ann. § 33–41–380(1) [U.P.A. (1914) § 16(1)]. . . .

Generally, partners are jointly and severally liable for everything chargeable to the partnership. . . . In South Carolina, a partnership is an entity separate and distinct from the individual partners who compose it. . . . Therefore, plaintiffs' argument is that if the court would find that PW-Bahamas and PW-US are partners by estoppel, PW-US would be jointly and severally liable with PW-Bahamas for everything chargeable to the partnership of the two firms. Moreover, if the two partnerships are partners by estoppel, the individual partners of PW-US would then be jointly and severally liable for the negligent acts of the PW-Bahamas partnership.

Plaintiffs maintain that Price Waterhouse holds itself out to be a partnership with offices around the world. According to the plaintiffs, the U.S. affiliate makes no distinction in its advertising between itself and entities situated in foreign jurisdictions. The foreign affiliates are permitted to use the Price Waterhouse name and trademark. Plaintiffs urge the conclusion of partnership by estoppel from the combination of facts that Price Waterhouse promotes its image as an organization affiliated with other Price Waterhouse offices around the world and that it is common knowledge that the accounting firm of Price Waterhouse operates as a partnership.

Plaintiffs offer for illustration that PW-Bahamas and PW-US hold themselves out to be partners with one another, a Price Waterhouse brochure, picked up by plaintiffs' counsel at a litigation services seminar, that describes Price Waterhouse as one of the "world's largest and most respected professional organizations." The brochure states: "[O]ver 28,000 Price Waterhouse professionals in 400 offices throughout the world can be called upon to provide support for your reorganization and litigation efforts." Plaintiffs assert that assurances like that contained in the brochure cast Price Waterhouse as an established international accounting firm and that the image, promoted by PW-US, is designed to gain public confidence in the firm's stability and expertise.

However, the plaintiffs do not contend that the brochure submitted was seen or relied on by them in making the decision to invest. In addition, plaintiffs point to nothing in the brochure that asserts that the affiliated entities of Price Waterhouse are liable for the acts of another, or that any of the affiliates operate within a single partnership.

Defendant PW-US supplied copies of the relevant Cross documents which showed that the order of Judge Pratt was later vacated. Furthermore, PW-US informs the court that during the period in question in the Cross case, there were licensing agreements between the U.S. partnership and the Bahamian partnership for use of the name and trademark on which the decision was based. Such licensing agreements are no longer in existence.

PW-US points out that the South Carolina statute, which was cited by plaintiffs in support of their argument for partnership by estoppel, speaks only to the creation of liability to third-persons who, in reliance upon representations as to the existence of a partnership, "[give] credit" to that partnership. . . . There is no evidence, neither has there been an allegation, that credit was extended on the basis of any representation of a partnership existing between PW-Bahamas and the South Carolina members of the PW-US partnership. There is no evidence of any extension of credit to either PW-Bahamas or PW-US, by plaintiffs. Thus, the facts do not support a finding of liability for partners by estoppel under the statutory law of South Carolina.

Further, there is no evidence that plaintiffs relied on any act or statement by any PW-US partner which indicated the existence of a partnership with the Bahamian partnership. Finally, there is no evidence, nor is there a single allegation that any member of the U.S. partnership had anything to do with the audit letter complained of by plaintiffs, or any other act related to the investment transaction.

The court cannot find any evidence to support a finding of partners by estoppel. Therefore, the allegations of negligence against PW-

Bahamas cannot serve to hold individual members of the PW-US partnership in the suit. . . .

ANALYSIS

1. **What Is in a Name?** Price Waterhouse was a leading accounting firm in the United States. At the time, its name would have been recognized by anyone with any knowledge of business or finance. How did the Bahamian firm become entitled to use the same name? Why would it have wanted to use the name? Should the answers to these questions be relevant to the outcome of the case?
2. **Different Theories, Different Proof.** What is the difference in proof required for the two separate theories on which the plaintiff relied?
3. **Another Theory?** Might the plaintiff also have relied on an agency theory?

2. PARTNERSHIP PROPERTY

In re Fulton

43 B.R. 273 (United States Bankruptcy Court 1984).

This matter is before the court on the plaintiff's claim that the debtor wrongfully scheduled a 1972 Great Dane 42 foot [trailer] as an asset. . . .

The plaintiff, Padgett Carroll, and the debtor [Walter Charles Fulton, Sr.] operated a trucking business under the name of C & F Trucking. Mr. Carroll contributed a semi-truck which the debtor drove for the business. The profits earned from the business were to be divided between the parties. In July 1982, Mr. Carroll's grandmother, Mattie Holcomb, wired him $9,000.00. He used $4,600.00 of these funds to purchase a used trailer from Fruehauf Corporation for C & F Trucking. The seller's invoice for the trailer listed C & F Trucking as the purchaser of the trailer. The Arkansas certificate of title for the trailer was signed by the debtor and listed C & F Trucking as the owner.

> **NOTE**
>
> Chapter 7 of the Bankruptcy Code provides for appointment of a trustee, sale of the debtor's assets, distribution of the proceeds to creditors, and discharge of the debtor (that is, relief from the claims of the creditors).

On December 16, 1982, the debtor filed a voluntary Chapter 7 bankruptcy petition. . . .

I.

The court must decide two main issues in this proceeding. First, the court must determine who owns the trailer in question. Second, the court must determine whether the Chapter 7 estate has any interest in the trailer.

. . .

The evidence at trial established that Padgett Carroll and the debtor were engaged in the business of C & F Trucking. Padgett Carroll agreed to provide the capital necessary to run the business while the debtor agreed to drive the truck. The profits earned from this business were to be divided between the parties. Based on this evidence, this court has no difficulty in determining that Padgett Carroll and the debtor were engaged in business as a partnership. . . .

In determining whether property is partnership property or property owned by an individual, the court must focus primarily on the intentions of the partners at the time the property was acquired.

"The intent of the partners determines what property shall be considered partnership property as distinguished from separate property. Such intention of the partners must be determined from their apparent intention at the time the property was acquired, as shown by the facts and circumstances surrounding the transaction of purchase, considered with the conduct of the parties toward the property after the purchase." 60 Am.Jur.2d Partnership § 92 at 21 (1972). . . .

The evidence produced at the trial of this matter establishes that the trailer in question is indeed partnership property. The trustee introduced both a sales invoice and a certificate of title listing the owner of the trailer as C & F Trucking. The testimony established that the trailer was purchased by Padgett Carroll for use in the C & F Trucking business and that the debtor actually used the trailer in furtherance of the business.

. . .

II.

Under [bankruptcy law], the estate consists of ". . . all legal or equitable interest of the debtor in property as of the commencement of the case." Since a partnership is a legal entity separate from its partners, a partner cannot claim title in partnership property. The partner may only claim the rights in specific partnership property as bestowed upon the partner under partnership law. When a partner files for bankruptcy, the partner's estate obtains whatever partnership interest was held by the filing partner.

When the debtor filed bankruptcy, the partnership of C & F Trucking if not already dissolved was dissolved by operation of law. See [UPA (1914) § 31(5)]. Upon dissolution, partnership property must be used to pay the liabilities of the partnership in the priority established in [UPA (1914) § 40(b)]. Debts to creditors other than partners are paid first, debts to partners for contributions other than for capital and profits are paid second, debts owing to partners in respect of capital contributions are paid third and finally, debts owing to partners in respect of profits are paid last.

In the present case, . . . [f]or purposes of this distribution, the court holds that the money loaned by the plaintiff, Mattie Holcomb, to the plaintiff, Padgett Carroll, was a loan to Padgett Carroll and not to the partnership of C & F Trucking. The purchase of the trailer by Padgett Carroll and his subsequent contribution of that trailer to C & F Trucking constitutes a capital contribution to the partnership of C & F Trucking.

Accordingly, the court ORDERS that the equity in the trailer shall be distributed in accordance with [UPA (1914) § 40(b)], as described above. . . .

NOTE

UPA (1997) § 204 codified the common law, laying out three rules:

1. Any asset acquired in the name of the partnership is partnership property, including:
    a. a transfer directly to the partnership in its own name; and
    b. a transfer to one or more partners acting in their capacity as partners and the name of the partnership appears on the transfer document.
2. If the partnership is not named, property acquired by one or more partners is partnership property if the document transferring title indicates the buyer was acting in his capacity as a partner.
3. Property purchased with partnership funds is presumed to be partnership property.

ANALYSIS

1. Assume that the trailer is sold for $4,000; that C & F Trucking has no other assets; that the only creditor of C & F Trucking is owed $1,000; and that Padgett Carroll has individual debts of $2,000 and no individual assets.
    a. Who gets what?
    b. What if the facts are the same except that C & F Trucking had assets, in addition to the trailer, that are sold for $9,000?
2. Does it seem fair that in the liquidation of the partnership Carroll gets $4,000 before Fulton gets anything and then they split the surplus, if any?

Putnam v. Shoaf

620 S.W.2d 510 (Ct.App. of Tenn., Western Section, at Jackson, 1981).

This dispute is over the sale of a partnership interest in the Frog Jump Gin Company.

The Frog Jump Gin had operated for a number of years showing losses in some years and profits in others. In the time immediately preceding February, 1976, it appears that the gin operated at a loss. Originally, the gin was operated as an equal partnership between E. C. Charlton, Louise H. Charlton, Lyle Putnam and Carolyn Putnam. In 1974 Mr. Putnam died and Mrs. Putnam, by agreement, succeeded to her husband's interest. The gin operated under that control and management until February 19, 1976, when Mrs. Putnam desired to sever her relationship with the other partners in Frog Jump Gin. At that time the gin was heavily indebted to the Bank of Trenton and Trust Company, and Mrs. Putnam desired to be relieved of this liability. John A. and Maurine H. Shoaf displayed an interest in obtaining Mrs. Putnam's one-half interest in the partnership. An examination by the Shoafs of the financial records of the gin, evidenced by a statement from the gin bookkeeper, indicated a negative financial position of approximately $90,000.00. The Shoafs agreed to take over Mrs. Putnam's position in the partnership if Mrs. Putnam and the Charltons would each pay $21,000.00 into the partnership account. The Shoafs agreed to assume personal liability for all partnership debts, including Putnam's share of any partnership debts made prior to their coming into the partnership, although the Uniform Partnership Act would only make him personally liable for debts made after his entry into the partnership unless he agreed to more.... Both the Charltons and Mrs. Putnam paid their respective amounts into the partnership account, and Shoaf assumed all partnership obligations as aforesaid.

At the time of his agreement the known assets of the Frog Jump Gin consisted primarily of the gin, its equipment, and the land upon which they were located. All gin assets, including the land, were held in the name of the partnership. Mrs. Putnam conveyed her interest in the partnership to the Shoafs by means of a quit claim deed. Upon Shoaf's assumption of the position of a partner, the services of the old bookkeeper were terminated and a new bookkeeper was hired.

In April, 1977, with the assistance of the new bookkeeper, it was learned that the old bookkeeper had engaged in a scheme of systematic embezzlement from the Frog Jump Gin Company from the time of Mr. Putnam's death until the bookkeeper's services were terminated. This disclosure led to suits being filed by the gin against the bookkeeper and the banks that had honored checks forged by the bookkeeper. There is no need to go into the details of all that litigation. Suffice it to say that Mrs.

Putnam was allowed to intervene claiming an interest in any fund paid by the banks and the upshot of it all was a judgment paid into Court by the banks in excess of $68,000.00. One-half of that sum, by agreement, has been paid to the Charltons as owners of a one-half interest in the gin, and the other half is the subject of this dispute between the Shoafs and Mrs. Putnam's estate. She has died pending this litigation and the case revived.

. . .

The conveyance between Mrs. Putnam and the Shoafs is evidenced by what is styled a "Quitclaim Deed" executed by Mrs. Putnam on February 19, 1976, which is as follows:

> "FOR AND IN CONSIDERATION of the sum of One Dollar ($1.00), cash in hand paid, the receipt of which is hereby acknowledged, and the assumption by Grantees of all Grantor's obligations arising or by virtue of her partnership interest in the Frog Jump Gin Company, including three notes to Bank of Tenton and Trust Company, I, CAROLYN B. PUTNAM, a widow, have this day bargained and sold and by these presents so hereby sell, transfer, convey and forever quitclaim unto JOHN A. SHOAF and wife, MAURINE H. SHOAF, their heirs and assigns, all the right, title and interest (it being a one-half (1/2) undivided interest) I have in and to the following described real and personal property located in the 25th Civil District of Gibson County, Tennessee, and described as follows; to-wit:"
>
> (The legal description of the real property follows.)
>
> "PERSONAL PROPERTY:
>
> "All of the personal property and machinery in said Frog Jump Gin Company's buildings and on said properties described and used in the operation of its cotton gin plant on the above-described parcel of land, including two Moss Gordin 75 saw gin stands; one Overhead incline cleaner; stick and green leaf machine; two Moss Gordin lint cleaners; two Mitchell Feeders; two Mitchell burners; one Hardwick Etter all steel press; condensers; fans; motors; pulleys; shafting; all piping; belting and machinery and appliances and other personal property, including all cotton trailers, on said parcel of land and used in connection with the operation of said cotton gin, accounts receivable, inventory and all other assets of Frog Jump Gin Company.
>
> "TO HAVE AND TO HOLD the said real and personal property with the appurtenances, estate, title and interest thereto belonging unto the said John A. Shoaf and wife, Maurine H. Shoaf, their heirs and assigns, forever.

"Witness my signature this the 19 day of February, 1976."

On the same day Mrs. Putnam and the Charltons executed the following agreement:

> "This Agreement made and entered into on this the 19th day of February, 1976, by and between E. C. Charlton and wife, Louise H. Charlton, party of one part, and Carolyn B. Putnam, party of the other part, all of Trenton, Gibson County, Tennessee;
>
> "WITNESSETH: THAT WHEREAS, the parties have heretofore been conducting a business, as partners, under the firm name and style of Frog Jump Gin Company; and
>
> "WHEREAS, Carolyn B. Putnam has agreed to pay into the partnership the sum of Twenty-one Thousand Dollars ($21,000.00), the receipt of which is hereby acknowledged, and has sold and conveyed her interest in the partnership to John A. Shoaf and wife, Maurine H. Shoaf.
>
> "NOW, THEREFORE, it is mutually agreed that the partnership be and hereby is dissolved. It is further mutually agreed that the parties do hereby release and forever discharge each other from any and all claims and demands on account of, connected with, or growing out of the said partnership, or the division of the assets thereof; and it is expressly understood and agreed that Carolyn B. Putnam is completely released and discharged from any and all liability, debts, or causes of action of the Frog Jump Gin Company, presently existing, contingent, or otherwise, including notes owed to Bank of Trenton and Trust Company, and that E. C. Charlton and wife, Louise H. Charlton assume all liability and indebtedness of the said partnership and covenant to indemnify and save harmless the said Carolyn B. Putnam in the premises.
>
> "In Witness Whereof, the parties have hereunto set their signatures, this day and date first above written."

At approximately the same time, Mrs. Putnam obtained from the Bank of Trenton a complete release from all personal liability for note indebtednesses to the Bank in the face amount of $105,000.00 in consideration of the Shoafs' assumption of all obligations of the Frog Jump Gin.

. . .

First, we must discover the nature of the ownership interest of Mrs. Putnam in that which she conveyed. Under the Uniform Partnership Act, . . . her partnership property rights consisted of her (1) rights in specific partnership property, (2) interest in the partnership and (3) right to participate in management. . . . The right in "specific partnership property" is the partnership tenancy possessory right of equal use or possession by partners for partnership purposes. This possessory right is incident to the partnership and the possessory right does not exist absent the partnership. The possessory right is not the partner's "interest" in the assets of the partnership. . . . The real interest of a partner, as opposed to that incidental possessory right before discussed, is the partner's interest in the partnership which is defined as "his share of the profits and surplus and the same is personal property." . . . Therefore, a co-partner owns no personal specific interest in any specific property or asset of the partnership. The partnership owns the property or the asset. . . . The partner's interest is an undivided interest, as a co-tenant in all partnership property. . . . That interest is the partner's pro rata share of the net value or deficit of the partnership. . . . For this reason a conveyance of partnership property held in the name of the partnership is made in the name of the partnership and not as a conveyance of the individual interests of the partners. . . .

This being true, all Mrs. Putnam had to convey was her interest in the partnership. Accordingly, she had no specific interest in the admittedly unknown choses in action to separately convey or retain. Therefore, the determinative question is: Did Mrs. Putnam intend to convey her interest in the partnership to the Shoafs? There can be no doubt that such was the intent of Mrs. Putnam, as she had no other interest to convey. . . . If we would say otherwise, that is that she intended to convey less, and thereby retain a partnership interest, Mrs. Putnam would have remained a partner unknown to the other parties and, in reality, unknown to herself. It is abundantly evident that the last thing Mrs. Putnam wanted was to remain a partner. She wanted out, and out she got.

. . . This situation is no different from a hypothetical oil discovery on the partnership real property after transfer of a partnership interest with neither party believing oil to be present at the time of the conveyance. The interest in the real property always was and remained in the partnership. Of course, the transferor would not have transferred his partnership interest had he known of the existence of oil on partnership property; but, mutual ignorance of the existence of the oil would not, in our opinion, warrant a "reformation" of the contract for sale of the partnership interest, or warrant a decree in favor of the transferor for a share of the value of the oil.

. . . We wonder what would be the position of Mrs. Putnam, or the estate, had the Frog Jump Gin failed, leaving a sizeable deficit, even after the influx of the bank's refund. Would she accept a partner's share of the Frog Jump Gin's liabilities for a share of the bank's refund? The question answers itself and we pose it only to show that she did not have a specific interest in any specific assets of the Frog Jump Gin, either to retain or convey. All she had was a partner's interest in a "share of the profits" (and losses) which she certainly intended to convey.

ANALYSIS

1. **Entity vs. Aggregate.** A partnership might be thought of as an entity—like a corporation, which is conceived of as a separate entity, in which individuals may own shares. Alternatively, it might be thought of as an aggregation of assets each of which is owned pro rata by the partners—just as, for example, an individual owning a hardware store might be thought to own directly and personally each and every item in the store's inventory. Does the court in the present case treat the partnership as an entity or an aggregate? Would it matter?
2. **Partners as Guarantors?** Suppose that after the change of ownership it was discovered, much to everyone's surprise, that an underground stream had undercut the land on which the gin was located and it was necessary to abandon the property. Could the Shoafs have recovered their loss from Ms. Putnam?

3. THE RIGHTS OF PARTNERS IN MANAGEMENT

INTRODUCTORY NOTE

In many, perhaps most, small partnerships, each of the partners expects to play a role in conducting the business of the partnership. The right of each partner to participate in the operation of the business in some way will be an implicit term of the partnership agreement. At the same time, disagreements may arise over various business decisions. Section 18(e) of the UPA (1914) provides that in the absence of an agreement to the contrary, "all partners have equal rights in the management and conduct of the partnership business," and § 18(h) provides that "any difference arising as to ordinary matters connected with the partnership business may be decided by a majority of the partners." (To the same effect is UPA (1997) § 401(h) and (k).) Thus, if there are three partners and they disagree as to an "ordinary" matter, the decision of the majority controls. For example, if the partnership operates a grocery store, and two of the partners, for business reasons, want to stop buying bread from a certain supplier, their decision is binding on the third partner. The majority can deprive the minority partner of the authority to buy bread from that supplier. If the supplier is made aware of the limitation, an order for bread from the minority partner would not bind the partnership or the other partners. If, however, there are only two partners, there can be no majority vote that will be effective to deprive either partner of authority to act for the partnership. Similar stalemates can, of course, arise in any partnership with an even number of partners.

National Biscuit Company v. Stroud

249 N.C. 467, 106 S.E.2d 692 (1959).

C.N. Stroud and Earl Freeman entered into a general partnership to sell groceries under the firm name of Stroud's Food Center. There is nothing in the agreed statement of facts to indicate or suggest that Freeman's power and authority as a general partner were in any way restricted or limited by the articles of partnership in respect to the ordinary and legitimate business of the partnership. Certainly, the purchase and sale of bread were ordinary and legitimate business of Stroud's Food Center during its continuance as a going concern.

Several months prior to February 1956 Stroud advised plaintiff that he personally would not be responsible for any additional bread sold by plaintiff to Stroud's Food Center. After such notice to plaintiff, it from 6 February 1956 to 25 February 1956, at the request of Freeman, sold and delivered bread in the amount of $171.04 to Stroud's Food Center.

In Johnson v. Bernheim, 76 N.C. 139, this Court said: "A and B are general partners to do some given business; the partnership is, by operation of law, a power to each to bind the partnership in any manner legitimate to the business. If one partner go to a third person to buy an article on time for the partnership, the other partner cannot prevent it by writing to the third person not to sell to him on time; or, if one party attempt to buy for cash, the other has no right to require that it shall be on time. And what is true in regard to buying is true in regard to selling. What either partner does with a third person is binding on the partnership. It is otherwise where the partnership is not general, but is upon special terms, as that purchases and sales must be with and for cash. There the power to each is special, in regard to all dealings with third persons at least who have notice of the terms." . . .

The General Assembly of North Carolina in 1941 enacted a Uniform Partnership Act, which became effective 15 March 1941. G.S. Ch. 59, Partnership, Art. 2.

G.S. § 59–39 is entitled "Partner Agent of Partnership as to Partnership Business," and subsection (1) reads: "Every partner is an agent of the partnership for the purpose of its business, and the act of every partner, including the execution in the partnership name of any instrument, for apparently carrying on in the usual way the business of the partnership of which he is a member binds the partnership, unless the partner so acting has in fact no authority to act for the partnership in the particular matter, and the person with whom he is dealing has knowledge of the fact that he has no such authority." G.S. § 59–39(4) states: "No act of a partner in contravention of a restriction on authority shall bind the partnership to persons having knowledge of the restriction."

G.S. § 59–45 provides that "all partners are jointly and severally liable for the acts and obligations of the partnership."

G.S. § 59–48 is captioned "Rules Determining Rights and Duties of Partners." Subsection (e) thereof reads: "All partners have equal rights in the management and conduct of the partnership business." Subsection (h) hereof is as follows: "Any difference arising as to ordinary matters connected with the partnership business may be decided by a majority of the partners; but no act in contravention of any agreement between the partners may be done rightfully without the consent of all the partners."

Freeman as a general partner with Stroud, with no restrictions on his authority to act within the scope of the partnership business so far as the agreed statement of facts shows, had under the Uniform Partnership Act "equal rights in the management and conduct of the partnership business." Under G.S. § 59–48(h) Stroud, his co-partner, could not restrict the power and authority of Freeman to buy bread for the partnership as a going concern, for such a purchase was an "ordinary matter connected with the partnership business," for the purpose of its business and within its scope, because in the very nature of things Stroud was not, and could not be, a majority of the partners. Therefore, Freeman's purchases of bread from plaintiff for Stroud's Food Center as a going concern bound the partnership and his co-partner Stroud. . . .

In Crane on Partnership, 2d Ed., p. 277, it is said: "In cases of an even division of the partners as to whether or not an act within the scope of the business should be done, of which disagreement a third person has knowledge, it seems that logically no restriction can be placed upon the power to act. The partnership being a going concern, activities within the scope of the business should not be limited, save by the expressed will of the majority deciding a disputed question; half of the members are not a majority."

. . .

At the close of business on 25 February 1956 Stroud and Freeman by agreement dissolved the partnership. By their dissolution agreement all of the partnership assets, including cash on hand, bank deposits and all accounts receivable, with a few exceptions, were assigned to Stroud, who bound himself by such written dissolution agreement to liquidate the firm's assets and discharge its liabilities. It would seem a fair inference from the agreed statement of facts that the partnership got the benefit of the bread sold and delivered by plaintiff to Stroud's Food Center, at Freeman's request, from 6 February 1956 to 25 February 1956. . . . But whether it did or not, Freeman's acts, as stated above, bound the partnership and Stroud.

The judgment of the court below is

Affirmed.

ANALYSIS

Protection from Liability. What could Stroud have done to protect himself from liability for obligations incurred by Freeman?

Summers v. Dooley

94 Idaho 87, 481 P.2d 318 (1971).

. . . Summers [plaintiff-appellant] entered a partnership agreement with Dooley (defendant-respondent) in 1958 for the purpose of operating a trash collection business. The business was operated by the two men and when either was unable to work, the non-working partner provided a replacement at his own expense. In 1962, Dooley became unable to work and, at his own expense, hired an employee to take his place. In July, 1966, Summers approached his partner Dooley regarding the hiring of an additional employee but Dooley refused. Nevertheless, on his own initiative, Summers hired the man and paid him out of his own pocket. Dooley, upon discovering that Summers had hired an additional man, objected, stating that he did not feel additional labor was necessary and refused to pay for the new employee out of the partnership funds. Summers continued to operate the business using the third man and in October of 1967 instituted suit in the district court for $6,000 against his partner, the gravamen of the complaint being that Summers has been required to pay out more than $11,000 in expenses, incurred in the hiring of the additional man, without any reimbursement from either the partnership funds or his partner. After trial before the court, sitting without a jury, Summers was granted only partial relief and he has appealed. . . .

The principal thrust of appellant's contention is that in spite of the fact that one of the two partners refused to consent to the hiring of additional help, nonetheless, the non-consenting partner retained profits earned by the labors of the third man and therefore the non-consenting partner should be estopped from denying the need and value of the employee, and has by his behavior ratified the act of the other partner who hired the additional man. . . .

An application of the relevant statutory provisions and pertinent case law to the factual situation presented by the instant case indicates that the trial court was correct in its disposal of the issue since a majority of the partners did not consent to the hiring of the third man. I.C. § 53–318(8) [UPA (1914 § 18(h))] provides:

"Any difference arising as to ordinary matters connected with the partnership business may be decided by a majority of the partners * * *."

> **NOTE**
>
> The court here quotes UPA (1914) § 18, which is set forth in the appendix to this chapter.

. . . A careful reading of the statutory provision indicates that subsection 5 [UPA (1914) § 18(e)] bestows equal rights in the management and conduct of the partnership business upon all of the partners.[2] The concept of equality between partners with respect to management of business affairs is a central theme and recurs throughout the Uniform Partnership law. . . . Thus the only reasonable interpretation of I.C. § 53–318(8) [UPA (1914) § 18(h)] is that business differences must be decided by a majority of the partners provided no other agreement between the partners speaks to the issues.

In the case at bar one of the partners continually voiced objection to the hiring of the third man. He did not sit idly by and acquiesce in the actions of his partner. Under these circumstances it is manifestly unjust to permit recovery of an expense which was incurred individually and not for the benefit of the partnership but rather for the benefit of one partner.

ANALYSIS

1. **Protecting Summers.** What should Summers have done?
2. **Protection by Agreement?** Could the partners have solved this problem by contract?
3. **Comparison to *Nabisco*.** Why could Freeman (in the *National Biscuit* case, supra) bind his partnership but Summers, in this case, could not?

> **PLANNING**
>
> Suppose Stroud and Freeman come to you before forming their partnership and ask you to draft a partnership agreement for them. What terms might you propose to avert or mitigate the problems that give rise to this sort of litigation?

Moren ex rel. Moren v. Jax Restaurant

679 N.W.2d 165 (Minn. App. 2004).

Remington Moren, through his father, commenced a negligence action against appellant Jax Restaurant for injures he sustained while on appellant's premises. The district court granted a summary judgment, dismissing appellant's third-party negligence complaint against respondent Nicole Moren, a partner in Jax Restaurant and the mother of Remington Moren. Because the court correctly determined that liability for Nicole Moren's negligence rested with the partnership, even if the partner's conduct partly served her personal interests, we affirm.

[2] In the absence of an agreement to the contrary. . . . In the case at bar, there is no such agreement and thus I.C. 53–318(5) [UPA (1914) § 18(e)] and each of the other subsections are applicable. . . .

Facts

Jax Restaurant, the partnership, operates its business in Foley, Minnesota. One afternoon in October 2000, Nicole Moren, one of the Jax partners, completed her day shift at Jax at 4:00 p.m. and left to pick up her two-year-old son Remington from day care. At about 5:30, Moren returned to the restaurant with Remington after learning that her sister and partner, Amy Benedetti, needed help. Moren called her husband who told her that he would pick Remington up in about 20 minutes.

Because Nicole Moren did not want Remington running around the restaurant, she brought him into the kitchen with her, set him on top of the counter, and began rolling out pizza dough using the dough-pressing machine. As she was making pizzas, Remington reached his hand into the dough press. His hand was crushed, and he sustained permanent injuries.

Through his father, Remington commenced a negligence action against the partnership. The partnership served a third-party complaint on Nicole Moren, arguing that, in the event it was obligated to compensate Remington, the partnership was entitled to indemnity or contribution from Moren for her negligence. The district court's summary judgment was premised on a legal conclusion that Moren has no obligation to indemnify Jax Restaurant so long as the injury occurred while she was engaged in ordinary business conduct. The district court rejected the partnership's argument that its obligation to compensate Remington is diminished in proportion to the predominating negligence of Moren as a mother, although it is responsible for her conduct as a business owner. This appeal followed. . . .

Issue

Does JAX Restaurant have an indemnity right against Nicole Moren in the circumstances of this case?

Analysis

. . .

Under Minnesota's Uniform Partnership Act of 1994 (UPA), a partnership is an entity distinct from its partners, and as such, a partnership may sue and be sued in the name of the partnership. [U.P.A. (1997) §§ 201 and 307.] "A partnership is liable for loss or injury caused to a person ... as a result of a wrongful act or omission, or other actionable conduct, of a partner acting in the ordinary course of business of the partnership or with authority of the partnership." [U.P.A (1997) § 305(a).] Accordingly, a "partnership shall ... indemnify a partner for liabilities incurred by the partner in the ordinary course of the business of the partnership . . . ." [U.P.A. (1997) § 401(c).] Stated conversely, an "act of a partner which is not apparently for carrying on in the ordinary course the partnership business or business of the kind carried on by the partnership binds the partnership only if the act was authorized by the other partners." [U.P.A. (1997) § 301(2)]. Thus, under the plain language of the UPA, a partner has a right to indemnity from the partnership, but the partnership's claim of indemnity from a partner is not authorized or required.

The district court correctly concluded that Nicole Moren's conduct was in the ordinary course of business of the partnership and, as a result, indemnity by the partner to the partnership was inappropriate. It is undisputed that one of the cooks scheduled to work that evening did not come in, and that Moren's partner asked her to help in the kitchen. It also is undisputed that Moren was making pizzas for the partnership when her son was injured. Because her conduct at the time of the injury was in the ordinary course of business of the partnership, under the UPA, her conduct bound the partnership . . . .

Appellant also claims that because Nicole Moren's action of bringing Remington into the kitchen was partly motivated by personal reasons, her conduct was outside the ordinary course of business. . . . [W]e conclude that the conduct of Nicole Moren was no less in the ordinary course of business because it also served personal purposes. It is undisputed that Moren was acting for the benefit of the partnership by making pizzas when her son was injured, and even though she was simultaneously acting in her role as a mother, her conduct remained in the ordinary course of the partnership business.

The district court determined, and appellant strenuously disputes, that Amy Benedetti authorized Nicole's conduct, or at least that her conduct of bringing Remington into the kitchen was not prohibited by the rules of the partnership. Because under Minnesota law authorization from the other partners is merely an alternative basis for establishing partnership liability, we decline to address the issue of whether Nicole Moren's partner authorized her conduct. . . .

Affirmed.

ANALYSIS

1. **The Defendant.** Why do you suppose Nicole's husband, Martin, acting on behalf of their son, Remington, sued the partnership of Nicole and her sister Amy?

2. **Partnership Law and Agency Law.** Why is partnership law important here? What if Amy, instead of calling in Nicole to help out, had called in a substitute cook? Suppose the cook had, of necessity, brought in her son and, because the cook failed to supervise properly, the son had been injured and sued the partnership. In the unlikely event of a third-party action against the cook, what would be the result of a motion to dismiss?

3. **Ordinary Course of Business.** What would the result have been if Martin had brought Remington to the restaurant during Nicole's normal working hours, to "see what mommy does at work"; that Martin had left Remington with Nicole while he went out for a quick beer; and that Remington had then been injured as in the actual case? Could Remington have recovered from the partnership (assuming Nicole was negligent in her supervision)? If so, could the partnership have recovered from Nicole in a third-party action?

PROBLEM

Alison, Bill, and Charles formed a partnership about two years ago to open and operate a grocery store. In accordance with their initial understanding, Alison has served as general manager, Bill has served as assistant general manager and produce manager, and Charles has run the meat department. About six months ago, Charles hired his son Don to work in the meat department. Alison and Bill believe that Don is surly and slow and that he is driving customers away. They have asked Charles to fire him, but Charles has refused to do so. He thinks Don is brash but lovable and that many customers like his style, and he is satisfied that he works fast enough to get his job done. The relationship of Alison and Bill with Charles and Don is unpleasant.

Alison and Bill come to you for advice. They ask whether they can fire Don and, if so, how they should go about it. What do you say?

RNR Investments Ltd. Partnership v. Peoples First Community Bank

812 So.2d 561 (Fla. App. 2002).

. . .

Factual and Procedural History

RNR is a Florida limited partnership formed pursuant to chapter 620, Florida Statutes, to purchase vacant land in Destin, Florida, and to construct a house on the land for resale. Bernard Roeger was RNR's general partner and Heinz Rapp, Claus North, and S.E. Waltz, Inc., were limited partners. The agreement of limited partnership provides for various restrictions on the authority of the general partner. Paragraph 4.1 of the agreement required the general partner to prepare a budget covering the cost of acquisition and construction of the project (defined as the "Approved Budget") and further provided, in pertinent part, as follows:

> The Approved Budget for the Partnership is attached hereto as Exhibit "C" and is approved by evidence of the signatures of the Partners on the signature pages of this Agreement. . . .

Paragraph 4.3 restricted the general partner's ability to borrow, spend partnership funds and encumber partnership assets, if not specifically provided for in the Approved Budget. Finally, with respect to the development of the partnership project, paragraph 2.2(b) provided:

> The General Partner shall not incur debts, liabilities or obligations of the Partnership which will cause any line item in the Approved Budget to be exceeded by more than ten percent (10%) or which will cause the aggregate Approved Budget to be exceed by more than five percent (5%) unless the General Partner shall receive the prior written consent of the Limited Partner.

In June 1998, RNR, through its general partner, entered into a construction loan agreement, note and mortgage in the principal amount of $990,000. From June 25, 1998 through Mar. 13, 2000, the bank disbursed the aggregate sum of $952,699, by transfers into RNR's bank account. . . . No representative of RNR objected to any draw of funds or asserted that the amounts disbursed were not associated with the construction of the house.

RNR defaulted under the terms of the note and mortgage by failing to make payments due in July 2000 and all monthly payments due thereafter. The Bank filed a complaint seeking foreclosure. . . . In its first affirmative defense, RNR alleged that the Bank had failed to review the limitations on the general partner's authority in RNR's limited partnership agreement. RNR asserted that the Bank had negligently failed to investigate and to realize that the general partner had no authority to execute notes, a mortgage and a construction loan agreement and was estopped from foreclosing. The Bank filed a motion for summary judgment with supporting affidavits attesting to the amounts due and owing and the amount of disbursements under the loan.

In opposition to the summary judgment motion, RNR filed the affidavit of Stephen E. Waltz, the president one of RNR's limited partners, S.E. Waltz, Inc. In that affidavit, Mr. Waltz stated that the partners anticipated that RNR would need to finance the construction of the residence, but that paragraph 2.2(b) of the partnership agreement limited the amount of any loan the general partner could obtain on behalf of RNR to an amount that would not exceed by more than 10% the approved budget on any one line item or exceed the aggregate approved budget by more than 5%, unless the general partner received the prior written consent of the limited partners. Waltz alleged that the limited partners understood and orally agreed that the general partner would seek financing in the approximate amount of $650,000. Further, Waltz stated:

> Even though the limited partners had orally agreed to this amount, a written consent was never memorialized, and to my surprise, the [Bank], either through its employees or attorney, . . . never requested the same from any of the limited partners at any time prior to [or] after the closing on the loan from the [Bank] to RNR.

Waltz alleged that the partners learned in the spring of 2000 that, instead of obtaining a loan for $650,000, Roeger had obtained a loan for $990,000, which was secured by RNR's property. He stated that the limited partners did not consent to Roeger obtaining a loan from the Bank in the amount of $990,000 either orally or in writing and that the limited partners were never contacted by the Bank as to whether they had consented to a loan amount of $990,000.

RNR asserts that a copy of the limited partnership agreement was maintained at its offices. Nevertheless, the record contains no copy of an Approved Budget of the partnership or any evidence that would show that a copy of RNR's partnership agreement or any partnership budget was given to the Bank or that any notice of the general partner's restricted authority was provided to the Bank.

A hearing on the motion for summary judgment was held, however, a transcript of that hearing is not contained in the record. Thereafter, the trial court entered a summary final judgment of foreclosure in favor of the Bank. . . .

Apparent Authority of the General Partner

Although the agency concept of apparent authority was applied to partnerships under the common law, . . . in Florida the extent to which the partnership is bound by the acts of a partner acting within the apparent authority is now governed by statute. [Section 402 of the Uniform Limited Partnership Act of 2001 provides:

> Each general partner is an agent of the limited partnership for the purposes of its activities. An act of a general partner, including the signing of a record in the partnership's name, for apparently carrying on in the ordinary course the limited partnership's activities or activities of the kind carried on by the limited partnership binds the limited partnership, unless the general partner did not have authority to act for the limited partnership in the particular matter and the person with which the general partner was dealing knew, had received a

notification, or had notice under Section 103(d) that the general partner lacked authority.]

Thus, even if a general partner's actual authority is restricted by the terms of the partnership agreement, the general partner possesses the apparent authority to bind the partnership in the ordinary course of partnership business or in the business of the kind carried on by the partnership, unless the third party ["knew, had received a notification, or had notice under Section 103(d) that the general partner lacked authority."] Id. . . . [A] third party has notice of a fact if that party ["(1) knows of it; (2) has received a notification of it; (3) has reason to know it exists from all of the facts known to the person at the time in question; or (4) has notice of it under subsection (c) or (d)." Section 103.] . . .

"Absent actual knowledge, third parties have no duty to inspect the partnership agreement or inquire otherwise to ascertain the extent of a partner's actual authority in the ordinary course of business, . . . even if they have some reason to question it." [Donald J. Weidner & John W. Larson, The Revised Uniform Partnership Act: The Reporters' Overview, 49 Bus. Law 1, 32 n.200 (1993).] The apparent authority provisions of section 620.8301(1), reflect a policy by the drafters that "the risk of loss from partner misconduct more appropriately belongs on the partnership than on third parties who do not knowingly participate in or take advantage of the misconduct . . ." J. Dennis Hayes, Notice and Notification Under the Revised Uniform Partnership Act: Some Suggested Changes, 2 J. Small & Emerging Bus. L. 299, 308 (1998).

Analysis

Under section [402], the determination of whether a partner is acting with authority to bind the partnership involves a two-step analysis. The first step is to determine whether the partner purporting to bind the partnership apparently is carrying on the partnership business in the usual way or a business of the kind carried on by the partnership. An affirmative answer on this step ends the inquiry, unless it is shown that the person with whom the partner is dealing actually knew or had received a notification that the partner lacked authority. . . . Here, it is undisputed that, in entering into the loan, the general partner was carrying on the business of RNR in the usual way. The dispositive question in this appeal is whether there are issues of material fact as to whether the Bank had actual knowledge or notice of restrictions on the general partner's authority.

RNR argues that, as a result of the restrictions on the general partner's authority in the partnership agreement, the Bank had constructive knowledge of the restrictions and was obligated to inquire as to the general partner's specific authority to bind RNR in the construction loan. We cannot agree. Under section [402], the Bank could rely on the general partner's apparent authority, unless it had actual knowledge or notice of restrictions on that authority. While the RNR partners may have agreed upon restrictions that would limit the general partner to borrowing no more than $650,000 on behalf of the partnership, RNR does not contend and nothing before us would show that the Bank had actual knowledge or notice of any restrictions on the general partner's authority. Here, the partnership could have protected itself by filing a statement . . . or by providing notice to the Bank of the specific restrictions on the authority of the general partner. . . .

ANALYSIS

1. **The Bank's Responsibility.** What would the bank have had to do to learn of Roeger's lack of authority?
2. **Protecting the Partnership.** What could the limited partners have done to protect themselves against a general partner who borrowed too much?

Day v. Sidley & Austin

394 F.Supp. 986 (D.D.C.1975), affirmed sub nom. Day v. Avery, 548 F.2d 1018 (D.C.Cir.1976), cert. denied, 431 U.S. 908, 97 S.Ct. 1706, 52 L.Ed.2d 394 (1977).

This case involves a dispute between a former senior partner of Sidley & Austin (S & A), a Chicago law firm, and some of his fellow partners. The controversy centers around the merger between that firm and another Chicago firm, Liebman, Williams, Bennett, Baird and Minow (Liebman firm), and the events subsequent to the merger which ultimately led to plaintiff's resignation. Plaintiff seeks damages claiming a substantial loss of income, damage to his professional reputation and personal embarrassment which resulted from his forced resignation.

The matter is now before the Court on defendants' motion for summary judgment. After consideration of the pre-and post-hearing memoranda of counsel, answers to interrogatories, affidavits, and oral arguments, this Court concludes that defendants' motion for summary judgment should be granted.

The Factual Background

The basic and material facts in this controversy may be briefly detailed.

Mr. Day was first associated with Sidley & Austin in 1938. His legal career was interrupted by World War II service in the Navy and by his tenure with both the Illinois state government and as Postmaster General of the United States. Upon leaving the federal government, he was instrumental in establishing a Washington office for the firm in 1963. As a senior underwriting partner, he was entitled to a certain percentage of the firm's profits, and was also privileged to vote on certain matters which were specified in the partnership agreement. He was never a member of the executive committee, however, which managed the firm's day-to-day business. He remained an underwriting partner with Sidley & Austin from 1963 until his resignation in December 1972.

At some time between February 1972 and July 12, 1972, S & A's executive committee explored the idea of a possible merger between that firm and the Liebman firm. S & A partners who were not on the executive committee were unaware of the proposal until it was revealed at a special meeting of its underwriting partners on July 17, 1972. At that meeting, each partner present, including plaintiff, voiced approval of the merger idea and favored pursuing further that possibility in such manner as the executive committee of S & A might think proper or advisable, with the understanding that any proposed agreement would first be submitted to all partners for their consideration before any binding commitments were made. The merger was further discussed at meetings of the underwriting partners held on September 6, September 22, September 26 and September 28. The plaintiff received timely notice of the meetings but did not attend.

The final Memorandum of Understanding dated September 29, 1972 and the final amended Partnership Agreement, dated October 16, 1972 were executed by all S & A partners, including plaintiff. The Memorandum incorporated a minor change requested by plaintiff.

At a meeting of the executive committee of the combined firm on October 16, 1972, it was decided that the Washington offices and the Washington office committees of the two predecessor firms would be consolidated. The former chairmen of the Washington office committees of the two firms were appointed co-chairmen of the new Washington Office Committee.

In late October of 1972, the new Washington Office Committee recommended to the Management Committee that a combined Washington office be set up at 1730 Pennsylvania Avenue, thus eliminating the old S & A Washington office in the Cafritz Building. A decision was then made to move to the new location despite plaintiff's objections.

Mr. Day resigned from Sidley & Austin effective December 31, 1972 claiming that the changes which occurred after the merger in the Washington office—the appointment of co-chairmen and the relocation of the office—made continued service with the firm intolerable for him.

. . .

Mr. Day contends that he had a contractual right to remain the sole chairman of the Washington office, and that the maintenance of this status was a condition precedent for his rejoining the firm in 1963 and opening the Washington office. According to plaintiff, the decision to appoint co-chairmen was made prior to the merger and defendants' concealment of that decision was a material omission and without that prior information his vote of approval for the merger would not have been given.

He further alleges that certain active misrepresentations about the results of the proposal also had the effect of voiding the approval of the merger. These other alleged misrepresentations were:

(1) that no Sidley partner would be worse off in any way as a result of the merger, including positions on committees;

(2) that two senior partners of the Liebman firm would soon be leaving law practice;

(3) that the merged firm would drop representation of a certain Liebman client whose interests might conflict with some Sidley clients;

(4) that the merger with Liebman would be advantageous to the Sidley partners and would add to the standing and prestige of the firm;

(5) that all aspects of the merger had been exhaustively investigated by defendants; and

(6) that there were good, sound, objective reasons which made the merger highly desirable.

Plaintiff also alleges that the fact that the Liebman firm had been shopping around for a merger partner for 10 years was concealed.

Events after the merger, allegedly void because of the mentioned omissions and misrepresentations, inevitably led to plaintiff's resignation. The loss of his status as sole chairman of the Washington office was viewed by plaintiff as a humiliating experience, especially as it was accompanied by harassment by the defendants. Day points to the method of handling the relocation of the consolidated firm as the most obvious manifestation of the defendants' intent to force his resignation. In an affidavit submitted by plaintiff, he asserts that the process of approving the office move entailed a series of meetings held and decisions made without consulting him, all in derogation of his former status as the final decision maker for the S & A Washington office.

Defendants do not concede that misrepresentations or omissions tainted the approval of the merger, nor do they admit engaging in harassment techniques intended to force plaintiff to resign. The thrust of defendants' argument for summary judgment is that plaintiff's factual allegations are not material because they fail to state a cause of action. Defendants contend that any possible taint of plaintiff's vote in favor of the merger is of no consequence because only a majority, and not unanimous consent, was required for the merger under the provisions of the partnership agreements. Defendants also contend that any diminution of status as perceived by plaintiff cannot have any legal consequences because he had no vested contractual right to remain the sole chairman. They rely on the terms of the partnership agreements to support this defense. Under the agreements, the Executive Committee had the authority to govern the composition of all other firm committees and no special provisions had been made as to plaintiff's vested right in the Washington office.

An analysis of the adequacy of each of plaintiff's causes of action follows.

Fraud

. . .

The key misrepresentation which forms the basis of plaintiff's complaint is that no Sidley partner would be worse off as a result of the merger. Plaintiff interpreted this to mean that he would continue to serve as the sole chairman of the Washington office and that he would wield the commanding authority regarding such matters as expanding office space. It was the change in plaintiff's status at the Washington office which directly precipitated his resignation.

This misrepresentation regarding plaintiff's status cannot support a cause of action for fraud, however, because plaintiff was not deprived of any *legal* right as a result of his reliance on this statement. The 1970 S & A Partnership Agreement, to which plaintiff was a party, sets forth in some detail the relationships among the partners and the structure of the firm. No mention is made of the Washington office or plaintiff's status therein, whereas special arrangements are specified for certain other partners. If chairmanship of the Washington office was of the importance now claimed, the absence of such a provision from the partnership agreement requires a measured explanation which Mr. Day does not supply. Plaintiff's allegations of an unwritten understanding cannot now be heard to contravene the provisions of the Partnership Agreement which seemingly embodied the complete intentions of the parties as to the manner in which the firm was to be operated and managed.

Nor can plaintiff have reasonably believed that no changes would be made in the Washington office since the S & A Agreement gave complete authority to the executive committee to decide questions of firm policy,[3]

---

[3] Both the 1970 and 1972 S & A Partnership Agreements contained the following language:

> 1. All questions of Firm policy, including determination of salaries, expense, Partners' participation, required balances of Partners, investment of funds, designation of Counsel, and the admission and severance of Partners, shall be decided by an Executive Committee . . . provided, however, that the determination of participation, admission and severance of Partners, shall require the approval of Partners (whether or not members of the Executive Committee) then holding a majority of all voting Percentages. The Committee shall advise and consult with other

which would clearly include establishment of committees and the appointment of members and chairpersons. Having read and signed the 1970 and 1972 S & A partnership agreements which implicitly authorized the Executive Committee to create, control or eliminate firm committees, plaintiff could not have reasonably believed that the status of the Washington Office Committee was inviolate and beyond the scope and operation of the Partnership Agreements. Thus, since plaintiff had no right to remain chairman of the Washington office, a misrepresentation regarding his chairmanship does not form the basis for a cause of action in fraud.

Breach of Contract, Conspiracy and Wrongful Dissolution or Ouster of Partner

As shown above, plaintiff had no contractual right to maintain his authority over the Washington office, and therefore he has not made out a case for breach of contract. Since he did not have a legal right to maintain his status in the firm, the conspiracy charge amounts to no more than an internal power sweep, executed and permitted under the provisions of the partnership agreement for which there is no legal remedy.

Similarly, there was no wrongful dissolution or ouster of plaintiff from the partnership because the merger of the two firms was authorized under the terms of the S & A partnership agreement. By the terms of the agreement, the executive committee was entrusted with "all questions of Firm policy."[4] Additionally, partners could be admitted and severed from the firm and the partnership agreement could be amended by majority approval by the partners. The merger of S & A with the Liebman firm could be considered either as the admission of new partners or the making of a new or amended agreement, and thus majority approval was all that was required, and a post facto change in plaintiff's vote would be of no effect.

Plaintiff contends that the merger was such a fundamental change in the nature of the partnership that unanimous approval was required and that had he known the personal consequences of the merger, he would have exercised a "veto" and the events which forced him to resign would not have occurred. This theory, however, runs counter to the prevailing law of partnership. Generally, common law and statutory

---

Partners to such an extent as the Committee may deem advisable and in the best interest of the Firm.

Any amendment of this Agreement or any subsequent agreement, if signed or initialed by Partners then holding a majority of all voting Percentages, shall be as effective as though signed or initialed by all Partners; provided, however, that any agreement providing for the incorporation of the Firm shall be signed by Partners then holding seventy five percent (75%) of all voting Percentages. . . .

[4] See note 3, supra. Management by an executive committee elected by a majority of the partners is a legally acceptable contractual arrangement. . . .

standards concerning relationships between partners can be overridden by an agreement reached by the parties themselves. The Uniform Partnership Act (adopted both in Illinois and the District of Columbia) specifically provides that statutory rules governing the rights and duties of the partners are "subject to any agreement between them."

Nor do the cases cited by plaintiff support the proposition that unanimous consent is needed for the merger of partnerships. In McCallum v. Asbury, 238 Or. 257, 393 P.2d 774 (1964), a partner sued to dissolve a partnership of medical doctors. Plaintiff challenged the amendment of the agreement by majority vote which provided for management by an executive committee. The court held that a majority could approve this change, even though the agreement provided that all partners were to have an equal share in management. Likewise, Fortugno v. Hudson Manure Co., 51 N.J.Super. 482, 144 A.2d 207 (1958), affords little support.

Fortugno basically held that a partner could not be effectively changed into a stockholder in a corporation without his consent. In that case, there had been no prior contract that the partnership agreement could be amended by majority vote. The S & A agreement, however, dealt specifically with incorporation of the firm, providing that incorporation would be effective if approved by three-fourths of the partners. Merger was a less dramatic change than incorporation, which would have eliminated the partnership entity. It cannot reasonably be argued, therefore, that the merger fell outside the purview of the Agreement, requiring unanimous consent for its approval. Amendments to the Agreement and admission of partners required only majority approval, and plaintiff's proposed "veto power" is nothing more than an expressed hope, incompatible with and contrary to the overall scheme and provisions of the S & A Agreement.

Breach of Fiduciary Duty

Plaintiff also alleges that defendants breached their fiduciary duty by beginning negotiations on a merger with the Liebman firm without consulting the other partners who were not on the executive committee and by not revealing information regarding changes that would occur as a result of the merger, such as the co-chairmen arrangement for the Washington office. An examination of the case law on a partner's fiduciary duties, however, reveals that courts have been primarily concerned with partners who make secret profits at the expense of the partnership. Partners have a duty to make a full and fair disclosure to other partners of all information which may be of value to the partnership. . . . The essence of a breach of fiduciary duty between partners is that one partner has advantaged himself at the expense of the firm. . . . The basic fiduciary duties are: 1) a partner must account for any profit acquired in a manner injurious to the interests of the partnership, such as commissions or purchases on the sale of partnership property; 2) a partner cannot without the consent of the other partners, acquire for himself a partnership asset, nor may he divert to his own use a partnership opportunity; and 3) he must not compete with the partnership within the scope of the business. . . .

A typical case of breach of fiduciary duty and fraud between partners cited by plaintiff is Bakalis v. Bressler, 1 Ill.2d 72, 115 N.E.2d 323 (1953). There, a defendant partner had surreptitiously purchased the building which housed the partnership's business and was collecting rents from the partnership for his own profit. What plaintiff is alleging in the instant case, however, concerns failure to reveal information regarding changes in the internal structure of the firm. No court has recognized a fiduciary duty to disclose this type of information, the concealment of which does not produce any profit for the offending partners nor any financial loss for the partnership as a whole. Not only was there no financial gain for defendants, but the remaining partners did not acquire any more power within the firm as the result of the alleged withholding of information from plaintiff. They were already members of the executive committee and as such had wide-ranging authority with regard to firm management. Thus plaintiff's claim of breach of fiduciary duty must fail.

What this Court perceives from Mr. Day's pleadings and affidavits is that he may be suffering from a bruised ego but that the facts fail to establish a legal cause of action. As an able and experienced attorney, it should have been clear that the differences and misunderstandings which developed with his former partners were business risks of the sort which cannot be resolved by judicial proceedings. Mr. Day, a knowledgeable, sophisticated and experienced businessman and a responsible member of a large law firm, bound himself to a well-defined contractual arrangement when he executed the 1970 Partnership Agreement. The contract clearly provided for management authority in the executive committee and for majority approval of the merger with the Liebman firm. Even if plaintiff had voted against the merger, he could not have stopped it. Furthermore, the partnership agreement, to which he freely consented denies the existence of a contractual right to any particular status within the firm for plaintiff. If plaintiff's partners did indeed combine against him, it is clear that their alleged activities did not amount to illegality, and that any personal humiliation or injury was a risk that he assumed when he joined with others in the partnership.

Accordingly it is this 29th of May, 1975.

Ordered that defendants' motion for summary judgment is granted and the complaint in this proceeding is dismissed with prejudice.

NOTE

Suppose a law partnership consists of 200 partners and that one of them retires. Obviously, the remaining 199 partners will continue to practice law without any noticeable change. Technically, however, under UPA (1914) §§ 29 and 31, the old partnership is dissolved by the retirement of any partner and when the remaining partners continue their practice a new partnership is formed. The partners may have a written partnership agreement that specifies what happens when a partner retires—most particularly, how that partner is paid off for her or his interest in the partnership. The agreement may also contain a provision specifying that the remaining partners will continue as partners under the existing agreement. That provision is a "continuation" agreement—that is, an agreement obligating the remaining partners to continue to associate with one another as partners under the existing agreement (or, perhaps, some variation of it). Thus, when Sidley & Austin and the Liebman firm merged, technically, the two firms dissolved (legally, they ceased to exist) and a new firm was formed. But the Sidley & Austin partnership agreement obligated all of its partners to become partners in the new firm. Any partner who objected to the merger could, before the merger, withdraw from the Sidley & Austin partnership, subject to the provisions of the Sidley & Austin agreement relating to withdrawal.

Under UPA (1997), if a partner retires (and in various other situations), there is a "dissociation" (§ 601) rather than a "dissolution" (§ 801). Where there has been a dissociation, the partnership continues as to the remaining partners and the dissociated partner is entitled, in the absence of an agreement to the contrary, to be paid an amount determined as if "on the date of dissociation, the assets of the partnership were sold at a price equal to the greater of the liquidation value or the value based on a sale of the entire business as a going concern without the dissociated partner," plus interest from the date of dissociation. § 701(a) and (b).

What is probably most important about Day v. Sidley & Austin is its illustration of the rule of partnership law that partners are free to make any agreement that suits them, without concern about niceties of partnership theory, and its illustration of the principle of contract law, "You made your bed, now you must lie in it."

ANALYSIS

1. **Control.** Before the merger, to what extent did Mr. Day have a legal right to share in control? Was there any difference in his legal right to share in control after the merger?
2. **Organization.** Does the Sidley & Austin system for control seem to you to be a sensible one? Why?

3. **Protecting a Partner.** What should Mr. Day have done, at the time he was about to join Sidley & Austin as manager of its Washington office, to protect himself from the mistreatment he claims he suffered?

4. **Specified Compensation for Expulsion.** Presumably the Sidley & Austin partnership agreement contained a provision allowing the firm to oust a partner and specifying a formula for determining the amount the ousted partner was to be paid for his or her share in partnership receivables, work in progress, office equipment, etc. Assuming that Mr. Day was correct in his assertion that he was forced out, in what circumstances, if any, should he be entitled to more than the amount so specified?

4. THE FIDUCIARY OBLIGATIONS OF PARTNERS

A. INTRODUCTION

Meinhard v. Salmon

249 N.Y. 458, 164 N.E. 545 (1928).

■ CARDOZO, CH. J.

On April 10, 1902, Louisa M. Gerry leased to the defendant Walter J. Salmon the premises known as the Hotel Bristol at the northwest corner of Forty-second street and Fifth avenue in the city of New York. The lease was for a term of twenty years, commencing May 1, 1902, and ending April 30, 1922. The lessee undertook to change the hotel building for use as shops and offices at a cost of $200,000. Alterations and additions were to be accretions to the land.

Salmon, while in course of treaty with the lessor as to the execution of the lease, was in course of treaty with Meinhard, the plaintiff, for the necessary funds. The result was a joint venture with terms embodied in a writing. Meinhard was to pay to Salmon half of the moneys requisite to reconstruct, alter, manage and operate the property. Salmon was to pay to Meinhard 40 per cent of the net profits for the first five years of the lease and 50 per cent for the years thereafter. If there were losses, each party was to bear them equally. Salmon, however, was to have sole power to "manage, lease, underlet and operate" the building. There were to be certain pre-emptive rights for each in the contingency of death.

The two were coadventurers, subject to fiduciary duties akin to those of partners. . . . As to this we are all agreed. The heavier weight of duty rested, however, upon Salmon. He was a coadventurer with Meinhard, but he was manager as well. During the early years of the enterprise, the building, reconstructed, was operated at a loss. If the relation had then ended, Meinhard as well as Salmon would have carried a heavy burden. Later the profits became large with the result that for each of the investors there came a rich return. For each, the venture had its phases of fair weather and of foul. The two were in it jointly, for better or for worse.

When the lease was near its end, Elbridge T. Gerry had become the owner of the reversion. He owned much other property in the neighborhood, one lot adjoining the Bristol Building on Fifth avenue and four lots on Forty-second street. He had a plan to lease the entire tract for a long term to someone who would destroy the buildings then existing, and put up another in their place. In the latter part of 1921, he submitted such a project to several capitalists and dealers. He was unable to carry it through with any of them. Then, in January, 1922, with less than four months of the lease to run, he approached the defendant Salmon. The result was a new lease to the Midpoint Realty Company, which is owned and controlled by Salmon, a lease covering the whole tract, and involving a huge outlay. The term is to be twenty years, but successive covenants for renewal will extend it to a maximum of eighty years at the will of either party. The existing buildings may remain unchanged for seven years. They are then to be torn down, and a new building to cost $3,000,000 is to be placed upon the site. The rental, which under the Bristol lease was only $55,000, is to be from $350,000 to $475,000 for the properties so combined. Salmon personally guaranteed the performance by the lessee of the covenants of the new lease until such time as the new building had been completed and fully paid for.

The lease between Gerry and the Midpoint Realty Company was signed and delivered on January 25, 1922. Salmon had not told Meinhard anything about it. Whatever his motive may have been, he had kept the negotiations to himself. Meinhard was not informed even of the bare existence of a project. The first that he knew of it was in February when the lease was an accomplished fact. He then made demand on the defendants that the lease be held in trust as an asset of the venture, making offer upon the trial to share the personal obligations incidental to the guaranty. The demand was followed by refusal, and later by this suit. A referee gave judgment for the plaintiff, limiting the plaintiff's interest in the lease, however, to 25 per cent. The limitation was on the theory that the plaintiff's equity was to be restricted to one-half of so much of the value of the lease as was contributed or represented by the occupation of the Bristol site. Upon cross-appeals to the Appellate Division, the judgment was modified so as to enlarge the equitable interest to one-half of the whole lease. With this enlargement of plaintiff's interest, there went, of course, a corresponding enlargement of his attendant obligations. The case is now here on an appeal by the defendants.

Joint adventurers, like copartners, owe to one another, while the enterprise continues, the duty of the finest loyalty. Many forms of conduct permissible in a workaday world for those acting at arm's length, are forbidden to those bound by fiduciary ties. A trustee is held to something stricter than the morals of the market place. Not honesty alone, but the punctilio of an honor the most sensitive, is then the standard of behavior. As to this there has developed a tradition that is unbending and inveterate. Uncompromising rigidity has been the attitude of courts of equity when petitioned to undermine the rule of undivided loyalty by the "disintegrating erosion" of particular exceptions (Wendt v. Fischer, 243 N.Y. 439, 444). Only thus has the level of conduct for fiduciaries been kept at a level higher than that trodden by the crowd. It will not consciously be lowered by any judgment of this court.

The owner of the reversion, Mr. Gerry, had vainly striven to find a tenant who would favor his ambitious scheme of demolition and construction. Baffled in the search, he turned to the defendant Salmon in possession of the Bristol, the keystone of the project. He figured to himself beyond a doubt that the man in possession would prove a likely customer. To the eye of an observer, Salmon held the lease as owner in his own right, for himself and no one else. In fact he held it as a fiduciary, for himself and another, sharers in a common venture. If this fact had been proclaimed, if the lease by its terms had run in favor of a partnership, Mr. Gerry, we may fairly assume, would have laid before the partners, and not merely before one of them, his plan of reconstruction. The pre-emptive privilege, or, better, the pre-emptive opportunity, that was thus an incident of the enterprise, Salmon appropriated to himself in secrecy and silence. He might have warned Meinhard that the plan had been submitted, and that either would be free to compete for the award. If he had done this, we do not need to say whether he would have been under a duty, if successful in the competition, to hold the lease so acquired for the benefit of a venture then about to end, and thus prolong by indirection its responsibilities and duties. The trouble about his conduct is that he excluded his coadventurer from any chance to compete, from any chance to enjoy the opportunity for benefit that had come to him alone by virtue of his agency. This chance, if nothing more, he was under a duty to concede. The price of its denial is an extension of the trust at the option and for the benefit of the one whom he excluded.

No answer is it to say that the chance would have been of little value even if seasonably offered. Such a calculus of probabilities is beyond the science of the chancery. Salmon, the real estate operator, might have been preferred to Meinhard, the woolen merchant. On the other hand, Meinhard might have offered better terms, or reinforced his offer by alliance with the wealth of others. Perhaps he might even have persuaded the lessor to renew the Bristol lease alone, postponing for a time, in return for higher rentals, the improvement of adjoining lots. We know that even under the lease as made the time for the enlargement of the building was delayed for seven years. All these opportunities were cut away from him through another's intervention. He knew that Salmon was the manager. As the time drew near for the expiration of the lease, he would naturally assume from silence, if from nothing else, that the lessor was willing to extend it for a term of years, or at least to let it stand as a lease from year to year. Not impossibly the lessor would have done so, whatever his protestations of unwillingness, if Salmon had not given assent to a project more attractive. At all events, notice of termination, even if not necessary, might seem, not unreasonably, to be something to be looked for, if the business was over and another tenant was to enter. In the absence of such notice, the matter of an extension was one that would naturally be attended to by the manager of the enterprise, and not neglected altogether. At least, there was nothing in the situation to give warning to anyone that while the lease was still in being, there had come to the manager an offer of extension which he had locked within his breast to be utilized by himself alone. The very fact that Salmon was in control with exclusive powers of direction charged him the more obviously with the duty of disclosure, since only through disclosure could opportunity be equalized. If he might cut off renewal by a purchase for his own benefit when four months were to pass before the lease would have an end, he might do so with equal right while there remained as many years. . . . He might steal a march on his comrade under cover of the darkness, and then hold the captured ground. Loyalty and comradeship are not so easily abjured.

. . .

We have no thought to hold that Salmon was guilty of a conscious purpose to defraud. Very likely he assumed in all good faith that with the approaching end of the venture he might ignore his coadventurer and take the extension for himself. He had given to the enterprise time and labor as well as money. He had made it a success. Meinhard, who had given money, but neither time nor labor, had already been richly paid. There might seem to be something grasping in his insistence upon more. Such recriminations are not unusual when coadventurers fall out. They are not without their force if conduct is to be judged by the common standards of competitors. That is not to say that they have pertinency here. Salmon had put himself in a position in which thought of self was to be renounced, however hard the abnegation. He was much more than a coadventurer. He was a managing coadventurer. . . . For him and for those like him, the rule of undivided loyalty is relentless and supreme. . . . A different question would be here if there were lacking any nexus of relation between the business conducted by the manager and the opportunity brought to him as an incident of management. . . . For this problem, as for most, there are distinctions of degree. If Salmon had received from Gerry a proposition to lease a building at a location far removed, he might have held for himself the privilege thus acquired, or so we shall assume. Here the subject-matter of the new lease was an extension and enlargement of the subject-matter of the old one. A managing coadventurer appropriating the benefit of such a lease without warning to his partner might fairly expect to be reproached with conduct that was underhand, or lacking, to say the least, in reasonable candor, if the partner were to surprise him in the act of signing the new instrument. Conduct subject to that reproach does not receive from equity a healing benediction.

A question remains as to the form and extent of the equitable interest to be allotted to the plaintiff. The trust as declared has been held to attach to the lease which was in the name of the defendant corporation. We think it ought to attach at the option of the defendant Salmon to the shares of stock which were owned by him or were under his control. The difference may be important if the lessee shall wish to execute an assignment of the lease, as it ought to be free to do with the consent of the lessor. On the other hand, an equal division of the shares might lead to other hardships. It might take away from Salmon the power of control and management which under the plan of the joint venture he was to have from first to last. The number of shares to be allotted to the plaintiff should, therefore, be reduced to such an extent as may be necessary to preserve to the defendant Salmon the expected measure of dominion. To that end an extra share should be added to his half.

Subject to this adjustment, we agree with the Appellate Division that the plaintiff's equitable interest is to be measured by the value of half of the entire lease, and not merely by half of some undivided part. A single building covers the whole area. Physical division is impracticable along the lines of the Bristol site, the keystone of the whole. Division of interests and burdens is equally impracticable. Salmon, as tenant under the new lease, or as guarantor of the performance of the tenant's obligations, might well protest if Meinhard, claiming an equitable interest, had offered to assume a liability not equal to Salmon's, but only half as great. He might justly insist that the lease must be accepted by his coadventurer in such form as it had been given, and not constructively divided into imaginary fragments. What must be yielded to the one may be demanded by the other. The lease as it has been executed is single and entire. If confusion has resulted from the union of adjoining parcels, the trustee who consented to the union must bear the inconvenience. . . .

The judgment should be modified by providing that at the option of the defendant Salmon there may be substituted for a trust attaching to the lease a trust attaching to the shares of stock, with the result that one-half of such shares together with one additional share will in that event be allotted to the defendant Salmon and the other shares to the plaintiff, and as so modified the judgment should be affirmed with costs.

PLANNING

1. **Drafting for Salmon.** Suppose you had represented Salmon at the outset of the initial investment transaction in 1902. What kind of provision would you have proposed to include in an agreement with Meinhard to cover the issue that arose in the case?

2. **Drafting for Meinhard.** If you had represented Meinhard what kind of provision would you have proposed?

3. **Who Prevails?** If you gave different answers to the preceding two questions, and if Meinhard and Salmon had been called upon to select one, which do you suppose they would have selected?

4. **A Legal Default Rule.** What does your answer to the preceding question tell you about what the legal rule should be in the absence of any discernible agreement?

5. **Current Law.** Consider UPA (1997) § 404, which is reprinted in the appendix to this chapter. How, if at all, would the outcome of Meinhard v. Salmon have been affected if the above provision had been the law? What do you suppose Judge Cardozo would have thought about § 101(b)? What do you think?

■ ANDREWS, J. (dissenting). . . .

Were this a general partnership between Mr. Salmon and Mr. Meinhard I should have little doubt as to the correctness of this result assuming the new lease to be an offshoot of the old. Such a situation involves questions of trust and confidence to a high degree; it involves questions of good will; many other considerations. As has been said, rarely if ever may one partner without the knowledge of the other acquire for himself the renewal of a lease held by the firm, even if the new lease is to begin after the firm is dissolved. Warning of such an intent, if he is managing partner, may not be sufficient to prevent the application of this rule.

We have here a different situation governed by less drastic principles. I assume that where parties engage in a joint enterprise each owes to the other the duty of the utmost good faith in all that relates to their common venture. Within its scope they stand in a fiduciary relationship. . . .

What then was the scope of the adventure into which the two men entered? . . .

It seems to me that the venture . . . had in view a limited object and was to end at a limited time. There was no intent to expand it into a far greater undertaking lasting for many years. The design was to exploit a particular lease. Doubtless in it Mr. Meinhard had an equitable interest, but in it alone. This interest terminated when the joint adventure terminated. There was no intent that for the benefit of both any advantage should be taken of the chance of renewal—that the adventure should be continued beyond that date. Mr. Salmon has done all he promised to do in return for Mr. Meinhard's undertaking when he distributed profits up to May 1, 1922. Suppose this lease, non-assignable without the consent of the lessor, had contained a renewal option. Could Mr. Meinhard have exercised it? Could he have insisted that Mr. Salmon do so? Had Mr. Salmon done so could he insist that the agreement to share losses still existed or could Mr. Meinhard have claimed that the joint adventure was still to continue for twenty or eighty years? I do not think so. The adventure by its express terms ended on May 1, 1922. The contract by its language and by its whole import excluded the idea that the tenant's expectancy was to subsist for the benefit of the plaintiff. On that date whatever there was left of value in the lease reverted to Mr. Salmon, as it would had the lease been for thirty years instead of twenty. Any equity which Mr. Meinhard possessed was in the particular lease itself, not in any possibility of renewal. There was nothing unfair in Mr. Salmon's conduct.

. . .

The judgment of the courts below should be reversed and a new trial ordered, with costs in all courts to abide the event.

■ POUND, CRANE and LEHMAN, JJ., concur with CARDOZO, CH. J., for modification of the judgment appealed from and affirmance as modified; ANDREWS, J., dissents in opinion in which KELLOGG and O'BRIEN, JJ., concur.

ANALYSIS

1. **Partnership Duration.** What was the agreement between Meinhard and Salmon? In particular, what was the agreement as to the duration of the relationship?
2. **Salmon's Obligation.** Did the court conclude that Salmon was obligated to share the new deal with Meinhard or only the opportunity or information? Why?
3. **More on Salmon's Obligation.** What if Salmon had read in the newspaper about Gerry's interest in developing his property and had approached Gerry with a proposal to participate in the development? Would he have had any obligation to notify Meinhard or let him in on the deal?

Sandvick v. LaCrosse

747 N.W.2d 519 (N.D. 2008).

I

In May 1996, Sandvick, Bragg, LaCrosse, and Haughton purchased three oil and gas leases in Golden Valley County, North Dakota. The leases were known as the Horn leases. The Horn leases were standard, paid-up leases with terms of five years and did not contain any provision for extending or renewing them. Empire Oil Company, owned by LaCrosse, held record title to the leases. The leases were purchased from the parties' credits in the Empire Oil Company JV checking account. Sandvick testified the parties' initial intent was to try to sell the leases during the five-year term.

Aside from the Horn leases, the parties had previously owned other oil and gas leases together. Haughton had owned other leases with Sandvick, and LaCrosse was also involved in some of these other leases. Some of the leases were purchased before the Horn leases, and some were purchased after.

In November 2000, Haughton and LaCrosse purchased three oil and gas leases on the Horn property. These leases were referred to as the "Horn Top Leases" and were set to begin at the expiration of the initial Horn Leases. The term "top lease" is defined in Howard R. Williams & Charles J. Meyers, Manual of Oil and Gas Terms 1285 (8th ed.1991), as a "lease granted by a landowner during the existence of a recorded mineral lease which is to become effective if and when the existing lease expires or is terminated." The top leases covered the same acreage as the Horn Leases and had a five-year term, with the title in the name of Empire Oil Company. The top leases were not recorded until December 2001. Prior to purchasing the top leases, LaCrosse and Haughton twice offered to purchase Sandvick's and Bragg's interests in the Horn leases, but Sandvick and Bragg refused. Haughton testified he did not inform either Sandvick or Bragg that he and LaCrosse had purchased the top leases.

In 2004, Sandvick and Bragg sued LaCrosse and Haughton, claiming they breached their fiduciary duties by not offering Sandvick and Bragg an opportunity to purchase the top leases with them. The trial was limited to the issues regarding the existence, life span, and scope of a partnership or joint venture. Following the bench trial, the district court concluded no partnership or joint venture existed.

. . .

II

On appeal, Sandvick and Bragg argue the district court erred in concluding the parties were not partners. In North Dakota, a partnership is "an association of two or more persons to carry on as co-owners a business for profit." [UPA (1997) § 102(11)]. The crucial elements of a partnership are (1) an intention to be partners, (2) co-ownership of the business, and (3) a profit motive. . . .

The district court concluded a partnership did not exist between the parties. In its memorandum opinion following trial, it found the parties were not co-owners of a business. It found the parties' undertaking was very limited and did not coincide with the definition of a business. It found that the parties entered into the leases for a set period of time and that their activity, rather than being a series of acts, was limited to that occurrence.

Under comment 1 to § 202 of the Revised Uniform Partnership Act, a "business" is defined as "a series of acts directed toward an end," and under [UPA (1997) § 102(1)], "includes every trade, occupation, and profession." . . .

In this case, the parties entered into the Horn leases for a specific period. The court found their intention was to try to sell the leases. . . . We conclude the purchase of the Horn leases was a separate act undertaken by the parties, not a series of acts. On the basis of the evidence in the record and the testimony at trial, we conclude the district court did not err in concluding a partnership did not exist.

III

Sandvick and Bragg argue the district court erred in concluding a joint venture did not exist. A joint venture is similar to a partnership but is more limited in scope and duration, and principles of partnership law apply to the joint venture relationship. SPW Associates, LLP v. Anderson, 2006 ND 159, ¶ 8, 718 N.W.2d 580. "For a business enterprise to constitute a joint venture, the following four elements must be present: (1) contribution by the parties of money, property, time, or skill in some common undertaking, but the contributions need not be equal or of the same nature; (2) a proprietary interest and right of mutual control over the engaged property; (3) an express or implied agreement for the sharing of profits, and usually, but not necessarily, of losses; and (4) an express or implied contract showing a joint venture was formed." Id. at ¶ 10 (citations omitted). . . .

The district court concluded the parties were not members of a joint venture when they acquired the Horn leases. It made the following findings of fact, which supported its conclusion:

> 7. Bragg never talked to Haughton about the investment in the Horn Leases and had no agreement with Haughton concerning the purchase of additional leases, the purchase of Horn minerals, or the purchase of leases on minerals adjacent to the Horn property. Sandvick had no written or oral agreement with either Haughton or Lacrosse concerning the acquisition of a new lease following the expiration of the Horn Leases.
>
> 8. At the time of the acquisition of the Horn Leases, Bragg had no agreement with Lacrosse concerning the development of those leases. Lacrosse never agreed to make Sandvick and

> Bragg a part of any subsequent lease of the Horn minerals. If Bragg had any expectations concerning the development of the Horn Leases, they were not communicated to Haughton.
>
> . . .
>
> 10. No agreement was entered into, express or implied, limiting the parties' abilities to continue activity which did not include the other parties to these proceedings.
>
> 11. None of the parties intended to be exclusively involved in this undertaking, and they knew that the other parties would continue to do business which would not include them.
>
> . . .
>
> 13. Under the circumstances, the parties had no expectations that the other parties would refrain from investing in the area without offering to the other parties an opportunity to join in the investment.

The court, however, also made findings that reflected a joint venture; specifically, the court found: (1) LaCrosse opened a checking account under the name Empire Oil JV Account; (2) the leases were purchased from the parties' credits in the Empire Oil Company JV account in equal shares; (3) title to the leases was held in Empire Oil Company's name; and (4) the parties' intent in acquiring the leases was to sell them. At trial, Bragg, LaCrosse, and Haughton testified that any profits would have been shared had the Horn leases been sold. This testimony, along with the court's findings above, demonstrates the existence of a joint venture. We conclude a joint venture did exist in regard to the parties' purchase of the Horn leases, because the leases were purchased out of the parties' checking account funds in equal shares, they were titled in Empire Oil's name rather than each of the parties' names, and profits were going to be shared if the leases were sold.

IV

Having concluded a joint venture exists, we look to the scope of the venture and decide whether any fiduciary duties were breached by LaCrosse and Haughton. "The existence and scope of a fiduciary duty depends upon the language of the parties' agreement." Grynberg v. Dome Petroleum Corp., 1999 ND 167, ¶ 21, 599 N.W.2d 261. "[P]rinciples of partnership law apply to the joint venture relationship." *Anderson*, 2006 ND 159, ¶ 8, 718 N.W.2d 580.

Under [UPA (1997) § 409(a)], a partner owes duties of loyalty and care to the other partners. The duty of loyalty is set forth in [UPA (1997) § 409(b):

a. To account to the partnership and hold as trustee for it any property, profit, or benefit derived by the partner in the conduct and winding up of the partnership business or derived from a use by the partner of partnership property, including the appropriation of a partnership opportunity;

b. To refrain from dealing with the partnership in the conduct or winding up of the partnership business as or on behalf of a party having an interest adverse to the partnership; and

c. To refrain from competing with the partnership in the conduct of the partnership business before the dissolution of the partnership.

"Joint adventurers, like copartners, owe to one another, while the enterprise continues, the duty of the finest loyalty." Svihl v. Gress, 216 N.W.2d 110, 115 (N.D.1974) (quoting Meinhard v. Salmon, 249 N.Y. 458, 164 N.E. 545, 546 (1928)); . . . .

In this case, the scope of the venture was to purchase and then attempt to sell the Horn leases. Approximately six months prior to the expiration of the leases, LaCrosse and Haughton purchased oil and gas leases, known as top leases, that were set to begin upon the expiration of the Horn leases. The top leases were nearly identical in all respects to the original Horn leases. The top leases had the same duration and acreage and were titled in Empire Oil Company's name. An important difference, however, between the original leases and the top leases was that Sandvick and Bragg were not informed of the acquisition of the top leases.

Although the original Horn leases did not contain an extension or renewal provision, the top leases purchased by LaCrosse and Haughton were effectively extensions of the original Horn leases. . . .

LaCrosse and Haughton created a conflict of interest by purchasing the top leases prior to the expiration of the original leases without notifying Sandvick and Bragg. It was in LaCrosse's and Haughton's best interest not to sell the original leases during the remaining six months of the original term. Having excluded Sandvick and Bragg, LaCrosse and Haughton potentially stood to benefit more by waiting to sell the leases until after the original term expired. We conclude LaCrosse and Haughton breached their fiduciary duties of loyalty by taking advantage of a joint venture opportunity when they purchased the top leases without informing Bragg and Sandvick. See Meinhard v. Salmon, 249 N.Y. 458, 164 N.E. 545, 548 (1928) (holding a co-venturer breached his duty of loyalty when he extended the lease on commercial property and excluded his co-venturer from the opportunity). Bragg and Sandvick should have had an opportunity to purchase the top leases with LaCrosse and Haughton. . . .

■ CROTHERS, JUSTICE, concurring in part and dissenting in part.

I concur with Part II of the Majority Opinion affirming the district court's findings and conclusion that the parties were not partners. I respectfully dissent from Parts III and IV where the Majority overlooks the district court's findings of fact and, therefore, overtakes the district court's fact-finding role.

. . .

Even accepting that the present facts require the conclusion that a joint venture was created, the Majority's ultimate decision that liability attaches to the "top leasing" activity is unpersuasive. Rather, North Dakota law allows partners (and therefore joint venturers) to limit the scope of their duty of loyalty to the remaining partners. [UPA (1997) § 105(d)]. This public policy is consistent with other jurisdictions examining the question in the context of mineral development. . . . This also means that, under North Dakota law, the parties could have limited their duty of loyalty. Nevertheless, the Majority presumes without question that the full duty of loyalty existed, and that it formed a basis for liability in this case.

There was no written contract in this case. The parameters of the transaction were unclear. A full trial occurred, with many witnesses testifying about their understanding of the business arrangement. From this, the district court made specific findings regarding the nature of the parties' enterprise, and the scope of their duties to each other [Ed.: Here this dissenting opinion quotes the same findings as those in the majority opinion plus the following two additional findings]:

> 9. The parties were all involved in other oil and gas related undertakings with various other parties, including, in some instances, the parties that are involved in these proceedings. These undertakings were separate and apart from the Horn Leases.
>
> 12. Haughton was interested in the area surrounding the Horn Leases and had various leasehold and mineral interests in the area dating from 1991. Sandvick, Bragg, and LaCrosse were aware of these facts and had reason to believe that he would continue to invest in the area.

Rather than ignoring the district court's findings, our standard of review requires that we respect the trier of fact's ability to see the witnesses, hear the testimony, and determine the scope of the obligations at issue in this case. I therefore would affirm the district court's judgment.

ANALYSIS

1. **Partnership vs. Joint Venture.** What is the difference between a partnership and a joint venture?
2. **Joint Venture: Existence and Scope.** The court asks, first, was there a joint venture, and, then, what was its scope? Are the two questions so clearly separate?
3. **The Business of the Joint Venture.** According to the majority, what was the "business" of the joint venture?
4. **Comparison to Meinhard v. Salmon.** The court invokes Meinhard v. Salmon. Is the argument for the plaintiff that a joint venture existed in that case stronger or weaker than the argument for the plaintiffs in this case?
5. **The Defendants' Obligation.** Just what was the obligation of the defendants? What did the Supreme Court think they did wrong?
6. **The Significance of Labels.** The investors' checking account was entitled "Empire Oil Company JV." According to the appellants' brief, citing the trial transcript, the parties referred to themselves as "partners" in the venture. What is the relevance of these labels?
7. **Fiduciary Duty.** During the term of the leases, Haughton investigated prospects in locations adjacent to the Horn leases and actually acquired leases in those locations. In doing so, did he violate his fiduciary obligations to his co-investors in the Horn leases?

Singer v. Singer

1981 Okla. Civ. App. 43, 634 P.2d 766 (Okla.Ct.App.1981).

This appeal is from an unusual judgment of district court declaring [that] land purchased by defendants is to be held in constructive trust for the benefit of persons not party to this suit. Suit was filed by Joe L. Singer, an individual, Singer Bros. partnership and MT Partnership against Stanley Singer (Stanley) and his sister Andrea Singer Pollack (Andrea). Judgment was rendered for Josaline Production Co., a partnership, and various members of the Trachtnberg family. The Trachtnbergs declined to participate in either the suit or to claim a share of the judgment. All parties to this action are related through family ties, intricate partnerships and trusts. Defendants borrowed and paid $1.5 million for the land and incurred $150,000 in interest expense. Trial judge refused to require plaintiffs to pay proportionate share of the $150,000 interest expense. . . .

Singer Family Business Relationship

The Singer family formed an oil production partnership in the late 1930's. . . . The original partnership was called Josaline Production Co. and was made up of the following partners prior to 1947:

Joseph B. Singer,

Joe L. Singer,

Alex Singer,

Trachtnberg brothers, and

Singer Bros. (Joe L. and Alex Singer).

In 1947, the partnership was dissolved and in the distribution in kind which followed the Trachtnbergs received 17 percent of the assets. The Singer family continued to operate as a partnership after the Trachtnbergs were excluded. However, it should be noted, the Trachtnbergs continued to invest in Josaline drilling programs on an ad hoc basis.

In 1962, a revised partnership contract was executed between the Singer family members. The new partnership consisted of essentially the same partners or their successors, except for the Trachtnbergs who remained legally aloof from Josaline. . . . In 1977, the parties re-drafted the partnership agreement, carefully defining duties and rights of the parties and restating the current ownership percentages. . . .

The 1977 restated partnership agreement contained the following paragraph:

> 8. Each partner shall be free to enter into business and other transactions for his or her own separate individual account, even though such business or other transaction may be in conflict with and/or competition with the business of this partnership. Neither the partnership nor any individual member of this partnership shall be entitled to claim or receive any part of or interest in such transactions. . . .

After 1947, the Trachtnbergs continued to hold a 17 percent undivided co-ownership in the oil and gas properties which had been distributed when they were dismissed from the partnership. Josaline continued to do business. As opportunities arose, in many cases, the Trachtnbergs were permitted to invest in Josaline projects to the same extent (17 percent) as their original holdings. It is important to note that profit from each leasehold estate was distributed to the Trachtnbergs as royalty owners, or as working interest co-owners, and not as a dividend from the Josaline partnership. Costs were assessed based on the same formula as would apply to any other leasehold estate co-owner, and they were not burdened with surcharge for partnership expenses, other than the usual cost of acquisition and drilling. . . .

The Dispute

On July 25, 1979, the Josaline partners held a meeting in Oklahoma City which was attended by several members of the Josaline partnership and by the Trachtnbergs. . . . One item of interest on the agenda was the possible purchase by the "group"[2] of 95 acres of land in the Britton area owned by Investors Diversified Services (IDS). . . . Prior to the meeting, Joe L. requested Stanley to look into the possibility of purchasing the land through the listing realtor. At the meeting the IDS land was briefly discussed but the decision of whether to purchase was deferred.

After the meeting, defendants Stanley and Andrea . . . purchased the IDS land. . . .

When the entire record is considered, we find this suit is prosecuted de facto by the individual members of Josaline for and on behalf of Josaline and its partners. The allegations of the petition aside, the case was tried on the theory that Josaline's individual partners have been simultaneously engaged in an "oral" partnership within the Josaline partnership. This "oral" partnership includes the Trachtnbergs and affects the partners' business dealings in the Britton area of interest. . . .

Partnership is a creature of voluntary agreement. A partnership relationship can be created by oral agreement but proof of the fact of partnership and its terms must be established, by "clear, unequivocal and decisive" evidence. . . . We find it significant that the Trachtnbergs refused to participate in this suit beyond giving depositions. They affirm doing business with Josaline, but offer no support for plaintiffs' material allegations concerning the fact or terms of the alleged oral partnership. Postjudgment, the Trachtnbergs even declined to accept the 17 percent windfall awarded to them by the court. Jack Trachtnberg denied being partners with Josaline, much less with Stanley and Andrea. . . .

We observe the manner of dealing between these highly sophisticated investors, partners and family members completely belies such a casual business relationship as contended by Joe L. It is noted that the various businesses owned by the parties . . . all were family partnerships and each was carefully reduced to writing. The agreements which have been placed of record in this case are detailed, thoughtfully prepared and comprehensive in setting forth the rights, duties and privileges of each of the parties. It is inconsistent that men of such sound business tradition would be party to an oral business relationship as extensive and pervasive as that claimed by plaintiffs without also reducing it to writing.

Rather, we believe there was, in fact, a traditional family business interest in the Britton area. For their common profit and convenience, they did business together. All such business was conducted through Josaline. However, outside the Josaline partnership, any interest offered to outsiders was treated as an ad hoc co-investment opportunity. These

[2] The term "group" has been used by plaintiffs throughout the trial to denote the individual partners of Josaline plus the Trachtnbergs.

outside investors included the Trachtnbergs, who retained the privilege of whether to accept or reject the investment opportunity. In other words, the parties outside Josaline were simply investors with a common area of interest.[11] Without the Trachtnbergs, suit is stripped to the unclouded, true dispute, i.e. Josaline against its own partners.[12]

The actions of Joe L. Singer were inconsistent with his theory that Stanley owed a fiduciary duty to either Josaline or the Trachtnbergs. After he discovered Stanley purchased the IDS land, he demanded 50 percent of the property for Singer Bros. . . . He seemed cavalierly unconcerned about protecting the other Josaline partners, who, according to his trial theory and the judgment, were entitled to 83 percent. Nor was he concerned for the rights of the Trachtnbergs who would have been entitled to a 17 percent share as partners. . . .

Plaintiffs' case is severely, if not fatally, weakened by the testimony of Joe L. Singer. He admitted having no personal oral agreement between himself, Stanley and Andrea. He testified the only conversation he had which gave him authority to include Andrea and Stanley in the "oral partnership" agreement was with Andrea and Stanley's father, Joseph B., in 1974. At the time Joe L. claimed to have obtained this proxy-like approval of the "oral partnership" covering the Britton area, Joseph B. and his son Stanley were seriously at odds over another business dispute. . . . Such a strained relationship logically militates against an important, binding business decision being made by one for the other. Even if such an agreement had been made by Joseph B., no proof was offered that he was acting as agent for his children. . . .

It is undisputed that between 1962 and 1979 Singer Bros. and Joe L. purchased other tracts of land and minerals within the Britton area.[14] At no time were these offered to the Josaline partners. . . .

After having identified the true parties in interest, resolution of the dispute—Josaline's contention that by reason of the fiduciary aspects of partnership it is entitled to participate in the purchase of the IDS land—is simplified. We would agree with Josaline's contention except for paragraph 8 of the partnership contract. . . .

---

[11] Investment in oil and gas leases as co tenants or co owners gives no presumption of the existence of partnership. . . . In fact, it is presumed, in the absence of a contrary showing, such ownership is merely a cotenancy. . . . It is well settled that the relationship of cotenancy is not a fiduciary relationship. . . . Further, co tenants deal with one another at arms length. . . .

[12] The testimony of Jack Trachtnberg leaves no doubt he did not consider himself to be a partner of anyone except his brother. On cross-examination, his response indicated bewilderment when counsel asked if he felt himself bound by any of the acts of Stanley, Andrea, Joseph B. or Joe L. In fact, he never really claimed to have anything more than an investor status with any of the parties involved.

[14] This defensive proof was brushed aside by Joe L. at trial as being small, inconsequential parcels of a much larger tract purchase. We note the "inconsequential" 10 acre mineral tract is the equivalent of 25 percent of the IDS minerals, it being conceded by both sides that the IDS minerals constitute the major value of the entire purchase.

We find paragraph 8 is designed to allow and is uniquely drafted to promote spirited, if not outright predatory competition between the partners. Its strong wording leaves no doubt in our minds that its drafters intended to effect such a result. . . .

From a fiduciary aspect, the permissible boundaries of intra-partnership competition, under paragraph 8, are limited only after the threshold of actual partnership acquisition has been crossed. Had Stanley and Andrea pirated an existing partnership asset or used partnership funds or encumbered Josaline financially, our decision would be different. . . .

We hereby reverse and remand to trial court with instructions to vacate the judgment rendered below and order judgment be rendered in favor of defendants.

ANALYSIS

1. **Fiduciary Duty.** What would have been the result, if the Josaline partnership agreement had not included Section 8?
2. **Result if a Corporation?** What would have been the result if Josaline had been a corporation?
3. **Creating a Partnership.** Even if there had been no oral agreement, why were not the Trachtnbergs partners by operation of law? Did they not share profits and control? Did they not intend to carry on the business as co-owners for profit?

Nemec v. Shrader

991 A.2d 1120 (Del. Sup. Ct. 2010).

■ STEELE, CHIEF JUSTICE, HOLLAND and RIDGELY, JUSTICES FOR THE MAJORITY.

. . .

Factual and Procedural Background

The Parties

Nemec retired from Booz Allen on March 31, 2006, after nearly 36 years of service with the Company. Nemec was elected three times to the Company's board of directors, where he served on the Finance and Professional Excellence Committees and chaired the Audit Committee. At the time of his retirement, Nemec ranked third in seniority among Booz Allen partners.

Wittkemper also retired from Booz Allen on March 31, 2006, after nearly 20 years of service with the Company. Wittkemper built the foundation for Booz Allen's German business and helped expand Booz Allen's business throughout Europe. For nine years Wittkemper was a member of Booz Allen's Worldwide Commercial Business Leadership Team. He also served as head of the Communications Media Technology practice, and later as head of Booz Allen's European Business.

Booz Allen, a Delaware corporation headquartered in McLean, Virginia, is a strategy and technology consulting firm. In July 2008, Booz Allen had approximately 300 shareholders, 21,000 employees, and annual revenues of approximately $4.8 billion. Booz Allen was founded as a partnership in 1914, but later changed its legal structure and became a Delaware corporation. Booz Allen retained, however, the attitude and culture of a partnership, owned and led by a relatively small cadre of corporate officers, who were referred to as the "partners."

The individual defendants were members of Booz Allen's board of directors at the time the plaintiffs' Booz Allen shares were redeemed, and at the time the Company sold Booz Allen's government business to The Carlyle Group. The Directors collectively owned about 11% of Booz Allen's outstanding common stock.

The Booz Allen Stock Rights Plan

Throughout their tenure, Nemec and Wittkemper, along with all other officers of the Company, were partially compensated with annual grants of stock rights that were convertible into common stock of the Company. Those rights were granted under the Booz, Allen & Hamilton Inc. Officers Stock Rights Plan. Under the Stock Plan, each retired officer had a "put" right, exercisable for a period of two years from the date of his or her retirement, to sell his or her shares back to the Company at book value. After that two-year period expired, the Company then had the right to redeem, at any time, part or all of the retired officer's stock at book value.

When they retired in March 2006, Nemec owned 76,000 shares of Booz Allen stock (representing about 2.6% of the Company's issued and outstanding common shares), and Wittkemper owned 28,000 shares (representing almost 1% of those shares). Nemec retained all of his Booz Allen stock during the two-year period following his retirement; Wittkemper sold most of his shares but retained some of them.

The Carlyle Transaction

In February 2007, Booz Allen reorganized its two principal lines of business into two separate business units: (i) a government unit, which provided consulting services to governments and governmental agencies, and (ii) a global commercial unit, which provided services to commercial and international businesses. At that time, Booz Allen's leadership began to consider spinning off one of those two businesses.

. . . In October 2007, Booz Allen and The Carlyle Group began negotiations, which culminated in The Carlyle Group's November 2007 offer to purchase Booz Allen's government business for $2.54 billion.

On January 16, 2008, the Wall Street Journal reported that Booz Allen was engaged "in discussions to sell its government-consulting business to private-equity firm Carlyle Group," and that "the sale price will likely be around $2 billion." They reported that the transaction was expected to close by March 31, 2008. At some point before March 31, 2008, however, Booz Allen's board and management learned that the Carlyle transaction would close later than planned.

In March 2008 . . . the purchase price of the Carlyle transaction had been agreed upon, and the Booz Allen board and stockholders knew that the transaction would generate over $700 per share to Booz Allen's stockholders.

On May 15, 2008, Booz Allen entered into (i) a formal merger agreement that would result in the sale of its government business to The Carlyle Group, and (ii) a spin-off agreement that would result in the transfer of its commercial business to Booz & Company, Inc. On May 16, 2008, Booz Allen publicly announced the sale of its government business to The Carlyle Group for $2.54 billion. That transaction closed on July 31, 2008—four months after the plaintiffs' put rights expired.

NOTE

This would have translated into a total of $53,200,000 for Nemec's 76,000 shares. The $2.54 billion paid by The Carlyle Group for the Booz Allen government business obviously was an accurate measure of the market value of that business. But that government business was presumably built up over the years with relatively little cash outlay that would be reflected on the firm's books. So its book value would be minimal. Once the division is sold, however, the $2.54 in cash is received and the book value reflects that amount. Thus, once the transaction with Carlyle is completed (but not before) the Booz Allen book value rises by just about the full $2.54 billion.

The Redemption of Plaintiffs' Booz Allen Stock

If allowed to participate in the Carlyle transaction, the plaintiffs would have received materially more than the March 2008 (pre-transaction) book value of their Booz Allen shares. In April 2008, the Company redeemed the plaintiffs' shares at their pre-transaction book value (approximately $162.46 per share).[6] The April 2008 redemption of the plaintiffs' shares added nearly $60 million to the proceeds received

[6] On March 10, 2008, Ralph Shrader, Booz Allen's chairman and CEO, told Nemec that allowing both Nemec and Wittkemper to retain their Booz Allen stock until the Carlyle transaction closed was an "easy moral decision." The Dissent construes this comment on "morality" as an indication of the parties' legal intent during contractual bargaining and signing 30 years earlier. [Ed.: The total for Nemec's 76,000 shares at $162.46 per share was $12,346,960.]

by Booz Allen working stockholders. At the time of the redemptions, Booz Allen was awaiting the receipt of an IRS private opinion letter regarding the tax treatment of the transaction, and the completion of an audit of financials for certain prior fiscal years (which had already been certified). None of the parties to the transaction expected that these events would present problems, and everyone anticipated that both would occur within a matter of days or weeks.

. . .

Procedural History

The plaintiffs' amended complaint asserted three separate claims. Count I alleged that by redeeming the plaintiffs' shares at a time when the Carlyle transaction was virtually certain to occur, Booz Allen breached its covenant of good faith and fair dealing implied in the Stock Plan. Count II claimed that the Directors breached their fiduciary duty of loyalty to the plaintiffs by causing the Company to redeem the plaintiffs' shares, in favor of the Directors' personal interests. Count III alleged that as a result of the improper redemptions, the Directors were unjustly enriched.

The defendants moved to dismiss the complaint for failure to state a claim upon which relief can be granted. The Chancellor granted the motion and dismissed the complaint in its entirety. This appeal followed.

Analysis

. . .

The Chancellor Properly Dismissed Count I

The implied covenant of good faith and fair dealing involves a "cautious enterprise," inferring contractual terms to handle developments or contractual gaps that the asserting party pleads neither party anticipated.[11] "[O]ne generally cannot base a claim for breach of the implied covenant on conduct authorized by the agreement."[12] We will only imply contract terms when the party asserting the implied covenant proves that the other party has acted arbitrarily or unreasonably, thereby frustrating the fruits of the bargain that the asserting party reasonably expected. When conducting this analysis, we must assess the parties' reasonable expectations at the time of contracting and not rewrite the contract to appease a party who later wishes to rewrite a contract he now believes to have been a bad deal. Parties have a right to enter into good and bad contracts; the law enforces both.

---

[11] Dunlap v. State Farm Fire & Cas. Co., 878 A.2d 434, 441 (Del.2005) (citing E.I. DuPont de Nemours & Co. v. Pressman, 679 A.2d 436, 443 (Del.1996); Cincinnati SMSA Ltd. P'ship v. Cincinatti Bell Cellular Sys. Co., 708 A.2d 989, 992 (Del.1998).

[12] *Dunlap*, 878 A.2d at 441.

The plaintiffs lacked "a reasonable expectation of participating in the benefits" of the Carlyle transaction.[15] Shrader's gratuitous, post-contracting remark and the Company's actions implementing the Company's contracted for redemption rights cannot outweigh the clearly written, express, contractual language.

The complaint's allegation that the Company . . . would not be for sale in whole or in part during the redemption period, and that no one at the time of drafting and adopting the Stock Plan could have anticipated that possibility (and if they had, all parties would have agreed to compensate retired stockholders as if they had contributed to the deal's value) stands naked, wholly unworthy of the inference that it is fully clothed. The implied covenant only applies to developments that could not be anticipated, not developments that the parties simply failed to consider—particularly where the contract authorizes the Company to act exactly as it did here.

. . .

. . . Our colleagues' thoughtful dissent suggests that we neglect to note that the challenged conduct (redeeming the retired stockholders shares) must "*further a legitimate interest of the party relying on the contract*" [emphasis supplied by the dissent]. The Company's directors, at the time of the decision to redeem owed fiduciary duties to the corporation and its stockholders. The redemption would not affect the Company directly. However, a failure to redeem the now retired stockholders' shares consistent with the Company's right under the stock plan would directly reduce the working stockholders' distribution by $60 million. If the Company's directors had not exercised the Company's absolute contractual right to redeem the retired stockholders shares, the working stockholders had a potential claim against the directors for favoring the retired stockholders to the detriment of the working stockholders.

. . . The fact that some directors were in the group of working stockholders who received a pro rata share of the $60 million did not make it an interested transaction because those director stockholders received the same pro rata benefit as all other stockholders similarly situated. The directors made a rational business judgment to exercise the Company's contractual right for the $60 million benefit to all working stockholders rather than to take no action and be accused of favoritism to the retired stockholders.

. . . The complaint alleges no facts that demonstrate that, at the time of contracting, both parties would reasonably have expected Nemec and Wittkemper to participate in the buy out. Nor does the complaint offer us a "cautious" approach to infer contractual terms. Rather, the plaintiffs

[15] [Continental Ins. Co. v. Rutledge & Co., 750 A.2d 1219,] 1234 [(Del. Ch. 2000).] . . .

would have us believe—without justification—that long term stockholders of a prestigious mergers and acquisition consulting firm would have no expectation that a future acquirer would be interested in purchasing all or part of the Company.

Crafting what is, in effect, a post contracting equitable amendment that shifts economic benefits from working to retired partners would vitiate the limited reach of the concept of the implied duty of good faith and fair dealing. Delaware's implied duty of good faith and fair dealing is not an equitable remedy for rebalancing economic interests after events that could have been anticipated, but were not, that later adversely affected one party to a contract. Rather the covenant is a limited and extraordinary legal remedy. . . . Accordingly, we affirm the Chancellor's dismissal of Count I.

The Chancellor Properly Dismissed Count II

Count II of the complaint alleges that by causing the Company to redeem the plaintiffs' shares before the Carlyle transaction closed, the Directors acted to further their own economic self-interest, at the expense and to the detriment of the plaintiffs, thereby breaching their fiduciary duty of loyalty. Those allegations, even if true, do not establish an enforceable breach of fiduciary duty claim in the specific circumstances alleged here.

The Chancellor held that the plaintiffs' fiduciary duty claim fails for two reasons. First, the claim seeks to enforce obligations that are expressly addressed by contract (the Stock Plan), and that, therefore, must be adjudicated within the analytical framework of a breach of contract claim. Stated differently, the Chancellor found that the Stock Plan created contract duties that superseded and negated any distinct fiduciary duties arising out of the same conduct that constituted the contractual breach. Second, the Chancellor held that the complaint did not adequately plead facts sufficient to establish that the timing of the Directors' redemption decision was contrary to the exercise of the Directors' sound and good faith business judgment. Because we affirm the dismissal of Count II on the first ground articulated by the Chancellor, we do not reach the second.

It is a well-settled principle that where a dispute arises from obligations that are expressly addressed by contract, that dispute will be treated as a breach of contract claim. In that specific context, any fiduciary claims arising out of the same facts that underlie the contract obligations would be foreclosed as superfluous.

. . .

The Chancellor Properly Dismissed Count III

Count III claims that the Directors were unjustly enriched by the pre-transaction redemption of the plaintiffs' Booz Allen shares. . . .

Unjust enrichment is "the unjust retention of a benefit to the loss of another, or the retention of money or property of another against the fundamental principles of justice or equity and good conscience."[36] . . .

. . . Just as the plaintiffs have failed on the merits of their breach of contract claim, they have failed to prove that the Directors' unjustly benefited from the pre-transaction redemption, in contravention of ". . . the fundamental principles of justice or equity and good conscience."[38]

. . . [T]he Chancellor properly dismissed Count III. . . .

Conclusion

For the foregoing reasons, the Court of Chancery's judgment is **AFFIRMED.**

■ JACOBS, JUSTICE, dissenting and BERGER, JUSTICE joining in dissent:

. . .

A party does not act in bad faith (the majority argues) by relying on contract provisions for which that party bargained, even if the result is to eliminate advantages the counterparty would otherwise receive. That is a correct, but incomplete, statement of the law. To avoid running afoul of the implied covenant, the challenged conduct must also further a legitimate interest of the party acting in reliance on the contract. Stated differently, under Delaware case law, a contracting party, even where expressly empowered to act, can breach the implied covenant if it exercises that contractual power arbitrarily or unreasonably. Here, the complaint adequately alleges that the Company's redemption of the plaintiffs' shares prejudiced the plaintiffs while serving no legitimate interest of the Company. In those circumstances, therefore, the redemption would have been arbitrary and unreasonable, for which reason the complaint stated a cognizable claim for breach of the implied covenant.

A. The Scope of the Implied Covenant

"The covenant is best understood as a way of implying terms in the agreement, whether employed to analyze unanticipated developments or to fill gaps in the contract's provisions."[42] As the majority opinion correctly states, ordinarily the implied covenant doctrine will not be employed to invalidate conduct expressly authorized by the contract itself. But, that principle is not global in its application. The grant of an

[36] Fleer Corp. v. Topps Chewing Gum, Inc., 539 A.2d 1060, 1062 (Del.1988).

[38] See Jackson Nat. Life. Ins. Co. [v. Kennedy], 741 A.2d [377, 394 Del. Ch. 1999)] . . . .

[42] [Dunlap v. State Farm Fire & Cas. Co., 878 A.2d 434,] 441 [(Del.2005)]. . . .

unqualified contractual right is not, nor can it be, a green light that authorizes the right holder to exercise its power in an arbitrary or unreasonable way. The exercise of any contractual right is limited by the implied duty to act reasonably and in good faith. Accordingly, a contracting party's conduct, even if in "literal compliance with [contract] and statutes," can breach the implied covenant if that party acts arbitrarily or unreasonably.[46]

The complaint alleges no facts from which it may reasonably be inferred that the plaintiffs contractually agreed to waive their implied right to be treated fairly by the Company in any redemption of their shares. Their claim that Booz Allen breached the implied covenant by exercising its power to redeem the plaintiffs' shares in the circumstances alleged here was, therefore, legally cognizable. Whether or not that claim will ultimately be validated must await the development of a factual record. That is why Count I was erroneously dismissed.

B. The Complaint Sufficiently Alleges That the Company Did Not Exercise Its Redemption Right in Good Faith

The majority concede that the Stock Plan does not address whether retired stockholders can share in any "locked in value" of the Company. They insist, however, that "[t]he complaint alleges no facts that demonstrate that, at the time of contracting, both parties would reasonably have expected [the plaintiffs] to participate in the buy out." We conclude otherwise.

The Carlyle transaction, as timed in relation to the redemptions effected here, was an unforeseen circumstance not provided for by the Stock Plan. That frames the issue, which is whether the complaint pleads facts from which one can infer that if the parties negotiating the Stock Plan had specifically addressed the circumstances presented here, they would have agreed that the Company could not exercise its redemption right before the transaction closed. A fair reading of the complaint requires an affirmative answer to that question.

. . .

The majority concedes that "[t]he redemption would not affect the Company directly." They suggest, however, that the Company had an indirect interest in eliminating the plaintiffs as shareholders, because a failure to redeem the plaintiffs' shares before the Carlyle transaction closed would reduce the working stockholders' distribution by $60 million. That, in turn, would give the working stockholders "a potential claim against the directors for favoring the retired stockholders to the detriment of the working stockholders."

---

[46] Dunlap, 878 A.2d at 444.

The demerit of this contention is twofold. First, the majority cites no authority, nor articulates any reasoning, to support its conclusory statement that the working stockholders would have a valid claim for breach of fiduciary duty against the directors for not redeeming the plaintiffs' shares. If that is so, then it is equally arguable that the plaintiffs would have had an identical fiduciary duty claim against the directors for causing their shares to be redeemed for the sole benefit of the working stockholders. Second, and more fundamentally, even if the working stockholders arguably had a legitimate economic interest in not being deprived of the $60 million the plaintiffs would otherwise have received, that is an interest that pertains only to the working stockholders-not the Company. Only by conflating the interest of the working shareholders with that of the Company is the majority then able to posit a legitimate corporate interest that the Company then became entitled (indeed, required) to further. This attribution of the working stockholders' interest to Booz Allen magically puts a second rabbit into the same hat.

At this stage, all that is before us, and before the Court of Chancery, is a motion to dismiss a complaint. At this stage, all that can be decided is whether the complaint states a cognizable legal claim. Whether or not that claim is factually supportable is a question to be resolved at a later stage. We therefore would reverse the dismissal of Count I of the complaint. Because the majority concludes otherwise, we respectfully dissent.

ANALYSIS

1. **The Directors' Duty.** Suppose the directors had decided not to redeem the Nemec and Wittkemper shares. Might the other shareholders have successfully sued the directors for waste?

2. **What Limits?** What if the deal with Carlyle was ready to close before the end of March but the directors deliberately delayed the closure in order to be able to redeem the Nemec and Wittkemper shares at the low book value?

3. **Partnership vs. Corporation.** Would the result be different if Booz Allen had been a partnership rather than a corporation?

4. **Why "Book Value"?** Note that even if the government business had not been sold it should have been obvious that it was worth far more than book value. Why would a shareholder/executive be willing to accept redemption at book value?

5. **"Legitimate Interest."** The dissent argues that for the redemption should have been permissible only if it "further[ed] a legitimate interest" of Booz Allen as an entity. What legitimate purpose might be imagined? Is "legitimate purpose" of the redemption really at issue in the case?

B. AFTER DISSOLUTION

Bane v. Ferguson

890 F.2d 11 (7th Cir.1989).

■ POSNER, CIRCUIT JUDGE.

The question presented by this appeal from the dismissal of the complaint . . . is whether a retired partner in a law firm has either a common law or a statutory claim against the firm's managing council for acts of negligence that, by causing the firm to dissolve, terminate his retirement benefits. . . .

Charles Bane practiced corporate and public utility law as a partner in the venerable Chicago law firm of Isham, Lincoln & Beale, founded more than a century ago by Abraham Lincoln's son Robert Todd Lincoln. In August 1985 the firm adopted a noncontributory retirement plan that entitled every retiring partner to a pension, the amount depending on his earnings from the firm on the eve of retirement. The plan instrument provided that the plan, and the payments under it, would end when and if the firm dissolved without a successor entity, and also that the amount paid out in pension benefits each year could not exceed five percent of the firm's net income in the preceding year. Four months after the plan was adopted, the plaintiff retired, moved to Florida with his wife, and began drawing his pension (to continue until his wife's death if he died first) of $27,483 a year. Bane was 72 years old when he retired. So far as appears, he had, apart from social security, no significant source of income other than the pension.

Several months after Bane's retirement, Isham, Lincoln & Beale merged with Reuben & Proctor, another large and successful Chicago firm. The merger proved to be a disaster, and the merged firm was dissolved in April 1988 without a successor—whereupon the payment of pension benefits to Bane ceased and he brought this suit. The suit alleges that the defendants were the members of the firm's managing council in the period leading up to the dissolution and that they acted unreasonably in deciding to merge the firm with Reuben & Procter, in purchasing computers and other office equipment, and in leaving the firm for greener pastures shortly before its dissolution. The suit does not allege that the defendants committed fraud, engaged in self-dealing, or deliberately sought to destroy or damage the law firm or harm the plaintiff; the charge is negligent mismanagement, not deliberate wrongdoing. The suit seeks damages, presumably the present value of the pension benefits to which the Banes would be entitled had the firm not dissolved.

. . .

[Bane's first theory of liability] is that the defendants, by committing acts of mismanagement that resulted in the dissolution of the firm, violated the Uniform Partnership Act, [UPA (1914) §] 9(3)(c), which provides that "unless authorized by the other partners . . . one or more but less than all the partners have no authority to: Do any . . . act which would make it impossible to carry on the ordinary business of the partnership." This provision is inapplicable. Its purpose is not to make negligent partners liable to persons with whom the partnership transacts (such as Bane), but to limit the liability of the other partners for the unauthorized act of one partner. . . . The purpose in other words is to protect partners. Bane ceased to be a partner when he retired in 1985.

Nor can Bane obtain legal relief on the theory that the defendants violated a fiduciary duty to him; they had none. A partner is a fiduciary of his partners, but not of his former partners, for the withdrawal of a partner terminates the partnership as to him. . . . Bane must look elsewhere for the grounds of a fiduciary obligation running from his former partners to himself. The pension plan did not establish a trust, and even if, notwithstanding the absence of one, the plan's managers were fiduciaries of its beneficiaries (there are myriad sources of fiduciary duty besides a trust), the mismanagement was not of the plan but of the firm. There is no suggestion that the defendants failed to inform the plaintiff of his rights under the plan or miscalculated his benefits or mismanaged or misapplied funds set aside for the plan's beneficiaries; no funds were set aside for them. Even if the defendants were fiduciaries of the plaintiff, moreover, the business-judgment rule would shield them from liability for mere negligence in the operation of the firm, just as it would shield a corporation's directors and officers, who are fiduciaries of the shareholders.

. . .

We are sorry about the financial blow to the Banes but we agree with the district judge that there is no remedy under the law of Illinois.

ANALYSIS

1. **Bane's Status.** At the time of the alleged injury, was Mr. Bane a partner in the firm that was liquidated? If not, what was his position?

2. **The Relevance of Negligence.** Since the lower court granted the defendants' motion to dismiss the complaint, we must assume for purposes of analysis that the defendants were in fact negligent in the way they ran the partnership and that it was this negligence that eventuated in the harm to Mr. and Mrs. Bane. Why is it that the defendants are not liable for the damages caused by their negligence? Was it the lack of any duty to Mr. Bane or was it that even if there was some sort of duty there is no cause of action?

3. **Comparison to Meinhard v. Salmon.** Review the language of Chief Judge Cardozo in Meinhard v. Salmon, describing the fiduciary duty of loyalty of partners toward one another. What outcome would that language seem to suggest in the present case (which involves the "duty of care")?

C. GRABBING AND LEAVING

Meehan v. Shaughnessy

404 Mass. 419, 535 N.E.2d 1255 (1989).

The plaintiffs, James F. Meehan (Meehan) and Leo V. Boyle (Boyle), were partners of the law firm, Parker, Coulter, Daley & White (Parker Coulter)....

... Parker, Coulter, Daley & White is a large partnership which specializes in litigation on behalf of both defendants and plaintiffs. Meehan joined the firm in 1959, and became a partner in 1963; his practice focuses primarily on complex tort litigation, such as product liability and aviation defense work. Boyle joined Parker Coulter in 1971, and became a partner in 1980; he has concentrated on plaintiffs' work. Both have developed outstanding reputations as trial lawyers in the Commonwealth. Meehan and Boyle each were active in the management of Parker Coulter.... At the time of their leaving, Meehan's interest in the partnership was 6% and Boyle's interest was 4.8%.

Meehan and Boyle had become dissatisfied at Parker Coulter. On June 27, 1984, after unsuccessfully opposing the adoption of a firm-wide pension plan, the two first discussed the possibility of leaving Parker Coulter. Another partner met with them to discuss leaving but told them their proposed firm would not be suitable for his type of practice. On July 1, Meehan and Boyle decided to leave Parker Coulter and form their own partnership.

Having decided to establish a new firm, Meehan and Boyle then focused on whom they would invite to join them. The two spoke with [Cynthia] Cohen, a junior partner and the de facto head of Parker Coulter's appellate department, about joining the new firm as a partner. They arranged to meet with her on July 5, and told her to keep their conversations confidential. The day before the July 5 meeting, Boyle prepared two lists of what he considered to be his cases. The lists contained approximately eighty to 100 cases, and for each case indicated the status, fee arrangement, estimated settlement value, and potential fee to MBC. Boyle gave these lists to Cohen for her to examine in preparation for the July 5 meeting.

At the July 5 meeting, Meehan and Boyle outlined to Cohen their plans for the new firm, including their intent to offer positions to [Steven]

Schafer, Peter Black (Black), and Warren Fitzgerald (Fitzgerald), who were associates at Parker Coulter. Boyle stated that he hoped the clients he had been representing would go with him to the new firm; Meehan said he would take the aviation work he had at Parker Coulter with him. Both stated that they felt others at Parker Coulter were getting paid as much as or more than they were, but were not working as hard. Cohen decided to consider the offer from Meehan and Boyle, and agreed to keep the plans confidential until formal notice of the separation was given to the partnership. Although the partnership agreement required a notice period of three months, the three decided to give only thirty days' notice. They chose to give shorter notice to avoid what they believed would be an uncomfortable situation at the firm, and possible retaliatory measures by the partnership. Meehan and Boyle had agreed that they would leave Parker Coulter on December 31, 1984, the end of Parker Coulter's fiscal year.

During the first week of August, Cohen accepted the offer to join the new firm as a partner. Her primary reason for leaving Parker Coulter to join MBC was that she enjoyed working with Meehan and Boyle.

In July, 1984, Boyle offered a position at MBC to Schafer, who worked closely with Boyle in the plaintiffs department. Boyle told Schafer to organize his cases, and "to keep an eye towards cases to be resolved in 1985 and to handle these cases for resolution in 1985 rather than 1984." He also told Schafer to make a list of cases he could take with him to MBC, and to keep all their conversations confidential.

Late in the summer of 1984, Meehan asked Black and Fitzgerald to become associates at MBC. Fitzgerald had worked with Meehan in the past on general defense work, and Black worked with Meehan, particularly in the aviation area. Meehan was instrumental in attracting Black, who had previously been employed by U.S. Aviation Underwriters (USAU), to Parker Coulter. Although Black had already considered leaving Parker Coulter, he was concerned about whether USAU would follow him to a small firm like MBC, and wanted to discuss his leaving Parker Coulter with the vice president of USAU. In October, 1984, Black and Meehan met with the USAU vice president in New York. They later received assurances from him that he would be interested in sending USAU business to the proposed new firm. Black then accepted the offer to join MBC. Fitzgerald also accepted. Schafer, Black, and Fitzgerald were the only associates Meehan, Boyle, and Cohen approached concerning the new firm.

During July and the following months, Meehan, Boyle, and Cohen made arrangements for their new practice apart from seeking associates. They began to look for office space and retained an architect. In early fall, a lease was executed on behalf of MBC in the name of MBC Realty Trust.

They also retained an attorney to advise them on the formation of the new firm.

. . .

Toward the end of November, Boyle prepared form letters to send to clients and referring attorneys as soon as Parker Coulter was notified of the separation. He also drafted a form for the clients to return to him at his home address authorizing him to remove cases to MBC. An outside agency typed these materials on Parker Coulter's letterhead. Schafer prepared similar letters and authorization forms.

While they were planning their departure, from July to approximately December, Meehan, Boyle, Cohen, Schafer, Black, and Fitzgerald all continued to work full schedules. They settled cases appropriately, made reasonable efforts to avoid continuances, tried cases, and worked on discovery. Each generally maintained his or her usual standard of performance.

Meehan and Boyle had originally intended to give notice to Parker Coulter on December 1, 1984. Rumors of their leaving, however, began to circulate before then. During the period from July to early fall, different Parker Coulter partners approached Meehan individually on three separate occasions and asked him if the rumors about his leaving were true. On each occasion, Meehan denied that he was leaving. On November 30, 1984, a partner, Maurice F. Shaughnessy (Shaughnessy), approached Boyle and asked him whether Meehan and Boyle intended to leave the firm. Shaughnessy interpreted Boyle's evasive response as an affirmation of the rumors. Meehan and Boyle then decided to distribute their notice that afternoon, which stated, as their proposed date for leaving, December 31, 1984. A notice was left on the desk of each partner. When Meehan, Boyle, and Cohen gave their notice, the atmosphere at Parker Coulter became "tense, emotional and unpleasant, if not adversarial."

On December 3, the Parker Coulter partners appointed a separation committee and decided to communicate with "important sources of business" to tell them of the separation and of Parker Coulter's desire to continue representing them. . . . Sometime during the week of December 3, the partners sent Boyle a list of cases and requested that he identify the cases he intended to take with him.

Boyle had begun to make telephone calls to referring attorneys on Saturday morning, December 1. He had spoken with three referring attorneys by that date and told them of his departure from Parker Coulter and his wish to continue handling their cases. On December 3, he mailed his previously typed letters and authorization forms, and by the end of the first two weeks of December he had spoken with a majority of referring attorneys, and had obtained authorizations from a majority of clients whose cases he planned to remove to MBC.

Although the partners previously were aware of Boyle's intention to communicate with clients, they did not become aware of the extent of his communications until December 12 or 13. Boyle did not provide his partners with the list they requested of cases he intended to remove until December 17. Throughout December, Meehan, Boyle, and Schafer continued to communicate with referring attorneys on cases they were currently handling to discuss authorizing their transfer to MBC. On December 19, 1984, one of the partners accepted on behalf of Parker Coulter the December 31 departure date and waived the three-month notice period provided for by the partnership agreement. Meehan, Boyle, and Cohen formalized their arrangement as a professional corporation on January 1, 1985.

MBC removed a number of cases from Parker Coulter. Of the roughly 350 contingent fee cases pending at Parker Coulter in 1984, Boyle, Schafer, and Meehan removed approximately 142 to MBC. Meehan advised Parker Coulter that the 4,000 asbestos cases he had attracted to the firm would remain, and he did not seek to take certain other major clients. Black removed thirty-five cases; Fitzgerald removed ten; and Cohen removed three. A provision in the partnership agreement in effect at the separation provided that a voluntarily retiring partner, upon the payment of a "fair charge," could remove "any matter in which the partnership had been representing a client who came to the firm through the personal effort or connection of the retiring partner," subject to the right of the client to stay with the firm. Approximately thirty-nine of the 142 contingent fee cases removed to MBC came to Parker Coulter at least in part through the personal efforts or connections of Parker Coulter attorneys other than Meehan, Boyle, Cohen, Schafer, Black, or Fitzgerald. In all the cases removed to MBC, however, MBC attorneys had direct, existing relationships with the clients. In all the removed cases, MBC attorneys communicated with the referring attorney or with the client directly by telephone or letter. In each case, the client signed an authorization.

. . .

Based on these findings, the [trial] judge determined that the MBC attorneys did not manipulate cases, or handle them differently as a result of their decision to leave Parker Coulter. He also determined that Parker Coulter failed to prove that the clients whose cases were removed did not freely choose to have MBC represent them. Consequently, he concluded that Meehan and Boyle neither violated the partnership agreement nor breached the fiduciary duty they owed to their partners. In addition, the judge also found that Meehan and Boyle did not tortiously interfere with

Parker Coulter's relations with clients or employees. He similarly rejected Parker Coulter's claims against Cohen and Schafer. . . .

We . . . consider Parker Coulter's claims of wrongdoing. Parker Coulter claims that the judge erred in finding that Meehan, Boyle, Cohen, and Schafer fulfilled their fiduciary duties to the former partnership. In particular, Parker Coulter argues that these attorneys breached their duties (1) by improperly handling cases for their own, and not the partnership's benefit, (2) by secretly competing with the partnership, and (3) by unfairly acquiring from clients and referring attorneys consent to withdraw cases to MBC.[12] We do not agree with Parker Coulter's first two arguments but agree with the third. . . .

It is well settled that partners owe each other a fiduciary duty of "the utmost good faith and loyalty." Cardullo v. Landau, 329 Mass. 5, 8 (1952). . . . As a fiduciary, a partner must consider his or her partners' welfare, and refrain from acting for purely private gain. . . . Meehan and Boyle owed their copartners at Parker Coulter a duty of the utmost good faith and loyalty, and were obliged to consider their copartners' welfare, and not merely their own.

Parker Coulter first argues that Meehan and Boyle violated their fiduciary duty by handling cases for their own benefit, and challenges the judge's finding that no manipulation occurred.[13] . . . The judge's determination was one of fact, and was based on the assessment of the credibility of individuals with personal knowledge of the facts about which they were testifying. . . .

Parker Coulter also claims that we should disregard the judge's finding of no manipulation because the finding is clearly contradicted by other subsidiary findings, namely that Boyle planned to, and told Schafer to, handle cases for resolution at MBC rather than at Parker Coulter; that Boyle reassigned a number of a departing attorney's cases to himself and Schafer; and that a number of cases which were ready to resolve at Parker Coulter were, in fact, not resolved there. We do not agree that there is a conflict. The judge's finding that Boyle spoke of engaging in improper conduct does not require the conclusion that this conduct actually took place. Similarly, his finding that the reassignment of cases did not establish manipulation is consistent with a determination that the reassignment was based on merit and workload. . . .

---

[12] Parker Coulter does not claim that Meehan and Boyle wrongfully dissolved the partnership by leaving prematurely. . . .

[13] The judge found, specifically, that: "MBC, Schafer, Black and Fitzgerald worked full schedules from July to November 30, 1984, and some beyond. There was no manipulation of the cases nor were the cases handled differently as a result of the decision by MBC to leave Parker Coulter. They tried cases, worked on discovery, settled cases and made reasonable efforts to avoid continuances, to try their cases when reached, and settle where appropriate and in general maintain the same level of industry and professionalism that they had always demonstrated."

Parker Coulter next argues that the judge's findings compel the conclusion that Meehan and Boyle breached their fiduciary duty not to compete with their partners by secretly setting up a new firm during their tenure at Parker Coulter. We disagree. We have stated that fiduciaries may plan to compete with the entity to which they owe allegiance, "provided that in the course of such arrangements they [do] not otherwise act in violation of their fiduciary duties." Chelsea Indus. v. Gaffney, 389 Mass. 1, 10, 11–12 (1983). Here, the judge found that Meehan and Boyle made certain logistical arrangements for the establishment of MBC. These arrangements included executing a lease for MBC's office, preparing lists of clients expected to leave Parker Coulter for MBC, and obtaining financing on the basis of these lists. We believe these logistical arrangements to establish a physical plant for the new firm were permissible. . . .

Lastly, Parker Coulter argues that the judge's findings compel the conclusion that Meehan and Boyle breached their fiduciary duties by unfairly acquiring consent from clients to remove cases from Parker Coulter. We agree that Meehan and Boyle, through their preparation for obtaining clients' consent, their secrecy concerning which clients they intended to take, and the substance and method of their communications with clients, obtained an unfair advantage over their former partners in breach of their fiduciary duties.

A partner has an obligation to "render on demand true and full information of all things affecting the partnership to any partner." G. L. c. 108A, [UPA (1914)] § 20. . . . On three separate occasions Meehan affirmatively denied to his partners, on their demand, that he had any plans for leaving the partnership. During this period of secrecy, Meehan and Boyle made preparations for obtaining removal authorizations from clients. Meehan traveled to New York to meet with a representative of USAU and interest him in the new firm. Boyle prepared form letters on Parker Coulter's letterhead for authorizations from prospective MBC clients. Thus, they were "ready to move" the instant they gave notice to their partners. . . .

On giving their notice, Meehan and Boyle continued to use their position of trust and confidence to the disadvantage of Parker Coulter. The two immediately began communicating with clients and referring attorneys. Boyle delayed providing his partners with a list of clients he intended to solicit until mid-December, by which time he had obtained authorization from a majority of the clients.

Finally, the content of the letter sent to the clients was unfairly prejudicial to Parker Coulter. The ABA Committee on Ethics and Professional Responsibility, in Informal Opinion 1457 (April 29, 1980), set forth ethical standards for attorneys announcing a change in professional association.[15] Because this standard is intended primarily to protect clients, proof by Parker Coulter of a technical violation of this standard does not aid them in their claims. We will, however, look to this standard for general guidelines as to what partners are entitled to expect from each other concerning their joint clients on the division of their practice. The ethical standard provides that any notice explain to a client that he or she has the right to decide who will continue the representation. Here, the judge found that the notice did not "clearly present to the clients the choice they had between remaining at Parker Coulter or moving to the new firm." By sending a one-sided announcement, on Parker Coulter letterhead, so soon after notice of their departure, Meehan and Boyle excluded their partners from effectively presenting their services as an alternative to those of Meehan and Boyle.

PROBLEM

Suppose Mark and Norma are lawyers and have practiced as partners for five years. One day Peter comes to the law offices of Mark and Norma, asks to see Mark, and tells Mark that he has a brother who has been seriously injured in an automobile accident and needs a lawyer. Peter says that he has heard that Mark is a good lawyer. Mark quickly concludes that Peter's brother has a strong case and is likely to be able to recover a large judgment. Mark concludes at that moment that it is time to end his partnership with Norma and begin practice on his own. If he does so, what are his obligations to Norma with respect to the representation of Peter's brother?

ANALYSIS

1. **Parker Coulter's Options.** On December 3, 1984, what options were available to Parker Coulter?
2. **Obligations of Departing Partners.** Once Meehan and Boyle decided to leave Parker Coulter, what were they free to do to establish their new practice? Did they have an obligation to inform their partners of their decision to leave as soon as that decision was "in concrete"? Even earlier, when it was a strong probability?

---

[15] These standards provide the following guidelines for notice to clients:

"(a) the notice is mailed; (b) the notice is sent only to persons with whom the lawyer had an active lawyer-client relationship immediately before the change in the lawyer's professional association; (c) the notice is clearly related to open and pending matters for which the lawyer had direct professional responsibility to the client immediately before the change; (d) the notice is sent promptly after the change; (e) the notice does not urge the client to sever a relationship with the lawyer's former firm and does not recommend the lawyer's employment (although it indicates the lawyer's willingness to continue his responsibility for the matters); (f) the notice makes it clear that the client has the right to decide who will complete or continue the matters; and (g) the notice is brief, dignified, and not disparaging of the lawyer's former firm."

See also ABA Committee on Ethics and Professional Responsibility Informal Opinion 1466 (Feb. 12, 1981) (extending Informal Opinion 1457 to departing associates as well as partners).

3. **Obligations of Departing Associates.** What about Schafer (the associate who left with Meehan and Boyle)? At some point before his departure, did he have an obligation to advise the Parker Coulter partners of the impending defection?

4. **The Possibility of Express Agreement.** Could, and should, any of the issues of fiduciary obligation have been settled by express prior agreement? If so, what might the agreement have stated?

Gibbs v. Breed, Abbott & Morgan

271 A.D.2d 180, 710 N.Y.S.2d 578 (N.Y.Sup.Ct.2000).

Plaintiffs Charles Gibbs and Robert Sheehan are former partners of Breed Abbott & Morgan ("BAM") who specialize in trust and estate law. They withdrew from BAM in July 1991 to join Chadbourne & Parke ("Chadbourne"), and brought this action for monies due to them under their BAM partnership agreement. Defendants asserted various counterclaims alleging that plaintiffs breached their fiduciary duties to BAM. . . . Plaintiffs appeal from the trial court's determination that, in the course of both partners' planning and eventually implementing their withdrawal from BAM, they breached their fiduciary duty to the partnership. Plaintiffs also appeal from the trial court's determination that $1,861,045 in damages resulted from these transgressions.

From January 1991 until July 1991, plaintiffs were the only partners in the Trusts and Estates department ("T/E") at BAM; plaintiff Gibbs was the head of the department. A third partner, Paul Lambert, had been the former head of the department, and he had obtained many, if not most, of the department's clients. In 1989 he had left the firm to become the United States Ambassador to Ecuador and was still on leave in 1991. Lambert intended to return to the firm upon completion of his term as ambassador. The BAM trusts and estates department also employed three associate attorneys, Warren Whitaker (fifteenth year), Austin Wilkie (fourth year), and Joseph Scorese (first year); two accountants, Lois Wetzel and Ellen Furst; and two paralegals, Lee Ann Riley and Ruth Kramer.

Gibbs had become dissatisfied with BAM, and in January 1991 he began interviews to locate a new affiliation. He also approached Sheehan to persuade him to move with him. Sheehan and Gibbs subsequently conducted a number of joint interviews with prospective employers. In May 1991, Ambassador Lambert visited BAM, and Gibbs told him that he had been interviewing. Lambert relayed this information to the other partners. In early June, plaintiffs informed the executive committee that they had received an offer from two firms: McDermott, Will & Emery and Bryan Cave.

On June 19, 1991, both plaintiffs informed Stephen Lang, BAM's presiding partner, that they had accepted offers to join Chadbourne. Lang asked Gibbs not to discuss his departure with any of the T/E associates, and Gibbs agreed not to do so. On June 20, 1991, Lawrence Warble, a BAM partner who was named temporary head of the T/E department, met with its associates and non-legal personnel to inform them that plaintiffs were leaving the firm.

On June 24, 1991, Gibbs and Sheehan sent Chadbourne a memo listing the names of the personnel in the T/E department at BAM, their respective salaries, their annual billable hours, and the rate at which BAM billed out these employees to clients. The memo included other information about the attorneys, including the colleges and law schools they attended, and their bar admissions. This list had been prepared by Sheehan on April 26, 1991, months before the partners announced they were leaving. Sheehan specifically testified that the memo was prepared in anticipation of discussions with prospective firms, and both Gibbs and Sheehan testified at trial that the recruitment of certain associates and support personnel was discussed with different firms between March and May, as the partners were considering various affiliations. While Gibbs and Sheehan were still partners at BAM, Chadbourne interviewed four BAM employees that Gibbs had indicated he was interested in bringing to Chadbourne with him. On June 27, 1991, plaintiffs submitted their written resignations. Before Gibbs and Sheehan left BAM, they wrote letters to clients served by them, advising that they were leaving BAM and that other attorneys at BAM could serve them. These letters did not mention the fact that the two partners were moving to Chadbourne. Although the partnership agreement required 45 days notice of an intention to withdraw, BAM waived this provision upon plaintiffs' production of their final billings for work previously performed.[1] Gibbs left BAM on July 9, 1991, and Sheehan left on July 11, 1991, both taking various documents, including their respective "chronology" or desk files.[2] With the assistance of his chronology file, Gibbs began to contact his former clients on July 11, 1991. On July 11th, Chadbourne made employment offers to Whitaker, Wilkie, Wetzel, and Riley. Wilkie, Wetzel, and Riley accepted that same day; Whitaker accepted on July 15,

[1] BAM did not attempt to prepare a joint letter with Gibbs and Sheehan, announcing their departure, as recommended by the American Bar Association Committee on Ethics and Professional Responsibility (see, ABA Comm. on Ethics and Professional Responsibility, Informal Op. 1457 (1980)).

[2] The "chronology" or desk files contained copies of every letter written by the respective attorneys during the previous years. The letters included those written to adversaries about pending legal matters, letters written to clients, and letters written to others about ongoing BAM matters. These letters were duplicates of those kept in BAM's regular client files, but defendants allege that due to the fact that the files are arranged chronologically, active matters are more easily referenced. The original correspondences, left with the firm, have been filed by client and are dispersed throughout the department.

1991. In the following weeks, 92 of the 201 BAM T/E clients moved their business to Chadbourne.

. . .

The members of a partnership owe each other a duty of loyalty and good faith, and "[a]s a fiduciary, a partner must consider his or her partners' welfare, and refrain from acting for purely private gain" (Meehan v. Shaughnessy, 404 Mass. 419, 434, 535 N.E.2d 1255). Partners are constrained by such duties throughout the life of the partnership and "[t]he manner in which partners plan for and implement withdrawals . . . is [still] subject to the constraints imposed on them by virtue of their status as fiduciaries" (Robert Hillman, Loyalty in the Firm: A Statement of General Principles on the Duties of Partners Withdrawing From Law Firms, 55 Wash. & Lee L. Rev. 997 [1998]). According the trial court's findings on issues of fact and credibility appropriate deference, we uphold that portion of the court's liability determination which found that plaintiffs breached their fiduciary duty as partners of the firm they were about to leave by supplying confidential employee information to Chadbourne while still partners at BAM . . . However, we find no breach with respect to Gibbs' interactions with Sheehan, or with respect to either partner's removal of his desk files from BAM.

Defendants did not establish that Gibbs breached any duty to BAM by discussing with Sheehan a joint move to another firm, or that Sheehan's decision was based upon anything other than his own personal interests. . . . In addition, while in certain situations "[a] lawyer's removal or copying, without the firm's consent, of materials from a law firm that do not belong to the lawyer, that are the property of the law firm, and that are intended by the lawyer to be used in his new affiliation, could constitute dishonesty, which is professional misconduct under [Model] Rule 8.4(c)" (D.C. Bar Legal Ethics Comm. Op. 273 at 192), here, the partners took their desk copies of recent correspondence with the good faith belief that they were entitled to do so. [These files] . . . were comprised of duplicates of material maintained in individual client files, the partnership agreement was silent as to these documents, and removal was apparently common practice for departing attorneys.

However, the record supports the court's finding that both partners committed a breach of their fiduciary duty to the BAM partners by supplying Chadbourne, and presumably the other partnerships they considered joining, with the April 26, 1991 memorandum describing the members of BAM's T/E department, their salaries, and other confidential information such as billing rates and average billable hours, taken from personnel files. Moreover, a closer examination of the record does not support the dissent's conclusion that these partners did not engage in surreptitious recruiting. The partners may not have discussed with firm employees the possibility of moving with them prior to June 20, 1991, but they indicated to Chadbourne the employees they were interested in prior to this date, and Gibbs specifically testified that he refrained from telling one of his partners, to whom he had a duty of loyalty, about his future plans to recruit specific associates and support staff from the partnership.

There is no evidence of improper client solicitation in this case, nor is it an issue on this appeal. Although the analogy could be useful in concluding that Gibbs did not breach his fiduciary duty to the partnership by working with Sheehan to find a new affiliation, the fiduciary restraints upon a partner with respect to client solicitation are not analogous to those applicable to employee recruitment. By contrast to the lawyer-client relationship, a partner does not have a fiduciary duty to the employees of a firm which would limit its duty of loyalty to the partnership. Thus, recruitment of firm employees has been viewed as distinct and "permissible on a more limited basis than . . . solicitation of clients" (Hillman, supra at 1031). Pre-withdrawal recruitment is generally allowed "only after the firm has been given notice of the lawyer's intention to withdraw" (id.).

However, here, Sheehan prepared a memo in April of 1991, well in advance of even deciding, much less informing his partners, of his intention to withdraw. There is ample support in the record for the trial court's finding that the preparation and sending of the April 26, 1991 memo, combined with the subsequent hiring of certain trusts and estates personnel, constituted an egregious breach of plaintiff's fiduciary duty to BAM. . . .

While partners may not be restrained from inviting qualified personnel to change firms with them . . ., here Gibbs and Sheehan began their recruiting while still members of the firm and prior to serving notice of their intent to withdraw. . . . The dissent's analysis, that once the firm was notified of the partners' departure, there was no breach of fiduciary duty, is flawed. The breach occurred in April of 1991 and could not be cured by any after-the-fact notification by the fiduciary who committed the breach that he was withdrawing from the firm. Chadbourne still had the unfair advantage of the confidential information from the April 1991 memo, and still had the upper hand, which was manifested by its ability to tailor its offers and incentives to the BAM recruits.

Contrary to the dissent, I would characterize the memo distributed to prospective competitors as confidential. The data was obtained from BAM personnel files which Sheehan had unique access to as a BAM partner. The dissent's statement that such financial information is generally known to "headhunters" is without foundation. While the broad outlines of the partners' profits at a select number of large New York firms and the incremental increases in the base compensation of young associates at some firms are published in professional publications such as the New York Law Journal, or known to some recruitment firms, the available figures often vary substantially from the actual compensation received by specific individuals.

. . .

The calculation of damages in cases such as this is difficult. . . . Here, the [trial] court based its damage award on what it believed to be a series of disloyal acts. Defendants did not establish how the only act of plaintiffs which this Court finds to be disloyal, that of supplying employee information to Chadbourne, in and of itself, was a substantial cause of BAM's lost profits . . . We therefore vacate the court's award to defendants of the total profits lost by BAM between the time of plaintiffs departure in July 1991 and BAM's dissolution in November 1993, and remand for consideration of the issue of whether plaintiffs' disloyal act of sending Chadbourne the April 26, 1991 memorandum was a significant cause of any identifiable loss, and, if so, the amount of such loss. . . .

■ SAXE, J. (concurring in part and dissenting in part)

. . .

Once it is recognized that partners in law firms do not breach their duty to the other members of their firm by speaking to colleagues about leaving the firm, there is no logic to prohibiting partners from inviting selected employees to apply for a position at the new firm as well, absent contractual obligations not at issue here. Support staff, like clients, are not the exclusive property of a firm with which they are affiliated.

Moreover, the paramount concern of ensuring that clients are completely free to choose which firm will best serve them . . . can only be protected if lawyers are able to take with them those willing members of their legal team who played an active and important role in the clients' work. . . . If departing partners are not free to solicit the employees who have served their clients, those partners may not be able to continue to offer the unhampered capability to serve those clients. . . .

Even assuming that a partner's duty of loyalty to the other members of his firm prohibits any recruitment of department support staff before the firm is notified of the partner's intended departure, here, there is no showing that members of the staff were contacted prior to the firm being notified. Once the firm is notified of the partners' planned withdrawal, both the firm and the departing partners are on equal footing in competing for these employees; the departing partners no longer have any unfair advantage.

Since plaintiffs were entitled to inform the department staff at issue of their move, and to invite these individuals to submit applications to Chadbourne themselves, there was no impropriety in the manner in which Chadbourne extended offers to members of plaintiffs' staff. The real damage to the firm, namely, the loss of the knowledgeable and experienced attorneys and support staff, was caused not by a breach of fiduciary duty, but simply by the departure of these people—an act that each one of them had an absolute right to do, despite the damage their joint departure would cause the firm. . . .

Under the circumstances, plaintiffs' preliminary compilation of information regarding the salaries, billable hours and standard billing rates of the employees they sought to bring with them, and their providing it to Chadbourne after giving notice to Breed, Abbott, provides no support for a liability determination against them.

First of all, there is no showing, nor did the trial court find, that the purportedly confidential information was provided to Chadbourne—or any other firm—during the period that plaintiffs were interviewing, or at any time before they gave notice to Breed, Abbott. The April 26, 1991 memo was simply a compilation of information of which a lead partner of a practice group is normally aware as a matter of course. . . .

Furthermore, although the salaries and bonuses paid to associates may be termed "confidential," in fact this information is often the greatest unkept secret in the legal profession. Unlike the earnings of law firm partners, which vary widely even within most firms, depending upon such factors as billable hours and "rainmaking" ability, the earnings of associates and support staff at large firms are relatively circumscribed, with each firm setting standard rates for both salaries and bonuses. Such information is widely known outside the firms themselves: the salary levels and bonuses paid to associates at large New York firms are regularly published in professional publications such as the New York Law Journal. Salary levels, bonuses and other financial information regarding employees' billing rates are well known to professional "headhunters," the agencies that specialize in recruiting and placing lawyers and law firm support staff, and associates' background information is available from sources such as the Martindale-Hubbell directory. Therefore, while plaintiffs obtained the salary information regarding the associates and staff in question through their position as partners at Breed, Abbott, it was information that could as easily been obtained elsewhere. The concept that this information is some sort of trade secret does not comport with the realities of the practice of law. . . .

ANALYSIS

1. **Written Partnership Agreements.** Should the partners in a law firm have a written agreement on what files or documents a departing lawyer is permitted to take with him or her? If so, what should it provide?

2. **Valuable Information?** The April 26, 1991, memo prepared by Sheehan contained detailed information on the salaries, bonuses, billable hours, etc. of associates and other employees of BAM. How important do you think this information was to Chadbourne? Should it matter that the memo was given to Chadbourne only after Gibbs and Sheehan told their partners at BAM that they were leaving?

3. **Judicial Notice?** The majority and dissent disagree as to whether the information in the April 26, 1991, memo was readily available from public sources. How did the judges arrive at their differing views on this seemingly important matter of fact?

4. **Who Won?** Which side won this case? On remand, is BAM likely to be able to prove it suffered damages, and the amount?

D. EXPULSION

Lawlis v. Kightlinger & Gray

562 N.E.2d 435 (Ind.App.1990).

. . .

The partnership [Kightlinger & Grey] for many years has practiced law in Indianapolis and Evansville under various firm names. [Gerald L.] Lawlis initially became an associate of the partnership in 1966 but resigned after three years to join the staff of Eli Lilly and Company as an attorney. In early 1971, the partnership offered Lawlis a position as a general partner and Lawlis accepted. He signed his first partnership agreement as a general partner in 1972. That agreement remained effective until a new one was executed by the partners, including Lawlis, in 1984. Both these agreements provided for partnership compensation based upon a unit system, i.e., partners participated in the profits according to the number of units assigned to them each year by the partnership. Lawlis became a senior partner in 1975 and continued to practice law with the firm without interruption until 1982.

In that year, Lawlis became an alcohol abuser, and due to that affliction did not practice law for several months in early 1983 and in mid 1984. During each of these periods, he sought treatment for his alcoholism. Lawlis did not reveal his problem with alcohol to the partnership until July of 1983 when he disclosed it to the partnership's Finance Committee. When he did so, it "promptly contacted and met as a group with a physician who had expertise in the area of alcoholism." It then drafted "a document entitled 'Program Outline' which set forth certain conditions for Lawlis's continuing relationship with the Partnership." That document, signed by Lawlis in August, 1983, contained the following understanding: "3. It must be set out and clearly understood that there is no second chance." By March, 1984, Lawlis had resumed the consumption of alcohol. Lawlis again sought treatment, and the firm gave Lawlis a second chance. Its Finance Committee then decided Lawlis would be required to meet specified conditions in order for his relationship with the partnership to continue. These conditions included meetings with specialists selected by the partnership, treatment and consultation regarding his problem, and the obtaining of favorable reports from the specialist as to the likelihood of a favorable treatment outcome. Lawlis was told he would be returned to full partnership status if he complied with the conditions imposed. He has not consumed any alcoholic beverages since his second treatment in an alcoholic clinic in March, 1984.

Two written partnership agreements embodying primarily the same provisions were in effect in 1982 and thereafter, executed in 1972 and 1984, respectively. Lawlis executed both agreements and each annual addendum thereto along with all the other partners of the firm. Under the 1984 agreement, the senior partners by majority vote were to determine (a) the units each partner annually received, (b) the involuntary expulsion of partners, and (c) the involuntary retirement of partners.

As Lawlis battled his problem, his units of participation yearly were reduced by the annual addendum to the partnership agreement. Because he had not consumed alcohol since his second trip to a clinic and had been congratulated by senior partner Wampler, a member of the Finance Committee, and several others as to his "100% turn around," Lawlis felt "a substantial restoration of my previous status was past due." So believing, he met with the Finance Committee on October 1, 1986, and proposed his units of participation be increased from his then 60 to 90 units in 1987.

On October 23, 1986, Wampler told Lawlis the firm's Finance Committee was going to recommend Lawlis's relationship as a senior partner be severed no later than June 30, 1987. Two days later, all the firm's files were removed from Lawlis's office. The severance recommendation was presented at the 1986 year-end senior partners meeting. All except Lawlis voted to accept the Finance Committee's recommendation. At that time, as the Finance Committee also had recommended, Lawlis was assigned one unit of participation for the first six months of 1987 to a maximum total value of $25,000 on a weekly draw. This arrangement permitted Lawlis to retain his status as a senior partner to facilitate transition to other employment and to give him continuing insurance coverage.

Lawlis refused to sign the 1987 addendum containing those provisions and retained counsel to represent his interests. In consequence, he was expelled by a seven to one vote of the senior partners at a meeting held on February 23, 1987. (Lawlis cast the lone dissenting vote.) Article X of the 1984 agreement requires a minimum two-thirds vote of the senior partners to accomplish the involuntary expulsion of a partner. Lawlis filed suit for damages for breach of contract. From the entry of an adverse summary judgment, Lawlis appeals.

. . .

Lawlis first claims his notification by Wampler on October 23, 1986, that the Finance Committee would recommend his severance as a partner coupled with the removal of all partnership files from his office two days later constituted [a] . . . dissolution of the partnership. At that time, he posits he ceased "to be associated in the carrying on as distinguished from the winding up of the business." Deeming such expulsion wrongful because not authorized by a two-thirds vote of the senior partners at that time, Lawlis asserts he has a claim for damages against the partners under IC 23–4–1–18(a)(2) [UPA (1914) § 38(a)(2)] for dissolution in contravention of the partnership agreement. We disagree.

It is readily apparent Wampler merely told Lawlis what the Finance Committee proposed to do in the future. No dissolution occurred on that account. That the firm's files were removed from Lawlis's office two days later is immaterial. After their removal, Lawlis still participated in the partnership's profits through a weekly draw even though he evidently had nothing to do. Finally, the undisputed facts clearly demonstrate there was a meeting of the minds he would remain a senior partner after October 23, 1986. The partnership continued to treat Lawlis as a senior partner after that date. The Finance Committee's memorandum of November 25, 1986, regarding Lawlis's partnership status, proposed for 1987 he be given a weekly draw on one unit of participation until June 30, 1987, at which time his relationship with the firm would terminate, unless he withdrew earlier. Further, that committee's minutes for its December 23, 1986 meeting regarding the change in letterhead show Lawlis's name was not to be removed from the letterhead; it was to be placed at the bottom of the list of partners.

Also, Lawlis considered himself to be a senior partner after October 26, 1986. He refused as a senior partner to sign the proposed 1987 addendum "which implemented the decisions made by the Finance Committee concerning Lawlis," Appellant's Brief, p. 8, and cast the lone dissenting vote on his expulsion at the meeting of the senior partners held on February 23, 1987. Article X of the partnership agreement provides:

Expulsion of a Partner

A two-thirds (2/3) majority of the Senior Partners, at any time, may expel any partner from the partnership upon such terms and conditions as set by said Senior Partners. . . . (Emphasis supplied).

Only a partner could refuse to sign the proposed 1987 addenda after its tender by the firm to Lawlis for signature, and only a senior partner could vote on the Finance Committee's proposal to expel a partner under the partnership agreement. The undisputed facts disclose Lawlis remained a senior partner of the firm until he was expelled as such by vote of the senior partners on February 23, 1987.

Further, the time a dissolution occurs under these circumstances is clearly defined by statute. The Indiana Uniform Partnership Act at IC 23–4–1–31 [UPA (1914) § 31] says:

> Sec. 31. Dissolution is caused: (1) Without violation of the agreement between the partners . . .
>
> (d) By the expulsion of any partner from the business bona fide in accordance with such a power conferred by the agreement between the partners.

Lawlis was expelled in accordance with the partnership agreement on February 23, 1987. Thus, dissolution occurred on that date, not when he was notified of the proposal to expel him. Lawlis has no claim for damages under IC 23–4–1–38(a)(2) [UPA (1914) § 38(a)(2)].

Lawlis next argues his expulsion contravened the agreement's implied duty of good faith and fair dealing because he was expelled for the "predatory purpose" of "increasing [the firm's] lawyer to partner ratio," as evidenced by the Finance Committee's proposal contained in its November 25, 1986, memo to partners regarding the 1986 year end meeting. The partnership, however, posits Indiana does not recognize a duty of good faith and fair dealing in the context of an at will relationship.

It would be a simple matter to extrapolate the principle that an employer may terminate an at will employee for any cause or no cause without liability and apply it to the roughly comparable at will business relationship we find here, namely, the relationship existing between the partnership as an entity and its individual partners. The Indiana Uniform Partnership Act, however, prevents us from so doing.

As noted above, when a partner is involuntarily expelled from a business, his expulsion must have been "bona fide" or in "good faith" for a dissolution to occur without violation of the partnership agreement. IC 23–4–1–31(1)(d). Said another way, if the power to involuntarily expel partners granted by a partnership agreement is exercised in bad faith or for a "predatory purpose," as Lawlis phrases it, the partnership agreement is violated, giving rise to an action for damages the affected partner has suffered as a result of his expulsion.

Lawlis finds a predatory purpose in the Finance Committee's November 25, 1986, memo to the partners by quoting portions of the memo's section "4. FIVE YEAR PLAN, Firm Growth and Financial Goals." He states:

> The five-year plan stated that, "The goal is to increase the top partners to at least $150,000 within the next two to three years. . . . In order to achieve the goal, we need to continue to improve our lawyer to partner ratio."
>
> Appellant's Brief, at 17. From that quote Lawlis reasons:
>
> Obviously, the easiest way for the Partnership to improve its lawyer to partner ratio, and thus increase the top partners' salaries, was to eliminate a senior partner. Lawlis's position in the Partnership had been weakened by his absences due to illness. The remaining partners knew this and pounced upon the opportunity to devour Lawlis's partnership interest.

Appellant's Brief, at 18. The undisputed facts demonstrate the total inaccuracy of the final sentence quoted from appellant's brief.

From the time Lawlis's addiction to alcohol became known to the partnership's Finance Committee, it sought to assist and aid him through his medical crisis, even though he was taking substantial amounts of time off from his work to attempt cures in sanatoriums and had concealed the fact of his alcoholism from his partners for many months. The firm permitted him to continue drawing on his partnership account even though he became increasingly unproductive in those years, as reflected by the continuing yearly drop in the number of units assigned him. After signing the Program Outline in August, 1983, which structured his business life by providing among other things for the monitoring of his work product by the firm for a period of one year, recommending he attend Alcoholics Anonymous meetings, setting the specific times he would arrive at and remain in the office, and containing a provision "3. . . . there is no second chance," Lawlis "resumed the consumption of alcohol" in March, 1984. Instead of expelling Lawlis at that time, the partnership acting through its Finance Committee continued to work with Lawlis by drawing up yet another set of conditions he was to meet to remain with the firm. Clearly, these undisputed facts present no "predatory purpose" on the firm's part, nor does the Finance Committee's Five Year Plan when that proposal is read in full. . . .

Lawlis next argues the firm's act of expelling him was constructively fraudulent because it constituted a breach of the fiduciary duty owed between partners which requires each to exercise good faith and fair dealing in partnership transactions and toward co-partners. . . . While we agree with Lawlis's bald statement of that concept, it has no application to the facts of this case.

The fiduciary relationship between partners to which the terms "bona fide" and "good faith" relate. . . concern the *business aspects or property of the partnership* and prohibit a partner, to wit a fiduciary, from taking any personal advantage touching those subjects.... Plaintiffs contend there was substantial evidence indicating the individual partner's breach of fiduciary duties they owed to plaintiffs as members of the bar. In view of our holding that the executive committee *had the right to expel plaintiffs without stating a reason or cause pursuant to the Partnership Agreement, there was no breach of any fiduciary duty.* (Emphasis supplied.)

Holman v. Coie (1974), 11 Wash.App. 195, 522 P.2d 515, 523–524. *Holman* concerned the expulsion of two partners from a law firm for no stated cause, but there was evidence a political speech by one of them had disgruntled the chief executive of one of the firm's major clients, the Boeing Corporation. Substantially the same consideration present in *Holman,* i.e., potential damage to partnership business, is present in this case.

...

All the parties involved in this litigation were legally competent and consenting adults well educated in the law who initially dealt at arm's length while negotiating the partnership agreements here involved. At the time the partners negotiated their contract, it is apparent they believed, as in *Holman,* the "guillotine method" of involuntary severance [that is, immediate termination by partnership vote without notice or hearing] would be in the best interests of the partnership. Their intent was to provide a simple, practical, and above all, a speedy method of separating a partner from the firm, if that ever became necessary for any reason. We find no fault with that approach to severance.

Where the remaining partners in a firm deem it necessary to expel a partner under a no cause expulsion clause in a partnership agreement freely negotiated and entered into, the expelling partners act in "good faith" regardless of motivation if that act does not cause a wrongful withholding of money or property legally due the expelled partner at the time he is expelled.... If we were to hold otherwise, we would be engrafting a "for cause" requirement upon this agreement when such was not the intent of the parties at the time they entered into their agreement....

Affirmed.

ANALYSIS

1. **The Timing of Expulsion.** What would the result have been if Lawlis had been expelled in July 1983 when his partners first discovered that he was suffering from alcoholism?
2. **Again, the Timing of Expulsion.** What if he had been expelled in August 1984?

3. **The Clients' Interests.** Suppose you had been a client of the partnership. What approach would you have wanted it to take?

Bohatch v. Butler & Binion

41 Tex.Sup.Ct.J. 308, 977 S.W.2d 543 (Tex.1998).

■ ENOCH, JUSTICE, delivered the opinion of the court, in which GONZALEZ, OWEN, BAKER, and HANKINSON, JUSTICES, join.

Partnerships exist by the agreement of the partners; partners have no duty to remain partners. The issue in this case is whether we should create an exception to this rule by holding that a partnership has a duty not to expel a partner for reporting suspected overbilling by another partner. The trial court rendered judgment for Colette Bohatch on her breach of fiduciary duty claim against Butler & Binion and several of its partners (collectively, "the firm"). The court of appeals held that there was no evidence that the firm breached a fiduciary duty and reversed the trial court's tort judgment; however, the court of appeals found evidence of a breach of the partnership agreement and rendered judgment for Bohatch on this ground. We affirm the court of appeals' judgment.

I. Facts

[The following statement of the facts is taken from the concurring opinion. It is more complete than the majority's statement, but otherwise the two statements are consistent with one another.]

John McDonald, an attorney licensed to practice in the District of Columbia and managing partner of the Washington, D.C. office of Butler & Binion, a Houston-based law firm, hired Colette Bohatch, also a D.C. lawyer, as a senior associate in January 1986. The firm's Washington office had only one other lawyer—Richard Powers, also a partner in the firm—and represented essentially one client—Pennzoil—before the Federal Energy Regulatory Commission. Bohatch, who had been deputy assistant general counsel of the FERC when she left to join Butler & Binion, worked for McDonald and Powers on Pennzoil matters.

In January 1989, Bohatch was made a partner in the firm on McDonald's recommendation, and as a partner she began receiving internal firm reports showing the number of hours each attorney worked, billed, and collected for. Reviewing these reports, Bohatch questioned how McDonald could bill as many hours as he reported, given her personal observations of his work habits. She and Powers discussed the subject on several occasions and even went so far as to look through McDonald's daily time diary surreptitiously and make a copy of it.

Bohatch never saw the bills to Pennzoil, which McDonald prepared and sent, so she did not know what fees Pennzoil was actually charged, or even what Butler & Binion's fee arrangement was with Pennzoil.

Nevertheless, from monthly internal reports consistently showing that McDonald billed far more hours than she saw him working, Bohatch concluded that McDonald was overbilling Pennzoil. Convinced that she was obliged by the District of Columbia Code of Professional Responsibility governing lawyer conduct to report her concerns to the firm's management, she discussed them with Butler & Binion's managing partner, Louis Paine, on July 15, 1990. Paine assured her that he would look into the matter.

Bohatch told Powers of her meeting with Paine, and Powers told McDonald. The next day, McDonald informed Bohatch that Pennzoil was dissatisfied with her work. Bohatch feared that McDonald was retaliating against her, and in fact, from that point forward neither McDonald nor Powers assigned Bohatch any other work for Pennzoil. McDonald also insinuated to other partners that Bohatch had complained of him because Pennzoil found her work unacceptable, even though Bohatch had contacted Paine before she was aware of any criticism of her work.

Bohatch called Paine to tell him of McDonald's retaliation, and Paine assured her that he was still investigating. Paine reviewed the firm's bills to Pennzoil and found that in all but one instance fewer hours were billed than were shown on internal computer printouts as having been worked. However, since the printouts merely reflected the time reported by attorneys, and Bohatch was claiming that McDonald reported more time than he actually worked, Paine determined that Pennzoil must be told of Bohatch's assertions so that it could itself evaluate the amounts charged.

Robert Burns, a member of Butler & Binion's management committee, told John Chapman, the Pennzoil in-house attorney who dealt most directly with Butler & Binion's Washington office, of Bohatch's assertions and asked him to review the firm's bills. Chapman confirmed to Burns that he had complained to McDonald several months earlier about the quality of Bohatch's work, and Burns intimated that Bohatch's assertions might have been in response to such complaints. Chapman discussed the matter with his immediate superior and with Pennzoil's general counsel. The three of them reviewed Butler & Binion's bills for the preceding year and concluded that they were reasonable. After Chapman's superior discussed their conclusions with Pennzoil's president and chief executive officer, Chapman told Burns that Pennzoil was satisfied that the firm's bills were reasonable.

Bohatch expected that Paine would ask her for additional information, and when he did not do so, she wrote him that she believed McDonald had overcharged Pennzoil $20,000 to $25,000 per month for his work. In fact, in the preceding six months McDonald had billed Pennzoil on average less than $24,000 per month for his work, so that if Bohatch had been correct, McDonald should have billed Pennzoil almost nothing. On August 23, 1990, a few weeks after their initial meeting, Paine told Bohatch that he had found no evidence of overbilling. Since he did not see how Bohatch could continue to work for McDonald or Pennzoil under the circumstances, given the rifts her allegations had caused, Paine suggested that she begin to look for other employment.

For more than nine months Butler & Binion continued to pay Bohatch a partner's monthly draw of $7,500 and allowed her to keep her office and benefits while she sought other employment. So as not to impair her prospects, the firm did not immediately expel her as a partner, but it did not pay her any partnership distribution other than her draw.... Bohatch left to join another firm in September, and Butler & Binion formally expelled her as a partner in October.

Bohatch sued Butler & Binion, Paine, Burns, and McDonald for breach of the firm partnership agreement and breach of fiduciary duty. A jury found [for her on both counts].

... The court of appeals held that defendants' only duty to Bohatch was not to expel her in bad faith. " 'Bad faith' in this context," the court of appeals wrote, "means only that partners cannot expel another partner for self-gain." Finding no evidence that defendants expelled Bohatch for self-gain, the court concluded that Bohatch could not recover for breach of fiduciary duty....

[The majority opinion follows.]

II. Breach of Fiduciary Duty

We have long recognized as a matter of common law that "[t]he relationship between ... partners ... is fiduciary in character, and imposes upon all the participants the obligation of loyalty to the joint concern and of the utmost good faith, fairness, and honesty in their dealings with each other with respect to matters pertaining to the enterprise." Fitz-Gerald v. Hull, 150 Tex. 39, 237 S.W.2d 256, 264 (Tex.1951) (quotation omitted). Yet, partners have no obligation to remain partners; "at the heart of the partnership concept is the principle that partners may choose with whom they wish to be associated." Gelder Med. Group v. Webber, 41 N.Y.2d 680, 394 N.Y.S.2d 867, 363 N.E.2d 573, 577 (N.Y.1977)....

[A]s provided by the partnership agreement, Bohatch's expulsion did not dissolve the partnership.... [T]he partnership agreement contemplates expulsion of a partner and prescribes procedures to be followed, but it does not specify or limit the grounds for expulsion. Thus, while Bohatch's claim that she was expelled in an improper way is governed by the partnership agreement, her claim that she was expelled for an improper reason is not. Therefore, we look to the common law to find the principles governing Bohatch's claim that the firm breached a duty when it expelled her.

Courts in other states have held that a partnership may expel a partner for purely business reasons. Further, courts recognize that a law firm can expel a partner to protect relationships both within the firm and with clients. Finally, many courts have held that a partnership can expel a partner without breaching any duty in order to resolve a "fundamental schism."

The fiduciary duty that partners owe one another does not encompass a duty to remain partners or else answer in tort damages. Nonetheless, Bohatch and several distinguished legal scholars urge this Court to recognize that public policy requires a limited duty to remain partners—i.e., a partnership must retain a whistleblower partner. They argue that such an extension of a partner's fiduciary duty is necessary because permitting a law firm to retaliate against a partner who in good faith reports suspected overbilling would discourage compliance with rules of professional conduct and thereby hurt clients.

While this argument is not without some force, we must reject it. A partnership exists solely because the partners choose to place personal confidence and trust in one another. . . . Just as a partner can be expelled, without a breach of any common law duty, over disagreements about firm policy or to resolve some other "fundamental schism," a partner can be expelled for accusing another partner of overbilling without subjecting the partnership to tort damages. Such charges, whether true or not, may have a profound effect on the personal confidence and trust essential to the partner relationship. Once such charges are made, partners may find it impossible to continue to work together to their mutual benefit and the benefit of their clients.

We are sensitive to the concern expressed by the dissenting Justices that "retaliation against a partner who tries in good faith to correct or report perceived misconduct virtually assures that others will not take these appropriate steps in the future." However, the dissenting Justices do not explain how the trust relationship necessary both for the firm's existence and for representing clients can survive such serious accusations by one partner against another. The threat of tort liability for expulsion would tend to force partners to remain in untenable circumstance—suspicious of and angry with each other—to their own detriment and that of their clients whose matters are neglected by lawyers distracted with intra-firm frictions.

Although concurring in the Court's judgment, Justice Hecht criticizes the Court for failing to "address amici's concerns that failing to impose liability will discourage attorneys from reporting unethical conduct." To address the scholars' concerns, he proposes that a whistleblower be protected from expulsion, but only if the report, irrespective of being made in good faith, is proved to be correct. We fail to see how such an approach encourages compliance with ethical rules more than the approach we adopt today. Furthermore, the amici's position is that a reporting attorney must be in good faith, not that the attorney must be right. In short, Justice Hecht's approach ignores the question Bohatch presents, the amici write about, and the firm challenges—whether a partnership violates a fiduciary duty when it expels a partner who in good faith reports suspected ethical violations. The concerns of the amici are best addressed by a rule that clearly demarcates an attorney's ethical duties and the parameters of tort liability, rather than redefining "whistleblower."

We emphasize that our refusal to create an exception to the at-will nature of partnerships in no way obviates the ethical duties of lawyers. Such duties sometimes necessitate difficult decisions, as when a lawyer suspects overbilling by a colleague. The fact that the ethical duty to report may create an irreparable schism between partners neither excuses failure to report nor transforms expulsion as a means of resolving that schism into a tort.

We hold that the firm did not owe Bohatch a duty not to expel her for reporting suspected overbilling by another partner.

. . .

■ HECHT, JUSTICE, concurring in the judgment.

The Court holds that partners in a law firm have no common-law liability for expelling one of their number for accusing another of unethical conduct. The dissent argues that partners in a law firm are liable for such conduct. Both views are unqualified; neither concedes or even considers whether "always" and "never" are separated by any distance. I think they must be. The Court's position is directly contrary to that of some of the leading scholars on the subject who have appeared here as amici curiae. The Court finds amici's arguments "not without some force," but rejects them completely. I do not believe amici's arguments can be rejected out of hand. The dissent, on the other hand, refuses even to acknowledge the serious impracticalities involved in maintaining the trust necessary between partners when one has accused another of unethical conduct. In the dissent's view, partners who would expel another for such accusations must simply either get over it or respond in damages. The dissent's view blinks reality.

. . .

This case does not force a choice between diametrically opposite views. Here, the report of unethical conduct, though made in good faith, was incorrect. That fact is significant to me because I think a law firm can always expel a partner for bad judgment, whether it relates to the representation of clients or the relationships with other partners, and whether it is in good faith. I would hold that Butler & Binion did not breach its fiduciary duty by expelling Colette Bohatch because she made a good-faith but nevertheless extremely serious charge against a senior partner that threatened the firm's relationship with an important client, her charge proved groundless, and her relationship with her partners was destroyed in the process. . . .

At least in the context of professional partnerships, the courts have uniformly recognized that a partner can be expelled to protect relationships both inside the firm and with clients. . . .

Despite statements in these cases that partners cannot expel one of their number for personal profit, in each instance the expelling partners believed that retaining the partner would hurt the firm financially and that the firm—and thus the partners themselves—stood to benefit from the expulsion. It is therefore far too simplistic to say, as the court of appeals held, that partners cannot expel a partner for personal financial benefit; if expulsion of a partner to protect the firm's reputation or preserve its relationship with a client benefits the firm financially, it perforce benefits the members of the firm. If expulsion of a partner can be in breach of a fiduciary duty, the circumstances must be more precisely defined.

. . .

Scholars are divided over not only how but whether partners' common-law fiduciary duty to each other limit expulsion of a partner. . . . Nine distinguished law professors—Professor Richard L. Abel of the University of California at Los Angeles School of Law, Professor Leonard Gross of the Southern Illinois University School of Law, Professor Robert W. Hamilton of the University of Texas School of Law, Professor David J. Luban of the University of Maryland School of Law, Professor Gary Minda of the Brooklyn Law School, Professor Ronald D. Rotunda of the University of Illinois College of Law, Professor Theodore J. Schneyer of the University of Arizona College of Law, Professor Clyde W. Summers of the University of Pennsylvania School of Law, and Professor Charles W. Wolfram of the Cornell Law School, the Reporter for the Restatement (Third) of Law, The Law Governing Lawyers—have argued in amicus curiae briefs that expulsion of a partner in bad faith is a breach of fiduciary duty, and that expulsion for self-gain is in bad faith, but so is expulsion for reporting unethical conduct. . . .

[I] am troubled by the arguments of the distinguished amici curiae that permitting a law firm to retaliate against a partner for reporting unethical behavior would discourage compliance with rules of conduct, hurt clients, and contravene public policy. . . .

This very difficult issue need not be finally resolved in this case. Bohatch did not report unethical conduct; she reported what she believed, presumably in good faith but nevertheless mistakenly, to be unethical conduct. . . .

Even if expulsion of a partner for reporting unethical conduct might be a breach of fiduciary duty, expulsion for mistakenly reporting unethical conduct cannot be a breach of fiduciary duty. At the very least, a mistake so serious indicates a lack of judgment warranting expulsion. No one would argue that an attorney could not be expelled from a firm for a serious error in judgment about a client's affairs or even the firm's affairs. . . . Reporting unethical conduct where none existed is no different. . . .

Butler & Binion's expulsion of Bohatch did not discourage ethical conduct; it discouraged errors of judgment, which ought to be discouraged. . . .

The dissent would hold that "law partners violate[ ] their fiduciary duty by retaliating against a fellow partner who ma[kes] a good-faith effort to alert her partners to the possible overbilling of a client." In fact, the dissent would adopt the broader proposition that a partner could not be expelled from a law firm for reporting any suspected ethical violation, regardless of how little evidence there might be for the suspicion. . . .

Bohatch was expelled not because she insisted on reporting admitted unethical actions, but because she insisted on complaining of actions that were not unethical.

. . .

■ SPECTOR, joined by PHILLIPS, CHIEF JUSTICE, dissenting.

. . .

I believe that the fiduciary relationship among law partners should incorporate the rules of the profession promulgated by this Court. . . . Although the evidence put on by Bohatch is by no means conclusive, applying the proper presumptions of a no-evidence review, this trial testimony amounts to some evidence that Bohatch made a good-faith report of suspected overbilling in an effort to comply with her professional duty. Further, it provides some evidence that the partners of Butler & Binion began a retaliatory course of action before any investigation of the allegation had begun.

. . . [R]etaliation against a partner who tries in good faith to correct or report perceived misconduct virtually assures that others will not take these appropriate steps in the future. Although I agree with the majority that partners have a right not to continue a partnership with someone against their will, they may still be liable for damages directly resulting from terminating that relationship.

. . .

The Court's writing in this case sends an inappropriate signal to lawyers and to the public that the rules of professional responsibility are subordinate to a law firm's other interests. . . . Accordingly, I respectfully dissent.

ANALYSIS

1. **Termination and Public Policy.** Although employment relationships at common law were regarded as "at will" in the absence of contrary agreement between the parties, and thus could be terminated at any time without cause, some courts have recently created a public policy-based exception to this rule forbidding firms from firing whistleblowers who call public or law enforcement attention to misconduct at the firm. If Bohatch had been an associate, rather than a partner, would the case for creating such a public policy-based rule forbidding her termination have been stronger? What about a public policy-based rule allowing her to be terminated, but imposing damages for doing so if her termination was done to retaliate against her for "blowing the whistle"? Would any of the three judges who wrote opinions in this case agree with you?

2. **Expulsion for Cause.** Partnership agreements sometimes permit expulsion of a partner only for "cause." If the partnership agreement in this case had contained such a limitation, would Bohatch's conduct have constituted "cause" for this purpose? Would any of the three judges who wrote opinions in this case agree with you?

3. **Partner's Liability to Partnership.** Suppose Pennzoil had "fired" the law firm as a result of the turmoil surrounding Bohatch's charges. Should Bohatch be liable to her fellow partners for making good faith but erroneous charges?

4. **Disparate Treatment.** Richard Powers was the third partner in Butler & Binion's Washington office. The dissent relates the following additional facts: Bohatch and Powers had each independently observed McDonald working only three to four hours a day. Powers approached Bohatch with his suspicions that McDonald might be over-billing Pennzoil. When Bohatch agreed that there was cause for concern, Powers urged Bohatch to "do something." When Bohatch did so, she was fired, but Powers was not. Given the emphasis in both the majority and concurring opinions on intra-firm trust, why wasn't Powers fired too? Given that Powers wasn't fired, does Butler & Binion's explanation for Bohatch's firing seem plausible?

5. **Law Practice: Profession or Business?** The dissent states: "The practice of law is a profession first, then a business." Do you agree? If so, what implications does that statement have for the doctrinal duties of lawyers? Would any of the cases studied so far have come out differently if they had involved law firms instead of "ordinary" businesses?

6. **You and Bohatch.** If you had been in Bohatch's position, what would you have done?

7. **Protecting the Firm.** What suggestions would you offer to a law firm to prevent the kind of problem that arose in this case?

8. **Justification for Termination?** Suppose that the managers of the firm had not expelled Bohatch; that McDonald had then quit in a huff and had taken the client, Pennzoil, with him; and that since the Washington office then had virtually no business, the firm decided to close it. Would the dissenters allow the firm to expel Bohatch without subjecting itself to an action for damages? Would the dissenters hold that Bohatch had a good cause of action against McDonald? Would the firm have a good cause of action against McDonald?

5. PARTNERS AT LOGGERHEADS: THE DISSOLUTION SOLUTION UNDER THE UPA (1914)

A. THE RIGHT TO DISSOLVE

Owen v. Cohen

19 Cal.2d 147, 119 P.2d 713 (1941).

This is an action in equity brought for the dissolution of a partnership and for the sale of the partnership assets in connection with the settlement of its affairs.

On or about January 2, 1940, plaintiff and defendant entered into an oral agreement whereby they contracted to become partners in the operation of a bowling-alley business in Burbank, California. The parties did not expressly fix any definite period of time for the duration of this undertaking. For the purpose of securing necessary equipment, plaintiff advanced the sum of $6,986.63 to the partnership, with the understanding that the amount so contributed was to be considered a loan to the partnership and was to be repaid to the plaintiff out of the prospective profits of the business as soon as it could reasonably do so. . . .

Plaintiff and defendant opened their partnership bowling-alley on March 15, 1940. From the day of its beginning until the institution of the present action on June 28, 1940—a period of approximately three and one-half months—the business was operated at a profit. During this time the partners paid off a part of the capital indebtedness and each took a salary of $50 per week. However, shortly after the business was begun differences arose between the partners with regard to the management of the partnership affairs and their respective rights and duties under their agreement. This continuing lack of harmonious relationship between the partners had its effect on the monthly gross receipts, which, though still substantial, were steadily declining, and at the date of the filing of this action much of the partnership indebtedness, including the aforementioned loan made by plaintiff, remained unpaid. On July 5,

1940, in response to plaintiff's complaint and upon order to show cause, the court appointed a receiver to take charge of the partnership business, which ever since has been under his control and management.

As the result of the trial of this action the court found . . . that the parties disagreed "on practically all matters essential to the operation of the partnership business and upon matters of policy in connection therewith"; that the defendant had "committed breaches of the partnership agreement" and had "so conducted himself in affairs relating to the business" that it was "not reasonably practicable to carry on the partnership business with him." From this finding it was concluded that the partnership was dissoluble by court decree in accordance with the provisions of section 2426 of the Civil Code.

Pursuant to these findings of fact and conclusions of law, the trial court rendered a decree adjudging the partnership dissolved and ordering the assets sold by the receiver. It was further decreed that the proceeds of such sale and of the receiver's operation of the business on hand upon the consummation of such sale be applied, after allowance for the receiver's fees and expenses, to payment of the partnership debts, including the amount of $6,986.63 loaned by plaintiff to the business; that one-half of the remainder of the proceeds be paid to plaintiff, together with the additional sum of $100.17 for his costs; and that defendant be given what was left. . . .

The principal question presented for consideration is whether or not the evidence warrants a decree of dissolution of the partnership. . . .

It is not necessary to enter into a detailed statement of the quarrel between the partners. Whether the disharmony was the result of a difference in disposition or other causes, the effect is the same. Most of the acts of which complaint is made are individually trivial, but from the aggregate the court found, and the record so indicates, that the breach between the partners was due in large measure to defendant's persistent endeavors to become the dominating figure of the enterprise and to humiliate plaintiff before the employees and customers of the bowling-alley. In this connection plaintiff testified that defendant declined to do any substantial amount of the work required for the successful operation of the business; that defendant informed him that he (defendant) "had not worked yet in 47 years and did not intend to start now"; and that he (plaintiff) "should do whatever manual work he could do on the premises, but that he (defendant) would act as manager and wear the dignity." The record also discloses that during the preparation and before the opening of the bowling-alley establishment, defendant told a mutual acquaintance that plaintiff would not be there very long. Corroborative of this evidence is plaintiff's testimony that a few weeks prior to the filing of this action, when he had concluded that he and defendant could not reconcile their differences, he asked defendant to make an offer either to buy out his (plaintiff's) interest in the business or to sell to him (plaintiff); that defendant replied, in effect, that when he was ready to sell to plaintiff, he would set the price himself and it would cost plaintiff plenty to get rid of him. In addition, there is considerable evidence demonstrating that the partners disagreed on matters of policy relating to the operation of the business. One cause of dispute in this connection was defendant's desire to open a gambling room on the second floor of the bowling-alley property and plaintiff's opposition to such move. Another was defendant's dissatisfaction with the agreed salary of $50 per week fixed for each partner to take from the business and his desire to withdraw additional amounts therefrom. This constant dissension over money affairs culminated in defendant's appropriation of small sums from the partnership's funds to his own use without plaintiff's knowledge, approval or consent. In justification of his conduct defendant claimed that on each occasion he set aside a like amount for plaintiff. This extenuating circumstance, however, does not serve to eliminate from the record the fact that monetary matters were a continual source of argument between the partners.

Defendant urges that the evidence shows only petty discord between the partners, and he advances, as applicable here, the general rule that trifling and minor differences and grievances which involve no permanent mischief will not authorize a court to decree a dissolution of a partnership. 20 R.C.L. 958, par. 182. However, as indicated by the same section in Ruling Case Law and previous sections, courts of equity may order the dissolution of a partnership where there are quarrels and disagreements of such a nature and to such extent that all confidence and cooperation between the parties has been destroyed or where one of the parties by his misbehavior materially hinders a proper conduct of the partnership business. It is not only large affairs which produce trouble. The continuance of overbearing and vexatious petty treatment of one partner by another frequently is more serious in its disruptive character than would be larger differences which would be discussed and settled. For the purpose of demonstrating his own preeminence in the business one partner cannot constantly minimize and deprecate the importance of the other without undermining the basic status upon which a successful partnership rests. In our opinion the court in the instant case was warranted in finding from the evidence that there was very bitter, antagonistic feeling between the parties; that under the arrangement made by the parties for the handling of the partnership business, the duties of these parties required cooperation, coordination and harmony; and that under the existent conditions the parties were incapable of carrying on the business to their mutual advantage. As the court concluded, plaintiff has made out a cause for judicial dissolution of the partnership under section 2426 of the Civil Code [U.P.A. § 32]:

"(1) On application by or for a partner the court shall decree a dissolution whenever:. . . .

"(c) A partner has been guilty of such conduct as tends to affect prejudicially the carrying on of the business,

"(d) A partner wilfully or persistently commits a breach of the partnership agreement, or otherwise so conducts himself in matters relating to the partnership business that it is not reasonably practicable to carry on the business in partnership with him,. . . .

"(f) Other circumstances render a dissolution equitable."

Defendant next questions the propriety of that portion of the decree which provides for the payment of plaintiff's loan to the business, to-wit, the sum of $6,986.63, from the proceeds realized upon the sale of the partnership assets. It is his contention that since the partners agreed that the amount so contributed was to be repaid from the profits of the business, which the evidence established to be a profitable enterprise, the court's order directing the discharge of this partnership obligation in a manner violative of the express understanding of the parties is unjustifiable. . . . That a party to a contract may absolutely limit his right to receive a sum of money from a specified source is indisputable. . . . But defendant's argument based upon this settled precept is of no avail here, for his above-described conduct, creative of a condition of disharmony in derogation of the best interests of the partnership, constituted ground for the court's decree of dissolution and its order directing the sale of the assets for the purpose of forwarding the settlement of the partnership affairs. Defendant, whose persistence in the commission of acts provocative of dissension and disagreement between the partners made it impossible for them to carry on the partnership business, is in no position now to insist on its continued operation. These circumstances not only render the assailed provision of the decree invulnerable to defendant's objection, but also establish its complete accord with established principles of equity jurisprudence.

. . .

The judgment is affirmed.

ANALYSIS

1. **Why the Lawsuit?** Why do you suppose the plaintiff filed a lawsuit seeking dissolution rather than simply giving notice of dissolution and demanding a winding up?
2. **Legal Effect.** What is the legal effect of the order for dissolution? What is the likely practical effect?

NOTE AND QUESTION

Under UPA (1997) § 801(5) a partnership is dissolved "on application by a partner, [by] a judicial decree that: (i) the economic purpose of the partnership is likely to be reasonably frustrated; (ii) another partner has engaged in conduct relating to the partnership business that makes it not reasonably practicable to carry on the business in partnership with that partner; or (iii) it is not otherwise reasonably practicable to carry on the partnership business in conformity with the partnership agreement." Do you think this is a change in the right direction?

Collins v. Lewis

283 S.W.2d 258 (Texas Court of Civil Appeals, 1955).

This suit was instituted in the District Court of Harris County by the appellants, who, as the owners of a fifty per cent (50%) interest in a partnership known as the L-C Cafeteria, sought a receivership of the partnership business, a judicial dissolution of the partnership, and foreclosure of a mortgage upon appellees' interest in the partnership assets. Appellees denied appellants' right to the relief sought, and filed a cross-action for damages for breach of contract in the event dissolution should be decreed. Appellants' petition for receivership having been denied after a hearing before the court, trial of the issues of dissolution and foreclosure, and of appellees' cross-action, proceeded before the court and a jury. At the conclusion of such trial, the jury, in response to special issues submitted, returned a verdict upon which the trial court entered judgment denying all relief sought by appellants.

The facts are substantially as follows:

In the latter part of 1948 appellee John L. Lewis obtained a commitment conditioned upon adequate financial backing from the Brown-Bellows-Smith Corporation for a lease on the basement space under the then projected San Jacinto Building for the purpose of constructing and operating a large cafeteria therein. Lewis contacted appellant Carr P. Collins, a resident of Dallas, proposing that he (Lewis) would furnish the lease, the experience and management ability for the operation of a cafeteria, and Collins would furnish the money; that all revenue of the business, except for an agreed salary to Lewis, would be applied to the repayment of such money, and that thereafter all profits would be divided equally between Lewis and Collins. These negotiations failed to materialize because of the inability of Lewis to conclude satisfactory terms with the building owners. Thereafter, in 1949, negotiations along substantially the same terms were reopened, and culminated in the execution between the building owners, as lessors, and Lewis and Collins, as lessees, of a lease upon such basement space for a term of 30 years. Thereafter Lewis and Collins entered into a partnership agreement to endure throughout the term of the lease contract. This agreement is in part evidenced by a formal contract between the parties, but both litigants concede that the complete agreement is ascertainable only from the verbal understandings and exchanges of letters between the principals. . . . The substance of the agreement was that Collins was to furnish all of the funds necessary to build, equip, and open the cafeteria for business. Lewis was to plan and supervise such construction, and, after opening for business, to manage the operation of the cafeteria. As a part of his undertaking, he guaranteed that moneys advanced by Collins would be repaid at the rate of at least $30,000, plus interest, in the first year of operation, and $60,000 per year, plus interest, thereafter, upon default of which Lewis would surrender his interest to Collins. In addition Lewis guaranteed Collins against loss to the extent of $100,000. In the partnership agreement fifty per cent interest therein is reflected to be owned by Collins and certain members of his family, in stated proportions, and the other fifty per cent is reflected to be owned by Lewis and members of his family. However, in their conduct of the business of the partnership, it is conceded by all litigants that Lewis and Collins completely controlled the respective equal fifty per cent interests in the business to the same extent as if the actual ownership were so vested. For the purpose of this opinion, they are treated as if that were in fact the case.

Immediately after the lease agreement had been executed Lewis began the preparation of detailed plans and specifications for the cafeteria. Initially Lewis had estimated, and had represented to Collins, that the cost of completing the cafeteria ready for operation would be approximately $300,000. Due to delays on the part of the building owners in completing the building, and delays in procuring the equipment deemed necessary to opening the cafeteria for business, the actual opening did not occur until September 18, 1952, some 2½ years after the lease had been executed. The innumerable problems which arose during that period are in part reflected in the exchange of correspondence between the partners. Such evidence reflects that as to the solution of most of such problems the partners were in entire agreement. It further reflects that such disagreements as did arise were satisfactorily resolved. It likewise appears that the actual costs incurred during that period greatly exceeded the amount previously estimated by Lewis to be necessary. The cause of such increase is disputed by the litigants. Appellants contend that it was brought about largely by the extravagance and mismanagement of appellee Lewis. Appellees contend that it resulted from inflation, increased labor and material costs, caused by the Korean War, and unanticipated but necessary expenses. Whatever may have been the reason, it clearly appears that Collins, while expressing concern over the increasing cost, and urging the employment of every possible economy, continued to advance funds and pay expenses, which, by the date of opening for business, had exceeded $600,000.

Collins' concern over the mounting costs of the cafeteria appears to have been considerably augmented by the fact that after opening for business the cafeteria showed expenses considerably in excess of receipts. Upon being informed, shortly after the cafeteria had opened for business, that there existed incurred but unpaid items of cost over and above those theretofore paid, Collins made demand upon Lewis that the cafeteria be placed immediately upon a profitable basis, failing which he (Collins) would advance no more funds for any purpose. There followed an exchange of recriminatory correspondence between the parties, Collins on the one hand charging Lewis with extravagant mismanagement, and Lewis on the other hand charging Collins with unauthorized interference with the management of the business. Futile attempts were made by Lewis to obtain financial backing to buy Collins' interest in the business. Numerous threats were made by Collins to cause Lewis to lose his interest in the business entirely. This suit was filed by Collins in January of 1953.

The involved factual background of this litigation was presented to the jury in a trial which extended over five weeks, and is reflected in a record consisting of a transcript of 370 pages, a statement of facts of 1,400 pages, and 163 original exhibits. At the conclusion of the evidence 23 special issues of fact were submitted to the jury. The controlling issues of fact, as to which a dispute existed, were resolved by the jury in their answers to Issues 1 to 5, inclusive, in which they found that Lewis was competent to manage the business of the L-C Cafeteria; that there is not a reasonable expectation of profit under the continued management of Lewis; that but for the conduct of Collins there would be a reasonable expectation of profit under the continued management of Lewis; that such conduct on the part of Collins was not that of a reasonably prudent person acting under the same or similar circumstances; and that such conduct on the part of Collins materially decreased the earnings of the cafeteria during the first year of its operation. . . .

We agree with appellants' premise that there is no such thing as an indissoluble partnership only in the sense that there always exists the power, as opposed to the right, of dissolution. But legal right to dissolution rests in equity, as does the right to relief from the provisions of any legal contract. The jury finding that there is not a reasonable expectation of profit from the L-C Cafeteria under the continued management of Lewis, must be read in connection with their findings that Lewis is competent to manage the business of L-C Cafeteria, and that but for the conduct of Collins there would be a reasonable expectation of profit therefrom. In our view those are the controlling findings upon the issue of dissolution. It was Collins' obligation to furnish the money; Lewis' to furnish the management, guaranteeing a stated minimum repayment of the money. The jury has found that he was competent, and could reasonably have performed his obligation but for the conduct of Collins. We know of no rule which grants Collins, under such circumstances, the right to dissolution of the partnership. . . .

The basic agreement between Lewis and Collins provided that Collins would furnish money in an amount sufficient to defray the cost of building, equipping and opening the L-C Cafeteria for operation. As a part of the agreement between Lewis and Collins, Lewis executed, and delivered to Collins, a mortgage upon Lewis' interest in the partnership "until the indebtedness incurred by the said Carr P. Collins . . . has been paid in full out of income derived from the said L-C Cafeteria, Houston, Texas."

The evidence shows that a substantial portion of the money used to build, equip and open the cafeteria was borrowed by Collins from the First National Bank in Dallas. The bank credit was admittedly extended upon Collins' financial responsibility. In the mechanics of arranging for such credit, however, Collins prepared and requested Lewis and his family to execute notes in the total sum of $175,000 payable to the First National Bank in Dallas on demand. Lewis expressed concern at creating an obligation payable on terms which he felt unable to meet, whereupon Collins addressed a signed letter to Lewis, containing language as follows: ". . . If you are apprehensive because of the fear that there might be a foreclosure of these notes or a failure to renew these notes for a sufficient period of time to liquidate them at a rate of not more than $2,500 per month the first year and $5,000 per month the second year, I can assure you that the notes will be renewed as often as is necessary to protect you on that point. . . ."

. . .

At about the time this suit was instituted, the First National Bank in Dallas made demand upon Lewis for payment of the notes described, thus maturing the liability of Collins upon his endorsement of the notes. The failure of Lewis to pay such notes on demand constitutes the default, by reason of which Collins seeks foreclosure of his mortgage on Lewis' interest in the partnership. We are unable to agree with appellants in this contention, and must overrule their points presenting it. Regardless of the legal relationship between Lewis and the First National Bank in Dallas, created by the notes described, Lewis' obligation to Collins is limited to repaying money advanced by Collins at the minimum rate of $30,000 the first year and $60,000 per year thereafter. Only upon default of that obligation does the right of foreclosure ripen. There is testimony in the record to the effect that Collins, as a director and stockholder in the Dallas Bank had induced the bank to make demand for payment in order to effect foreclosure. That proof appears to us to be entirely immaterial to the determination of the rights of these litigants. The proof is undisputed that the bank, after maturing the notes, took no further steps to effect collection. Aside from that, however, as we construe the partnership agreement, it was Collins' obligation to furnish all money needed to build, equip and open the cafeteria for business. With particular reference to the notes, it was Collins' obligation to protect Lewis against any demand for payment so long as Lewis met his obligation of repaying money advanced by Collins at the rate agreed upon. Failure on Collins' part to protect Lewis on his obligation to the bank would constitute a breach of contract by Collins.

Collins' right to foreclose, therefore, depends upon whether or not Lewis has met his basic obligation of repayment at the rate agreed upon. Appellees contend, we think correctly, that he has, in the following manner: the evidence shows that Collins advanced a total of $636,720 for the purpose of building, equipping and opening the cafeteria for business. The proof also shows that Lewis contended that the actual cost exceeded that amount by over $30,000. The litigants differed in regard to such excess, it being Collins' contention that it represented operating expense rather than cost of building, equipping and opening the cafeteria. The jury heard the conflicting proof relative to these contentions, and resolved the question by their answer to Special Issue 20, whereby they found that the minimum cost of building, equipping and opening the cafeteria for operation amounted to $697,603.36. Under the basic agreement of the partners, therefore, this excess was properly Collins' obligation. Upon the refusal of Collins to pay it, Lewis paid it out of earnings of the business during the first year of its operation. Thus it clearly appears that Lewis met his obligation, and the trial court properly denied foreclosure of the mortgage.

In their brief, appellants repeatedly complain that they should not be forced to endure a continuing partnership wherein there is no reasonable expectation of profit, which they say is the effect of the trial court's judgment. The proper and equitable solution of the differences which arise between partners is never an easy problem, especially where the relationship is as involved as this present one. We do not think it can properly be said, however, that the judgment of the trial court denying appellants the dissolution which they seek forces them to endure a partnership wherein there is no reasonable expectation of profit. We have already pointed out the ever present inherent power, as opposed to the legal right, of any partner to terminate the relationship. Pursuit of that course presents the problem of possible liability for such damages as flow from the breach of contract. The alternative course available to appellants seems clearly legible in the verdict of the jury, whose services in that connection were invoked by appellants.

Judgment affirmed.

NOTE

This case arose before Texas adopted its version of the UPA (1914) or, later, UPA (1997). The relevant provisions of these acts are essentially the same as the rules applied by the court in Collins v. Lewis.

ANALYSIS

1. **Effect of Decree of Dissolution.** What did Collins hope to gain by obtaining a decree of dissolution?
2. **What Next?** Where does the court's refusal to order dissolution leave Collins? What is likely to happen next?

PLANNING

What protection should Collins have had in the partnership agreement? If he had sought such protection, is it likely that Lewis would have objected?

INTRODUCTORY NOTE

The next case, Page v. Page, is an action for a declaratory judgment in which the plaintiff sought a declaration that the partnership was not for any definite term and therefore could be dissolved at the will of either partner. The California Supreme Court's discussion of implied agreements creating partnerships for a definite term is interesting and valuable. For present purposes, however, our focus is on the court's dictum about the process of dissolution. The business of the partnership was linen supply. After a long period of losses, it appeared that the business might finally be able to earn a profit. So why was the plaintiff anxious to have a declaratory judgment that the partnership was subject to dissolution at will?

Page v. Page

55 Cal.2d 192, 10 Cal.Rptr. 643, 359 P.2d 41 (1961).

■ TRAYNOR, JUSTICE.

Plaintiff and defendant are partners in a linen supply business in Santa Maria, California. Plaintiff appeals from a judgment declaring the partnership to be for a term rather than at will.

The partners entered into an oral partnership agreement in 1949. Within the first two years each partner contributed approximately $43,000 for the purchase of land, machinery, and linen needed to begin the business. From 1949 to 1957 the enterprise was unprofitable, losing approximately $62,000. The partnership's major creditor is a corporation, wholly owned by plaintiff, that supplies the linen and machinery necessary for the day-to-day operation of the business. This corporation holds a $47,000 demand note of the partnership. The partnership operations began to improve in 1958. The partnership earned $3,824.41 in that year and $2,282.30 in the first three months of 1959. Despite this improvement plaintiff wishes to terminate the partnership.

The Uniform Partnership Act provides that a partnership may be dissolved "By the express will of any partner when no definite term or particular undertaking is specified." Corp.Code, § 15031, subd. (1)(b). The trial court found that the partnership is for a term, namely, "such reasonable time as is necessary to enable said partnership to repay from partnership profits, indebtedness incurred for the purchase of land, buildings, laundry and delivery equipment and linen for the operation of such business. . . ." Plaintiff correctly contends that this finding is without support in the evidence.

Defendant testified that the terms of the partnership were to be similar to former partnerships of plaintiff and defendant, and that the understanding of these partnerships was that "we went into partnership to start the business and let the business operation pay for itself,—put in so much money, and let the business pay itself out." There was also testimony that one of the former partnership agreements provided in writing that the profits were to be retained until all obligations were paid.

Upon cross-examination defendant admitted that the former partnership in which the earnings were to be retained until the obligations were repaid was substantially different from the present partnership. The former partnership was a limited partnership and provided for a definite term of five years and a partnership at will thereafter. Defendant insists, however, that the method of operation of the former partnership showed an understanding that all obligations were to be repaid from profits. He nevertheless concedes that there was no understanding as to the term of the present partnership in the event of losses. He was asked: "[W]as there any discussion with reference to the continuation of the business in the event of losses?" He replied, "Not that I can remember." He was then asked, "Did you have any understanding with Mr. Page, your brother, the plaintiff in this action, as to how the obligations were to be paid if there were losses?" He replied, "Not that I can remember. I can't remember discussing that at all. We never figured on losing, I guess."

Viewing this evidence most favorably for defendant, it proves only that the partners expected to meet current expenses from current income and to recoup their investment if the business were successful.

Defendant contends that such an expectation is sufficient to create a partnership for a term under the rule of Owen v. Cohen, 19 Cal.2d 147, 150, 119 P.2d 713. In that case we held that when a partner advances a sum of money to a partnership with the understanding that the amount contributed was to be a loan to the partnership and was to be repaid as soon as feasible from the prospective profits of the business, the partnership is for the term reasonably required to repay the loan. It is true that Owen v. Cohen, supra, and other cases hold that partners may impliedly agree to continue in business until a certain sum of money is earned . . ., or one or more partners recoup their investments . . ., or until certain debts are paid . . ., or until certain property could be disposed of on favorable terms. . . . In each of these cases, however, the implied agreement found support in the evidence.

. . .

In the instant case, however, defendant failed to prove any facts from which an agreement to continue the partnership for a term may be implied. The understanding to which defendant testified was no more than a common hope that the partnership earnings would pay for all the necessary expenses. Such a hope does not establish even by implication a "definite term or particular undertaking" as required by section 15031, subdivision (1)(b) of the Corporations Code. All partnerships are ordinarily entered into with the hope that they will be profitable, but that alone does not make them all partnerships for a term and obligate the partners to continue in the partnerships until all of the losses over a period of many years have been recovered.

Defendant contends that plaintiff is acting in bad faith and is attempting to use his superior financial position to appropriate the now profitable business of the partnership. Defendant has invested \$43,000 in the firm, and owing to the long period of losses his interest in the partnership assets is very small. The fact that plaintiff's wholly-owned corporation holds a \$47,000 demand note of the partnership may make it difficult to sell the business as a going concern. Defendant fears that upon dissolution he will receive very little and that plaintiff, who is the managing partner and knows how to conduct the operations of the partnership, will receive a business that has become very profitable because of the establishment of Vandenberg Air Force Base in its vicinity. Defendant charges that plaintiff has been content to share the losses but now that the business has become profitable he wishes to keep all the gains.

There is no showing in the record of bad faith or that the improved profit situation is more than temporary. In any event these contentions are irrelevant to the issue whether the partnership is for a term or at will. Since, however, this action is for a declaratory judgment and will be the basis for future action by the parties, it is appropriate to point out that defendant is amply protected by the fiduciary duties of co-partners.

Even though the Uniform Partnership Act provides that a partnership at will may be dissolved by the express will of any partner (Corp.Code, § 15031, subd. (1)(b)), this power, like any other power held by a fiduciary, must be exercised in good faith.

. . .

A partner at will is not bound to remain in a partnership, regardless of whether the business is profitable or unprofitable. A partner may not, however, by use of adverse pressure "freeze out" a co-partner and appropriate the business to his own use. A partner may not dissolve a partnership to gain the benefits of the business for himself, unless he fully compensates his copartner for his share of the prospective business opportunity. . . .

[I]n the instant case, plaintiff has the power to dissolve the partnership by express notice to defendant. If, however, it is proved that plaintiff acted in bad faith and violated his fiduciary duties by attempting to appropriate to his own use the new prosperity of the partnership without adequate compensation to his copartner, the dissolution would be wrongful and the plaintiff would be liable as provided by subdivision (2)(a) of Corporations Code, § 15038 (rights of partners upon wrongful dissolution) for violation of the implied agreement not to exclude defendant wrongfully from the partnership business opportunity.

The judgment is reversed.

PROBLEMS

1. **Ousting a Partner.** Suppose the plaintiff wished to buy the assets of the partnership and continue its business with a new partner (who will take over as manager and will have a 25 percent share). How should he have proceeded?

2. **Liquidation of Partnership.** Suppose the plaintiff intended to liquidate the business (that is, shut it down and sell off its physical assets) and pick up its better accounts through his corporation. What advice would you have given?

B. THE CONSEQUENCES OF DISSOLUTION

Prentiss v. Sheffel

20 Ariz.App. 411, 513 P.2d 949 (1973).

The question presented by this appeal is whether two majority partners in a three-man partnership-at-will, who have excluded the third partner from partnership management and affairs, should be allowed to purchase the partnership assets at a judicially supervised dissolution sale. We hold that on the facts of this case, such a purchase is proper, and affirm the judgment entered by the trial court.

Suit was originally brought by plaintiffs-appellees seeking dissolution of a partnership they had formed with defendant-appellant. The partnership was created for the purpose of acquiring and operating the West Plaza Shopping Center located at Bethany Home Road and 35th Avenue in Phoenix, Arizona. (Hereinafter referred to as the Center).

As grounds for dissolution the plaintiffs contended that the defendant had in general been derelict in his partnership duties, and in particular that he had failed to contribute the balance of his proportionate share ($6,000) of the operating losses incurred by the Center. The plaintiffs also sought the trial court's permission to continue the partnership business both during the pendency of the suit and thereafter, and requested that a value be fixed on the defendant's interest in the partnership.

Defendant filed a counterclaim seeking a winding up of the partnership and the appointment of a receiver. He contended that his rights as a partner had been violated in that he had been wrongfully excluded from the partnership.

After an extended evidentiary hearing, the trial court made certain pertinent findings of fact which are here summarized:

1. That each of the plaintiffs owned a 42½% interest in the partnership, with an aggregate interest of 85%, while the defendant was the owner of a 15% interest.

2. That no detailed partnership agreement as to how the business would be supervised, how management decisions would be made, or the term of the partnership's existence, was ever made or entered into at any time between the parties, although there were frequent attempts to arrive at such an agreement.

3. That numerous unresolved disputes arose between the parties, most notably as to how title to the partnership property was to be held, and how management decisions should be made.

4. That as a result of these disputes the relationship between the parties deteriorated, culminating with plaintiffs notifying defendant that any further dealings between them should be through their attorney.

5. That defendant had never been denied physical access to the Center; that he visited there from time to time; and that he also engaged in conversations with the resident manager of the Center.

6. That because of his poor financial condition, defendant had not made payments of all of his pro-rata share of the deficits incurred by the Center when called upon to do so.

7. That since its acquisition, the Center's losses from operations had been materially reduced, and certain more advantageous lease provisions had been secured; that there had been no showing of waste nor detriment to the Center as a result of management operations.

8. That there was a freeze-out or exclusion of the defendant from partnership management and affairs.

Based upon these and other findings of fact the trial court concluded that a partnership-at-will existed between the plaintiffs and the defendant which was dissolved as a result of a freeze-out or exclusion of the defendant from the management and affairs of the partnership. A receiver was appointed by the court until the partnership property could be sold and a partition and distribution of assets could be made. The trial court expressly refused the defendant's request that an order be entered forbidding the plaintiffs from bidding at the contemplated judicial sale.

The receiver and the trial court proceeded with the liquidation and sale of the Center. The plaintiffs were the high bidders at the sale which was held in open court. Subsequently, the court entered an order confirming the sale of the Center to them. It is from this order that the defendant appeals.

The principal contention urged by the defendant is that he was *wrongfully* excluded from the management of the partnership, and therefore, because he would in some way be disadvantaged, the plaintiffs should not be allowed to purchase the partnership assets at a judicial sale. The record, however, does not support the defendant's position on two particulars. While the trial court did find that the defendant was excluded from the management of the partnership, there was no indication that such exclusion was done for the wrongful purpose of obtaining the partnership assets in bad faith rather than being merely the result of the inability of the partners to harmoniously function in a partnership relationship.

Moreover, the defendant has failed to demonstrate how he was injured by the participation of the plaintiffs in the judicial sale. To the contrary, from all the evidence it appears that if the plaintiffs had not participated, the sales price would have been considerably lower. Absent the plaintiffs' bid, there would have been only two qualified initial bids, which were $2,076,000 and $2,040,000 respectively. However, with the participation of plaintiffs, whose initial bid was $2,100,000, the final sales price was bid to $2,250,000. Thus it appears that defendant's 15% interest in the partnership was considerably *enhanced* by the plaintiffs' participation.

. . . The defendant characterizes the sale to plaintiffs as a forced sale of his partnership interest. However, defendant was not forced to sell his interest to the plaintiffs. He had the same right to purchase the partnership assets as they did, by submitting the highest bid at the judicial sale. His argument that the plaintiffs were bidding "paper" dollars due to their 85% partnership interest is without force. He too could have bid "paper" dollars to the extent of his 15% interest. Moreover, the fact that the plaintiffs could bid "paper" dollars made it possible, as defendant recognizes in his brief, for them to bid higher than outsiders.

As a consequence of this ability to enter a higher bid, the value of the defendant's 15% interest in the sale proceeds increased proportionately.

. . .

The defendant has cited no cases, nor has this court found any, which have prohibited a partner from bidding at a judicial sale of the partnership assets. . . .

It must be emphasized that on this appeal the defendant does not attack the fact that the trial court ordered a sale of the assets. The only area of attack is that plaintiffs have been allowed to participate and bid in that sale. . . .

The judgment of the superior court is affirmed.

ANALYSIS AND PLANNING

1. **Dealing with Bad Partners.** Prentiss v. Sheffel involves a partnership for the ownership and operation of a shopping center. Among the decisions that must be made for such a venture are the terms of rental agreements (amount of rent, duration of lease, etc.), selection and compensation of a manager, and the budget for advertising, repairs, and maintenance, and amounts to be spent on improvements. Suppose the two plaintiffs have found that the defendant is difficult to work with and generally uninformed and unhelpful. Their inclination is simply to avoid discussing partnership business with him at all, since they invariably outvote him whenever there is disagreement and they do not want to waste any more of their time trying to work with him. They come to you, asking what problems might be created for them if they proceed in accordance with this inclination and what suggestions you might have. What is your response?

2. **Two Rules for Auctions.** Property may be worth more to its current owners than to outsiders. One reason for this may be that the outsiders may fear that the owners are aware of some defect that the outsiders cannot observe. It may be that there are no such defects, but the owners may not be able to convince outsiders of that reality. Costs of transfer of ownership and management also may explain why property may be worth more to its current owners than to potential buyers.

   Suppose Amy, Bob, and Carol are equal partners in a firm that owns a shopping center. The partnership is terminable at will. Amy and Bob work together well. Their relationship with Carol is unpleasant and unproductive. They would like to buy Carol's one-third interest and would be willing to pay up to $700,000 for it, but they would prefer to pay less. They believe that the most an outsider would be willing to pay for the shopping center would be $1,800,000 ($600,000 for each partner). Consider two possible rules of law. Under Rule A (the rule of Prentiss v. Sheffel), Amy and Bob can dissolve the partnership, can insist on an auction, and can bid for the property themselves, using their interest in the partnership as partial payment. Under Rule B, Amy and Bob can dissolve the partnership, which will result in an auction of the property, but they will not be permitted to bid on the property. Suppose that Amy and Bob offer Carol $610,000 for her interest in the partnership. If Rule A is the law, how is Carol likely to respond? What if Rule B is the law? What do your answers to these questions tell you about which rule you would propose for a partnership agreement if you were advising the parties at the outset, at a time when all the partners anticipate cordial and productive relationships with one another? What are the results under each rule if the parties have different beliefs about what price an outsider would bid at an auction? For example, what if Amy and Bob think an outsider would bid at most $1,800,000, while Carol thinks an outsider would bid $2,400,000? What if these expectations are reversed?

Disotell v. Stiltner

100 P.3d 890 (Alaska 2004).

. . .

II. Fact and Proceedings

Carl Disotell is an Eagle River resident who develops properties as a general contractor. His construction company is Disotell Construction. Earl Stiltner is also an Eagle River resident. Stiltner owned and operated a real estate office and property management company in Eagle River from May 1990 until December 1997. In 1994 he . . . purchased [two lots] (the "hotel property") for $275,000. There was a two story commercial building on the property. . . .

Disotell and Stiltner met in 1997. They discussed Stiltner's property and agreed to form an equal partnership to develop, construct, and operate a hotel on the property. They never entered into a written partnership agreement. They intended to convert the two story commercial building on the property into a hotel that would open for business by May 15, 1998. Disotell Construction was to serve as general contractor; it was to provide its services on a cost only basis. Disotell was to use his experience as a developer to plan the project and obtain the necessary permits and licenses.

The parties agreed that Disotell would purchase a one half interest in the hotel property for $137,500, one half of Stiltner's cost. They also agreed that the funds from which Disotell would buy the one half interest would come only from the profits of the hotel. After Stiltner had recovered his original cost basis in the property and certain other costs, he and Disotell were to share profits on a fifty/fifty basis. . . .

Stiltner quitclaimed one half of his interest in the hotel property to Disotell on March 3, 1998. The parties disputed who was obligated to put up the cash for the project. Disotell later testified that Stiltner was to have provided all of the cash; Stiltner claimed they were to contribute equally to the expenses. The superior court later found that the partners jointly would provide for the project's cash needs. The parties agreed that neither would charge interest for the purchase of the hotel property or for cash expenses.

After learning that it could acquire a liquor license free of charge for a hotel of fifty or more rooms, the partnership agreed to convert the two story building into a four story hotel, bar, and restaurant. The partnership hired an architect, structural engineer, and a civil engineering firm. Disotell testified that he contributed hundreds of hours to developing the project.

. . .

The partnership never produced a profit. Stiltner has exclusively possessed the hotel property since May 15, 1998. He testified that he occupies the premises as his residence and has stored his personal possessions there.

. . .

III. Discussion

. . .

B. It Was Not Error to Give Stiltner a Buy-out Opportunity.

Disotell argues that the superior court failed to follow the [Alaska Uniform Partnership] Act when the court gave Stiltner the option to purchase Disotell's partnership interest for $73,213.50, the value of Disotell's interest as calculated by the court. The superior court proposed two alternative methods for winding up the partnership. The first alternative allowed Stiltner to purchase Disotell's partnership interest. The court reasoned that this would avoid the unnecessary cost of appointing a receiver and would reduce economic waste. The second alternative was available if Stiltner had insufficient funds to pay Disotell; the court would then "appoint a receiver to take possession of and to sell the partnership property, to pay the costs of the receiver, and distribute the remaining proceeds according to [its] findings of fact and conclusions of law.

Disotell claims that the Uniform Partnership Act made liquidation a matter of right. He argues that any partner who has not wrongfully caused dissolution of the partnership may demand liquidation. He asserts that the superior court erred when it concluded that "liquidation is not mandatory." He therefore seeks a remand with instructions for appointment of a receiver to take possession of the assets and liquidate them.

> Alaska Statute 32.05.320 [UPA (1914) § 37] provided that:
>
> "[u]nless otherwise agreed the partners who have not wrongfully dissolved the partnership ... may wind up the partnership affairs. . . ."
>
> Alaska Statute 32.05.330 [UPS (1914) § 38) provided in part:
>
> (a) When dissolution is caused in any way, except in contravention of the partnership agreement, each partner, as against the copartners and all persons claiming through them in respect of their interest in the partnership, unless otherwise agreed, may have the partnership property applied to discharge its liabilities, and the surplus applied to pay in cash the net amount owing to the respective partners. . . .
>
> (b) When dissolution is caused in contravention of the partnership agreement the rights of the partners are as follows:
>
> (1) each partner who has not caused dissolution wrongfully has
>
> (A) all the rights specified in (a) of this section, and
>
> (B) the right, as against each partner who has caused the dissolution wrongfully, to damages for breach of the agreement. . . .

Disotell argues that Stiltner breached the partnership agreement by dissolution; Stiltner maintains that the superior court's conclusion that "neither party was at fault in causing the dissolution of the partnership since ... either party could terminate it at will" was not clearly erroneous. Because neither party argues on appeal that Disotell wrongfully caused the dissolution, he may invoke the rights granted by AS 32.05.330(a).

Disotell argues that the most reasonable and "almost universally accepted" interpretation of AS 32.05.330(a) requires sale of partnership assets, absent a partnership agreement to the contrary. He claims that the Act "makes the policy choice that a sale is the most effective means of determining the fair market value of partnership assets." Although this remedy may seem harsh, he points out that partners are free to make alternative provisions in the partnership agreement. Because the partnership agreement did not address the consequences of dissolution, the statutory provisions govern by default.

. . .

In Dreifuerst v. Dreifuerst, cited by Disotell on appeal, the Wisconsin Court of Appeals, construing a statute identical to Alaska's, held that lawful dissolution gives each partner the right to force liquidation.[6] Other courts have recognized that the winding up that follows partnership dissolution generally involves liquidation of the partnership assets. . . .

Although the language of the Act and the general rule would seem to favor liquidation and cash distribution absent agreement to do otherwise, some courts construing statutes identical to section .330 have refused to compel liquidation.

We decline to follow the line of cases holding that the statute requires liquidation. We hold that the superior court did not err in reading subsection 330(a) to allow it to permit Stiltner to buy out Disotell's partnership interest. Careful reading of the text of AS 32.05.330(a) does not convince us that this subsection absolutely compels liquidation and forbids a buyout. Under appropriate, although perhaps limited, circumstances, a buyout seems a justifiable way of winding up a partnership. The superior court reasoned that a buyout would reduce economic waste by avoiding the cost of appointing a receiver and conducting a sale. Even though there was no ongoing business, the superior court noted that the expense of a sale could total as much as twelve percent of the property's value. This was a valid reason and potentially benefited both partners. The potential savings were significant. The court's effort to avoid further loss to both partners justifies its decision to offer Stiltner the buyout option. Further, properly conducted, a buyout guaranteed Disotell a fair value for his partnership interest. Liquidation exposed Disotell to the risk that no buyer would offer to pay fair market value for the property. A liquidation sale in which no other buyers participated might have given Stiltner an opportunity to buy the property for less than fair market value, to Disotell's disadvantage.

C. It Was Error to Permit a Buyout Without Objective Evidence of the Value of Disotell's Partnership Interest.

Although it was not error to grant Stiltner the option to buy out Disotell's partnership interest, it was error to permit the buyout without requiring some objective determination of the value of all of the partnership assets, particularly the land and building Stiltner contributed. The superior court used tax appraisals to establish the value of the hotel property and parking lot. The court relied on a report by an expert witness who, to explain the accounting methodology set out in AS 32.05.350, "assume[d], for illustrative purposes only," that the hotel property and parking lot would sell for their tax appraised values. The tax appraisals were not introduced into evidence. The expert discussed them only hypothetically to illustrate an entirely different point, not as support for an opinion of property values. Neither party introduced

[6] Dreifuerst v. Dreifuerst, 90 Wis.2d 566, 280 N.W.2d 335, 338 (App.1979).

evidence of any appraisal. Disotell and Stiltner both acknowledge that neither offered any evidence of value of the partnership assets.

Because a buyout is appropriate only if it is for fair market value, and there was no admissible evidence of fair market value, we must remand. It will be necessary on remand to determine the value of the assets before Stiltner attempts to buy out Disotell. . . .

D. It Was Error to Characterize as Partnership Debt Disotell's Obligation to Pay for His Capital Contribution.

Disotell argues that the court erred by characterizing as partnership debt the obligation he incurred to pay for his capital contribution. The parties stipulated that the partners had agreed that the funds from which Disotell would pay for his one half interest in the hotel property "would only come from the profits of the hotel." The superior court found:

> The partnership obligated itself to pay Stiltner "all the profits from the partnership until he had recovered his original cost basis of the Hotel property." . . . Further, the partnership took on Disotell's loan obligation, and promised to pay Stiltner the $137,500. Therefore, this court views the $137,500 as a loan obligation the partnership owes Stiltner.

The superior court classified the $137,500 as a partnership liability, deducting it from the net value of the partnership.

Our primary concern is determining the partners' intent. The partners' litigation stipulation stated that they had agreed that the funds from which Disotell would pay for his one half interest "would only come from the profits of the hotel." This stipulation is not reasonably susceptible to an interpretation that the partnership assumed Disotell's loan obligation. Stiltner's trial testimony is also inconsistent with any such interpretation:

> THE COURT: . . . [P]art of the stipulation, paragraph 7G, essentially says that you were then to receive all the profits of the partnership until you had recovered your original cost basis in the hotel property. Can you explain to me how that piece fits into your agreement?
>
> [STILTNER]: That's my purchase of the hotel.
>
> THE COURT: Mm hmm (affirmative).
>
> A: That him paying for that half of the hotel was delayed until the hotel started turning a profit.
>
> THE COURT: Okay.

> A: The 150 that he would owe me for a 50 percent interest in the hotel, that was delayed until the hotel started turning a profit.

This testimony implies that the loan obligation was Disotell's, not the partnership's. It is unlikely that Stiltner would have been willing to assume the obligation as a partnership debt and thereby effectively agree to pay half of Disotell's obligation. We conclude, therefore, that it was error to characterize the obligation as partnership debt.

The partners stipulated that Disotell had promised Stiltner: (1) to supply development and construction services on a cost only basis to construct a hotel and (2) to contribute his interest in the hotel property as capital and to subordinate his interest in profits until Stiltner had recovered his original cost basis in the hotel. The partners explicitly agreed that Disotell would pay for his one half interest "only" from profits. It is not clear, however, whether the parties contemplated the situation before us when they entered into the agreement. The superior court did not enter any findings as to whether the "repayment only out of profits" provision of the parties' agreement was intended to apply in the event that the partnership dissolved before making profits. We therefore remand the case with instructions to the superior court to determine whether the parties intended the provision to apply in this context.

If the superior court finds that the provision was not intended to apply in this situation, it may supply a provision that is reasonable under the circumstances. Under section 204 of the Restatement (Second) of Contracts, "[w]hen the parties to a bargain sufficiently defined to be a contract have not agreed with respect to a term which is essential to a determination of their rights and duties, a term which is reasonable in the circumstances is supplied by the court."[13] Comment d to Section 204 instructs on how the court should supply an omitted term:

> The process of supplying an omitted term has sometimes been disguised as a literal or purposive reading of contract language directed to a situation other than the situation that arises. Sometimes it is said that the search is for the term the parties would have agreed to if the question had been brought to their attention. Both the meaning of the words used and the probability that a particular term would have been used if the question had been raised may be factors in determining what term is reasonable in the circumstances. But where there is in fact no agreement, the court should supply a term which comports with community standards of fairness and policy

[13] Restatement (Second) of Contracts § 204 (1981).

rather than analyze a hypothetical model of the bargaining process.[14]

In considering what term is reasonable, the superior court should consider the risks and obligations each party assumed. In exchange for Stiltner's contribution of the hotel property to the partnership, Disotell agreed to renovate and build the hotel. The agreement obliged Disotell to supply his development and construction services to the hotel project. Those services were part of the consideration he offered for the one half interest in the hotel property that he purchased from Stiltner. If Disotell had completed construction of the hotel but the project had proven unprofitable, we doubt that fairness would demand that Disotell nevertheless repay the one half interest. In reality, however, the partnership dissolved before Disotell fulfilled his obligations under the agreement. The superior court has discretion to decide, therefore, that fairness requires that Disotell only repay the difference between the value of the services he contributed to the hotel property before the project became impossible and the value of what he was supposed to contribute.

E. The Superior Court Did Not Err by Refusing to Award Damages for Wrongful Dissolution of the Partnership.

Disotell claims that he is entitled to recover damages for Stiltner's wrongful dissolution of the partnership. . . .

. . . It was not clear error . . . for the superior court to find that neither party was at fault in causing the dissolution and that the dissolution arose out of disagreement on how the project was to proceed.

F. It Was Error to Deny Disotell Damages for Stiltner's Post Dissolution Use of the Property.

. . .

Stiltner is accountable to the partnership for any benefit he derived from his personal use of partnership property. Per Alaska Statute 32.05.160(a) [UPA (1914) § 21(1)],

> Every partner shall account to the partnership for any benefit, and hold as trustee for it any profits derived by the partner without the consent of the other partners from any transaction connected with the formation, conduct, or liquidation of the partnership or from any use by the partner of its property.

We therefore remand for determination of the value of Stiltner's personal use of the property.

---

[14] Id. at cmt. d (emphasis added).

IV. Conclusion

Because the Act did not prohibit the buyout option, it was not error to grant Stiltner the option to buy out Disotell's partnership interest. It was error, however, to permit a buyout without finding the fair market value of the property, based on admissible evidence. We therefore REMAND. We also REMAND for a determination of what each partner contributed to or took from the partnership. This determination should consider the value of the partnership assets and any difference between the services Disotell was to contribute to the project and those he actually contributed, but should not include the $137,500 loan obligation. It should also take into account the value of Stiltner's personal use of the hotel property during the windup period.

ANALYSIS

1. **Why Appeal?** Why do you suppose Disotell appealed? What is the likely outcome following the Supreme Court decision?
2. **Option Only to Disotell.** Why do you suppose the trial court gave Stiltner the option to buy out Disotell and did not give Disotell the option to buy out Stiltner?
3. **The Meaning of "Profits."** The parties agreed that Disotell was to pay Stiltner $137,500 out of "profits." What do you suppose they meant by "profits"? If you had been their lawyer, what issues would you have raised with them bearing on this aspect of their agreement?
4. **Avoiding Liquidation.** The court states that awarding Stiltner the option to buy out Disotell was justified because it "would reduce economic waste by avoiding the cost of appointing a receiver and conducting a sale." Do you agree? What do you suppose would have happened if the trial court had simply appointed a receiver and ordered a liquidation?
5. **Valuing Disotell's Interest.** How is the trial court supposed to determine the value of Disotell's interest? Suppose it is determined that the property has a current market value of $240,000; that if Disotell had performed all the services required to build the hotel, his services would have had a value of $100,00; and that in fact the services performed by Disotell had a value of $25,000. Ignore the value of Stiltner's use of the property. What is the value of Disotell's interest?
6. **Advice About Liquidation.** If the parties had sought your advice, what would you have suggested as the rule in the case of liquidation before any profits were realized?

Monin v. Monin

785 S.W.2d 499 (Ky.App.1989).

Discretionary Review Denied by Supreme Court 1990.

This is a partnership case. The parties, Charles Monin and Joseph Monin (a/k/a Sonny), are brothers who formed a partnership in 1967 for the purpose of hauling milk. In 1984 the relationship between Charles and Sonny deteriorated such that Sonny no longer desired to continue the partnership. Some efforts were made to resolve their affairs, to no avail. In July, 1984, Sonny notified Charles of his intention to dissolve the partnership, and the next day wrote to Dairymen Incorporated (DI) to notify them that he was canceling the partnership's contract with DI effective October 16, 1984, the annual renewal date of the hauling contract. Sonny also informed DI he wanted to apply for the right to haul milk for DI after the expiration of the partnership's contract. On September 24, 1984, Charles and Sonny executed an agreement to resolve their business arrangement. The document entitled "Partnership Sales Agreement" provided that they would hold a private auction between themselves for all the assets of the partnership "including equipment, and milk routes." As the contract with DI required approval of any sale or transfer of the milk hauling agreement, the sales agreement provided that such approval from DI would be sought and the sales agreement would be "null and void" if approval from DI was not forthcoming. The agreement also contained a covenant not to compete. Charles was the successful bidder at the auction, having bid $86,000.

On the same day as the auction, September 27, 1984, DI called a producers meeting at which time those present voted not to approve Charles as their hauler. Instead they voted to have Sonny haul their milk. Sonny accepted the offer and has since hauled milk for DI as Sonny Monin, Inc. As a result Sonny ended up with the major asset of the partnership, the milk hauling contract, at no cost to him.

On February 11, 1985, Charles commenced this action in the Nelson Circuit Court alleging that Sonny violated his fiduciary duty to the partnership and that he had tortiously interfered with the partnership's contractual relation with clients and customers. A bench trial was conducted in December, 1986. In its judgment for Sonny the trial court reasoned as follows:

> **NOTE**
>
> It would seem that Charles was entitled under the terms of the Sales Agreement to declare it "null and void" and recover the amount he paid for the partnership assets. Presumably he thought he could recover more by suing for damages for tortious breach of fiduciary duty.

When Charles was the high bidder at $86,000, the value of the partnership assets, including milk routes, was established as far as Charles was concerned. Sonny had no further say in establishing a value for such assets. When the producers and D.I. rejected Charles as a milk hauler, the value of the partnership assets became adjusted from $86,000 to $22,000 (the value of the milk hauling equipment).

When the producers voted for Sonny to haul their milk, they were not voting on a partnership matter. They were voting on Sonny's individual application. Furthermore, they were privileged to vote for some third person to haul their milk.

In summary, the affairs of the Monin Brothers partnership were finally settled on September 27, 1984. As a result of the actions of that date, the assets of the partnership were finally valued at $22,000. When Charles was rejected as the D.I.'s milk hauler on that date, the partnership had no interest in the milk routes and neither partner had any claim to same as part of their partnership interests.

We conclude the trial court's reasoning is flawed in that it ignores Sonny's duties to the partnership with respect to the most valuable asset of that entity, the milk hauling contract. As stated in Van Hooser v. Keenon, Ky., 271 S.W.2d 270, 273 (1954), "[T]here is no relation of trust or confidence known to the law that requires of the parties a higher degree of good faith than that of a partnership. *Nothing less than absolute fairness* will suffice." (Emphasis added.) Importantly, that decision holds that a partner's fiduciary duties extend beyond the partnership "to persons who have dissolved the partnership, and have not completely wound up and settled the partnership affairs." Sonny's continuing duty was especially applicable here as he agreed to sell his interest to Charles so Charles could continue the partnership business. . . . Nothing in the Uniform Partnership Act (KRS Chapter 362) changes the high degree of good faith partners must maintain in their relations with one another. . . .

Thus, when Sonny failed to withdraw his application with D.I. for the milk routes after agreeing to allow Charles to buy his interest in those routes and continue the partnership business, Sonny obviously breached his duties to the partnership. As the court found, the value of the partnership assets dropped from $86,000 to $22,000 when Sonny was awarded the contract by D.I. While it is possible D.I. would not have awarded the contract to Charles even if Sonny had withdrawn his name from contention, there is no evidence that any other person or entity was available or willing to take over the route. The law is clear that one partner cannot benefit at the expense of the partnership. . . . Sonny, by agreeing to sell his share of the assets to Charles and by actively pursuing those same assets from D.I., positioned himself such that whatever D.I. did, he could not lose. Understandably, Charles believes he was abused by the obvious conflict of interest. Thus, the trial court's dismissal of Charles's breach of fiduciary duty claim is reversed and remanded for entry of judgment in favor of Charles. We do not believe a new trial on damages is required; nor do we believe Charles is entitled to an accounting from Sonny for profits made since 1984. The value of the asset at issue was determined by the parties at or very near the time of Sonny's breach of duty to the partnership ($86,000 minus $22,000, or $64,000), and that should form the measure of damages to which Charles is entitled.

Finally, the trial court's findings concerning the tortious interference with contractual relations are supported by substantial evidence and will not be disturbed. CR 52.01. The evidence of Sonny's behind-the-back efforts to convince producers not to work with or accept Charles as their hauler was conflicting, and the trial court, as fact finder, could believe Sonny's version of the facts on that claim.

Accordingly, the judgment of the Nelson Circuit Court is reversed and remanded for entry of a new judgment consistent with this opinion.

■ EMBERTON, JUDGE, dissenting. I respectfully dissent.

I cannot agree with the majority that Sonny's actions constitute a breach of his fiduciary obligation to Charles. Evidence indicates that numerous efforts toward resolution of the problem—which efforts appeared to be made in good faith by Sonny—were summarily rebuffed by Charles. There is no evidence but that both parties were genuinely bidding at the September 27 private auction. Both understood that the successful bidder won equipment, the routes and the other assets only if DI approved the new contract.

Upon polling the affected producers, only 1 out of 12 indicated a preference for Charles. In fact, evidence was strong that most of the producers would not allow Charles to haul their milk; that the DI field representative stated DI could not work with Charles; and, that drivers stated they would quit before driving for Charles. The trial court, having heard the evidence, found that none of such positions taken by DI, or by the producers, were the result of actions taken (or statements made) by Sonny. DI, having such information, made a decision in its own best interest—not as a result of influence from Sonny.

I find nothing in the record to support a reversal of the trial court's decision. I would affirm.

ANALYSIS

1. **Comparison to Page v. Page.** How do you suppose the majority in *Monin* would have resolved the dispute in *Page*? What about the dissenter?

2. **What the Parties Would Have Agreed To.** Is *Monin* just a case of bad lawyering? If the issue presented by the case had been addressed by the Monin brothers at the time they were drafting the "Partnership Sales Agreement," what do you suppose they would have agreed to?

3. **Fiduciary Obligation vs. Contractual Obligation.** Do we really need the concept of fiduciary obligation to decide a case like Monin? Is the case properly viewed as a partnership-duty case rather than as a contract case?

Pav-Saver Corporation v. Vasso Corporation

143 Ill.App.3d 1013, 97 Ill.Dec. 760, 493 N.E.2d 423 (1986).

The matter before us arises out of the dissolution of the parties' partnership, the Pav-Saver Manufacturing Company. The facts are not in dispute, and only those needed to explain our disposition on the issues on appeal will be stated.

Plaintiff, Pav-Saver Corporation ("PSC") is the owner of the Pav-Saver trademark and certain patents for the design and marketing of concrete paving machines. Harry Dale is the inventor of the Pav-Saver "slip-form" paver and the majority shareholder of PSC, located in Moline, Illinois. H. Moss Meersman is an attorney who is also the owner and sole shareholder of Vasso Corporation. In 1974 Dale, individually, together with PSC and Meersman formed Pav-Saver Manufacturing Company for the manufacture and sale of Pav-Saver machines. Dale agreed to contribute his services, PSC contributed the patents and trademark necessary to the proposed operation, and Meersman agreed to obtain financing for it. The partnership agreement was drafted by Meersman and approved by Attorney Charles Peart, president of PSC. The agreement contained two paragraphs which lie at the heart of the appeal and cross-appeal before us:

> "3. The duties, obligations and functions of the respective partners shall be:
>
> A. Meersman shall provide whatever financing is necessary for the joint venture, as required.
>
> B. (1) PAV-SAVER shall grant to the partnership without charge the exclusive right to use on all machines manufactured and sold, its trademark 'PAV-SAVER' during the term of this Agreement. In order to preserve and maintain the good will and other values of the trademark PAV-SAVER, it is agreed between the parties that PAV-SAVER Corporation shall have the right to inspect from time to time the quality of machines upon which the licensed trademark PAV-SAVER is used. . . . Any significant changes in structure, materials or components shall be disclosed in writing or by drawings to PAV-SAVER Corporation.

> (2) PAV-SAVER grants to the partnership exclusive license without charge for its patent rights in and to its Patent #3,377,933 for the term of this agreement and exclusive license to use its specifications and drawings for the Slip-form paving machine known as Model MX 6–33, plus any specifications and drawings for any extensions, additions and attachments for said machine for said term. It [is] understood and agreed that same shall remain the property of PAV-SAVER and all copies shall be returned to PAV-SAVER at the expiration of this partnership. Further, PAV-SAVER, so long as this agreement is honored and is in force, grants a license under any patents of PAV-SAVER granted in the United States and/or other countries applicable to the Slip-Form paving machine.
>
> . . .
>
> "11. It is contemplated that this joint venture partnership shall be permanent, and same shall not be terminated or dissolved by either party except upon mutual approval of both parties. If, however, either party shall terminate or dissolve said relationship, the terminating party shall pay to the other party, as liquidated damages, a sum equal to four (4) times the gross royalties received by PAV-SAVER Corporation in the fiscal year ending July 31, 1973, as shown by their corporate financial statement. Said liquidated damages to be paid over a ten (10) year period next immediately following the termination, payable in equal installments."

In 1976, upon mutual consent, the PSC/Dale/Meersman partnership was dissolved and replaced with an identical one between PSC and Vasso, so as to eliminate the individual partners.

It appears that the Pav-Saver Manufacturing Company operated and thrived according to the parties' expectations until around 1981, when the economy slumped, sales of the heavy machines dropped off significantly, and the principals could not agree on the direction that the partnership should take to survive. On March 17, 1983, Attorney Charles Peart, on behalf of PSC, wrote a letter to Meersman terminating the partnership and invoking the provisions of paragraph 11 of the parties' agreement.

In response, Meersman moved into an office on the business premises of the Pav-Saver Manufacturing Company, physically ousted Dale, and assumed a position as the day-to-day manager of the business. PSC then sued in the circuit court of Rock Island County for a court-ordered dissolution of the partnership, return of its patents and trademark, and an accounting. Vasso counterclaimed for declaratory judgment that PSC had wrongfully terminated the partnership and that

Vasso was entitled to continue the partnership business, and other relief pursuant to the Illinois Uniform Partnership Act. . . . After protracted litigation, the trial court ruled that PSC had wrongfully terminated the partnership; that Vasso was entitled to continue the partnership business and to possess the partnership assets, including PSC's trademark and patents; that PSC's interest in the partnership was $165,000, based on a $330,000 valuation for the business; and that Vasso was entitled to liquidated damages in the amount of $384,612, payable pursuant to paragraph 11 of the partnership agreement. Judgment was entered accordingly.

Both parties appealed. PSC takes issue with the trial court's failure to order the return of its patents and trademark or, in the alternative, to assign a value to them in determining the value of the partnership assets. Further, neither party agrees with the trial court's enforcement of their agreement for liquidated damages. In its cross-appeal, PSC argues that the amount determined by the formula in paragraph 11 is a penalty. Vasso, on the other hand, contends in its appeal that the amount is unobjectionable, but the installment method of pay-out should not be enforced.

In addition to the afore-cited paragraphs of the parties' partnership agreement, the resolution of this case is controlled by the dissolution provision of the Uniform Partnership Act [§ 38] (Ill.Rev.Stat.1983, ch. 106–1/2, pars. 29–43). The Act provides:

> "(2). When dissolution is caused in contravention of the partnership agreement the rights of the partners shall be as follows:
>
> (a) Each partner who has not caused dissolution wrongfully shall have:
>
> . . .
>
> II. The right, as against each partner who has caused the dissolution wrongfully, to damage for breach of the agreement.
>
> (b) The partners who have not caused the dissolution wrongfully, if they all desire to continue the business in the same name, either by themselves or jointly with others, may do so, during the agreed term for the partnership and for that purpose may possess the partnership property, provided they secure the payment by bond approved by the court, or pay to any partner who has caused the dissolution wrongfully, the value of his interest in the partnership at the dissolution, less any damages recoverable under clause (2)(a)(II) of this section, and in like manner indemnify him against all present or future partnership liabilities.

> (c) A partner who has caused the dissolution wrongfully shall have:
>
> . . .
>
> II. If the business is continued under paragraph (2)(b) of this section the right as against his co-partners and all claiming through them in respect of their interests in the partnership, to have the value of his interest in the partnership, less any damages caused to his co-partners by the dissolution, ascertained and paid to him in cash, or the payment secured by bond approved by the court and to be released from all existing liabilities of the partnership; but in ascertaining the value of the partner's interest the value of the good will of the business shall not be considered."

Initially we must reject PSC's argument that the trial court erred in refusing to return Pav-Saver's patents and trademark pursuant to paragraph 3 of the partnership agreement, or in the alternative that the court erred in refusing to assign a value to PSC's property in valuing the partnership assets. The partnership agreement on its face contemplated a "permanent" partnership, terminable only upon mutual approval of the parties (paragraph 11). It is undisputed that PSC's unilateral termination was in contravention of the agreement. The wrongful termination necessarily invokes the provisions of the Uniform Partnership Act so far as they concern the rights of the partners. Upon PSC's notice terminating the partnership, Vasso elected to continue the business pursuant to section 38(2)(b) of the Uniform Partnership Act. As correctly noted by Vasso, the statute was enacted "to cover comprehensively the problem of dissolution . . . [and] to stabilize business." (Kurtzon v. Kurtzon (1st Dist.1950), 339 Ill.App. 431, 437, 90 N.E.2d 245, 248.) Ergo, despite the parties' contractual direction that PSC's patents would be returned to it upon the mutually approved expiration of the partnership (paragraph 3), the right to possess the partnership property and continue in business upon a wrongful termination must be derived from and is controlled by the statute. Evidence at trial clearly established that the Pav-Saver machines being manufactured by the partnership could not be produced or marketed without PSC's patents and trademark. Thus, to continue in business pursuant to the statutorily-granted right of the party not causing the wrongful dissolution, it is essential that paragraph 3 of the parties' agreement—the return to PSC of its patents—not be honored.

Similarly, we find no merit in PSC's argument that the trial court erred in not assigning a value to the patents and trademark. The only evidence adduced at trial to show the value of this property was testimony relating to good will. It was unrefuted that the name Pav-Saver enjoys a good reputation for a good product and reliable service.

However, inasmuch as the Uniform Partnership Act specifically states that "the value of the good will of the business shall not be considered" (Ill.Rev.Stat.1983, ch. 106–1/2, par. 38(2)(c)(II)), we find that the trial court properly rejected PSC's good will evidence of the value of its patents and trademark in valuing its interest in the partnership business.

[In the portion of the opinion omitted here the court rejects PSC's argument that the liquidated damages amount was an unenforceable "penalty." Among other observations, the court notes that the amount, $384,612, was payable in equal installments over a period of 10 years, which means that the present value, or current lump-sum equivalent, was substantially less.]

. . .

Affirmed.

■ JUSTICE STOUDER concurring in part—dissenting in part.

I generally agree with the result of the majority. I cannot, however, accept the majority's conclusion the defendant is entitled to retention of the patents.

. . .

The plaintiff (PSC) brought this action at law seeking dissolution of the partnership before expiration of the agreed term of its existence. Under the Uniform Partnership Act where dissolution is caused by an act in violation of the partnership agreement, the other partner(s) are accorded certain rights. The partnership agreement is a contract, and even though a partner may have the power to dissolve, he does not necessarily have the right to do so. Therefore, if the dissolution he causes is a violation of the agreement, he is liable for any damages sustained by the innocent partner(s) as a result thereof. The innocent partner(s) also have the option to continue the business in the firm name provided they pay the partner causing the dissolution the value of his interest in the partnership. (Ill.Rev.Stat.1983, ch. 106–1/2, par. 38(1), (2).)

The duties and obligations of partners arising from a partnership relation are regulated by the express contract as far as they are covered thereby. A written agreement is not necessary but where it does exist it constitutes the measure of the partners' rights and obligations. While the rights and duties of the partners in relation to the partnership are governed by the Uniform Partnership Act, the uniform act also provides that such rules are subject to any agreement between the parties. . . .

The partnership agreement entered into by PSC and Vasso in pertinent part provides:

> "3.B.(2) [PSC] grants to the partnership exclusive license without charge for its patent rights . . . for the term of this

> agreement. . . . [I]t being understood and agreed that same shall remain the property of [PSC] . . . and shall be returned to [PSC] at the expiration of this partnership. . . ."

The majority holds this provision in the contract is unenforceable. The only apparent reason for such holding is that its enforcement would affect defendant's option to continue the business. No authority is cited to support such a rule.

The partnership agreement further provides:

> "11. . . . If either party shall terminate or dissolve said [partnership], the terminating party shall pay to the other party as liquidated damages . . . [$384,612]."

This provision becomes operative at the same time as the provision relating to the return of the patents.

. . .

Here, [because] express terms of the partnership agreement deal with the status of the patents and measure of damages, the question is settled thereby. I think it clear the parties agreed the partnership only be allowed the use of the patents during the term of the agreement. The agreement having been terminated, the right to use the patents is terminated. The provisions in the contract do not conflict with the statutory option to continue the business and even if there were a conflict the provisions of the contract should prevail. The option to continue the business does not carry with it any guarantee or assurance of success and it may often well be that liquidation rather than continuation would be the better option for a partner not at fault.

As additional support for my conclusion, it appears the liquidated damages clause was insisted upon by the defendant because of earlier conduct of the plaintiff withdrawing from a former partnership. Thus, the existence of the liquidated damages clause recognizes the right of plaintiff to withdraw the use of his patents in accordance with the specific terms of the partnership agreement. Since liquidated damages depends on return of the patents, I would vacate that part of the judgment providing defendant is entitled to continue use of the patents and provide that use shall remain with plaintiff.

ANALYSIS AND PLANNING

1. **What Next?** Under the decision of the court, what happens next? Is PSC ever entitled to a cash distribution for its interest in the partnership?
2. **Planning for Exit.** This case provides a good illustration of a common problem in drafting agreements: the failure to think through and specify how the terms of the agreement are to be carried out. Here the

agreement provided for termination, and liquidated damages, but failed to specify, step by step, precisely what would happen following a notice of termination. If you had been called upon to draft the agreement, what questions of implementation, following termination, would you have raised with the parties? What possibilities for resolving those questions would you have been prepared to offer?

NOTE

Under § 701 of the UPA (1997), if a partner withdraws from a partnership in contravention of the partnership agreement, the partnership does not necessarily dissolve. If it does not, the partnership must buy out the withdrawing ("dissociated") partner for an amount equal to his or her share of the value of the assets of the partnership if "sold at a price equal to the greater of the liquidation value or the value based on a sale of the entire business as a going concern without the dissociated partner." This amount is reduced by any damages for wrongful withdrawal. Contrary to UPA (1914) § 38(2)(c)(II), however, there is no reduction for the value of goodwill.

C. THE SHARING OF LOSSES

Kovacik v. Reed

49 Cal.2d 166, 315 P.2d 314 (1957).

[Early in November 1952, Kovacik told Reed that he (Kovacik) had a chance to remodel some kitchens in San Francisco, and asked Reed to become his job superintendent and estimator. Kovacik explained that he had about $10,000.00 to invest and that, if Reed would superintend and estimate the jobs, he would share profits on a 50–50 basis. Kovacik did not ask Reed to share any losses that might result, and Reed did not offer to do so. Indeed, the two did not discuss possible losses at all. Reed accepted Kovacik's proposal and began work on the venture immediately. Through their venture, the two were able to obtain several remodeling jobs. Reed worked on all of the jobs as job superintendent, but contributed no funds. Instead, Kovacik provided the financing. In August, 1953, Kovacik (who kept all of the financial records) told Reed that the venture had lost money. He then demanded that Reed contribute to the amounts that he (Kovacik) had advanced beyond the income he received. Reed claimed that he never agreed to be liable for losses, and refused to pay.]

> **NOTE**
>
> The statement of facts is taken from a stipulated version relied upon by the court.

Kovacik thereafter instituted this proceeding, seeking an accounting of the affairs of the venture and to recover from Reed one half of the losses. Despite the evidence above set forth from the statement of the oral proceedings, showing that at no time had defendant agreed to be liable for any of the losses, the trial court "found"—more accurately, we think, concluded as a matter of law—that "plaintiff and defendant were to share equally all their joint venture profits and losses between them," and that defendant "agreed to share equally in the profits and losses of said joint venture." Following an accounting taken by a referee appointed by the court, judgment was rendered awarding plaintiff recovery against defendant of some $4,340, as one half the monetary losses[4] found by the referee to have been sustained by the joint venture.

It is the general rule that in the absence of an agreement to the contrary the law presumes that partners and joint adventurers intended to participate equally in the profits and losses of the common enterprise, irrespective of any inequality in the amounts each contributed to the capital employed in the venture, with the losses being shared by them in the same proportions as they share the profits. . . .

However, it appears that in the cases in which the above stated general rule has been applied, each of the parties had contributed capital consisting of either money or land or other tangible property, or else was to receive compensation for services rendered to the common undertaking which was to be paid before computation of the profits or losses.

Where, however, as in the present case, one partner or joint adventurer contributes the money capital as against the other's skill and labor, all the cases cited, and which our research has discovered, hold that neither party is liable to the other for contribution for any loss sustained. Thus, upon loss of the money the party who contributed it is not entitled to recover any part of it from the party who contributed only services.

The rationale of this rule . . . is that where one party contributes money and the other contributes services, then in the event of a loss each would lose his own capital—the one his money and the other his labor. Another view would be that in such a situation the parties have, by their agreement to share equally in profits, agreed that the values of their contributions—the money on the one hand and the labor on the other—were likewise equal; it would follow that upon the loss, as here, of both money and labor, the parties have shared equally in the losses. Actually,

---

[4] The record is silent as to the factors taken into account by the referee in determining the "loss" suffered by the venture. However, there is no contention that defendant's services were ascribed any value whatsoever. It may also be noted that the trial court "found" that "neither plaintiff nor defendant was to receive compensation for their services rendered to said joint venture, but plaintiff and defendant were to share equally all their joint venture profits and losses between them." Neither party suggests that plaintiff actually rendered services to the venture in the same sense that defendant did. And, as is clear from the settled statement, plaintiff's proposition to defendant was that plaintiff would provide the money as against defendant's contribution of services as estimator and superintendent.

of course, plaintiff here lost only some $8,680—or somewhat less than the $10,000 which he originally proposed and agreed to invest. . . .

The judgment is reversed.

NOTES AND QUESTIONS

1. **Inconsistency with UPA.** The relevant statutory provisions are UPA (1914) §§ 18(a) and 40, which are set forth in the appendix to this chapter. Is the holding in *Kovacik* consistent with the plain meaning, if any, of these provisions? The drafters of the revised UPA (1997) apparently did not believe so. Section 401(b) readopts the loss sharing rule of UPA section 18(a): "Each partner is entitled to an equal share of the partnership profits and is chargeable with a share of partnership losses in proportion to the partner's share of the profits." Even more to the point, the official comment thereto expressly rejects *Kovacik*:

    > Subsection (b) establishes the default rules for the sharing of partnership profits and losses. The UPA § 18(a) rules that profits are shared equally and that losses, whether capital or operating, are shared in proportion to each partner's share of the profits are continued. . . . The default rules apply, as does UPA § 18(a), where one or more of the partners contribute no capital, although there is case law to the contrary [citing, inter alia, *Kovacik*].

2. **Amount of Contribution.** What result if Reed had made even a nominal monetary contribution to the partnership's capital or had received some compensation for his services? What result if Kovacik had done as much work on the partnership's jobs as had Reed? What if Kovacik had done about half—or one quarter—as much work as Reed?

3. **Freedom of Contract?** Were Kovacik and Reed free to adopt any rule they wanted for sharing of losses? If so, why do you suppose they failed to do so?

4. **Effect of a Partner's Wealth.** Is it likely in this case that Kovacik was more wealthy than Reed? Is it more likely in most cases that the contributor of capital will be more wealthy than the contributor of services? If so, how should that affect the outcome of the case?

5. **Effect of Who Originated the Business.** Should the outcome in a case like *Kovacik* turn on which of the partners originated the project or business? If so, should the legal rule turn on the how this issue is resolved in each case or on how it is likely to turn out in most cases?

6. **Loss Sharing and Incentives.** Under the *Kovacik* rule, the services-only partner does not share in loss of the amount initially invested by the capital-only partner. What concern might the capital-only partner have about the effect of this rule on the job performance or the decisionmaking by the services-only partner? How might that concern affect the bargain over loss sharing?

7. **Bargaining Over Loss Allocation.** It appears that Kovacik and Reed had not bargained over, or even discussed, the question of allocating losses in the event the partnership failed. If they had bargained, what rule do you suppose they would have adopted? Would they have agreed that Reed had no obligation to contribute to partnership losses? Does your answer to that question inform your analysis of the merits of the rule announced in *Kovacik*?

D. LAW PARTNERSHIP DISSOLUTION

Meehan v. Shaughnessy

404 Mass. 419, 535 N.E.2d 1255 (1989).

[The fiduciary-obligation aspects of this case were presented earlier in this Chapter, where the statement of facts appears. Briefly, the court found that Meehan and Boyle, who had been partners in the law firm of Parker Coulter and left to form their own firm, had violated their fiduciary obligations to Parker Coulter by using impermissible methods to line up clients for their new firm before they left Parker Coulter. In the portion of the opinion presented here, the court addresses the legal rights of the Parker Coulter partners in case of dissolution. The court's analysis begins with a review of the provisions of the UPA (1914) (as embodied in Massachusetts law) bearing on dissolution—provisions considered in earlier cases in this Section of the casebook—and then turns to the effect of the Parker Coulter express agreement.]

The Parker Coulter partnership agreement provided for rights on a dissolution caused by the will of a partner which are different from those [the UPA] provides. Because going concerns are typically destroyed in the dissolution process of liquidation and windup, . . . the agreement minimizes the impact of this process. The agreement provides for an allocation to the departing partner of a share of the firm's current net income, and a return of his or her capital contributions. In addition, the agreement also recognizes that a major asset of a law firm is the expected fees it will receive from unfinished business currently being transacted. Instead of assigning a value to the departing partner's interest in this unfinished business, or waiting for the unfinished business to be "wound up" and liquidated, which is the method of division [the UPA] provides, the agreement gives the partner the right to remove any case which came to the firm "through the personal effort or connection" of the partner, if the partner compensates the dissolved partnership "for the services to and expenditures for the client."[7] Once the partner has removed a case, the agreement provides that the partner is entitled to retain all future

[7] The agreement expressly protects a client's right to choose his or her attorney, by providing that the right to remove a case is "subject to the right of the client to direct that the matter be retained by the continuing firm of remaining partners."

fees in the case, with the exception of the "fair charge" owed to the dissolved firm.[8]

Although the provision in the partnership agreement which divides the dissolved firm's unfinished business does not expressly apply to the removal of cases which did not come to Parker Coulter through the efforts of the departing partner, we believe that the parties intended this provision to apply to these cases also. We interpret this provision to cover these additional cases for two reasons. First, according to the Canons of Ethics and Disciplinary Rules Regulating the Practice of Law (S.J.C. Rule 3:07, Canon 2, as amended through 398 Mass. 1108 [1986]), a lawyer may not participate in an agreement which restricts the right of a lawyer to practice law after the termination of a relationship created by the agreement. One reason for this rule is to protect the public. . . . The strong public interest in allowing clients to retain counsel of their choice outweighs any professional benefits derived from a restrictive covenant. Thus, the Parker Coulter partners could not restrict a departing partner's right to remove any clients who freely choose to retain him or her as their legal counsel. Second, we believe the agreement's carefully drawn provisions governing dissolution and the division of assets indicate the partners' strong intent not to allow the provisions of [the UPA (1914)] concerning liquidation and windup to govern any portion of the dissolved firm's unfinished business. Therefore, based on the partners' intent, and on the prohibition against restrictive covenants between attorneys, we interpret the agreement to provide that, upon the payment of a fair charge, any case may be removed regardless of whether the case came to the firm through the personal efforts of the departing partner. This privilege to remove, as is shown in our later discussion, is of course dependent upon the partner's compliance with fiduciary obligations.

---

[8] The agreement provides that this "fair charge" is a "receivable account of the earlier partnership . . . and [is] divided between the remaining partners and the retiring partner on the basis of which they share in the profits of the firm at the time of the withdrawal." This fair charge is thus treated as an asset of the former partnership. Because the partnership, upon the receipt of the fair charge, gives up all future rights to income from the removed case, the partnership's collective interest in the case is effectively "wound up." The fair charge, therefore, is a method of valuing the partnership's unfinished business as it relates to the removed case.

Under the agreement, therefore, a partner who separates his or her practice from that of the firm receives (1) the right to his or her capital contribution, (2) the right to a share of the net income to which the dissolved partnership is currently entitled, and (3) the right to a portion of the firm's unfinished business, and in exchange gives up all other rights in the dissolved firm's remaining assets. As to (3) above, "unfinished business," the partner gives up all right to proceeds from any unfinished business of the dissolved firm which the new, surviving firm retains. Under the agreement, the old firm's unfinished business is, in effect, "wound up" immediately; the departing partner takes certain of the unfinished business of the old, dissolved Parker Coulter on the payment of a "fair charge," and the new, surviving Parker Coulter takes the remainder of the old partnership's unfinished business.[9] The two entities surviving after the dissolution possess "new business," unconnected with that of the old firm, and the former partners no longer have a continuing fiduciary obligation to windup for the benefit of each other the business they shared in their former partnership.

NOTE

By "capital contribution" apparently the court means "capital account." A partner's capital account is an accounting concept that reflects the partner's initial investment of cash or property, increased by any later such contributions, increased by profits over the years, decreased by losses, and decreased by amounts withdrawn (the "draw"). For example, suppose three equal partners each contribute $50,000 in cash upon the formation of the partnership, to get the firm started. In the first year of operation the firm earns $330,000, allocated $110,000 to each partner (since they are equal partners). Also, during the first year each partner draws (that is, receives from the partnership checking account) $90,000 for personal living expenses. The capital account of each partner at the end of the year would be $70,000: the initial $50,000 plus the $110,000 profit less the $90,000 draw.

In sum, the statute gives a partner the power to dissolve a partnership at any time. Under the statute, the assets of the dissolved partnership are divided among the former partners through the process of liquidation and windup. The statute, however, allows partners to design their own methods of dividing assets and, provided the dissolution is not premature, expressly states that the partners' method controls. Here, the partners have fashioned a division method which immediately winds up unfinished business, allows for a quick separation of the surviving practices, and minimizes the disruptive impact of a dissolution.

[9] A more equitable provision would require that the new, surviving partnership also pay a "fair charge" on the cases it takes from the dissolved partnership. This "fair charge" from the new firm, as is the "fair charge" from the departing partner, would be an asset of the dissolved partnership, in which the departing partner has an interest.

[The court next considers the damages owed by Meehan and Boyle to Parker Coulter for the violation of fiduciary obligation. The gist of the court's conclusion is that the defendants, Meehan and Boyle, have the burden of proving that clients who were improperly taken by them would have consented to the removal in the absence of the fiduciary breach. As to the nature of the proof, the court states:]

Circumstantial factors relevant to whether a client freely exercised his or her right to choose include the following: (1) who was responsible for initially attracting the client to the firm; (2) who managed the case at the firm; (3) how sophisticated the client was and whether the client made the decision with full knowledge; and (4) what was the reputation and skill of the removing attorneys.

[The court proceeds to specify the rule for determining damages:]

In those cases, if any, where the judge concludes, in accordance with the above analysis, that Meehan and Boyle have met their burden, we resolve the parties' dispute over fees solely under the partnership agreement. . . .

We [next] address the correct remedy in those cases, if any, which the judge determines Meehan and Boyle unfairly removed. In light of a conclusion that Meehan and Boyle have failed to prove that certain clients would not have preferred to stay with Parker Coulter, granting Parker Coulter merely a fair charge on these cases pursuant to the partnership agreement would not make it whole. We turn, therefore, to [UPA (1914) § 21]: "Every partner must account to the partnership for any benefit, and hold as trustee for it any profits derived by him without the consent of the other partners from any transaction connected with the formation, conduct or liquidation of the partnership. . . ." We have consistently applied this statute, and held that a partner must account for any profits which flow from a breach of fiduciary duty. . . .

Meehan and Boyle breached the duty they owed to Parker Coulter. If the judge determines that, as a result of this breach, certain clients left the firm, Meehan and Boyle must account to the partnership for any profits they receive on these cases pursuant to [the UPA (1914)], in addition to paying the partnership a fair charge on these cases pursuant to the agreement. The "profit" on a particular case is the amount by which the fee received from the case exceeds the sum of (1) any reasonable overhead expenses MBC [the firm formed by Meehan and Boyle, with Cohen also a partner] incurs in resolving the case, see Jewel v. Boxer, 156 Cal.App.3d 171, 180 (1984) . . ., and (2) the fair charge it owes under the partnership agreement. We emphasize that reasonable overhead expenses on a particular case are not the equivalent of the amount represented by the hours MBC attorneys have expended on the case multiplied by their hourly billing rate. Reasonable overhead expenses are to include only MBC's costs in generating the fee, and are not to include any profit margin for MBC. We treat this profit on a particular case as if it had been earned in the usual course of business of the partnership which included Meehan and Boyle as partners. . . . Failing to treat this profit as if it had been earned by Meehan or Boyle while at their former partnership would exclude Meehan and Boyle from participating in the fruits of their labors and, more importantly, would provide Parker Coulter with an unjustified windfall. Parker Coulter would receive a windfall because there is no guarantee that the profit would have been generated had the case not been handled at MBC. Meehan's and Boyle's former partners are thus entitled to their portion of the fair charge on each of the unfairly removed cases (89.2%), and to that amount of profit from an unfairly removed case which they would have enjoyed had the MBC attorneys handled the case at Parker Coulter (89.2%).

The MBC attorneys argue that any remedy which grants Parker Coulter a recovery in excess of a fair charge on cases removed impermissibly infringes on an attorney's relationship with clients and reduces his or her incentive to use best efforts on their behalf. We agree that punitive measures may infringe on a client's right to adequate representation, and to counsel of his or her own choosing. Cf. *Jewel*, supra at 178 (how fee distributed among former partners of no concern to client);. . . .

We believe, however, that the remedy we impose does not suffer from the MBC attorneys' claimed defects. Under the constructive trust we impose, Meehan and Boyle will receive a share of the fruits of their efforts in the unfairly removed cases which is the same as that which they would have enjoyed at Parker Coulter. We note, moreover, that incentives other than profit motivate attorneys. These incentives include an attorney's ethical obligations to the client and the profession, and a concern for his or her reputation. . . .

Furthermore, the MBC attorneys' argument would provide us with no mechanism to enforce the partners' fiduciary duties. Imposition of a narrowly tailored constructive trust will enforce the obligations resulting from a breach of duty and will not harm the innocent clients. We conclude, therefore, that Meehan and Boyle hold in a constructive trust for the benefit of the former partnership the profits they have derived or may derive from any cases which they unfairly removed.

ANALYSIS

1. **Consequences of Breach of Fiduciary Duty.** How much worse off are Meehan and Boyle by virtue of their breach of fiduciary duty than they would have been if Parker Coulter had had no agreement, there had been no such breach, and the rule of Jewel v. Boxer had been applied?

2. **Violation of Fiduciary Obligation.** The court in Meehan v. Shaughnessy does not consider whether Meehan and Boyle violated their fiduciary obligation to their Parker Coulter partners when, while still acting as partners of Parker Coulter, they talked Cohen (a junior partner at Parker Coulter) and Schafer (an associate) into joining their new firm. Assuming that this conduct was a violation of fiduciary obligation, what are the damages?

6. PARTNERS AT LOGGERHEADS: THE DISSOLUTION SOLUTION UNDER THE UPA (1997)

NOTE

The next case involves the Giles Land Company, which is a limited partnership rather than a general partnership. A limited partnership is like a general partnership except that it has two classes of partners, general partners and limited partners. The two classes have the same economic claims, but only the general partners have management control and only the general partners are personally liable for the debts of the partnership. But the parties, Norman Lee Giles and his wife Dolores N. Giles, and their seven children, paid no attention to this legal nicety; for them it was simply a family business, with Norman Lee Giles as patriarch and with son/brother Kelly viewed by the rest of the family as a nasty obstructionist. Technically, a proper remedy might have been to dissociate Kelly as a general partner, leaving him his limited-partnership interest. But the parties ignored this possibility and the court, quite sensibly, did the same, deciding the case as if the Giles Land Company was a general partnership.

Under UPA (1997) § 603, when a partner ceases to be associated with the firm, one of two things can happen. In most cases, the nondissociating partners, proceeding under Article 7 (§§ 701–704) will continue the partnership by buying out the dissociating partner's interest. Section 701 explains, in pertinent part, that:

> (a) If a person is dissociated from a partnership without resulting in a dissolution and winding up of the partnership business under Section 801, the partnership shall cause the person's interest in the partnership to be purchased for a buyout price determined pursuant to subsection (b).
>
> (b) The buyout price of the interest of a person dissociated as a partner is the amount that would have been distributable to the dissociating partner under Section 80 6(b) if, on the date of dissociation, the assets of the partnership were sold at a price equal to the greater of:
>
> (1) the liquidation value or;
>
> (2) the value based on a sale of the entire business as a going concern without the person.

(c) Interest accrues on the buyout price from the date of dissociation to the date of payment . . . .

In some cases, however, dissociation leads to a dissolution, in which case (and when a court has ordered dissolution) Article 8 (§§ 801–806) applies, and there is a "winding up" of the business. Winding up can result in a sale of the partnership assets and the ending of its business or in a sale of the business as a going concern, with the proceeds (after payment of debts) going pro rata to the partners. But if, for example, the partnership business as a going concern (assets including good will) is put up for sale at auction, some of the partners (e.g., the Giles family other than Kelly) may buy it at auction; they can use their interest in the partnership as consideration for the purchase while paying cash for the interests of the nonpurchasing partners (e.g., Kelly Giles). If there is an active market for the assets, however, as is true of some farm properties, there is a risk of the current owners (e.g., the Giles family) losing the property or of paying what they might consider a high price (e.g., for Kelly's interest) to keep it.

Giles v. Giles Land Company

47 Kan.App.2d 744, 279 P.3d 139 (2012).

Kelly Giles (Kelly), a general partner in a family farming partnership, filed suit against the partnership and his partners, arguing that he had not been provided access to partnership books and records. The remaining members of the partnership then filed a counterclaim requesting that Kelly be dissociated from the partnership. The trial court held that Kelly was not denied access to the partnership books and records. Kelly does not appeal from this decision. Moreover, the trial court held that Kelly should be dissociated from the partnership. Kelly, however, contends that the trial court's ruling regarding his dissociation from the partnership was improper. We disagree. Accordingly, we affirm.

The dispute in this case centers on a family owned and operated limited partnership, Giles Land Company, L.P. (partnership). On one side is the plaintiff, Kelly, the second youngest of seven children in the Giles family. On the other side are the defendants: the partnership; Norman Lee Giles and Dolores Giles, the mother and father of the seven children involved; and Kelly's six siblings: Norman Roger Giles (Roger), Lorie Giles Horacek, Trudy Giles Giard, Audry Giles Gates, Jody Giles Peintner, and Julie Giles Cox.

Kelly appeals from the trial court's judgment granting the counterclaim filed by the defendants, which included Norman and Dolores Giles along with their six other children, seeking the dissociation of Kelly from the partnership, under K.S.A. 56a–601 [UPA (1997) § 601]. The trial court also denied Kelly's claim that the defendants had failed to provide him full access to the partnership records, but Kelly does not appeal that judgment.

The record reveals the following facts. The partnership was formed in the mid-1990's. One-half of the assets in the partnership came from a trust held for the benefit of the children of Norman and Dolores, and the other half of the assets came from Norman. Over the years, Norman and Dolores transferred interests in the partnership to their children. The ownership in the partnership is as follows:

	General Partnership Interest	Limited Partnership Interest
Norman Lee Giles	4.634500	03.3357145
Dolores N. Giles	4.634500	03.3357145
Trudy Giles Giard		12.857143
Norman Roger Giles	.243667	12.857143
Audry Giles Gates		12.857143
Jody Giles Peintner		12.857143
Lorie Giles Horacek	.243666	12.857143
Kelly K. Giles	.243667	06.185714
Julie Giles Cox		12.857143
Totals:	10.00%	90.00%

The general partnership interests held by Roger, Lorie, and Kelly were gifted to them by their parents.

The partnership owns both ranchland and farmland. This partnership [Giles Land Company] is not the only Giles family business; there is also Giles Ranch Company and H.G. Land and Cattle Company. In 1999, Kelly was a partner in the Giles Ranch Company, but he became so overwhelmed with the debt he had incurred in the operations of the ranch company that he insisted that he be bought out of the ranch company and relieved of all debt. The other partners managed to buy out Kelly's interest in the ranch company. At the time of the lawsuit, Kelly only had an ownership interest in the partnership at issue, *i.e.*, Giles Land Company.

On March 26, 2007, the partnership held a meeting to discuss converting the partnership into a limited liability company. Kelly was unable to attend the meeting, but he later received a letter explaining the family's interest in converting the partnership to a limited liability company. Kelly did not sign the articles of organization for the proposed conversion and instead had his attorney request production of all of the partnership's books and records for his review. Kelly was not satisfied with the records that the partnership had provided, so he filed suit asking the court to force the partnership to turn over all of the documents he was requesting. In response, the defendants filed an answer and a counterclaim seeking to dissociate Kelly from the partnership.

After a 2-day trial, the trial court determined that the partnership had properly complied with the document requests. The trial court also held that Kelly should be dissociated from the partnership under K.S.A. 56a–601(e)(3) [UPA (1997) § 601(5)(C)] or, in the alternative, K.S.A. 56a–601(e)(1) [UPA (1997) § 601(5)(A)]. The trial court found that due to Kelly's threats and the total distrust between Kelly and his family, it was not practicable to carry on the business of the partnership so long as Kelly was a partner.

Did the Trial Court Err in Finding that Kelly Should Be Dissociated from the Partnership?

On appeal, Kelly argues that the trial court erred in finding that he should be dissociated from the partnership under K.S.A. 56a–601(e)(3) or, alternatively, K.S.A. 56a–601(e)(1). . . .

K.S.A. 56a–601 states the following:

> A partner is dissociated from a partnership upon the occurrence of any of the following events:
>
> . . . .
>
> (e) on application by the partnership or another partner, the partner's expulsion by judicial determination because:
>
> (1) The partner engaged in wrongful conduct that adversely and materially affected the partnership business;
>
> . . . .
>
> (3) the partner engaged in conduct relating to the partnership business which makes it not reasonably practicable to carry on the business in partnership with the partner."

The trial court relied primarily on K.S.A. 56a–601(e)(3) to dissociate Kelly; therefore, the record must demonstrate that (1) Kelly engaged in conduct relating to the partnership business and (2) such conduct makes it not reasonably practicable to carry on the business in partnership with Kelly. See K.S.A. 56a–601(e)(3).

NOTE

Section 801 reads, in pertinent part, as follows:

A partnership is dissolved, and its business must be wound up, upon the occurrence of any of the following:

. . .

(4) on application by a partner, the entry by [the appropriate court] of an order dissolving the partnership on the grounds that:

. . .

(C) another partner has engaged in conduct relating to the partnership business which makes it not reasonably practicable to carry on the business in partnership with that partner; or

(D) it is otherwise not reasonably practicable to carry on the partnership business in conformity with the partnership agreement . . . .

Kansas' partnership statutes were . . . changed on the enactment of the Kansas Revised Uniform Partnership Act in 1998. These changes brought about the concept of dissociation, which previously did not formally exist in our law. . . . The statutory dissociation language in K.S.A. 56a–601(e) is very similar to the dissolution provisions set out in K.S.A. 56a–801(e). The comment to § 601 of the UPA, which is the source of K.S.A. 56a–601(e), confirms that the dissociation provisions were based on the preexisting grounds for dissolution under the UPA. . . . Consequently, caselaw addressing the analogous UPA dissolution provisions is probative in analyzing the defendants' dissociation claim.

Kelly first contends that there is no evidence that he engaged in conduct relating to the partnership business. Kelly argues that the trial court erroneously relied on evidence that he had threatened his family members and that the familial relationship was broken. Kelly maintains that this evidence is not related to the partnership business and, therefore, it was not relevant.

Before we address Kelly's argument as to the trial court's use of this evidence in concluding that dissociation was proper, it is helpful to our review to set out some of the trial court's findings. . . .

First, the trial court found that Kelly did not trust the other general partners and that he did not trust some of his sisters who are limited partners in the partnership. The trial court also found that the general partners as well as all of the other partners did not trust Kelly.

The trial court further found that the relationship between Kelly and the other family members was irreparably broken. In reaching that conclusion, the trial court focused on a meeting between the partners in 2006. Kelly turned to each of the general partners and said that they would each die, in turn, and that he would be the last man standing and that he would then get to control the partnership. Although Kelly testified that this was not a threat and that he was simply trying to explain the right of survivorship, the trial court believed the testimony of the rest of the family that it was taken as a threat. The trial court also relied on evidence that Kelly had said that "paybacks are hell" and that he intended to get even with his partners. The trial court also found this to be a threat. Another fact that the trial court relied on in finding that the family relationship was irreparably broken was that it was impossible for any of the family members to communicate with Kelly regarding the partnership. Each family member testified that he or she believed that it was in the best interest of the partnership to not have Kelly remain a partner.

In finding that Kelly should no longer be a partner, the trial court stated:

> This court finds that the testimony of the counterclaimants regarding the plans of Kelly Giles to take over Giles Land Company, L.P., [the partnership], predicting the deaths of the other General Partners, the statement of Kelly Giles that 'paybacks are hell' and that he would get even, is credible. The Court finds that Kelly Giles' version of events as something close to the magnanimous savior of the family lacked credibility. The Court finds that Kelly Giles was not amenable to land acquisitions or working with the family. . . . The Court further finds that given the lack of trust between Kelly Giles and his siblings who are General Partners, the partnership cannot operate in a meaningful fashion, and certainly cannot operate as intended, as a family business where there is cooperation, as long as Kelly Giles is a partner in [the partnership].

. . .

Additionally, to support its argument that the trial court correctly applied K.S.A. 56a–601(e)(3), the defendants direct this court to consider Brennan v. Brennan Associates, 293 Conn. 60, 977 A. 2d 107 (2009). . . . The *Brennan* court held that "an irreparable deterioration of a relationship between partners is a valid basis to order dissolution, and, therefore, is a valid basis for the alternative remedy of dissociation." 293 Conn. at 81, 977 A. 2d 107.

Here, like in *Brennan,* Kelly argues that the evidence that the trial court relied on was not related to the partnership business. Reviewing the record as a whole, it is clear that the trial court found the evidence to be related to the partnership business because this was a family partnership and all of the alleged disputes were between family members in that partnership. It is also telling that both of the parents and all of the other siblings joined in this lawsuit seeking Kelly's dissociation. Clearly, the relationship between Kelly and his family was broken, and although Kelly attempted to argue that their personal issues were not interfering with the partnership, the trial court did not find his testimony to be credible.

In light of the animosity that Kelly harbors toward his partners and his distrust of them (which distrust is mutual), it is clear that Kelly can no longer do business with his partners and vice-versa. Indeed, the partnership has reached an impasse regarding important business because of a lack of communication between Kelly and his partners. The evidence indicated that most communications with Kelly had to be conducted through his attorney. Moreover, Kelly's statement predicting the deaths of his general partners, his statement that "paybacks are hell," and his statement that he would get even showed a naked ambition on his part to control the partnership, contrary to the interests of the other partners.

. . .

Alternative Theory for Dissociation

The trial court also found that there was enough evidence to dissociate Kelly under K.S.A. 56a–601(e)(1). . . .

Under this alternative theory of dissociation, the record must demonstrate (1) that Kelly engaged in wrongful conduct and (2) that the wrongful conduct adversely and materially affected the partnership business. . . .

Kelly first argues that he did not engage in wrongful conduct towards his parents, Norman and Dolores . . . Additionally, Kelly argues that even if his conduct was wrongful, it did not adversely or materially affect the partnership business. Kelly contends the record shows that the partnership continued to operate as it always had and that the partners failed to show how his conduct materially or adversely affected the business of the partnership.

. . .

Kelly had created a situation where the partnership could no longer carry on its business to the mutual advantage of the other partners. For example, Lorie testified that Kelly would berate and belittle Norman in an attempt to make Norman do what Kelly wanted. There was also testimony given by John Horacek, Lorie's husband, that in a phone conversation between Kelly and Norman, Kelly yelled and cursed at his father and his father was in tears by the end of the conversation. Norman further testified that it would be better for everyone if Kelly were no longer in the partnership because it was clear that Kelly did not agree with what the other partners were wanting to do with the future of the partnership. Norman testified: " 'Cause I think the route we're on now, Judge, if we continue on this, and we don't—we're just at a standstill on what we plan to do." There was also evidence that Kelly had frustrated the partnership's opportunities to purchase more land. . . .

Because this is a family partnership, the evidence of Kelly making threats or berating his parents to get them to give him what he wants qualifies as wrongful conduct. None of the partners were able to interact or communicate with Kelly. Additionally, Norman clearly testified that the partnership was at a standstill because of the disputes between Kelly and the rest of the partners. This is evidence that Kelly was materially or adversely affecting the partnership. Moreover, this evidence is clearly enough to support dissolution based on the caselaw listed earlier; therefore, it is also sufficient for dissociation. Based on this evidence, we determine that the trial court properly held that Kelly could also be dissociated under K.S.A. 56a–601(e)(1).

Affirmed.

ANALYSIS

1. **What Was Achieved?** What did UPA (1997) achieve by adding the possibility of dissociation found in § 601?
2. **Material Effect.** How did Kelly's actions "materially affect[ ] the partnership business" or "make[ ] it not reasonably practicable to carry on the business in partnership with the partner"?
3. **Appeal?** What advice might you have offered Kelly about whether to appeal the judgment of the trial court?
4. **Kelly's Conduct.** Was Kelly's conduct more or less reprehensible than that of defendant Cohen in Owen v. Cohen, supra, of defendant John Lewis in Collins v. Lewis, supra? Regardless of what you conclude on that question, would the plaintiff in either of those cases have been entitled to a dissolution under the principles applied in *Giles*?
5. UPA (1997) is mostly a set of default rules. That is, it provides rules where the partners have failed to provide their own; it leaves them free to change the UPA (1997) rules in their partnership agreement. This concept is made explicit in UPA (1997) § 601, which provides, in part:

   > A partner is dissociated from a partnership upon the occurrence of any of the following events:
   >
   > . . .
   >
   > (2) an event agreed to in the partnership agreement as causing the partner's dissociation;
   >
   > (3) the partner's expulsion pursuant to the partnership agreement . . . .

   The possibilities for agreements relating to ending a partnership relationship are illustrated by the *Lawlis* case above and are considered immediately below in in the section on Buyout Agreements.

Creel v. Lilly

354 Md. 77, 729 A.2d 385 (1999).

The primary issue presented in this appeal is whether Maryland's Uniform Partnership Act (UPA) . . . permits the estate of a deceased partner to demand liquidation of partnership assets in order to arrive at the true value of the business. Specifically, Petitioner (Anne Creel) maintains that the surviving partners have a duty to liquidate all partnership assets because (1) there is no provision in the partnership agreement providing for the continuation of the partnership upon a partner's death and (2) the estate has not consented to the continuation of the business. Respondents (Arnold Lilly and Roy Altizer) contend that because the surviving partners wound up the partnership in good faith, in that they conducted a full inventory, provided an accurate accounting to the estate for the value of the business as of the date of dissolution, and paid the estate its proportionate share of the surplus proceeds, they are under no duty to liquidate the partnership's assets upon demand of the deceased partner's estate. . . .

[The] UPA, which has governed partnerships in this State for the past 80 years, has been repealed since this litigation commenced. The Act that now governs Maryland partnerships is the UPA (1997) [UPA (1997)], . . . which was adopted in July 1998 with a phase-in period. Therefore, until December 31, 2002, both UPA and UPA (1997) will coexist, with § 9A–1204 determining which Act applies to a particular partnership's formation, termination, and any other conflict that may arise. . . .

For the reasons stated in this opinion, we concur in the finding of the courts below that Respondents are under no duty to "liquidate on demand" by Petitioner, as UPA does not mandate a forced sale of all partnership assets in order to ascertain the true value of the business. Winding up is not always synonymous with liquidation, which can be a harsh, drastic, and often unnecessary course of action. A preferred method in a good faith winding up, which was utilized in this case, is to pay the deceased partner's estate its proportionate share of the value of the partnership, derived from an accurate accounting, without having to resort to a full liquidation of the business. To hold otherwise vests excessive power and control in the deceased partner's estate, to the extreme disadvantage of the surviving partners. . . .

In this appeal, Petitioner also asks us to award the estate its share of the partnership profits generated by the Respondents' alleged continued use of the partnership assets for the period of time during which Petitioner claims the Respondents neither liquidated the business nor agreed to pay the estate its proper percentage share of the partnership.... We reject Petitioner's request and agree with the courts below that there is no basis for damages because Good Ole Boys Racing (Good Ole Boys) is a successor partnership and not a continuation of Joe's Racing, which was properly wound up and terminated before the new partnership began operations.

I. Background

On approximately June 1, 1993, Joseph Creel began a retail business selling NASCAR racing memorabilia. His business was originally located in a section of his wife Anne's florist shop, but after about a year and a half he decided to raise capital from partners so that he could expand and move into his own space. On September 20, 1994, Mr. Creel entered into a partnership agreement-apparently prepared without the assistance of counsel-with Arnold Lilly and Roy Altizer to form a general partnership called "Joe's Racing." ...

The three-man partnership operated a retail store in the St. Charles Towne Center Mall in Waldorf, Maryland. For their initial investment in Joe's Racing, Mr. Lilly and Mr. Altizer each paid $6,666 in capital contributions, with Mr. Creel contributing his inventory and supplies valued at $15,000. Pursuant to the partnership agreement, Mr. Lilly and Mr. Altizer also paid $6,666 to Mr. Creel ($3,333 each) "for the use and rights to the business known as Joe's Racing Collectables." The funds were placed in a partnership bank account with First Virginia Bank-Maryland. All three partners were signatories to this account, but on May 19, 1995, unknown to Mr. Lilly and Mr. Altizer, Mr. Creel altered the account so that only he had the authority to sign checks. It was only after Mr. Creel's death that Mr. Lilly and Mr. Altizer realized they could not access the account funds, which were frozen by the bank upon Mr. Creel's passing. Moreover, on approximately February 20, 1995, Mr. Creel paid a $5,000 retainer to an attorney without his partners' knowledge. He wanted the attorney to prepare documents for the marketing of franchises for retail stores dealing in racing memorabilia.

Joe's Racing had been in existence for almost nine months when Mr. Creel died on June 14, 1995. Mrs. Creel was appointed personal representative of his estate. In this capacity, and acting without the knowledge of the surviving partners, Mrs. Creel and the store's landlord agreed to shorten the lease by one month so that it expired on August 31, 1995. June, July, and August's rent was paid by Mr. Lilly and Mr. Altizer.

In accordance with § 9–602(4),[1] Joe's Racing was automatically dissolved upon Mr. Creel's death and because the partnership agreement

[1] Section 9–602 [of the UPA] states in pertinent part: "Dissolution is caused: . . . (4) By the death of any partner[.]"

did not expressly provide for continuation of the partnership nor did his estate consent to its continuation, the surviving partners were required under UPA to wind up the business. . . . In order to pay debts and efficiently wind up the partnership affairs, Mr. Lilly and Mr. Altizer requested that Mrs. Creel and the bank release the funds in the partnership account ($18,115.93 as of July 13, 1995). Their request was refused and it was at this point that litigation commenced. . . .

[The court below found] "that the surviving partners sought to wind up and close out the partnership and took all reasonable steps to do so, and that there was no breach by them of any fiduciary duty to the Estate. The lease on the store premises occupied by the partnership expired on 31 August 1995, and on that date Mr. Lilly conducted an inventory of all merchandise in the store. Based on that inventory, an accountant computed the value of the partnership business; Mrs. Creel was invited to review the books and records and retain her own accountant or appraiser if she questioned [Mr. Lilly or Mr. Altizer's] figures. She declined to do so. After 31 August 1995, Messrs. Lilly and Altizer ceased doing business as Joe's Racing and began doing business together under the name 'Good Ole Boys Racing.'

"The court accepted the valuation prepared by [Mr. Lilly and Mr. Altizer's] accountant as the correct value of the partnership assets as of 31 August 1995, and found that the surviving partners fully disclosed and delivered to the Estate all records of the financial affairs of the Joe's Racing partnership up to 31 August 1995, which the court took to be the end of the winding up period. Rejecting [Mrs. Creel's] assertions (1) that [Mr. Lilly and Mr. Altizer] were obligated to liquidate the partnership assets in order to wind up the partnership; (2) that [Mr. Lilly and Mr. Altizer], instead of winding up the partnership by liquidating its assets, misappropriated partnership assets, i.e., inventory to make a profit, for which they were obligated to account; and (3) that the Estate was entitled to 52% of such profits, the court declared that the Estate was entitled to a total of $21,631. . . . [orig. in ital.]

II. Discussion and Analysis

A.

. . . Section 9–101(g) [of the UPA] defines a partnership as "an association of two or more persons to carry on as co-owners [of] a business for profit." There is no requirement that the partnership be formally established with a writing; so long as this definition is met, a partnership exists whether the parties intend it to or not. However, the "general rule is that the partnership agreement governs the relations among the partners and between the partners and the partnership. The provisions of [UPA] govern to the extent the partnership agreement does not provide otherwise." John W. Larson et al., Revised Uniform Partnership Act

Reflects a Number of Significant Changes, 10 J. Partnership Tax'n 232, 233 (1993)(footnote omitted).

A partnership is either (1) for a definite term or a particular undertaking or (2) at will, which means the business has no definite term or particular undertaking.... An at-will partnership continues indefinitely and can be dissolved by the express will of any partner or automatically by the happening of a specific event as mandated by UPA, such as the death of a partner.... Under UPA, partners may avoid the automatic dissolution of the business upon the death of a partner by providing for its continuation in their partnership agreement.... Sophisticated partnerships virtually always use carefully drafted partnership agreements to protect the various partners' interests by providing for the continuation of the business, the distribution of partnership assets, etc., in the face of various contingencies such as death.... Less sophisticated partnerships, however, are often operating under oral terms or a "homemade" agreement that does not contain protections for the partners or the business.

While the death of a partner automatically dissolves the partnership unless there is an agreement stating otherwise, the partnership is not terminated until the winding-up process is complete.... Winding up is generally defined as "getting in the assets, settling with [the] debtors and creditors, and appropriating the amount of profit or loss [to the partners]." Comp. of Treas. v. Thompson Tr. Corp., 209 Md. 490, 501–02, 121 A.2d 850, 856 (1956)(quoting Lafayette Trust Co. v. Beggs, 213 N.Y. 280, 107 N.E. 644, 645 (1915)). The surviving partners have the right to wind up the partnership or the deceased partner's representative may obtain a winding up through the courts.... The winding-up procedure that applies in this case is found in § 9–609(a), which states in pertinent part: "When dissolution is caused in any way ... each partner ... unless otherwise agreed, may have the partnership property applied to discharge its liabilities, and the surplus applied to pay in cash the net amount owing to the respective partners."

Historically, under many courts and commentators' interpretation of UPA, when a partner died and the partnership automatically dissolved because there was no consent by the estate to continue the business nor was there a written agreement allowing for continuation, the estate had the right to compel liquidation of the partnership assets.... Reducing all of the partnership assets to cash through a liquidation was seen as the only way to obtain the true value of the business.... However, while winding up has often traditionally been regarded as synonymous with liquidation, this "fire sale" of assets has been viewed by many courts and commentators as a harsh and destructive measure. Consequently, to avoid the drastic result of a forced liquidation, many courts have adopted judicial alternatives to this potentially harmful measure....

Over time, the UPA rule requiring automatic dissolution of the partnership upon the death of a partner, in the absence of consent by the estate to continue the business or an agreement providing for continuation, with the possible result of a forced sale of all partnership assets was viewed as outmoded by many jurisdictions including Maryland. The development and adoption of UPA (1997) by the National Conference of Commissioners on Uniform State Laws (NCCUSL) mitigated this harsh UPA provision of automatic dissolution and compelled liquidation.

UPA (1997)'s underlying philosophy differs radically from UPA's, thus laying the foundation for many of its innovative measures. UPA (1997) adopts the "entity" theory of partnership as opposed to the "aggregate" theory that the UPA espouses. . . . Under the aggregate theory, a partnership is characterized by the collection of its individual members, with the result being that if one of the partners dies or withdraws, the partnership ceases to exist. . . . On the other hand, UPA (1997)'s entity theory allows for the partnership to continue even with the departure of a member because it views the partnership as "an entity distinct from its partners." Section 9A–201.

This adoption of the entity theory, which permits continuity of the partnership upon changes in partner identity, allows for several significant changes in UPA (1997). Of particular importance to the instant case is that under UPA (1997) "a partnership no longer automatically dissolves due to a change in its membership, but rather the existing partnership may be continued if the remaining partners elect to buy out the dissociating partner."[2] [Thomas R. Hurst,] Will the Revised Uniform Partnership Act (1994) Ever Be Uniformly Adopted?, 48 Fla. L.Rev. at 579 (emphasis added)(footnote omitted). In contrast to UPA, UPA (1997)'s "buy-out" option does not have to be expressly included in a written partnership agreement in order for it to be exercised; however, the surviving partners must still actively choose to exercise the option, as "continuation is not automatic as with a corporation." [Id.] at 579–80 . . . . Critically, under UPA (1997) the estate of the deceased partner no longer has to consent in order for the business to be continued nor does the estate have the right to compel liquidation.

Like UPA, UPA (1997) is a "gap filler" in that it only governs partnership affairs to the extent not otherwise agreed to by the partners in the partnership agreement. . . . There are certain UPA (1997) provisions, however, that partners cannot waive, such as unreasonably restricting the right of access to partnership books and records,

---

[2] UPA (1997) uses the term "dissociation" rather than dissolution. "Dissociation" is viewed as having a less significant impact on the partnership than dissolution, which is in line with UPA (1997)'s entity theory of partnership of continuing the business whenever possible. . . . Even after a dissociation leads to a dissolution, UPA (1997) offers a final opportunity for the partners to continue the partnership if they so choose. . . .

eliminating the duty of loyalty, unreasonably reducing the duty of care, and eliminating the obligation of good faith and fair dealing. . . .

B.

As discussed earlier, the traditional manner in which UPA allows for the continuation of the partnership upon the death of a partner is to either obtain the consent of the deceased partner's estate or include a continuation clause in the partnership agreement. . . . There have been several cases in other jurisdictions, however, where neither of these conditions was met and the court elected another option under UPA instead of a "fire sale" of all the partnership assets to ensure that the deceased partner's estate received its fair share of the partnership. . . . These jurisdictions have recognized the unfairness and harshness of a compelled liquidation and found other judicially acceptable means of winding up a partnership under UPA, such as ordering an in-kind distribution of the assets or allowing the remaining partners to buy out the withdrawing partner's share of the partnership [at its assessed value].

C.

In applying the law . . . to the facts of this case, we want to clarify that while UPA is the governing act, our holding is also consistent with UPA (1997) and its underlying policies. The legislature's recent adoption of UPA (1997) indicates that it views with disfavor the compelled liquidation of businesses and that it has elected to follow the trend in partnership law to allow the continuation of business without disruption, in either the original or successor form, if the surviving partners choose to do so through buying out the deceased partner's share. . . . [We now ask] whether the Creel estate has the right to demand liquidation of Joe's Racing where its partnership agreement does not expressly provide for continuation of the partnership and where the estate does not consent to continuation. . . . The pertinent paragraph and subsections of the Joe's Racing partnership agreement are as follows:

> "7. **Termination**
>
> (a) That, at the termination of this partnership a full and accurate inventory shall be prepared, and the assets, liabilities, and income, both in gross and net, shall be ascertained: the remaining debts or profits will be distributed according to the percentages shown above in the 6(e). . . .
>
> (d) Upon the death or illness of a partner, his share will go to his estate. If his estate wishes to sell his interest, they must offer it to the remaining partners first."

Even though the partnership agreement uses the word "termination," paragraph 7(a) is really discussing the dissolution of the partnership and the attendant winding-up process that ultimately led to termination. Paragraph 7(a) requires that the assets, liabilities, and income be "ascertained," but it in no way mandates that this must be accomplished by a forced sale of the partnership assets. . . .

In this case, the winding-up method outlined in 7(a) was followed exactly by the surviving partners: a full and accurate inventory was prepared on August 31, 1995; this information was given to an accountant, who ascertained the assets, liabilities, and income of the partnership; and finally, the remaining debt or profit was distributed according to the percentages listed in 6(e). . . .

In the instant case, per paragraph 7(a) of the partnership agreement and § 9–614 of UPA,[3] the Creel estate had the right to ask the surviving partners for an accounting of Mr. Creel's interest in Joe's Racing as of the date of dissolution. We agree with the Court of Special Appeals when it stated, however, that "[t]he right to an accounting is not a right to force the winding up partners to liquidate the assets. The personal representative of a deceased partner is entitled to receive, on behalf of the estate, as an ordinary creditor, the value of the decedent's partnership interest as of the date of dissolution, i.e., the date of the decedent's death." (Emphasis added). . . .

Finally, Mrs. Creel contends that the accountant's valuation improperly considered only the book value of the business and not its market value. "Book value" refers to the assets of the business, less its liabilities plus partner contributions or "equity." "Market value" includes the value of such intangibles as goodwill, the value of the business as an ongoing concern, and established vendor and supplier lines, among other factors. Again, we concur with the trial court's findings as to the valuation of Joe's Racing.

In making no finding of goodwill value, for example, the trial court likely considered the fact that Joe's Racing had only been operating a little over a year before the partnership was formed, and after Lilly and Altizer became partners with Mr. Creel the business was only in existence for nine months before Mr. Creel died. On these facts, it is reasonable for the trial court to conclude-without any evidence presented to the contrary-that a small business selling NASCAR memorabilia, which had been operating for barely two years, did not possess any goodwill value.

---

[3] Section 9–614, "Accrual of right to account," provides:

"The right to an account of his interest shall accrue to any partner, or his legal representative, as against the winding up partners or the surviving partners or the person or partnership continuing the business, at the date of dissolution, in the absence of any agreement to the contrary."

ANALYSIS

1. **Liquidation of Going-Concern Value.** The court seems worried that a partner with a right to force a "fire sale" of a firm's assets will destroy its going concern value. Suppose that a firm does have substantial going concern value. What will happen if a court orders its assets auctioned off?

2. **Avoiding Auction.** Suppose one of three partners dies and the dead partner's widow has a right to force the firm to auction its assets. If the other partners want to continue the firm, what can they do?

3. **The Right to Demand Liquidation.** Why did Mrs. Creel want the right to demand liquidation of the firm?

7. BUYOUT AGREEMENTS

INTRODUCTORY NOTE

A buy-out, or buy-sell, agreement is an agreement that allows a partner to end her or his relationship with the other partners and receive a cash payment, or series of payments, or some assets of the firm, in return for her or his interest in the firm. There are many possible approaches. A good buy-out agreement must be tailored to the needs and circumstances of each firm. Here is a brief outline of some of the issues and alternatives:

I. "Trigger" events
  - A. Death
  - B. Disability
  - C. Will of any partner

II. Obligation to buy versus option
  - A. Firm
  - B. Other investors
  - C. Consequences of refusal to buy
    - i. If there is an obligation
    - ii. If there is no obligation

III. Price
  - A. Book value
  - B. Appraisal
  - C. Formula (e.g., five times earnings)
  - D. Set price each year
  - E. Relation to duration (e.g., lower price in first five years)

IV. Method of payment

A. Cash

B. Installments (with interest?)

V. Protection against debts of partnership

VI. Procedure for offering either to buy or sell

A. First mover sets price to buy or sell

B. First mover forces others to set price

What terms would you propose for a buy-out agreement in the situations described in each of the cases presented in the preceding section?

G & S Investments v. Belman

145 Ariz. 258, 700 P.2d 1358 (Ct. App., Div. 2, 1984).

This case involves a partnership dispute arising out of the misconduct and subsequent death of Thomas N. Nordale. There are two principal issues in this case: whether the surviving general partner, G & S Investments, is entitled to continue the partnership after the death of Nordale, and how the value of Nordale's interest in partnership property is to be computed. The trial court, after making findings of fact and conclusions of law, entered judgment in favor of G & S Investments, finding that it had the right to continue the partnership and that the estate was owed $4,867.57. . . .

Century Park, Ltd., is a limited partnership which was formed to receive ownership of a 62-unit apartment complex in Tucson. In 1982 the general partners were G & S Investments (51 per cent) and Nordale (25.5 per cent). The remaining partnership interest was owned by the limited partners, Jones and Chapin.

In 1979 Nordale began using cocaine, which caused a personality change. He became suspicious of his partners and other people, and he could not communicate with other people. He stopped going to work and stopped keeping normal business hours. He stopped returning phone calls and became hyperactive, agitated and angry toward people for no reason. Commencing in 1980 he made threats to some of the other partners, stating that he was going to get them and fix them.

Nordale lived in the apartment complex. This led to several problems. He sexually solicited an underage female tenant of the complex. Despite repeated demands, he refused to give up possession or pay rent on an apartment that the partnership had allowed him to use temporarily during his divorce. His lifestyle in the apartment complex created a great deal of tension and disturbance and frightened the tenants. At least one tenant was lost because of the disturbances.

Fundamental business and management disputes also arose. Nordale irrationally insisted upon converting the apartment complex into condominiums despite adverse tax consequences and mortgage interest rates that were at an all-time high. He also insisted on raising the rents despite the fact that recent attempts to do so had resulted in mass vacancies which had a devastating economic effect on the partnership enterprise.

By 1981 Gary Gibson and Steven Smith (G & S Investments) had come to the conclusion that Nordale was incapable of making rational business decisions and that they should seek a dissolution of the partnership which would allow them to carry on the business and buy out Nordale's interest.

The original complaint, filed on September 11, 1981, sought a judicial dissolution and the right to carry on the business and buy out Nordale's interest as permitted by [UPA (1914) § 38].

. . .

After the filing of the complaint, on February 16, 1982, Nordale died. On June 28, 1982, appellees filed a supplemental complaint invoking their right to continue the partnership and acquire Nordale's interest under article 19 of the partnership's Articles of Limited Partnership. The key provisions of article 19 are as follows:

> "(a) In the interest of a continuity of the partnership it is agreed that upon the death, retirement, insanity or resignation of one of the general partners . . . *the surviving or remaining general partners may continue the partnership business. . . .*
>
> . . .
>
> (e) Rules as to resignation or retirement [which under Article 19(d) includes death].
>
> . . .
>
> (2) In the event the surviving or remaining general partner shall desire to continue the partnership business, *he shall purchase the interest of the retiring or resigning general partner. . . .*" (Emphasis added)

. . .

The Filing of the Original Complaint

Appellant contends that the mere filing of the complaint acted as a dissolution of the partnership, requiring the liquidation of the assets and distribution of the net proceeds to the partners. He takes this position because he believes the estate will receive more money under this theory than if the other partners are allowed to carry on the business upon payment of the amount which was due to Nordale under the partnership agreement. Appellees contend that the filing of the complaint did not cause a dissolution but that the wrongful conduct of Nordale, in contravention of the partnership agreement, gave the court the power to dissolve the partnership and allow them to carry on the business by themselves. See [UPA (1914) § 38.] We agree with appellees.

Contrary to appellant's contention, Nordale's conduct was in contravention of the partnership agreement. Nordale's conduct affected the carrying on of the business and made it impracticable to continue in partnership with him. His conduct was wrongful and was in contravention of the partnership agreement, thus allowing the court to permit appellees to carry on the business.... [UPA (1914) § 32] authorizes the court to dissolve a partnership when:

> "...
>
> (2) A partner becomes in any other way incapable of performing his part of the partnership contract.
>
> (3) A partner has been guilty of such conduct as tends to affect prejudicially the carrying on of the business.
>
> (4) A partner willfully or persistently commits a breach of the partnership agreement, or otherwise so conducts himself in matters relating to the partnership business that it is not reasonably practicable to carry on the business in partnership with him...."

In the case of Cooper v. Isaacs, 448 F.2d 1202 (D.C.Cir.1971) the court was met with the same contention made here, to-wit, that the mere filing of the complaint acted as a dissolution. The court rejected this contention. To paraphrase the reasoning of the court in Cooper v. Isaacs, supra, because the Uniform Partnership Act provides for dissolution for cause by decree of court and appellees have alleged facts which would entitle them to a dissolution on this ground if proven, their filing of the complaint cannot be said to effect a dissolution, wrongful or otherwise, under the act; dissolution would occur only when decreed by the court or when brought about by other acts.

Article 19 of the Articles of Partnership

Article 19 of the Articles of Partnership provides that upon the death, retirement, insanity or resignation of one of the general partners the surviving or remaining general partners may continue the partnership business. It further provides that should the surviving or remaining general partners desire to continue the partnership business, they must purchase the interest of the retiring or resigning general partner....

The Buy-out Formula

Article 19(e)(2)(i) contains the following buy-out provision:

"The amount shall be calculated as follows:

By the addition of the sums of the amount of the resigning or retiring general partner's *capital account* plus an amount equal to the average of the prior three years' profits and gains actually paid to the general partner, or as agreed upon by the general partners, provided said agreed sum does not exceed the calculated sum in dollars." (Emphasis added)

> **NOTE**
>
> The capital account is also reduced by the amount of any distributions. To illustrate, suppose the total cash amount initially contributed by the partners was $400,000; that Nordale contributed $100,000 (25 percent), which is his initial capital account; that there were no further contributions; that the partnership had net profits of $40,000 in each of its first three years (a total of $120,000). Nordale's share of the profit would be $30,000, which would increase his capital account to $130,000. If there had been a total distribution of $40,000 to the partners, Nordale would have received $10,000 and that would have reduced his capital account to $120,000. If there had been total losses of $500,000 in the first three years, and no distributions, Nordale's share of the losses would have been $125,000 and his capital account would have been a negative $25,000. Any change in the value of the partnerships real estate investment is ignored. Suppose, for example, that there had been total losses of $500,000, financed by borrowing against the security of the real estate, which had increased in fair market value by $1.3 million. The fair market value of Nordale's interest would have increased by $200,000 (25 percent of the $1.3 million increase in fair market value less 25 percent of the $500,000 loan). But his capital account would still be a negative $25,000. The court in the present case observes that "capital account" and "book value," though not "synonymous," are "functional equivalents."

Appellant claims that the term "capital account" in article 19(e)(2)(i) is ambiguous. The estate relies on the testimony of an accountant, Jon Young, that the term "capital account" is ambiguous merely because there is no definition of the term in the articles. He claimed that it was not clear whether the cost basis or the fair market value of the partnership's assets should be used in determining the capital account. Even on direct examination, however, Young admitted that read literally the buy-out formula takes the capital account of the deceased partner and adds to that amount the average of the prior three years' earnings. On cross-examination he admitted that generally accepted accounting principles require the partnership capital accounts be maintained on a cost basis and that he has never seen a partnership in which the capital accounts in the books and records were based on the fair market value. . . .

In contrast, Gibson and Smith testified that the parties actually intended and understood "capital account" to mean exactly what it literally says, the account which shows a partner's capital contribution to the partnership plus profits minus losses. Smith, an accountant, further testified that while there is a relationship between the capital accounts and valuation of the partnership assets, the valuation of the assets does not affect the actual entries made on the capital account.

There was no dispute that Nordale's capital account showed a negative balance of $44,510.09, . . . [while] the fair market value of his interest in the partnership . . . would have amounted to the sum of $76,714.24.

. . .

The words "capital account" are not ambiguous and clearly mean the partner's capital account as it appears on the books of the partnership. Our conclusion is further buttressed by the entire language of article 19(e)(2)(i) which requires, for a buy-out, the payment of the amount of the partner's capital account plus other sums. This is "capital account" language and not "fair market value" language.

. . .

Because partnerships result from contract, the rights and liabilities of the partners among themselves are subject to such agreements as they may make. . . .

Partnership buy-out agreements are valid and binding although the purchase price agreed upon is less or more than the actual value of the interest at the time of death. . . .

We do not have the power to rewrite article 19 based upon subjective notions of fairness arising long after the agreement was made or because the agreement did not turn out to be an advantageous one. Modern business practice mandates that the parties be bound by the contract they enter into, absent fraud or duress. . . . It is not the province of this court to act as a post-transaction guardian for either party.

8. LIMITED PARTNERSHIPS

Introduction

A limited partnership has two classes of partners—general partners, who have control of the partnership activities and operations, and limited partners, who do not have control—at least formally—and who are not liable for the debts and obligations of the partnership. Under earlier versions of the law, limited partners could become liable for the partnership's debts and obligations if they participated in control. Under the current version, Uniform Limited Partnership Act (2001, last amended in 2013), § 303(a), this risk of liability is substantially eliminated. Moreover, limited liability can be achieved for the people who will be running the business by using a corporation as the general partner, with the people running the business as the sole shareholders and the officers of the corporation. Corporations enjoy "limited liability"; shareholders and officers are not personally liable for the debts of the firm. The corporate general partner in a limited partnership typically has only a small equity interest in the limited partnership. This form of organization has been useful in activities such as real estate development; the developer will own and control the corporate general partner, the passive investors will be limited partners, and the developer may also be a limited partner. This choice of organizational form is driven in large part by tax considerations.

A more recent development (as of 2018) is the limited liability limited partnership (LLLP), which, for purposes of liability, in effect treats the general partners the same as limited partners. See Uniform Limited Partnership Act (2001) §§ 102(10) and 404(c).

In some states, partners in general partnerships can achieve limited liability by organizing as limited liability partnerships (LLP). See Uniform Partnership Act (UPA) (1997), §§ 102(9) and 306(c). This form of organization has been popular among legal, architectural, and accounting firms.

Frigidaire Sales Corporation v. Union Properties, Inc.

88 Wash.2d 400, 562 P.2d 244 (1977).

Petitioner, Frigidaire Sales Corporation, sought review of a Court of Appeals decision which held that limited partners do not incur general liability for the limited partnership's obligations simply because they are officers, directors, or shareholders of the corporate general partner. . . . We granted review, and now affirm the decision of the Court of Appeals.

. . . Petitioner entered into a contract with Commercial Investors (Commercial), a limited partnership. Respondents, Leonard Mannon and Raleigh Baxter, were limited partners of Commercial. Respondents were also officers, directors, and shareholders of Union Properties, Inc., the only general partner of Commercial. Respondents controlled Union Properties, and through their control of Union Properties they exercised the day-to-day control and management of Commercial. Commercial breached the contract, and petitioner brought suit against Union Properties and respondents. The trial court concluded that respondents did not incur general liability for Commercial's obligations by reason of their control of Commercial, and the Court of Appeals affirmed.

We first note that petitioner does not contend that respondents acted improperly by setting up the limited partnership with a corporation as the sole general partner. Limited partnerships are a statutory form of business organization, and parties creating a limited partnership must follow the statutory requirements. In Washington, parties may form a limited partnership with a corporation as the sole general partner. . . .

Petitioner's sole contention is that respondents should incur general liability for the limited partnership's obligations [under the Uniform Limited Partnership Act provision that removes the limitation of liability of a limited partner who "takes part in the control of the business"], because they exercised the day-to-day control and management of Commercial. Respondents, on the other hand, argue that Commercial was controlled by Union Properties, a separate legal entity, and not by respondents in their individual capacities.

[The court distinguishes Delaney v. Fidelity Lease Ltd., 526 S.W.2d 543 (Tex.1975), in which, among other things, the Texas Supreme Court expressed concern about the use of corporate general partners with "minimum capitalization and therefore minimum liability."]

However, we agree with our Court of Appeals analysis that this concern with minimum capitalization is not peculiar to limited partnerships with corporate general partners, but may arise anytime a creditor deals with a corporation. . . . Because our limited partnership statutes permit parties to form a limited partnership with a corporation as the sole general partner, this concern about minimal capitalization, standing by itself, does not justify a finding that the limited partners incur general liability for their control of the corporate general partner. . . . If a corporate general partner is inadequately capitalized, the rights of a creditor are adequately protected under the "piercing the corporate veil" doctrine of corporation law. . . .

Furthermore, petitioner was never led to believe that respondents were acting in any capacity other than in their corporate capacities. The parties stipulated at the trial that respondents never acted in any direct, personal capacity. When the shareholders of a corporation, who are also the corporation's officers and directors, conscientiously keep the affairs of the corporation separate from their personal affairs, and no fraud or manifest injustice is perpetrated upon third persons who deal with the corporation, the corporation's separate entity should be respected. . . .

For us to find that respondents incurred general liability for the limited partnership's obligations . . . would require us to . . . totally ignore the corporate entity of Union Properties, when petitioner knew it was dealing with that corporate entity. There can be no doubt that respondents, in fact, controlled the [partnership]. However, they did so only in their capacities as agents for their principal, the corporate general partner. Although the corporation was a separate entity, it could act only through its board of directors, officers, and agents. . . . Petitioner entered into the contract with Commercial. Respondents signed the contract in their capacities as president and secretary-treasurer of Union Properties, the general partner of Commercial. In the eyes of the law it was Union Properties, as a separate corporate entity, which entered into the contract with petitioner and controlled the limited partnership.

Further, because respondents scrupulously separated their actions on behalf of the corporation from their personal actions, petitioner never mistakenly assumed that respondents were general partners with general liability. . . . Petitioner knew Union Properties was the sole general partner and did not rely on respondents' control by assuming that they were also general partners. If petitioner had not wished to rely on the solvency of Union Properties as the only general partner, it could have insisted that respondents personally guarantee contractual performance. Because petitioner entered into the contract knowing that Union Properties was the only party with general liability, and because in the eyes of the law it was Union Properties, a separate entity, which controlled the limited partnership, there is no reason for us to find that respondents incurred general liability for their acts done as officers of the corporate general partner.

The decision of the Court of Appeals is affirmed.

ANALYSIS

1. **Liability if Not Limited Partners.** In *Frigidaire* the individual defendants were limited partners of Commercial Investors as well as officers, directors and shareholders of Union Properties, Inc., the general partner. If they had not been limited partners might they still have been personally liable (if they had not been so scrupulous about respecting the corporate form)? On what theory or theories? How would the proof differ, depending on whether they were or were not limited partners?

2. **Corporation as Sole General Partner.** Is there any good reason for practitioners not to use corporations as the sole general partners of limited partnerships—that is, any good reason not to shield general partners from liability by, in effect, incorporating them?

Jerman v. O'Leary

145 Ariz. 397, 701 P.2d 1205 (Ariz.App.1985).

This was an action by five per cent of the limited partners of Rincon Country Mobile Home Park, Ltd., against the general partners, appellants O'Leary [husband and wife], to impose a constructive trust or secure damages for an alleged breach of fiduciary duty when appellants secured for themselves 25 acres of unimproved land belonging to the partnership. The case was heard by the court, sitting without a jury, which awarded plaintiffs compensatory damages in the sum of $60,650, $10,000 punitive damages and attorney's fees in the sum of $13,125.

The Rincon Country Mobile Home Park, Ltd., was formed as an Arizona limited partnership in December 1974 with appellants O'Leary as the sole general partners. During the course of its operations the limited partnership acquired 36.46 acres of land adjacent to the mobile home park at a cost of $47,625. This land was not used in the construction of the mobile home park and is the focus of this lawsuit.

There were 38 investors in the limited partnership. The O'Learys owned 62.1 per cent of the limited partnership units. The remaining 47.9 per cent [sic] was held by the remaining 36 investors with the five-party appellees owning collectively a five per cent interest.

In December 1978 a sale was made of the mobile home park. The selling price was $4,000,000 on an installment sales basis and thus the limited partnership was not dissolved after the sale, but instead remained in existence with appellants O'Leary continuing to have responsibilities as general partners. The 36.46 acres of undeveloped real property were not included in the sale of the mobile home park and the partnership did not intend to develop the property.

The subject 36 acres were zoned SR, suburban ranch, which allowed placement of one residence for every four-acre area unless cluster development was used. Approximately 11 of the 36 acres were in the Pantano Wash and not usable.

In 1977 appellants filed an application with Pima County on behalf of the limited partnership to have the land rezoned from SR to TH, which permitted the land to be used for construction of a travel trailer park. It was necessary for the partnership, as part of the rezoning process, to convey to the county the 11 acres of land located in Pantano Wash. In August 1977 the county tentatively approved the change in zoning, subject to various conditions being met within two years, including the need to provide suitable sanitation facilities.

In August 1978 appellants became interested in purchasing the 25 acres from the limited partnership and hired an appraiser to determine the value of the land. However, appellants did not inform the appraiser of the zoning change. The land was appraised for $95,000 as SR property as of September 1978. Appellants then asked the accountant for the limited partnership to determine the monies they were entitled to receive in excess of their distributions as limited partners from the sale of the mobile home park and how payment could be made to the limited partnership which would permit the O'Learys to purchase the 25 acres that were to be sold. The accountant calculated that the limited partnership would receive not less than $110,125 in benefits if appellants forgave certain monies and deferred receipt of other payments. Appellants then offered to purchase the 25 acres from the limited partnership for the sum of $110,250. . . .

After the [offer] was mailed, appellee Jerman gave notice that he believed the land was worth $300,000 to $400,000 premised upon the conditional TH zoning and usage. In response to the Jerman objection, appellants had another letter prepared and mailed to the limited partners. That letter disclosed that the land had been rezoned and that appellees were asserting that the land was worth more money. Specifically, the letter provided:

> A small group of persons owning 22 of the total 464 units of the Limited Partnership have raised an objection to the transfer of the 25 acre parcel of vacant land to the General Partners, George and Brigid O'Leary for the sum of $110,250.00 as described in the previous letter. The unit holders objecting, allege that the land for which Mr. O'Leary has obtained re-zoning, is now worth more money than the price indicated.
>
> While it is possible that the property could be appraised for a higher figure, it was Mr. O'Leary's position that under the circumstances, the price at which the parcel was transferred to him was reasonable and was made in good faith. . . .

The letter also informed the members of the limited partnership that the O'Learys needed to invest substantial sums of money to develop the property. Consequently, they requested that each limited partner approve or disapprove of the sale so if there was a substantial disagreement the O'Learys could re-evaluate their decision to purchase. The members were informed that if a decision not to purchase was made by the O'Learys it would have an adverse impact on the distributions to be received from the sale of the mobile home park because the O'Learys would not be waiving certain payments owed them nor would certain payments to them be delayed. All the limited partners thereafter approved the sale except for appellees, who did not cast a ballot.

With this approval the O'Learys consummated the acquisition and a deed was issued on March 6, 1979. Appellees accepted the distributions from the sale of the mobile home park, which were more favorable because of the purchase price paid by the O'Learys.

[The court next summarizes trial testimony by various experts as to the value of the 25 acres. The estimates ranged widely, from a low of $100,000 to a high of $1,213,000.] . . .

I.

It was appellees' position in the trial court that appellants were wrongfully self-dealing in the partnership property in violation of A.R.S. § 29–309 which states in pertinent part:

> A general partner shall have all the rights and powers and be subject to all the restrictions and liabilities of a partner in a partnership without limited partners, except that without the written consent or ratification of the specific act by all the limited partners, a general partner or all of the general partners have no authority to:
>
> . . .
>
> 4. Possess partnership property, or assign their rights in specific partnership property, for other than a partnership purpose.

It was appellants' position that the articles of limited partnership that were signed by all the limited partners, including the appellees, gave the general partners the right to purchase the 25 acres. Article XVI(7) of the Articles of Limited Partnership states that the general partner may, without the consent of any limited partner,

> (7) acquire, hold and dispose of less than substantially all of the real property, interest therein, or appurtenance thereto, as well as personal or mixed property connected therewith, including the purchase, lease, development, improvement, maintenance, exchange, trade or sale of such properties at such price, rental or amount, for cash, securities or other property, and upon terms which the General Partner shall determine in its sole discretion.[1]

The record shows that by purchasing the 25 acres the general partners did not acquire substantially all the property of the partnership or the interest in real property in view of the interest owned by the partnership, as beneficiaries of the deed of trust involved in the sale of the mobile home park. See Dunlap Investors Ltd. v. Hogan, 133 Ariz. 130, 650 P.2d 432 (1982). The consent required by the statute can be found in the express provisions of a partnership agreement. See Mist Properties, Inc. v. Fitzsimmons Realty Co., 228 N.Y.S.2d 406 (N.Y.Sup.1962); Wasserman v. Wasserman, 7 Mass.App.Ct. 167, 386 N.E.2d 783 (1979). The rationale is stated in Wasserman v. Wasserman, supra:

---

[1] Appellees argue that paragraph 7 permits the general partner to acquire property for the partnership. However, that authority is granted by paragraph 3 of the agreement which states that the general partners may "from time to time purchase other lands as the General Partner, in his sole discretion, shall deem necessary or desirable for the conduct of the business of the Partnership."

> . . . in the absence of an express prohibition, the Act leaves the members of a limited partnership free to determine their rights with respect to each other by any contractual agreement which does not contravene public policy or run afoul of the common law. 228 N.Y.S.2d at 787.

Therefore, appellants had the right to purchase the 25 acres without the consent of any of the limited partners. However, this does not mean that the appellants' obligations toward the limited partners in regard to the property came to an end. A partner stands in a fiduciary relationship to his co-partner. Hurst v. Hurst, 1 Ariz.App. 603, 405 P.2d 913 (1965). . . . Here the appellants were obliged to pay fair market value for the 25 acres and not to conceal from their partners any facts in their possession which would bear upon the question of fair market value. Furthermore, appellants were obliged to reveal any other information regarding the purchase of this property which bore upon its value or the method they were utilizing to pay for it.

The record here discloses that appellants not only failed to advise the original appraiser as to the conditional zoning but that they accepted the use of his appraisal knowing that it was not based on current information. The subsequent letter informed the limited partners of the new zoning but the record does not disclose that appellants asked the appraiser to make a new appraisal before they resubmitted their proposal. These facts coupled with the great disparity of testimony between appellees' and appellants' witnesses on the issue of valuation, could justify a trier of fact in finding that appellants had not acted in good faith and breached their fiduciary duties in paying a price far below fair market value for the property.

. . .

Reversed and remanded for new trial.

ANALYSIS

1. **Waivable Duties.** The court holds that the general partners of a limited partnership owe fiduciary duties to the limited partners that, on the facts of this case, include a duty to disclose all material facts relating to the fair value of the property. A basic rule of contract law is that contracts entered into by a fiduciary that involve a breach of duty by the fiduciary are unenforceable as contrary to public policy. See Restatement (Second) of Contracts § 194. Should that rule extend to limited partnerships or should a limited partnership agreement that waives the fiduciary obligations of the general partner be enforceable?

2. **Contractual Language.** Assuming a limited partnership agreement could waive fiduciary duties, why didn't the contractual language permitting the general partners to acquire property, without the

consent of any limited partner, "upon terms which the General Partner shall determine in its sole discretion," constitute such a waiver?

3. **Permissible Waivers.** When are mandatory rules of business organization law appropriate, if ever?

4. **Ratification (I).** Note that the sale was approved by a majority of the limited partners. What effect should their approval of the sale have on the analysis, if any?

5. **Ratification (II).** In agency law, the retention of benefits from an unauthorized transaction generally constitutes a ratification of the transaction. Restatement (Third) of Agency § 4.01. Should not Jerman's acceptance of the limited partnership distribution, which apparently reflected the purchase price paid by the O'Learys, have constituted a ratification barring him from suit?

Sonet v. Plum Creek Timber Co., L.P.

24 Del.J.Corp.L. 771, 722 A.2d 319 (Del. Ch. 1998).

■ WILLIAM CHANDLER, CHANCELLOR.

This dispute arises out of a transaction in which a limited partnership organized under Delaware law seeks to convert itself into a real estate investment trust ("REIT"). The issue presented is this: . . . what controls the governance process in the context of limited partnerships—the partnership agreement or common law fiduciary duty doctrines? . . .

I. Background

> **NOTE**
>
> Publicly traded limited partnerships are relatively rare and confined mainly to the real estate and energy sectors. Under the Internal Revenue Code, a publicly traded limited partnership must receive at least 90% of its income from interest, dividends, real estate rents, gains from the sale or disposition of real property, commodities or commodity futures, and mineral, oil, or gas activities. Plum Creek Timber Co., LP, presumably was invested mainly in real estate, because it proposes to convert into a REIT by merging with a newly created trust.

Jerrold M. Sonet ("Plaintiff") is a holder of depository units ("Units") representing limited partnership interests in Plum Creek Timber Company, L.P., a Delaware limited partnership (the "Partnership"). The Partnership is registered with the Securities and Exchange Commission and the Units are publicly traded on the New York Stock Exchange. The Partnership and its corporate subsidiaries own, manage and operate approximately 2.4 million acres of timberland and twelve wood products conversion facilities in the Northwest and Southeast United States.

Defendant Plum Creek Management Company, L.P., a

Delaware limited partnership, is the general partner of the Partnership ("Management" or the "General Partner"). Defendant PC Advisory Corp. I, a Delaware corporation ("PC Advisory") (with the Partnership and Management, hereinafter referred to as "Defendants"), is the ultimate general partner of Management and, thus, might be considered the indirect general partner of the Partnership.

[Under] the limited partnership agreement (the "Partnership Agreement" or the "Agreement"), Management is required to make quarterly cash distributions of all "Available Cash," 98% of which goes to unitholders and 2% of which goes to Management. When the distribution of cash exceeds certain quarterly target levels, Management is entitled to receive an additional "incentive distribution" equal to a percentage of such excess, on a sliding scale which increases up to a maximum of 35% of distributions above the highest target level.

In June of 1998 the Partnership announced a plan to convert itself into a REIT by way of a merger with an entity specifically created for the purpose of conversion. Under the terms of that conversion Units would be converted into shares in the new REIT on a one-to-one basis. In addition, under the terms of the proposed conversion, in lieu of its 2% interest and its incentive distribution rights, Management would receive REIT shares equal to 27% of the total shares outstanding. The essence of Plaintiff's case is that the proposed allocation to Management of the new REIT is unfair and is the result of, among other things: 1) a self-dealing transaction between the General Partner and the Partnership; 2) improper manipulations of past distributions; 3) an attempt by PC Advisory to limit its exposure to upcoming losses; 4) unlawful entrenchment of PC Advisory and its principals, who will effectively control the new entity; and 5) manipulative timing of the transaction, which will shield unitholders from knowing of imminent losses caused by fundamental economic downturns. . . .

NOTE

A real estate investment trust (REIT) owns, and in many cases, operates commercial real estate. Under the tax laws, a REIT that distributes at least 90% of its taxable income to shareholders annually in the form of dividends, may deduct those dividends, from its income from its corporate income. This gives REITs a significant tax advantage over standard business corporations, for whom dividends are not deductible. This gives REITs a significant advantage over standard business corporations, for which dividends are not deductible.

. . .

III. Analysis

Delaware's limited partnership jurisprudence begins with the basic premise that, *unless limited by the partnership agreement,* the general partner has the fiduciary duty to manage the partnership in its interest and in the interests of the limited partners. That qualified statement necessarily marries common law fiduciary duties to contract theory when it comes to considering actions undertaken in the limited partnership context. Thus, I think it a correct statement of law that principles of contract preempt fiduciary principles where the parties to a limited partnership have made their intentions to do so plain.

For instance, in *Kahn v. Icahn,* this Court held that . . . "as a matter of statutory law, the traditional fiduciary duties among and between partners are defaults that may be modified by partnership agreements. This flexibility is precisely the reason why many choose the limited partnership form in Delaware." Delaware cases routinely uphold this view of limited partnership law. Those commentators who have addressed the subject at the deepest levels agree that the partnership form is particularly useful due to its contract theory-based structure.[8]

A. Limited Partnerships Generally

Limited partnerships have become the limited liability entity of choice for certain closely-held business ventures and are especially prevalent in enterprises where a general partner (or a corporate subsidiary) is actively engaged in investing the limited partners' passive investments. While originally used as a way of achieving preferential tax treatment, because of recent modifications to federal tax law, it is unclear that the limited partnership form provides significant tax benefits compared to other limited liability and so-called pass-through entities. Clearly some other relevant characteristic of the limited partnership must contribute to its increasing popularity. One might reasonably conclude that the statutory authority granted to limited partnerships to contract around—or to enhance—fiduciary duties goes a long way in explaining this popularity.

Although particularly well suited for closely-held businesses, limited partnerships have grown in popularity over the last forty years as publicly-traded entities (known as master limited partnerships) and are often designed to roll-up, or consolidate, a number of smaller limited

---

[8] See generally Frank H. Easterbrook & Daniel R. Fischel, The Economic Structure of Corporate Law 1–39 (1991); Henry N. Butler & Larry E. Ribstein, Opting Out of Fiduciary Duties: A Response to the Anti-Contractarians, 65 Wash. L.Rev. 1 (1990); Frank H. Easterbrook & Daniel R. Fischel, Contract and Fiduciary Duty, 36 J.L. & Econ. 425 (1993); Richard A. Epstein, Contract and Trust in Corporate Law: The Case of Corporate Opportunity, 21 Del. J. Corp. L. 1 (1996). For a contrary view, see Deborah A. DeMott, Beyond Metaphor: An Analysis of Fiduciary Obligation, 1988 Duke L.J. 879; Melvin Aron Eisenberg, The Limits of Cognition and the Limits of Contract, 47 Stan. L.Rev. 211 (1995); Lawrence E. Mitchell, The Death of Fiduciary Duty in Close Corporations, 138 U. Pa. L.Rev. 1675 (1990).

partnerships. If embodied in a security (*e.g.*, the Units in this case) which represents a transferable interest in the entity, limited partnership interests can become more liquid as a result of exchange listing, security registration, and more widely-known public information about a limited partnership. Such investment vehicles can greatly facilitate the accretion of capital for further expansion of a partnership's objectives.

. . . [T]he decision to adopt and operate under a particular limited liability structure is the sort of fundamental business decision that courts routinely protect. As a general matter, courts should be, and are, reluctant to import jurisprudence from one area of the law—which is loaded with notions of efficiency and fairness that are well developed for that particular context—into a separate area of the law—where many procedural and substantive aspects present in other legal regimes are only optional defaults. Mindful of that caution, I decline to rely unnecessarily on this Court's traditional analyses involving fiduciary duties in the corporate context. When a particular limited partnership has plainly opted out of the statutory default scheme, judicial review, in my opinion, must look to the limited partnership's distinct doctrinal foundation in contract theory. There is no reason, at least in the case before me, to depart from that source to further some highly generalized interest of equity.

In short, I think that under Delaware limited partnership law a claim of breach of fiduciary duty must first be analyzed in terms of the operative governing instrument—the partnership agreement—and only where that document is silent or ambiguous, or where principles of equity are implicated, will a Court begin to look for guidance from the statutory default rules, traditional notions of fiduciary duties, or other extrinsic evidence. In this case, my task is easy as I find that the partnership agreement in issue is clear on the threshold question of how the transaction in dispute should be governed.

B. The Partnership Agreement

The Agreement provides the General Partner with the discretion and power to manage virtually all of the affairs of the Partnership. To counterbalance the significant powers of the General Partner, the Agreement establishes an integrated framework of checks on that power. With respect to many of the day-to-day affairs of the Partnership, which are not subject to unitholder ratification, the General Partner's discretion is counterbalanced by the requirement that all of the General Partner's actions be fair and reasonable to the Partnership. With respect to certain extraordinary acts or transactions, such as mergers, the General Partner is given much broader latitude, namely "sole discretion." In the case of a merger in particular, however, the General Partner's sole discretion is checked by the Agreement's requirement that *a supermajority of unitholders (66 $^{2}/_{3}$ %) must approve the transaction.*

Plaintiff argues that under § 6.1 of the Agreement any merger proposed by the General Partner (*e.g.*, the merger used to effectuate the conversion to a REIT) must be fair and reasonable to the Partnership.[13] I understand Plaintiff to contend that since there is no language in § 6.1 that limits or expands the General Partner's discretion in the event of a merger, the fiduciary default rule that the terms of any transaction must be fair, reasonable, and aimed at furthering the interests of the partnership (and the limited partners) must apply. The problem with Plaintiff's argument is that it ignores the remainder of the Agreement. It also fails to recognize the rather practical problem of the impossibility of writing contract provisions that incorporate every bell and whistle all at once. As the following analysis shows, this Agreement is sufficient in communicating the intended governance structure. To understand that structure one needs to read the Agreement as a whole, and not just concentrate on one provision that mentions one of the "magic words."

The Agreement contemplates two fundamentally different types of managerial actions that may be taken: those that do not require unitholder approval and those that do. The requirement that the General Partner's action be "fair and reasonable" has no application where unitholder approval is required, such as with the proposed merger. Under the terms of § 6.9(a) of the Agreement, where unitholder approval is *not* required, *e.g.*, day-to-day management decisions of the Partnership, a requirement that the transaction be "fair and reasonable" is used as a surrogate check, in lieu of unitholder approval, on the General Partner's power. . . . In any event, pursuant to § 6(b) of the agreement, in situations where the General Partner is authorized to act according to its own discretion, there is no *requirement* that the General Partner consider the interests of the limited partners in resolution of a conflict of interest.

. . .

The procedures pursuant to which a merger may be effectuated are set forth under Article XVI of the Agreement, which is titled "Merger." Sections 16.2 and 16.3 provide the blueprint for proceeding with a merger transaction. First, the General Partner is permitted to enter into a

---

[13] Section 6.1 provides in relevant part:

> In addition to the powers now or hereafter granted a general partner of a limited partnership under applicable law or which are granted to the General Partners under any other provision of this Agreement, the General Partner . . . shall have full power and authority to do all things deemed necessary and desirable by it to conduct the business of the Partnership . . . including, without limitation, . . . (iii) the acquisition, disposition, mortgage, pledge, encumbrance, hypothecation or exchange of any assets of the Partnership or the merger or other combination of the Partnership with or into another entity (all of the foregoing subject to any prior approval which may be required by [66 2/3% of the outstanding Units, as provided by other sections in the agreement]).

Obviously, § 6.1 is simply a broad enabling provision that confers upon the General Partner the power and authority to manage the affairs of the Partnership.

merger in its sole discretion (*i.e.*, on the terms that the General Partner sees fit without required reference to the limited partners' interests). Second, the merger agreement is presented for a vote. Third, the merger agreement is approved upon receiving the endorsement of at least 66⅔% of the outstanding Units. This careful framework established by the Agreement confirms that to the extent that unitholders are unhappy with the proposed terms of the merger (and in this case the resultant conversion) their remedy is the ballot box, not the courthouse.

. . .

IV. Conclusion

The Partnership Agreement is clear and unambiguous. It provides that the General Partner can propose a merger on *any* terms, and that if the unitholders are displeased with those terms they are free to reject it. Since Plaintiff alleges only the mere potential for misleading disclosure, or only a possibility of disclosure that omits material information (*e.g.*, a change in the Partnership's underlying economic condition), I cannot entertain the claim that the proposed conversion is unfair or that its timing is manipulative. As Plaintiff has failed to state a claim upon which relief can be granted, the amended complaint is dismissed.

ANALYSIS

1. **Reconciling the Law.** Recall that in Jerman v. O'Leary, supra, the court held that the existence of a governing contract provision did "not mean that the appellants' obligations toward the limited partners in regard to the property came to an end. A partner stands in a fiduciary relationship to his co-partner. . . . Here the appellants were obliged to pay fair market value for the 25 acres and not to conceal from their partners any facts in their possession which would bear upon the question of fair market value."

   An alternative approach to the problem is taken in Section 105 of the Uniform Limited Partnership Act (2001), which provides, in pertinent part:

   > (a) Except as otherwise provided in subsection (c) and (d), the partnership agreement governs:
   >
   > > (1) relations among the partners and between the partners and the partnership.
   >
   > . . .
   >
   > (c) A partnership agreement may not:
   >
   > > . . .
   > >
   > > (6) alter or eliminate the duty of loyalty or the duty of care except as otherwise provided in subsection (d);

(d) . . .

(1) The partnership agreement may:

(A) specify the method by which a specific act or transaction that would otherwise violate the duty of loyalty may be authorized or ratified by one or more disinterested and independent persons after full disclosure of all material facts;

. . .

(2) If not manifestly unreasonable, the partnership agreement may:

. . .

(B) identify specific types or categories of activities that do not violate the duty of loyalty;

(C) alter the duty of care, but may not authorize conduct involving bad faith, willful or intentional misconduct, or knowing violation of law; and

(D) alter or eliminate any other fiduciary duty.

As a matter of sound policy, which of the three approaches—*Jerman, Sonet,* or the Uniform Act—seems preferable?

2. **Chandler's Approach.** How would Delaware Chancellor Chandler, who wrote the opinion in *Sonet,* likely have decided *Jerman*? In particular, consider whether the following language from the contract at issue in *Jerman* presents the situation Chancellor Chandler identified as a "document is silent or ambiguous, or where principles of equity are implicated, will a Court begin to look for guidance from the statutory default rules, traditional notions of fiduciary duties, or other extrinsic evidence":

> Article XVI(7) of the Articles of Limited Partnership states that the general partner may, without the consent of any limited partner,
>
> (7) acquire, hold and dispose of less than substantially all of the real property, interest therein, or appurtenance thereto, as well as personal or mixed property connected therewith, including the purchase, lease, development, improvement, maintenance, exchange, trade or sale of such properties at such price, rental or amount, for cash, securities or other property, and upon terms which the General Partner shall determine in its sole discretion.

3. **Traditional Notions.** Chancellor Chandler states that a court may look to "traditional notions of fiduciary duties" where "principles of equity are implicated." Can you give an example of such a case?

Cincinnati SMSA L.P. v. Cincinnati Bell Cellular Systems Co.

708 A.2d 989 (Del. 1998).

. . .

Facts

. . .

Cincinnati SMSA Limited Partnership is a Delaware Limited Partnership ("the Limited Partnership") formed in 1982 for the purpose of providing "Cellular Service" to Cincinnati, Columbus and Dayton, Ohio. Cincinnati Bell Cellular Systems Company ("Cincinnati Bell") is a limited partner.

When it was formed, the Limited Partnership was one of a number of partnerships around the country comprised of AT&T affiliates and other regional telephone companies. In response to the advent of cellular telecommunication service, the Federal Communications Commission ("FCC") divided the United States into separate market regions for licensing purposes. Urban market regions are called Standard Metropolitan Statistical Areas ("SMSAs"). Within each SMSA, the FCC authorizes the grant of two cellular service licenses—one to a wireline telephone company (the "B side license") and the other to any entity other than a telephone company (the "A side license").

Through their cellular service affiliates, the wireline telephone companies for Cincinnati, Columbus and Dayton agreed to pursue the B side license for all three areas as one entity—the Limited Partnership. At the center of the parties' dispute in this case are three provisions contained in the Limited Partnership Agreement ("the Agreement").

Section 10.4 of the Agreement contains a noncompete provision, which reads as follows:

> [S]hould any Limited Partner or an Affiliate thereof desire to provide Cellular Service in areas within the [Limited Partnership's] SMSAs, but not through the Partnership, then such Limited Partner . . . shall withdraw from the Partnership . . . . In no event shall any such Limited Partner or its Affiliate thereof directly or indirectly own, operate, or engage in any business rendering Cellular Service in the [Limited Partnership's] SMSAs within five years after the withdrawal of such Limited Partner . . . from the Partnership . . . .

Under Section 2.4 of the Agreement, "Cellular Service" is defined as:

> Any and all service authorized by the FCC under Part 22 of its cellular rules as promulgated under the Cellular Radio

> Decisions and provided pursuant to the terms of this Agreement.

Aside from Cellular Service, the Agreement allows partners to pursue independent interests under the following provision in Section 7.4:

> *Ownership or Conduct of Other Businesses.* Subject to the provisions of [Section 10.4], the Partners may engage in or possess an interest in other business ventures of every kind and description. Neither the Partnership nor any Partner shall have any rights by virtue of this Agreement in such independent business ventures or to the income or profits therefrom.

In the 1990s, the FCC began licensing a new band of radio stations for a type of mobile telephone service called Personal Communications Services ("PCS"). PCS is regulated under Part 24 of the FCC regulations.[3] In January 1997, Cincinnati Bell obtained a license to provide PCS and entered into an agreement to resell PCS offered by another provider.

. . .

Analysis

. . .

Delaware observes the well-established general principle that (absent grounds for reformation which are not present here) it is not the proper role of a court to rewrite or supply omitted provisions to a written agreement. In cases where obligations can be understood from the text of a written agreement but have nevertheless been omitted in the literal sense, a court's inquiry should focus on "what the parties likely would have done if they had considered the issue involved." In the narrow context governed by principles of good faith and fair dealing, this Court has recognized the occasional necessity of implying such terms in an agreement so as to honor the parties' reasonable expectations. But those cases should be rare and fact-intensive, turning on issues of compelling fairness.

The articulation of the standard for implying terms through application of the covenant of good faith and fair dealing represents an evolution from previous Delaware case law. In *Katz v. Oak Industries, Inc.,* the Court of Chancery stated that the legal test for implying contractual obligations was whether it was "*clear* from what was expressly agreed upon that the parties who negotiated the express terms of the contract would have agreed to proscribe the act later complained

---

[3] Whereas the cellular radiotelephone service governed by Part 22 of the FCC's regulations and designated in the Agreement uses radio bandwidths between both 825–845 MHz and 870–890 MHz, PCS uses the bandwidth between 1850–1990 MHz.

of as a breach of the implied covenant of good faith—had they thought to negotiate with respect to that matter."[11]

Delaware Supreme Court jurisprudence is developing along the general approach that implying obligations based on the covenant of good faith and fair dealing is a cautious enterprise. . . .

. . . In this case, the plaintiff articulates a policy argument, which is cogent at first blush, in support of implying an additional noncompete obligation with respect to PCS. The Limited Partnership sets forth two circumstances underlying its case: (1) the development and licensing of PCS was unforseen at the time the parties entered into the Agreement; and (2) from a subscriber's perspective, PCS and "Cellular Service" are indistinguishable.[18] The Limited Partnership concludes that, based on principles of good faith and fair dealing, partners are also forbidden to compete with the Limited Partnership through independent interests in PCS, even though PCS does not fall within the strict definition of "Cellular Service" in the Agreement. Cogent as this argument might have been *ex ante* when the Agreement was negotiated, it is not a persuasive argument to vary the Agreement *ex post*.

The unambiguous terms of the Agreement ultimately defeat the plaintiff's case. Section 2.4 defines "Cellular Service" in precise terms. Its meaning is confined to that service authorized by a discrete FCC regulation without room to include developing systems. On the other hand, Section 7.4 provides unambiguously and expansively that, so long as "Cellular Service" is not involved, partners "may engage in or possess an interest in other business ventures of every kind and description." Taken together, these provisions explicitly limit prohibited competition and provide generous leeway to partners with respect to other ventures. We are not compelled to conclude that, had they thought to address the subject, the partners more likely than not would have agreed to include PCS—which operates on different radio bandwidths than "Cellular Service" and is separately regulated by the FCC—in the Agreement's noncompete clause.

Further, the Court of Chancery's decision does not violate rules of contract construction. The Court's reading of the Agreement does not render ineffective the provisions in the Agreement. So long as partners are forbidden from competing with the Limited Partnership through "Cellular Service," declining to imply an additional obligation in the

[11] [Del.Ch., 508 A.2d 873, 880 (1986) (emphasis added)]; but see Schwartzberg, 685 A.2d at 376 (Katz standard may be "too high"). We need not, however, address in the abstract these general observations by the Court of Chancery because these issues are inherently fact-intensive.

[18] Like the mobile telephone service regulated by Part 22 of the FCC regulations, PCS operates through radio waves. When it first emerged as a competitor in the wireless service arena, however, PCS offered enhanced features such as paging, voice mail and caller ID that were not generally available with Cellular Service at the time.

noncompete provision does not render the restrictions in Section 10.4 "commercially meaningless or illusory," as contended by the Limited Partnership. Similarly, the fact that the Court of Chancery's strict reading of an unambiguous agreement is undesirable to the Limited Partnership does not make that reading unreasonable or arbitrary.

Conclusion

After reviewing the unambiguous terms of the Agreement, we conclude that, regardless of any set of facts that may be inferred from the pleadings, no restriction on the partners' independent ability to offer PCS service may be implied. Accordingly, we affirm the decision of the Court of Chancery.

ANALYSIS

1. **Implied Covenants.** Recall that in Sonet v. Timber Co., L.P., supra, Delaware Chancellor Chandler stated that where a "document is silent or ambiguous" a court may "begin to look for guidance from the statutory default rules, traditional notions of fiduciary duties, or other extrinsic evidence." In this case, the Delaware Supreme Court considered the implied covenant of good faith rather than "traditional notions of fiduciary duties."

   In Continental Ins. Co. v. Rutledge & Co., Inc., 750 A.2d 1219, 1234 (Del.Ch. 2000), the court stated:

   > The implied covenant of good faith "requires a party in a contractual relationship to refrain from arbitrary or unreasonable conduct which has the effect of preventing the other party to the contract from receiving the fruits of the contract." This doctrine emphasizes "faithfulness to an agreed common purpose and consistency with the justified expectations of the other party." The parties' reasonable expectations at the time of contract formation determine the reasonableness of the challenged conduct. I note that cases invoking the implied covenant of good faith and fair dealing should be rare and fact-intensive. Only where issues of compelling fairness arise will this Court embrace good faith and fair dealing and imply terms in an agreement.

   Why did the Supreme Court look to the implied covenant of good faith in *Cincinnati SMSA* rather than "traditional notions of fiduciary duties"? Conversely, why didn't Chancellor Chandler consider applying the implied covenant in *Sonet*?

2. **Potential Unstated Terms.** The Delaware Supreme Court rejected plaintiff's argument "that, had they thought to address the subject, the partners more likely than not would have agreed to include PCS . . . in the Agreement's noncompete clause." What do you think the partners would have done if they had "thought to address the subject"?

3. **Implied Covenants.** Why do the courts emphasize that they will only rarely use the implied covenant of good faith to fill gaps in an agreement?

4. **Contractual Alternative.** You are general counsel to Cincinnati SMSA Limited Partnership. The general partner wishes to amend the noncompete clause so as to prevent the limited partners from competing with Cincinnati SMSA using any technology developed in the future that competes with or complements the cellular phone technology currently covered by the noncompete provision. Rewrite the noncompete provision.

In re: El Paso Pipeline Partners, L.P. Derivative Litigation

2014 WL 2768782 (Del. Ch.).

. . .

I. FACTUAL BACKGROUND

. . .

A. The Partnership Structure

El Paso MLP is a Delaware limited partnership headquartered in Houston, Texas. El Paso MLP operates as a master limited partnership ("MLP"), a term that refers to a publicly traded limited partnership that is treated as a pass-through entity for federal income tax purposes. El Paso MLP owns interests in companies that operate natural gas pipelines, liquid natural gas ("LNG") terminals, and storage facilities throughout the United States. Its common units trade on the New York Stock Exchange under the symbol "EPB."

MLPs that focus on transporting and storing oil and natural gas, like El Paso MLP, are commonly referred to as midstream MLPs. Midstream MLPs are typically "sponsored" by a corporation with MLP-qualifying assets that generate stable cash flows. The sponsor seeks to maximize the market value of those assets by selling them to an MLP that can issue publicly traded securities on the strength of the cash flows and distribute the cash periodically to investors in a tax-efficient manner. In the typical structure, the sponsor owns 100% of the general partner of the MLP, giving the sponsor control over the MLP. The sponsor initially contributes a block of assets to the MLP and, over time, sells additional assets to the MLP. Because the assets move from the sponsor level down to the MLP level, the sales are referred to colloquially as "drop-downs."

In August 2007, El Paso Corporation ("El Paso Parent") formed El Paso MLP and contributed to El Paso MLP an initial set of MLP-qualifying assets. On November 15, El Paso MLP announced an initial public offering of 25,000,000 common units. The IPO prospectus cautioned that El Paso Parent would have no obligation to drop down additional assets into El Paso MLP. Despite this disclosure, El Paso Parent was plainly creating a sponsored MLP, implying that El Paso MLP over time would acquire assets from El Paso Parent.

Consistent with the typical MLP structure, El Paso Parent indirectly owns 100% of defendant El Paso Pipeline GP Company, L.L.C., . . . the general partner of El Paso MLP (the "General Partner"). The General Partner in turn owns a 2% general partner interest in El Paso MLP. By virtue of the general partner interest, El Paso Parent has a 2% economic interest in El Paso MLP and, more importantly, exercises control over El Paso MLP. . . . As is customary with sponsored MLPs, El Paso MLP has no employees of its own. Employees of El Paso Parent manage and operate El Paso MLP's business.

At the time of the March 2010 transaction, defendants Douglas L. Foshee, James C. Yardley, John R. Suit, D. Mark Leland, Ronald L. Kuehn, William A. Smith, and Arthur C. Reichstetter (together, the "Individual Defendants") constituted the board of directors of the General Partner (the "GP Board"). Four of the Individual Defendants [Foshee, Yardley, Suit, and Leland] held [all the top] management positions with El Paso Parent or the General Partner. . . . Each of the management directors beneficially owned equity stakes in El Paso Parent that dwarfed their equity stakes in El Paso MLP.

The other three members of the GP Board [Kuehn, Smith, and Reichstetter] were outside directors, although two had past ties to El Paso Parent. Kuehn was Interim CEO of El Paso Parent in 2003 and served as Chairman of the Board of El Paso Parent from 2003 until 2009, one year before the challenged transaction occurred. Smith was an Executive Vice President of El Paso Parent and Chairman of El Paso Merchant Energy's Global Gas Group until 2002. Reichstetter was the only director without past ties to El Paso Parent.

. . .

B. The Drop-Down Proposal

On February 9, 2010, El Paso Parent offered to sell to El Paso MLP . . . interests in Southern LNG and Elba Express . . . for . . . $1,053 billion. This decision refers to El Paso MLP's eventual purchase of . . . Southern LNG and Elba Express as the "Drop-Down."

Southern LNG owned an LNG terminal on Elba Island, a private 840-acre island off the coast of Georgia. Elba Express owned a 190-mile natural gas pipeline that connected the Elba Island terminal to four major interstate natural gas pipelines. . . .

By 2010, when El Paso Parent proposed the Drop-Down, domestic discoveries of shale gas and improved techniques for its extraction had led to higher levels of domestic production and lower gas prices. As a result, the market for imported LNG had weakened. Demand at the Elba Island facility fell to less than 10% of capacity. . . . At the time, the principal sources of revenue for Southern LNG and Elba Express were existing contracts with subsidiaries of Shell and British Gas (the "Service Agreements"). Under the Service Agreements, the subsidiaries had reserved 100% of the firm capacity of the Elba Island terminal and the Elba Express pipeline, guaranteeing that Shell and British Gas would have the capacity to transport or store gas at any time for a set charge. Because the Service Agreements were firm contracts, Southern LNG and Elba Express would charge fees to Shell and British Gas regardless of whether they actually stored or transported gas. The Service Agreements had terms of 25 to 30 years.

Despite their lengthy terms and firm pricing, the Service Agreements were not sure things. The Shell and British Gas counterparties were special purpose entities with no assets of their own. If the Service Agreements became sufficiently unprofitable, then Shell and British Gas could walk away from their subsidiaries, leaving Southern LNG and Elba Express to collect from judgment-proof shells. . . .

The plaintiffs believe that because of the weakened domestic market for imported LNG, El Paso Parent faced a significant risk that Shell and British Gas would choose to breach the Service Agreements, leaving Southern LNG and Elba Express with less than 20% of their anticipated revenue. The plaintiffs argue that through the Drop-Down, El Paso Parent sought to off-load these now-risky assets onto El Paso MLP at an inflated price.

C. The Conflicts Committee

Because El Paso Parent controlled El Paso MLP through the General Partner, and because El Paso Parent owned the assets that El Paso MLP would be acquiring, the Drop-Down created a conflict of interest for the General Partner. El Paso MLP's limited partnership agreement (the "LP Agreement" or "LPA") contemplated that El Paso MLP could proceed with a transaction that presented a conflict of interest for the General Partner . . . if the conflict-of-interest transaction received "Special Approval." The LP Agreement defined this form of approval as "approval by a majority of the members of the Conflicts Committee acting in good faith." LPA § 1.1. The LP Agreement in turn defined the Conflicts Committee as

> a committee of the Board of Directors of the General Partner composed of two or more directors, each of whom (a) is not a security holder, officer or employee of the General Partner, (b) is not an officer, director or employee of any Affiliate of the

> General Partner, (c) is not a holder of any ownership interest in the Partnership Group other than Common Units and awards that may be granted to such director under the Long Term Incentive Plan and (d) meets the independence standards required of directors who serve on an audit committee of a board of directors established by the Securities Exchange Act and the rules and regulations of the Commission thereunder and by the National Securities Exchange on which the Common Units are listed or admitted to trading.

Id.

At El Paso MLP, the Conflicts Committee was not a standing committee of the GP Board, but rather a committee constituted on an ad hoc basis to consider specific conflict-of-interest transactions. On February 12, 2010, the GP Board resolved to seek Special Approval for the Drop-Down. . . .

The resolution granted the Conflicts Committee, for the period of existence, the power and authority

> to evaluate and assess whether the [Drop-Down] is fair and reasonable to the Partnership and, if the Conflicts Committee so determines, (a) to approve the [Drop-Down] as provided by Section 7.9(a) of the Limited Partnership Agreement and (b) to make a recommendation to the [GP] Board whether or not to approve such terms and conditions of the [Drop-Down].
>
> . . .

The resolution named [the outside directors] Reichstetter, Kuehn, and Smith as the members of the committee. . . . At some point, the committee retained Akin Gump Strauss Hauer & Feld LLP ("Akin Gump") as its legal advisor and Tudor, Pickering, Holt & Co. ("Tudor") as its financial advisor. The engagements appear to have happened as a matter of course before the Conflicts Committee ever formally met.

As suggested by the ready hiring of Akin Gump and Tudor, the record reflects that El Paso Parent, the GP Board, and the individuals who served on the Conflicts Committee have developed a level of comfort with the Special Approval process:

- Between 2008 and 2012, El Paso Parent and El Paso MLP engaged in eight drop-down transactions. . . .
- El Paso Parent initiated each transaction. El Paso MLP never initiated a transaction.
- On each occasion, the General Partner opted to proceed by Special Approval and formed a Conflicts Committee.

- On each occasion, the members of the Conflicts Committee were Kuehn, Smith, and Reichstetter. . . .
- On each occasion, the committee hired Tudor as its financial advisor.
- On each occasion, the Conflicts Committee obtained some marginal improvement in the terms of El Paso Parent's original proposal.
- On each occasion, Tudor opined that the resulting deal was fair and collected a $500,000 fee plus expenses.

The Special Approval process for the Drop-Down fit this pattern.

D. Special Approval Is Granted

Over the course of the next month and a half, the Conflicts Committee met five times to review El Paso Parent's proposal. . . . El Paso Parent management gave Tudor a fifty-four page presentation that provided an overview of the proposed transaction and Southern LNG's and Elba Express's assets, including a summary of the Service Agreements. . . .

After the meeting on March 2, 2010, Reichstetter met with representatives of El Paso Parent to negotiate the transaction price. After some limited back and forth, they agreed upon consideration of $963 million,. . . .

On March 24, 2010, the Conflicts Committee met for the fifth and final time. . . . Tudor opined that the proposed transaction was "fair, from a financial point of view, to the holders of the Common Units of [El Paso MLP], other than [the General Partner] and its affiliates." The Conflicts Committee then unanimously approved resolutions recommending that El Paso MLP enter into the Drop-Down. . . .

E. El Paso Parent Declines To Exercise [An Option To Buy Other LNG Assets]

Unbeknownst to the Conflicts Committee, at the same time that El Paso Parent was proposing to sell LNG assets to El Paso MLP and touting their value, El Paso Parent was [declining to exercise its option] to buy LNG assets for itself [at a price that reflected] an EBITDA multiple of 9.1x . . .

During the negotiation of the Drop-Down, the Conflicts Committee did not know about [this] transaction . . . .

> **NOTE**
>
> EBITDA stands for annual Earnings Before Interest Taxes Depreciation and Amortization. In essence it is a measure of the annual net cash flow from an asset, independent of taxes and financing cost. EBITDA can be used in a number of ways to arrive at the value of the asset. One common, though crude, method is to multiply EBITDA by some widely accepted multiplier, which may vary, among other considerations, with the riskiness of the asset. For example, it the EBITDA (cash flow) of an asset is $10,000 and the appropriate multiplier for similar assets is 9, the value is $90,000. An asset with the same EBITDA but with greater risk would have a lower multiplier—say, 7, which would generate a value of $70,000. There is, of course, considerable uncertainty—one might say guesswork—in estimates of future EBITDA and in the choice of the appropriate multiplier.

According to the plaintiffs, the fact that El Paso Parent decided not to acquire an LNG asset at a lower implied EBITDA multiple while at the same time selling its own LNG assets to El Paso MLP for a higher implied EBITDA multiple was highly material information that should have been provided to the Conflicts Committee. The plaintiffs contend that the Gulf LNG deal illustrated arm's-length pricing for a comparable LNG asset, such that the Conflicts Committee's decision to buy a similar LNG asset at a significantly higher implied EBITDA multiple gives rise to an inference of bad faith. . . .

II. LEGAL ANALYSIS

. . .

A. Breach of the Express Terms of the LP Agreement

. . .

2. The Operative Contractual Framework

. . . Section 7.9(e) of the LP Agreement eliminates all common law duties that the General Partner and the Individual Defendants might otherwise owe to El Paso MLP and its limited partners, including fiduciary duties. The LP Agreement replaces those duties with contractual commitments. . . .

Under Section 7.9(a), if the General Partner takes action in its capacity as the General Partner, and the action involves a conflict of interest, then the action will be "permitted and deemed approved by all Partners" and "not constitute a breach" of the LP Agreement or "any duty stated or implied by law or equity" as long as the [action is (among other possibilities)] "approved by Special Approval." . . .

The LP Agreement defines Special Approval as "approval by a majority of the members of the Conflicts Committee acting in good faith." LPA § 1.1. The LP Agreement [further provides]:

> Whenever the Conflicts Committee makes a determination or takes or declines to take any other action, it shall make such

> determinations or take or decline to take such other action in good faith and shall not be subject to any other or different standards (including fiduciary standards).... In order for a determination or other action to be in "good faith" for purposes of this Agreement, the Person or Persons making such determination or taking or declining to take such other action must believe that the determination or other action is in the best interests of the Partnership.

Id. § 7.9(b).

Under Delaware law, the standard for good faith that applies to the Conflicts Committee requires a subjective belief that the determination or other action is in the best interests of El Paso MLP. . . .

3. The Application of the Subjective Good Faith Standard

Under the subjective good faith standard, "the ultimate inquiry must focus on the subjective belief of the specific directors accused of wrongful conduct." [Allen v.] Encore Energy [P'rs, P.P.], 72 A.3d [93], 107 [(Del. 2013)]. The Delaware Supreme Court has admonished that when applying the subjective belief standard, "[t]rial judges should avoid replacing the actual directors with hypothetical reasonable people." Id. Nevertheless, because science has not yet developed a reliable method of reading minds, objective facts are logically and legally relevant to the extent they permit an inference that the defendants lacked the necessary subjective belief. Id. The high court has provided illustrations of this concept:

> Some actions may objectively be so egregiously unreasonable . . . that they "seem[ ] essentially inexplicable on any ground other than [subjective] bad faith." It may also be reasonable to infer subjective bad faith in less egregious transactions when a plaintiff alleges objective facts indicating that a transaction was not in the best interests of the partnership and that the directors knew of those facts. Therefore, objective factors may inform an analysis of a defendant's subjective belief to the extent they bear on the defendant's credibility when asserting that belief. . . .

Id.

. . .

In this case, the plaintiffs contend that the members of the Conflicts Committee failed to appreciate how easy it would be for Shell and British Gas to walk away from the Service Agreements, that Shell and British Gas would have a significant economic incentive to do so given the weakness in the domestic gas market, and that the value of the projected revenue under the Service Agreements had to be discounted significantly in light of that risk. The plaintiffs also fault the Special Committee for failing to take into account the fact that on February 9, 2010, the same day El Paso Parent made its initial proposal to sell LNG assets to El Paso MLP at a multiple of 12.2x EBITDA, El Paso Parent was analyzing and later decided not to exercise a right to purchase a 30% interest in Gulf LNG at 9.1x EBITDA. As additional evidence of the Conflicts Committee's bad faith, the plaintiffs cite an email Kuehn sent early in the process in which he suggested an EBITDA multiple well below where the Conflicts Committee began negotiating and ultimately ended up. The plaintiffs also rely on two expert reports.

a. The Service Agreements

The plaintiffs focus primarily on the risk that Shell and British Gas would walk away from the Service Agreements.... The plaintiffs ... have introduced evidence establishing that the contractual counterparties to the Service Agreements were corporate shells and that only 17% of the projected revenue from the Service Agreements was guaranteed by entities with meaningful assets. Despite these limitations, the Conflicts Committee and Tudor valued the Service Agreements based on 100% of their projected revenue, without any discounting for the risk of breach.

The record establishes that there is no genuine dispute about whether the Conflicts Committee understood the state of the natural gas market. The members of the Conflicts Committee had extensive experience in the energy industry, and they received presentations about the condition of the natural gas market.

. . .

... Contrary to the plaintiffs' position, the record evidence establishes that the Conflicts Committee considered the revenue risk. Unlike the plaintiffs, the members of the Conflicts Committee believed that the guarantees were meaningful and that even if the guarantees covered only a portion of the Service Agreements' revenue, neither Shell nor British Gas would default. The Conflicts Committee saw little to no risk in the agreements because of El Paso MLP's ongoing relationships with Shell and British Gas, the interests that Shell and British Gas have in maintaining the availability of shipping and storage capacity, and the importance to Shell and British Gas of having a reputation for fulfilling their contracts.

What the plaintiffs really dispute is the weight the Conflicts Committee should have given to risks that both the Conflicts Committee and the plaintiffs identified. Reasonable minds could disagree about the judgment made by the Conflicts Committee, but the Conflicts Committee's judgment was not so extreme that it could support a potential finding of bad faith, nor was the committee's process sufficiently egregious to support such an inference....

b. El Paso Parent's Decision Not to Invest In Gulf LNG

. . .

The plaintiffs contend that El Paso Parent's decision not to acquire an LNG asset at a 9.1x EBITDA multiple while at the same time proposing to sell its own LNG assets to El Paso MLP at a 12.2x EBITDA multiple supports an inference that the Drop-Down was approved in bad faith. The plaintiffs first argue that because El Paso Parent concealed information from the Conflicts Committee, Special Approval for the Drop-Down was not properly obtained. But the subjective good faith of the members of the Conflicts Committee cannot be challenged based on information that the plaintiffs admit the members did not have. The contractual language of the Special Approval provision turns only on the subjective good faith of the Conflicts Committee. It does not address whether Special Approval is valid if the General Partner withholds information from the Conflicts Committee. That gap in the LP Agreement must be filled, if necessary, by the implied covenant of good faith and fair dealing.

NOTE

Several Delaware MLP decisions subsequent, and similar, to *El Paso Partners* have endorsed the notion that the language of the partnership agreement is to be respected and rejected invocation of fiduciary duty and the implied covenant of good faith and fair dealing. What, never? Well, hardly ever. In Dieckman v. Regency GP LP, 155 A.3d 358, the Delaware Supreme Court invoked the implied covenant in the special circumstances of the case in holding that approval of a conflicted transaction by a majority of the independent unitholders was insufficient to protect the transaction from attack. The language of the partnership agreement in the case disavowed fiduciary obligation, provided that approval by a majority of the independent unitholders was determinative, and relieved the general partner of any obligation to provide information about the transaction beyond its terms. However, the general partner in fact issued a proxy statement with allegedly misleading information. The court cited § 17-1101(d) of the Delaware limited partnership law, which expressly provides "that the partnership agreement may not eliminate the implied contractual covenant of good faith and fair dealing," and offered this common-sense observation (citations omitted):

> We find that implied in the language of the LP Agreement's conflict resolution provision is a requirement that the General Partner not act to undermine the protections afforded unitholders in the safe harbor process.

Partnership agreement drafters, whether drafting on their own, or sitting across the table in a competitive negotiation, do not include obvious and provocative conditions in an agreement like "the General Partner will not mislead unitholders when seeking Unaffiliated Unitholder Approval" or "the General Partner will not subvert the Special Approval process by appointing conflicted members to the Conflicts Committee." But the terms are easily implied because "the parties must have intended them and have only failed to express them because they are too obvious to need expression." Stated another way, "some aspects of the deal are so obvious to the participants that they never think, or see no need, to address them."

. . .

If the Conflicts Committee or its advisors knew about the Gulf LNG data point contemporaneously with the Drop-Down, then the pricing disparity might be sufficient to support an inference of bad faith when evaluated under the current procedural standard. Such a ruling would not mean that the defendants would lose and be held liable, only that a trial would be necessary to resolve a disputed question of fact as to their intent. In this case, however, the plaintiffs admit that the Conflicts Committee did not know about the Gulf LNG data point for purposes of the Drop-Down. That concession is dispositive.

. . .

e. Summary Judgment on Count I For the Drop-Down

. . . Summary judgment is therefore granted in favor of the General Partner, as well as the other defendants, . . . as to the claim that the Drop-Down violated the express requirements of the LP Agreement.

B. Breach Of The Implied Terms Of The LP Agreement

In addition to contending that the defendants breached their express contractual obligations under the LP Agreement, Count I of the First Complaint asserts that the defendants violated unwritten obligations supplied by the implied covenant of good faith and fair dealing. Because a claim for breach of the implied covenant of good faith and fair dealing is a claim for breach of contract, the General Partner is the only defendant potentially liable on this claim. [The court observes that the Limited Partnership Agreement does not expressly eliminate a good faith obligation of El Paso Parent to offer information, and that, consequently, the role of the court is to determine what the parties would have agreed to if they had addressed the issue. In this case, the court concludes, various terms of the actual Agreement suggest that had the parties addressed the issue, no such obligation would have been imposed. Thus, the court grants summary judgment to the defendants.]

ANALYSIS

1. **A Bad Investment?** Given the inherent conflict in the sale of assets from El Paso Parent to El Paso MLP, why would anyone invest in El Paso MLP?

2. **Nature of the Legal Relationship.** The court recognizes that the failure of El Paso Parent to purchase LNG assets at 9.1x EBITDA while selling similar assets to El Paso MLP at 12.2x EBITDA may have been relevant to the conflicts committee but that Parent had no obligation to offer that information to the committee. What does this tell you about the legal relationship between Parent and MLP?

3. **Deal Points.** Among the key "deal points" in any transaction are control (who's in charge and with what constraints?), returns (who gets what?), and duration (how long does it last and how can it be ended?). In this El Paso transaction, what are the terms as to each of these elements? How might the limited partners want to change these terms?

NOTE ON SUBSEQUENT RELATED DECISIONS

The plaintiffs in this case complained of two separate "dropdown" sales of assets by El Paso Parent (later acquired by Kinder Morgan) to El Paso MLP in 2010. In the "Spring Dropdown" Parent sold 51 percent of its Elba subsidiary to MLP, while in the "Fall Dropdown" Parent sold MLP the remaining 49 percent. In the 2014 decision presented here the court granted the defendants' motion for summary judgment with respect to the Spring Dropdown and dismissed that part of the case. The claim based on the Fall Dropdown went to trial, which resulted in a decision in April 2015 (2015 WL 1815846) in which the plaintiffs prevailed. In the following passage, the court summarized its lengthy, detailed discussion of the facts:

> I expected that at trial, the Committee members and their financial advisor would provide a credible account of how they evaluated the Fall Dropdown, negotiated with Parent, and ultimately determined that the transaction was in the best interests of El Paso MLP. It turned out that in most instances, the Committee members and their financial advisor had no explanation for what they did. The few explanations they had were conclusory or contradicted by contemporaneous documents. . . . The evidence at trial ultimately convinced me that when approving the Fall Dropdown, the Committee members went against their better judgment and did what Parent wanted, assisted by a financial advisor that presented each dropdown in the best possible light, regardless of whether the depictions conflicted with the advisor's work on similar transactions or made sense as a matter of valuation theory.
>
> This post-trial decision finds that the Committee members failed to form a subjective belief that the Fall Dropdown was in the best interests of El Paso MLP. The General Partner therefore breached

> the LP Agreement by causing El Paso MLP to engage in the Fall Dropdown.

There was, however, need for one more Chancery Court decision to resolve the dispute. In 2014, Kinder Morgan acquired ownership the portion of El Paso MLP that it did not already own and moved to dismiss on the ground that as a result of the acquisition it was in effect suing itself. This led to another opinion, in which the court—having observed that dismissal "would generate a windfall for [Kinder Morgan] at the expense of the [plaintiff] limited partners"—examined at considerable length doctrines (among others) relating to "direct" actions and "derivative" actions (see Chapter 5, Sec. 3). In the end the court found its way out of the legal tangle and denied the motion to dismiss. 2015 WL 7758609.

NOTE ON CONTRACTUAL NATURE OF PARTNERSHIPS

In The Haynes Family Trust v. Kinder Morgan G.P., Inc., 135 A.3d 76 (Del. 2016), the Delaware Supreme Court, in affirming a Chancery Court decision, had this to say about the contractual nature of partnership law (footnotes omitted):

> On appeal, the unitholders reiterate the arguments made below, which largely rest on their contention that they ought to be able to litigate this case as if they were investors in a corporation, whose directors had the traditional duties of loyalty and care. But, the unitholders were investors in a limited partnership under a statute that permits limited partnership agreements to eliminate fiduciary duties and restrict investors to relying upon the agreement's terms for protection. As we and the Court of Chancery have long noted, investors in these agreements must be careful to read those agreements and to understand the limitations on their rights. Here, the Court of Chancery properly held that there was no room for a substantive judicial review of the fairness of the transaction, because the general partner had complied with its contractual duties . . . and that compliance conclusively established the fairness of the transaction, precluding the judicial scrutiny that the unitholders now seek.
>
> . . . This case therefore stands as another reminder that with the benefits of investing in alternative entities often comes the limitation of looking to the contract as the exclusive source of protective rights.

9. APPENDICES

UNIFORM PARTNERSHIP ACT (1914)

Sec.		Page
§ 1.	Name of Act	418
§ 2.	Definition of Terms	418
§ 3.	Interpretation of Knowledge and Notice	418
§ 6.	Partnership Defined	418
§ 7.	Rules for Determining the Existence of a Partnership	419
§ 8.	Partnership Property	419
§ 9.	Partner Agent of Partnership as to Partnership Business	419
§ 10.	Conveyance of Real Property of the Partnership	420
§ 11.	Partnership Bound by Admission of Partner	421
§ 12.	Partnership Charged with Knowledge of or Notice to Partner	421
§ 13.	Partnership Bound by Partner's Wrongful Act	421
§ 14.	Partnership Bound by Partner's Breach of Trust	421
§ 15.	Nature of Partner's Liability	422
§ 16.	Partner by Estoppel	422
§ 17.	Liability of Incoming Partner	422
§ 18.	Rules Determining Rights and Duties of Partners	423
§ 19.	Partnership Books	423
§ 20.	Duty of Partners to Render Information	423
§ 21.	Partner Accountable as a Fiduciary	424
§ 22.	Right to an Account	424
§ 23.	Continuation of Partnership Beyond Fixed Term	424
§ 24.	Extent of Property Rights of a Partner	424
§ 25.	Nature of a Partner's Right in Specific Partnership Property	424
§ 26.	Nature of Partner's Interest in the Partnership	425
§ 27.	Assignment of Partner's Interest	425
§ 28.	Partner's Interest Subject to Charging Order	425
§ 29.	Dissolution Defined	426
§ 30.	Partnership not Terminated by Dissolution	426
§ 31.	Causes of Dissolution	426
§ 32.	Dissolution by Decree of Court	427
§ 33.	General Effect of Dissolution on Authority of Partner	427
§ 34.	Right of Partner to Contribution from Co-partners after Dissolution	428
§ 35.	Power of Partner to Bind Partnership to Third Persons after Dissolution	428
§ 36.	Effect of Dissolution on Partner's Existing Liability	429
§ 37.	Right to Wind Up	429
§ 38.	Rights of Partners to Application of Partnership Property	430
§ 39.	Rights Where Partnership is Dissolved for Fraud or Misrepresentation	431
§ 40.	Rules for Distribution	431

§ 41. Liability of Persons Continuing the Business in Certain Cases................432
§ 42. Rights of Retiring or Estate of Deceased Partner When the Business is Continued................433

---

§ 1. Name of Act

This act may be cited as Uniform Partnership Act.

§ 2. Definition of Terms

In this act, "Court" includes every court and judge having jurisdiction in the case.

"Business" includes every trade, occupation, or profession.

"Person" includes individuals, partnerships, corporations, and other associations.

"Bankrupt" includes bankrupt under the Federal Bankruptcy Act or insolvent under any state insolvent act.

"Conveyance" includes every assignment, lease, mortgage, or encumbrance.

"Real property" includes land and any interest or estate in land.

§ 3. Interpretation of Knowledge and Notice

(1) A person has "knowledge" of a fact within the meaning of this act not only when he has actual knowledge thereof, but also when he has knowledge of such other facts as in the circumstances shows bad faith.

(2) A person has "notice" of a fact within the meaning of this act when the person who claims the benefit of the notice:

(a) States the fact to such person, or

(b) Delivers through the mail, or by other means of communication, a written statement of the fact to such person or to a proper person at his place of business or residence.

§ 6. Partnership Defined

(1) A partnership is an association of two or more persons to carry on as co-owners a business for profit.

(2) But any association formed under any other statute of this state, or any statute adopted by authority, other than the authority of this state, is not a partnership under this act, unless such association would have been a partnership in this state prior to the adoption of this act; but this act shall apply to limited partnerships except in so far as the statutes relating to such partnerships are inconsistent herewith.

§ 7. Rules for Determining the Existence of a Partnership

In determining whether a partnership exists, these rules shall apply:

(1) Except as provided by section 16 persons who are not partners as to each other are not partners as to third persons.

(2) Joint tenancy, tenancy in common, tenancy by the entireties, joint property, common property, or part ownership does not of itself establish a partnership, whether such co-owners do or do not share any profits made by the use of the property.

(3) The sharing of gross returns does not of itself establish a partnership, whether or not the persons sharing them have a joint or common right or interest in any property from which the returns are derived.

(4) The receipt by a person of a share of the profits of a business is prima facie evidence that he is a partner in the business, but no such inference shall be drawn if such profits were received in payment:

(a) As a debt by installments or otherwise,

(b) As wages of an employee or rent to a landlord,

(c) As an annuity to a widow or representative of a deceased partner,

(d) As interest on a loan, though the amount of payment vary with the profits of the business,

(e) As the consideration for the sale of a good-will of a business or other property by installments or otherwise.

§ 8. Partnership Property

(1) All property originally brought into the partnership stock or subsequently acquired by purchase or otherwise, on account of the partnership, is partnership property.

(2) Unless the contrary intention appears, property acquired with partnership funds is partnership property.

(3) Any estate in real property may be acquired in the partnership name. Title so acquired can be conveyed only in the partnership name.

(4) A conveyance to a partnership in the partnership name, though without words of inheritance, passes the entire estate of the grantor unless a contrary intent appears.

§ 9. Partner Agent of Partnership as to Partnership Business

(1) Every partner is an agent of the partnership for the purpose of its business, and the act of every partner, including the execution in the partnership name of any instrument, for apparently carrying on in the usual way the business of the partnership of which he is a member binds

the partnership, unless the partner so acting has in fact no authority to act for the partnership in the particular matter, and the person with whom he is dealing has knowledge of the fact that he has no such authority.

(2) An act of a partner which is not apparently for the carrying on of the business of the partnership in the usual way does not bind the partnership unless authorized by the other partners.

(3) Unless authorized by the other partners or unless they have abandoned the business, one or more but less than all the partners have no authority to:

(a) Assign the partnership property in trust for creditors or on the assignee's promise to pay the debts of the partnership,

(b) Dispose of the good-will of the business,

(c) Do any other act which would make it impossible to carry on the ordinary business of a partnership,

(d) Confess a judgment,

(e) Submit a partnership claim or liability to arbitration or reference.

(4) No act of a partner in contravention of a restriction on authority shall bind the partnership to persons having knowledge of the restriction.

§ 10. Conveyance of Real Property of the Partnership

(1) Where title to real property is in the partnership name, any partner may convey title to such property by a conveyance executed in the partnership name; but the partnership may recover such property unless the partner's act binds the partnership under the provisions of paragraph (1) of section 9, or unless such property has been conveyed by the grantee or a person claiming through such grantee to a holder for value without knowledge that the partner, in making the conveyance, has exceeded his authority.

(2) Where title to real property is in the name of the partnership, a conveyance executed by a partner, in his own name, passes the equitable interest of the partnership, provided the act is one within the authority of the partner under the provisions of paragraph (1) of section 9.

(3) Where title to real property is in the name of one or more but not all the partners, and the record does not disclose the right of the partnership, the partners in whose name the title stands may convey title to such property, but the partnership may recover such property if the partners' act does not bind the partnership under the provisions of paragraph (1) of section 9, unless the purchaser or his assignee, is a holder for value, without knowledge.

(4) Where the title to real property is in the name of one or more or all the partners, or in a third person in trust for the partnership, a conveyance executed by a partner in the partnership name, or in his own name, passes the equitable interest of the partnership, provided the act is one within the authority of the partner under the provisions of paragraph (1) of section 9.

(5) Where the title to real property is in the names of all the partners a conveyance executed by all the partners passes all their rights in such property.

§ 11. Partnership Bound by Admission of Partner

An admission or representation made by any partner concerning partnership affairs within the scope of his authority as conferred by this act is evidence against the partnership.

§ 12. Partnership Charged with Knowledge of or Notice to Partner

Notice to any partner of any matter relating to partnership affairs, and the knowledge of the partner acting in the particular matter, acquired while a partner or then present to his mind, and the knowledge of any other partner who reasonably could and should have communicated it to the acting partner, operate as notice to or knowledge of the partnership, except in the case of a fraud on the partnership committed by or with the consent of that partner.

§ 13. Partnership Bound by Partner's Wrongful Act

Where, by any wrongful act or omission of any partner acting in the ordinary course of the business of the partnership or with the authority of his co-partners, loss or injury is caused to any person, not being a partner in the partnership, or any penalty is incurred, the partnership is liable therefor to the same extent as the partner so acting or omitting to act.

§ 14. Partnership Bound by Partner's Breach of Trust

The partnership is bound to make good the loss:

(a) Where one partner acting within the scope of his apparent authority receives money or property of a third person and misapplies it; and

(b) Where the partnership in the course of its business receives money or property of a third person and the money or property so received is misapplied by any partner while it is in the custody of the partnership.

§ 15. Nature of Partner's Liability

All partners are liable

(a) Jointly and severally for everything chargeable to the partnership under sections 13 and 14.

(b) Jointly for all other debts and obligations of the partnership; but any partner may enter into a separate obligation to perform a partnership contract.

§ 16. Partner by Estoppel

(1) When a person, by words spoken or written or by conduct, represents himself, or consents to another representing him to anyone, as a partner in an existing partnership or with one or more persons not actual partners, he is liable to any such person to whom such representation has been made, who has, on the faith of such representation, given credit to the actual or apparent partnership, and if he has made such representation or consented to its being made in a public manner he is liable to such person, whether the representation has or has not been made or communicated to such person so giving credit by or with the knowledge of the apparent partner making the representation or consenting to its being made.

(a) When a partnership liability results, he is liable as though he were an actual member of the partnership.

(b) When no partnership liability results, he is liable jointly with the other persons, if any, so consenting to the contract or representation as to incur liability, otherwise separately.

(2) When a person has been thus represented to be a partner in an existing partnership, or with one or more persons not actual partners, he is an agent of the persons consenting to such representation to bind them to the same extent and in the same manner as though he were a partner in fact, with respect to persons who rely upon the representation. Where all the members of the existing partnership consent to the representation, a partnership act or obligation results; but in all other cases it is the joint act or obligation of the person acting and the persons consenting to the representation.

§ 17. Liability of Incoming Partner

A person admitted as a partner into an existing partnership is liable for all the obligations of the partnership arising before his admission as though he had been a partner when such obligations were incurred, except that this liability shall be satisfied only out of partnership property.

§ 18. Rules Determining Rights and Duties of Partners

The rights and duties of the partners in relation to the partnership shall be determined, subject to any agreement between them, by the following rules:

(a) Each partner shall be repaid his contributions, whether by way of capital or advances to the partnership property and share equally in the profits and surplus remaining after all liabilities, including those to partners, are satisfied; and must contribute towards the losses, whether of capital or otherwise, sustained by the partnership according to his share in the profits.

(b) The partnership must indemnify every partner in respect of payments made and personal liabilities reasonably incurred by him in the ordinary and proper conduct of its business, or for the preservation of its business or property.

(c) A partner, who in aid of the partnership makes any payment or advance beyond the amount of capital which he agreed to contribute, shall be paid interest from the date of the payment or advance.

(d) A partner shall receive interest on the capital contributed by him only from the date when repayment should be made.

(e) All partners have equal rights in the management and conduct of the partnership business.

(f) No partner is entitled to remuneration for acting in the partnership business, except that a surviving partner is entitled to reasonable compensation for his services in winding up the partnership affairs.

(g) No person can become a member of a partnership without the consent of all the partners.

(h) Any difference arising as to ordinary matters connected with the partnership business may be decided by a majority of the partners; but no act in contravention of any agreement between the partners may be done rightfully without the consent of all the partners.

§ 19. Partnership Books

The partnership books shall be kept, subject to any agreement between the partners, at the principal place of business of the partnership, and every partner shall at all times have access to and may inspect and copy any of them.

§ 20. Duty of Partners to Render Information

Partners shall render on demand true and full information of all things affecting the partnership to any partner or the legal representative of any deceased partner or partner under legal disability.

§ 21. Partner Accountable as a Fiduciary

(1) Every partner must account to the partnership for any benefit, and hold as trustee for it any profits derived by him without the consent of the other partners from any transaction connected with the formation, conduct, or liquidation of the partnership or from any use by him of its property.

(2) This section applies also to the representatives of a deceased partner engaged in the liquidation of the affairs of the partnership as the personal representatives of the last surviving partner.

§ 22. Right to an Account

Any partner shall have the right to a formal account as to partnership affairs:

(a) If he is wrongfully excluded from the partnership business or possession of its property by his co-partners,

(b) If the right exists under the terms of any agreement,

(c) As provided by section 21,

(d) Whenever other circumstances render it just and reasonable.

§ 23. Continuation of Partnership Beyond Fixed Term

(1) When a partnership for a fixed term or particular undertaking is continued after the termination of such term or particular undertaking without any express agreement, the rights and duties of the partners remain the same as they were at such termination, so far as is consistent with a partnership at will.

(2) A continuation of the business by the partners or such of them as habitually acted therein during the term, without any settlement or liquidation of the partnership affairs, is prima facie evidence of a continuation of the partnership.

§ 24. Extent of Property Rights of a Partner

The property rights of a partner are (1) his rights in specific partnership property, (2) his interest in the partnership, and (3) his right to participate in the management.

§ 25. Nature of a Partner's Right in Specific Partnership Property

(1) A partner is co-owner with his partners of specific partnership property holding as a tenant in partnership.

(2) The incidents of this tenancy are such that:

(a) A partner, subject to the provisions of this act and to any agreement between the partners, has an equal right with his partners to possess specific partnership property for partnership purposes; but he has no right to possess such property for any other purpose without the consent of his partners.

(b) A partner's right in specific partnership property is not assignable except in connection with the assignment of rights of all the partners in the same property.

(c) A partner's right in specific partnership property is not subject to attachment or execution, except on a claim against the partnership. When partnership property is attached for a partnership debt the partners, or any of them, or the representatives of a deceased partner, cannot claim any right under the homestead or exemption laws.

(d) On the death of a partner his right in specific partnership property vests in the surviving partner or partners, except where the deceased was the last surviving partner, when his right in such property vests in his legal representative. Such surviving partner or partners, or the legal representative of the last surviving partner, has no right to possess the partnership property for any but a partnership purpose.

(e) A partner's right in specific partnership property is not subject to dower, curtesy, or allowances to widows, heirs, or next of kin.

§ 26. Nature of Partner's Interest in the Partnership

A partner's interest in the partnership is his share of the profits and surplus, and the same is personal property.

§ 27. Assignment of Partner's Interest

(1) A conveyance by a partner of his interest in the partnership does not of itself dissolve the partnership, nor, as against the other partners in the absence of agreement, entitle the assignee, during the continuance of the partnership, to interfere in the management or administration of the partnership business or affairs, or to require any information or account of partnership transactions, or to inspect the partnership books; but it merely entitles the assignee to receive in accordance with his contract the profits to which the assigning partner would otherwise be entitled.

(2) In case of a dissolution of the partnership, the assignee is entitled to receive his assignor's interest and may require an account from the date only of the last account agreed to by all the partners.

§ 28. Partner's Interest Subject to Charging Order

(1) On due application to a competent court by any judgment creditor of a partner, the court which entered the judgment, order, or decree, or any other court, may charge the interest of the debtor partner with payment of the unsatisfied amount of such judgment debt with

interest thereon; and may then or later appoint a receiver of his share of the profits, and of any other money due or to fall due to him in respect of the partnership, and make all other orders, directions, accounts and inquiries which the debtor partner might have made, or which the circumstances of the case may require.

(2) The interest charged may be redeemed at any time before foreclosure, or in case of a sale being directed by the court may be purchased without thereby causing a dissolution:

(a) With separate property, by any one or more of the partners, or

(b) With partnership property, by any one or more of the partners with the consent of all the partners whose interests are not so charged or sold.

(3) Nothing in this act shall be held to deprive a partner of his right, if any, under the exemption laws, as regards his interest in the partnership.

§ 29. Dissolution Defined

The dissolution of a partnership is the change in the relation of the partners caused by any partner ceasing to be associated in the carrying on as distinguished from the winding up of the business.

§ 30. Partnership not Terminated by Dissolution

On dissolution the partnership is not terminated, but continues until the winding up of partnership affairs is completed.

§ 31. Causes of Dissolution

Dissolution is caused:

(1) Without violation of the agreement between the partners,

(a) By the termination of the definite term or particular undertaking specified in the agreement,

(b) By the express will of any partner when no definite term or particular undertaking is specified,

(c) By the express will of all the partners who have not assigned their interests or suffered them to be charged for their separate debts, either before or after the termination of any specified term or particular undertaking,

(d) By the expulsion of any partner from the business bona fide in accordance with such a power conferred by the agreement between the partners;

(2) In contravention of the agreement between the partners, where the circumstances do not permit a dissolution under any other provision of this section, by the express will of any partner at any time;

(3) By any event which makes it unlawful for the business of the partnership to be carried on or for the members to carry it on in partnership;

(4) By the death of any partner;

(5) By the bankruptcy of any partner or the partnership;

(6) By decree of court under section 32.

§ 32. Dissolution by Decree of Court

(1) On application by or for a partner the court shall decree a dissolution whenever:

(a) A partner has been declared a lunatic in any judicial proceeding or is shown to be of unsound mind,

(b) A partner becomes in any other way incapable of performing his part of the partnership contract,

(c) A partner has been guilty of such conduct as tends to affect prejudicially the carrying on of the business,

(d) A partner wilfully or persistently commits a breach of the partnership agreement, or otherwise so conducts himself in matters relating to the partnership business that it is not reasonably practicable to carry on the business in partnership with him,

(e) The business of the partnership can only be carried on at a loss,

(f) Other circumstances render a dissolution equitable.

(2) On the application of the purchaser of a partner's interest under sections 28 or 29 [so in original; probably should read "sections 27 or 28."]:

(a) After the termination of the specified term or particular undertaking,

(b) At any time if the partnership was a partnership at will when the interest was assigned or when the charging order was issued.

§ 33. General Effect of Dissolution on Authority of Partner

Except so far as may be necessary to wind up partnership affairs or to complete transactions begun but not then finished, dissolution terminates all authority of any partner to act for the partnership,

(1) With respect to the partners,

(a) When the dissolution is not by the act, bankruptcy or death of a partner; or

(b) When the dissolution is by such act, bankruptcy or death of a partner, in cases where section 34 so requires.

(2) With respect to persons not partners, as declared in section 35.

§ 34. Right of Partner to Contribution from Co-partners after Dissolution

Where the dissolution is caused by the act, death or bankruptcy of a partner, each partner is liable to his co-partners for his share of any liability created by any partner acting for the partnership as if the partnership had not been dissolved unless

(a) The dissolution being by act of any partner, the partner acting for the partnership had knowledge of the dissolution, or

(b) The dissolution being by the death or bankruptcy of a partner, the partner acting for the partnership had knowledge or notice of the death or bankruptcy knowledge of the dissolution.

§ 35. Power of Partner to Bind Partnership to Third Persons after Dissolution

(1) After dissolution a partner can bind the partnership except as provided in Paragraph (3).

(a) By any act appropriate for winding up partnership affairs or completing transactions unfinished at dissolution;

(b) By any transaction which would bind the partnership if dissolution had not taken place, provided the other party to the transaction

(I) Had extended credit to the partnership prior to dissolution and had no knowledge or notice of the dissolution; or

(II) Though he had not so extended credit, had nevertheless known of the partnership prior to dissolution, and, having no knowledge or notice of dissolution, the fact of dissolution had not been advertised in a newspaper of general circulation in the place (or in each place if more than one) at which the partnership business was regularly carried on.

(2) The liability of a partner under Paragraph (1)(b) shall be satisfied out of partnership assets alone when such partner had been prior to dissolution

(a) Unknown as a partner to the person with whom the contract is made; and

(b) So far unknown and inactive in partnership affairs that the business reputation of the partnership could not be said to have been in any degree due to his connection with it.

(3) The partnership is in no case bound by any act of a partner after dissolution

(a) Where the partnership is dissolved because it is unlawful to carry on the business, unless the act is appropriate for winding up partnership affairs; or

(b) Where the partner has become bankrupt; or

(c) Where the partner has no authority to wind up partnership affairs; except by a transaction with one who

(I) Had extended credit to the partnership prior to dissolution and had no knowledge or notice of his want of authority; or

(II) Had not extended credit to the partnership prior to dissolution, and, having no knowledge or notice of his want of authority, the fact of his want of authority has not been advertised in the manner provided for advertising the fact of dissolution in Paragraph (1)(b)(II).

(4) Nothing in this section shall affect the liability under Section 16 of any person who after dissolution represents himself or consents to another representing him as a partner in a partnership engaged in carrying on business.

§ 36. Effect of Dissolution on Partner's Existing Liability

(1) The dissolution of the partnership does not of itself discharge the existing liability of any partner.

(2) A partner is discharged from any existing liability upon dissolution of the partnership by an agreement to that effect between himself, the partnership creditor and the person or partnership continuing the business; and such agreement may be inferred from the course of dealing between the creditor having knowledge of the dissolution and the person or partnership continuing the business.

(3) Where a person agrees to assume the existing obligations of a dissolved partnership, the partners whose obligations have been assumed shall be discharged from any liability to any creditor of the partnership who, knowing of the agreement, consents to a material alteration in the nature or time of payment of such obligations.

(4) The individual property of a deceased partner shall be liable for all obligations of the partnership incurred while he was a partner but subject to the prior payment of his separate debts.

§ 37. Right to Wind Up

Unless otherwise agreed the partners who have not wrongfully dissolved the partnership or the legal representative of the last surviving partner, not bankrupt, has the right to wind up the partnership affairs;

provided, however, that any partner, his legal representative or his assignee, upon cause shown, may obtain winding up by the court.

§ 38. Rights of Partners to Application of Partnership Property

(1) When dissolution is caused in any way, except in contravention of the partnership agreement, each partner, as against his co-partners and all persons claiming through them in respect of their interests in the partnership, unless otherwise agreed, may have the partnership property applied to discharge its liabilities, and the surplus applied to pay in cash the net amount owing to the respective partners. But if dissolution is caused by expulsion of a partner, bona fide under the partnership agreement and if the expelled partner is discharged from all partnership liabilities, either by payment or agreement under section 36(2), he shall receive in cash only the net amount due him from the partnership.

(2) When dissolution is caused in contravention of the partnership agreement the rights of the partners shall be as follows:

(a) Each partner who has not caused dissolution wrongfully shall have,

I. All the rights specified in paragraph (1) of this section, and

II. The right, as against each partner who has caused the dissolution wrongfully, to damages for breach of the agreement.

(b) The partners who have not caused the dissolution wrongfully, if they all desire to continue the business in the same name, either by themselves or jointly with others, may do so, during the agreed term for the partnership and for that purpose may possess the partnership property, provided they secure the payment by bond approved by the court, or pay to any partner who has caused the dissolution wrongfully, the value of his interest in the partnership at the dissolution, less any damages recoverable under clause (2)(a)(II) of this section, and in like manner indemnify him against all present or future partnership liabilities.

(c) A partner who has caused the dissolution wrongfully shall have:

I. If the business is not continued under the provisions of paragraph (2)(b) all the rights of a partner under paragraph (1), subject to clause (2)(a)(II), of this section,

II. If the business is continued under paragraph (2)(b) of this section the right as against his co-partners and all claiming through them in respect of their interests in the partnership, to have the value of his interest in the partnership, less any damages caused to his co-partners by the dissolution, ascertained and paid to him in cash, or the payment secured by bond approved by the court, and to be released from all existing liabilities of the partnership; but in ascertaining the value of the partner's interest the value of the good-will of the business shall not be considered.

§ 39. Rights Where Partnership is Dissolved for Fraud or Misrepresentation

Where a partnership contract is rescinded on the ground of the fraud or misrepresentation of one of the parties thereto, the party entitled to rescind is, without prejudice to any other right, entitled,

(a) To a lien on, or a right of retention of, the surplus of the partnership property after satisfying the partnership liabilities to third persons for any sum of money paid by him for the purchase of an interest in the partnership and for any capital or advances contributed by him; and

(b) To stand, after all liabilities to third persons have been satisfied, in the place of the creditors of the partnership for any payments made by him in respect of the partnership liabilities; and

(c) To be indemnified by the person guilty of the fraud or making the representation against all debts and liabilities of the partnership.

§ 40. Rules for Distribution

In settling accounts between the partners after dissolution, the following rules shall be observed, subject to any agreement to the contrary:

(a) The assets of the partnership are:

I. The partnership property,

II. The contributions of the partners necessary for the payment of all the liabilities specified in clause (b) of this paragraph.

(b) The liabilities of the partnership shall rank in order of payment, as follows:

I. Those owing to creditors other than partners,

II. Those owing to partners other than for capital and profits,

III. Those owing to partners in respect of capital,

IV. Those owing to partners in respect of profits.

(c) The assets shall be applied in order of their declaration in clause (a) of this paragraph to the satisfaction of the liabilities.

(d) The partners shall contribute, as provided by section 18(a) the amount necessary to satisfy the liabilities; but if any, but not all, of the partners are insolvent, or, not being subject to process, refuse to contribute, the other partners shall contribute their share of the liabilities, and, in the relative proportions in which they share the profits, the additional amount necessary to pay the liabilities.

(e) An assignee for the benefit of creditors or any person appointed by the court shall have the right to enforce the contributions specified in clause (d) of this paragraph.

(f) Any partner or his legal representative shall have the right to enforce the contributions specified in clause (d) of this paragraph, to the extent of the amount which he has paid in excess of his share of the liability.

(g) The individual property of a deceased partner shall be liable for the contributions specified in clause (d) of this paragraph.

(h) When partnership property and the individual properties of the partners are in possession of a court for distribution, partnership creditors shall have priority on partnership property and separate creditors on individual property, saving the rights of lien or secured creditors as heretofore.

(i) Where a partner has become bankrupt or his estate is insolvent the claims against his separate property shall rank in the following order:

I. Those owing to separate creditors,

II. Those owing to partnership creditors,

III. Those owing to partners by way of contribution.

§ 41. Liability of Persons Continuing the Business in Certain Cases

(1) When any new partner is admitted into an existing partnership, or when any partner retires and assigns (or the representative of the deceased partner assigns) his rights in partnership property to two or more of the partners, or to one or more of the partners and one or more third persons, if the business is continued without liquidation of the partnership affairs, creditors of the first or dissolved partnership are also creditors of the partnership so continuing the business.

(2) When all but one partner retire and assign(or the representative of a deceased partner assigns) their rights in partnership property to the remaining partner, who continues the business without liquidation of partnership affairs, either alone or with others, creditors of the dissolved partnership are also creditors of the person or partnership so continuing the business.

(3) When any partner retires or dies and the business of the dissolved partnership is continued as set forth in paragraphs (1) and (2) of this section, with the consent of the retired partners or the representative of the deceased partner, but without any assignment of his right in partnership property, rights of creditors of the dissolved

partnership and of the creditors of the person or partnership continuing the business shall be as if such assignment had been made.

(4) When all the partners or their representatives assign their rights in partnership property to one or more third persons who promise to pay the debts and who continue the business of the dissolved partnership, creditors of the dissolved partnership are also creditors of the person or partnership continuing the business.

(5) When any partner wrongfully causes a dissolution and the remaining partners continue the business under the provisions of section 38(2)(b), either alone or with others, and without liquidation of the partnership affairs, creditors of the dissolved partnership are also creditors of the person or partnership continuing the business.

(6) When a partner is expelled and the remaining partners continue the business either alone or with others, without liquidation of the partnership affairs, creditors of the dissolved partnership are also creditors of the person or partnership continuing the business.

(7) The liability of a third person becoming a partner in the partnership continuing the business, under this section, to the creditors of the dissolved partnership shall be satisfied out of partnership property only.

(8) When the business of a partnership after dissolution is continued under any conditions set forth in this section the creditors of the dissolved partnership, as against the separate creditors of the retiring or deceased partner or the representative of the deceased partner, have a prior right to any claim of the retired partner or the representative of the deceased partner against the person or partnership continuing the business, on account of the retired or deceased partner's interest in the dissolved partnership or on account of any consideration promised for such interest or for his right in partnership property.

(9) Nothing in this section shall be held to modify any right of creditors to set aside any assignment on the ground of fraud.

(10) The use by the person or partnership continuing the business of the partnership name, or the name of a deceased partner as part thereof, shall not of itself make the individual property of the deceased partner liable for any debts contracted by such person or partnership.

§ 42. Rights of Retiring or Estate of Deceased Partner When the Business is Continued

When any partner retires or dies, and the business is continued under any of the conditions set forth in section 41(1, 2, 3, 5, 6), or section 38(2)(b) without any settlement of accounts as between him or his estate and the person or partnership continuing the business, unless otherwise agreed, he or his legal representative as against such persons or partnership may have the value of his interest at the date of dissolution ascertained, and shall receive as an ordinary creditor an amount equal to the value of his interest in the dissolved partnership with interest, or, at his option or at the option of his legal representative, in lieu of interest, the profits attributable to the use of his right in the property of the dissolved partnership; provided that the creditors of the dissolved partnership as against the separate creditors, or the representative of the retired or deceased partner, shall have priority on any claim arising under this section, as provided by section 41(8) of this act.

UNIFORM PARTNERSHIP ACT (1997, Last Amended 2013) (selected provisions)

Article 1. General Provisions

Section 101. Short title.

This [act] may be cited as the Uniform Partnership Act.

Section 102. Definitions.

In this [act]:

(1) "Business" includes every trade, occupation, and profession.

(2) "Contribution", except in the phrase "right of contribution", means property or a benefit described in Section 403 which is provided by a person to a partnership to become a partner or in the person's capacity as a partner.

(3) "Debtor in bankruptcy" means a person that is the subject of:

(A) an order for relief under Title 11 of the United States Code or a comparable order under a successor statute of general application; or

(B) a comparable order under federal, state, or foreign law governing insolvency.

(4) "Distribution" means a transfer of money or other property from a partnership to a person on account of a transferable interest or in a person's capacity as a partner. The term:

(A) includes:

(i) a redemption or other purchase by a partnership of a transferable interest; and

(ii) a transfer to a partner in return for the partner's relinquishment of any right to participate as a partner in the management or conduct of the partnership's business or have access to records or other information concerning the partnership's business; and

(B) does not include amounts constituting reasonable compensation for present or past service or payments made in the ordinary course of business under a bona fide retirement plan or other bona fide benefits program.

(5) "Foreign limited liability partnership" means a foreign partnership whose partners have limited liability for the debts, obligations, or other liabilities of the foreign partnership under a provision similar to Section 306(c).

(6) "Foreign partnership" means an unincorporated entity formed under the law of a jurisdiction other than this state which would be a partnership if formed under the law of this state. The term includes a foreign limited liability partnership.

(7) "Jurisdiction", used to refer to a political entity, means the United States, a state, a foreign country, or a political subdivision of a foreign country.

(8) "Jurisdiction of formation" means the jurisdiction whose law governs the internal affairs of an entity.

(9) "Limited liability partnership", except in the phrase "foreign limited liability partnership" and in Article 11, means a partnership that has filed a statement of qualification under Section 901 and does not have a similar statement in effect in any other jurisdiction.

(10) "Partner" means a person that:

(A) has become a partner in a partnership under Section 402 or was a partner in a partnership when the partnership became subject to this [act] under Section 110; and

(B) has not dissociated as a partner under Section 601.

(11) "Partnership", except in Article 11, means an association of two or more persons to carry on as co-owners a business for profit formed under this [act] or that becomes subject to this [act] under Article 11 or Section 110. The term includes a limited liability partnership.

(12) "Partnership agreement" means the agreement, whether or not referred to as a partnership agreement and whether oral, implied, in a record, or in any combination thereof, of all the partners of a partnership concerning the matters described in Section 105(a). The term includes the agreement as amended or restated.

(13) "Partnership at will" means a partnership in which the partners have not agreed to remain partners until the expiration of a definite term or the completion of a particular undertaking.

(14) "Person" means an individual, business corporation, nonprofit corporation, partnership, limited partnership, limited liability company, [general cooperative association,] limited cooperative association,

unincorporated nonprofit association, statutory trust, business trust, common-law business trust, estate, trust, association, joint venture, public corporation, government or governmental subdivision, agency, or instrumentality, or any other legal or commercial entity.

(15) "Principal office" means the principal executive office of a partnership or a foreign limited liability partnership, whether or not the office is located in this state.

(16) "Property" means all property, whether real, personal, or mixed or tangible or intangible, or any right or interest therein.

(17) "Record", used as a noun, means information that is inscribed on a tangible medium or that is stored in an electronic or other medium and is retrievable in perceivable form.

(18) "Registered agent" means an agent of a limited liability partnership or foreign limited liability partnership which is authorized to receive service of any process, notice, or demand required or permitted by law to be served on the partnership.

(19) "Registered foreign limited liability partnership" means a foreign limited liability partnership that is registered to do business in this state pursuant to a statement of registration filed by the [Secretary of State].

(20) "Sign" means, with present intent to authenticate or adopt a record:

(A) to execute or adopt a tangible symbol; or

(B) to attach to or logically associate with the record an electronic symbol, sound, or process.

(21) "State" means a state of the United States, the District of Columbia, Puerto Rico, the United States Virgin Islands, or any territory or insular possession subject to the jurisdiction of the United States.

(22) "Transfer" includes:

(A) an assignment;

(B) a conveyance;

(C) a sale;

(D) a lease;

(E) an encumbrance, including a mortgage or security interest;

(F) a gift; and

(G) a transfer by operation of law.

(23) "Transferable interest" means the right, as initially owned by a person in the person's capacity as a partner, to receive distributions from a partnership, whether or not the person remains a partner or continues

to own any part of the right. The term applies to any fraction of the interest, by whomever owned.

(24) "Transferee" means a person to which all or part of a transferable interest has been transferred, whether or not the transferor is a partner.

Section 103. Knowledge; notice.

(a) A person knows a fact if the person:

(1) has actual knowledge of it; or

(2) is deemed to know it under subsection (d)(1) or law other than this [act].

(b) A person has notice of a fact if the person:

(1) has reason to know the fact from all the facts known to the person at the time in question; or

(2) is deemed to have notice of the fact under subsection (d)(2).

(c) Subject to Section 117(f), a person notifies another person of a fact by taking steps reasonably required to inform the other person in ordinary course, whether or not those steps cause the other person to know the fact.

(d) A person not a partner is deemed:

(1) to know of a limitation on authority to transfer real property as provided in Section 303(g); and

(2) to have notice of:

(A) a person's dissociation as a partner 90 days after a statement of dissociation under Section 704 becomes effective; and

(B) a partnership's:

(i) dissolution 90 days after a statement of dissolution under Section 802 becomes effective;

(ii) termination 90 days after a statement of termination under Section 802 becomes effective; and

(iii) participation in a merger, interest exchange, conversion, or domestication, 90 days after articles of merger, interest exchange, conversion, or domestication under Article 11 become effective.

(e) A partner's knowledge or notice of a fact relating to the partnership is effective immediately as knowledge of or notice to the partnership, except in the case of a fraud on the partnership committed by or with the consent of that partner.

Section 104. Governing law.

The internal affairs of a partnership and the liability of a partner as a partner for a debt, obligation, or other liability of the partnership are governed by:

(1) in the case of a limited liability partnership, the law of this state; and

(2) in the case of a partnership that is not a limited liability partnership, the law of the jurisdiction in which the partnership has its principal office.

Section 105. Partnership agreement; scope, function, and limitations.

(a) Except as otherwise provided in subsections (c) and (d), the partnership agreement governs:

(1) relations among the partners as partners and between the partners and the partnership;

(2) the business of the partnership and the conduct of that business; and

(3) the means and conditions for amending the partnership agreement.

(b) To the extent the partnership agreement does not provide for a matter described in subsection (a), this [act] governs the matter.

(c) A partnership agreement may not:

(1) vary the law applicable under Section 104(1);

(2) vary the provisions of Section 110;

(3) vary the provisions of Section 307;

(4) unreasonably restrict the duties and rights under Section 408, but the partnership agreement may impose reasonable restrictions on the availability and use of information obtained under that section and may define appropriate remedies, including liquidated damages, for a breach of any reasonable restriction on use;

(5) alter or eliminate the duty of loyalty or the duty of care, except as otherwise provided in subsection (d);

(6) eliminate the contractual obligation of good faith and fair dealing under Section 409(d), but the partnership agreement may prescribe the standards, if not manifestly unreasonable, by which the performance of the obligation is to be measured;

(7) unreasonably restrict the right of a person to maintain an action under Section 410(b);

(8) relieve or exonerate a person from liability for conduct involving bad faith, willful or intentional misconduct, or knowing violation of law;

(9) vary the power of a person to dissociate as a partner under Section 602(a), except to require that the notice under Section 601(1) to be in a record;

(10) vary the grounds for expulsion specified in Section 601(5);

(11) vary the causes of dissolution specified in Section 801(4) or (5);

(12) vary the requirement to wind up the partnership's business as specified in Section 802(a), (b)(1), and (d);

. . .

(d) Subject to subsection (c)(8), without limiting other terms that may be included in a partnership agreement, the following rules apply:

(1) The partnership agreement may:

(A) specify the method by which a specific act or transaction that would otherwise violate the duty of loyalty may be authorized or ratified by one or more disinterested and independent persons after full disclosure of all material facts; and

(B) alter the prohibition in Section 406(a)(2) so that the prohibition requires only that the partnership's total assets not be less than the sum of its total liabilities.

(2) To the extent the partnership agreement expressly relieves a partner of a responsibility that the partner would otherwise have under this [act] and imposes the responsibility on one or more other partners, the agreement also may eliminate or limit any fiduciary duty of the partner relieved of the responsibility which would have pertained to the responsibility.

(3) If not manifestly unreasonable, the partnership agreement may:

(A) alter or eliminate the aspects of the duty of loyalty stated in Section 409(b);

(B) identify specific types or categories of activities that do not violate the duty of loyalty;

(C) alter the duty of care, but may not authorize conduct involving bad faith, willful or intentional misconduct, or knowing violation of law; and

(D) alter or eliminate any other fiduciary duty.

(e) The court shall decide as a matter of law whether a term of a partnership agreement is manifestly unreasonable under subsection (c)(6) or (d)(3). The court:

(1) shall make its determination as of the time the challenged term became part of the partnership agreement and by considering only circumstances existing at that time; and

(2) may invalidate the term only if, in light of the purposes and business of the partnership, it is readily apparent that:

(A) the objective of the term is unreasonable; or

(B) the term is an unreasonable means to achieve the term's objective.

Section 106. Partnership agreement; effect on partnership and person becoming partner; preformation agreement.

(a) A partnership is bound by and may enforce the partnership agreement, whether or not the partnership has itself manifested assent to the agreement.

(b) A person that becomes a partner is deemed to assent to the partnership agreement.

(c) Two or more persons intending to become the initial partners of a partnership may make an agreement providing that upon the formation of the partnership the agreement will become the partnership agreement.

Article 2. Nature of Partnership

Section 201. Partnership as entity.

(a) A partnership is an entity distinct from its partners.

(b) A partnership is the same entity regardless of whether the partnership has a statement of qualification in effect under Section 901.

Section 202. Formation of partnership.

(a) Except as otherwise provided in subsection (b), the association of two or more persons to carry on as co-owners a business for profit forms a partnership, whether or not the persons intend to form a partnership.

(b) An association formed under a statute other than this [act], a predecessor statute, or a comparable statute of another jurisdiction is not a partnership under this [act].

(c) In determining whether a partnership is formed, the following rules apply:

(1) Joint tenancy, tenancy in common, tenancy by the entireties, joint property, common property, or part ownership does not by itself

establish a partnership, even if the co-owners share profits made by the use of the property.

(2) The sharing of gross returns does not by itself establish a partnership, even if the persons sharing them have a joint or common right or interest in property from which the returns are derived.

(3) A person who receives a share of the profits of a business is presumed to be a partner in the business, unless the profits were received in payment:

(A) of a debt by installments or otherwise;

(B) for services as an independent contractor or of wages or other compensation to an employee;

(C) of rent;

(D) of an annuity or other retirement or health benefit to a deceased or retired partner or a beneficiary, representative, or designee of a deceased or retired partner;

(E) of interest or other charge on a loan, even if the amount of payment varies with the profits of the business, including a direct or indirect present or future ownership of the collateral, or rights to income, proceeds, or increase in value derived from the collateral; or

(F) for the sale of the goodwill of a business or other property by installments or otherwise.

Section 203. Partnership property.

Property acquired by a partnership is property of the partnership and not of the partners individually.

Section 204. When property is partnership property.

(a) Property is partnership property if acquired in the name of:

(1) the partnership; or

(2) one or more partners with an indication in the instrument transferring title to the property of the person's capacity as a partner or of the existence of a partnership but without an indication of the name of the partnership.

(b) Property is acquired in the name of the partnership by a transfer to:

(1) the partnership in its name; or

(2) one or more partners in their capacity as partners in the partnership, if the name of the partnership is indicated in the instrument transferring title to the property.

(c) Property is presumed to be partnership property if purchased with partnership assets, even if not acquired in the name of the partnership or of one or more partners with an indication in the instrument transferring title to the property of the person's capacity as a partner or of the existence of a partnership.

(d) Property acquired in the name of one or more of the partners, without an indication in the instrument transferring title to the property of the person's capacity as a partner or of the existence of a partnership and without use of partnership assets, is presumed to be separate property, even if used for partnership purposes.

Article 3. Relations of Partners to Persons Dealing With Partnership

Section 301. Partner agent of partnership.

Subject to the effect of a statement of partnership authority under Section 303, the following rules apply:

(1) Each partner is an agent of the partnership for the purpose of its business. An act of a partner, including the signing of an instrument in the partnership name, for apparently carrying on in the ordinary course the partnership business or business of the kind carried on by the partnership binds the partnership, unless the partner did not have authority to act for the partnership in the particular matter and the person with which the partner was dealing knew or had notice that the partner lacked authority.

(2) An act of a partner which is not apparently for carrying on in the ordinary course the partnership's business or business of the kind carried on by the partnership binds the partnership only if the act was actually authorized by all the other partners.

Section 303. Statement of partnership authority.

(a) A partnership may deliver to the [Secretary of State] for filing a statement of partnership authority. The statement:

(1) must include the name of the partnership and:

(A) if the partnership is not a limited liability partnership, the street and mailing addresses of its principal office; or

(B) if the partnership is a limited liability partnership, the name and street and mailing addresses of its registered agent;

(2) with respect to any position that exists in or with respect to the partnership, may state the authority, or limitations on the authority, of all persons holding the position to:

(A) sign an instrument transferring real property held in the name of the partnership; or

(B) enter into other transactions on behalf of, or otherwise act for or bind, the partnership; and

(3) may state the authority, or limitations on the authority, of a specific person to:

(A) sign an instrument transferring real property held in the name of the partnership; or

(B) enter into other transactions on behalf of, or otherwise act for or bind, the partnership.

(b) To amend or cancel a statement of authority filed by the [Secretary of State], a partnership must deliver to the [Secretary of State] for filing an amendment or cancellation stating:

(1) the name of the partnership;

(2) if the partnership is not a limited liability partnership, the street and mailing addresses of the partnership's principal office;

(3) if the partnership is a limited liability partnership, the name and street and mailing addresses of its registered agent;

(4) the date the statement being affected became effective; and

(5) the contents of the amendment or a declaration that the statement is canceled.

(c) A statement of authority affects only the power of a person to bind a partnership to persons that are not partners.

(d) Subject to subsection (c) and Section 103(d)(1), and except as otherwise provided in subsections (f), (g), and (h), a limitation on the authority of a person or a position contained in an effective statement of authority is not by itself evidence of any person's knowledge or notice of the limitation.

(e) Subject to subsection (c), a grant of authority not pertaining to transfers of real property and contained in an effective statement of authority is conclusive in favor of a person that gives value in reliance on the grant, except to the extent that if the person gives value:

(1) the person has knowledge to the contrary;

(2) the statement has been canceled or restrictively amended under subsection (b); or

(3) a limitation on the grant is contained in another statement of authority that became effective after the statement containing the grant became effective.

(f) Subject to subsection (c), an effective statement of authority that grants authority to transfer real property held in the name of the partnership, a certified copy of which statement is recorded in the office for recording transfers of the real property, is conclusive in favor of a person that gives value in reliance on the grant without knowledge to the contrary, except to the extent that when the person gives value:

(1) the statement has been canceled or restrictively amended under subsection (b), and a certified copy of the cancellation or restrictive amendment has been recorded in the office for recording transfers of the real property; or

(2) a limitation on the grant is contained in another statement of authority that became effective after the statement containing the grant became effective, and a certified copy of the later-effective statement is recorded in the office for recording transfers of the real property.

(g) Subject to subsection (c), if a certified copy of an effective statement containing a limitation on the authority to transfer real property held in the name of a partnership is recorded in the office for recording transfers of that real property, all persons are deemed to know of the limitation.

Section 305. Partnership liable for partner's actionable conduct.

(a) A partnership is liable for loss or injury caused to a person, or for a penalty incurred, as a result of a wrongful act or omission, or other actionable conduct, of a partner acting in the ordinary course of business of the partnership or with the actual or apparent authority of the partnership.

(b) If, in the course of the partnership's business or while acting with actual or apparent authority of the partnership, a partner receives or causes the partnership to receive money or property of a person not a partner, and the money or property is misapplied by a partner, the partnership is liable for the loss.

Section 306. Partner's liability.

(a) Except as otherwise provided in subsections (b) and (c), all partners are liable jointly and severally for all debts, obligations, and other liabilities of the partnership unless otherwise agreed by the claimant or provided by law.

(b) A person that becomes a partner is not personally liable for a debt, obligation, or other liability of the partnership incurred before the person became a partner.

(c) A debt, obligation, or other liability of a partnership incurred while the partnership is a limited liability partnership is solely the debt, obligation, or other liability of the limited liability partnership. A partner is not personally liable, directly or indirectly, by way of contribution or otherwise, for a debt, obligation, or other liability of the limited liability partnership solely by reason of being or acting as a partner. This subsection applies:

(1) despite anything inconsistent in the partnership agreement that existed immediately before the vote or consent required to become a limited liability partnership under Section 901(b); and

(2) regardless of the dissolution of the limited liability partnership.

(d) The failure of a limited liability partnership to observe formalities relating to the exercise of its powers or management of its business is not a ground for imposing liability on a partner for a debt, obligation, or other liability of the partnership.

(e) The cancellation or administrative revocation of a limited liability partnership's statement of qualification does not affect the limitation in this section on the liability of a partner for a debt, obligation, or other liability of the partnership incurred while the statement was in effect.

Section 307. Actions by and against partnership and partners.

(a) A partnership may sue and be sued in the name of the partnership.

(b) To the extent not inconsistent with Section 306, a partner may be joined in an action against the partnership or named in a separate action.

(c) A judgment against a partnership is not by itself a judgment against a partner. A judgment against a partnership may not be satisfied from a partner's assets unless there is also a judgment against the partner.

(d) A judgment creditor of a partner may not levy execution against the assets of the partner to satisfy a judgment based on a claim against the partnership unless the partner is personally liable for the claim under Section 306 and:

(1) a judgment based on the same claim has been obtained against the partnership and a writ of execution on the judgment has been returned unsatisfied in whole or in part;

(2) the partnership is a debtor in bankruptcy;

(3) the partner has agreed that the creditor need not exhaust partnership assets;

(4) a court grants permission to the judgment creditor to levy execution against the assets of a partner based on a finding that partnership assets subject to execution are clearly insufficient to satisfy the judgment, that exhaustion of partnership assets is excessively burdensome, or that the grant of permission is an appropriate exercise of the court's equitable powers; or

(5) liability is imposed on the partner by law or contract independent of the existence of the partnership.

(e) This section applies to any debt, liability, or other obligation of a partnership which results from a representation by a partner or purported partner under Section 308.

Article 4. Relations of Partners to Each Other and to Partnership

Section 401. Partner's rights and duties.

(a) Each partner is entitled to an equal share of the partnership distributions and, except in the case of a limited liability partnership, is chargeable with a share of the partnership losses in proportion to the partner's share of the distributions.

(b) A partnership shall reimburse a partner for any payment made by the partner in the course of the partner's activities on behalf of the partnership, if the partner complied with this section and Section 409 in making the payment.

(c) A partnership shall indemnify and hold harmless a person with respect to any claim or demand against the person and any debt, obligation, or other liability incurred by the person by reason of the person's former or present capacity as a partner, if the claim, demand, debt, obligation, or other liability does not arise from the person's breach of this section or Section 407 or 409.

(d) In the ordinary course of its business, a partnership may advance reasonable expenses, including attorney's fees and costs, incurred by a person in connection with a claim or demand against the person by reason of the person's former or present capacity as a partner, if the person promises to repay the partnership if the person ultimately is determined not to be entitled to be indemnified under subsection (c).

(e) A partnership may purchase and maintain insurance on behalf of a partner against liability asserted against or incurred by the partner in that capacity or arising from that status even if, under Section 105(c)(7), the partnership agreement could not eliminate or limit the person's liability to the partnership for the conduct giving rise to the liability.

(f) A partnership shall reimburse a partner for an advance to the partnership beyond the amount of capital the partner agreed to contribute.

(g) A payment or advance made by a partner which gives rise to a partnership obligation under subsection (b) or (f) constitutes a loan to the partnership which accrues interest from the date of the payment or advance.

(h) Each partner has equal rights in the management and conduct of the partnership's business.

(i) A partner may use or possess partnership property only on behalf of the partnership.

(j) A partner is not entitled to remuneration for services performed for the partnership, except for reasonable compensation for services rendered in winding up the business of the partnership.

(k) A difference arising as to a matter in the ordinary course of business of a partnership may be decided by a majority of the partners. An act outside the ordinary course of business of a partnership and an amendment to the partnership agreement may be undertaken only with the affirmative vote or consent of all the partners.

Section 402. Becoming partner.

(a) Upon formation of a partnership, a person becomes a partner under Section 202(a).

(b) After formation of a partnership, a person becomes a partner:

(1) as provided in the partnership agreement;

(2) as a result of a transaction effective under Article 11; or

(3) with the affirmative vote or consent of all the partners.

(c) A person may become a partner without:

(1) acquiring a transferable interest; or

(2) making or being obligated to make a contribution to the partnership.

Section 403. Form of contribution.

A contribution may consist of property transferred to, services performed for, or another benefit provided to the partnership or an agreement to transfer property to, perform services for, or provide another benefit to the partnership.

Section 404. Liability for contribution.

(a) A person's obligation to make a contribution to a partnership is not excused by the person's death, disability, termination, or other inability to perform personally.

(b) If a person does not fulfill an obligation to make a contribution other than money, the person is obligated at the option of the partnership to contribute money equal to the value of the part of the contribution which has not been made.

(c) The obligation of a person to make a contribution may be compromised only by the affirmative vote or consent of all the partners. If a creditor of a limited liability partnership extends credit or otherwise acts in reliance on an obligation described in subsection (a) without knowledge or notice of a compromise under this subsection, the creditor may enforce the obligation.

Section 405. Sharing of and right to distributions before dissolution.

(a) Any distribution made by a partnership before its dissolution and winding up must be in equal shares among partners, except to the extent necessary to comply with a transfer effective under Section 503 or charging order in effect under Section 504.

(b) Subject to Section 701, a person has a right to a distribution before the dissolution and winding up of a partnership only if the partnership decides to make an interim distribution.

(c) A person does not have a right to demand or receive a distribution from a partnership in any form other than money. Except as otherwise provided in Section 806, a partnership may distribute an asset in kind only if each part of the asset is fungible with each other part and each person receives a percentage of the asset equal in value to the person's share of distributions.

(d) If a partner or transferee becomes entitled to receive a distribution, the partner or transferee has the status of, and is entitled to all remedies available to, a creditor of the partnership with respect to the distribution. However, the partnership's obligation to make a distribution is subject to offset for any amount owed to the partnership by the partner or a person dissociated as partner on whose account the distribution is made.

Section 406. Limitations on distributions by limited liability partnership.

(a) A limited liability partnership may not make a distribution, including a distribution under Section 806, if after the distribution:

(1) the partnership would not be able to pay its debts as they become due in the ordinary course of the partnership's business; or

(2) the partnership's total assets would be less than the sum of its total liabilities plus the amount that would be needed, if the partnership were to be dissolved and wound up at the time of the distribution, to satisfy the preferential rights upon dissolution and winding up of partners and transferees whose preferential rights are superior to the rights of persons receiving the distribution.

(b) A limited liability partnership may base a determination that a distribution is not prohibited under subsection (a) on:

(1) financial statements prepared on the basis of accounting practices and principles that are reasonable in the circumstances; or

(2) a fair valuation or other method that is reasonable under the circumstances.

. . .

Section 407. Liability for improper distributions by limited liability partnership.

(a) Except as otherwise provided in subsection (b), if a partner of a limited liability partnership consents to a distribution made in violation of Section 406 and in consenting to the distribution fails to comply with Section 409, the partner is personally liable to the partnership for the amount of the distribution which exceeds the amount that could have been distributed without the violation of Section 406.

(b) To the extent the partnership agreement of a limited liability partnership expressly relieves a partner of the authority and responsibility to consent to distributions and imposes that authority and responsibility on one or more other partners, the liability stated in subsection (a) applies to the other partners and not to the partner that the partnership agreement relieves of the authority and responsibility.

(c) A person that receives a distribution knowing that the distribution violated Section 406 is personally liable to the limited liability partnership but only to the extent that the distribution received by the person exceeded the amount that could have been properly paid under Section 406.

. . .

(e) An action under this section is barred unless commenced not later than two years after the distribution.

Section 409. Standards of conduct for partners.

(a) A partner owes to the partnership and the other partners the duties of loyalty and care stated in subsections (b) and (c).

(b) The fiduciary duty of loyalty of a partner includes the duties:

(1) to account to the partnership and hold as trustee for it any property, profit, or benefit derived by the partner:

(A) in the conduct or winding up of the partnership's business;

(B) from a use by the partner of the partnership's property; or

(C) from the appropriation of a partnership opportunity;

(2) to refrain from dealing with the partnership in the conduct or winding up of the partnership business as or on behalf of a person having an interest adverse to the partnership; and

(3) to refrain from competing with the partnership in the conduct of the partnership's business before the dissolution of the partnership.

(c) The duty of care of a partner in the conduct or winding up of the partnership business is to refrain from engaging in grossly negligent or reckless conduct, willful or intentional misconduct, or a knowing violation of law.

(d) A partner shall discharge the duties and obligations under this [act] or under the partnership agreement and exercise any rights consistently with the contractual obligation of good faith and fair dealing.

(e) A partner does not violate a duty or obligation under this [act] or under the partnership agreement solely because the partner's conduct furthers the partner's own interest.

(f) All the partners may authorize or ratify, after full disclosure of all material facts, a specific act or transaction by a partner that otherwise would violate the duty of loyalty.

(g) It is a defense to a claim under subsection (b)(2) and any comparable claim in equity or at common law that the transaction was fair to the partnership.

(h) If, as permitted by subsection (f) or the partnership agreement, a partner enters into a transaction with the partnership which otherwise would be prohibited by subsection (b)(2), the partner's rights and obligations arising from the transaction are the same as those of a person that is not a partner.

Article 5. Transferable Interests and Rights of Transferees and Creditors

Section 501. Partner not co-owner of partnership property.

A partner is not a co-owner of partnership property and has no interest in partnership property which can be transferred, either voluntarily or involuntarily.

Section 502. Nature of transferable interest.

A transferable interest is personal property.

Section 503. Transfer of transferable interest.

(a) A transfer, in whole or in part, of a transferable interest:

(1) is permissible;

(2) does not by itself cause a person's dissociation as a partner or a dissolution and winding up of the partnership business; and

(3) subject to Section 505, does not entitle the transferee to:

(A) participate in the management or conduct of the partnership's business; or

(B) except as otherwise provided in subsection (c), have access to records or other information concerning the partnership's business.

(b) A transferee has the right to:

(1) receive, in accordance with the transfer, distributions to which the transferor would otherwise be entitled; and

(2) seek under Section 801(5) a judicial determination that it is equitable to wind up the partnership business.

(c) In a dissolution and winding up of a partnership, a transferee is entitled to an account of the partnership's transactions only from the date of dissolution.

(d) A partnership need not give effect to a transferee's rights under this section until the partnership knows or has notice of the transfer.

(e) A transfer of a transferable interest in violation of a restriction on transfer contained in the partnership agreement is ineffective if the intended transferee has knowledge or notice of the restriction at the time of transfer.

(f) Except as otherwise provided in Section 601(4)(B), if a partner transfers a transferable interest, the transferor retains the rights of a partner other than the transferable interest transferred and retains all the duties and obligations of a partner.

(g) If a partner transfers a transferable interest to a person that becomes a partner with respect to the transferred interest, the transferee is liable for the partner's obligations under Sections 404 and 407 known to the transferee when the transferee becomes a partner.

Section 504. Charging order.

(a) On application by a judgment creditor of a partner or transferee, a court may enter a charging order against the transferable interest of the judgment debtor for the unsatisfied amount of the judgment. A charging order constitutes a lien on a judgment debtor's transferable interest and requires the partnership to pay over to the person to which the charging order was issued any distribution that otherwise would be paid to the judgment debtor.

(b) To the extent necessary to effectuate the collection of distributions pursuant to a charging order in effect under subsection (a), the court may:

(1) appoint a receiver of the distributions subject to the charging order, with the power to make all inquiries the judgment debtor might have made; and

(2) make all other orders necessary to give effect to the charging order.

. . .

Article 6. Dissociation

Section 601. Events causing dissociation.

A person is dissociated as a partner when:

(1) the partnership knows or has notice of the person's express will to withdraw as a partner, but, if the person has specified a withdrawal date later than the date the partnership knew or had notice, on that later date;

(2) an event stated in the partnership agreement as causing the person's dissociation occurs;

(3) the person is expelled as a partner pursuant to the partnership agreement;

(4) the person is expelled as a partner by the affirmative vote or consent of all the other partners if:

(A) it is unlawful to carry on the partnership business with the person as a partner;

(B) there has been a transfer of all of the person's transferable interest in the partnership, other than:

(i) a transfer for security purposes; or

(ii) a charging order in effect under Section 504 which has not been foreclosed;

(C) the person is an entity and:

(i) the partnership notifies the person that it will be expelled as a partner because the person has filed a statement of dissolution or the equivalent, the person has been administratively dissolved, the person's charter or the equivalent has been revoked, or the person's right to conduct business has been suspended by the person's jurisdiction of formation; and

(ii) not later than 90 days after the notification, the statement of dissolution or the equivalent has not been withdrawn, rescinded, or revoked, or the person's charter or the equivalent or right to conduct business has not been reinstated; or

(D) the person is an unincorporated entity that has been dissolved and whose activities and affairs are being wound up;

(5) on application by the partnership or another partner, the person is expelled as a partner by judicial order because the person:

(A) has engaged or is engaging in wrongful conduct that has affected adversely and materially, or will affect adversely and materially, the partnership's business;

(B) has committed willfully or persistently, or is committing willfully or persistently, a material breach of the partnership agreement or a duty or obligation under Section 409; or

(C) has engaged or is engaging in conduct relating to the partnership's business which makes it not reasonably practicable to carry on the business with the person as a partner;

(6) the person:

(A) becomes a debtor in bankruptcy;

(B) signs an assignment for the benefit of creditors; or

(C) seeks, consents to, or acquiesces in the appointment of a trustee, receiver, or liquidator of the person or of all or substantially all the person's property;

(7) in the case of an individual:

(A) the individual dies;

(B) a guardian or general conservator for the individual is appointed; or

(C) a court orders that the individual has otherwise become incapable of performing the individual's duties as a partner under this [act] or the partnership agreement;

(8) in the case of a person that is a testamentary or inter vivos trust or is acting as a partner by virtue of being a trustee of such a trust, the trust's entire transferable interest in the partnership is distributed;

(9) in the case of a person that is an estate or is acting as a partner by virtue of being a personal representative of an estate, the estate's entire transferable interest in the partnership is distributed;

(10) in the case of a person that is not an individual, the existence of the person terminates;

. . . or

(15) the partnership dissolves and completes winding up.

Section 602. Power to dissociate as partner; wrongful dissociation.

(a) A person has the power to dissociate as a partner at any time, rightfully or wrongfully, by withdrawing as a partner by express will under Section 601(1).

(b) A person's dissociation as a partner is wrongful only if the dissociation:

(1) is in breach of an express provision of the partnership agreement; or

(2) in the case of a partnership for a definite term or particular undertaking, occurs before the expiration of the term or the completion of the undertaking and:

(A) the person withdraws as a partner by express will, unless the withdrawal follows not later than 90 days after another person's dissociation by death or otherwise under Section 601(6) through (10) or wrongful dissociation under this subsection;

(B) the person is expelled as a partner by judicial order under Section 601(5);

(C) the person is dissociated under Section 601(6); or

(D) in the case of a person that is not a trust other than a business trust, an estate, or an individual, the person is expelled or otherwise dissociated because it willfully dissolved or terminated.

(c) A person that wrongfully dissociates as a partner is liable to the partnership and to the other partners for damages caused by the dissociation. The liability is in addition to any debt, obligation, or other liability of the partner to the partnership or the other partners.

Section 603. Effect of dissociation.

(a) If a person's dissociation results in a dissolution and winding up of the partnership business, Article 8 applies; otherwise, Article 7 applies.

(b) If a person is dissociated as a partner:

(1) the person's right to participate in the management and conduct of the partnership's business terminates, except as otherwise provided in Section 802(c); and

(2) the person's duties and obligations under Section 409 end with regard to matters arising and events occurring after the person's dissociation, except to the extent the partner participates in winding up the partnership's business pursuant to Section 802.

(c) A person's dissociation does not of itself discharge the person from any debt, obligation, or other liability to the partnership or the other partners which the person incurred while a partner.

Article 7. Person's Dissociation as a Partner When Business Not Wound Up

Section 701. Purchase of interest of person dissociated as partner.

(a) If a person is dissociated as a partner without the dissociation resulting in a dissolution and winding up of the partnership business under Section 801, the partnership shall cause the person's interest in the partnership to be purchased for a buyout price determined pursuant to subsection (b).

(b) The buyout price of the interest of a person dissociated as a partner is the amount that would have been distributable to the person under Section 806(b) if, on the date of dissociation, the assets of the partnership were sold and the partnership were wound up, with the sale price equal to the greater of:

(1) the liquidation value; or

(2) the value based on a sale of the entire business as a going concern without the person.

(c) Interest accrues on the buyout price from the date of dissociation to the date of payment, but damages for wrongful dissociation under Section 602(b), and all other amounts owing, whether or not presently due, from the person dissociated as a partner to the partnership, must be offset against the buyout price.

(d) A partnership shall defend, indemnify, and hold harmless a person dissociated as a partner whose interest is being purchased against all partnership liabilities, whether incurred before or after the dissociation, except liabilities incurred by an act of the person under Section 702.

(e) If no agreement for the purchase of the interest of a person dissociated as a partner is reached not later than 120 days after a written demand for payment, the partnership shall pay, or cause to be paid, in money to the person the amount the partnership estimates to be the buyout price and accrued interest, reduced by any offsets and accrued interest under subsection (c).

(f) If a deferred payment is authorized under subsection (h), the partnership may tender a written offer to pay the amount it estimates to be the buyout price and accrued interest, reduced by any offsets under subsection (c), stating the time of payment, the amount and type of security for payment, and the other terms and conditions of the obligation.

(g) The payment or tender required by subsection (e) or (f) must be accompanied by the following:

(1) a statement of partnership assets and liabilities as of the date of dissociation;

(2) the latest available partnership balance sheet and income statement, if any;

(3) an explanation of how the estimated amount of the payment was calculated; and

(4) written notice that the payment is in full satisfaction of the obligation to purchase unless, not later than 120 days after the

written notice, the person dissociated as a partner commences an action to determine the buyout price, any offsets under subsection (c), or other terms of the obligation to purchase.

(h) A person that wrongfully dissociates as a partner before the expiration of a definite term or the completion of a particular undertaking is not entitled to payment of any part of the buyout price until the expiration of the term or completion of the undertaking, unless the person establishes to the satisfaction of the court that earlier payment will not cause undue hardship to the business of the partnership. A deferred payment must be adequately secured and bear interest.

(i) A person dissociated as a partner may maintain an action against the partnership, pursuant to Section 410(b)(2), to determine the buyout price of that person's interest, any offsets under subsection (c), or other terms of the obligation to purchase. The action must be commenced not later than 120 days after the partnership has tendered payment or an offer to pay or within one year after written demand for payment if no payment or offer to pay is tendered. The court shall determine the buyout price of the person's interest, any offset due under subsection (c), and accrued interest, and enter judgment for any additional payment or refund. If deferred payment is authorized under subsection (h), the court shall also determine the security for payment and other terms of the obligation to purchase. The court may assess reasonable attorney's fees and the fees and expenses of appraisers or other experts for a party to the action, in amounts the court finds equitable, against a party that the court finds acted arbitrarily, vexatiously, or not in good faith. The finding may be based on the partnership's failure to tender payment or an offer to pay or to comply with subsection (g).

Section 702. Power to bind and liability of person dissociated as partner.

(a) After a person is dissociated as a partner without the dissociation resulting in a dissolution and winding up of the partnership business and before the partnership is merged out of existence, converted, or domesticated under Article 11, or dissolved, the partnership is bound by an act of the person only if:

(1) the act would have bound the partnership under Section 301 before dissociation; and

(2) at the time the other party enters into the transaction:

(A) less than two years has passed since the dissociation; and

(B) the other party does not know or have notice of the dissociation and reasonably believes that the person is a partner.

(b) If a partnership is bound under subsection (a), the person dissociated as a partner which caused the partnership to be bound is liable:

(1) to the partnership for any damage caused to the partnership arising from the obligation incurred under subsection (a); and

(2) if a partner or another person dissociated as a partner is liable for the obligation, to the partner or other person for any damage caused to the partner or other person arising from the liability.

Section 703. Liability of person dissociated as partner to other persons.

(a) Except as otherwise provided in subsection (b), a person dissociated as a partner is not liable for a partnership obligation incurred after dissociation.

(b) A person that is dissociated as a partner is liable on a transaction entered into by the partnership after the dissociation only if:

(1) a partner would be liable on the transaction; and

(2) at the time the other party enters into the transaction:

(A) less than two years has passed since the dissociation; and

(B) the other party does not have knowledge or notice of the dissociation and reasonably believes that the person is a partner.

(c) By agreement with a creditor of a partnership and the partnership, a person dissociated as a partner may be released from liability for a debt, obligation, or other liability of the partnership.

(d) A person dissociated as a partner is released from liability for a debt, obligation, or other liability of the partnership if the partnership's creditor, with knowledge or notice of the person's dissociation but without the person's consent, agrees to a material alteration in the nature or time of payment of the debt, obligation, or other liability.

Article 8. Dissolution and Winding Up

Section 801. Events causing dissolution.

A partnership is dissolved, and its business must be wound up, upon the occurrence of any of the following:

(1) in a partnership at will, the partnership knows or has notice of a person's express will to withdraw as a partner, other than a partner that has dissociated under Section 601(2) through (10), but, if the person has specified a withdrawal date later than the date the partnership knew or had notice, on the later date;

(2) in a partnership for a definite term or particular undertaking:

(A) within 90 days after a person's dissociation by death or otherwise under Section 601(6) through (10) or wrongful dissociation under Section 602(b), the affirmative vote or consent of at least half of the remaining partners to wind up the partnership business, for which purpose a person's rightful dissociation pursuant to Section 602(b)(2)(A) constitutes that partner's consent to wind up the partnership business;

(B) the affirmative vote or consent of all the partners to wind up the partnership business; or

(C) the expiration of the term or the completion of the undertaking;

(3) an event or circumstance that the partnership agreement states causes dissolution;

(4) on application by a partner, the entry by [the appropriate court] of an order dissolving the partnership on the grounds that:

(A) the conduct of all or substantially all the partnership's business is unlawful;

(B) the economic purpose of the partnership is likely to be unreasonably frustrated;

(C) another partner has engaged in conduct relating to the partnership business which makes it not reasonably practicable to carry on the business in partnership with that partner; or

(D) it is otherwise not reasonably practicable to carry on the partnership business in conformity with the partnership agreement;

(5) on application by a transferee, the entry by [the appropriate court] of an order dissolving the partnership on the ground that it is equitable to wind up the partnership business:

(A) after the expiration of the term or completion of the undertaking, if the partnership was for a definite term or particular undertaking at the time of the transfer or entry of the charging order that gave rise to the transfer; or

(B) at any time, if the partnership was a partnership at will at the time of the transfer or entry of the charging order that gave rise to the transfer; or

(6) the passage of 90 consecutive days during which the partnership does not have at least two partners.

Section 802. Winding up.

(a) A dissolved partnership shall wind up its business and, except as otherwise provided in Section 803, the partnership continues after dissolution only for the purpose of winding up.

(b) In winding up its business, the partnership:

(1) shall discharge the partnership's debts, obligations, and other liabilities, settle and close the partnership's business, and marshal and distribute the assets of the partnership; and

(2) may:

(A) deliver to the [Secretary of State] for filing a statement of dissolution stating the name of the partnership and that the partnership is dissolved;

(B) preserve the partnership business and property as a going concern for a reasonable time;

(C) prosecute and defend actions and proceedings, whether civil, criminal, or administrative;

(D) transfer the partnership's property;

(E) settle disputes by mediation or arbitration;

(F) deliver to the [Secretary of State] for filing a statement of termination stating the name of the partnership and that the partnership is terminated; and

(G) perform other acts necessary or appropriate to the winding up.

(c) A person whose dissociation as a partner resulted in dissolution may participate in winding up as if still a partner, unless the dissociation was wrongful.

(d) If a dissolved partnership does not have a partner and no person has the right to participate in winding up under subsection (c), the personal or legal representative of the last person to have been a partner may wind up the partnership's business. If the representative does not exercise that right, a person to wind up the partnership's business may be appointed by the affirmative vote or consent of transferees owning a majority of the rights to receive distributions at the time the consent is to be effective. A person appointed under this subsection has the powers of a partner under Section 804 but is not liable for the debts, obligations, and other liabilities of the partnership solely by reason of having or exercising those powers or otherwise acting to wind up the partnership's business.

. . .

Section 804. Power to bind partnership after dissolution.

(a) A partnership is bound by a partner's act after dissolution which:

(1) is appropriate for winding up the partnership business; or

(2) would have bound the partnership under Section 301 before dissolution if, at the time the other party enters into the transaction, the other party does not know or have notice of the dissolution.

(b) A person dissociated as a partner binds a partnership through an act occurring after dissolution if:

(1) at the time the other party enters into the transaction:

(A) less than two years has passed since the dissociation; and

(B) the other party does not know or have notice of the dissociation and reasonably believes that the person is a partner; and

(2) the act:

(A) is appropriate for winding up the partnership's business; or

(B) would have bound the partnership under Section 301 before dissolution and at the time the other party enters into the transaction the other party does not know or have notice of the dissolution.

Section 805. Liability after dissolution of partner and person dissociated as partner.

(a) If a partner having knowledge of the dissolution causes a partnership to incur an obligation under Section 804(a) by an act that is not appropriate for winding up the partnership business, the partner is liable:

(1) to the partnership for any damage caused to the partnership arising from the obligation; and

(2) if another partner or person dissociated as a partner is liable for the obligation, to that other partner or person for any damage caused to that other partner or person arising from the liability.

(b) Except as otherwise provided in subsection (c), if a person dissociated as a partner causes a partnership to incur an obligation under Section 804(b), the person is liable:

(1) to the partnership for any damage caused to the partnership arising from the obligation; and

(2) if a partner or another person dissociated as a partner is liable for the obligation, to the partner or other person for any damage caused to the partner or other person arising from the obligation.

(c) A person dissociated as a partner is not liable under subsection (b) if:

(1) Section 802(c) permits the person to participate in winding up; and

(2) the act that causes the partnership to be bound under Section 804(b) is appropriate for winding up the partnership's business.

Section 806. Disposition of assets in winding up; when contributions required.

(a) In winding up its business, a partnership shall apply its assets, including the contributions required by this section, to discharge the partnership's obligations to creditors, including partners that are creditors.

(b) After a partnership complies with subsection (a), any surplus must be distributed in the following order, subject to any charging order in effect under Section 504:

(1) to each person owning a transferable interest that reflects contributions made and not previously returned, an amount equal to the value of the unreturned contributions; and

(2) among persons owning transferable interests in proportion to their respective rights to share in distributions immediately before the dissolution of the partnership.

(c) If a partnership's assets are insufficient to satisfy all its obligations under subsection (a), with respect to each unsatisfied obligation incurred when the partnership was not a limited liability partnership, the following rules apply:

(1) Each person that was a partner when the obligation was incurred and that has not been released from the obligation under Section 703(c) and (d) shall contribute to the partnership for the purpose of enabling the partnership to satisfy the obligation. The contribution due from each of those persons is in proportion to the right to receive distributions in the capacity of a partner in effect for each of those persons when the obligation was incurred.

(2) If a person does not contribute the full amount required under paragraph (1) with respect to an unsatisfied obligation of the partnership, the other persons required to contribute by paragraph (1) on account of the obligation shall contribute the additional amount necessary to discharge the obligation. The additional contribution due from each of those other persons is in proportion to the right to receive distributions in the capacity of a partner in effect for each of those other persons when the obligation was incurred.

(3) If a person does not make the additional contribution required by paragraph (2), further additional contributions are determined and due in the same manner as provided in that paragraph.

(d) A person that makes an additional contribution under subsection (c)(2) or (3) may recover from any person whose failure to contribute under subsection (c)(1) or (2) necessitated the additional contribution. A person may not recover under this subsection more than the amount additionally contributed. A person's liability under this subsection may not exceed the amount the person failed to contribute.

(e) If a partnership does not have sufficient surplus to comply with subsection (b)(1), any surplus must be distributed among the owners of transferable interests in proportion to the value of the respective unreturned contributions.

(f) All distributions made under subsections (b) and (c) must be paid in money.

Article 9. Limited Liability Partnership

Section 901. Statement of qualification.

(a) A partnership may become a limited liability partnership pursuant to this section.

(b) The terms and conditions on which a partnership becomes a limited liability partnership must be approved by the affirmative vote or consent necessary to amend the partnership agreement except, in the case of a partnership agreement that expressly addresses obligations to contribute to the partnership, the affirmative vote or consent necessary to amend those provisions.

(c) After the approval required by subsection (b), a partnership may become a limited liability partnership by delivering to the [Secretary of State] for filing a statement of qualification. The statement must contain:

(1) the name of the partnership which must comply with Section 902;

(2) the street and mailing addresses of the partnership's principal office and, if different, the street address of an office in this state, if any;

(3) the name and street and mailing addresses in this state of the partnership's registered agent; and

(4) a statement that the partnership elects to become a limited liability partnership.

(d) A partnership's status as a limited liability partnership remains effective, regardless of changes in the partnership, until it is canceled pursuant to subsection (f) or administratively revoked pursuant to Section 903.

(e) The status of a partnership as a limited liability partnership and the protection against liability of its partners for the debts, obligations, or other liabilities of the partnership while it is a limited liability partnership is not affected by errors or later changes in the information required to be contained in the statement of qualification.

(f) A limited liability partnership may amend or cancel its statement of qualification by delivering to the [Secretary of State] for filing a statement of amendment or cancellation. The statement must be approved by the affirmative vote or consent of all the partners and state the name of the limited liability partnership and in the case of:

(1) an amendment, state the text of the amendment; and

(2) a cancellation, state that the statement of qualification is canceled.

UNIFORM LIMITED PARTNERSHIP ACT (2001) (Last Amended 2013)

[ARTICLE] 1

GENERAL PROVISIONS

SECTION 101. SHORT TITLE. This [act] may be cited as the Uniform Limited Partnership Act.

SECTION 102. DEFINITIONS. In this [act]:

(1) "Certificate of limited partnership" means the certificate required by Section 201. The term includes the certificate as amended or restated.

(2) "Contribution", except in the phrase "right of contribution", means property or a benefit described in Section 501 which is provided by a person to a limited partnership to become a partner or in the person's capacity as a partner.

(7) "General partner" means a person that:

(A) has become a general partner under Section 401 or was a general partner in a partnership when the partnership became subject to this [act] under Section 112; and

(B) has not dissociated as a general partner under Section 603.

(10) "Limited liability limited partnership", except in the phrase "foreign limited liability limited partnership" and in [Article] 11, means a limited partnership whose certificate of limited partnership states that the partnership is a limited liability limited partnership.

(11) "Limited partner" means a person that:

(A) has become a limited partner under Section 301 or was a limited partner in a limited partnership when the partnership became subject to this [act] under Section 112; and

(B) has not dissociated under Section 601.

(12) "Limited partnership", except in the phrase "foreign limited partnership" and in [Article] 11, means an entity formed under this [act] or which becomes subject to this [act] under [Article] 11 or Section 112. The term includes a limited liability limited partnership.

(13) "Partner" means a limited partner or general partner.

(14) "Partnership agreement" means the agreement, whether or not referred to as a partnership agreement and whether oral, implied, in a record, or in any combination thereof, of all the partners of a limited partnership concerning the matters described in Section 105(a). The term includes the agreement as amended or restated.

SECTION 104. GOVERNING LAW. The law of this state governs:

(1) the internal affairs of a limited partnership; and

(2) the liability of a partner as partner for a debt, obligation, or other liability of a limited partnership.

SECTION 105. PARTNERSHIP AGREEMENT; SCOPE, FUNCTION, AND LIMITATIONS.

(a) Except as otherwise provided in subsections (c) and (d), the partnership agreement governs:

(1) relations among the partners as partners and between the partners and the limited partnership;

(2) the activities and affairs of the partnership and the conduct of those activities and affairs; and

(3) the means and conditions for amending the partnership agreement.

(b) To the extent the partnership agreement does not provide for a matter described in subsection (a), this [act] governs the matter.

(c) A partnership agreement may not:

(1) vary the law applicable under Section 104;

(2) vary a limited partnership's capacity under Section 111 to sue and be sued in its own name;

(3) vary any requirement, procedure, or other provision of this [act] pertaining to:

(A) registered agents; or

(B) the [Secretary of State], including provisions pertaining to records authorized or required to be delivered to the [Secretary of State] for filing under this [act];

(4) vary the provisions of Section 204;

(5) vary the right of a general partner under Section 406(b)(2) to vote on or consent to an amendment to the certificate of limited partnership which deletes a statement that the limited partnership is a limited liability limited partnership;

(6) alter or eliminate the duty of loyalty or the duty of care except as otherwise provided in subsection (d);

(7) eliminate the contractual obligation of good faith and fair dealing under Sections 305(a) and 409(d), but the partnership agreement may prescribe the standards, if not manifestly unreasonable, by which the performance of the obligation is to be measured;

(8) relieve or exonerate a person from liability for conduct involving bad faith, willful or intentional misconduct, or knowing violation of law;

(9) vary the information required under Section 108 or unreasonably restrict the duties and rights under Section 304 or 407, but the partnership agreement may impose reasonable restrictions on the availability and use of information obtained under those sections and may define appropriate remedies, including liquidated damages, for a breach of any reasonable restriction on use;

(10) vary the grounds for expulsion specified in Section 603(5)(B);

(11) vary the power of a person to dissociate as a general partner under Section 604(a), except to require that the notice under Section 603(1) be in a record;

(12) vary the causes of dissolution specified in Section 801(a)(6);

(d) Subject to subsection (c)(8), without limiting other terms that may be included in a partnership agreement, the following rules apply:

(1) The partnership agreement may:

(A) specify the method by which a specific act or transaction that would otherwise violate the duty of loyalty may be authorized or ratified by one or more disinterested and independent persons after full disclosure of all material facts; and

(B) alter the prohibition in Section 504(a)(2) so that the prohibition requires only that the partnership's total assets not be less than the sum of its total liabilities.

(2) If not manifestly unreasonable, the partnership agreement may:

(A) alter or eliminate the aspects of the duty of loyalty stated in Section 409(b);

(B) identify specific types or categories of activities that do not violate the duty of loyalty;

(C) alter the duty of care, but may not authorize conduct involving bad faith, willful or intentional misconduct, or knowing violation of law; and

(D) alter or eliminate any other fiduciary duty.

SECTION 106. PARTNERSHIP AGREEMENT; EFFECT ON LIMITED PARTNERSHIP AND PERSON BECOMING PARTNER; PREFORMATION AGREEMENT.

(a) A limited partnership is bound by and may enforce the partnership agreement, whether or not the partnership has itself manifested assent to the agreement.

(b) A person that becomes a partner is deemed to assent to the partnership agreement.

(c) Two or more persons intending to become the initial partners of a limited partnership may make an agreement providing that upon the formation of the partnership the agreement will become the partnership agreement.

SECTION 107. PARTNERSHIP AGREEMENT; EFFECT ON THIRD PARTIES AND RELATIONSHIP TO RECORDS EFFECTIVE ON BEHALF OF LIMITED PARTNERSHIP.

(a) A partnership agreement may specify that its amendment requires the approval of a person that is not a party to the agreement or the satisfaction of a condition. An amendment is ineffective if its adoption does not include the required approval or satisfy the specified condition.

. . .

SECTION 110. NATURE, PURPOSE, AND DURATION OF LIMITED PARTNERSHIP.

(a) A limited partnership is an entity distinct from its partners. A limited partnership is the same entity regardless of whether its certificate states that the limited partnership is a limited liability limited partnership.

(b) A limited partnership may have any lawful purpose, regardless of whether for profit.

(c) A limited partnership has perpetual duration.

SECTION 111. POWERS. A limited partnership has the capacity to sue and be sued in the name of the partnership and the power to do all things necessary or convenient to carry on the partnership's activities and affairs.

SECTION 113. SUPPLEMENTAL PRINCIPLES OF LAW. Unless displaced by particular provisions of this [act], the principles of law and equity supplement this [act].

SECTION 114. PERMITTED NAMES.

(a) The name of a limited partnership may contain the name of any partner.

(b) The name of a limited partnership that is not a limited liability limited partnership must contain the phrase "limited partnership" or the abbreviation "LP" or "L.P." and may not contain the phrase "limited liability limited partnership" or the abbreviation "LLLP" or "L.L.L.P.".

(c) The name of a limited liability limited partnership must contain the phrase "limited liability limited partnership" or the abbreviation "LLLP" or "L.L.L.P." and must not contain the abbreviation "LP" or "L.P.".

[ARTICLE] 2

FORMATION; CERTIFICATE OF LIMITED PARTNERSHIP AND OTHER FILINGS

SECTION 201. FORMATION OF LIMITED PARTNERSHIP; CERTIFICATE OF LIMITED PARTNERSHIP.

(a) To form a limited partnership, a person must deliver a certificate of limited partnership to the [Secretary of State] for filing.

(b) A certificate of limited partnership must state:

(1) the name of the limited partnership, which must comply with Section 114;

(2) the street and mailing addresses of the partnership's principal office;

(3) the name and street and mailing addresses in this state of the partnership's registered agent;

(4) the name and street and mailing addresses of each general partner; and

(5) whether the limited partnership is a limited liability limited partnership.

(c) A certificate of limited partnership may contain statements as to matters other than those required by subsection (b), but may not vary or otherwise affect the provisions specified in Section 105(c) and (d) in a manner inconsistent with that section.

(d) A limited partnership is formed when:

(1) the certificate of limited partnership becomes effective;

(2) at least two persons have become partners;

(3) at least one person has become a general partner; and

(4) at least one person has become a limited partner.

SECTION 202. AMENDMENT OR RESTATEMENT OF CERTIFICATE OF LIMITED PARTNERSHIP.

(a) A certificate of limited partnership may be amended or restated at any time.

SECTION 212. [ANNUAL] [BIENNIAL] REPORT FOR [SECRETARY OF STATE].

(a) A limited partnership or registered foreign limited partnership shall deliver to the [Secretary of State] for filing [an annual] [a biennial] report that states:

(1) the name of the partnership or foreign partnership;

(2) the name and street and mailing addresses of its registered agent in this state;

(3) the street and mailing addresses of its principal office;

(4) the name of at least one general partner; and

(5) in the case of a foreign partnership, its jurisdiction of formation and any alternate name adopted under Section 1006(a).

[ARTICLE] 3

LIMITED PARTNERS

SECTION 301. BECOMING LIMITED PARTNER.

(a) Upon formation of a limited partnership, a person becomes a limited partner as agreed among the persons that are to be the initial partners.

(b) After formation, a person becomes a limited partner:

(1) as provided in the partnership agreement;

(2) as the result of a transaction effective under [Article] 11;

(3) with the affirmative vote or consent of all the partners; or

(4) as provided in Section 801(a)(4) or (a)(5).

(c) A person may become a limited partner without:

(1) acquiring a transferable interest; or

(2) making or being obligated to make a contribution to the limited partnership.

SECTION 302. NO AGENCY POWER OF LIMITED PARTNER AS LIMITED PARTNER.

(a) A limited partner is not an agent of a limited partnership solely by reason of being a limited partner.

(b) A person's status as a limited partner does not prevent or restrict law other than this [act] from imposing liability on a limited partnership because of the person's conduct.

SECTION 303. NO LIABILITY AS LIMITED PARTNER FOR LIMITED PARTNERSHIP OBLIGATIONS.

(a) A debt, obligation, or other liability of a limited partnership is not the debt, obligation, or other liability of a limited partner. A limited partner is not personally liable, directly or indirectly, by way of contribution or otherwise, for a debt, obligation, or other liability of the partnership solely by reason of being or acting as a limited partner, even if the limited partner participates in the management and control of the limited partnership. This subsection applies regardless of the dissolution of the partnership.

(b) The failure of a limited partnership to observe formalities relating to the exercise of its powers or management of its activities and affairs is not a ground for imposing liability on a limited partner for a debt, obligation, or other liability of the partnership.

SECTION 304. RIGHTS TO INFORMATION OF LIMITED PARTNER AND PERSON DISSOCIATED AS LIMITED PARTNER.

(a) On 10 days' demand, made in a record received by the limited partnership, a limited partner may inspect and copy required information during regular business hours in the limited partnership's principal office. The limited partner need not have any particular purpose for seeking the information.

SECTION 305. LIMITED DUTIES OF LIMITED PARTNERS.

(a) A limited partner shall discharge any duties to the partnership and the other partners under the partnership agreement and exercise any rights under this [act] or the partnership agreement consistently with the contractual obligation of good faith and fair dealing.

(b) Except as otherwise provided in subsection (a), a limited partner does not have any duty to the limited partnership or to any other partner solely by reason of acting as a limited partner.

(c) If a limited partner enters into a transaction with a limited partnership, the limited partner's rights and obligations arising from the transaction are the same as those of a person that is not a partner.

[ARTICLE] 4

GENERAL PARTNERS

SECTION 401. BECOMING GENERAL PARTNER.

(a) Upon formation of a limited partnership, a person becomes a general partner as agreed among the persons that are to be the initial partners.

(b) After formation of a limited partnership, a person becomes a general partner:

(1) as provided in the partnership agreement;

(2) as the result of a transaction effective under [Article] 11;

(3) with the affirmative vote or consent of all the partners; or

(4) as provided in Section 801(a)(3)(B).

(c) A person may become a general partner without:

(1) acquiring a transferable interest; or

(2) making or being obligated to make a contribution to the partnership.

SECTION 402. GENERAL PARTNER AGENT OF LIMITED PARTNERSHIP.

(a) Each general partner is an agent of the limited partnership for the purposes of its activities and affairs. An act of a general partner, including the signing of a record in the partnership's name, for apparently carrying on in the ordinary course the partnership's activities and affairs or activities and affairs of the kind carried on by the partnership binds the partnership, unless the general partner did not have authority to act for the partnership in the particular matter and the person with which the general partner was dealing knew or had notice that the general partner lacked authority.

(b) An act of a general partner which is not apparently for carrying on in the ordinary course the limited partnership's activities and affairs or activities and affairs of the kind carried on by the partnership binds the partnership only if the act was actually authorized by all the other partners.

SECTION 403. LIMITED PARTNERSHIP LIABLE FOR GENERAL PARTNER'S ACTIONABLE CONDUCT.

(a) A limited partnership is liable for loss or injury caused to a person, or for a penalty incurred, as a result of a wrongful act or omission, or other actionable conduct, of a general partner acting in the ordinary course of activities and affairs of the partnership or with the actual or apparent authority of the partnership.

(b) If, in the course of a limited partnership's activities and affairs or while acting with actual or apparent authority of the partnership, a general partner receives or causes the partnership to receive money or property of a person not a partner, and the money or property is misapplied by a general partner, the partnership is liable for the loss.

SECTION 404. GENERAL PARTNER'S LIABILITY.

(a) Except as otherwise provided in subsections (b) and (c), all general partners are liable jointly and severally for all debts, obligations, and other liabilities of the limited partnership unless otherwise agreed by the claimant or provided by law.

(b) A person that becomes a general partner is not personally liable for a debt, obligation, or other liability of the limited partnership incurred before the person became a general partner.

(c) A debt, obligation, or other liability of a limited partnership incurred while the partnership is a limited liability limited partnership is solely the debt, obligation, or other liability of the limited liability limited partnership. A general partner is not personally liable, directly or indirectly, by way of contribution or otherwise, for a debt, obligation, or other liability of the limited liability limited partnership solely by reason of being or acting as a general partner. This subsection applies:

(1) despite anything inconsistent in the partnership agreement that existed immediately before the vote or consent required to become a limited liability limited partnership under Section 406(b)(2); and

(2) regardless of the dissolution of the partnership.

(d) The failure of a limited liability limited partnership to observe formalities relating to the exercise of its powers or management of its activities and affairs is not a ground for imposing liability on a general partner for a debt, obligation, or other liability of the partnership.

(e) An amendment of a certificate of limited partnership which deletes a statement that the limited partnership is a limited liability limited partnership does not affect the limitation in this section on the liability of a general partner for a debt, obligation, or other liability of the limited partnership incurred before the amendment became effective.

SECTION 405. ACTIONS BY AND AGAINST PARTNERSHIP AND PARTNERS.

(a) To the extent not inconsistent with Section 404, a general partner may be joined in an action against the limited partnership or named in a separate action.

(b) A judgment against a limited partnership is not by itself a judgment against a general partner. A judgment against a partnership may not be satisfied from a general partner's assets unless there is also a judgment against the general partner.

(c) A judgment creditor of a general partner may not levy execution against the assets of the general partner to satisfy a judgment based on a claim against the limited partnership, unless the partner is personally liable for the claim under Section 404 and:

(1) a judgment based on the same claim has been obtained against the limited partnership and a writ of execution on the judgment has been returned unsatisfied in whole or in part;

(2) the partnership is a debtor in bankruptcy;

(3) the general partner has agreed that the creditor need not exhaust partnership assets;

(4) a court grants permission to the judgment creditor to levy execution against the assets of a general partner based on a finding that partnership assets subject to execution are clearly insufficient to satisfy the judgment, that exhaustion of assets is excessively burdensome, or that the grant of permission is an appropriate exercise of the court's equitable powers; or

(5) liability is imposed on the general partner by law or contract independent of the existence of the partnership

SECTION 406. MANAGEMENT RIGHTS OF GENERAL PARTNER.

(a) Each general partner has equal rights in the management and conduct of the limited partnership's activities and affairs. Except as otherwise provided in this [act], any matter relating to the activities and affairs of the partnership is decided exclusively by the general partner or, if there is more than one general partner, by a majority of the general partners.

(b) The affirmative vote or consent of all the partners is required to:

(1) amend the partnership agreement;

(2) amend the certificate of limited partnership to add or delete a statement that the limited partnership is a limited liability limited partnership; and

(3) sell, lease, exchange, or otherwise dispose of all, or substantially all, of the limited partnership's property, with or without the good will, other than in the usual and regular course of the limited partnership's activities and affairs.

(c) A limited partnership shall reimburse a general partner for an advance to the partnership beyond the amount of capital the general partner agreed to contribute.

(d) A payment or advance made by a general partner which gives rise to a limited partnership obligation under subsection (c) or Section 408(a) constitutes a loan to the limited partnership which accrues interest from the date of the payment or advance.

(e) A general partner is not entitled to remuneration for services performed for the limited partnership.

SECTION 407. RIGHTS TO INFORMATION OF GENERAL PARTNER AND PERSON DISSOCIATED AS GENERAL PARTNER.

(a) A general partner may inspect and copy required information during regular business hours in the limited partnership's principal office, without having any particular purpose for seeking the information.

SECTION 409. STANDARDS OF CONDUCT FOR GENERAL PARTNERS.

(a) A general partner owes to the limited partnership and, subject to Section 901, the other partners the duties of loyalty and care stated in subsections (b) and (c).

(b) The fiduciary duty of loyalty of a general partner includes the duties:

(1) to account to the limited partnership and hold as trustee for it any property, profit, or benefit derived by the general partner:

(A) in the conduct or winding up of the partnership's activities and affairs;

(B) from a use by the general partner of the partnership's property; or

(C) from the appropriation of a partnership opportunity;

(2) to refrain from dealing with the partnership in the conduct or winding up of the partnership's activities and affairs as or on behalf of a person having an interest adverse to the partnership; and

(3) to refrain from competing with the partnership in the conduct or winding up of the partnership's activities and affairs.

(c) The duty of care of a general partner in the conduct or winding up of the limited partnership's activities and affairs is to refrain from engaging in grossly negligent or reckless conduct, willful or intentional misconduct, or knowing violation of law.

(d) A general partner shall discharge the duties and obligations under this [act] or under the partnership agreement and exercise any rights consistently with the contractual obligation of good faith and fair dealing.

(e) A general partner does not violate a duty or obligation under this [act] or under the partnership agreement solely because the general partner's conduct furthers the general partner's own interest.

(f) All the partners of a limited partnership may authorize or ratify, after full disclosure of all material facts, a specific act or transaction by a general partner that otherwise would violate the duty of loyalty.

(g) It is a defense to a claim under subsection (b)(2) and any comparable claim in equity or at common law that the transaction was fair to the limited partnership.

(h) If, as permitted by subsection (f) or the partnership agreement, a general partner enters into a transaction with the limited partnership which otherwise would be prohibited by subsection (b)(2), the general partner's rights and obligations arising from the transaction are the same as those of a person that is not a general partner.

[ARTICLE] 6

DISSOCIATION

SECTION 601. DISSOCIATION AS LIMITED PARTNER.

(a) A person does not have a right to dissociate as a limited partner before the completion of the winding up of the limited partnership.

(b) A person is dissociated as a limited partner when:

(1) the limited partnership knows or has notice of the person's express will to withdraw as a limited partner, but, if the person has specified a withdrawal date later than the date the partnership knew or had notice, on that later date;

(2) an event stated in the partnership agreement as causing the person's dissociation as a limited partner occurs;

(3) the person is expelled as a limited partner pursuant to the partnership agreement;

. . .

(6) in the case of an individual, the individual dies;

(7) in the case of a person that is a testamentary or inter vivos trust or is acting as a limited partner by virtue of being a trustee of such a trust, the trust's entire transferable interest in the limited partnership is distributed;

(8) in the case of a person that is an estate or is acting as a limited partner by virtue of being a personal representative of an estate, the estate's entire transferable interest in the limited partnership is distributed;

(9) in the case of a person that is not an individual, the existence of the person terminates;

. . . or

(14) the limited partnership dissolves and completes winding up.

SECTION 603. DISSOCIATION AS GENERAL PARTNER. A person is dissociated as a general partner when:

(1) the limited partnership knows or has notice of the person's express will to withdraw as a general partner, but, if the person has specified a withdrawal date later than the date the partnership knew or had notice, on that later date;

(2) an event stated in the partnership agreement as causing the person's dissociation as a general partner occurs;

(3) the person is expelled as a general partner pursuant to the partnership agreement;

. . .

(6) in the case of an individual:

(A) the individual dies;

(B) a guardian or general conservator for the individual is appointed; or

(C) a court orders that the individual has otherwise become incapable of performing the individual's duties as a general partner under this [act] or the partnership agreement;

(7) the person:

(A) becomes a debtor in bankruptcy;

(B) executes an assignment for the benefit of creditors; or

(C) seeks, consents to, or acquiesces in the appointment of a trustee, receiver, or liquidator of the person or of all or substantially all the person's property;

(8) in the case of a person that is a testamentary or inter vivos trust or is acting as a general partner by virtue of being a trustee of such a trust, the trust's entire transferable interest in the limited partnership is distributed;

(9) in the case of a person that is an estate or is acting as a general partner by virtue of being a personal representative of an estate, the estate's entire transferable interest in the limited partnership is distributed;

(10) in the case of a person that is not an individual, the existence of the person terminates;

. . . or

(15) the limited partnership dissolves and completes winding up.

SECTION 604. POWER TO DISSOCIATE AS GENERAL PARTNER; WRONGFUL DISSOCIATION.

(a) A person has the power to dissociate as a general partner at any time, rightfully or wrongfully, by withdrawing as a general partner by express will under Section 603(1).

(b) A person's dissociation as a general partner is wrongful only if the dissociation:

(1) is in breach of an express provision of the partnership agreement; or

(2) occurs before the completion of the winding up of the limited partnership, and:

(A) the person withdraws as a general partner by express will;

(B) the person is expelled as a general partner by judicial order under Section 603(5);

(C) the person is dissociated as a general partner under Section 603(7); or

(D) in the case of a person that is not a trust other than a business trust, an estate, or an individual, the person is expelled or otherwise dissociated as a general partner because it willfully dissolved or terminated.

(c) A person that wrongfully dissociates as a general partner is liable to the limited partnership and, subject to Section 901, to the other partners for damages caused by the dissociation. The liability is in addition to any debt, obligation, or other liability of the general partner to the partnership or the other partners.

[ARTICLE] 8

DISSOLUTION AND WINDING UP

SECTION 801. EVENTS CAUSING DISSOLUTION.

(a) A limited partnership is dissolved, and its activities and affairs must be wound up, upon the occurrence of any of the following:

(1) an event or circumstance that the partnership agreement states causes dissolution;

(2) the affirmative vote or consent of all general partners and of limited partners owning a majority of the rights to receive distributions as limited partners at the time the vote or consent is to be effective;

(3) after the dissociation of a person as a general partner:

(A) if the partnership has at least one remaining general partner, the affirmative vote or consent to dissolve the partnership not later than 90 days after the dissociation by partners owning a majority of the rights to receive distributions as partners at the time the vote or consent is to be effective; or

(B) if the partnership does not have a remaining general partner, the passage of 90 days after the dissociation, unless before the end of the period:

(i) consent to continue the activities and affairs of the partnership and admit at least one general partner is given by limited partners owning a majority of the rights to receive distributions as limited partners at the time the consent is to be effective; and

(ii) at least one person is admitted as a general partner in accordance with the consent;

(4) the passage of 90 consecutive days after the dissociation of the partnership's last limited partner, unless before the end of the period the partnership admits at least one limited partner;

. . .

SECTION 802. WINDING UP.

(a) A dissolved limited partnership shall wind up its activities and affairs and, except as otherwise provided in Section 803, the partnership continues after dissolution only for the purpose of winding up.

CHAPTER 3

LIMITED LIABILITY ENTITIES

1. LIMITED LIABILITY COMPANIES

INTRODUCTORY NOTE

The limited liability company (LLC) is an unincorporated business organization that combines certain features of the corporate form with others more closely resembling general partnerships. In an LLC the investors are called "members." Like a corporation, the LLC offers limited liability for its members. It allows somewhat more flexibility than the corporation, however, in developing rules for management and control. The LLC may be managed by all its members (as in a partnership) or by managers, who may or may not be members (as in a corporation). The LLC also offers advantageous tax treatment as compared with a corporation. A corporation pays tax on its profits as earned and the shareholders (the equity investors) pay a second tax when those profits are distributed to them. Investors in an LLC are taxed, like partners, only once on its profits, as those profits are earned. Moreover, the investors in an LLC can take account, on their individual tax returns, of any losses of the LLC as those losses are incurred; the losses are said to "pass through." A corporation's losses can be carried forward to offset any future profits but cannot be used by its shareholders. In addition, the LLC allows greater freedom than a corporation in allocating profit and loss for tax purposes.

A. FORMATION

Water, Waste & Land, Inc. d/b/a Westec v. Lanham

955 P.2d 997 (Colo.1998).

This case requires us to decide whether the members or managers of a limited liability company (LLC) are excused from personal liability on a contract where the other party to the contract did not have notice that the members or managers were negotiating on behalf of a limited liability company at the time the contract was made.

I.

Water, Waste, & Land, Inc., the petitioner, is a land development and engineering company doing business under the name "Westec." At the time of the events in this case, Donald Lanham and Larry Clark were managers and also members of Preferred Income Investors, L.L.C. (Company or P.I.I.). The Company is a limited liability company organized under the Colorado Limited Liability Company Act, §§ 7–80–101 to –1101, 2 C.R.S. (1997) (the LLC Act).

In March 1995, Clark contacted Westec about the possibility of hiring Westec to perform engineering work in connection with a development project which involved the construction of a fast-food restaurant known as Taco Cabana. In the course of preliminary discussions, Clark gave his business card to representatives of Westec. The business card included Lanham's address, which was also the address listed as the Company's principal office and place of business in its articles of organization filed with the secretary of state. While the Company's name was not on the business card, the letters "P.I.I." appeared above the address on the card. However, there was no indication as to what the acronym meant or that P.I.I. was a limited liability company.

After further negotiations, an oral agreement was reached concerning Westec's involvement with the Company's restaurant project. Clark instructed Westec to send a written proposal of its work to Lanham and the proposal was sent in April 1995. On August 2, 1995, Westec sent Lanham a form of contract, which Lanham was to execute and return to Westec. Although Westec never received a signed contract, in mid-August it did receive verbal authorization from Clark to begin work. Westec completed the engineering work and sent a bill for $9,183.40 to Lanham. No payments were made on the bill.

Westec filed a claim in county court against Clark and Lanham individually as well as against the Company. At trial, the Company admitted liability for the amount claimed by Westec. The county court entered judgment in favor of Westec. The county court found that: (1) Clark had contacted Westec to do engineering work for Lanham; (2) it was "unknown" to Westec that Lanham had organized the Company as a limited liability company; and (3) the letters "P.I.I." on Clark's business card were insufficient to place Westec on notice that the Company was a limited liability company. Based on its findings, the county court ruled that: (1) Clark was an agent of both Lanham and the Company with "authority to obligate . . . Lanham and the Company"; (2) a valid and binding contract existed for the work; (3) Westec "did not have knowledge of any business entity" and only dealt with Clark and Lanham "on a personal basis"; and (4) Westec understood Clark to be Lanham's agent and therefore "Clark is not personally liable." Accordingly, the county court dismissed Clark from the suit, concluding he could not be held personally liable, and entered judgment in the amount of $9,183 against Lanham and the Company. Lanham appealed, seeking review in the Larimer County District Court (district court). The district court reversed, [relying in part on] the notice provision of § 7–80–208, of the LLC Act. . . ., which provides that the filing of the articles of organization serve as constructive notice of a company's status as a limited liability company. . . .

II.

Resolution of the controversy between Westec and Lanham requires us to analyze the relationship between the common law of agency and the reach of our statutes governing managers and members of a limited liability company. . . .

The limited liability company is a relatively recent innovation in the law governing business entities. . . . [T]he LLC has become a popular form of business organization because it offers members the limited liability protection of a corporation, together with the single-tier tax treatment of a partnership along with considerable flexibility in management and financing. The ability to avoid two levels of income taxation [that is, a tax collected from a corporation on its income plus a tax collected from the shareholders on dividend distributions by the corporation from the remaining income] is an especially attractive feature of organization as a limited liability company. . . .

III.

A.

The district court interpreted the LLC Act's notice provision, see § 7–80–208, as putting Westec on constructive notice of Lanham's agency relationship with the Company. In essence, this course of analysis assumed that the LLC Act displaced certain common law agency doctrines, at least insofar as these doctrines otherwise would be applicable to suits by third parties seeking to hold the agents of a limited liability company liable for their personal actions as agents.

We hold, however, that the statutory notice provision applies only where a third party seeks to impose liability on an LLC's members or managers simply due to their status as members or managers of the LLC. When a third party sues a manager or member of an LLC under an agency theory, the principles of agency law apply notwithstanding the LLC Act's statutory notice rules.

B.

Under the common law of agency, an agent is liable on a contract entered on behalf of a principal if the principal is not fully disclosed. In other words, an agent who negotiates a contract with a third party can be sued for any breach of the contract unless the agent discloses both the fact that he or she is acting on behalf of a principal and the identity of the principal. As a leading treatise explains:

> If both the existence and identity of the agent's principal are fully disclosed to the other party, the agent does not become a party to any contract which he negotiates. . . . But where the principal is partially disclosed (i.e. the existence of a principal is

> known but his identity is not), it is usually inferred that the agent is a party to the contract.
>
> Harold Gill Reuschlein and William A. Gregory, The Law of Agency and Partnership § 118 (2d ed.1990).

. . .

This somewhat counterintuitive proposition—that an agent is liable even when the third party knows that the agent is acting on behalf of an unidentified principal—has been recognized as sound by the courts of this state, and it is a well established rule under the common law.

C.

Whether a principal is partially or completely disclosed is a question of fact. . . . We are, therefore, bound to accept the county court's finding that Westec did not know Clark was acting as an agent for the Company or that the letters "P.I.I." stood for "Preferred Income Investors," a limited liability company registered under Colorado law. . . . The trial record was [also] sufficient to support the county court's finding that Clark was an agent for Lanham and this conclusion should not have been disturbed by the district court.

D.

In light of the partially disclosed principal doctrine, the county court's determination that Clark and Lanham failed to disclose the existence as well as the identity of the limited liability company they represented is dispositive under the common law of agency. Still, if the General Assembly has altered the common law rules applicable to this case by adopting the LLC Act, then these rules must yield in favor of the statute. We conclude, however, that the LLC Act's notice provision was not intended to alter the partially disclosed principal doctrine.

Section 7–80–208, C.R.S. (1997) states:

> The fact that the articles of organization are on file in the office of the secretary of state is notice that the limited liability company is a limited liability company and is notice of all other facts set forth therein which are required to be set forth in the articles of organization.

In order to relieve Lanham of liability, this provision would have to be read to establish a conclusive presumption that a third party who deals with the agent of a limited liability company always has constructive notice of the existence of the agent's principal. We are not persuaded that the statute can bear such an interpretation.

Such a construction exaggerates the plain meaning of the language in the statute. Section 7–80–208 could be read to state that third parties who deal with a limited liability company are always on constructive notice of the company's limited liability status, without regard to whether any part of the company's name or even the fact of its existence has been disclosed. However, an equally plausible interpretation of the words used in the statute is that once the limited liability company's name is known to the third party, constructive notice of the company's limited liability status has been given, as well as the fact that managers and members will not be liable simply due to their status as managers or members.

Moreover, the broad interpretation urged by Lanham would be an invitation to fraud, because it would leave the agent of a limited liability company free to mislead third parties into the belief that the agent would bear personal financial responsibility under any contract, when in fact, recovery would be limited to the assets of a limited liability company not known to the third party at the time the contract was made. While Westec has not alleged that Clark or Lanham deliberately tried to conceal the Company's identity or status as a limited liability company, Lanham's construction would open the door to sharp practices and outright fraud. We may presume that in adopting § 7–80–208, the General Assembly did not intend to create a safe harbor for deceit. . . .

In addition, statutes in derogation of the common law are to be strictly construed. . . .

Other LLC Act provisions reinforce the conclusion that the legislature did not intend the notice language of § 7–80–208 to relieve the agent of a limited liability company of the duty to disclose its identity in order to avoid personal liability. For example, § 7–80–201(1), 2 C.R.S. (1997), requires limited liability companies to use the words "Limited Liability Company" or the initials "LLC" as part of their names, implying that the legislature intended to compel any entity seeking to claim the benefits of the LLC Act to identify itself clearly as a limited liability company. By way of further support for our conclusion, § 7–80–107, 2 C.R.S. (1997), provides two bases of individual liability for members: (1) for "alleged improper actions," and (2) "the failure of a limited liability company to observe the formalities or requirements relating to the management of its business and affairs when coupled with some other wrongful conduct." . . .

If Clark or Lanham had told Westec's representatives that they were acting on behalf of an entity known as "Preferred Income Investors, LLC" the failure to disclose the fact that the entity was a limited liability company would be irrelevant by virtue of the statute, which provides that the articles of organization operate as constructive notice of the company's limited liability form. The county court, however, found that Lanham and Clark did not identify Preferred Income Investors, LLC, as the principal in the transaction. The "missing link" between the limited disclosure made by Clark and the protection of the notice statute was the failure to state that "P.I.I.," the Company, stood for "Preferred Income Investors, LLC."

ANALYSIS

1. **The Effect of Silence.** How far does the defendant's statutory argument go? Suppose that Lanham had contracted with Westec without giving any indication whatsoever that there was an LLC involved and that he was acting on its behalf. Would his argument still require that he be entitled to limited liability?
2. **Undisclosed Principal.** Suppose that an agent is acting on behalf of a principal who does not want his identity to be disclosed. What should the agent do to avoid his or her own personal liability?

B. THE OPERATING AGREEMENT

INTRODUCTORY NOTE

The following case, Elf Atochem North America, Inc. v. Jaffari, involves a unique procedural device known as the derivative lawsuit. Because the law regards an LLC as a legal person, the LLC is treated as an entity separate and distinct from its members. The LLC's status as a legal entity has numerous implications, one of which is that legal claims arising out of injuries done to the entity belong to the entity rather than its members. Put another way, the decision to bring a lawsuit on behalf of the entity is made by the entity. Of course, the entity has no mind or will of its own. The decision to sue or not in a given case will be made by the LLC's members acting collectively or, in the case of a manager-operated LLC, by its managers. The point, however, is that an individual LLC member acting alone generally may not bring suit on behalf of the entity.

Corporate law likewise treats claims arising out of an injury to the entity as belonging to the entity. Yet, corporate law has long recognized that there may be cases in which the corporation's managers may fail to pursue legitimate corporate claims. The most troubling class of such cases, of course, are those in which the claim would be brought against the corporation's managers themselves. Suppose the managers violated their fiduciary duties to the corporation. Would we expect them to bring suit against themselves?

The derivative suit was devised to permit shareholders to seek relief on behalf of the firm in those cases where the corporation's management has elected not to pursue the claim. A "direct" shareholder suit arises out of a cause of action belonging to the shareholder in his or her individual capacity. It is typically premised on an injury directly affecting the shareholder and must be brought by the shareholder in his or her own name. In contrast, a "derivative" suit is one brought by the shareholder on behalf of the corporation. The cause of action belongs to the corporation as an entity and arises out of an injury done to the corporation as an entity. The shareholder is thus merely acting as the firm's representative.

It can be difficult to tell to which type of action a particular case belongs. The basic tests are: (1) Who suffered the most immediate and direct injury? If the corporation, the suit is derivative. (2) To whom did the defendant's duty run? If the corporation, the suit is derivative.

The LLC statutes likewise adopted this procedural device. Section 1101 of the Uniform Limited Liability Company Act, for example, provides:

> A member of a limited liability company may maintain an action in the right of the company if the members or managers having authority to do so have refused to commence the action or an effort to cause those members or managers to commence the action is not likely to succeed.

Duray Development, LLC v. Perrin

288 Mich.App. 143, 792 N.W.2d 749 (2010).

. . .

I. BASIC FACTS AND PROCEDURAL HISTORY

Duray Development is a residential development company whose sole member is Robert Munger. . . . In 2004, Duray Development purchased 40 acres of undeveloped property . . . in Caledonia Township, Michigan.

On September 30, 2004, Duray Development entered into a contract with Perrin [and] Perrin Excavating, . . .for excavating [the property]. In that contract, . . . Perrin signed on behalf of himself and Perrin Excavating,. . . .

On October 27, 2004, Duray Development and Perrin entered into a new contract, intended to supersede the September 30, 2004 contract. The new contract contained the same language and provisions as the earlier contract. However, the new contract was between Duray Development and Outlaw [Excavating, LLC], and Perrin and Perrin Excavating . . . were not parties. Outlaw was an excavation company that Perrin . . . had recently formed. Perrin . . . signed the new contract on behalf of Outlaw, and held [himself] out to Duray Development as the owner . . . of the company. . . . Once [the contract was] signed, all parties proceeded under the contract as if Outlaw were the contractor for the Copper Corners development.

Two contracts were drafted because Perrin had not yet formed Outlaw at the time of the first contract. However, Duray Development did not want to wait for Perrin to finish forming the company before starting the excavation. . . . Therefore, the parties entered into the first contract on September 30, 2004, and then entered into the second contract once the parties thought Outlaw was a valid limited liability company.

Defendants began excavation and grading work pursuant to the contracts, but did not perform satisfactorily or on time. Duray Development then sued defendants for breach of contract. . . . Duray Development later learned through discovery that Outlaw did not obtain a "filed" status as a limited liability company until November 29, 2004, and therefore Outlaw was not a valid limited liability company at the time the parties executed the second contract.[1]

. . . After trial, the trial court ruled in favor of Duray Development, finding that Perrin was in breach of contract and owed $96,367.68 in damages to Duray Development.

In a posttrial memorandum, Perrin argued that he was not personally liable for Duray Development's damages. He asserted that, although Outlaw was not a valid limited liability company at the time of the execution of the second contract, Outlaw was nevertheless liable to Duray Development under the doctrine of de facto corporation. The trial court opined that if Outlaw were a corporation, then the de facto corporation doctrine most likely would have applied. However, the trial court concluded that the Limited Liability Company Act "clearly and specifically provides for the time that a limited liability company comes into existence and has powers to contract" and therefore superseded the de facto corporation doctrine and made it inapplicable to limited liability companies altogether. Perrin now appeals.

II. PERRIN'S PERSONAL LIABILITY

A. STANDARD OF REVIEW

. . . According to Perrin, even though Outlaw was not yet a properly formed limited liability company, the parties all treated the contract as though Outlaw was a properly formed limited liability company and, therefore, the doctrine of de facto corporation shielded Perrin from personal liability. He further argues that the doctrine of corporation by estoppel precluded Duray Development from arguing that he is personally liable.

. . .

THE LIMITED LIABILITY COMPANY ACT

The Limited Liability Company Act provides precisely when a limited liability company comes into existence. MCL 450.4202(2) provides that "[t]he existence of the limited liability company begins on the effective date of the articles of organization as provided in [MCL 450.4104]." MCL 450.4104(1) requires that the articles of organization be delivered to the administrator of the Michigan Department of Energy,

---

[1] According to the Limited Liability Company Act, MCL 450.4101 et seq., a limited liability company does not exist until the state administrator endorses the articles of organization with the word "filed." MCL 450.4104(2) and (6).

Labor and Economic Growth (DELEG). Under MCL 450.4104(2), after delivery of the articles of organization, "the administrator shall endorse upon it the word 'filed' with his or her official title and the date of receipt and of filing[.]" And under MCL 450.4104(6), "[a] document filed under [MCL 450.4104(2)] is effective at the time it is endorsed[.]"

. . .

In this case, Perrin signed the articles of organization for Outlaw on the same day as the second contract, October 27, 2004. Perrin then signed the October 27, 2004 contract on behalf of Outlaw. However, the DELEG administrator did not endorse the articles of organization until November 29, 2004. Therefore, pursuant to the Limited Liability Company Act, Outlaw was not in existence on October 27, 2004. And Outlaw did not adopt or ratify the second contract. Therefore, Perrin became personally liable for Outlaw's obligations unless a de facto limited liability company existed or limited liability company by estoppel applied.

C. DE FACTO CORPORATION AND CORPORATION BY ESTOPPEL

De facto corporation and corporation by estoppel are separate and distinct doctrines that warrant individual treatment. The de facto corporation doctrine provides that a defectively formed corporation—that is, one that fails to meet the technical requirements for forming a de jure corporation—may attain the legal status of a de facto corporation if certain requirements are met, as discussed later in this opinion. The most important aspect of a de facto corporation is that courts perceive and treat it in all respects as if it were a properly formed de jure corporation. . . .

Corporation by estoppel, on the other hand, is an equitable remedy and does not concern legal status. The general rule is: "Where a body assumes to be a corporation and acts under a particular name, a third party dealing with it under such assumed name is estopped to deny its corporate existence."[20] . . . [T]he de facto corporation doctrine establishes the legal existence of the corporation. By contrast, the corporation by estoppel doctrine merely prevents one from arguing against it, and does nothing to establish its actual existence in the eyes of the rest of the world.

. . .

D. THE DE FACTO CORPORATION DOCTRINE

The Michigan Supreme Court established the four elements for a de facto corporation long ago:

[20] [Estey Mfg. Co. v. Runnells, 55 Mich. 130, 133, 20 N.W. 823 (1884).]

> "When incorporators have [1] proceeded in good faith, [2] under a valid statute, [3] for an authorized purpose, and [4] have executed and acknowledged articles of association pursuant to that purpose, a corporation de facto instantly comes into being. A de facto corporation is an actual corporation. As to all the world, except the State, it enjoys the status and powers of a de jure corporation."[25]

Here, there is no question that elements (2), (3), and (4) were satisfied. . . .

It is less obvious whether the first element of the doctrine—good faith—was satisfied. There is little guidance in Michigan caselaw for a definition, or application, of this specific element. But in Newcomb-Endicott Co. v. Fee,[26] the Michigan Supreme Court, although applying a different set of elements, did state that in the absence of a claim or evidence of fraud or false representation on the part of the incorporators, and in light of a bona fide attempt to incorporate, there was no reason to deny a company the status of a de facto corporation.

Here, Duray Development does not allege that Perrin set up the corporation through fraud or false representations; that is, Duray Development does not allege that Perrin set up the corporation as a sham, for fraudulent purposes, or as a mere instrumentality under a theory of piercing the corporate veil. Rather, as the record indicates, Duray Development did not learn until after filing the complaint in this case that Outlaw was not a valid limited liability company on October 27, 2004. Duray Development at all times dealt with Outlaw as a valid corporation [sic] with which it contracted. Duray Development's sole member, Munger, testified that once the second contract took effect, Duray Development no longer considered Perrin or Perrin Excavating as parties to the contract, but instead considered Outlaw to be the new "contractor." There is no evidence whatsoever to suggest that Perrin formed Outlaw in anything other than good faith. Accordingly, the trial court was correct to conclude that, had Outlaw been formed as a corporation instead of a limited liability company, it would have been a de facto corporation for purposes of liability on the October 27, 2004 contract. Thus, all elements of a de facto corporation were present in this case.

The trial court, however, concluded that the de facto *corporation* doctrine does not apply to *limited liability companies* and therefore did not apply to Outlaw. It reasoned that the plain reading of the Limited Liability Company Act "clearly and specifically provides for the time that

---

[25] Tisch Auto Supply [Co. v. Nelson], 222 Mich. [196,] 200, 192 N.W. 600 [(1923)]. . . .

[26] 167 Mich. [574,] 582, 133 N.W. 540 [(1911)].

a limited liability company comes into existence and has powers to contract." . . .

Neither this Court nor the Supreme Court has addressed whether the de facto corporation doctrine can be extended or applied to a limited liability company. That is not to say, however, that the doctrine cannot be applied to a limited liability company. . . .

. . . [T]he similarities between the Business Corporation Act and the Limited Liability Company Act support the conclusion that the de facto corporation doctrine applies to both. The purposes for forming a limited liability company and a corporation are similar. Notably, the Limited Liability Company Act states, "A limited liability company may be formed under this act for any lawful purpose for which a domestic corporation or a domestic partnership could be formed, except as otherwise provided by law."[36] Further, both the Limited Liability Company Act and the Business Corporation Act contemplate the moment in time when a limited liability company or corporation comes into existence. Because the Business Corporation Act and the Limited Liability Company Act relate to the common purpose of forming a business and because both statutes contemplate the moment of existence for each, they should be interpreted in a consistent manner.

Accordingly, we conclude that the de facto corporation doctrine applies to Outlaw, a limited liability company. As a result, Outlaw, and not Perrin, individually, is liable for the breach of the October 27, 2004 contract.

E. CORPORATION BY ESTOPPEL

. . . The Supreme Court in Estey Mfg. Co. v. Runnells,[41] summarized the principle of corporation by estoppel as follows: "Where a body assumes to be a corporation and acts under a particular name, a third party dealing with it under such assumed name is estopped to deny its corporate existence."

As with the doctrine of de facto corporation, this Court has not addressed whether corporation by estoppel can be applied to limited liability companies. However, corporation by estoppel is an equitable remedy, and its purpose is to prevent one who contracts with a corporation from later denying its existence in order to hold the individual officers or partners liable. . . .

With this in mind, and in light of the purpose of corporation by estoppel, the corporate structure has little impact on the equitable principles at stake. In other words, there is no reason or purpose to draw a distinction on the basis of corporate form. Furthermore, like de facto

---

36 MCL 450.4201; see also MCL 450.1251(1).

41 [55 Mich. 130, 133, 20 N.W. 823 (1884).]

corporation, because corporation by estoppel coexists with the Business Corporation Act, so too can it coexist with the Limited Liability Company Act.

. . .

. . . [H]ere, the record clearly supports a finding of "limited liability company by estoppel" through the extension of the corporation by estoppel doctrine. Perrin was an individual party to the first contract, as was his limited liability company, Perrin Excavating. However, only Outlaw became a party to the second contract, which superseded the first. And all parties dealt with the second contract as though Outlaw were a party. After the second contract, Duray Development received billings from Outlaw, and not from Perrin. Duray Development also received a certificate of liability insurance for Outlaw. Munger testified that he dealt with Perrin, Perrin Excavating, and KDM Excavating before the second contract and only dealt with Outlaw after. Duray Development continued to assume Outlaw was a valid limited liability company after filing the lawsuit and only learned of the filing and contract discrepancies once litigation began in July 2006.

. . .

ANALYSIS

1. **De Facto LLCs and Estoppel.**

   a. Suppose that Perrin, chronically short of funds, finds it hard both to hire a lawyer to form a new firm and to keep his excavating equipment properly maintained. Perrin discusses this problem with Munger (Duray's owner), and Munger encourages him to defer hiring a lawyer. "Keep your equipment maintained," he tells Perrin. "You can always form your LLC later." Perrin takes his advice, and does not hire a lawyer. Does either the de facto or the estoppel doctrine apply? Does the analysis depend on whether Munger is suing Perrin, or the mechanic who worked on Perrin's excavating equipment is suing Perrin?

   b. Suppose that Perrin had failed to pay his legal bills and that, as a result his lawyer, after preparing initial drafts of the required documents for forming an LLC, refused to do any more work until Perrin finally paid, months later as the work on the Duray project was coming to an end. Would, and should, Perrin still be entitled to the benefit of the de facto LLC or estoppel doctrine?

2. **Policy Considerations.** Obviously, both the de facto corporation doctrine and the corporation by estoppel doctrine originated in corporate law. The drafters of the Model Business Corporation Act (MBCA) have

repeatedly tried to abolish these doctrines by statute. Section 50 of the 1969 MBCA required that a certificate of incorporation be issued in order for a de jure corporation to exist and § 139 imposed full personal liability on the promoters unless a de jure corporation existed. In the comments to § 50, the drafters stated that these provisions intended to abolish the de facto corporation doctrine.

The 1984 MBCA's drafters recognized that courts were resisting their predecessors' attempt to abolish the de facto corporation and corporation by estoppel doctrines. Accordingly, the drafters chose to relax the statutory standard slightly. MBCA § 2.04 provided: "All persons purporting to act as or on behalf of a corporation, knowing there was no incorporation under [the MBCA], are jointly and severally liable for all liabilities created while so acting." The 2016 version of the MBCA retains this rule. By negative inference, neither inactive investors nor active investors who are unaware of the defective incorporation may be held personally liable.

What policy arguments, if any, support the MBCA drafters' efforts to eliminate the common law doctrines?

Elf Atochem North America, Inc. v. Jaffari

727 A.2d 286 (Del.Sup.Ct.1999).

. . .

This is a purported derivative suit brought on behalf of a Delaware LLC calling into question whether: (1) the LLC, which did not itself execute the LLC agreement in this case ("the Agreement") defining its governance and operation, is nevertheless bound by the Agreement; and (2) contractual provisions directing that all disputes be resolved exclusively by arbitration or court proceedings in California are valid under the Act. Resolution of these issues requires us to examine the applicability and scope of certain provisions of the Act in light of the Agreement.

We hold that: (1) the Agreement is binding on the LLC as well as the members; and (2) since the Act does not prohibit the members of an LLC from vesting exclusive subject matter jurisdiction in arbitration proceedings (or court enforcement of arbitration) in California to resolve disputes, the contractual forum selection provisions must govern.

Accordingly, we affirm the judgment of the Court of Chancery dismissing the action brought in that court on the ground that the Agreement validly predetermined the fora in which disputes would be resolved, thus stripping the Court of Chancery of subject matter jurisdiction.

Facts

Plaintiff below-appellant Elf Atochem North America, Inc., a Pennsylvania Corporation ("Elf"), manufactures and distributes solvent-based maskants to the aerospace and aviation industries throughout the world. Defendant below-appellee Cyrus A. Jaffari is the president of Malek, Inc., a California Corporation. Jaffari had developed an innovative, environmentally-friendly alternative to the solvent-based maskants that presently dominate the market.

For decades, the aerospace and aviation industries have used solvent-based maskants in the chemical milling process.[3] Recently, however, the Environmental Protection Agency ("EPA") classified solvent-based maskants as hazardous chemicals and air contaminants. To avoid conflict with EPA regulations, Elf considered developing or distributing a maskant less harmful to the environment.

In the mid-nineties, Elf approached Jaffari and proposed investing in his product and assisting in its marketing. Jaffari found the proposal attractive since his company, Malek, Inc., possessed limited resources and little international sales expertise. Elf and Jaffari agreed to undertake a joint venture that was to be carried out using a limited liability company as the vehicle.

On October 29, 1996, Malek, Inc. caused to be filed a Certificate of Formation with the Delaware Secretary of State, thus forming Malek LLC, a Delaware limited liability company under the Act. The certificate of formation is a relatively brief and formal document that is the first statutory step in creating the LLC as a separate legal entity. The certificate does not contain a comprehensive agreement among the parties, and the statute contemplates that the certificate of formation is to be complemented by the terms of the Agreement.

Next, Elf, Jaffari and Malek, Inc. entered into a series of agreements providing for the governance and operation of the joint venture. Of particular importance to this litigation, Elf, Malek, Inc., and Jaffari entered into the Agreement, a comprehensive and integrated document of 38 single-spaced pages setting forth detailed provisions for the governance of Malek LLC, which is not itself a signatory to the Agreement. Elf and Malek LLC entered into an Exclusive Distributorship Agreement in which Elf would be the exclusive, worldwide distributor for Malek LLC. The Agreement provides that Jaffari will be the manager of Malek LLC. Jaffari and Malek LLC entered

[3] Manufactures of airplanes and missiles use maskants in the process of chemical milling in order to reduce the weight of their products. Chemical milling is a process where a caustic substance is placed on metal parts in order to dissolve the metal with which it comes into contact. Maskants are used to protect those areas of metal intended to be preserved.

into an employment agreement providing for Jaffari's employment as chief executive officer of Malek LLC.

The Agreement is the operative document for purposes of this Opinion, however. Under the Agreement, Elf contributed $1 million in exchange for a 30 percent interest in Malek LLC. Malek, Inc. contributed its rights to the water-based maskant in exchange for a 70 percent interest in Malek LLC. The Agreement contains an arbitration clause covering all disputes. The clause, Section 13.8, provides that "any controversy or dispute arising out of this Agreement, the interpretation of any of the provisions hereof, or the action or inaction of any Member or Manager hereunder shall be submitted to arbitration in San Francisco, California. . . ." Section 13.8 further provides: "No action . . . based upon any claim arising out of or related to this Agreement shall be instituted in any court by any Member except (a) an action to compel arbitration . . . or (b) an action to enforce an award obtained in an arbitration proceeding. . . ." The Agreement also contains a forum selection clause, Section 13.7, providing that all members consent to: "exclusive jurisdiction of the state and federal courts sitting in California in any action on a claim arising out of, under or in connection with this Agreement or the transactions contemplated by this Agreement, provided such claim is not required to be arbitrated pursuant to Section 13.8"; and personal jurisdiction in California. The Distribution Agreement contains no forum selection or arbitration clause.

Elf's Suit in the Court of Chancery

On April 27, 1998, Elf sued Jaffari and Malek LLC, individually and derivatively on behalf of Malek LLC, in the Delaware Court of Chancery, seeking equitable remedies. Among other claims, Elf alleged that Jaffari breached his fiduciary duty to Malek LLC, pushed Malek LLC to the brink of insolvency by withdrawing funds for personal use, interfered with business opportunities, failed to make disclosures to Elf, and threatened to make poor quality maskant and to violate environmental regulations. Elf also alleged breach of contract, tortious interference with prospective business relations, and (solely as to Jaffari) fraud.

The Court of Chancery granted defendants' motion to dismiss based on lack of subject matter jurisdiction. The court held that Elf's claims arose under the Agreement, or the transactions contemplated by the agreement, and were directly related to Jaffari's actions as manager of Malek LLC. Therefore, the court found that the Agreement governed the question of jurisdiction and that only a court of law or arbitrator in California is empowered to decide these claims. Elf now appeals the order of the Court of Chancery dismissing the complaint.

. . .

General Summary of Background of the Act

The phenomenon of business arrangements using "alternative entities" has been developing rapidly over the past several years. Long gone are the days when business planners were confined to corporate or partnership structures.

[The court describes the history of the adoption and amendment of the Delaware Limited Partnership (LP) Act, the present version of which is based on the Revised Uniform Limited Partnership Act (RULPA).]

The Delaware [LLC] Act was adopted in October 1992. . . . The LLC is an attractive form of business entity because it combines corporate-type limited liability with partnership-type flexibility and tax advantages. The Act can be characterized as a "flexible statute" because it generally permits members to engage in private ordering with substantial freedom of contract to govern their relationship, provided they do not contravene any mandatory provisions of the Act. . . .

The Delaware Act has been modeled on the popular Delaware LP Act. In fact, its architecture and much of its wording is almost identical to that of the Delaware LP Act. Under the Act, a member of an LLC is treated much like a limited partner under the LP Act. The policy of freedom of contract underlies both the Act and the LP Act.

. . .

Policy of the Delaware Act

The basic approach of the Delaware Act is to provide members with broad discretion in drafting the Agreement and to furnish default provisions when the members' agreement is silent. The Act is replete with fundamental provisions made subject to modification in the Agreement (e.g. "unless otherwise provided in a limited liability company agreement. . . .").[26]

Although business planners may find comfort in working with the Act in structuring transactions and relationships, it is a somewhat awkward document for this Court to construe and apply in this case. To understand the overall structure and thrust of the Act, one must wade through provisions that are prolix, sometimes oddly organized, and do not always flow evenly. Be that as it may as a problem in mastering the Act as a whole, one returns to the narrow and discrete issues presented in this case.

[26] . . . For example, members are free to contract among themselves concerning management of the LLC, including who is to manage the LLC, the establishment of classes of members, voting, procedures for holding meetings of members, or considering matters without a meeting.

Freedom of Contract

Section 18–1101(b) of the Act, like the essentially identical Section 17–1101(c) of the LP Act, provides that "[i]t is the policy of [the Act] to give the maximum effect to the principle of freedom of contract and to the enforceability of limited liability company agreements." Accordingly, the following observation relating to limited partnerships applies as well to limited liability companies:

> The Act's basic approach is to permit partners to have the broadest possible discretion in drafting their partnership agreements and to furnish answers only in situations where the partners have not expressly made provisions in their partnership agreement. Truly, the partnership agreement is the cornerstone of a Delaware limited partnership, and effectively constitutes the entire agreement among the partners with respect to the admission of partners to, and the creation, operation and termination of, the limited partnership. Once partners exercise their contractual freedom in their partnership agreement, the partners have a great deal of certainty that their partnership agreement will be enforced in accordance with its terms.[27]

In general, the commentators observe that only where the agreement is inconsistent with mandatory statutory provisions will the members' agreement be invalidated. Such statutory provisions are likely to be those intended to protect third parties, not necessarily the contracting members. As a framework for decision, we apply that principle to the issues before us, without expressing any views more broadly.

The Arbitration and Forum Selection Clauses in the Agreement are a Bar to Jurisdiction in the Court of Chancery

In vesting the Court of Chancery with jurisdiction, the Act accomplished at least three purposes: (1) it assured that the Court of Chancery has jurisdiction it might not otherwise have because it is a court of limited jurisdiction that requires traditional equitable relief or specific legislation to act; (2) it established the Court of Chancery as the default forum in the event the members did not provide another choice of forum or dispute resolution mechanism; and (3) it tends to center interpretive litigation in Delaware courts with the expectation of uniformity. Nevertheless, the arbitration provision of the Agreement in this case fosters the Delaware policy favoring alternate dispute

---

[27] Martin I. Lubaroff & Paul Altman, Delaware Limited Partnerships § 1.2 (1999) (footnote omitted). . . .

resolution mechanisms, including arbitration. Such mechanisms are an important goal of Delaware legislation, court rules, and jurisprudence.

Malek LLC's Failure to Sign the Agreement Does Not Affect the Members' Agreement Governing Dispute Resolution

Elf argues that because Malek LLC, on whose behalf Elf allegedly brings these claims, is not a party to the Agreement, the derivative claims it brought on behalf of Malek LLC are not governed by the arbitration and forum selection clauses of the Agreement.

. . .

We are not persuaded by this argument. Section 18–101(7) defines the limited liability company agreement as "any agreement, written or oral, of the member or members as to the affairs of a limited liability company and the conduct of its business." Here, Malek, Inc. and Elf, the members of Malek LLC, executed the Agreement to carry out the affairs and business of Malek LLC and to provide for arbitration and forum selection.

Notwithstanding Malek LLC's failure to sign the Agreement, Elf's claims are subject to the arbitration and forum selection clauses of the Agreement. The Act is a statute designed to permit members maximum flexibility in entering into an agreement to govern their relationship. It is the members who are the real parties in interest. The LLC is simply their joint business vehicle. This is the contemplation of the statute in prescribing the outlines of a limited liability company agreement.

Classification by Elf of its Claims as Derivative is Irrelevant

Elf argues that the Court of Chancery erred in failing to classify its claims against Malek LLC as derivative. Elf contends that, had the court properly characterized its claims as derivative instead of direct, the arbitration and forum selection clauses would not have applied to bar adjudication in Delaware.

. . .

Although Elf correctly points out that Delaware law allows for derivative suits against management of an LLC, Elf contracted away its right to bring such an action in Delaware and agreed instead to dispute resolution in California. That is, Section 13.8 of the Agreement specifically provides that the parties (i.e., Elf) agree to institute "[n]o action at law or in equity based upon any claim arising out of or related to this Agreement" except an action to compel arbitration or to enforce an arbitration award. Furthermore, under Section 13.7 of the Agreement, each member (i.e., Elf) "consent[ed] to the exclusive jurisdiction of the state and federal courts sitting in California in any action on a claim arising out of, under or in connection with this Agreement or the transactions contemplated by this Agreement."

Sections 13.7 and 13.8 of the Agreement do not distinguish between direct and derivative claims. They simply state that the members may not initiate any claims outside of California. Elf initiated this action in the Court of Chancery in contravention of its own contractual agreement. As a result, the Court of Chancery correctly held that all claims, whether derivative or direct, arose under, out of or in connection with the Agreement, and thus are covered by the arbitration and forum selection clauses.

This prohibition is so broad that it is dispositive of Elf's claims . . . that purport to be under the Distributorship Agreement that has no choice of forum provision. Notwithstanding the fact that the Distributorship Agreement is a separate document, in reality these counts are all subsumed under the rubric of the Agreement's forum selection clause for any claim "arising out of" and those that are "in connection with" the Agreement or transactions "contemplated by" or "related to" that Agreement under Sections 13.7 and 13.8. . . .

The Court of Chancery was correct in holding that Elf's claims bear directly on Jaffari's duties and obligations under the Agreement. Thus, we decline to disturb its holding.

The Argument that Chancery Has "Special" Jurisdiction for Derivative Claims Must Fail

Elf claims that 6 Del.C. §§ 18–110(a), 18–111 and 18–1001 vest the Court of Chancery with subject matter jurisdiction over this dispute. According to Elf, the Act grants the Court of Chancery subject matter jurisdiction over its claims for breach of fiduciary duty and removal of Jaffari, even though the parties contracted to arbitrate all such claims in California. In effect, Elf argues that the Act affords the Court of Chancery "special" jurisdiction to adjudicate its claims, notwithstanding a clear contractual agreement to the contrary.

Again, we are not persuaded by Elf's argument. Elf is correct that 6 Del.C. §§ 18–110(a) and 18–111 vest jurisdiction with the Court of Chancery in actions involving removal of managers and interpreting, applying or enforcing LLC agreements respectively. As noted above, Section 18–1001 provides that a party may bring derivative actions in the Court of Chancery. Such a grant of jurisdiction may have been constitutionally necessary if the claims do not fall within the traditional equity jurisdiction. Nevertheless, for the purpose of designating a more convenient forum, we find no reason why the members cannot alter the default jurisdictional provisions of the statute and contract away their right to file suit in Delaware.

. . . [B]ecause the policy of the Act is to give the maximum effect to the principle of freedom of contract and to the enforceability of LLC agreements, the parties may contract to avoid the applicability of Sections 18–110(a), 18–111, and 18–1001. . . .

Our conclusion is bolstered by the fact that Delaware recognizes a strong public policy in favor of arbitration. Normally, doubts on the issue of whether a particular issue is arbitrable will be resolved in favor of arbitration. . . . If we were to hold otherwise, arbitration clauses in existing LLC agreements could be rendered meaningless. By resorting to the alleged "special" jurisdiction 296 of the Court of Chancery, future plaintiffs could avoid their own arbitration agreements simply by couching their claims as derivative. Such a result could adversely affect many arbitration agreements already in existence in Delaware.

. . .

ANALYSIS

1. **Why Agree to Arbitrate?** Elf obviously objected to arbitration in California (or perhaps anywhere). So why did it originally agree to the arbitration clause?

2. **Effect of Waiver.** Suppose that the parties had included in their LLC operating agreement a provision of the following sort:

   > Each member agrees that the other shall be relieved of and immune to liability for any act against the other or against the LLC, whether in tort or contract or in law or equity, regardless of any allegation of willfulness, intention, or gross negligence.

   What result?

3. **Contractual Choice.** Is there any good reason why the parties should not be allowed to contract as to jurisdiction and arbitration?

Fisk Ventures, LLC v. Segal

2008 WL 1961156 (Del. Ch.), aff'd sub nom.,
Segal v. Fisk Ventures, LLC, 984 A.2d 124 (Del. 2009).

. . .

I. Background

. . .

A. The Company, its Structure, and the LLC Agreement

Genitrix, LLC, is a Delaware limited liability company formed to develop and market biomedical technology. Dr. Segal founded the Company in 1996 following his postdoctoral fellowship at the Whitehead Institute for Biomedical Research [at MIT]. Originally formed as a

Maryland limited liability company, Genitrix was moved in 1997 to Delaware at the behest of Dr. H. Fisk Johnson, who invested heavily.

Equity in Genitrix is divided into three classes of membership. In exchange for the patent rights he obtained from the Whitehead Institute, Segal's capital account was credited with $500,000. This allowed him to retain approximately 55% of the Class A membership interest. The remainder of the Class A interest was apparently granted to other individuals not involved in this suit. In the initial round of investment, Johnson contributed $843,000 in return for a sizeable portion of the Class B membership interest. The remainder of the Class B interest is held by Fisk Ventures, LLC, and Stephen Rose. Finally, various other investors contributed over $1 million for membership interests in Class C. These Class C investors are apparently mostly passive; the power in the LLC is essentially divided by the LLC Agreement (the "Agreement") between the Class A and Class B members.

Under the Agreement, the Board of Member Representatives (the "Board") manages the business and affairs of the Company. As originally contemplated by the Agreement, the Board consisted of four members: two of whom were appointed by Johnson and two of whom were appointed by Segal. In early 2007, however, the balance of power seemingly shifted. Because the Company failed to meet certain benchmarks, the Board expanded to five seats and the Class B members were able to appoint a representative to the newly created seat. Nevertheless, because the Agreement requires the approval of 75% of the Board for most actions, the combined 60% stake of Fisk Ventures and Johnson is insufficient to control the Company. In other words, the LLC Agreement was drafted in such a way as to require the cooperation of the Class A and B members.

B. The Parties . . .

Dr. Andrew Segal, fresh out of residency training, worked for the Whitehead Institute for Biomedical Research in Cambridge, Massachusetts from 1994 to early 1996. While there, Segal researched and worked on projects relating to how the human immune system could be manipulated effectively to attack cancer and infectious diseases. In early 1996, Dr. Segal left the Whitehead Institute and obtained a license to certain patent rights related to his research.

With these patent rights in hand, Dr. Segal formed Genitrix. Intellectual property rights alone, however, could not fund the research, testing, and trials necessary to bring Dr. Segal's ideas to some sort of profitable fruition. Consequently, Segal sought and obtained capital for the Company. Originally, Segal served as both President and Chief Executive Officer, and the terms of his employment were governed by contract (the "Segal Employment Agreement"). Under the Segal Employment Agreement, any intellectual property rights developed by

Dr. Segal during his tenure with Genitrix would be assigned to the Company. . . .

Fisk Ventures is a Delaware limited liability company controlled by Dr. H. Fisk Johnson, who owns 99% of it. Fisk is a Class B member and is entitled to appoint one person to the Board. Fisk filed the initial petition in this action seeking dissolution of the Company. . . .

Dr. Johnson is the controlling member of Fisk and is himself a Class B shareholder in the Company who is personally now entitled to appoint two members to the Board. . . .

Stephen Rose and William Freund are Class B Members of the Company and are Class B Representatives on the Board who were appointed by Johnson. Johnson also employs both Rose and Freund in a number of capacities outside of Genitrix, and Segal alleges that they are therefore dependant on Johnson or his affiliates for their livelihood.

C. The Company's Woes . . .

1. Early Difficulties, the Fisk Ventures Note, and the Class B Put Right

From its inception, Genitrix found itself strapped for cash. Segal's allegations contain numerous references to the tight budget and reminders that he worked for the Company for little or no pay in order to ease Genitrix's financial pain. In the earliest part of this decade, the Company hobbled along on grants from the National Institutes of Health and a series of relatively small financing transactions. Between November 2000 and August 2002, Johnson contributed another $550,000 in convertible debt, much of which was subsequently converted to Class B equity, and other investors provided $100,000 in convertible debt that was subsequently converted to Class C equity.

> **NOTE**
>
> Convertible debt is debt that is convertible into equity, generally at the option of the holder of the debt (that is, the lender). It gives an investor some downside advantage—that is, a priority over other investors in the event of insolvency. It also offers upside potential in that it can be converted to equity if the firm prospers. In addition, it offers an "exit" possibility in that there will usually be some date when the debt must be repaid.

This influx of financing was insufficient, however. In the summer of 2003, Segal communicated to the Board that the Company would require $2.6 million to allow for human trials of the technology. Johnson, who by that point had contributed about $1.4 million, stated that he was unwilling to be the sole financier of the Company. Nevertheless, Johnson and Fisk Ventures agreed to contribute another $2 million in convertible debt if the Company agreed to try to raise an additional $5 million from other investors over the following two years.

Over the course of negotiating the terms of the Fisk Ventures note, Segal proposed that the "Put Right" of the Class B investors be suspended to allow him to more easily woo other investors. [The Put Right provided that] the Class B Members may, at any time, force the Company to purchase any or all of their Class B membership interests at a price determined by an independent appraisal. If the purchase price exceeds 50% of the Company's tangible assets, the Members who exercised the Put Right would receive notes secured by all of the assets of the Company. In other words, the Put—if exercised—would subrogate what would otherwise be senior claims of new investors. Though Segal believed this right would scare off potential investors, the Class B Members refused to suspend or relinquish their contractual rights, though they did communicate that they had no immediate or foreseeable intention of exercising the right. Segal alleges that, based on his conversations with Rose, he believed the Class B Members would be "more flexible with respect to the Put" once there was a prospective investment "on the table."

2. Failed Efforts to Raise Money from New Investors

To meet the $5 million challenge put forth in the Fisk Ventures Note, the Company retained an investment banking consultant to help it raise money from venture capital funds. This effort failed to generate any investment. By the summer of 2005—almost two years after the creation of the Fisk Ventures Note—the Company had failed to raise the needed $5 million, ...

. . . Dr. Segal turned his attention to individual, high-net-worth investors. Early indications were positive, but, Segal alleges, several potential investors complained about the Class B Put Right, one of whom called it a "deal killer." Thus, Segal again asked the Class B members to relinquish or suspend the Put Right. The Class B members again refused.

3. The Private Placement Memorandum, . . .

Meanwhile, in August 2005, Segal took it upon himself to [draft a document, a "private placement memorandum," that he could use to seek funds from] high-net-worth individuals. . . . When he attempted to get the approval of the Board in December, the Class B representatives refused to consent, citing the haste with which Segal was then acting. Once again, moreover, Segal wanted the Class B members to suspend or relinquish their Put Right. . . .

Segal stressed the Company's need to quickly secure additional funding and encouraged the Class B members to [approve], but the Class B Members instead offered a counterproposal of $500,000 in convertible debt from Fisk Ventures. The terms of that note would have required the Company to meet certain benchmarks. If the Company failed to meet them, the Class B members would obtain control of the Board. . . .

[Segal next sought funds from Scott Tilson, a Class C investor, who was prepared to provide the funds only if the Class B members suspended their Put Right for three years, which they refused to do.]

4. Segal's Removal as CEO

The LLC Agreement contains a provision that allows the Class B members to replace Segal's Board representatives if the Company fails to adhere to certain covenants while Segal serves as CEO. Concerned that the Company was dangerously close to breaching those covenants and worried that he would lose his Board representation, Segal circulated to the Board in March 2006 a proposal to remove himself as CEO. Instead of discussing and approving this resolution, however, the Class B representatives, who represented over 50% of the Board, executed and circulated their own resolution, which replaced Segal with Chris Pugh, another employee of Genitrix, as "interim" CEO. . . .

5. The Company's Current State

In March 2006, the Company ran out of operating cash. Fisk Ventures provided another $125,000 capital contribution to pay the remaining employees and to cover some expenses, but larger problems loomed. The Board met in the third week of April to discuss its options.

Keeping with the common theme in this case, Dr. Segal and the Class B members had different ideas of what the Company should do. Dr. Segal proposed splitting Genitrix in two; the Class B members flatly rejected this proposal. The Class B members advocated a "buy down" proposal in which the Company would raise $3.5 million, in exchange for which the Class B members would find their interest in the Company reduced to 25% and would become largely passive investors. Although Dr. Segal initially expressed some interest in this proposal, he rejected it when he saw the actual terms set forth in writing by the Class B members about a month later.

In August 2006, Pugh left Genitrix to work for another firm, leaving the Company with just two employees (including Dr. Segal). That other employee left in May 2007. The Company has no office, no capital funds, no grant funds, and generates no revenue. The Board has not met since the fall of 2006 because the Class A representatives have refused to participate in any meetings. In May 2007 and at the invitation of the Class B members, Dr. Segal proposed terms under which the Class B members might purchase his interest in the Company. The Class B members rejected those terms in June 2007 and subsequently Fisk Ventures initiated this suit, seeking dissolution of Genitrix.

D. The Counterclaims/Third-Party Claims and the Parties' Contentions

. . . Segal contends that the counterclaim/third-party defendants breached the LLC Agreement, breached the implied covenant of good faith and fair dealing implicit in the LLC Agreement, breached their fiduciary duties to the Company, and tortiously interfered with the Segal Employment Agreement. Segal passionately contends that the Class B defendants failed to comply with their duties to Segal and to the Company by standing in the way of proposed financing. . . .

III. Failure to State a Claim

. . . Because Segal has not stated facts that either show he is entitled or from which I can infer he is entitled to relief, I dismiss his claims.

A. Breach of Contract

. . . Dr. Segal's counterclaims and third-party claims contend—perhaps reasonably—that Genitrix suffered because the Class B members refused to accede to Segal's proposals with respect to research, financing, and other matters. It may very well be that Genitrix would be a thriving company today if only the Class B members had seen things Segal's way. However, it may very well be that Genitrix would also be a thriving company today if only Dr. Segal had gone along with what the Class B members wanted. Indeed, the LLC Agreement endows both the Class A and Class B members with certain rights and protections. In no way does it obligate one class to acquiesce to the wishes of the other simply because the other believes its approach is superior or in the best interests of the Company. To find otherwise—that is, to find that the Court must decide whose business judgment was more in keeping with the LLC's best interests—would cripple the policy underlying the LLC Act promoting freedom of contract. . . .

B. Breach of the Implied Covenant of Good Faith and Fair Dealing

Every contract contains an implied covenant of good faith and fair dealing that "requires a 'party in a contractual relationship to refrain from arbitrary or unreasonable conduct which has the effect of preventing the other party to the contract from receiving the fruits' of the bargain."[45] Although occasionally described in broad terms, the implied covenant is not a panacea for the disgruntled litigant. In fact, it is clear that "a court cannot and should not use the implied covenant of good faith and fair dealing to fill a gap in a contract with an implied term unless it is clear from the contract that the parties would have agreed to that term

[45] Dunlap v. State Farm Fire & Cas. Co., 878 A.2d 434, 442 (Del.2005) (quoting Wilgus v. Salt Pond Inv. Co., 498 A.2d 151, 159 (Del.Ch.1985)).

had they thought to negotiate the matter."[47] Only rarely invoked successfully, the implied covenant of good faith and fair dealing protects the spirit of what was *actually bargained and negotiated for* in the contract. Moreover, because the implied covenant is, by definition, *implied,* and because it protects the *spirit* of the agreement rather than the form, it cannot be invoked where the contract itself expressly covers the subject at issue.

Here, Segal argues that Fisk, Rose, and Freund breached the implied covenant of good faith and fair dealing by frustrating or blocking the financing opportunities proposed by Segal. However, neither the LLC Agreement nor any other contract endowed him with the right to unilaterally decide what fundraising or financing opportunities the Company should pursue, and his argument is "another in a long line of cases in which a plaintiff has tried, unsuccessfully, to argue that the implied covenant grants [him] a substantive right that [he] did not extract during negotiation."[51] Moreover, the LLC Agreement *does* address the subject of financing, and it specifically requires the approval of 75% of the Board. Implicit in such a requirement is the right of the Class B Board representatives to disapprove of and therefore block Segal's proposals. As this Court has previously noted, "[t]he mere exercise of one's contractual rights, without more, cannot constitute . . . a breach [of the implied covenant of good faith and fair dealing]."[52] Negotiating forcefully and within the bounds of rights granted by the LLC agreement does not translate to a breach of the implied covenant on the part of the Class B members. . . .

NOTE

In a subsequent stage of the litigation, the Chancery Court granted Fisk Ventures' motion for a judicial order of dissolution, on the statutory ground that it was no longer "reasonably practicable to carry on the business." The opinion in the dissolution portion of the proceedings is reprinted in Subsection 2G below.

ANALYSIS

1. **Veto Power?** What does this case teach us about the wisdom of a provision that, in effect, gave each of the principal parties a veto power over all decisions? Why do well-advised entrepreneurs and investors agree to such a provision? In this case, did either party benefit from the veto power? Should the parties have anticipated some sort of stalemate

[47] Corporate Prop. Assocs. 14 Inc. v. CHR Holding Corp., C.A. No. 3231–VCS, 2008 WL 963048 at *5 Del. Ch. Apr. 10, 2008) . . . .

[51] Allied Capital [Corp. v. GC-Sun Holding, LP], 910 A.2d [1020], 1024 [(Del. Ch. 2006)].

[52] Shenandoah Life Ins. Co. v. Valero Energy Corp., C.A. No. 9032, 1988 WL 63491, at *8 (Del. Ch. June 21, 1988).

and included a tie-breaker in the LLC agreement? If so, what sort of tie breaker?

2. **"Put Right."** What was the function of the "Put Right"? Why would a new investor insist on waiver of that right and why was Dr. Johnson unwilling to provide the waiver?

3. **Additional Investments?** Suppose there was clear and convincing evidence that Genitrix's financial problems could be solved by an additional investment of $1 million. Further suppose that the holders of the Class B membership interests could easily afford to make such an investment. Should the court have ordered them to do so? If so, on what terms?

C. PIERCING THE LLC VEIL

INTRODUCTORY NOTE

Sole proprietors and members of a general partnership put all of their personal assets at risk. As we saw in Chapter 1's discussion of the principal's liability for an agent's conduct, the law simply does not distinguish between the personal and business assets of a sole proprietor. As we saw in Chapter 2, the law acknowledges some distinctions between partnership and personal property, but partners are subject to joint and several liability for all firm obligations, which leaves their personal assets vulnerable to the claims of firm creditors.

In contrast, corporate law insulates shareholders from personal liability. Under the doctrine of limited liability, shareholders of a corporation generally are not liable for debts incurred or torts committed by the firm. Shareholder losses when the firm faces financial difficulties are limited to the amount the shareholder has invested in the firm—the amount initially paid by the shareholder to purchase his or her stock. One can think of limited liability as being a corollary the corporation's status as a separate legal person—in the eyes of the law, it is the corporation that incurs the debt or commits the tort and the corporation which must bear the responsibility for its actions.

Model Business Corporation Act (2016) § 6.22(b) offers a typical statutory formulation of the doctrine: "A shareholder of a corporation is not personally liable for any liabilities of the corporation . . . except . . . (ii) that a shareholder may become personally liable by reason of that shareholder's own acts or conduct." Notice the proviso, which encompasses the equitable remedy known as piercing the corporate veil. "The 'veil' of the 'corporate fiction,' or the 'artificial personality' of the corporation is 'pierced,' and the individual or corporate shareholder exposed to personal or corporate liability, as the case may be, when a court determines that the debt in question is not really a debt of the corporation, but ought, in fairness, to be viewed as a debt of the individual or corporate shareholder or shareholders." STEPHEN B. PRESSER, PIERCING THE CORPORATE VEIL § 1.01 at 1–6 (1991 and supp.) (footnotes and emphasis omitted). Or, as a seminal 1912 law review article put it: "When the conception of corporate entity is employed to defraud creditors, to evade an existing obligation, to circumvent a statute, to achieve or perpetuate monopoly, or to protect knavery or crime, the courts will draw aside the web [i.e., veil] of entity, will regard the corporate company as an association of live, up-and-doing, men and women shareholders, and will do justice between real persons." I. Maurice Wormser, *Piercing the Veil of Corporate Entity*, 12 COLUM. L. REV. 496, 517 (1912).

LLCs similarly provide limited liability for their members. Uniform Limited Liability Company Act (1997) § 304 thus provides: "A debt, obligation, or other liability of a limited liability company is solely the debt, obligation, or liability of the company. A member or manager is not personally liable . . . for a debt, obligation, or other liability of the company solely by reason of being or acting as a member or manager." Query, however, whether corporate law's veil piercing rules carry over to the LLC context. In the following case, that question is resolved (affirmatively) by statute. How should a court rule in the absence of such a statute?

Tom Thumb Food Markets, Inc. v. TLH Properties, LLC

1999 WL 31168 (Minn.App.) (unpublished opinion).

Facts

. . .

Hartmann, who has been a commercial developer since 1984, testified that in 1993, Jerry Smith, the part owner of land in Zimmerman, Minnesota, asked Hartmann to develop a commercial site. After Tom Thumb indicated interest, Hartmann sent a letter dated March 18, 1993, stating, "I have the land purchased and am presently undertaking the re-zoning and permit process." At that time, however, Hartmann had not purchased the land but was operating under an oral agreement with Smith to develop the site, which included only Smith's offer to extend a written option to purchase the land.

On December 4, 1995, the parties signed a "Lease Agreement." Hartmann signed on behalf of the landlord, TLH Properties.2 The agreement required TLH to construct a building agreed to by the parties. TLH agreed "to deliver possession of the Leased Premises to Tenant on or before May 31, 1996." The lease term was 12 years, with two four-year renewal options. TLH represented and warranted that "no other person, corporation, partnership or other entity has the right to lease or occupy the Leased Premises." The lease contained no contingencies and included the following integration clause:

> This lease * * * set[s] forth all the covenants, promises, agreements, conditions and understandings between Landlord

> and Tenant concerning the Leased Premises and there are no covenants, promises, agreements, conditions or understandings, either oral or written, between them other than are herein set forth.

When Hartmann attempted to obtain a construction loan for the project through his bank, the bank required underwriting for the risk of the tenancy and requested financial information from Tom Thumb. Tom Thumb ignored a series of such requests, but finally, on March 25, 1996, the bank informed Hartmann that after reviewing information it had recently received from Tom Thumb, it was "unable to underwrite the proposed tenant, Tom Thumb, to [its] satisfaction" and for that reason denied Hartmann's financing request.

Smith then withdrew from the venture because of the risk presented by Tom Thumb. Tom Thumb attempted to assist Hartmann in obtaining financing, but the property was sold to SuperAmerica in the meantime. Tom Thumb later discovered that Hartmann had never owned the property.

After Tom Thumb presented its proof at the court trial, it moved to . . . add a claim that Hartmann should be held personally liable under the theory of piercing the corporate veil. The district court allowed the amendment and concluded after trial that Hartmann was personally liable. The district court found that Hartmann breached the lease and Tom Thumb was entitled to 12 years of lost profits at a present value of $492,000. The district court found that Tom Thumb failed to prove damages based on fraud and misrepresentation. . . .

Decision

I.

Hartmann argues that the lease was conditional because it was subject to a financing contingency and that he was unable to acquire financing only because of Tom Thumb. The district court ruled that because the parties did not agree to or include any contingencies in their lease, it was not conditional.

. . .

Here, two experienced parties to a commercial lease stated that their entire agreement was contained in the written lease. The lease contains no financing contingency or any express requirement that Tom Thumb provide financial information or otherwise qualify as a tenant. Nor does the language of the lease imply that the agreement was contingent on Hartmann's ability to obtain financing. . . . Further, even when parties include a written contingency, performance is not excused unless it is impossible because of the failure of the contingency. . . . The refusal of one bank to finance Hartmann's project did not excuse his performance for lack of financing. . . . Therefore, the district court properly ruled that the lease was not subject to a contingency.

II.

Hartmann argues that the district court erred by piercing the TLH corporate veil and holding him personally liable for damages.

> [C]ase law that states the conditions and circumstances under which the corporate veil of a corporation may be pierced under Minnesota law also applies to limited liability companies.

Minn.Stat. § 322B.303, subd. 2 (1996). . . .

Courts will pierce the corporate veil if (1) an entity ignores corporate formalities and acts as the alter ego or instrumentality of a shareholder and (2) the liability limitations of the corporate forum results in injustice or is fundamentally unfair.

This record fails to establish the injustice or fundamental unfairness required to pierce TLH's corporate veil. The district court found that "Hartmann and TLH intentionally misled Tom Thumb as to the ownership of the property." Although the record establishes that Hartmann misrepresented his ownership in the property, it does not support a finding that those statements were intended to mislead Tom Thumb. Hartmann's undisputed testimony and the testimony of Smith, one of the landowners, was that they planned to form the limited liability company to develop the land for Tom Thumb. Far from creating the company to perpetrate a fraud, the undisputed testimony was that the company was formed to achieve development of a Tom Thumb store.

Furthermore, a party seeking equity "must come with clean hands." Edin [v. Josten's, Inc.] 343 N.W.2d [691], 694 [Minn.App. (1984)]. . . . The record is undisputed that when Hartmann attempted to obtain financing for the project, Tom Thumb delayed sending financial statements to Hartmann's bank. The record is also undisputed that when the bank ultimately received Tom Thumb's financial information, it refused to finance the project because Tom Thumb had a negative net worth. Tom Thumb's conduct contributed to the delay and ultimately caused the bank to refuse financing. This conduct contributed to breach of the lease, and it would be unjust to allow Tom Thumb to recover against Hartmann personally. . . . We therefore reverse the district court's decision to pierce the corporate veil.

ANALYSIS

1. **LLCs vs. Corporations.** Absent a statute mandating the use of corporate veil piercing precedents in determining the personal liability of members of an LLC, should a court rely on such precedents? Is there

any good reason to treat LLCs differently than corporations in this regard?

2. **Relevance of Experience.** What is the relevance, if any, of the court's description of the litigants as "two experienced parties" to a contract?

3. **Formalities.** The court opines that corporate law permits veil piercing where "an entity ignores corporate formalities and acts as the alter ego or instrumentality of a shareholder." Under that rubric, courts take into account such factors as commingling of personal and organizations funds and other assets, the failure to maintain minutes or adequate organizational records, the failure to adequately capitalize a firm, and the disregard of other legal formalities. Uniform Limited Liability Company Act (1997) § 304(b) provides, however: "The failure of a limited liability company to observe formalities relating to the exercise of its company powers or management of its activities and affairs is not a ground for imposing liability on a member or manager for a debt, obligation, or other liability of the company." In the absence of such a statute, what weight, if any, should a court give to evidence tending to show that the LLC's members failed to observe the sorts of organizational formalities referred to above?

NetJets Aviation, Inc. v. LHC Communications, LLC

537 F.3d 168 (2d Cir. 2008).

. . .

I. BACKGROUND

NetJets is engaged in the business of leasing fractional interests in airplanes and providing related air-travel services. LHC is a Delaware limited liability company whose sole member-owner is Zimmerman. . . .

A. The Contracts Between NetJets and LHC

On August 1, 1999, LHC entered into two contracts with NetJets. In the first (the "Lease Agreement"), NetJets leased to LHC a 12.5 percent interest in an airplane, for which LHC was to pay NetJets a fixed monthly rental fee. The lease term was five years, with LHC having a qualified right of early termination. The second contract (the "Management Agreement") required NetJets to manage LHC's interest in the leased airplane and to provide services such as maintenance and piloting with

> **NOTE**
>
> NetJets is a leading provider of private-jet services. In 1998 it was acquired by Berkshire Hathaway Inc., which was founded and is headed by greatly admired Warren Buffett, and which holds investments in a wide variety of businesses. Buffett, through his investment in the company, became one of the world's wealthiest people.

respect to that airplane, or substitute aircraft, at specified hourly rates. It required LHC to pay a monthly management fee, as well as fuel charges, taxes, and other fees associated with LHC's air travel. The Management Agreement allotted to LHC use of the airplane for an average of 100 hours per year for the five-year term of the lease ("LHC air hours"), and it provided that if the leased airplane were unavailable at a time when LHC wished to use it, NetJets would provide substitute aircraft. NetJets regularly sent LHC invoices for the services provided under the Lease and Management Agreements.

. . .

In July 2000, LHC terminated its agreements with NetJets. LHC's chief financial officer ("CFO") James P. Whittier sent a letter, addressed to a NetJets vice president, stating, in pertinent part, that "[t]he present outstanding is $440,840.39 and we are requesting that you apply the deposit of $100,000 against the outstanding and contact this office to resolve the balance.". . .

As requested, NetJets contacted LHC and applied the $100,000 deposit against LHC's debt; however, it did not receive payment of the remaining balance of $340,840.39. In 2001, LHC ceased operations.

B. The Present Action and the Decision of the District Court

NetJets commenced the present diversity action in 2002, asserting claims against LHC and Zimmerman for breach of contract, account stated, and unjust enrichment. . . .

Following a period of discovery, NetJets moved for summary judgment against both defendants on the breach-of-contract and account-stated claims. NetJets contended that Zimmerman should be held liable for the debts of LHC as its alter ego based on evidence, described in greater detail in Part II.B. below, of, inter alia, (a) the frequent use of LHC air hours for personal travel by Zimmerman and his friends and family, (b) the frequent transfers of funds between LHC and Zimmerman's other companies, (c) Zimmerman's frequent withdrawal of funds from LHC for his own personal use, and (d) the fact that LHC is no longer in business and has no assets with which to pay its debt to NetJets, a condition that NetJets contends was caused by Zimmerman's withdrawals.

In a Memorandum and Order dated June 12, 2006, the district court granted NetJets's summary judgment motion in part, awarding it $340,840.39 against LHC on the account-stated claims. . . .

Although Zimmerman had not moved for summary judgment in his favor, the court *sua sponte* granted summary judgment dismissing all of NetJets's claims against him.

II. DISCUSSION

. . .

For the reasons that follow, we conclude . . . that NetJets is entitled to trial on its contract and account-stated claims against Zimmerman as LHC's alter ego.

. . .

B. NetJets's Claims Against Zimmerman

1. Limitations on Limited Liability

. . . The shareholders of a corporation and the members of an LLC generally are not liable for the debts of the entity, and a plaintiff seeking to persuade a Delaware court to disregard the corporate structure faces "a difficult task," Harco National Insurance Co. v. Green Farms, Inc., No. CIV. A. 1331, 1989 WL 110537, at *4 (Del. Ch. Sept. 19, 1989) ("Harco").

Nonetheless, in appropriate circumstances, the distinction between the entity and its owner "may be disregarded" to require an owner to answer for the entity's debts. Pauley Petroleum Inc. v. Continental Oil Co., 239 A.2d 629, 633 (Del. 968). In general, with respect to the limited liability of owners of a corporation, Delaware law permits a court to pierce the corporate veil "where there is fraud or where [the corporation] is in fact a mere instrumentality or alter ego of its owner." Geyer v. Ingersoll Publications Co., 621 A.2d 784, 793 (Del.Ch.1992); . . .

To prevail under the alter-ego theory of piercing the veil, a plaintiff need not prove that there was actual fraud but must show a mingling of the operations of the entity and its owner plus an "overall element of injustice or unfairness." Harco, 1989 WL 110537, at *4.

> "[A]n alter ego analysis must start with an examination of factors which reveal how the corporation operates and the particular defendant's relationship to that operation. These factors include whether the corporation was adequately capitalized for the corporate undertaking; whether the corporation was solvent; whether dividends were paid, corporate records kept, officers and directors functioned properly, and other corporate formalities were observed; whether the dominant shareholder siphoned corporate funds; and whether, in general, the corporation simply functioned as a facade for the dominant shareholder."

Id. at *4. . . .

> "[N]o single factor c[an] justify a decision to disregard the corporate entity, but . . . some combination of them [i]s required, and . . . *an overall element of injustice or unfairness must always*

> *be present, as well.*" Harco, [1989 WL 110537, at *5] (quoting Golden Acres, 702 F.Supp. at 1104).

Harper v. Delaware Valley Broadcasters, Inc., 743 F.Supp. 1076, 1085 (D.Del.1990) ("Harper") (emphasis added), aff'd, 932 F.2d 959 (3d Cir.1991).

. . . Our Court has stated this as a two-pronged test focusing on (1) whether the entities in question operated as a single economic entity, and (2) whether there was an overall element of injustice or unfairness. . . .

These principles are generally applicable as well where one of the entities in question is an LLC rather than a corporation. In the alter-ego analysis of an LLC, somewhat less emphasis is placed on whether the LLC observed internal formalities because fewer such formalities are legally required. . . .

3. The Evidence that LHC and Zimmerman Operated as One

With respect to the question of whether LHC and Zimmerman operated as a single entity, the record contains, inter alia, financial records of LHC and deposition testimony from Zimmerman and LHC's CFO, Whittier. The evidence discussed below, taken in the light most favorable to NetJets, shows, inter alia, that LHC, of which Zimmerman is the sole member-owner, was started with a capitalization of no more than $20,100; that LHC proceeded to invest millions of dollars supplied by Zimmerman, including some $22 million in an internet technology company eventually called Bazillion, Inc. ("Bazillion"); and that Zimmerman put money into LHC as LHC needed it, and took money out of LHC as Zimmerman needed it.

Whittier, who had known Zimmerman since 1980 and worked with him full time from 1996 until April 2002, was LHC's only officer other than Zimmerman. In addition to LHC, Zimmerman directly or indirectly owned or controlled a number of companies, including Landover Telecom Corporation ("Landover Telecom"), LandTel N.V. ("LandTel"), IP II Partners, LP ("IP II"),. . . . Whittier acted as CFO for each of those companies. During most of the period 1996 to April 2002, Whittier "got paid from either Mr. Zimmerman or one of his corporations."

Zimmerman formed LHC in 1998; for most of its operating life, it shared office space with some of Zimmerman's other companies; LHC employed no more than five-to-seven people at any given time; and some of its employees worked for both LHC and Zimmerman's other companies or for LHC and Zimmerman personally. Whittier ran much of LHC's day-to-day operations based on instructions, general or specific, received from Zimmerman.

Zimmerman formed LHC "to be used as an investment vehicle for Mr. Zimmerman for him to make investments." "With regards to investments, Mr. Zimmerman reviewed investments. If he decided to go forward after his review, he would make an investment through [LHC] to an investment corporation he wanted to invest in." Although Zimmerman sought Whittier's advice as to the best way of accomplishing something he had decided he wanted to do, the ultimate decisions were always made by Zimmerman. "There were no decisions, financial decisions, made with regard to LHC without Mr. Zimmerman's approval."

Whittier testified that LHC also "was an operating company which maintained a consulting agreement with another entity called Landtel NV." But LandTel, which was wholly owned by Zimmerman's Landover Telecom—and was apparently LHC's only paying client—did not come into existence until January 2000, and LHC records do not show receipt of any consulting fees from LandTel until July 2000. Until LandTel was formed, therefore, the day-to-day LHC operations run by Whittier apparently consisted only of making Zimmerman's investments and carrying on Zimmerman's personal business. . . .

Whittier's compensation was paid sometimes by LHC and sometimes by Zimmerman personally.

In connection with Zimmerman's personal business, LHC's records show numerous transfers of money by Zimmerman to LHC, as well as numerous transfers of money from LHC to Zimmerman. Some of the transfers by Zimmerman to LHC were for the purpose of having LHC make investments,. . . . Other transfers by Zimmerman to LHC were made for the purpose of meeting LHC's operating expenses. . . .

Whittier testified that Zimmerman would transfer funds to LHC "as needed." ("Monies would go in . . . LHC based on the need."). Often those funds would come from Zimmerman's personal bank accounts. However, because Zimmerman generally waited until the eleventh hour to provide money to meet LHC's operating needs, sometimes "shortcuts" were taken by having the money come to LHC directly from one of Zimmerman's other companies . . ., none of which had any business relationship with LHC.

Whittier testified also that "[m]onies would go . . . out of LHC based on the need." For example, Zimmerman would take money out of LHC to "mak[e] an investment in another entity." In addition, at several brokerage firms, Zimmerman had personal accounts that were unrelated to LHC's operations; he had many margin calls in those accounts because he "utilized margin debt very aggressively," especially with respect to two stocks whose market prices dropped sharply in 2000 (one "from a high of above 90 down to the 60s" and the other "from a high of 93 down to 3"). Zimmerman had LHC make payments to meet some of these margin calls in his personal accounts. On May 15 and 16, 2000, for example, LHC wired a total of $2 million to Salomon Smith Barney to meet margin calls or reduce the margin debt on Zimmerman's personal brokerage accounts. On August 22 and October 6, 2000, LHC sent Paine Webber, another firm at which Zimmerman personally had "big brokerage accounts," checks totaling $2 million. . . .

LHC also transferred money to Zimmerman, or to third persons on his behalf, in connection with his living expenses. For example, LHC made payments to Fox Lair (consistently called "Fox Liar" in LHC's general ledger), a Zimmerman corporation that owned a $15 million New York apartment on Park Avenue, which was characterized by Zimmerman as "a corporate residence" but was used by no one other than Zimmerman and his family. Fox Lair needed money "to pay phone bills and cleaning people and things of that nature"; according to LHC's ledgers, from December 5, 2000, through July 2, 2001, Fox Lair received some $70,000 from LHC. In addition, LHC made periodic payments to the Screen Actors Guild (of which Zimmerman's wife was a member) for health insurance for Zimmerman and his family; LHC purchased a Bentley automobile at a cost of approximately $350,000 for Zimmerman's personal use, placing title in his name; and LHC made a payment of $110,000, characterized in its general ledger as "Loan receivable" and in its check register as "Interest Expense," to a person who had no connection with LHC but who held a mortgage on a property owned by Zimmerman personally.

In addition, many of the air hours to which LHC was entitled under its agreements with NetJets were used by Zimmerman personally. Of the 40-odd LHC flights invoiced by NetJets, Zimmerman acknowledges that "approximately 6" were for vacations for himself and/or his wife. But in addition to those six, there were at least an equal number of flights that apparently had no relation to LHC's business. These flights included several that transported Zimmerman's family to and from Europe or to and from one of Zimmerman's five homes. Zimmerman contends that use of LHC air hours for these purposes was "part of [his compensation] package" and "[o]ne of the perks of being the chairman." That may be; but for purposes of determining whether Zimmerman and LHC were alter egos, it is pertinent that Zimmerman made all of LHC's financial decisions; Zimmerman alone decided what his perks and package would be.

In LHC's general ledger, each of the transfers of money between LHC and Zimmerman—in either direction—is labeled "Loan receivable." They were also so labeled regardless of whether Zimmerman's payment to LHC was to be used to make an investment or was to be used for operating expenses. . . . The decision that those transactions would be labeled loans or loan repayments was made by Zimmerman.

"There were no written agreements" with regard to any of Zimmerman's loans; nor were there any "set repayment program" or agreements as to repayment terms: "Money was put in as needed and when money was not needed and Mr. Zimmerman needed money elsewhere, he might transfer it out. That was his decision to make." "There was no procedure. Money was put in and taken out as needed."

In all, LHC's financial records for the period January 1, 2000, through June 18, 2002, show—in addition to some two dozen transactions between LHC and Zimmerman's other companies—approximately 60 transfers of money directly from Zimmerman to LHC and approximately 60 transfers of money out of LHC directly to Zimmerman. In sum, there is evidence that, inter alia, Zimmerman created LHC to be one of his personal investment vehicles; that he was the sole decisionmaker with respect to LHC's financial actions; that Zimmerman frequently put money into LHC as LHC needed it to meet operating expenses; that LHC used some of that money, as well as some moneys it received from selling shares of one of its assets, to pay more than $4.5 million to third persons for Zimmerman's personal expenses including margin calls, mortgage payments, apartment expenses, and automobiles; and that with no written agreements or documentation or procedures in place, Zimmerman directly, on the average of twice a month for 2½ years, took money out of LHC at will in order to make other investments or to meet his other personal expenses. This evidence is ample to permit a reasonable factfinder to find that Zimmerman completely dominated LHC and that he essentially treated LHC's bank account as one of his pockets, into which he reached when he needed or desired funds for his personal use. Accordingly, we reject Zimmerman's contention that the district court should have granted summary judgment in his favor on the ground that he and LHC did not operate as a single economic entity.

4. The Evidence of Fraud, Illegality, or Injustice

. . . NetJets adduced sufficient evidence of fraud, illegality, or unfairness to warrant a trial on its contract and account-stated claims against Zimmerman as LHC's alter ego. For example, in an effort to parry NetJets's contention that LHC was undercapitalized, Zimmerman submitted an affidavit from LHC's accountant [Balaban] stating that "it was not intended by Zimmerman to treat the monies paid into LHC as loans" and that all of Zimmerman's payments into LHC were in fact capital contributions. Yet, as discussed above, Whittier testified that Zimmerman instructed him that those payments were to be characterized as loans, in order to allow Zimmerman to take money out of LHC at will and to do so without tax consequences.

Further, although the Balaban affidavit stops short of giving an opinion as to how to characterize Zimmerman's withdrawals of money from LHC, it would appear that, if his payments to LHC were capital contributions as the Balaban affidavit opines, LHC's payments to Zimmerman would be properly characterized as distributions. Yet the DLLCA provides generally, with some qualifications, that an LLC "shall not make a distribution to a member to the extent that at the time of the distribution, after giving effect to the distribution, all liabilities of the limited liability company . . . exceed the fair value of the assets of the limited liability company." Del.Code tit. 6, § 18–607(a). Given that LHC ceased operating and was unable to pay its debt to NetJets, if Zimmerman's withdrawals left LHC in that condition those withdrawals may well have been prohibited by § 18–607(a). A factfinder could infer that Zimmerman's payments to LHC were deliberately mischaracterized as loans in order to mask the fact that Zimmerman was making withdrawals from LHC that were forbidden by law, and could thereby properly find fraud or an unfair siphoning of LHC's assets.

The record also includes other evidence from which a reasonable factfinder could find that Zimmerman operated LHC in his own self-interest in a manner that unfairly disregarded the rights of LHC's creditors. For example, it could find

— that although LHC was apparently unable in 2000 to pay its $340,840.39 (net of LHC's deposit) debt to NetJets, in that year LHC bought, and gave Zimmerman title to, a Bentley automobile for $350,210.95;

— that LHC's only paying client for its consulting services began paying LHC for those services in July 2000 (the month in which LHC terminated its agreements with NetJets), sending LHC a first payment of approximately $675,000 on July 9, and that on that day Zimmerman withdrew that amount and more from LHC;

— that from the point at which LHC terminated its relationship with NetJets in July 2000 until the end of 2001—the year in which NetJets ceased operations—LHC's records of its transactions directly with Zimmerman indicate that Zimmerman withdrew from LHC approximately $750,000 more than he put in;

— and that, excluding moneys put into LHC solely for its investments in Bazillion, the total amount of money taken out of LHC by Zimmerman and his other companies appears to exceed the amount that he and those companies put into LHC by some $3 million.

From this record, a reasonable factfinder could properly find that there was an overall element of injustice in Zimmerman's operation of LHC. . . .

CONCLUSION

. . . For the reasons stated above, the judgment of the district court is vacated . . . [and] the case is remanded for further proceedings not inconsistent with this opinion.

ANALYSIS

1. **How to Protect NetJets.** What should NetJets have done before the LHC default to protect its interests?
2. **Windfall?** Is it fair to say that NetJets got a windfall—that is, more than it bargained for?
3. **How to Protect Zimmerman.** What should Zimmerman have done to protect himself from personal liability?
4. **The Reality of LHC.** What is the relevance of the fact that Zimmerman made all the decisions, including the amount of his own compensation, and that LHC was purely an investment company?
5. **Observation of Formalities.** Uniform Limited Liability Company Act § 303(b) provides that: "The failure of a limited liability company to observe the usual company formalities or requirements relating to the exercise of its company powers or management of its business is not a ground for imposing personal liability on the members or managers for liabilities of the company." In the absence of such a statute, what weight, if any, should a court give to evidence tending to show that the LLC's members failed to observe the sorts of organizational formalities referred to above? Put another way, what are the important differences between an LLC and a corporation that are relevant to piercing?

D. FIDUCIARY OBLIGATION

McConnell v. Hunt Sports Enterprises

132 Ohio App.3d 657, 725 N.E.2d 1193 (1999).

[On October 31, 1996, several wealthy individuals and their controlled entities formed Columbus Hockey Limited, L.L.C. (CHL) for the purpose of seeking a National Hockey League franchise for Columbus Ohio. The two leading figures in the story that unfolded were John H. McConnell and Lamar Hunt, who were investors in CHL and wound up on opposite sides of the present lawsuit. To secure the NHL franchise, CHL needed an arena and sought public financing through an increase in the countywide sales tax. Unfortunately for CHL, the voters rejected the sales tax increase. Shortly thereafter, Nationwide Insurance Enterprise developed an interest in building the arena and leasing it to the holder of the franchise. With this in mind, Dimon McPherson, Nationwide's chairman and chief executive officer, met with Hunt, who purported to act for CHL, but without consulting with the other CHL investors. Nationwide made a proposal for the lease, which Hunt rejected. Meanwhile, an NHL deadline was fast approaching. Having received several rebuffs from Hunt, McPherson approached McConnell, who said that if Hunt would not agree to lease the arena, he would. McPherson conveyed this information to the Nationwide board of directors. Thereafter, Hunt again stated to Nationwide's representatives that he found the lease unacceptable, but was still interested in pursuing the matter.

On June 4, 1997, the NHL franchise expansion committee was advised of McConnell's unconditional backup offer and recommended to the NHL board of governors that a franchise be awarded for the city of Columbus.

On June 9, the CHL investors met. Hunt and his allies stated that they found Nationwide's lease offer unacceptable. McConnell and his allies, on the other hand, accepted the lease offer and signed an agreement in their own names (after the elimination of "Columbus Hockey Limited" from the signature line). On June 17, 1997, the NHL expansion committee recommended that the Columbus franchise be awarded to McConnell's group. On the same date the McConnell group filed the present law suit seeking a declaratory judgment to establish its legal right to the franchise without inclusion of Hunt or CHL. The suit relied on the express language of the CHL operating agreement that is discussed by the court below. The Hunt group filed an answer and counterclaim on behalf of itself and CHL and also filed a suit on behalf of CHL against McConnell and some of his group in a New York state court.

On June 25, 1997, the NHL board of governors awarded a franchise to Columbus with McConnell's group as owner.

In the present Ohio declaratory judgment action there was a flurry of motions and countermotions, a jury trial, and finally, on May 18, 1998, a directed verdict in favor of McConnell on the main counts. On appeal, the court issued a lengthy opinion, parts of which follow, beginning with a response to the Hunt group's argument that the lower court erred in refusing to allow introduction of extrinsic evidence of the meaning of the crucial language in the CHL operating agreement.]

The construction of written contracts is a matter of law. . . . If a contract is clear and unambiguous, there is no issue of fact to be determined,. . . . Only where the language of a contract is unclear or ambiguous or when the circumstances surrounding the agreement invest the language of the contract with a special meaning, will extrinsic evidence be considered in an effort to give effect to the parties' intentions. . . .

The test for determining whether a term is ambiguous is that common words in a written contract will be given their ordinary meaning unless manifest absurdity results or unless some other meaning is clearly evidenced from the face or overall content of the contract.... For the reasons that follow, we conclude that section 3.3 is plain and unambiguous and allowed members of CHL to compete against CHL for an NHL franchise.

Section 3.3 of the operating agreement states:

> "Members May Compete. Members shall not in any way be prohibited from or restricted in engaging or owning an interest in any other business venture of any nature, including any venture which might be competitive with the business of the Company."

Appellant emphasizes the word "other" in the above language and states, in essence, that it means any business venture that is different from the business of the company....

Appellant's interpretation of section 3.3 goes beyond the plain language of the agreement and adds words or meanings not stated in the provision. Section 3.3, for example, does not state "[m]embers shall not be prohibited from or restricted in engaging or owning an interest in any other business venture that is different from the business of the company." Rather, section 3.3 states: "any other business venture of any nature." (Emphasis added.) It then adds to this statement: "including any venture which might be competitive with the business of the Company." The words "any nature" could not be broader, and the inclusion of the words "any venture which might be competitive with the business of the Company" makes it clear that members were not prohibited from engaging in a venture that was competitive with CHL's investing in and operating an NHL franchise....

[The court next turns to the trial court's direction to the jury that the McConnell group] did not violate any [fiduciary] duty by forming and joining COLHOC [Limited Partnership], by allegedly excluding appellant from participating in an NHL franchise, by preparing to compete against CHL and in not providing additional capital for CHL.

Such instruction was proper because, as discussed [above], appellees [the McConnell group] were permitted to compete against CHL for a hockey franchise, and there was no requirement that CHL members contribute additional capital. As will be addressed in more detail infra, these acts in and of themselves would not constitute breach of fiduciary duty because the operating agreement allowed such acts....

Before we can review the propriety of the directed verdict in this case, the law on fiduciary duty and interference with a prospective business relationship must be addressed. The term "fiduciary relationship" has been defined as a relationship in which special confidence and trust is reposed in the integrity and fidelity of another, and there is a resulting position of superiority or influence acquired by virtue of this special trust. . . . In the case at bar, a limited liability company is involved which, like a partnership, involves a fiduciary relationship. Normally, the presence of such a relationship would preclude direct competition between members of the company. However, here we have an operating agreement that by its very terms allows members to compete with the business of the company. Hence, the question we are presented with is whether an operating agreement of a limited liability company may, in essence, limit or define the scope of the fiduciary duties imposed upon its members. We answer this question in the affirmative.

. . .

. . . In becoming members of CHL, appellant and appellees agreed to abide by the terms of the operating agreement, and such agreement specifically allowed competition with the company by its members. As such, the duties created pursuant to such undertaking did not include a duty not to compete. Therefore, there was no duty on the part of appellees to refrain from subjecting appellant to the injury complained of herein.

We find further support for our conclusion in case law concerning close corporations and partnerships. . . .

Given the above, we conclude as a matter of law that it was not a breach of fiduciary duty for appellees to form COLHOC and obtain an NHL franchise to the exclusion of CHL. In so concluding, we are not stating that no act related to such obtainment could be considered a breach of fiduciary duty. In general terms, members of limited liability companies owe one another the duty of utmost trust and loyalty. However, such general duty in this case must be considered in the context of members' ability, pursuant to operating agreement, to compete with the company.

We now turn to the elements of tortious interference with a prospective business relationship. The tort of interference with a business relationship occurs when a person, without a privilege to do so, induces or otherwise purposely causes a third person not to enter into or continue a business relationship with another. . . .

[A]ppellees were permitted under the operating agreement to compete with CHL and, as discussed above, this in and of itself cannot constitute a breach of fiduciary duty. Further, in so competing, appellees did not engage in any acts that would otherwise constitute wrongful behavior. Nationwide contacted McConnell only after appellant indicated the lease terms were unacceptable. Even then, McConnell stated he would accept the lease terms and obtain the franchise on his own only if appellant did not. There is no evidence that McConnell acted in any secretive manner in his actions leading up to the franchise award or that he used CHL assets for personal gain. In short, the evidence shows that appellees obtained the NHL franchise to the exclusion of CHL. Appellees did nothing beyond this that could constitute a breach of fiduciary duty.

Likewise, the evidence does not show that appellees tortiously interfered with appellant's prospective business relationships with Nationwide and the NHL. The evidence does not show that appellees induced or otherwise purposely caused Nationwide and the NHL not to enter into or continue a business relationship with appellant. Indeed, and as indicated above, the evidence shows that McConnell stated he would lease the arena and obtain the franchise only if appellant did not. It was only after appellant rejected the lease proposal on several occasions that McConnell stepped in. Appellant had yet another opportunity on June 9, 1997 to participate in the Nationwide arena lease and the NHL franchise. Appellant again found the lease proposal unacceptable, and without a signed lease term sheet, there would have been no franchise from the NHL. McPherson testified that Nationwide would accept a lease agreement with whomever the successful franchise applicant was. In addition, it is clear . . . that the NHL was still considering appellant as a potential franchise owner up until the last moment. Again, the evidence does not show that appellees' actions constituted an intentional interference with appellant's business relationships. It must be noted that appellees had the right to compete against CHL. However, even given such right, McConnell did not approach Nationwide or the NHL. Nationwide approached McConnell only after appellant indicated the lease terms were unacceptable. In short, it was appellant's actions that caused the termination of any relationship or potential relationship it had with Nationwide and the NHL. In conclusion, there was not sufficient material evidence presented at trial so as to create a factual question for the jury on the issues of breach of fiduciary duty and tortious interference with business relationships. Therefore, a directed verdict in favor of appellees . . . was appropriate.

[The court next addresses the trial court's directed verdict in favor of the McConnell group on its claim of the Hunt group's] breach of contract in unilaterally rejecting the Nationwide lease proposal, in failing to negotiate with Nationwide in good faith, in allowing Nationwide's deadline to expire without response, and in wrongfully and unlawfully usurping control of CHL. In granting appellees' motion for a directed verdict, the trial court found appellant violated the CHL operating agreement in failing to ask for and obtain the authorization of CHL members, other than appellees, prior to filing the answer and counterclaim in this action and the suit in New York. . . . The trial court awarded appellees $1.00 in damages.

. . . Appellant [Hunt's firm] contends that under the operating agreement, it could only be liable for willful misconduct. In addition, appellant contends it was the "operating member" of CHL and, therefore, had full authority to act on CHL's behalf. For the reasons that follow, we conclude that a directed verdict in favor of appellees . . . was appropriate.

First, there was no evidence at trial that appellant was the operating member of CHL. The operating agreement, which sets forth the entire agreement between the members of CHL, does not name any person or entity the operating or managing member of CHL. Instead, all members of CHL had an equal number of units in CHL, as reflected by the amount of their capital contributions shown on Schedule A of the operating agreement. Pursuant to section 4.1 of the operating agreement, no member was permitted to take any action on behalf of the company unless such action was approved by the specified number of members, which was, at the very least, a majority of the units allocated.

This brings us to the question of whether appellant breached the operating agreement by failing to obtain the approval of the other CHL members prior to filing, in CHL's name, the answer and counterclaim in this suit [and] the suit in New York. . . . Again, section 4.1(b) of the operating agreement requires at least majority approval prior to taking any action on behalf of CHL. Further, the approval of the members as to any action on behalf of CHL must have been evidenced by minutes of a meeting properly noticed and held or by an action in writing signed by the requisite number of members. . . .

There is no evidence that appellant obtained the approval of CHL members prior to filing the actions listed above. Indeed, there is no evidence that appellant even asked permission of any member to file the actions, let alone held a meeting or requested approval in writing. The evidence does show that appellant, in the name of CHL, filed the answer and counterclaim in the present suit [and] the action in New York. . . . This was contrary to sections 4.1 and 4.2 of the operating agreement and constituted breach of such agreement.

Appellant points to section 4.4 of the operating agreement and contends appellees had to show willful misconduct on its part in filing such actions. Section 4.4 states:

> "Exculpation of Members; Indemnity. In carrying out their duties hereunder, the Members shall not be liable to the Company or to any other Member for their good faith actions, or failure to act, or for any errors of judgment, or for any act or omission believed in good faith to be within the scope of authority conferred by this Agreement, but only for their own willful misconduct in the performance of their obligations under this Agreement. Actions or omissions taken in reliance upon the advice of legal counsel as being within the scope of authority conferred by this Agreement shall be conclusive evidence of such

good faith; however, good faith may be determined without obtaining such advice."

Section 4.4's provisions are in the context of members carrying out their duties under the operating agreement. There was no duty on appellant's part to unilaterally file the actions at issue. Indeed, we have determined that appellant did not act properly under the operating agreement in filing such actions. Hence, the provision in section 4.4 indicating members were only liable to other members for their own willful misconduct in the performance of their obligations under the operating agreement does not even apply to the actions taken by appellant.

However, even if we applied this provision, the evidence shows appellant engaged in willful misconduct in filing the actions at issue. As indicated above, appellant was a member of CHL at the time of its formation. As a member of CHL, appellant agreed to be bound by the terms of the operating agreement. Hunt read the operating agreement prior to signing it. The agreement required a majority vote prior to taking any action on behalf of CHL, such as the filing of the actions at issue.

ANALYSIS

1. **An Alternative.** Suppose that Hunt, with the approval of all the other members of CHL, had been negotiating with Nationwide and was near an agreement and that McConnell had then made a good offer to Nationwide and secured the right to lease the arena and, with that in hand, had secured the franchise. What result?
2. **Contracting Around the Case.** Do you agree that the language of Section 3.3 of the operating agreement was clear and unambiguous? How might it have been drafted to remove all possible doubt in its application to this case?

VGS, Inc. v. Castiel

2000 WL 1277372 (Del.Ch.).

One entity controlled by a single individual forms a one "member" limited liability company. Shortly thereafter, two other entities, one of which is controlled by the owner of the original member, become members of the LLC. The LLC Agreement creates a three-member Board of Managers with sweeping authority to govern the LLC. The individual owning the original member has the authority to name and remove two of the three managers. He also acts as CEO. The unaffiliated third member becomes disenchanted with the original member's leadership. Ultimately the third member's owner, also the third manager, convinces the original member's owner's appointed manager to join him in a clandestine strategic move to merge the LLC into a Delaware corporation. The appointed manager and the disaffected third member do not give the original member's owner, still a member of the LLC's board of managers, notice of their strategic move. After the merger, the original member finds himself relegated to a minority position in the surviving corporation. While a majority of the board acted by written consent, as all involved surely knew, had the original member's manager received notice beforehand that his appointed manager contemplated action against his interests he would have promptly attempted to remove him. Because the two managers acted without notice to the third manager under circumstances where they knew that with notice that he could have acted to protect his majority interest, they breached their duty of loyalty to the original member and their fellow manager by failing to act in good faith. The purported merger must therefore be declared invalid.

. . .

I. Facts

David Castiel formed Virtual Geosatellite LLC (the "LLC") on January 6, 1999 in order to pursue a Federal Communications Commission ("FCC") license to build and operate a satellite system which its proponents claim could dramatically increase the "real estate" in outer space capable of transmitting high speed internet traffic and other communications. When originally formed, it had only one MemberVirtual Geosatellite Holdings, Inc. ("Holdings"). On January 8, 1999, Ellipso, Inc. ("Ellipso") joined the LLC as its second Member. Several weeks later, on January 29, 1999, Sahagen Satellite Technology Group LLC ("Sahagen Satellite") became the third Member of the LLC. David Castiel controls both Holdings and Ellipso. Peter Sahagen, an aggressive and apparently successful venture capitalist, controls Sahagen Satellite.

Pursuant to the LLC Agreement, Holdings received 660 units (representing 63.46% of the total equity in the LLC), Sahagen Satellite received 260 units (representing 25%), and Ellipso received 120 units (representing 11.54%). The founders vested management of the LLC in a Board of Managers. As the majority unitholder, Castiel had the power to appoint, remove, and replace two of the three members of the Board of Managers. Castiel, therefore, had the power to prevent any Board decision with which he disagreed. Castiel named himself and Tom Quinn to the Board of Managers. Sahagen named himself as the third member of the Board.

Not long after the formation of the LLC, Castiel and Sahagen were at odds. Castiel contends that Sahagen wanted to control the LLC ever since he became involved, and that Sahagen repeatedly offered, unsuccessfully, to buy control of the LLC. Sahagen maintains that Castiel ran the LLC so poorly that its mission had become untracked, additional necessary capital could not be raised, and competent managers could not be attracted to join the enterprise. Further, Sahagen claims that Castiel directed LLC assets to Ellipso in order to prop up a failing, cash-strapped Ellipso. At trial, these issues and other similar accusations from both sides were explored in great detail. For our purposes here, all that need be concluded is the unarguable fact that Castiel and Sahagen had very different ideas about how the LLC should be managed and operated.

Sahagen ultimately convinced Quinn that Castiel must be ousted from leadership in order for the LLC to prosper. As a result, Quinn (Castiel's nominee) covertly "defected" to Sahagen's camp, and he and Sahagen decided to wrest control of the LLC from Castiel. Many LLC employees and even some of Castiel's lieutenants testified that they believed it to be in the LLC's best interest to take control from Castiel.

On April 14, 2000, without notice to Castiel, Quinn and Sahagen acted by written consent to merge the LLC under Delaware law into VGS, Inc. ("VGS"), a Delaware corporation. Accordingly, the LLC ceased to exist, its assets and liabilities passed to VGS, and VGS became the LLC's legal successor-in-interest. VGS's Board of Directors is comprised of Sahagen, Quinn, and Neel Howard. Of course, the incorporators did not name Castiel to VGS's Board.

On the day of the merger, Sahagen executed a promissory note to VGS in the amount of $10 million plus interest. In return, he received two million shares of VGS Series A Preferred Stock. VGS also issued 1,269,200 shares of common stock to Holdings, 230,800 shares of common stock to Ellipso, and 500,000 shares of common stock to Sahagen Satellite. Once one does the math, it is apparent that Holdings and Ellipso went from having a 75% controlling combined ownership interest in the LLC to having only a 37.5% interest in VGS. On the other hand, Sahagen and Sahagen Satellite went from owning 25% of the LLC to owning 62.5% of VGS.

There can be no doubt why Sahagen and Quinn, acting as a majority of the LLC's board of managers did not notify Castiel of the merger plan. Notice to Castiel would have immediately resulted in Quinn's removal from the board and a newly constituted majority which would thwart the effort to strip Castiel of control. Had he known in advance, Castiel surely would have attempted to replace Quinn with someone loyal to Castiel who would agree with his views. Clandestine machinations were, therefore, essential to the success of Quinn and Sahagen's plan.

II. Analysis

A. The Board of Managers did have authority to act by majority vote

The LLC Agreement does not expressly state whether the Board of Managers must act unanimously or by majority vote. Sahagen and Quinn contend that because a number of provisions would be rendered meaningless if a unanimous vote was required, a majority vote is implied. Castiel, however, maintains that a unanimous vote must be implied when the majority owner has blocking power.

Section 8.01(b)(i) of the LLC Agreement states that, "[t]he Board of Managers shall initially be composed of three (3) Managers." Sahagen Satellite has the right to designate one member of the initial board, and if the Board of Managers increased in number, Sahagen Satellite could "designate a number of representatives on the Board of Managers that is less than Sahagen's then current Percentage Interest." If unanimity were required, the number of managers would be irrelevant. Sahagen, and his minority interest, would have veto power in any event. The existence of language in the LLC Agreement discussing expansion of the Board is therefore quite telling.

Also persuasive is the fact that Section 8.01(c) of the LLC Agreement, entitled "Matters Requiring Consent of Sahagen," provides that Sahagen's approval is needed for a merger, consolidation, or reorganization of the LLC. If a unanimity requirement indeed existed, there would have been no need to expressly list matters on which Sahagen's minority interest had veto power.

Section 12.01(a)(i) of the LLC Agreement also supports Sahagen's argument. This section provides that the LLC may be dissolved by written consent by either the Board of Managers or by Members holding two-thirds of the Common Units. The effect of this Section is to allow any combination of Holdings and Sahagen Satellite, or Holdings and Ellipso, as Members, to dissolve the LLC. It seems unlikely that the Members designed the LLC Agreement to permit Members holding two-thirds of the Common Units to dissolve the LLC but denied their appointed Managers the power to reach the same result unless the minority manager agreed.

Castiel takes the position that while the Members can act by majority vote, the Board of Managers can act only by unanimous vote. He maintains that if the Board fails to agree unanimously on an issue the issue should be put to an LLC Members' vote with the majority controlling. The practical effect of Castiel's interpretation would be that whenever Castiel and Sahagen disagreed, Castiel would prevail because the issue would be submitted to the Members where Castiel's controlling interest would carry the vote. If that were the case, both Sahagen's Board position and Quinn's Board position would be superfluous. I am confident that the parties never intended that result, or if they had so intended, that they would have included plain and simple language in the agreement spelling it out clearly.

B. By failing to give notice of their proposed action, Sahagen and Quinn failed to discharge their duty of loyalty to Castiel in good faith

Section 18–404(d) of the LLC Act states in pertinent part:

> Unless otherwise provided in a limited liability company agreement, on any matter that is to be voted on by managers, the managers may take such action without a meeting, without prior notice and without a vote if a consent or consents in writing, setting forth the action so taken, shall be signed by the managers having not less than the minimum number of votes that would be necessary to authorize such action at a meeting.

Therefore, the LLC Act, read literally, does not require notice to Castiel before Sahagen and Quinn could act by written consent. The LLC Agreement does not purport to modify the statute in this regard.

Those observations cannot complete the analysis of Sahagen and Quinn's actions, however. Sahagen and Quinn knew what would happen if they notified Castiel of their intention to act by written consent to merge the LLC into VGS, Inc. Castiel would have attempted to remove Quinn, and block the planned action. Regardless of his motivation in doing so, removal of Quinn in that circumstance would have been within Castiel's rights as the LLC's controlling owner under the Agreement. Section 18–404(d) has yet to be interpreted by this Court or the Supreme Court. Nonetheless, it seems clear that the purpose of permitting action by written consent without notice is to enable LLC managers to take quick, efficient action in situations where a minority of managers could not block or adversely affect the course set by the majority even if they were notified of the proposed action and objected to it. The General Assembly never intended, I am quite confident, to enable two managers to deprive, clandestinely and surreptitiously, a third manager representing the majority interest in the LLC of an opportunity to protect that interest by taking an action that the third manager's member would surely have opposed if he had knowledge of it. My reading of Section 18–404(d) is grounded in a classic maxim of equity—"Equity looks to the intent rather than to the form."[3] In this hopefully unique situation, this application of the maxim requires construction of the statute to allow action without notice only by a constant or fixed majority. It cannot apply to an illusory, will-of-the wisp majority which would implode should notice be given. Nothing in the statute suggests that this court of equity should blind its eyes to a shallow, too clever by half, manipulative

[3] DONALD J. WOLFE, JR. & MICHAEL A. PITTENGER, CORPORATE AND COMMERCIAL PRACTICE IN THE DELAWARE COURT OF CHANCERY, at vii (1998) (listing the maxims of equity). . . .

attempt to restructure an enterprise through an action taken by a "majority" that existed only so long as it could act in secrecy.

Sahagen and Quinn each owed a duty of loyalty to the LLC, its investors and Castiel, their fellow manager. Castiel or his entities owned a majority interest in the LLC and he sat as a member of the board representing entities and interests empowered by the Agreement to control the majority membership of the board. The majority investor protected his equity interest in the LLC through the mechanism of appointment to the board rather than by the statutorily sanctioned mechanism of approval by members owning a majority of the LLC's equity interests. It may seem somewhat incongruous, but this Agreement allows the action to merge, dissolve or change to corporate status to be taken by a simple majority vote of the board of managers rather than rely upon the default position of the statute which requires a majority vote of the equity interest. Instead the drafters made the critical assumption, known to all the players here, that the holder of the majority equity interest has the right to appoint and remove two managers, ostensibly guaranteeing control over a three member board. When Sahagen and Quinn, fully recognizing that this was Castiel's protection against actions adverse to his majority interest, acted in secret, without notice, they failed to discharge their duty of loyalty to him in good faith. They owed Castiel a duty to give him prior notice even if he would have interfered with a plan that they conscientiously believed to be in the best interest of the LLC.[4] Instead, they launched a preemptive strike that furtively converted Castiel's controlling interest in the LLC to a minority interest in VGS without affording Castiel a level playing field on which to defend his interest. "[Another] traditional maxim of equity holds that equity regards and treats that as done which in good conscience ought to be done."[5] In good conscience, under these circumstances, Sahagen and Quinn should have given Castiel prior notice.

Many hours were spent at trial focusing on contentions that Castiel has proved to be an ineffective leader in whom employees and investors have lost confidence. I listened to testimony regarding delayed FCC licensing, a suggested new management team for the LLC, and the alleged unlocked value of the LLC. A substantial record exists fully flushing out the rancorous relationships of the members and their wildly disparate views on the existing state of affairs as well as the LLC's prospects for the future. But the issue of who is best suited to run the LLC should not be resolved here but in board meetings where all

[4] I make no ruling here as to whether I believe the merger and the resulting recapitalization of the LLC was in the LLC's best interests, nor do I rule here regarding the wisdom of Castiel's actions had he in fact been able to remove Quinn before the merger.

[5] WOLFE & PITTENGER, supra, at § 2–3(b)(1)(i), citing 2 JOHN NORTON POMEROY, A TREATISE ON EQUITY JURISPRUDENCE § 363 et seq. (5th ed. (1941)).

managers are present and all members appropriately represented, and/or in future litigation, if it unfortunately becomes necessary.

Likewise, the parties spent much time and effort arguing over the standard to be applied to the actions taken by Sahagen and Quinn. Specifically, the parties debated whether the standard should be entire fairness or the business judgment rule. It should be clear that the actions of Sahagen and Quinn, in their capacity as managers constituted a breach of their duty of loyalty and that those actions do not, therefore, entitle them to the benefit or protection of the business judgment rule. They intentionally used a flawed process to merge the LLC into VGS, Inc., in an attempt to prevent the member with majority equity interest in the LLC from protecting his interests in the manner contemplated by the very LLC Agreement under which they purported to act. Analysis beyond a look at the process is clearly unnecessary. Perhaps, had notice been given and an attempt then made to block Castiel's anticipated action to replace Quinn, the allegedly disinterested and independent member that Castiel himself had appointed, the analysis might be different. However, this, as all cases must be reviewed as it is presented, not as it might have been.

III. Conclusion

For the reasons stated above, I find that a majority vote of the LLC's Board of Managers could properly effect a merger. But, I also find that Sahagen and Quinn failed to discharge their duty of loyalty to Castiel in good faith by failing to give him advance notice of their merger plans under the unique circumstances of this case and the structure of this LLC Agreement. Accordingly, I declare that the acts taken to merge the LLC into VGS, Inc. to be invalid and the merger is ordered rescinded. . . .

ANALYSIS

1. **Why Grant Veto Rights?** The court states that "Section 8.01(c) of the LLC Agreement, entitled 'Matters Requiring Consent of Sahagen,' provides that Sahagen's approval is needed for a merger, consolidation, or reorganization of the LLC." Castiel did not have a similar veto power. Why not?

2. **The Role of the Board.** On the court's view of how the Board of Managers should operate, what is Quinn, a potted plant?

3. **What Does a Fiduciary Duty Entail?** The court states that "Sahagen and Quinn each owed a duty of loyalty to the LLC, its investors and Castiel, their fellow manager." Suppose that Sahagen and Quinn firmly and sincerely believed that ousting Castiel from control was essential for the financial well-being of the LLC and Castiel and that the plan for taking control from Castiel that they adopted was the only feasible one.

If they failed to adopt that plan would they have failed in their duty of loyalty?

Gottsacker v. Monnier

281 Wis.2d 361, 697 N.W.2d 436 (2005).

. . .

On September 4, 1998, Julie Monnier (hereinafter Monnier) formed New Jersey LLC as a vehicle to own investment real estate. Ten days later, the company acquired a 40,000-square-foot warehouse located at 2005 New Jersey Avenue in Sheboygan, Wisconsin. . . . New Jersey LLC purchased the property for $510,000, with the financing arranged for and guaranteed by Monnier.

> **NOTE**
>
> The paragraphs in the original are numbered, but the numbers have been removed for reading ease.

Brothers Paul Gottsacker (hereinafter Paul) and Gregory Gottsacker (hereinafter Gregory) became members of New Jersey LLC in January 1999. They entered into a Member's Agreement, which expressed their intent to operate under Wisconsin's limited liability company laws. That document stated in relevant part:

> (4) Julie A. Monnier shall own a 50% interest in the capital, profits and losses of Company and shall have 50% of the voting rights of Company.
>
> (5) Paul Gottsacker and Gregory Gottsacker, collectively, shall own a 50% interest in the capital, profits and losses of Company and shall have 50% of the voting rights of Company.

New Jersey LLC later purchased additional property in Sheboygan on Wilson Avenue. When it was sold, the proceeds were distributed to the members as follows: 50% to Julie, 25% to Paul, and 25% to Gregory. After the sale of the Wilson Avenue property, the only remaining asset of New Jersey LLC was the warehouse on New Jersey Avenue.

Relationships among the members of New Jersey LLC subsequently became strained. In May 2000, Paul and Gregory had a falling-out, allegedly due to Gregory's lack of contribution to the enterprise. Thereafter, communication between the brothers was virtually nonexistent. Monnier also testified that she had not spoken with Gregory since 1998.

On June 7, 2001, Monnier executed a warranty deed transferring the warehouse property owned by New Jersey LLC to a new limited liability company called 2005 New Jersey LLC for $510,000, the same amount as the original purchase price. The new limited liability company consisted of two members: Monnier with a 60% ownership interest and Paul with a 40% ownership interest. Neither one had discussed the transfer with Gregory before it occurred.

Following the transfer, Monnier sent a check to Gregory for $22,000, which purportedly represented his 25% interest in the warehouse property previously owned by New Jersey LLC. Gregory did not cash the check. Monnier and Paul, meanwhile, did not receive any cash payment but instead left their equity in the recently created 2005 New Jersey LLC.

> **NOTE**
>
> How Monnier might have derived this figure is unclear, though the first paragraph suggests that the property may have been subject to a loan.

Gregory commenced suit against Monnier, Paul, and 2005 New Jersey LLC, alleging that they had engaged in an illegal transaction under Wis. Stat. Ch. 183. After a bench trial, the circuit court agreed, noting that the sole purpose of the transfer of the warehouse property was to eliminate Gregory's ownership interest in the asset.

Because the transfer served no legitimate business purpose, and because Monnier and Paul both profited from it, the circuit court determined that Monnier and Paul were precluded by the conflict of interest rules under Wis. Stat. Ch. 183 from voting to authorize the transfer. In the alternative, it concluded that Paul did not have authority to act without the assent of Gregory because the two brothers held a "collective" interest in the ownership. Ultimately, the circuit court ordered that 2005 New Jersey LLC return the warehouse property to New Jersey LLC. Monnier, Paul, and 2005 New Jersey LLC appealed.

The court of appeals affirmed the decision of the circuit court on different grounds. Contrary to the circuit court, the court of appeals reasoned that the provisions of Wis. Stat. Ch. 183, specifically Wis. Stat. §§ 183.0402 and 183.0404, do not prevent a member who has a material conflict of interest from dealing with matters of the LLC. . . . Rather, those statutes prohibit a member who has a material conflict of interest from dealing unfairly with the LLC or its members. . . . Thus, a member with a material conflict of interest can vote to transfer property but is required to do so fairly. . . .

Applying this standard to the present case, the court of appeals held that the transfer of property was unfair in two respects. First, the conveyance was not an "arm's length transaction" because it did not occur on the open market. . . . Second, the sale made it impracticable for New Jersey LLC to carry on with its intended business (i.e., to hold the commercial property as a long-term investment). . . . Accordingly, the court of appeals did not reach the issue of whether Paul and Gregory each held a 25% ownership interest or whether the term "collectively" in the

Member's Agreement required both brothers to jointly vote the entire 50%. . . .

The first issue we address is whether the petitioners possessed the majority necessary to authorize the transfer in question. Gregory submits that they did not. He notes that under the Member's Agreement for New Jersey LLC, Monnier had 50% of the voting rights, while he and his brother "collectively" had the other 50%. Thus, Gregory asserts, Monnier needed the approval of both brothers in order to transfer the commercial real estate.

The petitioners, meanwhile, maintain that Paul and Gregory each possessed 25% of the voting rights. They argue that there is nothing in the Member's Agreement to indicate that the brothers could not vote independently. Furthermore, they contend that the term "collectively" simply refers to the sum of the brothers' individual interests, which are 25% each. . . .

. . . [W]e are satisfied that the term "collectively" refers to the sum of the brothers' individual 25% interests. To conclude otherwise would require unanimous approval by the members in order to perform any act that concerns the business of the company. Here, there is no express language indicating that the parties intended such a result. Construing the Member's Agreement to allow one minority member to effectively deadlock the LLC is unreasonable absent express language. . . .

Having determined that the petitioners possessed the majority necessary to authorize the transaction, we consider next whether they were nonetheless prohibited from voting to transfer the property because of a material conflict of interest. Here, the circuit court found that "[t]he conveyance of the property by Julie Monnier and Paul Gottsacker to themselves in the guise of a newly created LLC, unquestionably, represents a material conflict of interest." This finding is supported by the facts of the case. Not only did Monnier and Paul engage in self-dealing, but in doing so they also increased their individual interests in the new LLC which received the property. . . .

The question therefore becomes what, if any, impact did this conflict of interest have on Monnier and Paul's ability to vote to transfer the property. Wisconsin Stat. § 183.0404 governs voting in LLCs and contemplates situations that would prevent a member from exercising that voting power. Subsection (3) of the statute explicitly states that members can be "precluded from voting." However, that subsection does not address how or when that preclusion would occur. Wisconsin Stat. § 183.0404 provides in relevant part:

> (1) Unless otherwise provided in an operating agreement or this chapter . . . an affirmative vote, approval or consent as

> follows shall be required to decide any matter connected with the business of a limited liability company:
>
> > (a) If management of a limited liability company is reserved to the members, an affirmative vote, approval or consent by members whose interests in the limited liability company represent contributions to the limited liability company of more than 50% of the value. . . .
>
> (3) Unless otherwise provided in an operating agreement, if any member is precluded from voting with respect to a given matter, then the value of the contribution represented by the interest in the limited liability company with respect to which the member would otherwise have been entitled to vote shall be excluded from the total contributions made to the limited liability company for purposes of determining the 50% threshold under sub. (1)(a) for that matter. . . .

Because Wis. Stat. § 183.0404 does not address how or when a member is precluded from voting, Gregory asks that we look to Wis. Stat. § 183.1101 for guidance. Wisconsin Stat. § 183.1101 pertains to the authority to sue on behalf of an LLC. It states that, "the vote of any member who has an interest in the outcome of the action that is adverse to the interest of the limited liability company shall be excluded." Wis. Stat. § 183.1101(1). According to Gregory, if one wishes to harmonize this section with Wis. Stat. § 183.0404, then it must follow that a member who has an interest adverse to the interest of the LLC is precluded from voting.

The petitioners, however, contend that members are not precluded from voting on a matter affecting the LLC, even if they have a material conflict of interest. For support, the petitioners rely upon Wis. Stat. § 183.0402, the statute defining duties of managers and members. That statute anticipates members having a material conflict of interest and requires them to "deal fairly" with the LLC and its other members. Wisconsin Stat. § 183.0402(1)(a) provides: . . .

> (1) No member or manager shall act or fail to act in a manner that constitutes any of the following:
>
> > (a) A willful failure to deal fairly with the limited liability company or its members in connection with a matter in which the member or manager has a material conflict of interest. . . .

Reading Wis. Stat. §§ 183.0404 and 183.0402 together in harmony, we determine that the WLLCL does not preclude members with a material conflict of interest from voting their ownership interest with respect to a given matter. Rather, it prohibits members with a material conflict of interest from acting in a manner that constitutes a willful failure to deal fairly with the LLC or its other members. We interpret this requirement to mean that members with a material conflict of interest may not willfully act or fail to act in a manner that will have the effect of injuring the LLC or its other members. . . .

Here, the circuit court made no express determination as to whether the petitioners willfully failed to deal fairly in spite of the conflict of interest. Under the circuit court's analysis, there was no need to reach this issue because the court reasoned that a material conflict of interest precluded any vote to transfer the property.

The court of appeals did address the question of whether the petitioners dealt fairly. In doing so, it found that the transfer was unfair in two respects. First, the conveyance was not an "arm's length transaction" because it did not occur on the open market. . . . Second, the sale made it impracticable for New Jersey LLC to carry on with its intended business (i.e., to hold the commercial property as a long-term investment). . . .

> We agree with the petitioners that the court of appeals improperly made findings of fact in this case. As we explained in Wurtz v. Fleischman, 97 Wis.2d 100, 107, n. 3, 293 N.W.2d 155 (1980), the court of appeals is not empowered to make such determinations:

The court of appeals is by Constitution limited to appellate jurisdiction. Art. VII, sec. 5(3), Wis. Const. This precludes it from making any factual determination where the evidence is in dispute. . . .

Accordingly, we remand the cause to the circuit court for further findings and application of the foregoing standard. Consistent with Wis. Stat. § 183.0402(2), Monnier and Paul on remand shall also "account to the limited liability company and hold as trustee . . . any improper personal profit derived by that member . . . without the consent of a majority of the disinterested members" for the transfer in question. . . .

■ LOUIS B. BUTLER, JR., J. (dissenting). . . .

Because there was no affirmative vote, approval, or consent to transfer the warehouse property owned by New Jersey LLC to a new limited liability company called 2005 New Jersey LLC, as required by the Member's Agreement and Wis. Stat. § 183.0404(1) (2001–02), no legal transfer of the property took place. . . .

The meaning of the Member's Agreement signed on January 13, 1999, by Julie Monnier, Paul Gottsacker, and Gregory Gottsacker is at issue here. The relevant portion of the agreement is as follows: [Paragraphs (4) and (5), given in majority opinion.]

Part (4) of the agreement clearly states that Julie Monnier owns a 50 percent interest in the Company, and shall have 50 percent of the voting rights of Company. Part (5) clearly provides that the Gottsacker brothers collectively own a 50 percent interest in the Company and "shall have 50% of the voting rights of Company." . . . There is no ambiguity in the construction of this agreement. Part (4) defines a separate 50 percent interest and voting right, and part (5) defines a separate 50 percent interest and voting right. Part (5) could have been written to provide each brother with a 25 percent share of the collective interest and voting right, but it was not drafted in that manner. Instead, the interest and the voting right were created as a collective. . . .

If the parties choose to set forth an agreement that requires the brothers to vote together as one interest, this court should not stand in their way. . . . [T]he trial court got it right when it concluded that Paul Gottsacker lacked the authority to act without the assent of his brother. . . .

ANALYSIS

1. **Contractual Language.** If Paul and Gregory thought they should agree about how to vote their 50% before they voted, what should they have written? If they wanted to indicate that they could each vote 25%, what should they have written?
2. **Duty of Fairness.** Where does the member's duty of fairness come from?
3. **What Standard of Review?** What standard of review should a court use to review a transaction like this?

E. ADDITIONAL CAPITAL

Racing Investment Fund 2000, LLC v. Clay Ward Agency, Inc.

320 S.W.3d 654 (Ky. 2010).

Racing Investment Fund 2000, LLC is a limited liability company created in August 2000, to purchase, train and race thoroughbred horses. [Pursuant to the Operating Agreement, investors would buy 50 units at $100,000 per unit.] In May, 2004, Racing Investment entered into an agreed judgment with its former equine insurance firm, Clay Ward Agency, Inc., for past-due insurance premiums. Shortly thereafter, Racing Investment partially paid the judgment by tendering all of the remaining assets of the then-defunct limited liability company. When Racing Investment failed to pay the remainder of the amount owed, Clay Ward succeeded in having Racing Investment held in contempt of court for its failure to pay the entire judgment amount. Specifically, the trial court ruled that a provision in Racing Investment's Operating Agreement which allowed the limited liability company's Manager to call for additional capital contributions, as needed, from all members on a pro rata basis for "operating, administrative or other business expenses" provided a means of satisfying the Clay Ward judgment [for $57,139.68]. The trial court ordered that Racing Investment "act accordingly to satisfy the Judgment within a reasonable period of time" or face other sanctions. After the Court of Appeals affirmed, this Court granted discretionary review to consider whether the capital call provision can be invoked by a court to obtain funds from the limited liability company's members in order to satisfy a judgment against the limited liability company. Having concluded that KRS 275.150 provides for immunity from personal liability for a limited liability company's debts unless a member agrees otherwise and, further, that members of Racing Investment did not, by signing an operating agreement allowing for periodic capital calls from the Manager, subject themselves to personal liability, we reverse. . . .

Analysis

In 1994, Kentucky joined a growing national trend by recognizing limited liability companies (LLCs) through the adoption of the "Kentucky Limited Liability Company Act" codified at KRS Chapter 275. As early commentators noted, the hallmark of this new form of business entity is its combination of the income tax advantages of a partnership with the business advantages of a corporation. Thomas Rutledge and Lady Booth, The Limited Liability Company Act: Understanding Kentucky's New Organizational Option, 83 Ky. L.J. 1 (1994–95). The "centerpiece" of a limited liability company is its "provision for limited liability of its members and managers in regard to the debts and obligations of the LLC. . . ." *Id.* at 6. . . . One indicia of the strength of that limited liability protection is the Internal Revenue Service's recognition that federal employment tax liabilities incurred by an LLC cannot be collected from the LLC's members. *Id. citing* Rev. Rul. 2004–41, 2004–1 C.B. 845.[1]

Kentucky codified the limited liability feature of a limited liability company at KRS 275.150—"Immunity from personal liability":

> (1) Except as provided in subsection (2) of this section or as otherwise specifically set forth in other sections in this chapter, no member, manager, employee, or agent of a limited liability company, including a professional limited liability company, shall be personally liable by reason of being a member, manager, employee, or agent of the limited liability company, under a judgment, decree, or order of a court, agency, or tribunal of any type, or in any other manner, in this or any other state, or on any other basis, for a debt, obligation, or liability of the limited liability company, whether arising in contract, tort, or

[1] Kentucky has made exceptions, however, for state taxes owed by an LLC: there can be personal liability on the part of members for sales taxes, payroll taxes and other state taxes. . . .

> otherwise. The status of a person as a member, manager, employee, or agent of a limited liability company, including a professional limited liability company, shall not subject the person to personal liability for the acts or omissions, including any negligence, wrongful act, or actionable misconduct, of any other member, manager, agent, or employee of the limited liability company.
>
> (2) Notwithstanding the provisions of subsection (1) of this section, under a written operating agreement or under another written agreement, a member or manager may agree to be obligated personally for any of the debts, obligations, and liabilities of the limited liability company.

Notably, the statute contains a strong, detailed declaration of personal immunity followed by recognition in subsection (2) that a member or members may agree in writing to be personally liable for the LLC's debts, obligations and liabilities. As one national commentator has noted, "[s]ince most LLCs are created for the purpose of obtaining limited liability, few LLCs take advantage of the opportunity to allow their members to waive limited liability under the act." Steven C. Alberty, Limited Liability Companies: A Planning and Drafting Guide § 3.06(b)(2) (2003).

. . .

Section 4.3(a) of the Racing Investment Operating Agreement, entitled "Additional Capital Contributions" provides:

The Investor Members ... shall be obligated to contribute to the capital of the Company, on a prorata basis in accordance with their respective Percentage Interests, such amounts as may be reasonably deemed advisable by the Manager from time to time in order to pay operating, administrative, or other business expenses of the Company which have been incurred, or which the Manager reasonably anticipates will be incurred, by the Company. *Except* under unusual circumstances, such additional capital contributions ("Additional Capital Contributions") shall not be required more often than quarterly and shall be due and payable by each Investor Member ... within fifteen (15) days after such Investor Member receives written notice from the Company of the amount due (a "Quarterly Bill"), The Manager shall not be required to make any additional capital contributions.

This is the provision relied upon by Clay Ward in contending that Racing Investment was in contempt of court for not having paid the agreed judgment in full. Under Clay Ward's interpretation, Racing Investment incurred a legitimate business expense for the equine insurance premiums prior to its dissolution and the members of the LLC, by agreeing to the periodic capital contribution provision, are subject to a "last call" to satisfy the outstanding balance on the judgment. In accepting this construction, the trial court and Court of Appeals essentially concluded that, by agreeing to make periodic capital contributions pursuant to Section 4.3(a), individual members of Racing Investment are legally responsible for their pro rata share of the entity's business debt. Indeed, under this theory, any outstanding debt that remains unpaid by the LLC can be satisfied through application for a court-ordered capital call. We reject this construction as contrary to the plain terms of the Operating Agreement and the letter and spirit of the Kentucky Limited Liability Company Act.

As discussed above, an operating agreement providing for future capital contributions by the LLC's members is neither "unique" as suggested by Clay Ward nor "atypical" as described by the Court of Appeals. Many businesses choosing the limited liability company form have circumstances that require periodic capital infusion. . . . Section 4.3(a) is a provision designed to assure members will contribute additional capital, as deemed necessary by the Manager, to advance Racing Investment's thoroughbred racing venture. While Clay Ward's insurance premiums were indeed a legitimate business expense for which the Manager could have made a capital call, that premise alone does not lead . . . to the relief ordered by the trial court. Simply put, Section 4.3(a) is a not-uncommon, on-going capital infusion provision, not a debt-collection mechanism by which a court can order a capital call and, by doing so, impose personal liability on the LLC's members for the entity's outstanding debt. Clay Ward insists that its quest to be paid is not about individual member liability, but there is no other way to construe what occurs when a court orders a capital call be made to pay for a particular LLC debt. From any viewpoint, the shield of limited liability has been lifted and the LLC's members have been held individually liable for its debt.

KRS 275.150 emphatically rejects personal liability for an LLC's debt unless the member or members, as the case may be, have agreed through the operating agreement or another written agreement to assume personal liability. Any such assumption of personal liability, which is contrary to the very business advantage reflected in the name "limited liability company," must be stated clearly in unequivocal language which leaves no room for doubt about the parties' intent. Section 4.3(a) of Racing Investment's Operating Agreement does not begin to meet this standard. A provision designed to provide on-going capital infusion as necessary, at the Manager's discretion, for the conduct of the entity's business affairs is simply not an agreement "to be obligated personally for any of the debts, obligations and liabilities of the limited liability company." KRS 275.150(2). To reiterate, assumption of personal liability by a member of an LLC is so antithetical to the purpose of a limited liability company that any such assumption must be stated in unequivocal terms leaving no doubt that the member or members intended to forego a principal advantage of this form of business entity. On this score, Section 4.3(a) simply does not qualify.

. . .

ANALYSIS

1. **Litigation Strategy.** The defendant in the case is Racing Investment. The members are not joined as defendants. Why not? Why does the court focus on the limited liability of the members?

2. **Failure to Contribute.** What is the function of the following provision in the Operating Agreement (quoted in the Racing Investment brief but not referred to in the court's opinion) concerning the possibility of a member failing to respond to a call for a contribution, and how does it work?

   > The Managing Member:
   >
   > may notify all Investor Members . . . of such default and disclose any information with respect thereto as the Manager deems advisable, and/or (ii) may, but shall not be obligated to, borrow the amount of the Additional Capital Contribution which the Defaulting Investor Member failed or neglected to pay from the Manager, any member, any officer, any Affiliate of the Manager, or any member or officer, any bank, or any other source on such terms and conditions . . . as the Manager, in the Manager's sole discretion, may deem advisable.

   If the Managing Member calls for additional contributions and some or all the members fail to contribute, what are the next steps?

3. **Negotiating the Operating Agreement.** If you had represented a potential investor in Racing Investment and had been asked for your opinion on the Operating Agreement, what would you have said about the provision on calls for additional contributions (Section 4.3(a))?

PLANNING: ADDITIONAL CAPITAL

Suppose that in the Racing Investment Fund situation there were 10 members, each of whom had initially invested $500,000 for 10 units and had been making periodic additional contributions for several years. Now suppose that the manager sends to each of the investors a letter stating:

> I regret to report that our horses have not done well, but I have high hopes for the future. We are out of money and need an additional contribution from each of you of $20,000, a total of $200,000. This sum is needed to continue operations for another season and sell the horses in an orderly manner. My best estimate is that if we have a successful racing season the orderly sale will

result in net proceeds (after payment of debts) of as much as $5,000,000; if we have a bad season, the net will be zero. Our consultants, who are the best in the business, say that the probability of netting the $5,000,000 is about 50 %, with an equal probability of netting nothing. Without the additional contribution I will be obliged to take the best offer I can get right now for all the horses, which I firmly believe will be barely enough to pay off our debts. Thus, if each of you contributes $20,000 you can expect, within the next year or so, liquidating distribution of $500,000, if all goes well. Without the additional contributions you will probably receive nothing. As you all know, it is presently impossible for us to borrow the needed funds from a bank or other third party without personal guarantees from each of you, and my understanding is that few if any of you would be willing to provide such a guarantee.

A week after this letter is received by the members, eight of the ten members have agreed to contribute the additional $20,000, but the other two have refused. The manager goes back to the eight members who have agreed to contribute and asks them to commit to an additional $5,000. These additional amounts would be recoverable from the liquidating distribution (if any) of the members who have refused to contribute.

1. **The Dilemma.** If you are a member who has agreed to contribute $20,000 and you are now asked for the additional $5,000, what is your reaction?

2. **Solution?** How might the operating agreement have been drafted to mitigate the problem suggested by the immediately preceding question?

F. EXPULSION

Walker v. Resource Development Co.

27 Del.J.Corp.L. 463, 791 A.2d 799 (Del.Ch.2000).

I. Introduction

This is a post-trial opinion concerning the power of the members of a majority in interest of a Delaware limited liability company to remove the entity's other member and declare his interest forfeited. . . .

II. Background

A. The Parties

Plaintiff Randolph T. Walker is a cousin of former President Bush. Walker testified to having attended Windham College[2] and to having participated in several courses offered by the Commercial Investment

[2] Walker claims that this school shut down after his graduation and although he earned a degree, he never obtained a diploma.

Real Estate Association. Walker also testified that his presence at various banking conferences as a non-attendee gave him experience in sophisticated financial consulting.[3]

Defendant William J. Cox, Jr., before the events described herein, was an intelligence officer in the United States Navy. Defendant William C. Baron met Cox while serving as an intelligence officer for the Department of Defense. Prior to leaving the service, they spent time serving in the former Soviet Republic of Moldova. Both had certain technical expertise that would help them in working in the oil and gas industry, but had no significant business experience. Defendant William C. Liedtke, III, is an oil and gas attorney and is the son of William C. Liedtke, Jr. The elder Liedtke, along with his brother J. Hugh Liedtke, were partners and close associates of former President Bush in various oil and gas related business ventures. Liedtke has considerable legal and business sophistication, especially in the oil and gas industry.

Defendant Resource Development Company, Limited, L.L.C. ("REDECO") is a Delaware limited liability company founded by Cox and Baron. Between April 4 and August 23, 1995, at the very least, REDECO's members were defendants Cox, Baron and Liedtke (collectively, the "three Bills") and plaintiff Walker. . . .

B. Walker Meets Cox and Baron and Joins REDECO

On December 16, 1994, Bill Cox negotiated and secured a Letter of Intent signed by the Prime Minister of Moldova, pursuant to which REDECO would obtain an oil and gas exploration and production concession from the Moldovan Government. It contemplated that the parties would enter into a formal concession when final documents were negotiated and final approvals obtained. The Letter of Intent provided that, REDECO, an entity Cox and Baron established, would have a five-year drilling commitment in Moldova beginning in 1995. REDECO needed to raise approximately $5 million per year to fund its operations under the commitment.

At the end of 1994, Walker was involved in difficult divorce proceedings and was experiencing various personal problems, including a bout of alcohol abuse. In early February 1995, he planned a vacation to Hawaii to "get a break" but a snowstorm in Washington, D.C. delayed his departure. Walker booked a room at the Four Seasons Hotel and visited

[3] On cross-examination, defendants' counsel asked Walker to elaborate on his experience. Walker explained, "I think I had reached the point in my life whereby working with the European Institute and the Aspen Institute on banking conferences . . . I had the contacts with international banks to assist in [financing transactions]." Tr. at 134. Explaining the capacity in which he attended, Walker stated, "I was invited by the assistant to the president because I wanted to attend—we live near the Aspen Institute and they were very expensive meetings, and so they acknowledged that I could attend without paying . . . if I photographed." Tr. at 135–36. Also, Walker attended the European Institute "as a guest with a camera, and they paid [him] for it." Tr. at 137.

the bar. Walker overheard Baron telling the bartender about his venture in Moldova. Walker chimed in, noting that he is the first cousin of the former President. Walker stated that he had access to valuable business connections and was known for a strong personal reputation.

At trial, Baron explained his initial contact with Walker:

> And Mr. Walker claimed that he had not only the prior knowledge and ability to provide financing but he had done these sort of things in the past. For the amount of money we were looking for, it was not a big deal. He could do it right away. He knew all sorts of people, all over the world.
>
> I mean, he literally walked the walk and talked the talk, like financiers do. And he presented a great image. And he was very believable, to the point where I said, well, I would like you to meet the managing partner of our company. It seemed to me like a wonderful opportunity that presented itself.

Baron scheduled a meeting between Walker and Cox. When they met, Cox was equally taken in by Walker's apparent sophistication. Walker commented on the need to improve REDECO's business plan presentation, which he thought was "very unprofessional." Walker also contacted representatives of several potentially interested parties known to him through family connections, although none of these parties expressed immediate interest in REDECO.

Walker next introduced Cox and Baron to Stephen L. Norris, the founder of an investment fund called The Appian Group. Walker told Cox that the Appian Group "was a merchant bank with considerable financial resources, large investors from the Middle East, and just huge amounts of money behind it." Norris was a high-level appointee during the Bush Administration. Norris expressed some interest.

Because they needed money to develop the Moldovan concession, and believing that a partnership with Walker could be useful, Cox and Baron suggested that Walker and REDECO establish a close relationship. On February 6, 1995, REDECO signed an agency agreement . . . through which Walker would "act as agent for REDECO for the limited purpose of negotiating with potential investors in REDECO's business projects in Moldova." . . .

Except for the survival of the arbitration clause, this agreement provided that it would terminate automatically if Walker failed to close a financing transaction by March 30, 1995. Further, REDECO retained a right to terminate the agreement at any time following the occurrence of, inter alia:

> breach by Walker of any material term of this Agreement, and of any agreement executed and delivered pursuant to the terms

of this Agreement, if not cured by Walker within thirty (30) days after receipt by Walker of written notice of such breach from REDECO, which notice shall set forth in reasonable detail the facts forming the basis of the breach.

C. Liedtke Joins the Business and Walker Travels with Norris

Walker introduced Cox and Baron to Bill Liedtke, an experienced oil and gas attorney and consultant. Leidtke first met Cox and Baron at the end of February when they presented the Moldovan opportunity to POGO Petroleum, a company with which Liedtke's family is involved. Although POGO declined to invest, from that point on, Liedtke personally spent a good deal of time working with Cox, Baron and Walker.

Before Walker could leave for Hawaii, Norris invited him to Europe and Walker accepted. While travelling in Europe, Walker and Norris shared expenses, but it appears that Norris paid the vast majority of those costs, to the extent that [by] May, Walker owed Norris about $13,000.

During these travels, Walker discussed REDECO with Norris. Walker wanted Norris to finance the concession project, which the parties termed the "upstream" aspect of the business. Norris expressed interest but wanted to structure a companion deal in which AGIP Petroli, Italy's national oil company, would invest money in a series of gas stations inside Moldova, referred to as the "downstream" aspect of the business. In connection with this AGIP deal, Norris sent a brochure to Liedtke, apparently seeking an investment by him or his uncle. Since Liedtke "was a little perplexed" by this unsolicited contact (and troubled by Walker's involvement in it), Liedtke never gave the brochure further consideration. In any event, Norris eventually made clear that any financing he might provide for the upstream operations would be contingent on his and REDECO's involvement in the downstream operations.

As of March 30, 1995, Walker had not obtained the promised $5 million for REDECO. Thus, the February 8, 1995 Agreement expired by its own terms.

While Walker was with Norris in Europe, the three Bills were busy putting together the business plan and trying to get final documentation for the Moldovan concession. At first, Liedtke worked for REDECO solely as a consultant. According to Liedtke, "I treated it as a consulting arrangement even after being given an interest in the LLC later. It was just a side venture in my office." By April, however, Liedtke formally joined REDECO to assist with preparing the documentation for REDECO's transactions. According to Liedtke, "I did not request the interest. That was something that was just, that was brought up by Mr. Cox."

Cox distributed an April 4 letter to Walker, Liedtke and Baron, detailing the progress of the venture and explaining the new ownership structure of REDECO. The letter stated that the partnership had grown to four members, with the following proportionate ownership breakdown: 51% for Cox, 21% for Baron, 18% for Walker and 10% for Liedtke. Cox wrote that "the partnership is now closed." An April 24 memorandum from Cox to Liedtke, Baron and Walker explained that there are two categories of partners, full-time and part time. Cox wrote that "full time partners . . . work only for REDECO. Besides their ownership, they will receive a salary." In contrast, "part time partners may pursue other interests. Besides their ownership, they will receive an annual stipend of $48,000.00, or $4,000.00 per month." Presumably, Baron and Cox were full-time partners while Walker and Liedtke were part-time.

D. Walker is Removed From His Position as Fundraiser

The evidence at trial showed that each of the three Bills duly performed his job responsibilities for REDECO, under the direction of Cox, acting as Managing Member of the LLC. Further, on May 10, 1995, Cox requested a capital contribution by each of the members. Baron paid in his contribution by paying expenses incurred by him on the company's behalf and not seeking reimbursement. Liedtke originally paid in his contribution by forwarding expenses, but testified that he wrote "one check," on "approximately August 21st for about $1,800." At some point in July, Walker paid in $700. The record does not detail how, precisely, Cox made his contributions.

Walker failed to secure any financing. Indeed, aside from those initial telephone calls and his efforts with Norris, there is no evidence that Walker actually sought financing on REDECO's behalf. Rather, he was travelling partly for business but mostly for pleasure, sometimes with Norris and sometimes on his own, keeping in touch with the three Bills primarily to discuss the progress of negotiations with the Appian Group.

In the meanwhile, Cox and Baron were still negotiating the terms of the Moldovan concession. In order to show REDECO's ability to finance the business, Norris sent Cox and Baron a letter dated April 5, 1995, describing the possibility of his participation in both the upstream and downstream ventures. Cox and Baron explained Walker's involvement in the venture to the Moldovan representatives.[18] Impressed, the

[18] Just as Walker uses his contacts to impress others and make himself appear to be experienced in fields in which he is not, Cox and Baron gave themselves an air of credibility by using Walker's name and influential family connections.

Moldovans working on the deal asked to meet the cousin of the former President of the United States.

Cox contacted Walker, who was in Vienna, and asked him to join them in Moldova. Walker initially agreed to make the trip, but on three separate occasions, failed to travel from Vienna to Moldova where his arrival was eagerly awaited. . . .

Walker testified unpersuasively that he refused to go to Moldova because Cox insisted that he enter the country illegally, without a visa, and bring a large amount of cash with him. Cox denies this, and I find Walker's testimony on this point to be incredible. According to Cox, Walker was inebriated when they spoke by telephone and explained his failure to appear in Moldova on the fact that his credit cards had been seized. Walker adamantly insisted that Cox use his own credit card to get Walker out of Vienna. After discussing the matter with Baron and Liedtke, however, the three Bills decided to refuse Walker's request because of his financial irresponsibility.

Shortly after this incident, Cox called Norris to inquire into the situation. Cox testified that "[Norris] stated that Mr. Walker would have to be removed as the point of contact with him. He would no longer deal with Mr. Walker." . . . According to Cox, when he called Norris,

> Steve told me at that point he was very glad that I called up because he was at wit's end with Randy and that Randy now owed him a lot of money, and Randy had been causing him problems, and Steve told me, he said if Randy remains in the deal, I am not going to conclude anything with you, and I asked him to repeat that, and I said—I gave him assurance at that point that I would make sure that Randy was removed from any further negotiations with the Appian Group or from the project, as per Steve Norris' request.[24]

Apart from Norris' demand that he not deal with Walker, the three Bills had other concerns about Walker, including his evident drinking problem, financial irresponsibility, indebtedness to Norris, and failure to appear in Moldova.

Accordingly, Cox removed Walker from his official duties with REDECO. . . .

The letter states that Walker would be removed "from all official duties as a Member of REDECO Ltd." The letter explains that the decision:

---

[24] Cox Dep. of Jan. 21, 1999, at 76–77 (emphasis added). Surprisingly, defendants argue in their post-trial briefs that prior to July 25, 1995, the three Bills did not know of Walker's indebtedness to Norris.

> comes about after a series of unfortunately embarrassing actions by Mr. Walker that bring our current oil and gas exploration projects into jeopardy. As stipulated in our operating agreement, personal bankruptcy, inability to meet personal financial commitments to the partnership, and failure to perform assigned duties and tasks are all reasons for removal. . . . A vote of the remaining Members regarding this action will be taken in our June meeting.

Walker contacted REDECO to determine the letter's meaning. In response, Baron sent him a letter dated May 18, 1995, explaining that "Bill Cox, as the Managing Member, still intends to authorize your 18% of the Management Fee, as originally agreed. In this respect, you are still being 'included.'" In other words, Walker lost his job, but Cox did not purport to eliminate Walker's ownership interest in REDECO.[26]

E. Norris Insists on Walker's Reinstatement

A few weeks later, Walker contacted Cox and, according to Cox, stated that "he had a problem with alcohol. . . . He had cleaned up his act. He was on the wagon. And he told me he was back in good graces with Mr. Norris."[27] Walker also told Cox that the "financing with the Appian Group, which was going to happen very soon, would only happen if [Walker] were involved in the transaction." When Cox sought to confirm this representation, Norris "demanded that Randy be back in the deal or he would not close any financing with [REDECO]."

With REDECO's need to secure financing becoming ever more urgent and the Appian Group the only live possibility, the three Bills decided to allow Walker back into his job. Through June and July 1995, however, it was Cox—not Walker—who worked with Norris to close the deal.

In order to get the financing needed to begin the upstream project, REDECO was willing to agree to Appian's insistence on pursuing the downstream project involving AGIP. In that regard, a meeting was held in Rome, Italy, attended by Cox and Walker, Norris and other Appian representatives, and representatives of AGIP. In light of the ongoing

---

[26] At some point during this time period, Liedtke contacted members of the Bush family to inquire about Walker. He did this on his own and not at the request of Cox or Baron. He was told that Walker was a generally unpleasant person. Liedtke did not inquire into Walker's business reputation. Further, despite the fact, thoroughly obvious at trial, that Walker is not what he originally represented himself to be, neither Cox nor Baron, who knew of Liedtke's close ties with the Bush family, asked Liedtke to inquire as to Walker's business experience or reputation.

[27] Walker made similar representations to Stephen Norris to win back his "good graces," stating in a letter to Norris dated June 30, 1995: "I am enjoying my new mindset without the wine, in fact I don't miss it a bit." JE 40. Norris later testified that he too was deceived and that Walker regrettably did not stop drinking during this period. JE 76 (Norris Dep. at 151).

negotiations, Cox testified that "it looked like with the Appian Group we had a closing that was imminent."

F. The Concession and Operating Agreement are Signed

On July 6, 1995, REDECO and the Prime Minister of Moldova finally executed the concession. Walker played no role in negotiating this agreement.

Also during June and July, Walker and the three Bills negotiated a form of operating agreement for REDECO. REDECO needed to have in place a formal operating agreement prior to finalizing any investment by Appian. The agreement was also needed because to ensure that the three Bills would be protected from liability from Walker's actions. On July 25, 1995, the three Bills and Walker entered into the REDECO LLC Operating Agreement. Despite their knowledge of Walker's personal problems, fiscal irresponsibility, debts to Norris and likely inability to offer financing opportunities other than Norris, the three Bills agreed to give Walker an 18% stake in the entity.

Liedtke testified at his deposition that, when Walker was first reinstated, he was still "on probation." The July 25 Agreement, however, fails to treat Walker differently from the other members. In particular, there is no provision making Walker's continued equity participation contingent either on his performance or closing a deal with the Appian Group.

Several provisions detail the powers and obligations of Cox as Manager. Article X provides for removal of the Manager by the members "whenever in their judgment the best interest of the Company will be served thereby. Such removal shall be without prejudice to the contract rights, if any, of any person so removed." Thus, removal as a Manager would not impair Cox's ownership rights in REDECO.

Article XII(c), which sets out the same proportionate ownership as was agreed to in April, provides that "all Company costs and benefits (and the deductions of any tax credits or deductions attributable thereto) shall be allocated to the members in their Sharing Ratios." Article XIX provides that "a member of record has an absolute obligation to perform an enforceable promise to make a contribution, or otherwise pay cash or transfer property owned by the Company."

The honoring of commitments to contribute is enforced solely by Article XX, which provides that "in the event a member fails to make a contribution to the Company required by an enforceable promise, the Company is entitled to reduce the defaulting member's ownership in a proportion that the amount of the default bears to the total contribution of the member." . . .

Critically, Article XXII provides for the withdrawal of members. As to involuntary withdrawal, section (b) states that:

> "[a] member of the Company ceases to be a member, and is deemed to have withdrawn from the Company, on the occurrence of any of the following events:
>
> > (i) When the member files a voluntary bankruptcy petition.
> >
> > (ii) If the member is a natural person, the death of the member or an adjudication of a court of competent jurisdiction that the member is incompetent to manage his or her person or property.
> >
> > (iii) If the member is a corporation, in the filing of a certificate of dissolution for the corporation or the revocation of the corporation's charter.
> >
> > (iv) If the member is an estate, on the personal representative's distribution of the estate's entire interest in the Company."

. . .

G. The Appian Deal Falls Apart and Cox Removes Walker

1. The Events of August 23–24, 1995

REDECO and the Appian Group were scheduled to meet on August 23, 1995 at Appian's offices. To Cox's surprise, Norris did not attend that meeting, sending, instead, a subordinate who did not have authority to close the deal. Also, this subordinate presented an offer that materially differed from that anticipated by Cox. Instead of investing its own funds, Appian proposed to commit only to seek out a syndicate of outside investors in the Moldovan concession venture. After Cox sent Walker to bring Norris to the meeting and Norris refused, Cox, in Walker's words, "started going ballistic."

Walker tried to calm Cox down, but Cox stormed out of the meeting, furious that after months of negotiations, no deal would be struck with the Appian Group. Walker followed him out. Cox stated at trial, "After I left the offices Mr. Walker stopped me and said, 'Bill, listen we are going to close this deal. We are going to get the financing. I know we are, because Steve Norris is going to compensate me when we get this deal closed.' "

According to Cox, this was a startling admission that Walker was working for or controlled by Norris, with whom he was supposed to be conducting arm's-length negotiations on REDECO's behalf. Cox asserts that he explained and discussed this admission with Baron and Liedtke. With their assent, he removed Walker.

The removal letter, entitled "Severance Arrangement," "set[ ] forth the arrangement [the three Bills] reached concerning [Walker's] withdrawal as a member of [REDECO]." The letter does not refer directly to Walker's alleged admission or to his relationship with Norris. Instead, it refers in general terms to Walker's poor performance and misconduct, as follows:

> Your actions have constituted a breach of trust and have resulted in a loss of faith in your abilities to continue as a member of the Firm. Your actions over the past few months appear to violate Firm policies and prevent us from fulfilling our normal business responsibilities. Accordingly, we have mutually agreed that your membership must terminate immediately so it is clear you are not and cannot be acting on behalf of the Firm.
>
> . . . We hereby terminate your ownership interest in the Firm. In addition to the numerous actions constituting breach of trust, your financial obligations to the Firm remain outstanding. To this end, we have calculated your share of the Firm's total debt to be $4,179.43. Please pay this sum to the Firm on or before September 1, 1995.

Walker never acknowledged or returned the document to Cox. Instead, his counsel sent Cox a letter dated September 22, 1995, stating that because the Operating Agreement does not provide for involuntary withdrawal of a member, Walker remained an 18% owner of the business. With respect to amounts due, Walker's counsel explained that the Agreement does not require additional capital contributions except pursuant to an "enforceable promise" to pay. This letter requested "documentation of this alleged obligation." Cox made no response.

2. Did Walker Make this Admission?

For his part, Walker denies having any "side deal" with Norris and denies ever saying that he did. Norris's deposition testimony on the matter also does not support Cox's recollection. When asked whether Walker would be entitled to some commission or payment if the REDECO transaction had come to fruition, Norris stated, "I honestly don't have any specific recollection of what kind of arrangement, if any—I emphasize that—that we would have had with Mr. Walker for introducing us to REDECO."

The testimony of Baron and Liedtke also fails to support Cox's version of events. Instead, it shows that the decision to terminate Walker was the result of the failure of the negotiations with Norris and The

Appian Group, not some newly revealed impropriety of Walker's financial dealings with Norris.

. . .

H. The Escrowed Stock of a Canadian Corporation Represents the Three Bills' REDECO Interest

REDECO eventually obtained financing from Costilla Corp., a company with which Liedtke's brother was affiliated. . . .

A series of financing transactions eventually led to the exchange of the three Bills' REDECO holdings (via interests in other companies) into shares of a Canadian corporation holding a 12.5% interest in any future profits that might be earned by REDECO from the Moldovan concession after various other investors receive their return. Specifically, REDECO Energy, Inc., a publicly traded corporation listed on the Alberta stock exchange, holds the 12.5% future profits interest. The three Bills' only remaining connection with REDECO is through shares in REDECO Energy. . . .

III. The Parties' Contentions

Walker contends that the three Bills had no right or power to deprive him of his 18% membership interest in REDECO. He also argues that he had no side deal with Norris and never said otherwise to Cox. Thus, he claims, there is no basis on which to argue that the Operating Agreement was the product of fraud or misrepresentation.

Walker's remedy analysis is less complete. Despite a full and fair opportunity to do so, he made no effort at trial to prove the fair value of his 18% interest in REDECO. Thus, there is no basis in the record on which to consider an award of money damages. He also made no effort to challenge the bona fides of any of the transactions that have taken place since 1995 and that have substantially altered REDECO's financial structure and the three Bills' interest in it. . . .

These failures of proof do not leave Walker without a remedy. The trial testimony did prove that the stock interests now held by the three Bills in REDECO Energy represent 100% of the original membership interest in REDECO. Thus, while it is not possible to "unscramble the eggs" due to the multiple intervening transactions with third parties, it is still possible to trace Walker's 18% interest in REDECO to the shares now owned by the three Bills in REDECO Energy. This provides a framework on which to consider an award in equity—such as the imposition of a constructive trust on a portion of those shares.

. . .

IV. Analysis

Defendants focus on Walker's alleged admission that he stood to be paid by Norris when the deal with Appian closed. They say that this admission caused them to remove him from the company. I conclude, however, that the failure of negotiations with Norris—not any "admission" by Walker—was the actual cause of Walker's removal. The fact is that the three Bills willingly overlooked a multitude of issues relating to Walker's participation in the deal as long as they thought The Appian Group would provide financing. It is only because that prospect vanished and Walker's relationship to Norris no longer mattered that Cox and the others decided to throw him out.

A. Walker Was Removed Because He Failed to Obtain Financing

Cox and Baron brought Walker into REDECO for the sole purpose of raising money. . . .

So long as a deal with Norris was likely, which Cox believed was the case until August 23, 1995, the three Bills were willing to look beyond Walker's weaknesses and problems. Ironically, the testimony is that they executed the Operating Agreement confirming his membership interest, in part, to ensure that the LLC would be recognized as a legal entity in order to shield them from liability for Walker's conduct. In this way, Walker could provide the benefit of introducing REDECO to a financing source without exposing his "partners" to personal liability for his misconduct.

Cox went to the August 23 meeting thinking he had "a closing that was imminent" with the Appian Group. Cox was furious when Norris refused to appear and had his lieutenant propose a new deal. Cox stormed out of the meeting. The next day, Cox delivered to Walker a letter purporting to remove Walker from REDECO. From my review of the evidence as a whole, I conclude that Cox and the others took this step solely or primarily because Walker failed to deliver a source of financing.

B. The August 24, 1995 Removal Letter Did Not Remove Walker From His Membership In REDECO

The three Bills had no authority to unilaterally remove Walker from the LLC on August 24, 1995. Neither the Operating Agreement nor the law provides any mechanism for removal of a member in these circumstances.

1. The Operating Agreement Does Not Provide For Removal

. . . "The basic approach of the Delaware Act is to provide members with broad discretion in drafting the [Operating] Agreement and to furnish default provisions when the members' agreement is silent."[48] "Once members exercise their contractual freedom in their limited liability company agreement, they can be virtually certain that the agreement will be enforced in accordance with its terms."[49]

. . .

Thus, LLC members' rights begin with and typically end with the Operating Agreement. The Operating Agreement includes no provision that can be read to allow the three Bills to deprive Walker of his ownership interest in the circumstances presented in this case. Article X deals with removal of the Manager but makes clear that "removal shall be without prejudice to the [Manager's] contract rights," implicitly including his ownership rights. Article XXII, does address the voluntary and involuntary withdrawal from membership but identifies no instance even arguably applicable in this case. The absence of such a provision is surprising, considering what the three Bills knew about Walker at the time they entered into this agreement. They knew that he had embarrassed the company, experienced bouts of drunkenness and alcohol abuse, misrepresented his sophistication in financing transactions and borrowed money from the very person with whom he was supposed to be negotiating on REDECO's behalf. Most importantly, they knew or had every reason to know that if the Appian deal fell through, they could not rely on Walker to find an alternative source of financing for REDECO.

Thus, the three Bills could easily have protected themselves in the Operating Agreement against the failure of negotiations with Norris by simply making Walker's REDECO interest contingent on successfully closing a deal with Appian. They failed to do so for reasons that are unexplained. Since the Operating Agreement does not justify Walker's removal, defendants are left to the default rules.

2. There is No Basis in the Law for Unilateral Removal of an LLC Member

Defendants make the troubling argument that, although there is no basis for doing so in the Operating Agreement, under applicable law the three Bills had the inherent power to remove Walker from the entity, taking away his ownership interests therein, due to his alleged breach of fiduciary duty. In their post-trial brief, defendants identified virtually no legal support for this proposition. . . .

Defendants also claim that "both the Delaware statutes and authority from other jurisdictions provide that a Chancery Court should uphold the removal of a member or partner when the equities so dictate." For this they cite 8 Del. C. § 18–1104, which simply states that the rules

[48] Elf Atochem North America, Inc. v. Jaffari, Del. Supr., 727 A.2d 286, 291 (1999).

[49] R. F. Balotti & J.A. Finkelstein, The Delaware Law of Corporations & Business Organizations, § 20.4 (2000) (hereinafter "Balotti & Finkelstein").

of law and equity govern where the statute is silent, and two plainly distinguishable cases decided by New York state and federal courts. None of these authorities vary the fundamental principle under Delaware law that a majority of the members (or stockholders) of a business entity, unless expressly granted such power by contract, have no right to take the property of other members (or stockholders). Other mechanisms may be available to them to recast their business relations to eliminate persons from the enterprise, such as the merger provisions of the various business entity laws. But, these provisions do not provide for the forfeiture of economic rights, requiring instead that the persons whose interests are eliminated are entitled to receive fair value therefor.

C. Walker's Interest in REDECO Was Never Diluted to Zero

Defendants also argue that even if Walker's alleged failure to disclose his conflict of interest did not warrant his removal, his failure to make capital contributions did. Defendants point out that under Article XII(c) of the Operating Agreement, each member was required to contribute to the company's costs and expenses. Defendants then assert that under Article XIX, a member has an absolute obligation "to perform an enforceable promise" to make contributions. Under Article XX, failure to honor such an "enforceable promise" entitles to entity "to reduce the defaulting member's ownership in a proportion that the amount of the default bears to the total contribution of the member." Hence, defendants argue that Walker's total capital contribution of $700 was far outweighed by the contributions that he refused to make and the "cost, time and disruption that he caused."

Defendants' problem is two-fold. First, the term "enforceable promise" is undefined. I assume it does not mean that anytime Cox made a call for contributions, all of the members were required to pay immediately. Defendants failed to show that Walker ignored an enforceable promise by not making the capital contributions, principally because they provided little or no evidence of how the three Bills made their own contributions. Baron testified that at least part of his own contribution consisted of expenses for which he sought no reimbursement, and conceded that he did not keep receipts of those expenses. Although Cox (and, perhaps, Liedtke) contributed his own funds to REDECO before August 24, 1995, defendants have not explained when the other members made an "enforceable promise" to contribute a particular amount of money by a particular date.

Defendants' second problem is more important. The August 24, 1995 Removal Letter never mentions Walker's failure to honor any such promise as a basis for his removal. Rather, his alleged "breach of trust" is the basis for the removal. . . . For these reasons, even if defendants could reduce Walker's interest on account of his owing money to the company, they did not purport to do so and will not now be heard to rely on that ground as a justification for their actions.

. . .

E. Walker's Remedy

. . . The evidence shows that the three Bills contributed $139,000 "net of everything" since August 24, 1995. Had Walker been allowed to retain his 18% share in REDECO, he would have had to pay his share of REDECO's accrued debt, both the $4,179.43 he owed prior to August 24, 1995, plus an additional $25,020.00, representing 18% of the $139,000 expended by the three Bills after that date, for a total of $29,199.43 plus interest. If he is to recover his proportionate share of the REDECO Energy stock, he will be required to pay that amount in exchange therefor.

V. Conclusion

For the reasons and to the extent set forth herein, I will enter judgment in favor of plaintiff and against the defendants. . . .

ANALYSIS

1. **When *Is* Expulsion Permissible?** In Chapter 2, we saw a number of cases in which partners were validly expelled from their partnerships. (E.g., Lawlis v. Kightlinger & Gray, and Bohatch v. Butler & Binion.) Why were the partners in those firms allowed to expel a member, while the "three Bills" were not allowed to expel Walker?

2. **If Termination Can Be Bought.** Assuming Walker was willing to be removed, at a price, how could the "three Bills" have validly terminated their relationship with him?

3. **If Termination Cannot Be Bought.** Assuming Walker was not willing to be removed, how could the "three Bills" have validly terminated their relationship with him?

4. **The Effect of the Uniform Act.** Uniform Limited Liability Company Act (1997) § 602 provides, in pertinent part:

    > A person is dissociated as a member when:
    >
    > (6) on application by the limited liability company or a member in a direct action under Section 801, the person is expelled as a member by judicial order because the person:
    >
    > (A) has engaged or is engaging in wrongful conduct that has affected adversely and materially, or will affect adversely and materially, the company's activities and affairs;
    >
    > (B) has committed willfully or persistently, or is committing willfully or persistently, a material breach of the operating agreement or a duty or obligation under Section 409; or

(C) has engaged or is engaging in conduct relating to the company's activities and affairs which makes it not reasonably practicable to carry on the activities and affairs with the person as a member;

The Delaware LLC statute lacks such a provision. If REDECO had been formed in a ULLCA jurisdiction, would the "three Bills" likely have prevailed in a suit seeking judicial disassociation of Walker's interest? If so, what consequences would have followed? See ULLCA §§ 701–02.

5. **Additional Capital.** Provisions for additional capital contributions by the members are an essential component of any agreement for the operation of a closely held business. REDECO's Operating Agreement had a provision for requiring LLC members to contribute additional capital, but that clause proved unavailing as a ground for expelling Walker. Setting aside defendants' self-serving attempt to use the clause for that purpose, was the additional capital provision otherwise well-drafted? Put another way, suppose REDECO had run out of money. Could Cox, in his capacity as managing member, have validly forced the other LLC members to contribute additional capital?

G. DISSOLUTION

The Dunbar Group, LLC v. Tignor

267 Va. 361, 593 S.E.2d 216 (2004).

... XpertCTI, LLC (Xpert), is a limited liability company that provides "computer telephony integration" (CTI) software to dealers and manufacturers for installation in certain telephone systems and equipment. CTI software enables the use of computers to "interface" with and control telephone systems.

Xpert was formed in March 2000, by The Dunbar Group, LLC (Dunbar), and Archie F. Tignor, who each owned a membership interest of 50 percent in Xpert. Edward D. Robertson, Jr., a computer software developer and consultant, was the sole member and manager of Dunbar.

Tignor, a commercial telephone and telecommunications equipment dealer and installer, owned 50 percent of the stock of X-tel, Inc. (X-tel), a telecommunications sales firm. Tignor served as the president of X-tel, which was a dealer in equipment for Samsung Telecommunications America, Inc. (Samsung), a manufacturer, distributor, and seller of telecommunications equipment.

Dunbar and Tignor executed an "Operating Agreement" for Xpert under which they were the sole managers of Xpert. Dunbar created Xpert's proprietary software, or "source code," and conducted the daily operations of the company. Tignor's main function was to provide Xpert with access to his business contacts in the telecommunications industry, including Samsung.

Xpert's operating agreement provided a procedure for a company member to assert a breach of the agreement by another company member. The agreement specified that if the breach was not timely cured by the defaulting member, the complaining member had the "right to petition a court of competent jurisdiction for dissolution of the Company." The agreement also stated that the "dissolution of a [m]ember or occurrence of any other event that terminates the continued membership of a [m]ember in the Company shall not cause the dissolution of the Company."

In December 2000, Xpert entered into a contract with Samsung to supply Samsung with software-driven security devices called "dongles," which were to be included in all telecommunications systems sold by Samsung. Xpert received about $20,000 per month from the Samsung contract. The Samsung contract contained a provision specifying the contract's duration:

> This Agreement shall come into force and effect on the date written above [December 5, 2000] and shall remain in full force and effect for consecutive periods of thirty-six (36) months thereafter .... After this time the contract will continue on an annual basis unless terminated by either party giving 90 days notice before the anniversary of the contract date.

Certain disputes arose between Robertson and Tignor over matters primarily related to the management and disbursement of Xpert's assets. In May 2002, Dunbar's counsel sent a letter to Tignor's counsel stating that it was apparent to Robertson that "his continued working relationship with Mr. Tignor [was] no longer possible." Dunbar's counsel further stated that "Mr. Robertson is of the opinion that it is in the parties' best interest to sever their ties as fully and quickly as possible."

In September 2002, Dunbar, Xpert, and Robertson, in his capacity as a manager of Xpert, (collectively, Dunbar) filed an amended bill of complaint against Tignor and X-tel requesting, among other things, entry of an order "expelling and dissociating Tignor as a member of Xpert pursuant to Virginia Code § 13.1–1040.1(5)." Dunbar alleged that Tignor engaged in "numerous acts of misconduct as a member and manager of Xpert," including the commingling of Xpert's funds with the funds of Tignor and "his corporate alter ego, X-tel."

Code § 13.1–1040.1, which provides for a court-ordered expulsion of a member of a limited liability company, states in relevant part:

> [A] member is dissociated from a limited liability company upon the occurrence of any of the following events:

5. On application by the limited liability company or another member, the member's expulsion by judicial determination because:

a. The member engaged in wrongful conduct that adversely and materially affected the business of the limited liability company;

b. The member willfully or persistently committed a material breach of the articles of organization or an operating agreement; or

c. The member engaged in conduct relating to the business of the limited liability company which makes it not reasonably practicable to carry on the business with the member.

Tignor filed a separate "Application for Judicial Dissolution" against Dunbar and Xpert. Tignor requested, among other things, the dissolution of Xpert under Code § 13.11047 on the ground that "it is not reasonably practicable to carry on the business of [Xpert] in conformity with the Articles of Organization and [the] Operating Agreement." Tignor alleged that "serious differences of opinion as to company management have arisen between the members and managers" of Xpert, and that the company was "deadlocked" in its ability to conduct its business affairs, including contracting with customers for goods and services and the "receipt and disbursement of [Xpert's] assets and company funds."

The chancellor consolidated for trial Dunbar's amended bill of complaint and Tignor's application for judicial dissolution. At a hearing, the chancellor received evidence relating to both pleadings.

The evidence showed that Tignor commingled Xpert's funds with X-tel's funds by placing several checks, which were made payable to Xpert, into X-tel's bank account. Tignor provided inaccurate information to Robertson concerning one of those checks, which was made payable to Xpert in the amount of about $47,000. Tignor used the proceeds from that check to pay some of X-tel's expenses and to meet X-tel's payroll, including the payment of Tignor's own salary.

Without informing Robertson, Tignor also authorized a change in the status of Xpert's checking account that prevented checks from being written on the account. When Robertson, who was unaware of the change, wrote a check payable to one of Xpert's vendors, the check "bounced."

Although Dunbar had been renting office space from X-tel, Tignor evicted Robertson from X-tel's premises. Tignor also restricted Robertson's access to various testing equipment located in X-tel's offices, reducing Robertson's ability to test Xpert's products. Robertson needed access to this equipment to ensure the quality of Xpert's products before they were delivered to Xpert's customers. Due to Robertson's restricted ability to test Xpert's products, Xpert's customers did not receive their orders in a timely manner and products were sent to customers "in less than quality condition."

Tignor also terminated Robertson's e-mail account with Xpert without giving him prior notice. This sudden termination of Robertson's e-mail account created "a lot of confusion" among Xpert's customers, giving the appearance that Xpert had "gone out of business."

In December 2002, the chancellor entered an order in which he found that Tignor commingled Xpert's funds with his own funds and the funds of X-tel. The chancellor also concluded that Tignor's actions had been contrary to Xpert's best interests and had "adversely affected Xpert's ability to carry on its business." The chancellor further determined that Tignor had acted "in violation of subparagraph five of Code § 13.11040.1.

The chancellor ordered that Tignor be "immediately expelled as an active member of Xpert" and that Robertson "shall continue to operate Xpert" and provide to Tignor a monthly accounting of Xpert's finances. The chancellor also ordered:

> Xpert . . . shall continue the arrangement pursuant to this order until its contract with [Samsung] expires or otherwise terminates, including any extensions. Following the fulfillment or non-renewal of the [Samsung] contract, the court orders that Xpert . . . be dissolved and its assets distributed pursuant to the Virginia Code and the operating agreement of Xpert.

Dunbar appeals.

Dunbar does not challenge that part of the chancellor's order expelling Tignor as a member of Xpert, but attacks only the portion of the order providing for the dissolution of Xpert. Dunbar argues that the evidence is insufficient to support the dissolution of Xpert because the evidence did not satisfy the standard required by Code § 13.1–1047 for the judicial dissolution of a limited liability company. In support of this argument, Dunbar primarily asserts that the record fails to show that after the expulsion of Tignor as a member of Xpert, it would not be reasonably practicable to carry on Xpert's business. . . .

This appeal presents our first opportunity to consider the statutory standard provided in Code § 13.1–1047 for the judicial dissolution of a limited liability company. The statute states that

> [o]n application by or for a member, the circuit court of the locality in which the registered office of the limited liability company is located may decree dissolution of a limited liability company if it is not reasonably practicable to carry on the

> business in conformity with the articles of organization and any operating agreement.

Id.

Because this statutory language is plain and unambiguous, we apply the plain meaning of that language.... Only when a circuit court concludes that present circumstances show that it is not reasonably practicable to carry on the company's business in accord with its articles of organization and any operating agreement, may the court order a dissolution of the company.

The record here, however, does not show that the chancellor evaluated the evidence in light of the fact that Tignor was being expelled as a member and manager of Xpert. Although Tignor's actions in those capacities had created numerous problems in the operation of Xpert, his expulsion as a member changed his role from one of an active participant in the management of Xpert to the more passive role of an investor in the company. The record fails to show that after this change in the daily management of Xpert, it would not be reasonably practicable for Xpert to carry on its business pursuant to its operating authority.

Moreover, we observe that the terms of the chancellor's dissolution order refute a conclusion that dissolution was appropriate under the statutory standard of Code § 1.3.11.047. While the chancellor concluded that judicial dissolution of Xpert was warranted, he nevertheless ordered that Xpert continue operating as a limited liability company for as long as the Samsung contract remained in effect. This provision in the chancellor's order indicates that he concluded that Tignor's expulsion from Xpert would make it reasonably practicable for Xpert to continue to operate for an extended period of time.

For these reasons, we will affirm that part of the chancellor's judgment expelling Tignor as a member of Xpert, reverse that part of the judgment ordering the dissolution of Xpert, and enter final judgment. Affirmed in part, reversed in part, and final judgment.

ANALYSIS

1. **Reconciling the Case.** Recall two cases in Chapter 2, Section 6.A, on dissolution of partnerships: Owen v. Cohen and Collins v. Lewis. In *Owen*, the California court ordered dissolution while in *Collins* the Texas court refused to do so. What differences between the two cases explain the different outcomes? Is the present case more like *Owen* or *Collins*?
2. **What Should Tignor Have Done?** Where does the decision leave Tignor? Has he been treated fairly? In retrospect, was it unwise of him to accept a contract under which he (or Dunbar) could be turned into a

passive investor (that is, could be dissociated without dissolution of the LLC)?

Investcorp, L.P. v. Simpson Investment Co.

267 Kan. 840, 983 P.2d 265, modified, 267 Kan. 875 (1999).

This summary judgment case involves a family controversy over the dissolution of a Limited Liability Company (LLC). . . .

The Simpson Investment Company, L.C. (Company) members were deadlocked on important management issues. Several members withdrew to effect dissolution of the Company. The parties dispute whether these withdrawing members may now participate in dissolution, including liquidation of the Company's assets. The issue is control of dissolution. Both family factions rely on the Company's operating agreement to support their positions. The plaintiffs are the withdrawing Simpsons. The defendant Company is comprised of the remaining Simpsons.

. . .

The district court, in entering partial summary judgment for the Company, held that dissolution is properly controlled by the defendant Company and its remaining members. Under the district court's ruling, the withdrawing Simpsons are no longer members of the Company.

. . . [W]e disagree with the district court's definition of "members." The withdrawing members, whose action triggered dissolution, remain "members" during dissolution.

Facts

The Company was formed in 1991 by two brothers, Donald and Alfred Simpson, to manage various land holdings of the Simpson family.

The operations of the Company are governed by an Amended and Restated Operating Agreement (operating agreement). Presently, the sole asset of the Company is 104 acres of commercial property in Johnson County. . . . Its worth is estimated at over $10 million. . . .

The Donald Simpson family (the remaining Simpsons) hold a 50% ownership, and the Alfred Simpson family (the withdrawing Simpsons and the Christopher A. Moran Trust [Moran Trust]) hold the other 50%. The Moran Trust, Mark Simpson, trustee, is aligned with the Alfred Simpson family but did not withdraw. The election of the Moran Trust to remain was strategically significant. Section 9.3 of the operating agreement required unanimous consent of the remaining members to continue the Company when dissolution is initiated by a member's resignation. The Moran Trust did not consent to continue the Company. The result was dissolution.

Each family had contradictory ideas about the disposition of the 104 acres. The plaintiffs claim they attempted to resolve the stalemate, offering, among other things, to divide the property. The operating agreement does not allow partition. . . .

Family differences were not resolved. Alfred's family (spearheaded by Mark) decided to force dissolution by withdrawing as members. They did so according to the terms of the operating agreement, which directed that any member could resign after giving 6 months' notice. The withdrawing members noticed their resignations on April 10, 1996.

Under the operating agreement, the Company could elect to purchase a withdrawing member's interest. The remaining members (the Donald Simpsons plus the Moran Trust) declined to do so. The Company refused to proceed with dissolution even though the operating agreement required unanimous consent to continue. The withdrawing members then sued the Company seeking dissolution. . . .

The district court ruled that the Company was dissolved because unanimous consent by the remaining members to continue was not obtained. The Company had argued that the Company was not dissolved because a majority in interest of the remaining members had agreed to continue the business. The district court, in ordering dissolution, relied on the version of K.S.A. 17–7622(a)(3) existing in 1991 when the Company was formed. Under that statute, consent of all remaining members was required to continue the Company unless the articles of organization otherwise provided a right to continue. K.S.A. 17–7622(a)(3) was amended in 1995 to permit an LLC to continue by consent of a majority in interest of the remaining members. . . .

Discussion

. . .

We first examine the operating agreement. A key section provides:

> "9.2 Effect of Dissolution. Except as provided in Section 9.3 below, upon the dissolution of the Company, the Members shall proceed to wind up, liquidate and terminate the business and affairs of the Company. In connection with such winding up, the Members shall liquidate and reduce to cash (to the extent necessary or appropriate) the assets of the Company as promptly as is consistent with obtaining a fair value therefor, satisfy and compromise the liabilities of the Company . . ., make distributions, in cash or in kind, to the Members and do any and all acts and things authorized by, and in accordance with, the Act and other applicable laws for the purpose of winding up and liquidation." . . .

The district court construed Section 9.2 as excluding the withdrawing members from participating in dissolution. The district judge looked to the definition of "Members" in the operating agreement. Members are defined as "those persons who are members of the Company from time to time, including any Substitute Members." . . . He reasoned, ". . . the term 'Members' as used in Section 9.2 of the Operating Agreement is to be construed as meaning the members of the Company as of the relevant time of examination of the document. That time is now. . . ."

. . .

We find only moderate assistance in resolving the question of who may participate in dissolution (winding up) by looking to either the ULLCA or the law of other states. The ULLCA § 803(a) excludes managers or members who dissolved wrongfully. Kansas does not distinguish between wrongful and rightful dissolving members. Some states take the ULLCA approach; however, there is a lack of consensus on the question and states have chosen different courses. . . .

Resolution of the Simpson family dispute is fact driven. Each Simpson faction advances a reasonable view of the operating agreement's meaning of "member." However, we are persuaded that the plaintiffs' view should prevail. The use of "remaining Member" in § 9.3 and also in Section 8.7 is significant in view of the fact that the term "remaining Member" is not found in Section 9.2. Section 8.7 says:

> **NOTE**
>
> Section 9.3 of the Operating Agreement provided: "Continuation. Notwithstanding the provisions of Section 9.1 and 9.2 above, the death, retirement, resignation, expulsion, bankruptcy or dissolution of a Member or the occurrence of any other event which terminates the continued membership of a Member in the Company, shall not cause the Company to be wound up, liquidated or terminated, in the event all of the remaining Members unanimously consent to the continuation of the Company." (Emphasis supplied.)

"Adjustment of Percentage Interests.

"Upon the purchase by the Company of a Selling Member's Interest in accordance with Section 8.5 above, the Percentage Interests of each remaining Member shall be adjusted in accordance with the provisions of this Section effective as of the Valuation Date. The Percentage Interest of each *remaining Member* shall be adjusted to that percentage determined by dividing the Percentage Interest of such Member prior to such adjustment by the total Percentage Interest of all Members (other than the Selling Member) prior to such adjustment." (Emphasis supplied.)

. . . The parties did not make use of the word "remaining" in Section 9.2, but they did so elsewhere.

The many references to "member" in the Act when coupled with the operating agreement suggest the better view is that, in dissolution, "member" includes a withdrawing member having a financial interest in the Company's assets. For example, we note that Section 4.1 of the operating agreement, entitled Allocations and Distributions, provides in part:

> "(b) Liquidation proceeds shall be distributed in the following order of priority:
>
> > "(i) To the payment of debts and liabilities of the Company (including those to the Members) and the expenses of liquidation; then
> >
> > "(ii) To the Managers in payment of the Manager Additional Contributions (if any) and any return thereon; then
> >
> > "(iii) The remainder to the Members in accordance with their respective positive Capital Account balances." (Emphasis added.)

Withdrawal as a dissolution trigger is contemplated by the operating agreement. Withdrawal here was proper. The operating agreement defined "members" as "those persons who are members of the Company from time to time, including any Substitute Members." Each plaintiff has a financial interest in the company. Until dissolution has run its course, plaintiffs are members. . . .

ANALYSIS

1. **Why Did This Happen?** The withdrawing members found themselves in a difficult situation, which required some fancy footwork on their part. Who is to blame for the mess in which the parties found themselves?
2. **A Better Contract.** What should the Operating Agreement have provided?

AFTERMATH

While the litigation between the withdrawing and remaining members dragged on, the LLC continued doing business and incurring expenses. A dispute thus arose between the withdrawing and remaining members as to sharing of expenses between October 21, 1996 and May 30, 2002 (the dates on which, respectively, the withdrawing members first filed suit seeking dissolution and the date on which the withdrawing members filed a motion for a declaratory judgment that they were not liable for sharing the expenses during that period). In holding that the withdrawing members in fact were required to share ratably in paying those expenses, the court opined that nothing in the Operating Agreement negated the statutory provisions under which all LLC members are liable for expenses incurred in the post-dissolution winding up process. Because the withdrawing members had failed to challenge the reasonableness or propriety of the expenses in question, they therefore had no basis for avoiding liability for them. 85 P.3d 1140 (Kan. 2003).

R & R Capital, LLC v. Buck & Doe Run Valley Farms, LLC

2008 WL 3846318 (Del.Ch.).

. . .

I. Background

. . . Generally, the respondent entities were formed years ago with capital contributions from the Russet brothers (presumably the Rs in R & R Capital) and Linda Merritt. The bulk of the capital (over $9.7 million) was provided by the petitioners, but Merritt had the sole and exclusive power to manage the entities. These respondent entities own land and race horses. Unfortunately, the relationship between the financiers, the Russets, and their appointed manager, Merritt, has deteriorated, and, perhaps predictably, the parties have turned to the courts. . . .

The June 2 petition for dissolution seeks, in the alternative, the winding up and dissolution of the respondent entities or the appointment of a receiver. The petitioners allege that most of the respondent entities have had their certificates of formation canceled for failing to designate a registered agent, for failing to pay annual taxes, or for both. They further allege that Merritt's attempts to revive the cancelled certificates are ineffective as a matter of law, that Merritt has refused to provide an accounting of the canceled entities, and that Merritt—along with her "longtime boyfriend" Leonard Pelullo—has defrauded the entities and orchestrated self-dealing transactions. . . .

II. Analysis

. . .

B. The Waiver Entities

Petitioners are members of . . . seven respondent entities . . . . [These entities] (collectively, the "Waiver Entities") contend that the petitioners cannot pursue this action because they have waived their rights to seek dissolution or the appointment of a liquidator. . . . Because neither Delaware's LLC Act nor its policy precludes such a waiver, and because the waiver of such rights would not leave an LLC member inequitably remediless, this Court concludes that petitioners have indeed waived these rights and grants the Waiver Entities' motion to dismiss.

1. The LLC Agreements

The seven Waiver Entities have identical LLC Agreements and each one addresses dissolution explicitly. Specifically, . . . [they each] contain the following provision:

> Waiver of Dissolution Rights. The Members agree that irreparable damage would occur if any member should bring an action for judicial dissolution of the Company. Accordingly each member accepts the provisions under this Agreement as such Member's sole entitlement on Dissolution of the Company and waives and renounces such Member's right to seek a court decree of dissolution or to seek the appointment by a court of a liquidator for the Company.

. . .

2. Freedom of Contract and Limited Liability Companies

As this Court has noted, "Limited Liability Companies are creatures of contract, 'designed to afford the maximum amount of freedom of contract, private ordering and flexibility to the parties involved.' "[18] Delaware's LLC Act leaves to the members of a limited liability company the task of "arrang[ing] a manager/investor governance relationship;" the Act generally provides defaults that can be modified by contract.[19] Indeed, the Act itself explicitly provides that "[i]t is the policy of this chapter to give the maximum effect to the principle of freedom of contract and to the enforceability of limited liability company agreements."[20] It is this flexibility that gives "uncorporate" entities like limited liability companies their allure; "a principle [sic] attraction of the LLC form of entity is the statutory freedom granted to members to shape, by contract, their own approach to common business 'relationship' problems."[22] . . .

3. The LLC Act Does Not Prohibit Waiver of these Rights

. . . Petitioner's . . . statutory argument is based on the principle that certain provisions of the LLC Act are mandatory and non-waivable. As the Supreme Court has explained, "[t]he Act can be characterized as a 'flexible statute' because it generally permits members to engage in private ordering with substantial freedom of contract to govern their

[18] TravelCenters of Am., LLC v. Brog, C.A. No. 3516–CC, 2008 WL 1746987, at *1 (Del.Ch. Apr.3, 2008) . . . .

[19] See Myron T. Steele, Judicial Scrutiny of Fiduciary Duties in Delaware Limited Partnerships and Limited Liability Companies, 32 DEL. J. CORP. L. 1, 5 (2007) (concluding that courts should not "superimpose[e] their view ex post on how that relationship should be structured and scrutinized").

[20] 6 Del. C. S 18–1101(b); . . . .

[22] Haley v. Talcott, 864 A.2d 86, 88 (Del.Ch.2004).

relationship, provided they do not contravene any mandatory provisions of the Act."[29] Generally, the mandatory provisions of the Act are "those intended to protect third parties, not necessarily the contracting members."[30]

Sections 18–802, 18–803, and 18–805 are not mandatory provisions of the LLC Act that cannot be modified by contract. First, the Act does not expressly say that these provisions cannot be supplanted by agreement, and, in fact, section 18–803 does include the "unless otherwise provided" phrase. Second, the provisions employ permissive rather than mandatory language. Section 18–802 states that the "Court of Chancery may decree dissolution" . . . Finally, and most importantly, none of the rights conferred by these provisions that are waived in the LLC Agreement is designed to protect third parties. This Court has recognized that third parties have no interest in dissolution under section 18–802 . . . .

NOTE

Delaware Limited Liability Company Act, 6 Del. Code Sec. 18-802 provides:

> On application by or for a member or manager, the Court of Chancery may decree dissolution of a limited liability company whenever it is not reasonably practicable to carry on the business in conformity with a limited liability company agreement.

Sec. 18-803(a) provides:

> Unless otherwise provided in a limited liability company agreement, a manager who has not wrongfully dissolved a limited liability company or, if none, the members or a person approved by the members . . . who own more than 50 percent of the then current percentage or other interest in the profits of the limited liability company . . . may wind up the limited liability company's affairs; but the Court of Chancery, upon cause shown, may wind up the limited liability company's affairs upon application of any member or manager . . . .

4. Public Policy Does Not Prohibit Waiver of these Rights

Finally, petitioners argue that the Court should refuse to enforce their knowing, voluntary waiver of their right to seek dissolution or the appointment of a receiver because such waivers violate the public policy of Delaware and offend notions of equity. This argument too must fail. First, as discussed throughout this Opinion and others, in treatises, and in the LLC Act itself, the public policy of Delaware with respect to limited liability companies is freedom of contract. Second, there are legitimate business reasons why a firm would want to set up its governance structure so that its members could not petition the Court for dissolution. Finally, the LLC Act provides protections that cannot be waived; this Court need

[29] Elf Atochem N. Am., Inc. v. Jaffari, 727 A.2d 286, 290 (Del.1999).

[30] Id. at 292 . . . .

not exercise its equitable discretion and disregard a negotiated agreement among sophisticated parties to allow this action to proceed.

The hunt for legislative intent with respect to Delaware's LLC Act is rather simple, because the General Assembly explicitly stated that the "policy" of the Act is "to give the maximum effect to the principle of freedom of contract and to the enforceability of limited liability company agreements."[40] The LLC Act provides members with "the broadest possible discretion in drafting their [LLC] agreements" and assures that "once [members] exercise their contractual freedom in their [LLC] agreement, the [members] have a great deal of certainty that their [LLC] agreement will be enforced in accordance with its terms."[41] One treatise concludes that "[f]lexibility lies at the core of the DLLC Act. . . .

Chief Justice Steele has powerfully argued that the freedom of contract principle must be assiduously guarded lest the courts erode the primary attraction of limited liability companies. . . . Professor Larry Ribstein, whose scholarship on limited liability companies has been frequently cited by both this Court and the Supreme Court, emphasizes that it is the rigor with which Delaware courts apply the contractual language of LLC Agreements that makes limited liability companies successful.[44] Indeed, "Delaware is a freedom of contract state, with a policy of enforcing the voluntary agreements of sophisticated parties in commerce."[45] Here, the LLC Agreement is a contract between sophisticated parties. The business relationships between the individuals behind the petitioners and Lynda Merritt is extensive; clearly these were parties who knew how to make use of the law of alternative entities. The mere fact that the business relationship has now soured cannot justify the petitioners' attempt to disregard the agreement they made. Therefore, contrary to petitioners' argument that Delaware's public policy will not countenance their unambiguous contractual waiver, the state's policy mandates that this Court respect and enforce the parties' agreement.

In addition to Delaware's general policy promoting the freedom of contract, there are legitimate business reasons why members of a limited liability company may wish to waive their right to seek dissolution or the appointment of a receiver. For example, it is common for lenders to deem in loan agreements with limited liability companies that the filing of a petition for judicial dissolution will constitute a noncurable event of

---

[40] 6 Del. C. § 18–1101(b).

[41] Elf Atochem N. Am., Inc. v. Jaffari, 727 A.2d 286, 291 (Del.1999) (quoting MARTIN I. LUBAROFF AND PAUL ALTMAN, DELAWARE LIMITED PARTNERSHIPS § 1.2 (1999)).

[44] See generally Larry E. Ribstein, The Uncorporation and Corporate Indeterminacy (Ill. Law and Econ. Research Paper Series, Research Paper No. LE08–012, 2008), available at http://papers.ssrn.com/pape.tar?abstract_id=1115876 . . . .

[45] Personnel Decisions, Inc. v. Bus. Planning Sys., Inc., C.A. No. 3213–VCS, 2008 WL 1932404, at *6 (Del.Ch. May 5, 2008).

default. In such instances, it is necessary for all members to prospectively agree to waive their rights to judicial dissolution to protect the limited liability company. Otherwise, a disgruntled member could push the limited liability company into default on all of its outstanding loans simply by filing a petition with this Court. . . .

Finally, petitioners' plea to this Court's sense of equity is misplaced. . . . [T]he LLC Act preserves the implied covenant of good faith and fair dealing. . . . It is [this] unwaivable protection of the implied covenant that allows the vast majority of the remainder of the LLC Act to be so flexible. There is no threat to equity in allowing members to waive their right to seek dissolution, because there is no chance that some members will be trapped in a limited liability company at the mercy of others acting unfairly and in bad faith.

III. Conclusion

When parties wish to launch a new enterprise, the form of the limited liability company offers a highly customizable vehicle in which to do so. The flexibility of such an entity springs from its roots in contract . . . . The allure of the limited liability company, however, would be eviscerated if the parties could simply petition this court to renegotiate their agreements when relationships sour. Here, the sophisticated members of the seven Waiver Entities knowingly, voluntarily, and unambiguously waived their rights to petition this Court for dissolution or the appointment of a receiver under the LLC Act. This waiver is permissible and enforceable because it contravenes neither the Act itself nor the public policy of the state. . . .

ANALYSIS

1. **Good Faith and Fair Dealing.** Should Delaware courts allow members to waive the requirements of good faith and fair dealing as well?
2. **"Freedom of Contract."** Is the importance of "freedom of contract" any less for corporations than for LLCs?
3. **What Result?** Where does the decision of the court leave the petitioners?

Fisk Ventures, LLC v. Segal

2009 WL 73957 (Del.Ch.).

This case presents the narrow question of whether it is "reasonably practicable," under 6 Del. C. § 18–802, for a Delaware limited liability company to continue to operate. . . .

I. Background

Genitrix, LLC ("Genitrix" or the "Company") . . . was formed by Dr. Andrew Segal in 1996 to commercialize his biotechnology concepts of directing the human immune system to attack cancer and infectious diseases. Although initially promising, the Company's financial condition has deteriorated to the point where currently Genitrix is in critical financial straits.

. . . As this Court stated in a previous opinion, "[t]he Company has no office, no capital funds, no grant funds, and generates no revenue."[2]

. . . In 1997, Genitrix entered into a Patent License Agreement (the "Whitehead Agreement") with Whitehead and Massachusetts Institute of Technology.

. . . As set forth in Article 2 of the Whitehead Agreement, the license gives Genitrix the worldwide right to develop, sell and commercialize Licensed Products and Licensed Services derived from the patent rights. Article 11 of the Whitehead Agreement provides that the license is not assignable, except in limited circumstances including "in connection with the sale or transfer of all or substantially all of Genitrix's equity and assets."

In September 1997, H. Fisk Johnson, head of Fisk Ventures, LLC, . . . contributed $842,000 in cash in exchange for Class B interests in Genitrix. Investments by other Class C investors brought the total cash investment in Genitrix to $1.1 million. Segal received a $500,000 Class A investment credit in exchange for his contribution of patent rights that he obtained from Whitehead. . . .

As a Class B member of Genitrix, Fisk Ventures negotiated a "Put Right" with respect to the Class B membership interests, found in § 11.5 of the LLC Agreement. Section 11.5(a) allows "the holders of the Class B Interests . . . to sell any or all of such Member's Class B Interests to the Company on such terms as are set forth herein," at any time after "the fourth anniversary of the date of this Agreement." [Under § 11.5, the amount to be paid to the Class B investors is to be determined by an independent valuation. If the price exceeds 50% of the value of Genitrix's tangible assets, they will gain creditor status, giving their holder greater security and a higher priority than they currently have as purely equity members.] . . .

Fisk Ventures has been free to exercise the Put Right ever since September 11, 2001—the fourth anniversary date of the LLC Agreement. The Put Right permits Fisk Ventures, at their sole discretion, to exit their

---

[2] Fisk Ventures v. Segal, C.A. No. 3017–CC, 2008 WL 1961156, at *6 (Del. Ch. July 3, 2008).

investment in Genitrix—for fair market value—for any reason or for no reason.

Soon after formation, a four-person Board was organized to manage the affairs of Genitrix, with Segal and Johnson each appointing two representatives. The Genitrix Board now consists of five representatives. Under § 7.5 of the LLC Agreement, the Genitrix Board can only act pursuant to approval of 75% of its members, whether by vote or by written consent.

Segal was originally appointed as both President and Chief Executive Officer of Genitrix. Segal ceased to be CEO of the Company in March 2006, but continues to serve as President.

. . .

II. Analysis

. . .

2. Freedom of Contract and Limited Liability Companies

> "Limited Liability Companies are creatures of contract, 'designed to afford the maximum amount of freedom of contract, private ordering and flexibility to the parties involved.' "[9] Delaware's LLC Act thus allows LLC members to " 'arrange a manager/investor governance relationship;' the LLC Act provides defaults that can be modified by contract" as deemed appropriate by the LLC's managing members.[10] The LLC Act explicitly states that "[i]t is the policy of this chapter to give the maximum effect to the principle of freedom of contract and to the enforceability of limited liability company agreements."[11]

Genitrix's LLC Agreement provides that the Company "shall be dissolved and its affairs wound up only on the first to occur of the following: (a) the written consent of Members holding at least 75% of the Membership Interests, voting as provided in § 3.5; and (b) the entry of a decree of judicial dissolution of the Company under Section 18–802 of the Act." Segal, as the controlling member of Genitrix's Class A membership interest, opposes dissolution. Since the managing members are hopelessly deadlocked to the extent that 75% of the membership interest in Genitrix will not be voted in favor of dissolution, the only other

---

[9] R & R Capital, LLC v. Buck & Doe Run Valley Farms, LLC, C.A. No. 3803–CC, 2008 WL 3846318, at *4 (Del. Ch. Aug. 19, 2008) (quoting TravelCenters of Am., LLC v. Brog, C.A. No. 3516–CC, 2008 WL 1746987, at *1 (Del. Ch. Apr. 3, 2008)).

[10] R & R Capital, LLC v. Buck & Doe Run Valley Farms, LLC, C.A. No. 3803–CC, 2008 WL 3846318, at *4 . . . .

[11] 6 Del. C. § 18–1101(b).

opportunity for members seeking dissolution would be through a decree of judicial dissolution in accordance with the LLC agreement.

3. Standard for Dissolution of a Limited Liability Company

The Court of Chancery may decree judicial dissolution of a Delaware limited liability company "whenever it is not reasonably practicable to carry on the business in conformity with a limited liability company agreement."[13]

In interpreting § 18–802, this Court has by analogy often looked to the dissolution statute for limited partnerships, [§ 17–802.15, under which the test] is whether it is 'reasonably practicable' to carry on the business of a limited partnership, and not whether it is impossible."[16] To decide whether to dissolve a partnership pursuant to § 17–802, the courts have historically looked to the "business of the partnership and the general partner's ability to achieve that purpose in conformity with the partnership agreement."[17] . . .

The text of § 18–802 does not specify what a court must consider in evaluating the "reasonably practicable" standard, but several convincing factual circumstances have pervaded the case law: (1) the members' vote is deadlocked at the Board level; (2) the operating agreement gives no means of navigating around the deadlock; and (3) due to the financial condition of the company, there is effectively no business to operate.

These factual circumstances are not individually dispositive; nor must they all exist for a court to find it no longer reasonably practicable for a business to continue operating. In fact, the Court in *Haley v. Talcott* found that although the limited liability company was "technically functioning" and "financially stable," meaning that it received rent checks and paid a mortgage, it should be dissolved because the company's activity was "purely a residual, inertial status quo that just happens to exclusively benefit one of the 50% members."[22] If a board deadlock prevents the limited liability company from operating or from furthering its stated business purpose, it is not reasonably practicable for the company to carry on its business.

4. Judicial Dissolution of a Limited Liability Company

a. Genitrix's Board is Deadlocked

Under the LLC Agreement, Genitrix's Board has the exclusive power to manage the business and affairs of the company. The Board is unable

---

[13] 6 Del. C. § 18–802.

[16] PC Tower Ctr., Inc. v. Tower Ctr. Dev. Assoc. Ltd. P'ship, C.A. No. 10788, 1989 WL 63901, at *6 (Del. Ch. June 8, 1989).

[17] Id.

[22] Haley v. Talcott, 864 A.2d [86, 91, 96 (Del. Ch. 2004)].

to act unless both the Class B and the Class A shareholders agree on a course of action. The LLC Agreement imposes a 75% voting requirement for business issues: "Approval of at least 75% of the Representatives shall be required to authorize any of the actions . . . specified in this Agreement as requiring the authorization of the Board." The LLC Agreement requires the cooperation of the Board's managing members in order to accomplish or overcome any issue facing Genitrix. This type of charter provision, unless a "tie-breaking" clause exists, is almost always a recipe for disaster. In this case, unfortunately, the parties are behaving true to form.

Although Genitrix's Board is charged to run the Company, the Board is unable to act and is hopelessly deadlocked. Fisk Ventures and Segal have a long history of disagreement and discord over a wide range of issues concerning the direction and operation of Genitrix. On one of the most important issues facing the Company, the raising and use of operating capital, the Board is unable to negotiate acceptable terms to all involved parties. Additionally, the Board has even been considerably deadlocked over whether to have Board meetings. The parties have a history of discord and disagreement on almost every issue facing the Company. There exists almost a five-year track record of perpetual deadlock. Indeed, concerning the current issue, dissolution, the Board is equally deadlocked.

. . .

b. Navigating the Deadlock in The LLC Agreement

In examining the four corners of Genitrix's LLC Agreement I conclude that no provision exists that would allow the Board to circumvent the deadlocked stalemate. The document was negotiated by sophisticated parties engaged in an arm's length negotiation. The product of that negotiation, the LLC Agreement, was carefully drafted in such a way that solved one problem but lead directly to the deadlock now gripping the Company. The provision requiring a 75% vote for Board action was agreed upon by the parties to specifically prohibit board domination by one party over another. The provision has certainly accomplished its intended purpose. Unfortunately, it has also led to a stalemate, and the LLC Agreement on its face provides no means of remedying the situation.

Segal argues that since Fisk Ventures owns a Put Right, provided for in § 11.5 of the LLC Agreement, which allows Fisk Ventures to exit its investment by forcing Genitrix to buy out Fisk Ventures for the fair value of its investment, the LLC Agreement contains a provision that will resolve the Board's deadlock. Segal points to Fisk Ventures' Put Right as a proper "exit mechanism" and as an alternative to judicial dissolution. . . .

Segal ignores the fact, however, that the Put Right contemplated in the LLC Agreement grants its owner an option, to be freely exercised at the will and pleasure of its holder. Nowhere in § 11.5 or in the entire LLC Agreement does the Company have the right to force a buyout if it considers one of its members belligerent or uncooperative. Fisk Ventures holds the option, not Genitrix. Fisk Ventures negotiated for and obtained the Put Right as consideration for its original investment in Genitrix and it would be inequitable for this Court to force a party to exercise its option when that party deems it in its best interests not to do so. I am not permitted to second guess a party's business decision in choosing whether or not to exercise its previously negotiated option rights.

c. Not Reasonably Practicable to Carry on the Business

As noted previously, Genitrix is in dire financial condition. "The Company has no office, no capital funds, no grant funds, and generates no revenue."[27] . . .

Segal argues that one of the major sources of Board contention and deadlock has been Fisk Ventures' unwillingness to allow further capital infusion without significant anti-dilution protections. For this reason alone, Segal argues, Genitrix has been unable to raise additional funds. Segal further contends that if Fisk Ventures is forced to exercise its Put Right then Genitrix will be free to raise funds to effect the buy-back. But again, Segal fails to realize that Fisk Ventures has the right to protect itself against what it perceives as Company actions that would diminish the value of its stake in Genitrix. . . .

. . . The LLC Agreement is a negotiated contract and Fisk Ventures has the right to attempt to maximize its position in accordance with the LLC Agreement's terms. If Fisk Ventures chooses to exercise its leverage under the LLC Agreement to benefit itself, it is perfectly within its right to do so. . . .

Ultimately, even if the financial progress of Genitrix is impeded by the deadlock in the boardroom, if that deadlock cannot be remedied through a legal mechanism set forth within the four corners of the operating agreement, dissolution becomes the only remedy available as a matter of law. The Court is in no position to redraft the LLC Agreement for these sophisticated and well-represented parties.

III. Conclusion

This case involves a long-lived corporate dispute that resulted in devastating deadlock to Genitrix's Board and the loss of significant value to all involved. . . . Because Genitrix's dire financial straits leave the Company with no reasonably practical means to operate its business, I

[27] Fisk Ventures v. Segal, C.A. No. 3017–CC, 2008 WL 1961156, at *6 (Del. Ch. July 3, 2008).

conclude judicial dissolution in accordance with the LLC Agreement is the best and only option for these parties. For the foregoing reasons, I grant the motion seeking judgment in favor of petitioner on the petition for dissolution. . . .

ANALYSIS

1. **Additional Investment?** Suppose there was clear and convincing evidence that Genitrix's financial problems could be solved by an additional investment of $1 million. Further suppose that there was clear and convincing evidence that the holders of the Class B membership interests could easily afford to make such an investment. Should the court have ordered them to do so? If so, on what terms?

2. **Reconciling *Collins*.** Can the result in this case be reconciled with that of Collins v. Lewis (Chapter 2, Sec. 6A)?

3. **Consider *Callier*.** The following are the facts of Callier v. Callier, 378 N.E.2d 405 (Ill.App. 1978): All Steel Pipe and Tube is a close corporation formed in 1969 to engage in the business of selling steel pipes and tubes. The two equal shareholders, plaintiff-appellee Leo Callier and defendant-appellant Scott Callier, each made an initial investment of $500 in the corporation. Scott is Leo's uncle. Defendant-appellant Felix Callier, one of the two directors of the corporation, is Scott's father and Leo's grandfather. It is undisputed that Felix, who is in his 80's, is the "nominee" of Scott on the board of directors, and that he has never taken an active role in the day-to-day management of the business. Leo is the other director, and is president of the corporation. Scott's title is general manager; he was appointed to that position by unanimous resolution of the board, and can only be removed by the board.

   Increasingly over the years of their business association, Scott and Leo had differences of opinion about various aspects of the operation of the company. Despite the steady deterioration of the owners' relationship, the company flourished. From about $200,000 in 1970, gross sales had increased to $25,000,000 a year in 1974.

   In early 1975, the series of events leading to this litigation took place. Scott was involved in preparing and sending to each employee of the corporation, and each employee's spouse, a letter warning that "social and/or emotional and/or physical relationships between male and female employees for other than business purposes" would thenceforth be grounds for immediate dismissal. This so called "fraternization letter" created a furor within the company, and resulted in Leo's informing Scott that he no longer wanted to be associated with him.

   Negotiations looking towards the redemption of Scott's shares by Leo began immediately, but despite the diligent efforts of their attorneys the parties could not reach an agreement. In April 1975, the discussion turned to voluntary dissolution and liquidation of the corporation, but still no agreement could be reached.

Leo thereupon sued for dissolution on grounds of deadlock under Ill.Rev.Stat.1975, ch. 32, par. 157–86(a)(1), which authorizes courts to dissolve a corporation where "the directors are deadlocked in the management of the corporate affairs and the shareholders are unable to break the deadlock, and that irreparable injury to the corporation is suffered or threatened by reason thereof. . . ." The court refused to grant a dissolution, holding that:

> What the evidence shows . . . is two equal shareholders who were unable to get along and unable to reach agreement within a four-month period as to the redemption of one's shares by the other or to the terms of voluntary dissolution. This is not equivalent to an inability of the corporation to perform the functions for which it was created. . . .
>
> It appears to us that Leo Callier simply decided that he was not going to have anything more to do with Scott Callier, and when their redemption-liquidation negotiations stalled, he made a unilateral decision without consulting the other director or shareholder to shut down the corporation. . . . [At that time,] corporate affairs were being managed, and quite successfully. In fact, the company appeared on its way to the second best year of its history, despite a general downturn in the pipe industry.

Would the Delaware court have reached the same result? Should courts make it easier for parties who can no longer stand working with one another to get a "no fault" business "divorce"?

2. SECURITIES REGULATION ISSUES

INTRODUCTORY NOTE

An important question with respect to these new business forms is whether ownership interests therein will be deemed securities for purposes of federal and state securities law.

Regulation of the primary market in this country began with the passage of the first state "blue sky law" by Kansas in 1911. These statutes had a limited jurisdictional reach, they contained many special interest exemptions, and the states had limited enforcement resources. In the aftermath of the Great Crash of 1929 and subsequent Great Depression, there was general agreement that the time had come for federal regulation of the securities markets. Between 1933 and 1940 Congress passed 7 statutes regulating various aspects of the industry. Of these, the most important for our purposes are the Securities Act of 1933 and the Securities Exchange Act of 1934.

The Securities Act is principally concerned with the primary market. In drafting it, Congress rejected proposals for federal merit review of securities. Instead, Congress concentrated on two goals: mandating disclosure of material information to investors and prevention of fraud. As to disclosure, the Securities Act follows a transactional disclosure model—i.e. mandating disclosures by issuers in connection with primary market transactions.

The Securities Exchange Act ("Exchange Act") is principally concerned with secondary market transactions. A whole host of issues fall within its purview, including a number that figure prominently in this course: insider trading and other forms of securities fraud, short-swing profits by corporate insiders, regulation of shareholder voting via proxy solicitations, and regulation of tender offers. Another important element of the Exchange Act is its requirement of periodic disclosures by publicly held corporations.

The Exchange Act is also important because it created the Securities and Exchange Commission as the primary federal agency charged with administering the various securities laws. There are five Commissioners, who must be confirmed by the Senate and no more than three of whom can belong to the same political party. Most of the work, of course, is done not by the Commissioners but by the professional staff. The staff is mainly comprised of lawyers, although there are a fair number of accountants and other specialists, and is organized into Divisions and Offices having various responsibilities. The staff has three primary functions: it provides interpretative guidance to private parties raising questions about the application of the securities laws to a particular transaction; it advises the Commission as to new rules or revisions of existing rules; and it investigates and prosecutes violations of the securities laws. Those of you who ultimately decide to practice in this area will spend most of your careers dealing with the staff; only very rarely will you actually have occasion to deal with the Commissioners.

It is perhaps a cheap way of getting your attention, but it is nevertheless worth pointing out that securities regulation issues reportedly are the single most common source of legal malpractice claims against business lawyers. Why? Put bluntly, because there are so many ways the lawyer can go awry. One of the easiest mistakes a lawyer can make is to fail to recognize that he or she is dealing with a security. This typically has adverse consequences for the client, which often turns out to have adverse consequences for the lawyer.

Knowing whether or not a particular type of instrument or investment will be deemed to be a security is important for at least two reasons. First, it tells you whether the registration requirements of the Securities Act apply to the transaction. The Securities Act prohibits the sale of securities unless the company issuing the securities (the issuer) has "registered" them with the § More specifically, § 5 of the Act imposes three basic rules: (1) a security may not be offered for sale through the mails or by use of other means of interstate commerce unless a registration statement has been filed with the SEC; (2) securities may not be sold until the registration statement has become effective; and (3) the prospectus (a disclosure document) must be delivered to the purchaser before a sale.

To register securities, the issuer must give the Commission extensive information about its finances and business. A large company about to sell stock to the public for the first time will need to file a registration statement that can easily exceed a hundred pages. In the process, it will involve its general counsel and outside accountants. The lawyers' fees alone can exceed $100,000, and the investment banking firm that underwrites the issue (i.e., attempts to find buyers for the stock) will charge a fee several times that amount.

For present purposes, the key point is that one need only go through the registration process if the thing your client is selling is a security. If the SEC or a private plaintiff sues your client for failing to register securities, your first response thus might be that what you sold is not a security. If that doesn't work, you will next argue that one of the exemptions from registration is available. And if that doesn't work, you'll try to settle the case on the best terms you can get.

The other reason the definition of a security is important relates to the antifraud provisions of the Acts. In general, plaintiffs have a much easier time when they bring suit under the securities laws than they would if they had to bring suit under state common law fraud rules. For one thing, the elements of federal securities fraud are less demanding and thus easier to prove. For another thing, there are certain procedural advantages, such as liberal venue and service of process provisions. As a result, plaintiffs defrauded in what looks like a garden variety fraud often allege that a security is present in the scheme so as to bring their claims under the federal securities laws. Such attempts not infrequently succeed, because the securities laws apply to lots of things that don't look very much like securities at first glance. For example, investments in worm farms. Smith v. Gross, 604 F.2d 639 (9th Cir.1979).

The statutory definition of a security in § 2(1) of the Securities Act is divided into two broad categories. (The Exchange Act definitional section is substantially identical and the two are usually interpreted as in pari materia.) First, a list of rather specific instruments, including "stock," "notes," and "bonds." Second, a list of general, catch-all phrases, such as "evidence of indebtedness," "investment contracts" and, in perhaps the most general description of them all, "any instrument commonly known as a 'security.' " The situation is further complicated by the first sentence of § 2, which provides that the terms used in the Act shall be defined in accordance with the various provisions of § 2, "unless the context otherwise requires." This "context" clause is an escape hatch. Courts have sometimes used it to hold that although an instrument appears to fall within one of the listed types of securities, the instrument shall not be held to constitute a security for purposes of the securities laws if "the context otherwise requires." In other words, the "context" clause can be used to say: yes, this thing looks like a security, but given the nature of the transaction we're going to hold that it does not come within the Securities Act. And vice-versa.

Most of the litigation involving atypical instruments claimed to be securities turns on whether the instrument in question falls within one of the catch-all phrases in § 2, especially the term "investment contract." The following cases provides good examples of the issues business lawyers often face in this context.

Great Lakes Chemical Corp. v. Monsanto Co.

96 F.Supp.2d 376 (D.Del.2000).

. . . Plaintiff Great Lakes Chemical Corporation is a Delaware corporation with its principal place of business in Indianapolis, Indiana. Defendants Monsanto Company and its wholly owned subsidiary, Sweet Technologies, Inc. ("STI"), are Delaware corporations with their principal places of business in St. Louis, Missouri.

On May 3, 1999, Great Lakes purchased NSC Technologies Company, LLC ("NSC"), from Monsanto and STI. NSC is a Delaware limited liability company with its principal place of business in Mount Prospect, Illinois.

On January 4, 2000, Great Lakes filed the complaint in this action, alleging that Monsanto and STI violated § 10(b) of the Securities Exchange Act of 1934, . . . and Rule 10b–5 promulgated thereunder . . ., by failing to disclose material information in conjunction with the sale of NSC. . . .

On March 9, 2000, Monsanto and STI moved to dismiss the complaint pursuant to Fed.R.Civ.P. . . . 12(b)(6), . . . for failure to state a claim upon which relief may be granted. Among their assertions, Monsanto and STI argue that the interests sold to Great Lakes were not "securities," as defined by § 2(a)(1) of the Securities Act of 1933. . . .

I. Factual and Procedural Background . . .

A. The Formation of NSC

1. Creation of the NSC Unit within Monsanto

Monsanto is the world's largest manufacturer and distributor of L-phenylalanine ("L-phe"), an amino acid that is a principal ingredient in the sweetener aspartame. Monsanto manufactures and sells aspartame as the product NutraSweet. L-phe is also useful in the production of numerous pharmaceutical products.

In approximately 1985, Monsanto created the NSC Unit within its NutraSweet division to develop specialized pharmaceutical intermediates and pharmaceutical active compounds derived from L-phe. . . . By 1998, the NSC Unit's principal business was based on the development and sale of L-phe and Tic-D, a pharmaceutical intermediate derived from L-phe.

2. Creation of NSC as a Limited Liability Company

On September 25, 1998, Monsanto entered into an agreement (the "LLC Agreement") with STI to establish the NSC Unit as a limited liability company called NSC Technologies Company, LLC ("NSC"), pursuant to the Delaware Limited Liability Company Act . . .

a. Members and Interests

The LLC Agreement names Monsanto and STI as the Members of NSC, and provides that each Member shall have an Interest in NSC. The LLC Agreement defines "Interest" as "[a] Member's Percentage Interest, right to distributions under Section 4.1 of this Agreement, and any other rights which such Member has in the Company." A Member's Percentage Interest is determined according to the Member's capital contributions to NSC. Pursuant to the LLC Agreement, Monsanto contributed assets to NSC totaling $162.9 million, and STI contributed assets totaling $37.1 million, giving the firms an 81.5% and 18.5% Percentage Interest, respectively, in NSC. . . .

b. Net Cash Flow and other distributions

The Members are entitled to receive distributions of Net Cash Flow and allocations of profits and losses. Net Cash Flow is defined, essentially, as all cash receipts of NSC, excluding members' capital contributions, less all cash expenditures, accrued expenses, and loan payments due. . . . The LLC Agreement also provides that NSC's income, profits, gains, losses, deductions, and credits shall be allocated to the Members pro rata in accordance with their respective Percentage Interests.

c. Board of Managers

The LLC Agreement provides that the business and affairs of NSC shall be managed by a Board of Managers. As noted above, the Board, in its sole discretion, shall determine the Net Cash Flow of NSC, and shall distribute the Net Cash Flow to the Members on a pro rata basis. Except as otherwise provided for in the LLC Agreement, the Board of Managers has exclusive authority to bind NSC, and to manage and control NSC's business and affairs. . . . The Members of NSC may remove the Managers with or without cause.

d. Members' voting rights

The Members of NSC are entitled to vote on certain matters, including on all incurrences of indebtedness or guarantees thereof. The LLC Agreement specifies that a Majority in Interest, which is defined as

51% of the Percentage Interests owned by the Members, is required to constitute a quorum, or to amend the LLC Agreement.

e. Transfer of Interests

The LLC Agreement restricts the ability of Members to transfer or otherwise dispose of their Interests in NSC absent consent of the Board. Moreover, Members are prohibited from disposing of their Interests in NSC when the disposition would cause NSC to be taxable as a corporation, would violate federal or state securities laws, or would violate other laws or commitments binding on NSC. . . .

B. The Sale of NSC

1. Solicitation of Great Lakes

In October 1998, BancBoston Robertson Stephens, an investment bank, prepared a Confidential Descriptive Memorandum (the "Offering Memorandum") on behalf of Monsanto and STI to promote the sale of NSC. The Offering Memorandum provides an overview of NSC's business, identifies potential growth opportunities and strategies for NSC, and reports NSC's financial performance. . . .

On November 10, 1998, Monsanto and STI presented the Offering Memorandum to Great Lakes. . . . On November 12, 1998, Great Lakes responded to the solicitation with a letter indicating its interest in submitting a bid. . . .

2. Changes in the Market for L-phe and Tic-D

In early 1999, as negotiations over the sale of NSC [to Great Lakes] continued, a number of events were occurring that may have impacted the business prospects of NSC. Monsanto and other competing producers of L-phe, in particular the Korean firm Daesang, began discounting the sale price of L-phe in the sweetener market. . . . Moreover, an Italian firm, Archimica, was producing Tic-D, a pharmaceutical intermediate derived from L-phe, by a manufacturing process that allegedly infringed the claims of a United States patent assigned to NSC. . . .

3. Great Lakes' Offer to Purchase NSC . . .

On January 15, 1999, [Monsanto] provided representatives of Great Lakes with revised sales projections for NSC, reducing the forecast of $93.2 million originally stated in the Offering Memorandum to $78 million.

The following week, Great Lakes offered to acquire defendants' Interests in NSC for approximately $130 million. [After further discussions about NSC's financial prospects,] the parties adjusted the purchase price for NSC from $130 million to $125 million. On April 8, 1999, the parties entered into an Ownership Interest Purchase

Agreement (the "Purchase Agreement"). . . . The parties closed the transaction on May 3, 1999. . . .

D. The Lawsuit

. . . On January 20, 2000, Great Lakes filed an eight count complaint in this court. Count I asserts that Monsanto and STI violated § 10(b) of the Securities Exchange Act of 1934, . . . and Rule 10b–5 . . ., by making material misrepresentations and by failing to disclose material facts in connection with the sale of securities. . . .

II. Discussion

A. What Is an LLC?

In Delaware, LLCs are formed pursuant to the Delaware Limited Liability Company Act, 6 Del.C. § 18–101 et seq. LLCs are hybrid entities that combine desirable characteristics of corporations, limited partnerships, and general partnerships. LLCs are entitled to partnership status for federal income tax purposes under certain circumstances, which permits LLC members to avoid double taxation, i.e., taxation of the entity as well as taxation of the members' incomes. . . . Moreover, LLCs members, unlike partners in general partnerships, may have limited liability, such that LLC members who are involved in managing the LLC may avoid becoming personally liable for its debts and obligations. See 6 Del.C. § 18–303. In addition, LLCs have greater flexibility than corporations in terms of organizational structure. The Delaware Limited Liability Company Act, for example, establishes the default rule that management of an LLC shall be vested in its members, but permits members to establish other forms of governance in their LLC agreements. See 6 Del.C. § 18–402. . . .

B. Are the Interests in NSC . . . "Securities" Under Federal Law?

. . . Defendants contend that plaintiff's claim fails as a matter of law because the Interests in NSC do not constitute securities.

Section 2(a)(1) of the Securities Act of 1933 lists financial instruments that qualify as securities, as follows:

The term "security" means any note, stock, treasury stock, bond, debenture, evidence of indebtedness, certificate of interest or participation in any profit-sharing agreement, . . . investment contract, voting trust certificate, . . . any put, call, straddle, option, or privilege on any security, certificate of deposit, or group or index of securities . . ., or, in general, any interest or instrument commonly known as a "security," or any certificate of interest or participation in, temporary or interim certificate for, receipt for, guarantee of, or warrant or right to subscribe to or purchase, any of the foregoing.

. . . Among the securities enumerated in § 2(a)(1) of the Securities Act, Great Lakes contends that the Interests in NSC constitute either "stock," an "investment contract," or "any interest or instrument commonly known as a 'security.' "

1. Key Cases Governing the Characterization of Novel Instruments

a. SEC v. W.J. Howey

The Supreme Court defined the parameters of an "investment contract" for the purposes of federal securities law in the case of SEC v. W.J. Howey Co., 328 U.S. 293, 298, 66 S.Ct. 1100, 90 L.Ed. 1244 (1946). *Howey* concerned a Florida corporation, the Howey Company, that sold small tracts of land in a citrus grove to forty-two purchasers, many of whom were patrons of a resort hotel. . . . For the most part, the purchasers lacked the knowledge, skill, and equipment necessary for the care and cultivation of citrus trees. They invested in the enterprise for profit. The purchasers were free to contract with a number of companies to service the tracts, but the sales contract stressed the superiority of Howey-in-the-Hills Service, Inc., which the purchasers chose to service 85% of the acreage sold. The service contracts granted Howey-in-the-Hills full and complete possession of the acreage, and the individual purchasers had no right of entry to market the crop. Purchasers of tracts shared in the profits of the enterprise, which amounted to 20% in the 1943–44 growing season. The Howey Company did not register the interests in the enterprise as securities.

. . . Because the interests at issue did not constitute any of the traditional kinds of securities enumerated in § 2(a)(1) of the Securities Act, the SEC argued that the interests were "investment contracts." Noting that the term "investment contract" was not defined by Congress, but that the term was widely used in state securities laws, the Court largely adopted the definition used at the time by state courts. The Court stated that "an investment contract for purposes of the Securities Act means a contract, transaction or scheme whereby a person invests his money in a common enterprise and is led to expect profits solely from the efforts of the promoter or a third party." *Howey*, 328 U.S. at 298–99, 66 S.Ct. 1100. Thus, the three requirements for establishing an investment contract are: (1) "an investment of money," (2) "in a common enterprise," (3) "with profits to come solely from the efforts of others." Id. at 301, 66 S.Ct. 1100. In articulating this test, the Supreme Court stated that this definition "embodies a flexible rather than a static principle, one that is capable of adaptation to meet the countless and variable schemes devised by those who seek the use of the money of others on the promise of profits." Id. at 299, 66 S.Ct. 1100.

b. United Housing Foundation, Inc. v. Forman

The Supreme Court established guidelines for whether non-traditional instruments labeled "stock" constitute securities in United Housing Foundation, Inc. v. Forman, 421 U.S. 837, 95 S.Ct. 2051, 44 L.Ed.2d 621 (1975). *Forman* concerned a nonprofit housing cooperative that sold shares of "stock" to prospective tenants. The sole purpose of acquiring the shares was to enable the purchaser to occupy an apartment in the cooperative. The shares essentially represented a recoverable deposit on the apartment. The shares were explicitly tied to the apartment, as they could not be transferred to a non-tenant. Nor could they be pledged or encumbered. No voting rights attached to the shares.

After the housing cooperative raised rental charges, the residents sued the cooperative under § 17(a) of the Securities Act, . . . asserting that the cooperative falsely represented that it would bear all subsequent cost increases due to factors such as inflation. The Supreme Court held that the "stock" issued by the cooperative did not constitute a security. The shares, the Court found, lacked the five most common features of stock: (1) the right to receive dividends contingent upon an apportionment of profits; (2) negotiability; (3) the ability to be pledged or hypothecated; (4) voting rights in proportion to the number of shares owned; and (5) the ability to appreciate in value. Id. at 851, 95 S.Ct. 2051. Finding that the purchasers obtained the shares in order to acquire subsidized low-cost living space, not to invest for profit, the Court ruled that the "stock" issued by the cooperative was not a security. . . .

c. Landreth Timber Co. v. Landreth

Following the issuance of *Forman*, a number of lower courts began to apply the *Howey* test to distinguish between investment transactions, which were covered by the securities laws, and commercial transactions, which were not. . . . In *Landreth*, the Ninth Circuit addressed whether a single individual who purchased 100% of the stock in a lumber corporation, and who had the power to actively manage the acquired business, could state a claim under the securities laws for alleged fraud in the sale of the business. The Ninth Circuit found that the purchaser bought full control of the corporation, and that the economic reality of the transaction was the purchase of a business, and not an investment in a security. . . . The court held that the sale of 100% of the stock of a closely held corporation was not a transaction involving a "security."

Reversing the Ninth Circuit, the Supreme Court reasoned that it would be burdensome to apply the *Howey* test to transactions involving traditional stock. See Landreth Timber Co. v. Landreth, 471 U.S. 681, 686–88 (1985). The Court held that, insofar as a transaction involves the sale of an instrument called "stock," and the stock bears the five common attributes of stock enumerated in *Forman*, the transaction is governed by the securities laws. . . . The financial instrument involved in the case, the Court reasoned, "is traditional stock, plainly within the statutory definition." Id. at 690. "There is no need here," the Court continued, "to look beyond the characteristics of the instrument to determine whether the [Securities] Acts apply." Id. The Court stated that the *Howey* test should only be applied to determine whether an instrument is an "investment contract," and should not be applied in the context of other instruments enumerated in § 2(a)(1) of the Securities Act. See id. at 691–92. . . .

2. Prior Cases Concerning . . . LLCs . . .

The present case raises novel issues regarding the regulation of transactions involving interests in LLCs. The court has identified three cases in which other courts have determined whether interests in LLCs constitute securities.

a. Keith v. Black Diamond Advisors, Inc.

In Keith v. Black Diamond Advisors, Inc., 48 F.Supp.2d 326 (S.D.N.Y.1999), the plaintiff, Keith, founded a sub-prime mortgage lending firm, Eagle Corp., and brought it to profitability. Milton was an original investor in Eagle. Black Diamond, a venture capital firm, proposed a joint venture in which it would contribute $150,000 in cash, and Keith and Milton would each contribute their interests in Eagle, to form a New York limited liability company, Pace LLC. Through this transaction, Black Diamond acquired 50% of the interests in Pace, and Keith and Milton each received a 25% stake. Keith alleged that Black Diamond subsequently used its majority position to strip him of control of Pace. Keith sued Black Diamond for federal securities fraud.

The court applied the *Howey* test, and found that Keith had invested money in a common enterprise. The court, however, found that Keith had retained substantial control over the enterprise, such that he did not have an expectation of profits "solely from the efforts of others." As such, the court concluded that the LLC interests were not investment contracts. . . .

b. SEC v. Parkersburg Wireless LLC

SEC v. Parkersburg Wireless LLC, 991 F.Supp. 6 (D.D.C.1997), involves a LLC that was established to provide wireless cable services. The promoters of the company sold "memberships" in the company to over 700 individuals in 43 states. . . .

The SEC sought to enjoin the sale of the membership interests. The court found that the interests sold in the LLC "easily satisfy" the *Howey* test for investment contracts. The investors' $10,000 minimum contribution constituted an "investment of money." Because the 700 individuals were to receive a pro rata share of the company's revenues, the court found there was a common enterprise. Moreover, the investors had little, if any, input into the company, so their profits were to come solely from the efforts of others.

c. SEC v. Shreveport Wireless Cable Television Partnership

SEC v. Shreveport Wireless Cable Television Partnership, 1998 WL 892948 (D.D.C.1998), involves three entities: Reading Partnership and Shreveport Partnership, which are both general partnerships, and Baton Rouge LLC. All three entities were established to provide wireless cable services. Each entity engaged the services of a corporation to develop the telecommunications services and to solicit public investment in the enterprises. The promoters sold memberships in the three entities to approximately 2000 investors.

The SEC sought to enjoin the sale of interests in the ventures. . . . The court found that the purchasers of the interests had invested money in a common enterprise. The court found, however, that there was a question of fact as to whether the investors exercised significant control over the management of the corporation, and denied defendants' motion for summary judgment. . . .

3. Are the Interests In NSC "Stock"?

Great Lakes contends that NSC is the functional equivalent of a corporation, and that the Interests in NSC should be treated as stock. Great Lakes notes that the LLC Agreement refers to the Interests as "equity securities," and that the LLC Agreement prohibits the transfer of the Interests in such a way as would "violate the provisions of any federal or state securities laws."

Monsanto and STI, on the other hand, contend that the Interests cannot be stock because NSC is not a corporation. . . .

[T]he Supreme Court has described the five most common characteristics of stock as follows: [see *Forman* list above.] As noted by plaintiffs, these attributes of stock also characterize, at least to some degree, the Interests in NSC. NSC's Members are entitled to share, pro rata, in distributions of Net Cash Flow, contingent upon its distribution by the Board of Managers. The Interests are negotiable and may be pledged or hypothecated, subject to approval by the Board of Managers. . . . Members in NSC have voting rights in proportion to their Percentage Interest in the company. And, the Interests in NSC have the capacity to appreciate in value. The Interests in NSC are undoubtedly stock-like in character, but the question remains if the Interests can be characterized as "stock" for the purposes of the federal securities laws.

The primary goal of the securities laws is to regulate investments, and not commercial ventures. . . . In transactions involving traditional stock, lower courts had attempted to distinguish between investment transactions and commercial transactions. . . . The Supreme Court, as discussed above, held that it is unnecessary to attempt to distinguish between commercial and investment transactions when the financial instrument in question is traditional stock. . . .

In the present case, the LLC Interests, although they are "stock-like" in nature, are not traditional stock. *Landreth,* thus, is inapplicable to this case, and the court must determine whether the sale of NSC was essentially an investment transaction, in which case the securities laws apply, or whether it was a commercial transaction, in which case they do not. To make this determination, the court will apply the *Howey* test for investment contracts. . . . The court will also consider whether the Interests can be characterized as "any interest or instrument commonly known as a security."

4. Are the Interests in NSC an "Investment Contract"?

As stated above, to constitute an "investment contract," the instruments purchased by Great Lakes must involve: (1) "an investment of money," (2) "in a common enterprise," (3) "with profits to come solely from the efforts of others." Howey, 328 U.S. at 301. The parties do not dispute that the first prong of the *Howey* test—an investment of money—is satisfied by the facts of this case. . . .

a. Did Great Lakes invest in a "common enterprise"?

To determine whether a party has invested funds in a common enterprise, courts look to whether there is horizontal commonality between investors, or vertical commonality between a promoter and an investor. Horizontal commonality requires a pooling of investors' contributions and distribution of profits and losses on a pro-rata basis among investors. . . . The vertical commonality test is less stringent, and requires that an investor and promoter be engaged in a common enterprise, with the "fortunes of the investors linked with those of the promoters." Securities and Exchange Commission v. R.G. Reynolds Enterprises, Inc., 952 F.2d 1125, 1130 (9th Cir.1991). . . .

In this case, Great Lakes bought 100% of the Interests of NSC from Monsanto and STI. Great Lakes, accordingly, did not pool its contributions with those of other investors, as is required for horizontal commonality. After the sale, Monsanto and STI retained no interest in NSC, so it cannot be said that the fortunes of Great Lakes were linked to those of defendants, as is required for vertical commonality.

Great Lakes urges that when the Interests in NSC were created, Monsanto and STI pooled their contributions in a common enterprise. Great Lakes contends that Monsanto's and STI's Interests were securities when they were created, and that they did not cease to be securities when conveyed to Great Lakes. . . .

In this case, the challenged transaction is the sale of NSC by defendants to Great Lakes, and not the formation of NSC. Thus, the fact that Monsanto and STI pooled their contributions in the formation of NSC does not change the character of the sale of NSC to Great Lakes. The court concludes that Great Lakes did not invest in a common enterprise.

b. Were Great Lakes' Profits in NSC To Come "Solely from the Efforts of Others"?

Monsanto and STI argue that the profits in NSC did not come solely from the efforts of others, as would support a finding that the Interests in NSC were securities. . . . Rather, defendants contend that Great Lakes had the power to control NSC through its authority to remove managers with or without cause, and to dissolve the entity.

Great Lakes argues, on the other hand, that it depended solely on the efforts of others to profit from NSC, as the LLC Agreement provides that the Members would retain no authority, right, or power to manage or control the operations of the company. . . .

There is little caselaw establishing guidelines for determining whether a member in an LLC is sufficiently passive that he is dependent solely on the efforts of others for profits. In the context of general partnerships and limited partnerships, by contrast, there has been extensive litigation on whether partnership interests may qualify as securities. . . . Because partners have equal rights in the management of general partnerships, and because they are not protected by limited liability, courts consistently state that partners in general partnerships are unlikely to be passive investors who profit solely on the efforts of others. Some courts have adopted per se rules that partnership interests are not securities. . . . Other courts have adopted a presumption that partnership interests are not securities, but permit a finding that partnership interests are securities when a partner has so little control over the management as to be a passive investor. . . .

Limited partnerships are comprised of general partners and limited partners. General partners in limited partnerships have all the powers and duties of general partners in general partnerships, and are liable for the debts of the partnership. . . . Limited partners have limited liability, but become liable as general partners if they take part in the control of the business. . . . A limited partner may advise a general partner with respect to the business of the limited partnership, or cause a general partner to take action by voting or otherwise, without losing his limited liability. . . . In cases involving transactions of interests in limited partnerships, wherein the limited partners exercised no managerial role in the partnership's affairs, courts treat the limited partners as passive investors, and find that the membership interests of limited partners constitute securities under federal law. . . . Where, however, a limited partner is found to have exercised substantial control over the management of the partnership, courts find that the limited partner has not profited solely from the efforts of others, and rule that the interest in the partnership is not a security. . . .

In comparison with limited partnerships, the Delaware Limited Liability Company Act permits a member in an LLC to be an active participant in management and still to retain limited liability. 6 Del.C. § 18–303. Thus, there is no statutory basis, as with limited partnerships, to presume that LLC members are passive investors entitled to protection under the federal securities laws.

The Delaware Limited Liability Company Act grants parties substantial flexibility in determining the character of an LLC. Accordingly, the terms of the operating agreement of each LLC will determine whether its membership interests constitute securities. The presumptions that courts have articulated with respect to general partnerships and limited partnerships do not apply to LLCs. Rather, to determine whether a member's profits are to come solely from the efforts of others, it is necessary to consider the structure of the particular LLC at issue, as provided in its operating agreement.

In the present case, the Members of NSC had no authority to directly manage NSC's business and affairs. . . . The Members, however, had the power to remove any Manager with or without cause, and to dissolve the company. . . . Great Lakes' authority to remove managers gave it the power to directly affect the profits it received from NSC. Thus, the court finds that Great Lakes' profits from NSC did not come solely from the efforts of others. . . .

5. Are the Interests in NSC "Any Interest or Instrument Commonly Known as a Security"?

Great Lakes argues that, even if the Interests in NSC do not otherwise satisfy the *Howey* test for investment contracts, they should be deemed to be "any interest or instrument commonly known as a security," as provided for in § 2(a)(1) of the Securities Act. Great Lakes notes that the LLC Agreement refers to the Interests at issue as "equity securities," and that the LLC Agreement prohibits the transfer of the Interests in such a way as would "violate the provisions of any federal or state securities laws." . . .

The Supreme Court has indicated that the term "any interest or instrument commonly known as a security" covers the same financial instruments as referred to by the term "investment contract." In United Housing Foundation, Inc. v. Forman, 421 U.S. 837 (1975), the Court stated that "[w]e perceive no distinction, for present purposes, between an 'investment contract' and an 'instrument' commonly known as a 'security.' In either case, the basic test for distinguishing the transaction from other commercial dealings is 'whether the scheme involves an investment of money in a common enterprise with profits to come solely from the efforts of others.'" Id. at 852 (quoting *Howey*, 328 U.S. at 301).... The *Howey* test, the Court explained, "embodies the essential attributes that run through all of the Court's decisions defining a security." *Forman*, 421 U.S. at 852.

When confronted with novel financial instruments, numerous courts have considered whether to distinguish between an "investment contract" and "any interest or instrument commonly known as a security," and have declined to do so.... In this case, too, the court finds that it would be improper to extend the definition of a security by reinterpreting the term "any interest or instrument commonly known as a security."

In sum, the court finds that the Interests in NSC constitute neither "stock," nor an "investment contract," nor "any interest or instrument commonly known as a security." ...

III. Conclusion

For the forgoing reasons, the court will grant defendants' motion to dismiss all counts of plaintiff's complaint....

ANALYSIS

1. **Close Corporation.** Suppose that Monsanto and STI had organized NSC as a close corporation. Would the transaction have been subject to Rule 10b–5?
2. **General Partnership.** Suppose they had organized it as a general partnership. What result?

Koch v. Hankins

928 F.2d 1471 (9th Cir.1991).

The plaintiff-investors ("investors") appeal from the district court's summary judgment that the investments did not constitute securities within the meaning of the Securities Exchange Act of 1934....

The investors are primarily doctors [and] dentists ... who invested between $23,000 and $500,000 each in general partnerships formed to purchase land for the production of jojoba. [Defendants included a number of plaintiffs' accountants and lawyers who promoted the partnerships.] The investments were undertaken in part for tax purposes and allegedly were promoted to the [investors] on that basis.

> **NOTE**
>
> Jojoba is a shrub whose seeds produce a commercially valuable wax.

The overall investment scheme involved thirty-five different general partnerships, each of which purchased eighty acres of land from "selling corporations" owned by the promoters, which in turn purchased land from a common seller. In all, approximately 2700 acres and 160 investors were involved in the various general partnerships. Although the promoters present the general partnerships as independent entities, the investors assert that the promoters told them at the outset that it was not economically feasible to farm jojoba in eighty-acre parcels; that they never regarded their general partnerships as separate eighty-acre farms but rather as part of a 2700-acre plantation; and indeed that the promoters themselves did not view the general partnerships as separate farms with the capability of operating independently. . . . [T]he thirty-five general partnerships all specified identically that the general partners would initially employ Franklin W. Rogers as foreman to carry out the onsite farming cultural practices . . .; that [each] partnership would execute an irrigation lease for a term of five years for an annual rental of $2,800; and that [each] partnership would purchase from the promoters by bill of sale a supply of jojoba seeds, fertilizer, weed control and other materials at a cost of $300 per acre. In addition, the thirty-five partnerships shared a common field office financed by an administrative fund to which all the partnerships contributed. At a minimum, therefore, whether the eighty-acre partnerships could or were intended to operate independently from the 2700-acre Great Western Jojoba plantation is a disputed question of fact.

Each general partnership was comprised of one operating general partner and a number of general partners. The thirty-five partnership agreements detail identically the rights and responsibilities of the partners. The operating general partners have responsibility for executing the general partners' decisions about the management and control of partnership business. Within each partnership, the general partners have full and exclusive control of the business of the partnership and can take action in that regard only upon a majority vote. Within each partnership, the general partners have the ability to remove any person from a management position by majority vote and have access to the partnership's books and records.

The degree of actual participation by the general partners and operating general partners and its significance to the endeavor is a matter of considerable dispute. The promoters point out that some investors have voted on such partnership business decisions as whether to pay additional assessments to meet operating budgets, a proposed sale of partnership assets in response to an offer by a third party, whether to interplant alfalfa between rows of jojoba, whether to join a marketing cooperative, whether to amend the partnership agreement, water district elections, and whether to stop farming their parcel or section. In addition, some investors have visited the property their partnerships purchased and tested the soil. There are also letters and memoranda in the record from operating general partners and general partners which suggest that the operating general partners paid careful attention to the status of their particular farms and kept the general partners informed in some detail as to the status of particular plots.

The investors argue, on the other hand, that their role was essentially passive. It is undisputed that none of them had any experience in jojoba farming. It appears that even those investors who nominally held the role of operating general partner usually acted as conduits for materials created by the promoters. The investors assert that the operating general partners did not even generate the pro rata assessments for operating expenses for each general partner. Those figures were determined by the promoters. Finally, the investors assert that any voting they did was largely pro forma in light of their lack of expertise, their inability to devote time to direct participation in the project, and their ability at best to shape decisionmaking only for the eighty acres owned by their particular general partnership. It is even disputed in the record whether, had investors actively exercised decisionmaking regarding the farming of their particular parcels of land, their decisions would have been implemented.

As one might guess from the fact that the parties are now in court, the investments proved less than successful. . . .

. . . Both § 2 of the Securities Act of 1933, and § 3 of the Securities Exchange Act of 1934, define the term "security" to include, inter alia, any "investment contract." Since the investments involved in this case do not constitute any of the other types of securities protected by the Acts, the critical threshold inquiry is whether the general partnerships constitute "investment contracts" within the meaning of the Acts.

The term "investment contract" has been interpreted by the Supreme Court broadly to reach "novel, uncommon, or irregular devices, whatever they appear to be . . ." SEC v. C.M. Joiner Leasing Corp., 320 U.S. 344, 351 (1943). "It embodies a flexible rather than a static principle, one that is capable of adaptation to meet the countless and variable schemes devised by those who seek the use of the money of others on the promise of profits." SEC v. W.J. Howey Co., 328 U.S. 293, 299 (1946) (holding that a combined sale of units of a citrus grove development coupled with a contract for cultivating, marketing and remitting the net proceeds to the investor was an "investment contract"). . . . Thus, the fact that the investments here are structured as "general partnerships" is not determinative of their status as securities; rather, we must examine the economic realities of the transactions to determine whether they are, in fact, investment contracts.

The Supreme Court in *Howey* set out the classic three-part definition of an investment contract: "An investment contract for purposes of the Securities Act means a contract, transaction or scheme whereby a person [1] invests his money in [2] a common enterprise and is led to [3] expect profits solely from the efforts of the promoter or a third party." 328 U.S. at 298–99. The Ninth Circuit has held that "the word 'solely' should not be read as a strict or literal limitation on the definition of an investment contract." SEC v. Glenn W. Turner Enters., Inc., 474 F.2d 476, 482 (9th Cir.), cert. denied, 414 U.S. 821 (1973). Instead, this circuit looks to whether "the efforts made by those other than the investor are the undeniably significant ones, those essential managerial efforts which affect the failure or success of the enterprise." Id. Here, as in most cases dealing with the *Howey* test, the inquiry revolves around the third, "control," element of the test—whether the investors had an expectation of profits which would be produced in essential part through the efforts of others.

. . .

The Fifth Circuit held in [Williamson v. Tucker, 645 F.2d 404, 424 (5th Cir.1981)] that:

A general partnership or joint venture interest can be designated a security if the investor can establish, for example, that (1) an agreement among the parties leaves so little power in the hands of the partner or venturer that the arrangement in fact distributes power as would a limited partnership; or (2) the partner or venturer is so inexperienced and unknowledgeable in business affairs that he is incapable of intelligently exercising his partnership or venture powers; or (3) the partner or venturer is so dependent on some unique entrepreneurial or managerial ability of the promoter or manager that he cannot replace the manager of the enterprise or otherwise exercise meaningful partnership or venture powers.

According to *Williamson* the critical determination is whether, although "on the face of a partnership agreement, the investor retains substantial control over his investment and an ability to protect himself from the managing partner or hired manager . . ., [the investor can demonstrate that] he was so dependent on the promoter or on a third party that he was in fact unable to exercise meaningful partnership powers." Id. The *Williamson* opinion made clear that the three factors are not exclusive and that "other factors could . . . also give rise to such a dependence." Id. at 424, n.15. *Williamson* likewise specified that the inquiry is not directed to what actually transpires after the investment is made, i.e., whether the investor later decides to be passive or to delegate all powers and duties to a promoter or managing partner; rather, "one would have to show that the reliance on the manager which forms the basis of the partner's expectations was an understanding in the original transaction." Id. at 424, n. 14. [The court next held that Ninth Circuit's en banc opinion in Hocking v. Dubois, 885 F.2d 1449 (9th Cir.1989) (en banc), had adopted *Williamson* as a controlling precedent.]

> **NOTE**
>
> In *Hocking*, the plaintiff purchased a condominium in a resort community. The purchaser hoped to generate rental income rather than to acquire a place to live. Plaintiff also entered into a rental agreement pursuant to which an agent recommended by the promoter handled all aspects of renting the condo to vacationers. Rents generated by the condo were not paid directly to the purchaser, but were pooled with the rentals generated by all condos in the facility and then shared out among their owners on a pro rata basis. The Hocking court held that the condo purchase and its associated rent pooling agreements constituted a security. 885 F.2d 1449 (9th Cir.1989).

In determining whether the investors relied on the efforts of others, we look not only to the partnership agreement itself, but also to other documents structuring the investment, to promotional materials, to oral representations made by the promoters at the time of the investment, and to the practical possibility of the investors exercising the powers they possessed pursuant to the partnership agreements. . . .

Assuming the disputed facts in favor of the nonmoving party (the investors), . . . none of the investors knew anything about jojoba farming and, taking their allegations as true, none of them intended to engage actively in the business of jojoba farming. Rather, they relied substantially on the knowledge of the promoters and experts, and on the services to be provided by the on-site manager. . . .

The investors argue that all three *Williamson* factors tilt in favor of a finding that the investments here were securities. Because of the reliance of the individual partnerships on participation in the larger plantation, the investors contend that the power of the partnership is distributed as is the power in a limited partnership, thus implicating the first *Williamson* factor. The investors, however, are jumping ahead to the third factor and ignoring the crux of the first. It is clear from both *Williamson* itself and from *Hocking* that the first factor is addressed to the legal powers afforded the investor by the formal documents without regard to the practical impossibility of the investors invoking them. Here, the partnership agreement clearly affords the partners significant legal powers.

As a legal matter, the partners have the responsibility and authority to control every aspect of the jojoba cultivation process. Additional assessments of capital must be approved by 75 percent of the partnership units; a majority of the partnership units can remove any person from a management position; decisions regarding the management and control of the business must be made by a majority vote.[1] . . . Like the condominium purchaser in *Hocking*, who was free to terminate the rental pooling agreement, occupy the unit himself, rent the unit out on his own, or sell the unit, the investors here could—theoretically, at least—vote to cease farming, replace the operating general partner, terminate services by the on-site manager, vote to interplant rows of alfalfa, etc. Compare *Howey*, 328 U.S. 293 (orange grove investment gave the management company a leasehold interest and full and complete possession of the acreage, along with full discretion and authority over the cultivation, harvest and marketing of the crops such that investors had no right of entry to market the crop without the consent of the company). Under these facts, as in *Hocking*, the investors have not demonstrated that their partnership agreements leave them "with so little power as to place [them] in a position analogous to a limited partner." 885 F.2d at 1461. It therefore appears that the first *Williamson* factor tilts in favor of the promoters.

Under the second *Williamson* factor we consider the investors' sophistication and expertise. . . . Under *Williamson*, the relevant inquiry is whether "the partner or venturer is so inexperienced and unknowledgeable in business affairs that he is incapable of intelligently exercising his partnership or venture powers." 645 F.2d at 424. Here, while the investors were doctors and dentists as opposed to business people, all of them had at least $23,000 to invest in the venture and some had considerably more. The record indicates that some of the investors had prior experience in pistachio ventures and other tax shelters at the time of their investment. However, since the district court focused exclusively on the investors' formal status, the record is not fully developed on this issue and we simply have no basis for evaluating the sophistication of many of the investors. The question of the investors' expertise or lack thereof and its effect on their ability to exercise their powers intelligently is a question of fact which should be resolved in the first instance by the trial court. Since the record is insufficiently developed on this issue, we remand to the district court to determine whether the investors have raised a genuine issue of fact as to whether

---

[1] Although an investor participating in a general partnership obviously relinquishes some control since decisions must be made by majority vote, this type of diminution in control by itself would not satisfy the third prong of *Howey* unless the numbers of partners became so large "that a partnership vote would be more like a corporate vote, each partner's role having been diluted to the level of a single shareholder." *Williamson*, 645 F.2d at 423. Such is not the case here. Even though each investor's absolute control is reduced by the voting structure, the general partners as a legal matter "do have the sort of influence [within the partnership] which generally provides them with access to important information and protection against a dependence on others." Id. at 422.

their lack of expertise prevented them from exercising meaningful control over their investment.

We turn finally to the third *Williamson* factor, which involves whether "the partner or venturer is so dependent on some unique entrepreneurial or managerial ability of the promoter or manager that he cannot replace the manager of the enterprise or otherwise exercise meaningful partnership or venture powers." 645 F.2d at 424. In this case, the investors' reliance on participation in the larger, 2700-acre jojoba plantation is analogous to, and arguably more extreme than, Hocking's reliance on the rental pooling agreement. In *Hocking*, the en banc panel noted that while the investor enjoyed complete legal control over his particular condominium unit, he had made the investment in anticipation of receiving income from the rental pooling agreement, and in order for him to replace the management of that agreement he would have had to gain the votes of 75 percent of participating investors. The court in *Hocking* held that "[those] facts alone create[d] a real question of whether Hocking was stuck with HCP as a rental manager." 885 F.2d at 1461. Because the rental pooling agreement resulted in the condominiums being managed as a resort hotel, and "the commercial viability of a one-room hotel [did] not strongly argue for separate management," the court found that "the individual investor may have [had] no choice but to place his condominium in the rental pool, if he [were] to receive significant rental income." Id. It thus reversed the district court's summary judgment that the investment was not a security.

Here, as in *Hocking*, there is a question of fact as to whether the investors could, as a practical matter, pull out of the larger enterprise and still receive the income they had contemplated when they made the investment. The promoters focus on the significant management powers and access to information afforded the general partners by the partnership agreements. The partnership agreement, however, only provides for the exercise of general partner control and decisionmaking within each partnership, and as to the land controlled by each partnership, not as to issues concerning the entire plantation. Likewise, the access to information provisions of the partnership agreement apply only to information related to the partnership and available to the partnership or the operating general partner. . . .

As in *Hocking*, while the investors here could readily order the on-site manager to cease cultivating their particular plot, it would be difficult if not impossible for an investor to affect the management of the plantation as a whole. There is not even a formalized mechanism in the partnership agreements for attempting to effect change on behalf of all thirty-five partnerships. Therefore, to replace the on-site manager for the entire plantation, an investor would have to catalyze a vote in each of the thirty-five partnerships (an endeavor which would be rendered difficult if not impossible by the fact that many of the investors did not even know the names of their own partners, much less have such information regarding the other thirty-four partnerships) and obtain the approval of a significant enough bloc of the partnerships to make it impracticable for the on-site manager to continue farming the remaining sections. In addition, the ready availability of alternative jojoba farm managers is more questionable than the availability of alternative realtors to manage a rental pool agreement in Hawaii, the situation presented in *Hocking*.

The fact that some investors were provided with detailed information about the status of their eighty acres and that some investors visited the land and even offered evaluations and suggestions to the on-site managers is not dispositive. . . . In this case, even if a general partner vigorously exercised his or her rights under the partnership agreement, he or she arguably could have no impact on the investment (other than to ensure its failure by withdrawing from the larger plantation).

Thus, the investors here have at least raised an issue of fact as to the necessity of participating in the 2700-acre plantation in order to produce income from the general partnership acreage, and as to their ability to affect decisionmaking regarding that larger plantation. They have not, as did the plaintiff-investors in *Williamson*, made only vague statements that they relied and were dependent upon the efforts of the promoters. Having raised a genuine question as to the third *Williamson* factor, they likewise have created a genuine question for the trier of fact as to whether at the time of their investment they expected any profit to arise essentially through the efforts of others. The district court's grant of summary judgment in favor of the promoters must therefore be reversed.

. . .

3. APPENDIX

UNIFORM LIMITED LIABILITY COMPANY ACT (1997, Last Amended 2013)

ARTICLE 1. GENERAL PROVISIONS

Section 101. Short title.

This [act] may be cited as the Uniform Limited Liability Company Act.

Section 102. Definitions.

In this [act]:

(1) "Certificate of organization" means the certificate required by Section 201. The term includes the certificate as amended or restated.

(2) "Contribution", except in the phrase "right of contribution", means property or a benefit described in Section 402 which is provided by a person to a limited liability company to become a member or in the person's capacity as a member.

(3) "Debtor in bankruptcy" means a person that is the subject of:

(A) an order for relief under Title 11 of the United States Code or a comparable order under a successor statute of general application; or

(B) a comparable order under federal, state, or foreign law governing insolvency.

(4) "Distribution" means a transfer of money or other property from a limited liability company to a person on account of a transferable interest or in the person's capacity as a member. The term:

(A) includes:

(i) a redemption or other purchase by a limited liability company of a transferable interest; and

(ii) a transfer to a member in return for the member's relinquishment of any right to participate as a member in the management or conduct of the company's activities and affairs or to have access to records or other information concerning the company's activities and affairs; and

(B) does not include amounts constituting reasonable compensation for present or past service or payments made in the ordinary course of business under a bona fide retirement plan or other bona fide benefits program.

(5) "Foreign limited liability company" means an unincorporated entity formed under the law of a jurisdiction other than this state which would be a limited liability company if formed under the law of this state.

(6) "Jurisdiction", used to refer to a political entity, means the United States, a state, a foreign county, or a political subdivision of a foreign country.

(7) "Jurisdiction of formation" means the jurisdiction whose law governs the internal affairs of an entity.

(8) "Limited liability company", except in the phrase "foreign limited liability company" and in [Article] 10, means an entity formed

under this [act] or which becomes subject to this [act] under [Article] 10 or Section 110.

(9) "Manager" means a person that under the operating agreement of a manager-managed limited liability company is responsible, alone or in concert with others, for performing the management functions stated in Section 407(c).

(10) "Manager-managed limited liability company" means a limited liability company that qualifies under Section 407(a).

(11) "Member" means a person that:

(A) has become a member of a limited liability company under Section 401 or was a member in a company when the company became subject to this [act] under Section 110; and

(B) has not dissociated under Section 602.

(12) "Member-managed limited liability company" means a limited liability company that is not a manager-managed limited liability company.

(13) "Operating agreement" means the agreement, whether or not referred to as an operating agreement and whether oral, implied, in a record, or in any combination thereof, of all the members of a limited liability company, including a sole member, concerning the matters described in Section 105(a). The term includes the agreement as amended or restated.

(14) "Organizer" means a person that acts under Section 201 to form a limited liability company.

(15) "Person" means an individual, business corporation, nonprofit corporation, partnership, limited partnership, limited liability company, [general cooperative association,] limited cooperative association, unincorporated nonprofit association, statutory trust, business trust, common-law business trust, estate, trust, association, joint venture, public corporation, government or governmental subdivision, agency, or instrumentality, or any other legal or commercial entity.

(16) "Principal office" means the principal executive office of a limited liability company or foreign limited liability company, whether or not the office is located in this state.

(17) "Property" means all property, whether real, personal, or mixed or tangible or intangible, or any right or interest therein.

(18) "Record", used as a noun, means information that is inscribed on a tangible medium or that is stored in an electronic or other medium and is retrievable in perceivable form.

(19) "Registered agent" means an agent of a limited liability company or foreign limited liability company which is authorized to receive service of any process, notice, or demand required or permitted by law to be served on the company.

(20) "Registered foreign limited liability company" means a foreign limited liability company that is registered to do business in this state pursuant to a statement of registration filed by the [Secretary of State].

(21) "Sign" means, with present intent to authenticate or adopt a record:

(A) to execute or adopt a tangible symbol; or

(B) to attach to or logically associate with the record an electronic symbol, sound, or process.

(22) "State" means a state of the United States, the District of Columbia, Puerto Rico, the United States Virgin Islands, or any territory or insular possession subject to the jurisdiction of the United States.

(23) "Transfer" includes:

(A) an assignment;

(B) a conveyance;

(C) a sale;

(D) a lease;

(E) an encumbrance, including a mortgage or security interest;

(F) a gift; and

(G) a transfer by operation of law.

(24) "Transferable interest" means the right, as initially owned by a person in the person's capacity as a member, to receive distributions from a limited liability company, whether or not the person remains a member or continues to own any part of the right. The term applies to any fraction of the interest, by whomever owned.

(25) "Transferee" means a person to which all or part of a transferable interest has been transferred, whether or not the transferor is a member. The term includes a person that owns a transferable interest under Section 603(a)(3).

Section 103. Knowledge; notice.

(a) A person knows a fact if the person:

(1) has actual knowledge of it; or

(2) is deemed to know it under subsection (d)(1) or law other than this [act].

(b) A person has notice of a fact if the person:

(1) has reason to know the fact from all the facts known to the person at the time in question; or

(2) is deemed to have notice of the fact under subsection (d)(2).

(c) Subject to Section 210(f), a person notifies another person of a fact by taking steps reasonably required to inform the other person in ordinary course, whether or not those steps cause the other person to know the fact.

(d) A person not a member is deemed:

(1) to know of a limitation on authority to transfer real property as provided in Section 302(g); and

(2) to have notice of a limited liability company's:

(A) dissolution 90 days after a statement of dissolution under Section 702(b)(2)(A) becomes effective;

(B) termination 90 days after a statement of termination under Section 702(b)(2)(F) becomes effective; and

(C) participation in a merger, interest exchange, conversion, or domestication, 90 days after articles of merger, interest exchange, conversion, or domestication under [Article] 10 become effective.

Section 104. Governing law.

The law of this state governs:

(1) the internal affairs of a limited liability company; and

(2) the liability of a member as member and a manager as manager for a debt, obligation, or other liability of a limited liability company.

Section 105. Operating agreement; scope, function, and limitations.

(a) Except as otherwise provided in subsections (c) and (d), the operating agreement governs:

(1) relations among the members as members and between the members and the limited liability company;

(2) the rights and duties under this [act] of a person in the capacity of manager;

(3) the activities and affairs of the company and the conduct of those activities and affairs; and

(4) the means and conditions for amending the operating agreement.

(b) To the extent the operating agreement does not provide for a matter described in subsection (a), this [act] governs the matter.

(c) An operating agreement may not:

(1) vary the law applicable under Section 104;

(2) vary a limited liability company's capacity under Section 109 to sue and be sued in its own name;

(3) vary any requirement, procedure, or other provision of this [act] pertaining to:

(A) registered agents; or

(B) the [Secretary of State], including provisions pertaining to records authorized or required to be delivered to the [Secretary of State] for filing under this [act];

(4) vary the provisions of Section 204;

(5) alter or eliminate the duty of loyalty or the duty of care, except as otherwise provided in subsection (d);

(6) eliminate the contractual obligation of good faith and fair dealing under Section 409(d), but the operating agreement may prescribe the standards, if not manifestly unreasonable, by which the performance of the obligation is to be measured;

(7) relieve or exonerate a person from liability for conduct involving bad faith, willful or intentional misconduct, or knowing violation of law;

(8) unreasonably restrict the duties and rights under Section 410, but the operating agreement may impose reasonable restrictions on the availability and use of information obtained under that section and may define appropriate remedies, including liquidated damages, for a breach of any reasonable restriction on use;

(9) vary the causes of dissolution specified in Section 701(a)(4);

(10) vary the requirement to wind up the company's activities and affairs as specified in Section 702(a), (b)(1), and (e);

(11) unreasonably restrict the right of a member to maintain an action under [Article] 8;

(12) vary the provisions of Section 805, but the operating agreement may provide that the company may not have a special litigation committee;

(13) vary the right of a member to approve a merger, interest exchange, conversion, or domestication under Section 1023(a)(2), 1033(a)(2), 1043(a)(2), or 1053(a)(2);

(14) vary the required contents of a plan of merger under Section 1022(a), plan of interest exchange under Section 1032(a), plan of conversion under Section 1042(a), or plan of domestication under Section 1052(a); or

(15) except as otherwise provided in Sections 106 and 107(b), restrict the rights under this [act] of a person other than a member or manager.

(d) Subject to subsection (c)(7), without limiting other terms that may be included in an operating agreement, the following rules apply:

(1) The operating agreement may:

(A) specify the method by which a specific act or transaction that would otherwise violate the duty of loyalty may be authorized or ratified by one or more disinterested and independent persons after full disclosure of all material facts; and

(B) alter the prohibition in Section 405(a)(2) so that the prohibition requires only that the company's total assets not be less than the sum of its total liabilities.

(2) To the extent the operating agreement of a member-managed limited liability company expressly relieves a member of a responsibility that the member otherwise would have under this [act] and imposes the responsibility on one or more other members, the agreement also may eliminate or limit any fiduciary duty of the member relieved of the responsibility which would have pertained to the responsibility.

(3) If not manifestly unreasonable, the operating agreement may:

(A) alter or eliminate the aspects of the duty of loyalty stated in Section 409(b) and (i);

(B) identify specific types or categories of activities that do not violate the duty of loyalty;

(C) alter the duty of care, but may not authorize conduct involving bad faith, willful or intentional misconduct, or knowing violation of law; and

(D) alter or eliminate any other fiduciary duty.

(e) The court shall decide as a matter of law whether a term of an operating agreement is manifestly unreasonable under subsection (c)(6) or (d)(3). The court:

(1) shall make its determination as of the time the challenged term became part of the operating agreement and by considering only circumstances existing at that time; and

(2) may invalidate the term only if, in light of the purposes, activities, and affairs of the limited liability company, it is readily apparent that:

(A) the objective of the term is unreasonable; or

(B) the term is an unreasonable means to achieve the term's objective.

Section 106. Operating agreement; effect on limited liability company and person becoming member; preformation agreement.

(a) A limited liability company is bound by and may enforce the operating agreement, whether or not the company has itself manifested assent to the operating agreement.

(b) A person that becomes a member is deemed to assent to the operating agreement.

(c) Two or more persons intending to become the initial members of a limited liability company may make an agreement providing that upon the formation of the company the agreement will become the operating agreement. One person intending to become the initial member of a limited liability company may assent to terms providing that upon the formation of the company the terms will become the operating agreement.

Section 108. Nature, purpose, and duration of limited liability company.

(a) A limited liability company is an entity distinct from its member or members.

(b) A limited liability company may have any lawful purpose, regardless of whether for profit.

(c) A limited liability company has perpetual duration.

Section 109. Powers.

A limited liability company has the capacity to sue and be sued in its own name and the power to do all things necessary or convenient to carry on its activities and affairs.

ARTICLE 2. FORMATION; CERTIFICATE OF ORGANIZATION AND OTHER FILINGS

Section 201. Formation of limited liability company; certificate of organization.

(a) One or more persons may act as organizers to form a limited liability company by delivering to the [Secretary of State] for filing a certificate of organization.

(b) A certificate of organization must state:

(1) the name of the limited liability company, which must comply with Section 112;

(2) the street and mailing addresses of the company's principal office; and

(3) the name and street and mailing addresses in this state of the company's registered agent.

(c) A certificate of organization may contain statements as to matters other than those required by subsection (b), but may not vary or otherwise affect the provisions specified in Section 105(c) and (d) in a manner inconsistent with that section. However, a statement in a certificate of organization is not effective as a statement of authority.

(d) A limited liability company is formed when the certificate of organization becomes effective and at least one person has become a member.

Section 202. Amendment or restatement of certificate of organization.

(a) A certificate of organization may be amended or restated at any time.

(b) To amend its certificate of organization, a limited liability company must deliver to the [Secretary of State] for filing an amendment stating:

(1) the name of the company;

(2) the date of filing of its initial certificate; and

(3) the text of the amendment.

(c) To restate its certificate of organization, a limited liability company must deliver to the [Secretary of State] for filing a restatement, designated as such in its heading.

(d) If a member of a member-managed limited liability company, or a manager of a manager-managed limited liability company, knows that any information in a filed certificate of organization was inaccurate when the certificate was filed or has become inaccurate due to changed circumstances, the member or manager shall promptly:

(1) cause the certificate to be amended; or

(2) if appropriate, deliver to the [Secretary of State] for filing a statement of change under Section 116 or a statement of correction under Section 209.

ARTICLE 3. RELATIONS OF MEMBERS AND MANAGERS TO PERSONS DEALING WITH LIMITED LIABILITY COMPANY

Section 301. No agency power of member as member.

(a) A member is not an agent of a limited liability company solely by reason of being a member.

(b) A person's status as a member does not prevent or restrict law other than this [act] from imposing liability on a limited liability company because of the person's conduct.

Section 302. Statement of limited liability company authority.

(a) A limited liability company may deliver to the [Secretary of State] for filing a statement of authority. The statement:

(1) must include the name of the company and the name and street and mailing addresses of its registered agent;

(2) with respect to any position that exists in or with respect to the company, may state the authority, or limitations on the authority, of all persons holding the position to:

(A) sign an instrument transferring real property held in the name of the company; or

(B) enter into other transactions on behalf of, or otherwise act for or bind, the company; and

(3) may state the authority, or limitations on the authority, of a specific person to:

(A) sign an instrument transferring real property held in the name of the company; or

(B) enter into other transactions on behalf of, or otherwise act for or bind, the company.

(b) To amend or cancel a statement of authority filed by the [Secretary of State], a limited liability company must deliver to the [Secretary of State] for filing an amendment or cancellation stating:

(1) the name of the company;

(2) the name and street and mailing addresses of the company's registered agent;

(3) the date the statement being affected became effective; and

(4) the contents of the amendment or a declaration that the statement is canceled.

(c) A statement of authority affects only the power of a person to bind a limited liability company to persons that are not members.

(d) Subject to subsection (c) and Section 103(d), and except as otherwise provided in subsections (f), (g), and (h), a limitation on the authority of a person or a position contained in an effective statement of authority is not by itself evidence of any person's knowledge or notice of the limitation.

(e) Subject to subsection (c), a grant of authority not pertaining to transfers of real property and contained in an effective statement of authority is conclusive in favor of a person that gives value in reliance on the grant, except to the extent that when the person gives value:

(1) the person has knowledge to the contrary;

(2) the statement has been canceled or restrictively amended under subsection (b); or

(3) a limitation on the grant is contained in another statement of authority that became effective after the statement containing the grant became effective.

. . .

Section 303. Statement of denial.

A person named in a filed statement of authority granting that person authority may deliver to the [Secretary of State] for filing a statement of denial that:

(1) provides the name of the limited liability company and the caption of the statement of authority to which the statement of denial pertains; and

(2) denies the grant of authority.

Section 304. Liability of members and managers.

(a) A debt, obligation, or other liability of a limited liability company is solely the debt, obligation, or other liability of the company. A member or manager is not personally liable, directly or indirectly, by way of contribution or otherwise, for a debt, obligation, or other liability of the company solely by reason of being or acting as a member or manager. This subsection applies regardless of the dissolution of the company.

(b) The failure of a limited liability company to observe formalities relating to the exercise of its powers or management of its activities and affairs is not a ground for imposing liability on a member or manager for a debt, obligation, or other liability of the company.

ARTICLE 4. RELATIONS OF MEMBERS TO EACH OTHER AND TO LIMITED LIABILITY COMPANY

Section 401. Becoming member.

(a) If a limited liability company is to have only one member upon formation, the person becomes a member as agreed by that person and the organizer of the company. That person and the organizer may be, but need not be, different persons. If different, the organizer acts on behalf of the initial member.

(b) If a limited liability company is to have more than one member upon formation, those persons become members as agreed by the persons before the formation of the company. The organizer acts on behalf of the persons in forming the company and may be, but need not be, one of the persons.

(c) After formation of a limited liability company, a person becomes a member:

(1) as provided in the operating agreement;

(2) as the result of a transaction effective under [Article] 10;

(3) with the affirmative vote or consent of all the members; or

(4) as provided in Section 701(a)(3).

(d) A person may become a member without:

(1) acquiring a transferable interest; or

(2) making or being obligated to make a contribution to the limited liability company.

Section 402. Form of contribution.

A contribution may consist of property transferred to, services performed for, or another benefit provided to the limited liability company or an agreement to transfer property to, perform services for, or provide another benefit to the company.

Section 403. Liability for contributions.

(a) A person's obligation to make a contribution to a limited liability company is not excused by the person's death, disability, termination, or other inability to perform personally.

(b) If a person does not fulfill an obligation to make a contribution other than money, the person is obligated at the option of the limited liability company to contribute money equal to the value of the part of the contribution which has not been made.

(c) The obligation of a person to make a contribution may be compromised only by the affirmative vote or consent of all the members. If a creditor of a limited liability company extends credit or otherwise acts in reliance on an obligation described in subsection (a) without knowledge or notice of a compromise under this subsection, the creditor may enforce the obligation.

Section 404. Sharing of and right to distributions before dissolution.

(a) Any distribution made by a limited liability company before its dissolution and winding up must be in equal shares among members and persons dissociated as members, except to the extent necessary to comply with a transfer effective under Section 502 or charging order in effect under Section 503.

(b) A person has a right to a distribution before the dissolution and winding up of a limited liability company only if the company decides to make an interim distribution. A person's dissociation does not entitle the person to a distribution.

(c) A person does not have a right to demand or receive a distribution from a limited liability company in any form other than money. Except as otherwise provided in Section 707(d), a company may distribute an asset in kind only if each part of the asset is fungible with each other part and each person receives a percentage of the asset equal in value to the person's share of distributions.

(d) If a member or transferee becomes entitled to receive a distribution, the member or transferee has the status of, and is entitled to all remedies available to, a creditor of the limited liability company with respect to the distribution. However, the company's obligation to make a distribution is subject to offset for any amount owed to the company by the member or a person dissociated as a member on whose account the distribution is made.

Section 405. Limitations on distributions.

(a) A limited liability company may not make a distribution, including a distribution under Section 707, if after the distribution:

(1) the company would not be able to pay its debts as they become due in the ordinary course of the company's activities and affairs; or

(2) the company's total assets would be less than the sum of its total liabilities plus the amount that would be needed, if the company were to be dissolved and wound up at the time of the distribution, to satisfy the preferential rights upon dissolution and winding up of members and transferees whose preferential rights are superior to the rights of persons receiving the distribution.

(b) A limited liability company may base a determination that a distribution is not prohibited under subsection (a) on:

(1) financial statements prepared on the basis of accounting practices and principles that are reasonable in the circumstances; or

(2) a fair valuation or other method that is reasonable under the circumstances.

. . .

Section 406. Liability for improper distributions.

(a) Except as otherwise provided in subsection (b), if a member of a member-managed limited liability company or manager of a manager-managed limited liability company consents to a distribution made in violation of Section 405 and in consenting to the distribution fails to comply with Section 409, the member or manager is personally liable to the company for the amount of the distribution which exceeds the amount that could have been distributed without the violation of Section 405.

(b) To the extent the operating agreement of a member-managed limited liability company expressly relieves a member of the authority and responsibility to consent to distributions and imposes that authority and responsibility on one or more other members, the liability stated in subsection (a) applies to the other members and not the member that the operating agreement relieves of the authority and responsibility.

(c) A person that receives a distribution knowing that the distribution violated Section 405 is personally liable to the limited liability company but only to the extent that the distribution received by the person exceeded the amount that could have been properly paid under Section 405.

. . .

Section 407. Management of limited liability company.

(a) A limited liability company is a member-managed limited liability company unless the operating agreement:

(1) expressly provides that:

(A) the company is or will be "manager-managed";

(B) the company is or will be "managed by managers"; or

(C) management of the company is or will be "vested in managers"; or

(2) includes words of similar import.

(b) In a member-managed limited liability company, the following rules apply:

(1) Except as expressly provided in this [act], the management and conduct of the company are vested in the members.

(2) Each member has equal rights in the management and conduct of the company's activities and affairs.

(3) A difference arising among members as to a matter in the ordinary course of the activities and affairs of the company may be decided by a majority of the members.

(4) The affirmative vote or consent of all the members is required to:

(A) undertake an act outside the ordinary course of the activities and affairs of the company; or

(B) amend the operating agreement.

(c) In a manager-managed limited liability company, the following rules apply:

(1) Except as expressly provided in this [act], any matter relating to the activities and affairs of the company is decided exclusively by the manager, or, if there is more than one manager, by a majority of the managers.

(2) Each manager has equal rights in the management and conduct of the company's activities and affairs.

(3) The affirmative vote or consent of all members is required to:

(A) undertake an act outside the ordinary course of the company's activities and affairs; or

(B) amend the operating agreement.

(4) A manager may be chosen at any time by the affirmative vote or consent of a majority of the members and remains a manager until a successor has been chosen, unless the manager at an earlier time resigns, is removed, or dies, or, in the case of a manager that is not an individual, terminates. A manager may be removed at any time by the affirmative vote or consent of a majority of the members without notice or cause.

(5) A person need not be a member to be a manager, but the dissociation of a member that is also a manager removes the person as a manager. If a person that is both a manager and a member ceases to be a manager, that cessation does not by itself dissociate the person as a member.

(6) A person's ceasing to be a manager does not discharge any debt, obligation, or other liability to the limited liability company or members which the person incurred while a manager.

(d) An action requiring the vote or consent of members under this [act] may be taken without a meeting, and a member may appoint a proxy or other agent to vote, consent, or otherwise act for the member by signing an appointing record, personally or by the member's agent.

(e) The dissolution of a limited liability company does not affect the applicability of this section. However, a person that wrongfully causes dissolution of the company loses the right to participate in management as a member and a manager.

(f) A limited liability company shall reimburse a member for an advance to the company beyond the amount of capital the member agreed to contribute.

(g) A payment or advance made by a member which gives rise to a limited liability company obligation under subsection (f) or Section 408(a) constitutes a loan to the company which accrues interest from the date of the payment or advance.

(h) A member is not entitled to remuneration for services performed for a member-managed limited liability company, except for reasonable compensation for services rendered in winding up the activities of the company.

Section 408. Reimbursement; indemnification; advancement; and insurance.

(a) A limited liability company shall reimburse a member of a member-managed company or the manager of a manager-managed company for any payment made by the member or manager in the course of the member's or manager's activities on behalf of the company, if the member or manager complied with Sections 405, 407, and 409 in making the payment.

(b) A limited liability company shall indemnify and hold harmless a person with respect to any claim or demand against the person and any debt, obligation, or other liability incurred by the person by reason of the person's former or present capacity as a member or manager, if the claim, demand, debt, obligation, or other liability does not arise from the person's breach of Section 405, 407, or 409.

(c) In the ordinary course of its activities and affairs, a limited liability company may advance reasonable expenses, including attorney's fees and costs, incurred by a person in connection with a claim or demand against the person by reason of the person's former or present capacity as a member or manager, if the person promises to repay the company if the person ultimately is determined not to be entitled to be indemnified under subsection (b).

(d) A limited liability company may purchase and maintain insurance on behalf of a member or manager against liability asserted against or incurred by the member or manager in that capacity or arising from that status even if, under Section 105(c)(7), the operating agreement could not eliminate or limit the person's liability to the company for the conduct giving rise to the liability.

Section 409. Standards of conduct for members and managers.

(a) A member of a member-managed limited liability company owes to the company and, subject to Section 801, the other members the duties of loyalty and care stated in subsections (b) and (c).

(b) The fiduciary duty of loyalty of a member in a member-managed limited liability company includes the duties:

(1) to account to the company and hold as trustee for it any property, profit, or benefit derived by the member:

(A) in the conduct or winding up of the company's activities and affairs;

(B) from a use by the member of the company's property; or

(C) from the appropriation of a company opportunity;

(2) to refrain from dealing with the company in the conduct or winding up of the company's activities and affairs as or on behalf of a person having an interest adverse to the company; and

(3) to refrain from competing with the company in the conduct of the company's activities and affairs before the dissolution of the company.

(c) The duty of care of a member of a member-managed limited liability company in the conduct or winding up of the company's activities and affairs is to refrain from engaging in grossly negligent or reckless conduct, willful or intentional misconduct, or knowing violation of law.

(d) A member shall discharge the duties and obligations under this [act] or under the operating agreement and exercise any rights consistently with the contractual obligation of good faith and fair dealing.

(e) A member does not violate a duty or obligation under this [act] or under the operating agreement solely because the member's conduct furthers the member's own interest.

(f) All the members of a member-managed limited liability company or a manager-managed limited liability company may authorize or ratify, after full disclosure of all material facts, a specific act or transaction that otherwise would violate the duty of loyalty.

(g) It is a defense to a claim under subsection (b)(2) and any comparable claim in equity or at common law that the transaction was fair to the limited liability company.

(h) If, as permitted by subsection (f) or (i)(6) or the operating agreement, a member enters into a transaction with the limited liability company which otherwise would be prohibited by subsection (b)(2), the member's rights and obligations arising from the transaction are the same as those of a person that is not a member.

(i) In a manager-managed limited liability company, the following rules apply:

(1) Subsections (a), (b), (c), and (g) apply to the manager or managers and not the members.

(2) The duty stated under subsection (b)(3) continues until winding up is completed.

(3) Subsection (d) applies to managers and members.

(4) Subsection (e) applies only to members.

(5) The power to ratify under subsection (f) applies only to the members.

(6) Subject to subsection (d), a member does not have any duty to the company or to any other member solely by reason of being a member.

Section 410. Rights to information of member, manager, and person dissociated as member.

(a) In a member-managed limited liability company, the following rules apply:

(1) On reasonable notice, a member may inspect and copy during regular business hours, at a reasonable location specified by the company, any record maintained by the company regarding the company's activities, affairs, financial condition, and other circumstances, to the extent the information is material to the member's rights and duties under the operating agreement or this [act].

(2) The company shall furnish to each member:

(A) without demand, any information concerning the company's activities, affairs, financial condition, and other circumstances which the company knows and is material to the proper exercise of the member's rights and duties under the operating agreement or this [act], except to the extent the company can establish that it reasonably believes the member already knows the information; and

(B) on demand, any other information concerning the company's activities, affairs, financial condition, and other circumstances, except to the extent the demand for the information demanded is unreasonable or otherwise improper under the circumstances.

(3) The duty to furnish information under paragraph (2) also applies to each member to the extent the member knows any of the information described in paragraph (2).

(b) In a manager-managed limited liability company, the following rules apply:

(1) The informational rights stated in subsection (a) and the duty stated in subsection (a)(3) apply to the managers and not the members.

(2) During regular business hours and at a reasonable location specified by the company, a member may inspect and copy information regarding the activities, affairs, financial condition, and other circumstances of the company as is just and reasonable if:

(A) the member seeks the information for a purpose reasonably related to the member's interest as a member;

(B) the member makes a demand in a record received by the company, describing with reasonable particularity the information sought and the purpose for seeking the information; and

(C) the information sought is directly connected to the member's purpose.

(3) Not later than 10 days after receiving a demand pursuant to paragraph (2)(B), the company shall inform in a record the member that made the demand of:

(A) what information the company will provide in response to the demand and when and where the company will provide the information; and

(B) the company's reasons for declining, if the company declines to provide any demanded information.

(4) Whenever this [act] or an operating agreement provides for a member to vote on or give or withhold consent to a matter, before the vote is cast or consent is given or withheld, the company shall, without demand, provide the member with all information that is known to the company and is material to the member's decision.

(c) Subject to subsection (h), on 10 days' demand made in a record received by a limited liability company, a person dissociated as a member may have access to the information to which the person was entitled while a member if:

(1) the information pertains to the period during which the person was a member;

(2) the person seeks the information in good faith; and

(3) the person satisfies the requirements imposed on a member by subsection (b)(2).

(d) A limited liability company shall respond to a demand made pursuant to subsection (c) in the manner provided in subsection (b)(3).

(e) A limited liability company may charge a person that makes a demand under this section the reasonable costs of copying, limited to the costs of labor and material.

(f) A member or person dissociated as a member may exercise the rights under this section through an agent or, in the case of an individual under legal disability, a legal representative. Any restriction or condition imposed by the operating agreement or under subsection (h) applies both to the agent or legal representative and to the member or person dissociated as a member.

(g) Subject to Section 504, the rights under this section do not extend to a person as transferee.

(h) In addition to any restriction or condition stated in its operating agreement, a limited liability company, as a matter within the ordinary course of its activities and affairs, may impose reasonable restrictions and conditions on access to and use of information to be furnished under this section, including designating information confidential and imposing nondisclosure and safeguarding obligations on the recipient. In a dispute concerning the reasonableness of a restriction under this subsection, the company has the burden of proving reasonableness.

ARTICLE 5. TRANSFERABLE INTERESTS AND RIGHTS OF TRANSFEREES AND CREDITORS

Section 501. Nature of transferable interest.

A transferable interest is personal property.

Section 502. Transfer of transferable interest.

(a) Subject to Section 503(f), a transfer, in whole or in part, of a transferable interest:

(1) is permissible;

(2) does not by itself cause a person's dissociation as a member or a dissolution and winding up of the limited liability company's activities and affairs; and

(3) subject to Section 504, does not entitle the transferee to:

(A) participate in the management or conduct of the company's activities and affairs; or

(B) except as otherwise provided in subsection (c), have access to records or other information concerning the company's activities and affairs.

(b) A transferee has the right to receive, in accordance with the transfer, distributions to which the transferor would otherwise be entitled.

(c) In a dissolution and winding up of a limited liability company, a transferee is entitled to an account of the company's transactions only from the date of dissolution.

(d) A transferable interest may be evidenced by a certificate of the interest issued by a limited liability company in a record, and, subject to this section, the interest represented by the certificate may be transferred by a transfer of the certificate.

(e) A limited liability company need not give effect to a transferee's rights under this section until the company knows or has notice of the transfer.

(f) A transfer of a transferable interest in violation of a restriction on transfer contained in the operating agreement is ineffective if the intended transferee has knowledge or notice of the restriction at the time of transfer.

(g) Except as otherwise provided in Section 602(5)(B), if a member transfers a transferable interest, the transferor retains the rights of a member other than the transferable interest transferred and retains all the duties and obligations of a member.

(h) If a member transfers a transferable interest to a person that becomes a member with respect to the transferred interest, the transferee is liable for the member's obligations under Sections 403 and 406 known to the transferee when the transferee becomes a member.

ARTICLE 6. DISSOCIATION

Section 601. Power to dissociate as member; wrongful dissociation.

(a) A person has the power to dissociate as a member at any time, rightfully or wrongfully, by withdrawing as a member by express will under Section 602(1).

(b) A person's dissociation as a member is wrongful only if the dissociation:

(1) is in breach of an express provision of the operating agreement; or

(2) occurs before the completion of the winding up of the limited liability company and:

(A) the person withdraws as a member by express will;

(B) the person is expelled as a member by judicial order under Section 602(6);

(C) the person is dissociated under Section 602(8); or

(D) in the case of a person that is not a trust other than a business trust, an estate, or an individual, the person is expelled or otherwise dissociated as a member because it willfully dissolved or terminated.

(c) A person that wrongfully dissociates as a member is liable to the limited liability company and, subject to Section 801, to the other members for damages caused by the dissociation. The liability is in addition to any debt, obligation, or other liability of the member to the company or the other members.

Section 602. Events causing dissociation.

A person is dissociated as a member when:

(1) the limited liability company knows or has notice of the person's express will to withdraw as a member, but, if the person has specified a withdrawal date later than the date the company knew or had notice, on that later date;

(2) an event stated in the operating agreement as causing the person's dissociation occurs;

(3) the person's entire interest is transferred in a foreclosure sale under Section 503(f);

(4) the person is expelled as a member pursuant to the operating agreement;

(5) the person is expelled as a member by the affirmative vote or consent of all the other members if:

(A) it is unlawful to carry on the limited liability company's activities and affairs with the person as a member;

(B) there has been a transfer of all the person's transferable interest in the company, other than:

(i) a transfer for security purposes; or

(ii) a charging order in effect under Section 503 which has not been foreclosed;

(C) the person is an entity and:

(i) the company notifies the person that it will be expelled as a member because the person has filed a statement of dissolution or the equivalent, the person has been administratively dissolved, the person's charter or the equivalent has been revoked, or the person's right to conduct business has been suspended by the person's jurisdiction of formation; and

(ii) not later than 90 days after the notification, the statement of dissolution or the equivalent has not been withdrawn, rescinded, or revoked, the person has not been reinstated, or the person's charter or the equivalent or right to conduct business has not been reinstated; or

(D) the person is an unincorporated entity that has been dissolved and whose activities and affairs are being wound up;

(6) on application by the limited liability company or a member in a direct action under Section 801, the person is expelled as a member by judicial order because the person:

(A) has engaged or is engaging in wrongful conduct that has affected adversely and materially, or will affect adversely and materially, the company's activities and affairs;

(B) has committed willfully or persistently, or is committing willfully or persistently, a material breach of the operating agreement or a duty or obligation under Section 409; or

(C) has engaged or is engaging in conduct relating to the company's activities and affairs which makes it not reasonably practicable to carry on the activities and affairs with the person as a member;

(7) in the case of an individual:

(A) the individual dies; or

(B) in a member-managed limited liability company:

(i) a guardian or general conservator for the individual is appointed; or

(ii) a court orders that the individual has otherwise become incapable of performing the individual's duties as a member under this [act] or the operating agreement;

(8) in a member-managed limited liability company, the person:

(A) becomes a debtor in bankruptcy;

(B) signs an assignment for the benefit of creditors; or

(C) seeks, consents to, or acquiesces in the appointment of a trustee, receiver, or liquidator of the person or of all or substantially all the person's property;

(9) in the case of a person that is a testamentary or inter vivos trust or is acting as a member by virtue of being a trustee of such a trust, the trust's entire transferable interest in the limited liability company is distributed;

(10) in the case of a person that is an estate or is acting as a member by virtue of being a personal representative of an estate, the estate's entire transferable interest in the limited liability company is distributed;

(11) in the case of a person that is not an individual, the existence of the person terminates;

(12) the limited liability company participates in a merger under [Article] 10 and:

(A) the company is not the surviving entity; or

(B) otherwise as a result of the merger, the person ceases to be a member;

(13) the limited liability company participates in an interest exchange under [Article] 10 and, as a result of the interest exchange, the person ceases to be a member;

(14) the limited liability company participates in a conversion under [Article] 10;

(15) the limited liability company participates in a domestication under [Article] 10 and, as a result of the domestication, the person ceases to be a member; or

(16) the limited liability company dissolves and completes winding up.

Section 603. Effect of dissociation.

(a) If a person is dissociated as a member:

(1) the person's right to participate as a member in the management and conduct of the limited liability company's activities and affairs terminates;

(2) the person's duties and obligations under Section 409 as a member end with regard to matters arising and events occurring after the person's dissociation; and

(3) subject to Section 504 and [Article] 10, any transferable interest owned by the person in the person's capacity as a member

immediately before dissociation is owned by the person solely as a transferee.

(b) A person's dissociation as a member does not of itself discharge the person from any debt, obligation, or other liability to the limited liability company or the other members which the person incurred while a member.

ARTICLE 7. DISSOLUTION AND WINDING UP

Section 701. Events causing dissolution.

(a) A limited liability company is dissolved, and its activities and affairs must be wound up, upon the occurrence of any of the following:

(1) an event or circumstance that the operating agreement states causes dissolution;

(2) the affirmative vote or consent of all the members;

(3) the passage of 90 consecutive days during which the company has no members unless before the end of the period:

(A) consent to admit at least one specified person as a member is given by transferees owning the rights to receive a majority of distributions as transferees at the time the consent is to be effective; and

(B) at least one person becomes a member in accordance with the consent;

(4) on application by a member, the entry by [the appropriate court] of an order dissolving the company on the grounds that:

(A) the conduct of all or substantially all the company's activities and affairs is unlawful;

(B) it is not reasonably practicable to carry on the company's activities and affairs in conformity with the certificate of organization and the operating agreement; or

(C) the managers or those members in control of the company:

(i) have acted, are acting, or will act in a manner that is illegal or fraudulent; or

(ii) have acted or are acting in a manner that is oppressive and was, is, or will be directly harmful to the applicant; or

(5) the signing and filing of a statement of administrative dissolution by the [Secretary of State] under Section 708.

(b) In a proceeding brought under subsection (a)(4)(C), the court may order a remedy other than dissolution.

Section 702. Winding up.

(a) A dissolved limited liability company shall wind up its activities and affairs and, except as otherwise provided in Section 703, the company continues after dissolution only for the purpose of winding up.

(b) In winding up its activities and affairs, a limited liability company:

(1) shall discharge the company's debts, obligations, and other liabilities, settle and close the company's activities and affairs, and marshal and distribute the assets of the company; and

(2) may:

(A) deliver to the [Secretary of State] for filing a statement of dissolution stating the name of the company and that the company is dissolved;

(B) preserve the company activities, affairs, and property as a going concern for a reasonable time;

(C) prosecute and defend actions and proceedings, whether civil, criminal, or administrative;

(D) transfer the company's property;

(E) settle disputes by mediation or arbitration;

(F) deliver to the [Secretary of State] for filing a statement of termination stating the name of the company and that the company is terminated; and

(G) perform other acts necessary or appropriate to the winding up.

(c) If a dissolved limited liability company has no members, the legal representative of the last person to have been a member may wind up the activities and affairs of the company. If the person does so, the person has the powers of a sole manager under Section 407(c) and is deemed to be a manager for the purposes of Section 304(a).

(d) If the legal representative under subsection (c) declines or fails to wind up the limited liability company's activities and affairs, a person may be appointed to do so by the consent of transferees owning a majority of the rights to receive distributions as transferees at the time the consent is to be effective. A person appointed under this subsection:

(1) has the powers of a sole manager under Section 407(c) and is deemed to be a manager for the purposes of Section 304(a); and

(2) shall deliver promptly to the [Secretary of State] for filing an amendment to the company's certificate of organization stating:

(A) that the company has no members;

(B) the name and street and mailing addresses of the person; and

(C) that the person has been appointed pursuant to this subsection to wind up the company.

(e) [The appropriate court] may order judicial supervision of the winding up of a dissolved limited liability company, including the appointment of a person to wind up the company's activities and affairs:

(1) on the application of a member, if the applicant establishes good cause;

(2) on the application of a transferee, if:

(A) the company does not have any members;

(B) the legal representative of the last person to have been a member declines or fails to wind up the company's activities; and

(C) within a reasonable time following the dissolution a person has not been appointed pursuant to subsection (c); or

(3) in connection with a proceeding under Section 701(a)(4).

Section 704. Known claims against dissolved limited liability company.

(a) Except as otherwise provided in subsection (d), a dissolved limited liability company may give notice of a known claim under subsection (b), which has the effect provided in subsection (c).

(b) A dissolved limited liability company may in a record notify its known claimants of the dissolution. The notice must:

(1) specify the information required to be included in a claim;

(2) state that a claim must be in writing and provide a mailing address to which the claim is to be sent;

(3) state the deadline for receipt of a claim, which may not be less than 120 days after the date the notice is received by the claimant; and

(4) state that the claim will be barred if not received by the deadline.

(c) A claim against a dissolved limited liability company is barred if the requirements of subsection (b) are met and:

(1) the claim is not received by the specified deadline; or

(2) if the claim is timely received but rejected by the company:

(A) the company causes the claimant to receive a notice in a record stating that the claim is rejected and will be barred unless the claimant commences an action against the company to enforce the claim not later than 90 days after the claimant receives the notice; and

(B) the claimant does not commence the required action not later than 90 days after the claimant receives the notice.

(d) This section does not apply to a claim based on an event occurring after the date of dissolution or a liability that on that date is contingent.

Section 705. Other claims against dissolved limited liability company.

(a) A dissolved limited liability company may publish notice of its dissolution and request persons having claims against the company to present them in accordance with the notice.

. . .

Section 707. Disposition of assets in winding up.

(a) In winding up its activities and affairs, a limited liability company shall apply its assets to discharge the company's obligations to creditors, including members that are creditors.

(b) After a limited liability company complies with subsection (a), any surplus must be distributed in the following order, subject to any charging order in effect under Section 503:

(1) to each person owning a transferable interest that reflects contributions made and not previously returned, an amount equal to the value of the unreturned contributions; and

(2) among persons owning transferable interests in proportion to their respective rights to share in distributions immediately before the dissolution of the company.

(c) If a limited liability company does not have sufficient surplus to comply with subsection (b)(1), any surplus must be distributed among the owners of transferable interests in proportion to the value of the respective unreturned contributions.

(d) All distributions made under subsections (b) and (c) must be paid in money.

ARTICLE 8. ACTIONS BY MEMBERS

Section 801. Direct action by member.

(a) Subject to subsection (b), a member may maintain a direct action against another member, a manager, or the limited liability company to enforce the member's rights and protect the member's interests, including rights and interests under the operating agreement or this [act] or arising independently of the membership relationship.

(b) A member maintaining a direct action under this section must plead and prove an actual or threatened injury that is not solely the result of an injury suffered or threatened to be suffered by the limited liability company.

Section 802. Derivative action.

A member may maintain a derivative action to enforce a right of a limited liability company if:

(1) the member first makes a demand on the other members in a member-managed limited liability company, or the managers of a manager-managed limited liability company, requesting that they cause the company to bring an action to enforce the right, and the managers or other members do not bring the action within a reasonable time; or

(2) a demand under paragraph (1) would be futile.

Section 803. Proper plaintiff.

A derivative action to enforce a right of a limited liability company may be maintained only by a person that is a member at the time the action is commenced and:

(1) was a member when the conduct giving rise to the action occurred; or

(2) whose status as a member devolved on the person by operation of law or pursuant to the terms of the operating agreement from a person that was a member at the time of the conduct.

Section 804. Pleading.

In a derivative action, the complaint must state with particularity:

(1) the date and content of plaintiff's demand and the response to the demand by the managers or other members; or

(2) why demand should be excused as futile.

Section 805. Special litigation committee.

(a) If a limited liability company is named as or made a party in a derivative proceeding, the company may appoint a special litigation committee to investigate the claims asserted in the proceeding and determine whether pursuing the action is in the best interests of the company. If the company appoints a special litigation committee, on motion by the committee made in the name of the company, except for good cause shown, the court shall stay discovery for the time reasonably necessary to permit the committee to make its investigation. This subsection does not prevent the court from:

(1) enforcing a person's right to information under Section 410; or

(2) granting extraordinary relief in the form of a temporary restraining order or preliminary injunction.

(b) A special litigation committee must be composed of one or more disinterested and independent individuals, who may be members.

(c) A special litigation committee may be appointed:

(1) in a member-managed limited liability company:

(A) by the affirmative vote or consent of a majority of the members not named as parties in the proceeding; or

(B) if all members are named as parties in the proceeding, by a majority of the members named as defendants; or

(2) in a manager-managed limited liability company:

(A) by a majority of the managers not named as parties in the proceeding;

or

(B) if all managers are named as parties in the proceeding, by a majority of the managers named as defendants.

(d) After appropriate investigation, a special litigation committee may determine that it is in the best interests of the limited liability company that the proceeding:

(1) continue under the control of the plaintiff;

(2) continue under the control of the committee;

(3) be settled on terms approved by the committee; or

(4) be dismissed.

(e) After making a determination under subsection (d), a special litigation committee shall file with the court a statement of its determination and its report supporting its determination and shall serve each party with a copy of the determination and report. The court shall determine whether the members of the committee were disinterested and independent and whether the committee conducted its investigation and made its recommendation in good faith, independently, and with reasonable care, with the committee having the burden of proof. If the court finds that the members of the committee were disinterested and independent and that the committee acted in good faith, independently, and with reasonable care, the court shall enforce the determination of the committee. Otherwise, the court shall dissolve the stay of discovery entered under subsection (a) and allow the action to continue under the control of the plaintiff.

Section 806. Proceeds and expenses.

(a) Except as otherwise provided in subsection (b):

(1) any proceeds or other benefits of a derivative action, whether by judgment, compromise, or settlement, belong to the limited liability company and not to the plaintiff; and

(2) if the plaintiff receives any proceeds, the plaintiff shall remit them immediately to the company.

(b) If a derivative action is successful in whole or in part, the court may award the plaintiff reasonable expenses, including reasonable attorney's fees and costs, from the recovery of the limited liability company.

(c) A derivative action on behalf of a limited liability company may not be voluntarily dismissed or settled without the court's approval.

ARTICLE 9. FOREIGN LIMITED LIABILITY COMPANIES

Section 901. Governing law.

(a) The law of the jurisdiction of formation of a foreign limited liability company governs:

(1) the internal affairs of the company;

(2) the liability of a member as member and a manager as manager for a debt, obligation, or other liability of the company; and

(3) the liability of a series of the company.

(b) A foreign limited liability company is not precluded from registering to do business in this state because of any difference between the law of its jurisdiction of formation and the law of this state.

(c) Registration of a foreign limited liability company to do business in this state does not authorize the foreign company to engage in any activities and affairs or exercise any power that a limited liability company may not engage in or exercise in this state.

INDEX

References are to Pages

ACCORD AND SATISFACTION
Ratification and, principles compared, 80

ACCOUNTING ACTIONS
Agents, 153, 239
Contract liabilities of principals
 Sales contracts, 42
Grabbing and leaving, accounting actions, 167
Partnerships, 228, 336
Principals' remedy of, 190

AGENCY RELATIONSHIPS
Accountings, 239
Actual agency, consensual relationship, 93
Agreements creating and contracts distinguished, 22
Apparent agency
 Restatement of Agency, 39
 Tort liabilities of principals, 101
Authority issues
  See also Authority, this index
 Apparent authority, clothing of agent with, 50
 Burden of proof, 28
 Ratification of authority, 35
 Scope of authority, 35
 Status as agent, 2, 4
Best efforts, contract calling for, 148, 154
Bidding against principal, fiduciary duties, 153
Burden of proof
  Generally, 33, 73
 Authority, 27
Care Duties, this index
Circumstantial evidence, 22
Clothing of agent with apparent authority, 50
Compensation as factor, 2
Competing with principal, 149
Confidentiality Duties, this index
Conflicts of interest violating fiduciary duties, 146, 149
Consensual nature of actual agency, 93
Consent of principal to creation, 22
Contract liabilities of agents, undisclosed principal, 50, 481
Contract liabilities of principals
  Generally, 26 et seq.
  See also Liabilities, this index
 General agent, 61
 Inherent agency, 42
 Partially disclosed principal, 61
 Scope of agency, 50
 Secret instructions, 50
 Undisclosed principal, 50, 481
Contracts and agreements creating distinguished, 22
Contractual and noncontractual, 2, 6
Control
 Agent status, 18, 22
 Nine control factors, 23, 26
Corporate principals, 142
Course of dealing creating, 22
Creditor as agent, 19, 22
Definitions
  Generally, 2, 23
 Restatement of Agency, 64
 Status as agent, below
Disclosure, fiduciary duties of, 151
Distributorship contracts, 123
Employment, 2
Estoppel, agency by, 74
Evidence, 22, 33
Fact and law questions, 33, 64
Fiduciary duties
  See also Fiduciary Duties, this index
 Agency status issues, 6
Franchises, 95
General agents, 61
Good Faith Duties, this index
Grabbing and Leaving, this index
Implied agency, 34
Implied authority and inherent agency distinguished, 39
Independent contractors
 Agent and non-agent, 86
 Agents distinguished, 6
Inherent agency
 Contract liabilities of principals, 42
 Implied authority distinguished, 39
Inherent Agency Power, this index
Intent to create, 22
Joint ownership and, 64
Liabilities
  See also Liabilities, this index
 Status issues, 1
Licensed franchises, 93
Limited liability companies, 481
Loyalty Duties, this index
Marital status and, 64
Master and servant, 2
Non-delegable duties, 139
Ostensible principal, agent acting as, 50
Partially disclosed principals
  Generally, 481
 Contract liabilities, 61
Partners as agents, 253
Practical or economic vs legal relationships, 12
Presumptions, 33
Recitals denying authority, 125
Recitals disclaiming agency status, 12, 18
Sales contracts, liabilities of principals, 42
Sales relationships distinguished, 23
Scope of agency, contract liabilities of principals, 50
Scope of authority, 35

Scope of Employment, this index
Scope of relationships, 1
Secret instructions, contract liabilities of principals, 50
Side business of agent, secret profits, 148
Status determinations
Generally, 1
Authority issues, 2, 4
Compensation as factor, 2
Control factors, 18, 19, 23
Creditors, 19, 22
Fact and law questions, 33
Fiduciary duty issues, 6
Independent contract status distinguished, 6
Liabilities issues, 1
Recitals disclaiming agency status, 12, 18
Risk bearing, 90
Sales persons, 23, 42, 50
Subagents, 12
Three elements creating, 64
Three kinds of relationships, 2
Subagents
Generally, 27
Authority of agent to create, 27
Status, 12
Three elements creating, 64
Three kinds of relationships, 2
Tort liabilities of principals
Generally, 85 et seq.
See also Liabilities, this index
Apparent agency, 101
Non-delegable duties, 139
Unauthorized contracts, agent liability on, 67, 82
Undisclosed principal
Contract liabilities, 50, 481
Partially disclosed principal, 481
Restatement of Agency, 42
Unincorporated nonprofit associations, 32
Who is an agent. Status as agent, above

AGGREGATE THEORY
See Entity and Aggregate Theories, this index

ALTER EGO THEORY
Veil piercing, 508

ARBITRATION
LLC operating agreement provisions, 491

ATTORNEYS
See also Law Firms, this index
Ethical standards
Profession/business distinctions, 324
Whistleblower expulsion case, 317
Withdrawing partners, 306
Fiduciary duties
Client relationships, 151
Inter se of law firm partners, 301
Securities regulation practice, malpractice risks, 576

AT-WILL EMPLOYMENT DOCTRINE
Generally, 156
Whistleblower protections, 324

AUTHORITY
Active and dormant partners, 52
Acts constituting ratification, 66
Actual authority
Apparent authority distinguished, 39
Definition, 39
Implied authority distinguished, 39
Inherent authority distinguished, 60
Restatement of Agency, 36
Agents
See also Agency Relationships, this index
Apparent agency, 39
Liability on unauthorized contract, 67, 82
Ratification of authority, 35
Apparent authority
Actual authority distinguished, 39
Clothing of agent with, 50
Contract liabilities of principals, 37
Criticisms of doctrine, 55
Definition, 27, 39
Definitional confusion, 61
Equitable estoppel and, 77
Estoppel principle, 56, 74
General partners, 260
Implied authority distinguished, 27
Inherent agency power distinguished, 57, 61
Inherent authority distinguished, 60
Manifestations creating, 42, 54
Partners, 231
Reliance on, 79
Assurances of, 62
Belief in existence of, 28
Burden of proof, 28
Clothing of agent with apparent authority, 50
Conduct, ratification by, 65
Contract liabilities of principals
Generally, 26
See also Liabilities, this index
Apparent authority, 37
Estoppel, 72
Inherent agency, 42
Inherent authority, 50, 57
Ratification, 35, 63
Contractual limitations, 12
Customary, 54, 56
Death of principal, 174
Dormant and active partners, 52
Effect of ratification, 66
Estoppel
Apparent authority, 74
Contract liabilities of principals, 72
Ratification and, 68
Expulsion of LLC members, 551
General partners, 260
Implied agency relationships, 34
Implied authority
Actual authority distinguished, 39

Apparent authority distinguished, 27
Definition, 27
Independent contractors, tort liabilities of principals, 85
Inherent agency distinguished, 39
Inherent agency, implied authority distinguished, 39
Inherent authority
Actual authority distinguished, 60
Apparent authority distinguished, 60
Contract liabilities of principals, 50, 57
LLC members, 552
Inherent power
Generally, 42
See also Inherent Agency Power, this index
Limited liability companies, 532, 552
Manifestations creating apparent authority, 42, 54
Partners
Active and dormant, 52
Apparent authority, 231
Management rights, 252
Restrictions on authority of, 252
Prompt repudiation principle, 71
Protection through assurances of, 62
Ratification
Generally, 35
Accord and satisfaction and, principles, compared, 80
Acts constituting, 66
Conduct, ratification by, 62
Contract liabilities of principals, 63
Effect of, 66
Estoppel and, 68
Fact and law questions, 68
Failure to act as affirmance, 68
Implied affirmation cases, 66
Recitals denying authority, 125
Reliance on apparent authority, 79
Restrictions on authority of partners, 252
Revocable authority, 15
Sales, 42
Scope of authority, 35
Servants, tort liabilities of principals, 86
Subagent, authority of agent to create, 27
Subjective belief in existence of, 28
Tort liabilities of principals
Generally, 85 et seq.
Civil rights statute claims, 121
Independent contractors, 85
Policy considerations, 92
Servants, 86
Statutory claims, 120
Unauthorized contracts, agent liability on, 67, 82
Warranties of, 76

BRIBERY
Fiduciary duties, 142

BURDEN OF PROOF
Agency relationships, 33, 73
Authority, 27

BUSINESSES
Definition, 279

BUY-OUT AGREEMENTS
Generally, 381
Calculations, 385
Court ordered buy-outs
Generally, 384
Receivership alternative, 344, 348
Dissociation of partner, 358
Fiduciary duties, 345
Partnerships
Generally, 381
Court orders, 384
Fiduciary duties, 345
UPA, 378
Partnerships, liquidation/buy-out alternatives, 344

CAPITAL ACCOUNTS
Generally, 363, 385

CARE DUTIES
Abnormally dangerous activities, 136
Business owners, 74
Independent contractor relationships, 130
Land owners, 296
Partners, 280, 296
Ultrahazardous activities, 132
Uniform Limited Partnership Act, 399
Waivers, 378

CHOICE OF LAW
Generally, 32

CIRCUMSTANTIAL EVIDENCE
Agency relationships, 22

CIVIL RIGHTS STATUTES
See also Labor Law, this index
Employee definitions, 226
Partner protections, 220
Partners as employers or employees, 221
Partnership promotion decisions as subject to protection, 222
Professional corporation shareholders as employees, 214
Tort liabilities of principals, 121

COMPENSATION
Agent status, compensation as factor, 2
Expulsion, compensation issues, 271
Fiduciary duties, 288
Law firms
Fair charge payments for cases taken by departing partners, 301
Partnerships, voting as to shares, 312

COMPETITION BY FIDUCIARY
See also Conflicts of Interest, this index
Bidding against principal, fiduciary duties, 153
Contractually permitted competition among partners, 285

Disclosure duties
Agents, as to competitive activities, 148
Preparation to compete, 162
General partners of limited partnerships
Generally, 399
Contract drafting considerations, 405
Grabbing and leaving
Generally, 298
See also Grabbing and Leaving, this index
Limited partnerships
Generally, 399
Contract drafting considerations, 405
Generally, 399
LLC operating agreements, competition provisions, 519
Noncompetition covenants, 170
Partners
Generally, 271, 277
Contractually permitted competition, 285
Principals
Disclosure of, 162
Limited partnerships, 399
Secret profits, 142, 146, 148
Side business of agent, 148
Unfair competition
Generally, 167
See also Unfair Competition, this index

CONFIDENTIAL INFORMATION
Agent's misuse, 163
Breach of confidence as unfair competition, 171
Customer lists as
Generally, 169, 171
See also Grabbing and Leaving, this index
Misappropriations by departing members of law firm, 307, 308
Misuse by agent, 162
Trade secrets or processes, 170

CONFLICTS OF INTEREST
See also Competition by Fiduciary, this index
Agents, 146, 148
Contract drafting considerations, 149
Fiduciary and contractual duties, conflicts of, 293
Fiduciary duties, 281, 529
Interested transactions, 291
LLC members
Generally, 533
Voting, 533
Secret profits, 146

CONSTRUCTIVE TRUST REMEDIES
Limited partnerships, 389
Partnerships, 143, 283

CONTRACT DRAFTING CONSIDERATIONS
See also Default Rules, this index; Freedom of Contract, this index
Agents' conflicting business activities, 151
Authority of officers, 36
Buy-Out Agreements, this index
Competition among partners, 285
Control factors affecting partner/employee distinctions, 213
Control provisions affecting tort liabilities, 91
Expulsions of partners, 313
Grabbing and leaving, 304, 310
Independent contractors undertaking inherently dangerous activities, 132
Law partnership dissolutions, 361
Loss sharing factors affecting partner/ employee distinctions, 214
Partner/employee distinctions, control factors affecting, 214
Partnerships
Competition among, 285
Continuation agreements, 270, 378
Dissolution, 333, 358, 378
Expulsion, 313
Management rights, 256
Retirements, 270
Withdrawals, 304, 311
Tort liabilities, control provisions affecting, 91

CONTRACTS
Agency relationships, agreements creating and contracts distinguished, 22
Ambiguities, construction, 518
Best efforts, contract calling for, 148, 154
Construction, 518
Fiduciary and contractual duty conflicts, 293
Freedom of Contract, this index
Implied Covenant of Good Faith and Fair Dealing, this index
Implied terms, limited partnerships, 402
Investment contracts, 576, 591
Liabilities of principals
Generally, 26 et seq.
See also Liabilities, this index
Limited partnerships
Agreements creating, 397
Implied terms, 402
Noncompetition covenants, 170
Offer and acceptance, 68
Partnership dissolution, contractual limitations, 353
Sales contracts, liabilities of principals, 42

CONTROL
See also Management Rights, this index
Agent status, 18, 22
Convertible debt holdings in entities, 500
Creditor's control of debtor's business operations, 20

Franchise relationships, 100
Franchisee operations, 96
General partners of limited partnerships
Limited partners compared, 587
Independent contractor and master-servant relationships distinguished, 86, 100
Legal vs de facto control, partnerships, 231
Lenders and partners distinguished, 232
Limited and general partners compared, 587
Limited liability company stalemates, 504
Limited partners
General and limited partners compared, 587
Master-servant and independent contractor relationships distinguished, 86, 100
Nine control factors, 23, 26
Partners and lenders distinguished
Generally, 232
See also Creditors, this index
Partnerships
Executive committee partners, powers of, 221
Legal vs de facto control, 231
Partner/employee distinctions, 213
Risk and, 140
Securities regulations, control as factor in determining applicability, 592
Tort liabilities of principals, 88, 96
Vicarious liability and, 138

COOPERATION DUTIES
See also Deadlock, this index; Veto Rights, this index
Dissolution of partnership for failures of cooperation, 325

CORPORATIONS
Agency relationships involving corporate principals, 142
Derivative Suits, this index
Fiduciary duties of corporate officers, 154, 162
Fiduciary duties of directors, 291
Good faith duties of corporate officers, 162
Liability
See also Limited Liability Principle, this index
Corporate officers and directors of general partners, 387
LLCs
Compared, 479
General partners, corporate officers and directors as, liability, 387
Veil piercing, 508
Partnership management in corporate form, 288
Professional Corporations, this index
Veil Piercing, this index

COURSE OF DEALING
Agency relationships created by, 22

COURT ORDERS
Buy-outs, court ordered
Generally, 384
Receivership alternative, 344, 348
Dissolution
Generally, 563
Breach of LLC operating agreement, petition rights, 556
Deadlock, 572
Financing deadlock, 504
Reasonable practicability of continued operations, 571
Statutory standards, LLCs, 558
Waivers of right to seek, 564
Waivers of right to seek, LLC members, 564
Expulsion, limited liability companies, 556
Receiver Appointments, this index

COVENANT OF GOOD FAITH AND FAIR DEALING
See Implied Covenant of Good Faith and Fair Dealing, this index

CREDITORS
Convertible debt holdings in entities, 500
Management intervention rights, 22, 234
Open account financing, 20
Partners and lenders distinguished
Generally, 232 et seq.
Control factors, 231
Crop mortgages, 239, 240
Profit sharing by lenders, 232, 240
Priorities of claims, 500
Profit sharing by lenders, 232, 240
Securities Regulation, this index
Veil Piercing, this index
Veto powers, 23, 234

DAMAGE REMEDY
Fiduciary duty violations, 364
Grabbing and leaving disputes, 309

DEADLOCK
See also Veto Powers, this index
Court orders, 572
Dissolution for
Generally, 572
See also Dissolution, this index
Equal rights partnerships, 252
Financing deadlock, 504
LLCs
Generally, 560, 571
Stalemates, 504

DEATH
Buy-sell agreements, 382
LLC member, 548
Partner, 374, 381
Principal, termination of authority, 174

DEFAULT RULES
Generally, 150, 177
See also Contract Drafting Considerations, this index; Freedom of Contract, this index

Fiduciary duties
Generally, 277
Mandatory provisions, 394
LLCs, mandatory provisions, 565
Partnerships
Mandatory provisions, 378
Voting rights, 231
Uniform Partnership Act, 229

DEFINITIONS
Actual authority, 39
Agency
Generally, 2, 22
See also Agency Relationships, this index
Apparent authority
Generally, 27, 39
Definitional confusion, 61
Book value, 231
Business, 279
Capital account, 385, 363
Convertible debt, 500
Employee, 215, 226
Franchisee, 86
General agent, 61
Implied authority, 27
Independent contractor, 85
Inherent agency power, 42, 52
Investment contract, 576, 591
Master-servant relationship, 216
Open account, 20
Partnership
Generally, 209 et seq.
See also Partnerships, this index
Put rights, 500
Ratification, 65
Respondeat superior, 86
Subagent, 27
Top lease, 278
Trade secret, 176
Unjust enrichment, 293
Winding up, 561

DERIVATIVE LIABILITY
Employment relationships, 109, 117

DERIVATIVE SUITS
Generally, 484
Arbitration of, 491
Direct shareholder suits distinguished, 491
Entity vs aggregate status, 483
Parties, 484
Uniform Limited Liability Company Act, 491

DISCLOSURE DUTIES
Agents, as to competitive activities, 148
Competition with principal, 162
Fiduciary duties, 303
Fiduciary duties as including, 151
Partnerships, 151, 303
Preparation to compete, 162
Securities regulation federal statues, 575

DISCRIMINATION
See Civil Rights Statutes, this index

DISGORGEMENT REMEDY
Secret profits, 142, 146

DISSOLUTION
See also Deadlock, this index
Articles of dissolution, limited liability companies, 557
Breach of operating agreement, petition rights, 556
Contract drafting considerations, 357
Court ordered
Generally, 563
See also Court Orders, this index
Deadlock, 572
Waivers of right to seek, LLC members, 564
Financing deadlock, court orders, 504
LLCs
Generally, 555 et seq.
See also Limited Liability Companies, this index
Partnership compared, 571
Partnership dissolution standards compared, 571
Partnerships
Generally, 271 et seq.
See also Partnerships, this index
LLCs compared, 571
Reasonable practicability of continued operations, court orders, 571
Statutory standards, 558
Uniform Limited Liability Company Act, 562
Uniform Partnership Act, 335, 377
Waiver of right to seek, LLCs, 564
Withdrawal of LLC member to effect, 560

DISTRIBUTORSHIPS
Agency relationships, 123
Liabilities, 85, 123

DUTIES
Care Duties, this index
Confidentiality Duties, this index
Cooperation Duties, this index
Disclosure Duties, this index
Fiduciary Duties, this index
Good Faith Duties, this index
Implied Covenant of Good Faith and Fair Dealing, this index
Loyalty Duties, this index

ECONOMIC ANALYSES
Tort liability of principals, 138

EMPLOYMENT RELATIONSHIPS
See also Master-Servant Relationships, this index
Agency relationships as, 2
At-Will Employment Doctrine, this index
Best efforts provisions in contracts, 154
Civil Rights Statutes, this index
Contractual vs at-will, 156
Control factors, partner/employee distinctions, 213

Definitions of employee, 226
Derivative liability, 109, 117
Deviations from scope of employment, 114
Discrimination, statutory, 125
Fiduciary duties, officer compensation, 288
Foreseeable acts of employees, 112, 125
Grabbing and Leaving, this index
Intentional torts, scope of employment, 116
Labor Law, this index
Liabilities, this index
Motive test, scope of employment, 111
Non-delegable duties, scope of employment, 127
Officer compensation, fiduciary duties, 288
Partnerships distinguished, 209 et seq.
Restatement of Agency, 100
Risk attributable to employers business, scope of employment, 119
Scope of Employment, this index

ENTITY AND AGGREGATE THEORIES
Generally, 252
Derivative suits, 484
Limited liability companies, 483
Limited liability principle, 506
Partnerships
Generally, 252
Property conveyances, 403
UPA, 307
Veil piercing, 505

ESTOPPEL
Agency by, 74
Apparent authority, equitable estoppel and, 56, 77
Authority to contract, estoppel to deny, 72
Customary authority, 56
Equitable estoppel and apparent authority, 77
Holding out, partnership by estoppel, 243
Inherent agency power theories compared, 52
Partnership by, 232, 242
Ratification and, 68
Reliance and, 244

ETHICAL STANDARDS
Profession/business distinctions, 324
Whistleblower expulsion case, 320
Withdrawing partners, 306

EVIDENCE
Agency relationships, 22, 33
Burden of Proof, this index
Circumstantial evidence of agency relationship, 22
Course of dealing, agency relationships created by, 22
Fact and Law Questions, this index
Partnership status, 232, 285

EXECUTORS
Fiduciary duties, 151

EXPULSION
At-will employment doctrine, applicability to partner expulsions, 314
Bad faith expulsion
Generally, 313, 317
Fiduciary duties, 322
Cause expulsion of partner, 324
Compensation, 271
Contract drafting considerations, 314
Court ordered, 556
Dissolution effected by, 313
Fairness duties, partner expulsions, 314
Fiduciary duties, partner expulsions, 315, 319, 322
Good faith and fair dealing duties, 314
Inherent authority to expel, LLC members, 552
Law Firms, this index
LLC members
Generally, 540 et seq.
See also Limited Liability Companies, this index
No cause expulsion clause, 316
Predatory purpose, 314
Public policy considerations, 324
Uniform Limited Liability Company Act, 554
Uniform Partnership Act, 314
Whistleblower case, 320
Wrongful, 267, 311

FACT AND LAW QUESTIONS
Agency relationships, 33, 64
Ratification of authority, 68

FAIRNESS DUTIES
See also Implied Covenant of Good Faith and Fair Dealing, this index
Fiduciary duties as including, 153
Limited liability companies, 535
Partnership expulsions, 313
Waivers, 567

FIDUCIARY DUTIES
Generally, 142 et seq.
Accounting for profits, 152
Agency status determinations, 6
Attorneys, 151
Best efforts, contractual obligations, 148, 154
Bidding against principal, 153
Bribery, 142
Buy-outs, 348
Cardozo statement, 271, 298
Care duties of partners, 296
Compensation policies, 288
Competition by Fiduciary, this index
Confidential information misuse, 163
Conflicts of Interest, this index
Constructive Trust Remedy, this index
Contract duty conflicts, 291
Corporate directors, 291
Corporate officers, 154, 162
Damages for violations, 364
Default and mandatory rules, 394
Disclosure Duties, this index

Disgorgement Remedy, this index
Duration
See also Grabbing and Leaving, this index
Dissolution, duties after, 296
During agency relationship, 142 et seq.
During and after termination of agency, 154 et seq.
Partnerships, 296
Executors, 151
Existence of fiduciary relationship, 151
Fair dealing, 152
Fairness Duties, this index
Freeze outs, 337
General partners of limited partnerships, 389
Good faith duties included, 143, 148
Grabbing and leaving
Generally, 298 et seq., 361
See also Grabbing and Leaving, this index
Honesty, 143
Implied covenant of good faith distinguished, 404
Interference with business relationships, 519
Joint ventures, 271
Lawyers in firms, duties inter se
Generally, 301
See also Law Firms, this index
Limited partnerships
Competition, 399
General partners, 389
Uniform Limited Partnership Act, 399
Waivers, 393
LLCs
Generally, 517 et seq.
See also Limited Liability Companies, this index
Loyalty duties included, 147, 148, 530
Managers, LLC, 523
Merger decisions, 268
Misrepresentations to principal, 163
Partnerships, this index
Profits, accounting for, 152
Public policy and waivers, 393
Ratification, self dealing, 392
Scope of, 151
Secret profits
Competing side business of agent, 148
Disgorgement of, 142, 146
Self dealing
Limited partnerships, 392
Ratification, 392
Side business of agent, competing, 148
Statutory mandates, partnerships, 378
Trustees, 151
Types of fiduciary relationship, 151
Undivided loyalty, 274
Uniform Limited Partnership Act, 399
Uniform Partnership Act, 276
Waivers
Limited partnerships, 393
Public policy, 393

FORMAL REQUIREMENTS OF ENTITIES
Failure to observe, 483
Formation of LLCs, 479
Partnerships, 221, 228, 376
Registered agents of LLCs, 564
Veil piercing, failure to observe corporate formalities, 508

FRANCHISES
Agency nature of franchise relationships, 95
Control factors, 101
Independent contractor status, 86
Liabilities
Generally, 85
Employees of franchisee, 96
License relationships, 93
Risk bearing, 95

FREEDOM OF CONTRACT
See also Contract Drafting Considerations, this index
Default Rules, this index
Limited partnerships, 494
LLCs
Generally, 551
Dissolution, 565
Operating agreements, 495
Public policy, 566
Waivers of rights, 564

FREEZE OUTS
Partnerships, 337, 338

FUNDAMENTAL CHANGES IN ENTITIES
Veto powers, 267, 529

GOOD FAITH DUTIES
At will relationships, 314
Corporate officers, 162
Fiduciary duties including, 143, 148
Implied Covenant of Good Faith and Fair Dealing, this index
Partnership expulsions
Generally, 313
Bad faith
Generally, 319
Fiduciary duties, 322
Waivers of good faith and fair dealing, 567

GRABBING AND LEAVING
Generally, 154 et seq.
Accountings actions, 167
Client relationships after dissolution of law firms, 365
Competition with partners, 298
Confidential information, misappropriations, 163, 307, 308
Confidentiality duties, 167
Contract drafting considerations, 305, 311
Customer list appropriations, 170
Damages
Fiduciary duty violations, 364
Law firms, 309

Fiduciary duties
Generally, 298 et seq., 361
Damages for violations, 364
Departing law firm partners, 301
Interference with contractual relationships, 301
Law firms
Generally, 298 et seq., 361
Client relationships after dissolution, 365
Confidential information misappropriations by leaving members, 307, 308
Damages, 309
Restatement of Agency, 162
Solicitation
Associates of law firms, 301
Clients of law firms, 298 et seq., 361
Customers of principal, 167, 169
Employees of principal, 155, 158
Trade secrets, appropriating, 170
Unfair competition, 187

GUARANTORS
Partners as, 252

HAZARDOUS ACTIVITIES
Independent contractors, tort liabilities, 130

HOLDING OUT
Partnership by estoppel, 242

HONESTY
Fiduciary duties, 143

IMPLIED COVENANT OF GOOD FAITH AND FAIR DEALING
Generally, 290, 293, 404, 503
Fiduciary duties distinguished, 404
Limited partnerships agreements, 402
LLC operating agreements, 503
Waivers of good faith and fair dealing obligations, 568

INCAPACITY
Partnership dissolution for incapacity of partner, 384

INDEMNIFICATION
Partners by partnerships, 257

INDEPENDENT CONTRACTORS
Abnormally dangerous activities, tort liabilities, 134, 138
Agent and non-agent, 86
Agents distinguished, 6
Care duties, 130
Control factors, 86
Economic analysis of tort liability responsibilities, 138
Employees distinguished, labor law protections, 215
Employees of independent contracts, principal liabilities to, 132
Financial responsibility issues, tort liabilities, 134
Franchisees as, 86
Hazardous activities, tort liabilities, 130
Incompetent contractor, 138
Inherently dangerous activities, 132, 138
Labor laws, independent contractors and employees distinguished, 215
Liabilities
Generally, 85
Restatement of Agency, 100
Tort Liabilities, below
Master-servant relationships distinguished, 86, 100
Negligent selection, 139
Non-delegable duties, 139
Partners distinguished, 213
Scope of Employment, this index
Tort liabilities
Generally, 129 et seq.
Abnormally dangerous activities, 135, 138
Employees of independent contracts, principal liabilities to, 132
Financial responsibility issues, 132
Hazardous activities, 130
Inherently dangerous activities, 132, 138
Negligent selection, 139
Non-delegable duties, 139
Policy considerations, 135
Principal's liabilities, 129 et seq.

INHERENT AGENCY POWER
Generally, 42
Apparent authority distinguished, 57, 61
Estoppel theories compared, 52
Implied authority and inherent agency distinguished, 39
Restatement of Agency, 52, 60

INTERESTED TRANSACTIONS
Generally, 291
See also Conflicts of Interest, this index

INTERFERENCE
Business relationships, fiduciary obligations, 519
Contractual relationships, grabbing and leaving, 301

INVESTMENTS
Active and passive investors
LLC members, 586, 588
Tax considerations, 396
Dilution protections, 500, 573
Partners and common interest investors distinguished, 285
Risk/return calculations, 236
Securities Regulation, this index
Subrogation of senior claims, 500

JOINT OWNERS
Agency relationships, 64

JOINT TENANCIES
Partnerships distinguished, 240

JOINT VENTURES
Fiduciary duties, 271
Partnership for a term, dissolution, 333

Partnerships compared, 278
Securities regulations applicable to joint venture interests, 592
Status determinations, 279

JUDICIAL REVIEW
Court Orders, this index
Damages Remedy, this index
Disgorgement Remedy, this index
Public Policy, this index

LABOR LAW
Civil Rights Statutes, this index
Independent contractors and employees distinguished, 215
Partners and employees distinguished, 209
Professional corporation shareholders as employees, 214
Whistleblower protections, 320

LAW FIRMS
Associates
 Duties to partners, 305
 Solicitation by departing law firm partners, 301
Client relationships after dissolution
 Grabbing and leaving, 365
Compensation
 Expulsion, 271
Confidential information misappropriations by leaving members, 307, 308
Contingent fee cases, grabbing and leaving, 301
Counsel, partner status, 220
Dissolutions
 Fiduciary duties after, 296
 Retirement of partner and, 270
Ethical standards
 Profession/business distinctions, 324
 Whistleblower expulsion case, 320
 Withdrawing partners, 306
Executive committees
 Management rights, 263
 Powers, 221
Expulsions
  Generally, 311 et seq.
 Bad faith, 319
 Cause, 324
 Compensation, 271
 Whistleblower case, 317
Fair charge payments for cases taken by departing partners, 301
Fiduciary duties inter se
 Damages for violations, 364
 Dissolutions, 296
 Merger decisions, 268
 Of departing law firm partners, 301
Grabbing and leaving
  Generally, 298 et seq., 361
 Client relationships after dissolution, 365
 Confidential information misappropriations by leaving members, 307, 308
 Damages, 309
 Fiduciary duties of departing partners, 301
 Solicitation of associates, 301
Income partner status, 219
Management rights
 Executive committees, 264
 Merger decisions, 263
Mergers
 Fiduciary duties, 268
 Management rights, 263
Other members, raiding of, 298 et seq., 361
Partner status, of counsel attorneys, 220
Profession/business distinctions, 324
Referring attorneys, solicitation of by members leaving, 301
Retirement of partner and dissolution, 270
Solicitation of associates, 301
Solicitation of clients, 298 et seq., 361
Solicitation of referring attorneys, 301
Whistleblower case, bad faith expulsion claim, 319
Withdrawals, ethical standards, 306
Wrongful expulsion of partner, 311

LENDERS
See Creditors, this index

LIABILITIES
  Generally, 26 et seq.
 See also Limited Liability Principle, this index
Abnormally dangerous activities, 135, 138
Agent liability on unauthorized contract
 Generally, 67, 82
Agent liability on unauthorized contracts, LLCs, 481
Apparent agency, 101
Apparent authority, 37
Business enterprise theory of tort law, 111
Contract liabilities of agents
  Generally, 67, 82
 Undisclosed principal, 50, 481
Contract liabilities of principals
  Generally, 26 et seq.
 Apparent authority, 37, 42
 Authority, 26
 Definiteness of contract terms, 39
 Disclosed principal, 61
 Estoppel, 72
 General agent, 61
 Inherent agency, 42
 Inherent authority, 50, 57
 Offer and acceptance, 68
 Partially disclosed principal, 61
 Partially disclosed principle doctrine, 481
 Ratification of agent's authority, 35, 63
 Sales contracts, 42
 Scope of agency, 50
 Secret instructions, 50
 Undisclosed principal, 50, 481

Unincorporated nonprofit associations, 32
Control factors and tort liabilities, 88, 96
Derivative liability, employment relationships, 109, 117
Deviations from scope of employment, 114
Disclosed principals, contract liabilities, 61
Discrimination, statutory, 125
Distributorships, 85, 123
Economic analysis of tort liability responsibilities, 138
Employees of independent contractors, principal liabilities to, 132
Employment relationships, derivative liability, 109, 117
Estoppel, contract liabilities of principals, 72
Franchise operations
Generally, 86
Employees of franchisee, 96
General agents, 61
Guarantors, partners as, 252
Hazardous activities of independent contractors, 130
Indemnification of partners by partnerships, 257
Independent Contractors, this index
Inherent agency, 42
Inherent authority, 50, 57
Inherently dangerous activities, 132, 138
Intentional torts, scope of employment, 116
Limited partnerships
Officers and directors of corporate general partners, 387
LLCs
Agent liability on unauthorized contracts, 481
Formal requirements, failure to observe, 483
Losses, this index
Management rights and, 259
Master-servant relationships, 86
Negligent selection of independent contractor, 139
Non-delegable duties
Independent contractors, 139
Scope of employment, 127
Officers and directors of corporate general partners of limited partnerships, 387
Ordinary course of business, 258
Partially disclosed principal doctrine, 61, 481
Partner indemnification by partnerships, 257
Partners as guarantors, 252
Policy considerations, independent contractor torts, 135
Principal for debts of agent, 21
Ratification, contract liabilities of principals, 35, 63
Respondeat Superior, this index
Risk attributable to employer's business, 119
Sales contracts, 42
Scope of agency, contract liabilities of principals, 50
Scope of Employment, this index
Secret instructions, contract liabilities of principals, 50
Securities regulation litigation, 577
Servants' torts, 86
Statutory claims, 120
Tort liabilities of principals
Generally, 85 et seq.
Abnormally dangerous activities, 135, 138
Apparent agency, 101
Business enterprise theory, 111
Civil rights statute claims, 121
Control factors, 88, 96
Economic analysis, 138
Employees of independent contractors, liabilities to, 133
Financial responsibility of independent contractors, 132
Foreseeable acts of employees, 112, 125
Hazardous activities of independent contractors, 130
Independent Contractors, this index
Inherently dangerous activities, 132, 138
Negligent selection of independent contractor, 139
Non-delegable duties independent contractors, 139
Policy considerations, 92
Scope of employment liability, above
Servants, 86
Statutory claims, 120
Undisclosed principals
Contract liabilities, 50, 481
Partially disclosed principals, 61, 481
Restatement of Agency, 53
Unincorporated nonprofit associations, 32
Veil Piercing, this index
Vicarious Liability, this index

LIMITED LIABILITY COMPANIES (LLC)
Generally, 479 et seq.
Additional capital
Generally, 535
Expulsion for failure to honor call for, 553
Advantages of form, 580
Agency relationships, 481
Arbitration provisions in operating agreements, 491
Authority
Generally, 533
Expulsions of members, 551
Classes of members, 499
Collective interest members, 531
Conflicts of interest, fiduciary obligations, 529
Control stalemates, 504

Corporations compared
Generally, 479
Veil piercing, 508
Court orders
Dissolution, below
Expulsion, 556
Deadlock, dissolution for, 560, 571
Derivative Suits, this index
Disclosure of LLC relationships, 479
Dissolution
Generally, 555 et seq., 563
Articles of dissolution, 557
Court ordered
Generally, 564
Breach of operating agreement, petition rights, 556
Financing deadlock, 504
Reasonable practicability of continued operations, 571
Statutory standards, 558
Waivers of right to seek, 564
Deadlock, 560, 571
Freedom of contract as to, 565
Members, dissolution of, 556
Member's withdrawal to effect, 560
Operating agreement breaches, 556, 558
Operating agreement provisions, 560
Partnership dissolution standards compared, 571
Reasonable practicability of continued operations, 571
Uniform Limited Liability Company Act, 562
Waiver of right to seek, 564
Winding up, 561
Withdrawal of member to effect, 560
Dissolution on, 560
Entity vs aggregate status, 484
Expulsion of members
Generally, 540 et seq.
Additional capital contributions, expulsion for failure to make, 553
Authority, 551
Court ordered, 556
Inherent authority, 552
Operating agreement provisions, 547, 551
Uniform Limited Liability Company Act, 554
Fairness duties, 535
Fiduciary obligations
Generally, 517 et seq.
Conflicts of interest, 529
Managers, 523
Formal requirements
Failure to observe, 483
Formation, 479
Freedom of contract principle
Generally, 551, 565
Dissolution, 565
Operating agreements, 495
Inherent authority to remove members, 552
Interests in LLCs as regulated securities, 577
Investments, active and passive, 587
Liabilities
Formal requirements, failure to observe, 483
Veil piercing, 508
Limited liability
Notice of, 480
Waivers by members, 537
Loss sharing, 479
Loyalty duties, 520
Management rights
Generally, 479
Classes of members, 499
Managers
Generally, 479
Fiduciary obligations, 523
Limited liability, 479
Members
Generally, 479
Active and passive, 587
Additional capital, calls for, 535
Classes of members, 499
Collective interest, 531
Dissolution of a member, 556
Exculpation agreements, 522
Expulsion of members, above
Interests as regulated securities, 577
Limited liability, 479
One member, LLCs, 523
Remaining members, 562
Withdrawal of member to effect dissolution, 560
Notice of limited liability, 480
One member, LLCs, 523
Operating agreements
Generally, 484 et seq.
Additional capital, 535
Amendments and restatements, 560
Arbitration provisions, 491
Breaches, 556, 558
Competition provisions, 519
Dissolution provisions, 560
Dissolution rights, waivers, 564
Exculpation of members, 522
Expulsion of members provisions, 547, 551
Freedom of contract, above
Implied covenant of good faith and fair dealing, 503
Veto powers, 504
Veto rights, 529
Voting rights, 534
Waivers of dissolution rights, 564
Partnerships compared
Generally, 479
Remaining members, 562
Self-dealing, 532
Sharing of profits and losses, 479
Tax considerations, 479, 536, 580
Veil piercing, 505, 506
Veto rights, 529

Voting rights
Generally, 494
Conflicts of interest, 531
Operating agreements, 535
Scope, 579
Waiver of right to seek dissolution, 564
Winding up, 561
Withdrawal of member, 560

LIMITED LIABILITY PRINCIPLE
Corporate officers and directors of general partners of limited partnerships, 388
Corporations, 388, 505
Entity and aggregate theories, 506
Limited partnerships, 388
LLCs
Members and managers, 479
Notice of limitations, 480
Waivers by members, 537
Notice of limitations, 480
Officers and directors of corporate general partners of limited partnerships, 388
Tax obligations, 536
Veil Piercing, this index
Waivers, LLC members, 537

LIMITED PARTNERSHIPS
Agreements creating, 397
Apparent authority of general partners, 260
Business activities, 396
Competition
Fiduciary duties, 399
General partners with partnership
Generally, 399
Contract drafting considerations, 405
Control
General and limited partners compared, 587
Corporate officers and directors of general partners, liability, 388
Fiduciary duties
Competition, 399
General partners, 389
Self dealing, 392
Uniform Limited Partnership Act, 399
Waivers, 393
Freedom of contract, 494
General partners
Apparent authority, 260
Competition with partnership
Generally, 399
Contract drafting considerations, 405
Corporate officers and directors of general partners, liability, 387
Fiduciary duties, 389
Limited partners compared, 587
Officers and directors of corporate general partners, liability, 387
Liabilities
Corporate officers and directors of general partners, 387
Management exercises, 259
Limited liability principle, 388
Limited partners
See also Investments, this index
General partners compared, 587
Management rights, 259
Master limited partnerships, 396
Officers and directors of corporate general partners, liability, 387
Publicly traded interests, security regulations, 394
Securities regulation, partnership interests as securities, 587
Security regulations, 394
Tax considerations, 396
Waivers of fiduciary duties, 393

LIQUIDATION
Partnerships, 337
Winding up distinguished, 344, 374

LOSS SHARING
See also Sharing of Profits and Losses, this index
Dissolving partnership, 358
Limited liability companies, 479
Partners as guarantors, 252
Partnerships
Dissolution, 358
Service partners, 360
Underwater partnerships, obligations of partners, 248
Profit sharing as implying, 358

LOYALTY DUTIES
Competition, disloyal. See Competition by Fiduciary, this index
Fiduciary duties as including, 147, 148
Fiduciary nature of, 530
Limited liability companies, 520
Undivided loyalty owed by fiduciaries, 274
Uniform Limited Partnership Act, 399

MANAGEMENT RIGHTS
See also Control, this index
Active and passive investors. See Investments, this index
Creditor power to exercise, 23, 234
Equal rights partnerships, 252
Fiduciary obligations of managers, 523
Limited partnerships, 259
LLCs
Generally, 479
See also Limited Liability Companies, this index
Classes of members, 499
Partners
Generally, 252 et seq.
See also Partnerships, this index

MARITAL STATUS
Agency relationships, 64

MASTER-SERVANT RELATIONSHIPS
See also Employment Relationships, this index
Agency relationships as, 2
Common law's definition of the, 216
Independent contractor relationships distinguished, 86, 100
Liabilities, 86
Restatement of Agency, 216
Tort liabilities of principals, 86

MODEL BUSINESS CORPORATION ACT
Veil piercing, 505

MOTIVE
Scope of employment, motive test, 111

NEGLIGENCE
Care Duties, this index
Liabilities, this index

OPEN ACCOUNT FINANCING
Generally, 19

ORDINARY COURSE OF BUSINESS
Generally, 258
Partnership business, liabilities, 257

OUSTER
See Expulsion, this index

OWNERSHIP
Agency relationships between joint owners, 64
Partnerships distinguished, 240, 279, 285

PARTIES
Derivative suits, 484

PARTNERSHIPS
Generally, 209 et seq.
Accounting rights, 228
Accountings, 374
Active and dormant partners, 52
Admission of partners, 230
Agents, partners as, 253
Apparent authority of general partners, 260
Apparent authority of partners, 231
At will employment doctrine, applicability to partner expulsions, 314
Auctions of property of partnership on dissolution, 340
Authority limitations, management rights, 252
Authority restrictions and management rights, 252
Bad faith expulsion claim
Generally, 313, 319
Fiduciary duties, 322
Buy-out agreements
Generally, 381
Court-ordered, 340
Fiduciary duties, 345
Liquidation compared, 344
UPA, 378
Capital accounts, 363, 385
Care duties
Generally, 280
Fiduciary nature of, 296
Choses in action as property of partnership, 251
Civil rights statutes
Partner protections, 220
Promotion decisions as subject to protection, 222
Compensation
Expelled partner, 271
Fiduciary duties, 288
Voting as to shares, 312
Competition with partner
See also Competition by Fiduciary, this index
Fiduciary duties, 271, 277
Grabbing and leaving, 298
Confidential information misappropriations by leaving members of law firm, 307, 308
Consequences of dissolution
Generally, 348 et seq.
Auctions, 340
Buy-outs, above
Liquidation and buy-out compared, 344
Valuation of partnership property, 344
Contract drafting considerations
Continuation agreements, 270, 378
Dissolution, 333, 358, 378
Expulsion, 313
Retirements, 270
Withdrawals, 304, 311
Contractual limitations on dissolution, 353
Contributions, sharing of profits and losses, contributions as factor, 360
Control
Executive committee partners, powers of, 221
Legal vs de facto control, 231
Lenders and partners distinguished, 232
Partner/employee distinctions, 213
Conveyances of partnership property, 250
Cooperation duties
Generally, 327
Failures resulting in dissolution, 325
Corporations distinguished, 236
Corporations managed as, 288
Court orders
Buy-outs, 340, 384
Dissolution, 325
Damages for violations of fiduciary duties, 364
Death of partners, 374
Definitions
Generally, 209, 213
Status determinations, below
Disclosure duties, 303
Dissociation
Buy-outs, 358
Dissolution distinguished, 270, 378

Dissolution
Generally, 325 et seq.
Auctions, 340
Buy-outs, above
Consequences of dissolution, above
Contract drafting considerations, 333, 357, 378
Contractual limitations on rights of, 353
Cooperation duty failures, 325
Court ordered, 326
Death of partner, 374
Dissociation distinguished, 270, 378
Events of, 214
Expulsion as effecting, 313
Fiduciary duties after, 296
Incapacity of partner, 384
Law Firms, this index
Liquidation, 337
LLCs compared, 571
Loss sharing, 358
Partnership for a term, 333
Powers and rights of, 329, 331
Receiver appointments, 326
Retirement of partner and, 270
Right to dissolve, 325
Stalemated management rights, 252
UPA, 314, 329, 335
Valuation of partnership property, 344
Wrongful, 267, 353
Distributions, 385
Dormant and active partners, 52
Duration of fiduciary duties, 296
Employer vs employee status of partners for purposes of civil rights statutes, 221
Employment decisions, management rights as to, 255
Employment relationships distinguished, 209 et seq.
Equal rights of management, 252
Estoppel, partnership by, 232, 242
Evidence of existence, 285
Evidence of status, 231
Executive committee partners, powers of, 221
Expulsion
Generally, 311 et seq.
Bad faith claims
Generally, 314, 319
Fiduciary duties, 322
Cause expulsions, 324
Compensation, 271
Contract drafting considerations, 314
Dissolution effected by, 313
Fiduciary duties
Generally, 315, 319
Bad faith claim, 322
Good faith and fair dealing duties, 314
Law partners, 311
No cause expulsion clause, 319
Predatory purpose, 314
Public policy considerations, 324
Uniform Partnership Act, 314
Whistleblower case, 317
Wrongful, 267, 311
Expulsion of partners, 230
Fiduciary duties
Generally, 151, 271 et seq.
Buy-outs, 348
Care, 296
Compensation, 288
Competition with partner, 271, 277
Constructive trust remedy, 283
Damages for violations, 364
Disclosure, 303
Dissolution, duties after, 296
Duration, 296
Expulsion
Generally, 315, 319
Bad faith claim, 322
Freeze outs, 337
Law partners, 301
Merger decisions, 268
Statutory mandates, 378
Freeze outs, 337
Fundamental changes, management rights, 268
General partners, operating general partners distinguished, 590
Good faith and fair dealing duties, expulsion, 314
Goodwill valuation, 355
Grabbing and Leaving, this index
Guarantors, partners as, 252
Incapacity of partner, dissolution for, 384
Income partner status, 219
Indemnification of partners, 257
Independent contractor/partner distinctions, 214
Intent to create, 238
Investments in, securities regulation, 588
Investors with common interest and partners distinguished, 285
Joint tenancies relationships distinguished, 240
Joint ventures compared, 278
Judicial orders. Court orders, above
Junior partners, 219
Labor laws, applicability to partners, 209
Law. See Law Firms, this index
Lenders and partners distinguished
Generally, 232 et seq.
Control factors, 231
Crop mortgages, 239, 240
Profit sharing lenders, 232, 240
Liabilities
Indemnification of partners, 257
Ordinary course of business, 257
Underwater partnership, 248
Limited liability companies compared, 479
Limited Partnerships, this index
Liquidation
Generally, 228, 337
Buy-out alternatives, 344
Loggerheads, partners at. Stalemates, below

Loss sharing
Generally, 214, 385
Dissolution, 358
Service partners, 360
Management rights
Authority restrictions and, 252
Contract drafting considerations, 256
Employment decisions, 255
Equal rights, 252
Executive committees, 264
Fundamental changes, 268
Liability, 259
Limited partnerships, 259
Merger decisions, 263
Ordinary matters, 252, 255
Receiver appointments, 326
Stalemates, below
UPA, 255
Merger decisions
Fiduciary duties, 268
Management rights, 263
Negative financial positions, liabilities of partners, 249
Operating general partners, 590
Ordinary matters, management rights as to, 252, 255
Other members of law firm, raiding of, 298 et seq., 361
Ouster. Expulsion, above
Ownership relationships distinguished, 240, 278, 285
Powers and rights of dissolution, 329, 331
Predatory purpose for expulsion, 314
Professional corporations distinguished, 214
Profit sharing
Generally, 209
Lenders, 232, 240
Promotion decisions as subject to civil rights statutes protections, 222
Property of partnership
Generally, 248
Auctions on dissolution, 340
Capital accounts, 385
Choses in action, 251
Conveyances, 250
Dissolution
Valuation, 344
Entity and aggregate theories, 252
Goodwill valuation, 355
Guarantors, partners as, 252
Negative financial positions, 249
Underwater partnership, 248
Valuation on dissolution, 344
Receiver appointments, 326
Retirement of partner, 270
Right of dissolution, 325
Risks, 227, 505
Securities regulation of investments in, 587, 588, 592
Service partners, loss sharing, 360
Settling of accounts, 230
Sharing of profits and losses
Generally, 358
Contributions as factor, 360
Income partner status, 219
Uniform Partnership Act, 219, 227
Solicitation of clients by departing partners, 298 et seq., 361
Stalemates
Generally, 325 et seq.
See also Deadlock, this index
Cooperation duties, 327
Deadlocks, this index
Dissolution, above
Management rights problems, 252
Status determinations
Generally, 209 et seq.
Agents, partners as, 253
Evidence, 232
Lenders and partners distinguished, above
Ownership relationships distinguished, 240, 278, 285
UPA, 240, 253
Statutory mandates, fiduciary duties, 378
Tenancy relationships distinguished, 240, 285
Term, dissolution of partnership for, 333
Uniform Partnership Act, this index
Valuation of partnership property on dissolution, 344
Vicarious liability of partners, 219
Whistleblower case, bad faith expulsion claim, 319
Who are partners
Generally, 209 et seq.
Status determinations, above
Withdrawals
Generally, 298 et seq.
Contract drafting considerations, 305, 311
Ethical standards for withdrawing law partners, 306
Wrongful dissolution, 267
Wrongful expulsion, 267, 311
Wrongful termination, 353

PIERCING THE CORPORATE VEIL
See Veil Piercing, this index

PLANNING
See Contract Drafting Considerations, this index

POLICY CONSIDERATIONS
See also Public Policy, this index
Business enterprise theory of tort law, 111
Independent contractor torts, 135
Respondeat superior, 111
Tort liabilities of principals, 91
Veto powers of entity members, 504
Vicarious liability, 111

POWER
Authority, this index
Inherent Agency Power, this index

PROFESSIONAL CORPORATIONS
See also Law Firms, this index
Partnerships distinguished, 214
Shareholders as employees for purposes of civil rights statutes, 214

PROFIT SHARING
Generally, 209
See also Sharing of Profits and Losses, this index
Accounting duties of fiduciaries, 153
Loss sharing implied by, 358
Secret Profits, this index

PUBLIC POLICY
See also Policy Considerations, this index
At-will employment, whistleblowers, 324
Fiduciary duty waivers, 393, 566
Freedom of contract, 566

RATIFICATION
Generally, 63, 394
See also Authority, this index
Definition, 65
Restatement of Agency, 394
Self dealing, 392

REAL ESTATE INVESTMENT TRUSTS
Security regulations, 394

RECEIVER APPOINTMENTS
See also Court Orders, this index
Buy-out orders to avoid, 344, 348
Costs, 342
Limited liability companies, 564
Partnerships, 326, 329, 339
Waivers of rights to seek, 567

RELIANCE
Estoppel elements, 244

RESPONDEAT SUPERIOR
Generally, 86
Loss spreading function, 111
Policy considerations, 111
Vicariously liability under theory of, 119

RESTATEMENT OF AGENCY
Generally, 178 et seq.
See also Default Rules, this index
Actual authority, 36
Agency defined, 64
Apparent agency, 39
Competition, disloyal, 162
Employment relationships
Generally, 100
Scope of employment, 114
Grabbing and leaving, 162
Independent contractor liabilities, 100
Inherent agency power, 52, 60
Liabilities
Independent contractors, 100
Undisclosed principal, 53
Master-servant relationship, 216
Ratification, 394
Scope of employment, 114
Undisclosed principal, 53

RISK
Abnormally dangerous jobs, 136
Agency status determinations, risk bearing, 90
Control and, 140
Franchise operations, risk bearing, 95
Inherently dangerous activities, 132
Investments, this index
Partners, 227, 505
Scope of employment, risk attributable to employer's business, 119
Securities regulation, legal malpractice risks, 576
Sole proprietors, 505
Tort risks, respondeat superior assignment, 111

SALES
Agency and sales relationships distinguished, 23
Agents, sales persons as, 23, 42, 50
Authority to sell, 42
Distributorships, this index
Franchise Operations, this index
Securities Regulation, this index

SCOPE OF EMPLOYMENT
Generally, 106 et seq.
Agency, scope of, 50
Deviations, 114
Discrimination, statutory, 125
Foreseeable acts of employees, 112, 125
Intentional torts, 116
Motive test, 111
Non-delegable duties, 127
Restatement of Agency, 114
Risk attributable to employer's business, 119
Tort liabilities, 106 et seq.

SECRET PROFITS
Generally, 148
See Fiduciary Duties, this index
Disgorgement, 142, 146

SECURITIES REGULATION
Generally, 575 et seq.
Acquisitions subject to, 577
Active and passive investors, 587
Blue sky laws, 575
Control as factor in determining applicability, 592
Disclosure model of federal statues, 565
Fraud litigation, 577
General partnership interests, 592
Howey test of scope of regulations, 582, 591
Investment contracts, 576, 591
Joint venture interests, 592
Legal malpractice risks, 576
Limited partnership interests as securities, 394
LLCs
Active and passive investors, 587
Interests in as securities, 577

Partnership interests as securities, 587, 588, 592
Primary and secondary markets, 576
Real estate investment trusts, 394
Scope of regulation, 577
SEC organization, 576
Stock, 583
Underwriters, 577

SELF-DEALING
Limited liability companies, 532

SERVANTS
See Master-Servant Relationships, this index

SHARING OF PROFITS AND LOSSES
Contributions as factor, 360
Income partner status, 219
Limited liability companies, 479
Loss Sharing, this index
Partnerships
Generally, 358
Contributions as factor, 360
Profit Sharing, this index
Uniform Partnership Act, 219
UPA, 360

SOLE PROPRIETORS
Risks, 505

STALEMATE
See Deadlock, this index

TAX CONSIDERATIONS
Investors, active and passive, 396
Limited liability companies, 479, 536, 580
Limited partnerships, 396

TENANCIES IN COMMON
Partnerships distinguished, 240, 285

TRADE SECRETS
Definition, 176
Grabbing and leaving violations of fiduciary duties, 170

TRUSTEES
Fiduciary duties, 151

UNFAIR COMPETITION
See also Competition by Fiduciary, this index
Confidences, breach of, 171
Customer lists, taking of, 169
Elements, 171
Grabbing and leaving, 167

UNIFORM LIMITED LIABILITY COMPANY ACT
Derivative suits, 491
Dissolution, 562
Expulsion of members, 554
Veil piercing, 508

UNIFORM LIMITED PARTNERSHIP ACT
Care duties, 399
Fiduciary duties, 399

UNIFORM PARTNERSHIP ACT
Generally, 417 et seq.
See also Default Rules, this index
Agents, partners as, 253
Apparent authority of partners, 231
Buy-out options, 378
Death of partner, dissolution on, 377
Default rules, 229
Definition of partnership, 213
Dissociation of partner
Generally, 270, 378
Buy-outs, 358
Dissolution
Generally, 313, 329, 335
Entity and aggregate theories, 257
Expulsion, 313
Fiduciary duties, 277
Goodwill valuation, 355
Management rights, 256
Ordinary matters, management rights as to, 255
Partnership status determinations
Generally, 240
Agents, partners as, 253
Profit and loss sharing, 219, 227
Sharing of profits and losses, 360
Winding up, 281, 380

UNINCORPORATED NONPROFIT ASSOCIATIONS
Contract liabilities, 32

UNJUST ENRICHMENT
Generally, 293

VEIL PIERCING
Generally, 505
Alter ego theory, 508
Corporate formalities, failure to observe, 508
Inadequate capitalization, 388
LLCs
Generally, 505, 506
Corporations compared, 508
Model Business Corporation Act, 505

VETO POWERS
See also Deadlock, this index
Creditors, 23, 234
Fundamental changes in entity, 268, 529
LLC operating agreements, 504, 529
Policy considerations, 504

VICARIOUS LIABILITY
Control and, 138
Partnerships, 219
Policy considerations, 111
Respondeat superior theory creating, 119

VOTING RIGHTS
Law partnerships, income members, 219
LLC members
Generally, 494
Conflicts of interest, 531
Operating agreements, 535
Scope, 579
One partner, one vote as default rule, 231
Partner compensation, 312

Partner status determinations, 224
Percentage voting arrangements
LLCs, 585
Partnerships, 266

WAIVERS
Care duties, 378
Dissolution of LLC, waiver of right to seek dissolution, 564
Fiduciary duties
Limited partnerships, 393
Public policy, 393
Freedom of contract and waivers of rights, 565
Good faith and fair dealing, 567
Limited partnerships, fiduciary duties, 393
Mandatory rules, 565
Public policy
Fiduciary duties, 393
Limitations, 566

WINDING UP
Generally, 313
Buy-out alternatives, 342
Costs, 423
Limited liability companies, 561
Liquidation distinguished, 344, 374
LLCs, 562
UPA, 281, 380

WITHDRAWAL
Contract drafting considerations, 305, 311
Dissolution, LLC member's withdrawal to effect, 560
Law firms, ethical standards, 306
LLCs
Dissolution on, 560
Remaining members, 562
Withdrawal of member to effect dissolution, 560

WRONGFUL TERMINATION
Partnerships, 353